P9-CFW-966

chology, psychiatry, social work, occupational therapy, pedagogy, and education will find this book to be most useful as they work with children in an educational or "correctional" context. For students of deviant behavior and the psychology of the exceptional child as well as general child psychology it will serve as an excellent supplementary textbook. Parents will profit from this book especially if they have children in need of special education.

About the Editors . . .

Beatrice A. Ashem

(Ph. D., University of Waterloo, Waterloo, Ontario, Canada) was Assistant Director of the Behavior Therapy Unit, Douglas Hospital, Montreal, Canada and Consultant to the Day Nursery of the Montreal Children's Hospital, Montreal. She has also served on the staffs of the Lakeshore Psychiatric Hospital, Toronto and the Psychiatric Unit of the Kingston General Hospital. More recently she has served on the faculty of the University of Lagos, Nigeria. Miss Ashem's articles on behavior modification with adults have appeared in several psychological journals.

Ernest G. Poser

(Ph.D., University of London, England) is Professor of Psychology at McGill University and Director of the Behavior Therapy Unit at Douglas Hospital in Montreal. He was trained in Behavior Therapy at the Academic Unit of Psychiatry, Middlesex Hospital, London and is a Diplomate in Clinical Psychology of the American Board of Examiners in Professional Psychology. He established one of the first training centers for behavior therapists in a hospital setting and is currently engaged in extending the application of learning principles to the prevention of maladaptive behavior.

PERGAMON GENERAL PSYCHOLOGY SERIES

Editors: Arnold P. Goldstein, *Syracuse University*
Leonard Krasner, *SUNY, Stony Brook*

Adaptive Learning:
Behavior Modification with Children

PGPS-29

Adaptive Learning: Behavior Modification with Children

Beatrice A. Ashem

and

Ernest G. Poser

Behavior Therapy Unit
Douglas Hospital, Montreal

PERGAMON PRESS INC.

New York · Toronto · Oxford · Sydney · Braunschweig

CARNEGIE LIBRARY
LIVINGSTONE COLLEGE
SALISBURY, N. C. 28144

PERGAMON PRESS INC.
Maxwell House, Fairview Park, Elmsford, N.Y. 10523

PERGAMON OF CANADA LTD.
207 Queen's Quay West, Toronto 117, Ontario

PERGAMON PRESS LTD.
Headington Hill Hall, Oxford

PERGAMON PRESS (AUST.) PTY. LTD.
Rushcutters Bay, Sydney, N.S.W.

VIEWEG & SOHN GmbH
Burgplatz 1, Braunschweig

Copyright © 1973, Pergamon Press Inc.
Library of Congress Catalog Card No. 72-156903

All Rights Reserved. No part of this publication may be reproduced, stored in a retrieval system or transmitted in any form, or by any means, electronic, mechanical, photocopying, recording or otherwise, without prior permission of Pergamon Press Inc.

Printed in the United States of America
08 016822 1

370.152
as 824

Contents

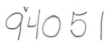
94051

Contributors

Abramovitz, Arnold
Azerrad, Jacob
Baer, Donald M.
Bailey, Jon
Baker, Bruce L.
Bandura, Albert
Becker, W.C.
Bowers, Kenneth S.
Brigham, Thomas A.
Broden, Marcia
Brodsky, G.
Brown, Richard A.
Bushell, Jr., Don
Clark, Robert
Davison, Gerald C.
Dunlap, Ann
England, G.
Erickson, Marie
Evans, M.B.
Freitag, Gilbert
Gold, Vivian J.
Goodwin, William
Grusec, Joan E.
Guess, Doug
Hall, R. Vance
Hallsten, Jr., Edwin A.
Hawkins, Nancy
Holland, Cornelius J.
Jackson, Deloris
Jehu, Derek
Johnson, Stephen M.
Kaprowy, E.
Kassorla, Irene C.
Keutzer, Carolin
Kilgour, K.
Kolvin, Israel
Kondas, O.
Landeen, Julie
Lazarus, Arnold A.
Lovaas, O. Ivar
Lund, Diane

Martin, G.L.
McConnell Owen, L.
McKerracher, D.W.
McNeal, Shirley A.
McReynolds, Leija V.
Mees, Hayden L.
Meichenbaum, Donald H.
Menlove, Frances L.
Metz, J. Richard
Meyerson, Lee
Michaelis, Mary Louise
Minke, Karl A.
Montenegro, Hernan
Neale, D.H.
O'Leary, K. Daniel
Pascal, Charles E.
Patterson, G.R.
Peterson, Linda R.
Peterson, Robert F.
Phelps, Richard E.
Pilek, V.
Polefka, David A.
Reid, John B.
Reid, Kathleen M.
Risley, Todd
Ritter, Brunhilde
Ross, Robert R.
Russell, C.D.
Rutherford, Gorin
Sailor, Wayne
Sherman, James A.
Staats, Arthur W.
Stafford, Richard L.
Saudergas, R.A.
Tasto, Donald L.
Wahler, Robert G.
Wolf, Montrose
Wrobel, Patricia Ann
Zimmerman, Elaine H.
Zimmerman, J.

Preface

Ever since becoming involved in the operation of a Behavior Therapy Unit we have received numerous requests from educators, psychologists, psychiatrists, social workers, occupational therapists and nurses for reference material to guide them in doing behavior modification with children. This has posed certain problems.

First, queries have concerned widely disparate behaviors of children, ranging from the normal to those with gross emotional disturbances or physical handicaps. As articles describing behavior modification techniques with children have been published in a variety of journals, covering numerous disciplines, many articles are not readily available to practicing personnel. Secondly, when one attempts to explain behavior modification techniques to individuals in widely differing disciplines, one cannot assume that all are equally familiar with the terminology normally used to describe these methods. Hence, it is frequently necessary to define basic nomenclature.

Our first purpose then was to provide a Source Book of behavior therapy and behavior modification techniques to which personnel in various disciplines can refer. We felt that the scope of such a book should be broad enough to be of interest to anyone working with children. It is our hope that it will stimulate the development of behavior modification programmes in schools, hospitals and the community in general. For this reason articles were selected to meet two criteria: the material presented had to be theoretically sound and efficacious in practice. While every attempt was made to include the best designed studies in each area we did not exclude exploratory studies addressing themselves to problems which, by their very nature, are not yet amenable to rigorous experimental control.

To provide further guidelines to those interested in establishing behavior modification programmes with children we have shared our own experience primarily in terms of how such programmes might be put into operation and maintained within an institutional setting. It is further hoped that by outlining some of the problems we have encountered, others might be helped to avoid these in their own endeavors.

We wish to thank all authors who permitted their articles to be included in this volume and gratefully acknowledge permission to reprint these papers, received from the following publishers: Academic Press, American Psychological Association, The British Journal of Psychiatry, The Canadian Psychiatric Association Journal, The Council for Exceptional Children, Pergamon Press, and The Society for the Experimental Analysis of Behavior.

Introduction

BEHAVIOR CHANGE IN CHILDHOOD:
THEORETICAL ISSUES

Definition

In a literal sense the term behavior modification is applicable to any attempt at behavior change whatever its theoretical orientation. Historically, however, the term has evolved to refer to those remedial and management procedures which are based on learning theory.

Attempts to modify behavior are sometimes referred to as behavior therapy, remedial learning or conditioning therapy. Some aspect of learning theory is basic to them all, but the psychology of learning is also relevant to many other vehicles of behavior change not encompassed by the papers presented in this book.

What then is the difference between the methods which concern us here and those traditionally used in child guidance and orthopsychiatry? It is to be found both in the therapist's theoretical orientation and in the methods he uses. Knowledge of the former is not enough, for the therapist's theoretical position is not necessarily a good predictor of what he will do; nor is the method he uses always indicative of his theoretical position. Thus, relaxation techniques are used by behavior therapists and by practitioners of autogenic training, but for very different theoretical reasons. Similarly, Freudians, Rogerians and eclectic psychotherapists, despite their conceptual differences, all rely on what Schofield (1964) has called "conversational" methods.

There are obvious differences between the behavioral and psychodynamic approaches to clinical problems. The subject of discussion fundamental to all dynamic therapies is the significance to the patient of past or present interpersonal relationships. Whether this relationship is viewed as the central process in therapy as, for instance, in the analysis of a transference, or as a prerequisite for therapeutic behavior change, as in the Rogerian model, is not crucial in the present context.

Behavior therapy, by contrast, is derived from the experimental tradition in psychology with particular reference to studies based on theories of learning. Much of the early work in this field dealt with the experimental investigation of behavior disorders in individual cases. More recently some behavior therapy techniques have become the method of choice for treating certain forms of maladaptive behavior.

Most but not all treatment methods derived from learning theory make use of conditioning techniques. In this regard they resemble either the Pavlovian (classical) or Skinnerian (operant) paradigm, although in practice each technique tends to encompass elements of both conditioning models.

All behavior therapists share a concern for what maintains a disorder rather than what caused it. This is not because a knowledge of etiology is considered superfluous, but because it is often unrelated to an experimental analysis of behavior. Circumstances responsible for causing a particular maladjustment may be very different from those responsible for maintaining it. Consequently, the focus of most behavior modifiers is on the client's presenting problem in the here and now. Once this has been defined the therapist's aim is to identify those aspects of the environment which control the occurrence, exacerbation and remission of the deviant behavior. The systematic manipulation of relevant environmental events, so that they come to elicit more adaptive responses, is the goal of most behavior modification. The extent to which this aim is achieved in any particular case is typically assessed by reference to a pretreatment baseline of the behavior to be modified.

Taken singly, none of these defining characteristics of behavior modification are unique to that form of treatment, but in combination they describe an approach quite distinct from that of dynamically-oriented psychotherapy, client-centered therapy or any other treatment method based primarily on verbal interchange.

Implicit in the process of applied behavior analysis, on which the conditioning therapies are based, is the quest for control of all variables relevant to behavior change. Baer, Wolf, and Risley (1968) have described this process as involving the application of: "Sometimes tentative principles of behavior to the improvement of specific behaviors, and simultaneously evaluating whether or not any changes noted are indeed attributable to the process of application — and if so, to what parts of the process. In short, analytic behavioral application is a self-examining, self-evaluating, discovery-oriented research procedure for studying behavior."

Behavior Therapy vs. Behavior Modification

It is useful within the general area of the conditioning therapies to reserve the phrase "behavior modification" for those endeavors where the target behavior to be modified is self-limiting and well within the normal range. Crying in young children, inattentiveness in the classroom or littering behavior are cases in point.

The term "behavior therapy" is more appropriate for those conditions in which it is attempted to counteract forms of maladaptive behavior which in some way impede the child's normal development. Enuresis, school phobias and self-destructive behavior would fall into this second category.

Distinction between Behavior Therapy with Children and with Adults

The procedures used to effect behavior change in children most often involve operant conditioning. This is because the behavior problems of children, unlike those of adults, frequently present overt manifestations of disturbed or disturbing motor responses. Hence, it is relatively easy to arrange appropriate contingencies to control that behavior. Also in the case of young children there are obvious limitations to the use of verbal techniques in effecting behavior change. In this regard, operant conditioning resembles the pediatric approach which places much greater reliance than does adult medicine on the observation of signs rather than verbally reported symptoms. It is also the case that operant methods follow more naturally from the usual controls adults exercise over young children, namely reward and punishment. Because of this it is not difficult to persuade, and teach, parents as well as teachers to apply contingency principles.

The success of operant procedures with children or adults depends on the degree to which the therapist can (a) control the reward system, and (b) consistently apply the prescribed reinforcement. However, while rewards are the fundamental motivating force in learning, habits of responding are only acquired over time. Reinforcement consistently applied enhances learning; inconsistent reinforcement not only hinders learning but helps to produce interpersonal anxieties.

One of the great advantages in using behavior therapy techniques with children is that *all* authority figures in contact with the child can be programmed to apply reinforcements consistently. As response patterns are not firmly established in childhood, intervention, by a therapist, to modify maladaptive responding at this stage can be more easily accomplished than similar intervention years later.

The control a therapist imposes on a patient when using operant techniques raises ethical questions. The community at large is agreed that children must learn; and for the most part welcomes methods which maximize learning. However, when methods used to maximize learning in adults involve elements of control, dismay is frequently expressed at depriving the individual of his freedom of choice. This is especially the case where treatment is carried out against the patient's wishes. (This occasionally happens with psychotics or criminal offenders.) In point of fact there is less deprivation of individual freedom with operant techniques than with many other forms of therapy. Operant conditioning is a method most often aimed at the facilitation of self-control, speech development, increased self-confidence, or sociability, and these are the very attributes recognized by society as necessary vehicles for the attainment of personal freedom. In fact, operant techniques characteristically deal with "happenings" in the child's life rather than "feelings." Hence, these methods often avoid interpersonal and emotional conflicts between parent and child by allowing the latter to obtain some desired reward contingent upon pro-social behavior. The same *process* of learning is involved whether appropriate or inappropriate responses are acquired.

BEHAVIOR CHANGE IN CHILDHOOD: PRACTICAL ISSUES

Orientation: Research, Teaching or Service

It has been our experience that in setting up a behavior modification facility the relative importance assigned to research, teaching or service will, to a large extent, determine the format of the programme. Ideally any setting in which behavior modification is practiced should provide opportunities for the development of each of these functions. Emphasis on one to the exclusion of another automatically imposes restraints on what can be accomplished.

Because of the emphasis academic courses in psychology place upon research the first concern of psychologists is often for those endeavors which contribute to knowledge. However, it must be recognized that the demands of a research-oriented programme are not always compatible with those of a good teaching unit. Again, in a research unit the criteria for patient selection are sometimes incompatible with the institutions' service demands. Hence in this field, as in all other clinical enterprises, there are conflicts of commitment to be resolved.

Let us consider the implications of developing each of these programmes. Knowing their relative merits will make it easier for psychologists setting up new units to reach a decision with regard to their own programme.

1. *Requirements for a Research Programme*
   a. Large populations from which to draw a sufficient number of similar cases so that groups can be matched.
   b. University trained personnel to devote time to such research.
   c. Adequate control over setting and subjects. This is necessary to ensure that the environment during treatment is essentially the same for all patients undergoing a particular therapy and to know what other interventions occurred between the termination of treatment and follow-up.

As many patients have multiple behavior problems rather than a single symptom, a research programme sometimes denies patients treatment for symptoms not currently under investigation.

2. *Requirements for a Teaching Programme*
   a. A variety of patients, rather than homogeneity of subjects, is required to provide adequate coverage.

This militates against easy comparison of treatment techniques for any particular disorder. It does permit single case studies.

   b. Ample opportunity for students to learn behavior therapy techniques.

Students in training may make errors of judgment. Consequently, teaching programmes cannot provide the tight control necessary to assess the effectiveness of treatment. Furthermore, because students are transitory several persons may be involved in the treatment, or treatments, of a single patient.

   c. Provision of an adequate interdisciplinary service where trainees can experience the operation of a multi-service approach to the care and treatment of the patient.

3. *Requirements for a Service Programme*
   a. A well trained staff to give the best possible treatment within the shortest period of time.
   b. A mobile staff that can reach into the home and into the community to tap all available resources.
   c. Certain gratifications for staff in the work situation to compensate for heavy demands made upon them. These rewards should be an integral part of existing programmes for all levels of staff.
   d. The development of a system showing patient progress is a primary need of a service programme. It can also provide an important source of reinforcement for staff.
   e. An autonomous programme which permits staff complete freedom to implement all procedures necessary for a comprehensive behavior modification programme. This will place responsibility for administration of the service upon the professional person most familiar with behavior therapy techniques.

Facilities

Like all other technologies, that of behavior modification requires special facilities and equipment. Also the setting in which behavior modification is to be undertaken differs from that of other therapeutic milieus in various ways. Most of these have to do with staff, record keeping, apparatus and follow-up services.

The present authors have described elsewhere some of the requirements for establishing an adult behavior therapy service in a mental hospital (Poser, 1967, 1969; Poser & Ashem, 1969).[1] In a setting suitable for children the following requirements deserve particular attention.

Staff.   In the absence of nurses trained in behavior modification, nursing staff or a children's unit should preferably be drawn from those with special training in pediatric nursing. That type of background is often more relevant than that of psychiatric nursing because the nurse with pediatric experience tends to be more attuned to the principles of contingency management fundamental to all operant conditioning techniques.

---

[1]Reprints available from authors on request.

Functions of the nurse unique to a behavior therapy programme relate primarily to record keeping. Required observations will focus not merely on eating, sleeping and general ward behavior, as is the usual nursing procedure, but on the diurnal and sometimes hourly fluctuations in the behavior to be modified. The nurse, by virtue of her past experience in making disciplined observations, providing quantitative recordings and dealing with minor manifestations of physical illness, is admirably suited to participate in behavior therapy. Her attention should at all times be specifically directed toward the relevant aspects of each patient's behavior.

A second important function of the nurse is her role as the primary dispenser of reinforcement in the hospital setting. As patients see more of the nursing staff than of any other hospital personnel, the importance of her role as a purveyor of consistent reinforcement in the social environment cannot be over-emphasized.

Training. The very nature of a behavior modification programme makes it essential that all staff dealing with patients be proficient in applying operant reinforcement schedules. To become a competent behavior therapist the individual should have some knowledge of:

a. Learning principles as they relate to psychopathology.
b. Aims involved in the observation of behavior.
c. Applied behavior analysis.
d. Conditioning principles.
e. The methods used in behavior modification.

For professional persons to acquire proficiency in all these areas would require from six months to a year. It has been our experience, however, that some behavior therapy procedures can readily be mastered by subprofessional personnel provided they are given adequate supervision.

The articles appearing in this book specifically relate to some of these procedures. In addition to having mastered the techniques, trainees must be observed in action either directly or through video recordings. It is very difficult for an unskilled person (or even a skilled one) who is conditioning speech in an autistic child for instance, to know whether the reinforcement occurred quickly enough after the response for the child to make the association. Small errors may occur, and unwittingly children are reinforced for other than the required responses. If an observer can draw these errors to the attention of a trainee immediately, they can be corrected before learning is impaired.

Space and equipment. For in-service work with children, the most important space requirements call for one-way vision observation rooms, and areas suitable for the temporary isolation of patients during timeout from positive reinforcement. Depending on the type of problem to be treated, it is also useful to set aside a "lever room" in which children have to perform a repetitive motor act, such as depressing a lever, in order to get out of the room. In this way the child learns that termination of punishment comes not merely as a result of elapsed time but also requires a certain degree of physical effort. For extreme cases of behavior pathology, such as self-destructive behavior or physical aggressiveness, various shock generators, particularly those operating by remote control, should be available. In conjunction with these negative reinforcers, closed circuit T.V. installations to facilitate observations by the nursing staff are desirable, though not essential.

Even more important than devices for restraint and negative reinforcement are mechanisms for the prompt dispensation of rewards for appropriate behavior. In working with children this is not a major difficulty. People, objects, situations and events, experienced as effective reinforcers by children, are much more ubiquitous than positive reinforcers for adults. This is equally true for in-patient and out-patient populations.

When dealing with out-patients it is useful to provide simple "behavioral prescriptions" for the guidance of parents and other significant adults in the child's home or school environment. These instructions should be sufficiently specific to enable the adult to respond appropriately not only when the child's maladaptive behavior occurs but also when it does not occur. For this purpose token reinforcers as well as portable devices such as interval timers, frequency counters and auditory signals helpful in teaching children to discriminate right from wrong responses could be made available to parents or teachers.

Record keeping.   The purpose of progress notes used in behavior modification programmes is to provide a flow chart of changes in target symptoms being treated. Records should be kept in such a way that these changes can be depicted graphically. This demands quantitative measures of specific behavior during each of the different phases of treatment: pre-treatment, treatment, post-treatment and follow-up. We have used different colored sheets to identify each phase more readily.

PROCEDURAL ISSUES

Preliminary Assessment of Suitability

The disproportion between the multitude of referrals for behavioral therapy with children, and the available professional staff to deal with these imposes a stringent need for selection of those cases most likely to benefit from conditioning treatment. Unfortunately, there are as yet few objective guidelines. Except for a few relatively minor behavior disorders in children no comparative studies on the outcome of behavioral versus traditional therapy have been done. From the available information it would appear that, just as in adult disorders, those conditions in which the symptoms are readily observable lend themselves to behavior therapy better than those in which symptoms are sporadic and vague. The latter would include anti-social behavior and the mood disorders for which it is often difficult to arrange contingency management. Symptomatic behaviors elicitable only in unusual surroundings or under extra-ordinary circumstances are not, as a rule, amenable to conditioning therapies. The more observable the behavior is, in a wide variety of situations including the clinic or hospital setting, the easier it is to arrive at a behavioral analysis relevant to isolating the factors which maintain such behavior. In our experience every case in which such an analysis can be made stands to benefit from behavior therapy even though other methods might be equally appropriate for certain cases.

Observation of Behavior

Again and again we have noted that satisfactory assessment of outcome is a direct function of the specificity and scope of pre-treatment observations. Accurate observations provide the basis for an analysis of behavior which must precede every adequate behavior modification programme. If treatment fails it need not necessarily mean that the behavior therapy was ineffective, but that the observations failed to provide the kind of data from which appropriate methods could be derived.

There are different kinds of observations to be made, depending on the nature of the presenting behavior disorder. Roughly these are of two kinds, i.e., behaviors disturbing to the patient or others in his environment, and behaviors which are deficient, such as speech retardation or paucity of pro-social responses. Relevant observations must be made for each class. In addition, observations may have to be made specific to a presenting symptom.

For classes of behavior which are disturbing to the patient it is necessary to ascertain the antecedent conditions, as well as the consequence associated with the response. For instance, in observing a child with phobic behaviors, it is not only essential to determine the environmental conditions provoking the anxiety, it is equally important to ascertain the nature of the responses the child has learned to reduce or avoid anxiety. Even more important is the need to determine if these responses do in fact relieve him of anxiety. Often this whole stimulus-response configuration is fairly complex, and may not be readily observable. To develop an effective treatment programme it is important to isolate the very diverse aspects of the environment which currently maintain the response. When the behavior is disturbing to others, and not to the patient, there is usually immediate response gratification involved for the patient. During the observation period an assessment of these rewards must be made; it is also important to note events that are unpleasant and aversive to the child.

Quantification of deficient behavior is a fairly straightforward procedure. It will be important to know which components of the response *to be conditioned* are already part of the child's repertoire. Let us assume speech is to be conditioned. Questions typically asked will be: (a) Does he look at persons, if so, at whom? (b) Does he imitate, if so, what and how much? (c) What sounds, words or sentences does he use? Under what conditions, and how frequently? (d) Does he follow verbal instruction? When the task is to build in behaviors, the whole reward system of the patient must be explored. Rewards habituate with repetition. For this reason a hierarchy of rewards should be obtained.

Observations of idiosyncratic behavior may require special sets of observations. Psychomotor retardation in schizophrenic children is a fairly frequent symptom; yet difficult to quantify. The therapist may have to devise unusual kinds of measures to obtain frequency data, or to determine if the behavior is under external stimulus control.

Basis for Selecting Therapeutic Strategies

From his analysis of the observational data the therapist will be able to choose between operant techniques, modelling, reciprocal inhibition or other methods. If the condition being dealt with implies a behavioral deficit, then examination of the kind and amount of deficit will help to identify the most appropriate type of operant programme. When the behavior to be conditioned is not, and possibly never has been, part of the individual's repertoire, modelling techniques are often indicated. Sometimes it is useful to combine these with operant conditioning of the subject's imitative responses. If, on the other hand, the deviant behavior provides considerable gain for the child, then an operant programme which aims at reversing the consequences of his existing response pattern would be the treatment of choice.

The literature suggests that children rarely suffer the incapacitating anxieties of adults. For this reason operant programmes which alter the consequences of maladaptive behavior would be favored over some of the treatments normally given adults, such as desensitization or flooding.

Participation of Parents in a Re-education Programme

One of the great advantages in doing behavior therapy with children is that parents very frequently expect to be involved in their children's treatment programme. Unfortunately, there has, so far, been little effort on the part of traditional therapists or educationists to have parents carry out therapeutic programmes. With behavior modification techniques such participation is *de rigueur*. Effective behavior modification with children calls for parental involvement from the first day of treatment.

If, as has been stated earlier, comprehensive observations are prerequisite to effective therapy, the importance of the parents' role becomes self-evident. The parents are undoubtedly best situated to observe the child. The question is: How can parents be trained to observe and analyze these interactions when they themselves are involved?

The most efficient method of training parents is to videotape normal family interactions. Videotaping is best done in the home but if this is not possible the clinic setting would do.

Parents can be taught to recognize and evaluate their own characteristic responses to their child's behavior and detect their consequences. Instruction can then be given to promote contingent management of behavior. If no videotape is available parents might be trained to make frequency charts at home of behavior which must be changed, and to determine the environmental variables which elicit or maintain these behaviors.

Once therapy begins, parents should be allowed to observe and then do therapy under supervision. After a few training sessions they should be able to carry out contingent reinforcement with their children fairly well. Many will realize for the first time that there is a lawful relation between their behavior and that of their children!

Assessment of Progress

Certain basic data are gathered during an observation period. The frequency of observed behavior serves as the baseline from which to assess therapeutic progress. Assessment of progress may be done at regular intervals — set by the therapist — or it may be done at the conclusion of treatment. When it is done at regular intervals, say every six weeks, therapy should be suspended for a time while further baseline observations are made. In view of the growing body of evidence that experimenter demand variables affect the outcome of psychological research, observations should be made by an independent observer. Ideally, this would be an associate who knows nothing of the goals of treatment. In practice this is difficult, if not impossible, to do.

Evaluations of outcome typically use the patient as his own control. The question is how much has he changed relative to what he was — not relative to others. For children on operant programmes frequency data are relatively easy to obtain. It is merely a matter of measuring the increase (e.g., amount of speech production) or decrease (e.g., number of temper tantrums) of these observed behaviors. For some cases information can only be obtained from the patient or his family. Particularly in the case of patients with anxiety symptoms, self-reports must be carefully assessed. In addition, behavioral evidence can be obtained indicating the degree to which the patient shows freedom from fears.

Questionnaire data may be of value if the child is old enough to read and to understand the questions. Pre- and post-treatment tests can be administered, but these are rarely as convincing as behavioral indices from which it is apparent if a child's performance level has improved following therapy.

Assessment of progress cannot be considered complete at termination of treatment. Follow-up data obtained over a prolonged period after treatment are essential in evaluating the overall effectiveness of therapy.

Follow-up

Follow-up studies of patients treated by conditioning techniques are still too few, and rare indeed are reports covering more than a period of five years after termination of treatment. Such studies as are available too often fail to provide objective indices of behavior change in which the assessment is made by reference to a control group and by observers other than the therapist. The increased availability of videotape recordings provides opportunity for showing changes in the interactions between parent and child or child and therapist at various stages of treatment and follow-up. These tapes could then be evaluated by independent observers yielding a clinical assessment of behavior change. Since many symptoms treated by behavior therapy lend themselves to video recording it should be possible to use this technique for the objectification of follow-up studies.

PROBLEMS IN APPLICATION

Cooperation of Parents

Getting parental cooperation in child behavior therapy can present problems. For one thing the parents of disturbed children are often themselves disturbed. Interactions with their children are frequently inconsistent or manipulative. They may be unable to impose any kind of structure upon the child's behavior. The child can learn no other way to satisfy his needs than through primitive behaviors (e.g., temper tantrums), which ultimately force the parent to comply.

Part of the parents' reluctance to participate in programmes designed to structure their child's behavior comes from an awareness of their own limitations. Even if they verbally agree to carry out treatment, they sometimes cannot be relied upon to do so consistently. Thus the child may be placed on a partial reinforcement schedule — a condition which could effectively maintain maladaptive behaviors for long periods of time.

Occasionally parents turn their children over to an institution and virtually wash their hands of further responsibility. Disinterested parents of this kind are hard to motivate. If their cooperation is required for success of treatment, it may be necessary to point out that life will be easier for them if they can learn to deal effectively with their children. Much supervision and training must be given to insure that parents really understand the principles involved, and not just the specific manipulation required of them.

Control of the Environment

If children are out-patients it is especially difficult to ensure that all behaviors emitted meet with optimal and prescribed consequences. It is often hard enough to get parents (who are the most involved with the patient) to cooperate. To enlist the help of teachers and siblings is even more difficult. To modify reactions of peers to the patient requires the greatest ingenuity, but it can be done, at least in structured settings where cooperation of a teacher has also been gained. Once a behavior modification programme goes into operation, changes in the child's behavior are often so dramatic that the child gets more positive social reinforcement than he has ever had. Not only does life become significantly less abrasive for the child, but the consequences thereof frequently provide enormous gratification for parents and teachers alike.

A difficulty encountered in institutional settings is the sheer size of groups that one person is required to handle. However, it has been shown that the actual time it takes to reward behaviors such as "attention" or "study habits" contingently through social approval or tokens, is not as great as that required for less efficient methods. The improvement in behavior which results makes this time well spent.

While operant programmes have been found manageable for large groups, they do not sustain themselves. Particularly, if key personnel in charge of the programme leave, the whole enterprise may disintegrate. Another problem arises when the patient is removed from the environment in which he has been reinforced. Behavior gains may not be maintained in the absence of reinforcement.

These problems require separate solutions. How does one create institutions where behavior modification programmes once elaborated can be maintained without extra staff? Again, how does one maintain desired behaviors when reinforcement is no longer forthcoming, or is infrequent? For the first problem there may well have to be a massive education programme of personnel. Techniques may have to be devised whereby implementation of remedial programmes in hospitals or schools becomes as routinized as the giving of medication or the holding of assemblies. As for the second, it seems that greater attention must be paid to modifying the social environment from which these young patients come and to which they must necessarily return.

Sub-optimal Behaviors within the Normal Range

INTRODUCTION

Most of the papers in this section deal with the use of contingent reinforcement techniques intended to facilitate learning in young children endowed with average mental ability. Methods to expedite the acquisition of speech and reading skills are discussed. The last three papers, in the sub-section "Control of Fear Responses," concern themselves with the management of maladaptive fear responses often seen in otherwise well-adjusted children.

Common to all these investigations is an experimental paradigm in which a baseline for the behavior to be modified is clearly established prior to any intervention. The target behavior is then observed under treatment conditions. At that stage controls are introduced either by the "reversal" method, as in the work of Hall *et al.*, and Bushell *et al.*, or by the multiple baseline technique.

In the "reversal" method the experimental variable is alternately applied and withdrawn to see whether the desired behavior change depends on it. In the multiple baseline technique the experimental variable is applied to only one of several baseline behaviors to demonstrate the specific effect of treatment. Though generally used with an experimental design in which each subject acts as his own control the multiple baseline method also lends itself to other strategies.

Brigham and Sherman's study relates to the interaction between reinforcement and generalization in language learning and makes the point that it is not necessary to reinforce differentially every imitative verbal response to obtain generalized improvement in the accuracy of verbal imitation. This represents an extension to normal children of similar findings earlier reported for children with speech deficits. The second paper in this section describes an approach useful in the treatment of stammerers and provides a two- to five-year follow-up of the cases treated.

Research on contingency management in education is sometimes impeded by the complexity and cost of equipment. The papers in the sub-section "Cognitive Learning Development" describe some simple techniques whereby objective data on classroom behavior can be obtained. These data suggest that systematic application of reinforcement procedures do enhance the child's performance. Several authors describe the operation of token systems. Usually the dispensation of tokens is controlled by the experimenter but Johnson and Martin, in an original contribution to this volume, find that children managing their own token reward system by contingently reinforcing themselves, maintained discrimination behavior at as high a rate and accuracy level as did children receiving externally administered reinforcers.

Articles in the sub-section "Control of Fear Responses" address problems approached in the form of "analogue studies" in that the experimental variables are more stringently controlled than is usually possible when these remedial techniques are applied to more severe behavior disorders. In addition to a paper on modelling (Bandura *et al.*), there are two reports on group desensitization; a technique so far rarely used with children.

Wherever possible those studies have been included in which some follow-up data on the effect of a given procedure are reported. These show that in many instances the behavior change obtained is demonstrable well after termination of the formal training or treatment programme.

Speech Development

An Experimental Analysis of Verbal Imitation in Preschool Children*†

THOMAS A. BRIGHAM and JAMES A. SHERMAN

University of Kansas

Abstract: A model presented English words to three preschool children and reinforced accurate imitation of these words. The model also presented novel Russian words but the subjects' imitation of these words was never reinforced. As long as the subjects' imitation of English words was reinforced, their accuracy of imitating non-reinforced Russian words increased. When reinforcement was not contingent upon imitation of English words, accuracy of imitating both the English and the Russian words decreased. These results support and extend previous work on imitation.

Imitation as a class of behaviors has become increasingly important, both as a potential method of producing socially significant behavioral changes (Metz, 1965; Lovaas, Berberich, Perloff, & Schaeffer, 1966; Baer, Peterson, & Sherman, 1967) and as a key concept in theoretical analyses of language development and socialization (Lovaas *et al.*, 1966; Bandura & Walters, 1963; Bijou & Baer, 1965). Recent experimental studies of imitation have produced two consistent findings: if a class of imitative responses is developed in a child, then a relatively novel response can be taught by demonstration without direct shaping of that response (Metz, 1965; Lovaas *et al.*, 1966; Baer *et al.*, 1967); if some imitative responses directly produce reinforcement, then other imitative responses may be maintained even though they never directly produce reinforcement (Baer & Sherman, 1964; Metz, 1965; Lovaas *et al.*, 1966; Baer *et al.*, 1967).

Lovaas *et al.* (1966) reported another related finding in the area of verbal imitation beyond that reported in other recent studies of imitation. Their subjects were two autistic children who were taught imitative speech through a long process of imitative training. After imitation of English words had been established, novel Norwegian words, interspersed with English words, were presented. Imitation of English words was reinforced, but imitation of Norwegian words was not. In spite of non-reinforcement, the subjects attempted to mimic the novel Norwegian words and improved in accuracy of imitation on these words. These findings have important implications for theories of language learning and methods of speech therapy. However, the study by Lovaas *et al.* did not include procedures specifically designed to examine whether or not continued reinforcement of English imitations was necessary to develop and maintain imitative accuracy of Norwegian words. The purpose of the present study was to

*This report was based on an MA Thesis by the senior author, Department of Human Development, University of Kansas. This research was supported by the Office of Economic Opportunity, Executive Office of the President, Washington, D.C. 20506 and the Headstart E & R Center, University of Kansas, grant # OEO 1410, and by PHS Research Grant # HD 02674 from the National Institute of Child Health and Human Development. Reprints may be obtained from either author, Department of Human Development, University of Kansas, Lawrence, Kansas 66044.

†Reprinted from the *Journal of Applied Behavior Analysis*, 1968, 1, 2, 151–158. Copyright 1968 with permission from the Society for the Experimental Analysis of Behavior, Inc., and Dr. T. A. Brigham.

replicate, with normal children, the Lovaas *et al.* study and to examine the relationship between reinforcement of some imitative responses and the improvement of other unreinforced imitative responses.

METHOD

Subjects

The three subjects were four-year-old boys of normal linguistic and physical development; all attended the Human Development Laboratory Preschool of the University of Kansas.

Procedure

In each of several experimental conditions, English and Russian words were presented. The experimental manipulations consisted of reinforcement of accurate English imitations, reinforcement of behavior other than English imitations, and pairing of English words with reinforcement. Imitation of Russian words was never reinforced and accuracy of imitation of these words was examined as a function of the operations performed on English imitations.

Training was conducted four days a week in the morning, Monday through Thursday, each session lasting approximately twenty minutes. The reinforcers for Subject 1 were assorted candies such as M & Ms and after-dinner mints. For Subjects 2 and 3, assorted candies were used in three of the four weekly sessions, and once a week the children were able to earn tokens which they could trade for a toy.

The first session for each subject tested whether he imitated the experimenter's verbal cues. The subject was seated at a low table across from the experimenter. He was told that the experimenter would read a list of words one at a time and that the child could earn candy (or tokens) if he correctly repeated the word after the experimenter said it. The stimulus words for the first session were fifteen English words of varying complexity such as apple, capital, reverse, cartoon, represent, and dog. Each word was presented twice in an unsystematic order. Each time the child correctly reproduced the stimulus word, he was immediately given a token or candy, and also praised for his performance (e.g., "Good," "Very good"). If the child failed to repeat the word correctly, the experimenter said nothing, and then presented the next stimulus word. The criterion for reinforcement of the subject's imitation was based simply on the experimenter's ability to understand the subject. This allowed for a small variance from a hypothetical exact pronunciation. (For example, a slight elongation of the last vowel sound in "cartoon" was acceptable, but the substitution of a "g" for the "s" in "represent" was unacceptable.) During the first session, each subject attempted to imitate all of the experimenter's verbal models and thus was continued in the program.

Reinforcement for imitation of English words. The procedures in Sessions 2 through 6 for Subject 1 and Sessions 2 through 5 for Subjects 2 and 3 were basically the same as those for the first session, with two major exceptions. The instructions at the beginning of the sessions were deleted (the subjects were given no further instructions throughout the study). In addition, Russian stimulus words were added. The Russian words were presented in the same manner as the English words; however, the Russian words were never followed by reinforcement. When a Russian word was represented, if the subject responded the experimenter presented a new stimulus word no sooner than ten seconds after the subject's response. If the subject did not respond, the next stimulus word was presented no sooner than ten seconds after the experimenter's demonstration. Fifteen different stimulus words (English and Russian) were presented to subjects in all sessions, with each word being presented twice in an unsystematic order. The number of sessions for each procedure and the Russian words presented to each subject per session are summarized in Table 1. As shown in Table 1, the number of different Russian words was increased over sessions. This was done to minimize the possibility that the results obtained might be a function of the specific Russian words employed. Since the number of different words presented each session was always fifteen (each word presented twice), the increase in Russian words was accomplished by a decrease in the proportion of English words.

Table 1. Summary of Russian words presented to each subject per session. The Russian spellings are approximate as the Cyrillic alphabet differs from the Roman. The letters in the representations of the Russian words were chosen for their similarity in shape to the Cyrillic letter and have little to do with the pronunciation of the letter.

	Subject 1		Subjects 2 and 3	
Procedure	Sessions	Russian Words*	Sessions	Russian Words*
Reinforcement of English	1	none	1	none
imitation	2	1, 2, 3	2	1, 2, 3, 7
	3	1, 2, 3	3	1, 2, 3, 7
	4	1, 2, 4, 5	4	1, 2, 3, 5, 7
	5	1, 2, 3, 4, 5	5	1, 2, 3, 5, 7
	6	1, 2, 3, 4, 5		
Reinforcement of behavior	7	1, 2, 3, 4, 5	6	1, 2, 3, 5, 7
other than imitation (DRO)	8	1, 2, 3, 4, 5	7	1, 2, 3, 5, 7
	9	1, 2, 5, 6, 7	8	1, 2, 3, 6, 7
	10	1, 2, 5, 6, 7	9	1, 2, 3, 5, 6
Reinforcement of English	11	1, 2, 5, 6, 7	10	1, 3, 5, 6, 7
imitation	12	1, 2, 4, 6, 7	11	1, 2, 5, 6, 7
	13	1, 2, 4, 6, 7	12	1, 2, 3, 5, 6
			13	1, 2, 3, 5, 7
Pairing of English words			14	1, 2, 3, 4, 5, 8
with reinforcement			15	2, 3, 4, 5, 6, 8
			16	2, 4, 5, 6, 7, 8
			17	2, 4, 5, 6, 7, 8
Reinforcement of English			18	1, 2, 3, 4, 7, 8
imitation			19	1, 2, 3, 4, 5, 6
			20	1, 2, 3, 4, 5, 6, 8

*1. tabapaw; 2. kapandaw; 3. moloko; 4. knuga; 5. clobap; 6. deborka; 7. malruk; 8. ctena.

Reinforcement of behavior other than imitation: DRO. Following reinforcement of English imitations, a schedule of differential reinforcement of behavior other than imitation of English words (DRO) was used. During the DRO procedure, none of the subjects' imitations was reinforced. Instead, reinforcement was delivered at least five seconds after the last imitation of each English word. No reinforcement was presented after Russian words. That is, the experimenter presented an English word; if the subject imitated it, reinforcement was delivered no sooner than five seconds after the response. If the subject repeated his imitation, reinforcement was delivered at least five seconds after the last imitation. If the subject did not respond, reinforcement was delivered at least five seconds after the stimulus word was presented. The actual time between response and reinforcement varied from five to twenty seconds with a mean of approximately ten seconds. After this DRO interval had elapsed, but before the next stimulus word was presented, the experimenter occasionally delivered additional praise to the subjects non-contingently. This was done to keep the rate of praise approximately constant over the different experimental procedures.

In the third session of the DRO period for Subject 1, two new Russian words were added. One new Russian word was introduced in the third session of DRO for Subjects 2 and 3. The Russian stimulus words added during the DRO are labelled Russian$_2$; the Russian stimulus words introduced previously are labelled Russian$_1$. Since the number of Russian words presented during DRO sessions for each subject was held constant, the introduction of the Russian$_2$ words required that the number of Russian$_1$ words be reduced. To avoid any biasing of the sample, all Russian$_1$ words were continued as possible stimuli, and those used in each session were selected randomly. The purpose of adding Russian$_2$ words was to investigate whether the DRO procedure affected the acquisition of accurate pronunciation of Russian words as well as maintenance of accurate pronunciation. Due to an error in the preparation of the list of stimulus words, the Russian$_2$ word was not presented in Sessions 13 and 14 for Subjects 2 and 3.

Reinforcement for imitation of English words II.   After four sessions of the DRO procedure, imitation of English words was again reinforced. Again, only the imitation of English was reinforced; the imitation of Russian words was not.

Pairing of English words and reinforcement.   Subjects 2 and 3 were presented with a procedure in which English words were paired with reinforcement (similar to a classical conditioning paradigm). The experimenter presented an English stimulus word and at the same time delivered candy or tokens to the subject. Whether the subject responded correctly, incorrectly, or not at all, the experimenter waited approximately twenty seconds and then presented the next stimulus word. Only the English words were paired with reinforcement. After the twenty-seconds interval following reinforcement had elapsed, but before the next stimulus presentation, the experimenter occasionally delivered praise to subjects non-contingently. Two new Russian words were added during this procedure, as a probe for the effects of this new condition on the acquisition of accurate pronunciation of new Russian words. These new words were labelled Russian$_3$. The Russian$_2$ word was continued, and, as before, the Russian$_1$ words presented in each session were selected randomly.

Reinforcement for imitation of English words III.   Contingent reinforcement of correct imitation of the English stimulus words was reinstated. As in the two reinforcement procedures before, the subjects' responses to the Russian words were never followed by experimental reinforcement.

Scoring of verbal responses.   The data from all sessions were tape recorded. The Russian words were analyzed and scored in detail for pronunciation. The English words were not; the English scores presented in the Results section are based simply on the number of English words correctly pronounced divided by the total number presented. Correctness was determined by the experimenter's immediate judgment of accuracy during sessions.

Scoring of the Russian words was done by two analysts working independently. One analyst scored all of the sessions; the second analyst scored a random but representative half of the sessions for reliability determinations. The scoring of the Russian words was carried out in a manner similar to that used by Lovaas *et al.* (1966). Each letter pronounced correctly was given one point; each syllable pronounced correctly was given three points. The points were totaled and divided by the total number of points possible, yielding a degree of correctness score expressed as a percentage. A reliability score for each Russian stimulus word in a session was determined by dividing the highest point score assigned by one analyst into the point score assigned by the other analyst. These reliability scores for individual words were summed and divided by the number of Russian words presented to give an average reliability score for that session. Another measure of analyst reliability was computed in which the analysts' judgments of whether the Russian pronunciation was correct or incorrect were compared. When the two analysts agreed that a word was either correct or incorrect, it was scored as one point; if they disagreed, it was scored as zero. The total was then divided by the total number of agreements possible to give a per cent-agreement score for that session. Table 2 contains a list of all the Russian stimulus words used in the experiment, the approximate Russian spelling of each word, the phonetic spelling, and the points assigned to each word.

RESULTS

The results for the two measures of analyst reliability, degree of correctness and per cent-agreement, yielded scores ranging from 80 per cent to 100 per cent with a mean of 93 per cent for the degree of correctness score and a mean of 93 per cent for the per cent-agreement score. Further, reliability of scoring did not appear to differ across the various experimental conditions or across different Russian words. The high scores for analyst reliability over the sessions sampled indicate that the changes in the subjects' imitation of Russian stimulus words were clearly observable and objectively scoreable.

The major results of the study are graphically presented in Figs. 1, 2, and 3.

The subjects' performances throughout the experiment were very similar. All improved steadily in their Russian pronunciation during the initial reinforcement period. The subjects' English imitation, although scored in a less precise manner, showed a parallel improvement.

When the DRO condition was introduced, performances of all subjects on the Russian words promptly decreased. The initial drop was to a point approximately equal to the subjects' scores for imitation of Russian words at the beginning of the study. In the third session

Table 2. Russian stimulus words used in the experiment.

Approximation of Spelling	Approximate Phonetic Spelling	Points Letters + Syllables = Total	
1. tabapaw	tah var ish	12 345 67 + 9	16 points
2. kapandaw	care an dash	123 45 678 + 9	17 points
3. moloko	mal a koy	123 4 567 + 9	16 points
4. knuga	kuh nee guh	12 34 56 + 9	15 points
5. clobap	slo var	123 456 + 6	12 points
6. deborka	da borch ka	12 3456 78 + 9	17 points
7. malruk	mal chick	123 456 + 6	12 points
8. ctena	sten na	1234 56 + 6	12 points

of the DRO period, two new Russian words were presented to Subject 1 and a single new Russian word was presented to Subjects 2 and 3. The scores for the Russian$_2$ words were below the initial scores for Russian$_1$ imitation during the first reinforcement period and also below the scores for the Russian$_1$ words during the third session of the DRO. For Subjects 1 and 3, English imitation scores again closely paralleled the scores for Russian imitation.

When reinforcement of English imitation was reinstated, subjects' imitation of both English and Russian promptly improved. All subjects again reached a high level of performance on the English and Russian$_1$ words, but their scores on the Russian$_2$ words remained somewhat lower.

In the first session of stimulus pairing, the subjects' imitation of the Russian$_3$ words added

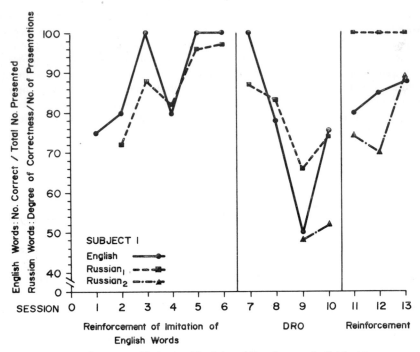

Fig. 1. Accuracy of imitation, English and Russian words, Subject 1.

during this session was very accurate, and the imitation of the Russian₁ words dropped only slightly. However, as the procedure was continued, performances on all Russian words again dropped to a level lower than the preceding reinforcement period. Imitation of the English words followed a similar course, eventually deteriorating to the lowest level of the experiment in the last session of the stimulus pairing procedure.

The second reinstatement of reinforcement for English imitations again resulted in a pronounced improvement in the subjects' imitation of all Russian words. The Russian scores during this procedure were among the highest of the experiment, and near the scoring ceiling. Once again, the improvement in the Russian imitation was closely associated with a parallel improvement in imitation of the English words.

The changes in the accuracy of imitation scores represent a change in the topography of the imitative responses, not a failure to make imitative responses. Subjects 1 and 3 made a vocal response after every Russian stimulus presentation throughout the experiment. Subject 2 failed to make a vocal response to Russian words twice in Session 15 and once in Session 17. Although these failures to respond were scored as zero for the presentation, if they were left out of the scoring it would not change the basic shape or direction of the curves. Some examples of the decrease in accuracy after very accurate imitation of the same stimulus words are the responses: "to pot" for the stimulus word "slovar," "borsha" for "deborchka," and "keyliga" for "kaneega."

DISCUSSION

The results of this study replicate and extend the initial findings of Lovaas *et al.* (1966) related to improvement in imitation of unreinforced stimulus words. Possibly most important

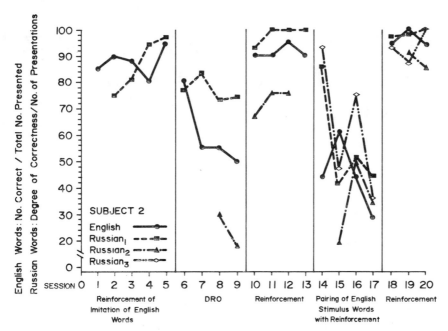

Fig. 2. Accuracy of imitation, English and Russian words, Subject 2.

for the extension of the findings of Lovaas *et al.* (1966) to the problem of normal speech development is the fact that the subjects for this experiment were normal speakers. That is, their language behavior was apparently the result of normal processes of speech development, not of extensive experimental procedures designed to teach them speech. Also, these subjects were of an age when their vocabulary was rapidly increasing in size and complexity. Thus, their extensive imitative skills (first session English imitation scores of seventy-five, eighty-five, and ninety-five per cent correct) may be very important in the process or processes of vocabulary elaboration. This possibility is further strengthened by the main findings: the subjects improved in their never-reinforced imitation of the Russian words, indicating that it was not necessary to reinforce differentially every imitative verbal response to obtain generalized improvement in accuracy. Studies by Baer and Sherman (1964) and Baer *et al.* (1967) have reported similar results. They demonstrated that it was possible to maintain imitative responses which were never reinforced, as long as some of the subjects' imitative responses were reinforced. These studies also reported that if reinforcement was discontinued for all imitative responses, and delivered contingent on the occurrence of other responses instead (DRO), then the probability of occurrence of all imitative responses decreased. The present study extends these results to accuracy of verbal imitation. During reinforcement for behavior other than verbal imitation, the accuracy of both the formerly reinforced and non-reinforced imitative responses decreased. When reinforcement of the imitation of English words was reinstated, both the reinforced and non-reinforced imitative responses again increased in accuracy.

The stimulus pairing procedure also involved discontinuing contingent reinforcement of all imitative responses. The data from the last two sessions of this procedure show a similar decrement in accuracy of imitative responding. Since the amount of reinforcement delivered to the subjects remained fairly constant over the experiment, it is probable that the difference in performances was the result of the way the reinforcers were delivered. When the

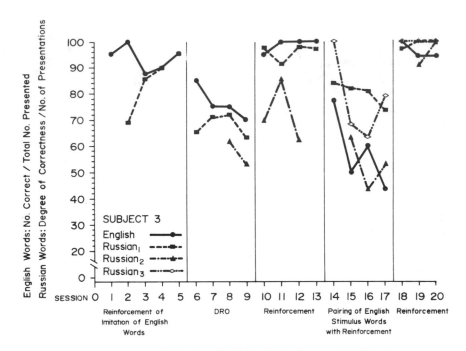

Fig. 3. Accuracy of imitation, English and Russian words, Subject 3.

experimental procedures and results are considered together, it appears that, under conditions where some imitative responses are directly reinforced, all imitative responses increase in accuracy; under conditions where this direct reinforcement is discontinued, all imitative responses are inaccurate or decrease in accuracy.

There are several possible explanations of these results. A number of recent papers on imitation have suggested that the development of non-reinforced imitative behavior can be analyzed as a result of the experimentally developed reinforcing properties of behavior similar to a model (Lovaas *et al.*, 1966; Baer *et al.*, 1967). A corresponding account may be applied to findings of the present study. During reinforcement of English imitation, vocal productions which matched those of the experimenter were reinforced. Since vocal matching (similar auditory stimuli) preceded and was discriminative for reinforcement, it may have become a conditioned reinforcer. If this were the case, improvement on the Russian words could have been a function of the increased amounts of conditioned reinforcement involved in closer approximations to a good pronunciation (thus producing more closely matched auditory stimuli). When the relationship between matching vocal productions and reinforcement was withdrawn in the DRO and stimulus pairing procedures, the conditioned reinforcing effects of matching auditory stimuli should decrease, accounting for the decreased accuracy of matching the unreinforced Russian words found during these two procedures. However, since the auditory consequences to the subjects of their own vocalizations were not directly manipulated, it is not possible to state definitely that the present findings were a result of the indirect manipulation of the conditioned reinforcement value of auditory similarity.

An alternative analysis of the improvement in Russian imitations is that subjects failed to discriminate the differential consequences between the English words and Russian words. If this were the case, the general improvement of accuracy of Russian imitations may be accounted for on the basis of a variable-ratio schedule of reinforcement for imitative responding. That is, the procedures which reinforced accurate English imitations may have functionally reinforced accurate verbal imitation in general. Similarly, the converse may have been true of the DRO and pairing procedures.

REFERENCES

Baer, D. M., Peterson, R. F. & Sherman, J. A. The development of imitation by reinforcing behavioral similarity to a model. *Journal of the Experimental Analysis of Behavior*, 1967, **10**, 405–416.

Baer, D. M. & Sherman, J. A. Reinforcement control of generalized imitation in young children. *Journal of Experimental Child Psychology*, 1964, **1**, 37–49.

Bandura, A. & Walters, R. H. *Social Learning and Personality Development*. New York: Holt, Rinehart & Winston, 1963.

Bijou, S. W. & Baer, D. M. *Child Development II: Universal stage of infancy*. New York: Appleton-Century-Crofts, 1965.

Lovaas, O. I., Berberich, J. P., Perloff, B. F. & Schaeffer, B. Acquisition of imitative speech by schizophrenic children. *Science*, 1966, **151**, 705–707.

Metz, J. R. Conditioning generalized imitation in autistic children. *Journal of Experimental Child Psychology*, 1965, **2**, 389–399.

The Treatment of Stammering in Children by the Shadowing Method*

O. KONDAŠ†

Department of Psychology, Comenius University, Bratislava, Czechoslovakia

Abstract: There are very few reports about the application of behavior therapy to child stammering and these are not encouraging. Remedial education treatment is followed by frequent relapses. The present work gives data about the methods, effects and long-term results in nineteen child stammerers treated by the shadowing technique. A discussion of some of the theoretical problems involved is given and shows how the theoretical analysis influences treatment procedures. Seventy per cent of the cases were successfully treated by the shadowing technique and subsidiary procedures; relapses occurred in only twelve per cent of the cases.

INTRODUCTION

The experiments of Cherry and Sayers (1956) on chronic stammerers have shown that the transference of the auditory perceptions of proper speech might provide a technique for reducing stammering. They concluded that "some of the experiments have suggested methods for training, and show some therapeutic promise." However, there have been few clinical accounts of their method and follow-up evaluations of the treatment effects have been neglected. Both Cherry and Sayers and Maclaren (1960) examined the immediate influence of "shadowing" on speech fluency in adult stammerers.

The application of learning theory to the treatment of childhood stammering is very rare. In his survey on behavior therapy in children, Rachman (1962) mentions two unsuccessfully treated stammerers; the results in a further three children under operant control were more encouraging. Case (1960) used the method of negative practice in the treatment of stammering in adults with eighty per cent success, and another study was conducted by Walton & Black (1958). The remedial education treatment of child stammering is accompanied by frequent relapses which generally take place during the first months after treatment. For example, Chmelková (1956) recorded a forty per cent relapse rate; as relapses seem to be one of the most important problems in treating stammering, the present work emphasizes the durability of the (re-)acquired fluent speech.

METHOD

Subjects

The sample consisted of sixteen children aged between eight and sixteen ($\bar{X} = 10.9$), one twenty-year-old student and three children between the ages of five and six. In addition to

---

*Reprinted from *Behavior Research and Therapy*, 1967, **5**, 325–329. Copyright 1967 with permission from Pergamon Press Publishing Company and Dr. O. Kondaš.
†Now at: Bratislava, Exnárova 17, Czechoslovakia.

severe stammering, twelve of the children had frequent speech spasms accompanied by extraneous movements and grimaces. Four of them were unable to speak one whole sentence (they could not communicate verbally and had to write their answers).

Treatment Procedure[1]

Since pneumographic records of stammerers show irregular and shallow breathing when speaking (Kondaš, 1964, p. 160), breathing exercises were carried out during the first two sessions. The exercises consist of a combination of deep and slow inspirations. At the second or third session, exercises in relaxed breathing (similar to those used in autogenic training) were given.

The main part of the procedure used in treating the eight- to sixteen-year-old children was the speech shadowing technique (Cherry & Sayers, 1956). Training in shadowing began in the second or third session. The therapist read an unknown text which was then repeated exactly ('shadowed') by the stammerer, one or two words later. One session consisted of two or three short exercises (three to five minutes in duration) accompanied by short breaks. As soon as the technique was mastered, daily home-exercises were provided by the parents for about five minutes. To maintain the child's interest and motivation alternative forms of shadowing (by telephone and by a voice-cue technique) were used. The modifications were introduced only after the fifth session and thereafter the two forms of shadowing exercises were alternated in the following sessions. At the sixth or seventh session, various aspects of stammering were discussed individually with eight of the older stammerers.

In four cases there was insufficient progress towards achieving fluency after ten to fifteen treatment sessions (plus eight to fourteen weeks of home-exercises) and desensitization treatment was substituted. In the anxiety hierarchies, stress was placed on everyday talking situations such as talking with schoolfellows, parents, teachers, strangers, answering questions etc.

For three young children the shadowing technique was adapted into a play form. Using a puppet-show the child was told that we were going to teach him how to play with puppets. After a short training in puppet-movements, the therapist functioned as a prompter and the little stammerer as an actor who spoke for the puppet. "Scenes" were used at home, too, three times a week, and the parents were asked not to pay attention to stuttering moments. The results from this group are evaluated separately. All the treatment was provided on an out-patient basis.

Criteria for Evaluation

The main criterion of evaluation was the frequency of stammers and hesitations (= errors) during shadowing and natural talking. Additional information was obtained from a clinical evaluation of the patient's speech as judged by the following scheme.

0. No effect, i.e. some changes in stammering frequency, but stammering still frequent and speech still not fluent.
1. Little improved — frequency of stammers decreased after treatment but fluent speech was still absent.
2. Much improved — stammering disappeared from current speech; patient speaks fluently most of the time with occasional loss of fluency.

---

[1]The main characteristics of the procedure are the same as described formerly in Slovak (Kondaš, 1964).

3. Cured — speech is completely fluent; people cannot tell that the child was a stammerer (some slowness of speech may eventually appear).

The same scheme was used in the follow-up evaluation. All but four cases were assessed one to two months after the termination of treatment. In a follow-up evaluation five cases were assessed by the therapist, and the speech of the others was described by parents and by school-teachers. In all but one case the follow-up evaluation lasted over three years with five years as the maximal interval.

The average duration of the follow-up was 3.2 years; four cases were followed for five years, eight cases for from three to four years, four cases for two years, and the last case one year. The three young children (not included in Table 1) were followed for from one to four years.

RESULTS

Only one patient experienced difficulty in learning the shadowing method which was mastered quickly by most of the children. Mild cases (three to five stammers per minute) showed some improvement in talking within three weeks of shadowing practice. In nine cases, two months of practice was needed before improvements emerged but in five cases the duration of treatment was six to nine months. The frequency of therapeutic sessions was however decreased from once a week to once a fortnight or once every three weeks.

A reduction in stammering frequency during shadowing appears from the very beginning of practice. The difference in frequency of errors between the first and fifth session with shadowing are statistically significant ($p < 0.005$).

At the termination of therapy, or one month later, the frequency of stammers and hesitations decreased from 12.2 to 2.2. The difference is statistically significant ($t = 3.478$, $p < 0.005$). When considered individually, the decrement was observed in all but two cases. The eight subjects who also had the extra interview did not differ from the others, and nor did the desensitization subgroup.

The effects of the treatment according to the criterion of current talking fluency and the follow-up assessments are summarized in Table 1. For comparative purposes data on more intensive, in-patient treatment (daily remedial exercises in combination with drug-induced sleep therapy over the course of four weeks (Zahálková-Pavlová & Zima, 1956) are included in the Table.

The data in Table 1 show that seventy per cent of cases were successfully treated by the shadowing technique and subsidiary procedures. This is seventeen per cent more than the

Table 1. Comparison of treatment effects.

Group	Cured	Much improved	Combined %	Slightly improved	Un-improved	Combined %
Shadowing method ($n = 17$)						
(a) after therapy	9	3	70.6	3	2	29.4
(b) follow-up	8	2	58.8	2	5	41.2
Remedial and sleep therapy ($n = 41$)*						
(a) after therapy	7	15	53.7	19	—	46.3

*Follow-up evaluation was not given.

figure obtained with intensive in-patient remedial treatment combined with sleep therapy. Only "cured" and "much improved" cases are taken as successful. It should be mentioned that one of our unimproved cases was feeble-minded (IQ 58).

The follow-up evaluation shows that the successful effects of the treatment are markedly stable. Only one of the nine "cured" patients showed some slight relapse two years and five months after the end of the treatment. He ascribed it to an excessive fear of a class-teacher at technical school. In the "much improved" group, one case became worse ten months after treatment, and further treatment over the course of a month produced another temporary improvement. The case of the university student is interesting in one respect. He finished his studies, speaking fluently except when he drank wine – this was not considered to be a relapse. In the whole group relapses appeared in twelve per cent of cases, while Zahálková & Zima (1956) mentioned one relapse shortly after termination and three cases who relapsed while still in hospital.

The group of three young children treated by a modified form of shadowing were much improved or cured after only three to five sessions with the therapist and three to six weeks of home-exercises. Their speech was quite fluent and is unchanged after periods from one to three years post-treatment.

DISCUSSION AND CONCLUSIONS

Cherry & Sayers (1956) and other authors have studied the inhibition of stammering by the transference of auditory perceptions. Their work supports the hypothesis that stammering is related to delayed auditory feedback and that "the determining defects here involved are perceptual rather than motor." Shadowing and other techniques of auditory perceptual distraction were shown to have a positive effect on stammering. Cherry & Sayers suggested that some of their techniques might provide a means for treating stammering and the present data support their claim. The inhibition of stammering became evident in the course of the first few exercises. The transfer of speech fluency from the shadowing condition to the normal speech behavior follows somewhat later, and in this connection some problems arise.

From the learning standpoint, the speech-shadowing technique seems to represent a method of positive practice. The fluent speech which develops during shadowing is self-reinforced and fluent verbal behavior is thereby established. The transfer of fluent speech from shadowing to the conditions of natural talking still remains a serious problem because speech in the shadowing situation does not provide for the active formulation of proper sentences or the communicative character of speech. Another obstacle may arise from the patient's fear of some speech situations. Shadowing in the presence of another person, the training of regular breathing while reading and speaking, desensitization treatment and some negative practice, too, may be considered as helpful means for overcoming some of these problems and for ensuring successful transfer.

A fear of talking and the subsequent approach–avoidance conflict which may arise are well-known features of the secondary stammering. It is also known that the stammerer avoids words which have become cues for stammering or fluency failure. These cues probably play a role in the generalization of stammer errors and specific word cues of past disfluency may (according to Brutten & Gray, 1961) "elicit adjacent stuttering where it had not previously existed." In one of our previous cases who had had considerable word-cue-connected stammers even during shadowing practice, some special shadowing exercises were provided in Latin and this type of failure then disappeared (Kondaš, 1964, p. 162).

The durability of improved speech depends on the gradient of generalization, and on subsequent reinforcement of speech fluency by everyday events. Therefore, the fluency of current talking (and not of shadowing) was used as a criterion for terminating treatment. Shadowing-speech fluency was reflected in the decreasing frequency of exercises required. Home-exercises were, however, continued once a week during the month following the completion of the treatment. Under these arrangements the effect of the treatment seems to be satisfactory from the standpoint of its durability. The relapses were substantially less than under remedial education treatment. Although the critical interval for relapses is the first year after treatment they sometimes occur even later.

In Cherry & Sayer's (Eysenck, 1960) article, Marland included seven child stammerers among her case illustrations. Fifty-seven per cent of them were successfully treated. Our results (seventy per cent) are better.

Thus, the shadowing technique seems to be a useful form of treatment for stammering in children. The play-form modification of shadowing has proved to be a feasible, natural and successful method for very young children. The durability of the improvements achieved by the above procedures is considered to be one of the most important results of the present work. The results confirm Eysenck & Rachman's (1965) belief that "some method used in treating this condition in adults may prove more successful" in children than the reported attempts to overcome stuttering by desensitization.

REFERENCES

Brutten, E. J. & Gray, B. B. (1961) Effect of word cue removal on adaptation and adjacency: A clinical paradigm. *J. Speech Hearing Dis.* **26**, 385–389.

Case, H. W. (1960) Therapeutic methods in stuttering and speech blocking. In *Behaviour Therapy and the Neuroses*, (Ed. Eysenck, H. J.). Pergamon Press, Oxford.

Cherry, C. & Sayers, B. McA. (1956) Experiments upon the total inhibition of stammering by external control and some clinical results. *J. psychosom. Res.* **1**, 233–246. Reprinted in *Behaviour Therapy and the Neuroses*, (Ed. Eysenck, H. J.). Pergamon Press, Oxford (1960).

Chmelková, A. (1956) Skupinová terapie koktavosti (Group therapy of stammering). *Cs. Logopedie*, 202–203, Stat. Pedagog. Naklad., Praha.

Eysenck, H. J. (1960) *Behaviour Therapy and the Neuroses*. Pergamon Press, Oxford.

Eysenck, H. J. & Rachman, S. (1965) *The Causes and Cures of Neurosis*. Routledge & Kegan Paul, London.

Kondaš, O. (1964) Podiel ucenia v psychoterapii (*The Role of Learning in Psychotherapy*). Vyd. Slov. Akademie vied. Bratislava.

Kondaš, O. (1965) Princip interferencie v discentnej reedukacii balbuties a dyslexie (Principle of inter-ference in discent correction of stammering and reading disability). *Psychologica*, Sborn. FFUK, 57–68, Bratislava.

Maclaren, J. (1960) The treatment of a stammering by the Cherry-Sayers method: Clinical impressions. In *Behaviour Therapy and the Neuroses*, (Ed. Eysenck, H. J.), pp. 457–460. Pergamon Press, Oxford (1960).

Rachman, S. (1962) Learning theory and child psychology: Therapeutic possibilities. *J. Child Psychol. Psychiat.* **3**, 149–163. Reprinted in *Experiments in Behaviour Therapy*, (Ed. Eysenck, H. J.). Pergamon Press, Oxford (1964).

Walton, D. & Black, D. A. (1958) The application of learning theory to the treatment of stammering. *J. psychosom. Res.* **3**, 170–179. Reprinted in *Behaviour Therapy and the Neuroses*, (Ed. Eysenck, H. J.). Pergamon Press, Oxford (1960).

Zahálková-Pavlová, A. & Zima, J. (1956) Výsledky komplexní léčby spánken u koktavosti (Results of complex sleep therapy in stammering). *Cs. Logopedie*, 197–201. Stat. Pedagog. Naklad., Praha.

Cognitive Learning Development

A General Apparatus for the Investigation of Complex Learning in Children*

ARTHUR W. STAATS

Departments of Psychology and Educational Psychology, University of Hawaii, U.S.A.

Abstract: In a long term experimental project the author has been working with complex learning in children. One of the goals of the research has been the development of an apparatus and reinforcement procedure which is easy to construct and apply, is "generally" applicable to various types of complex learning, and which will maintain the participation and learning of children of various ages and types over long periods of time while engaged in arduous learning tasks. The apparatus which the author developed and tested has been used with normal children of various ages down to two years, with educable and trainable mental retardates, with children with emotional and behavior problems, with culturally deprived children. Reading, writing, number concept learning, concept formation, complex discrimination learning, and speech acquisition have been investigated using this type of apparatus.

INTRODUCTION

One of the paths of progress in an area of research involves the development of apparatus and procedures by which new types of objective data may be collected. Much early work on instrumental conditioning utilized various adaptations of the maze and the apparatus devised by Skinner for work with animals also represented a significant step forward. The latter apparatus offered a situation in which the dependent variable of the animal's behavior was easily obtained, and objective data produced. Furthermore, the dependent variable was sensitive to the manipulation of independent variables of various kinds.

The apparatus also was adaptable for the study of different types of behavior and different principles of learning. That is, it could be adapted for bar-pressing behavior in rats, key-pecking in pigeons, knob-pulling in primates, and so on. And, in addition to the principle of reinforcement, the principles involving discrimination learning, stimulus generalization, schedules, superstitious behavior, and so on, could also be objectively isolated and studied.

There is an implicit motivational aspect of animal research apparatus which is not easily reproduced with children, however, especially the very young or children with various behavioral difficulties. The participation and hard-working behaviors of the lab-animal may be guaranteed by deprivation operations, or by the use of aversive stimulation and negative reinforcement. Those procedures are undesirable with children. Thus, an apparatus and reinforcement procedure of similar generality, in which complex learning can be studied objectively over the long durations necessary is not derivable from the animal procedures. The straightforward presentation of edibles (especially candy) to children has been useful for some research and treatment purposes, but it is restricted. There is a limit to how much can be given to a child under ordinary conditions, with the parents' consent. Furthermore,

*Reprinted from *Behaviour Research and Therapy*, 1968, **6**, 45–50. Copyright 1968 with permission from Pergamon Press Publishing Company and Dr. A. W. Staats.

while edibles are effective over short periods, the production of comparable participation and cooperation is a problem in long-term research with children under such a reinforcement system.

The author has been working with complex (cognitive) learning in children for some time (*see* Staats, 1965; Staats, Finley, Minke & Wolf, 1964; Staats, Minke, Finley, Wolf & Brooks, 1964; Staats, Staats, Schutz & Wolf, 1962). One of the lines of progress of this research has been the development of an experimental situation within which children could be run in long-term research, involved in complex learning tasks, without deprivation or the use of aversive stimulation. A primary goal of this research has been the development of a simple, easy to apply, generally applicable, and effective apparatus and reinforcement system that will maintain good experimental behavior and voluntary participation with children, including those who are very young, over long periods of time while involved in arduous learning tasks. The apparatus has to be economical and easy to construct, and be capable of adaptation to the study of various types of learning with children of various age groups. Earlier laboratory procedures of the author (Staats *et al.*, 1962, 1964, 1964) lacked some of the necessary characteristics stated above, especially those of simplicity, ease and economy of construction, and generality of application.

The author has, however, designed and tested an apparatus that does fulfill the needs stated. This apparatus was developed in long-term research with the author's daughter beginning when she was two years of age. In this research, reading, writing, and number concept learning were studied. The apparatus and methods developed have since been applied by additional Es in working with other children, and the apparatus and findings are now being used in further replications and extensions, involving other experimenters and additional subjects. The apparatus and reinforcement procedures have functioned consistently well with various types of Ss, various experimenters, and various types of learning.

Since the apparatus and reinforcement procedures have such wide applicability in a variety of types of significant child learning, they will be described for general use.

APPARATUS

The apparatus can be constructed so that it has legs on it, or it can be constructed without legs and placed upon a table built for a child. The apparatus is schematized in Fig. 1.

In front of the child there is a shute, which is just below the window in which the stimuli are displayed. When the child makes a correct response a marble is delivered by the experimenter. The E simply takes a marble out of the container fixed to the back of the partition separating the E and the S, and drops the marble down the shute. The marble falls into the container below the shute.

The child then takes the marble and deposits it in one of five places. He can put it in the hole to the right and above the shute, in which case the marble drops into the container on the other side of the partition that holds the marbles for E. When the child does deposit a marble through that hole, the E will drop an item from the trinket-edible mixture down the shute and this constitutes one of the types of back-up reinforcers that establishes the marble as a token reinforcer. The trinket-edible mixture is composed of small plastic trinkets made by the Paul A. Price company as well as a mixture of edibles such as peanuts, raisins, and M and M candies.

Or, rather than depositing the marble in that manner, the child may place the marble into one of the four tubes to his left. The first tube holds ten marbles, the second thirty, the third eighty and the fourth 150. When a tube is full the child gets the toy hung above the tube, and the tube is emptied by the E into the marble container. The four tubes are fixed on a board

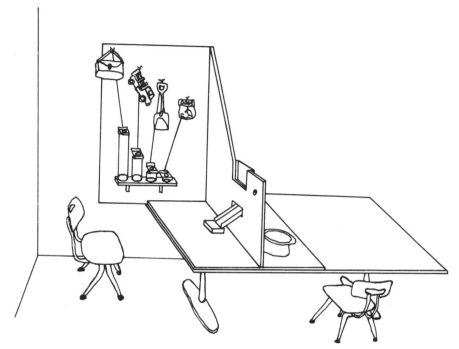

Fig. 1. The child learning apparatus.

that is on a track so that the board may be removed by the experimenter and a tube emptied when it is full. One further point here, there is a black line drawn from the top of the tube to the hook upon which the toy is hung for that tube.

In the procedure the child selects his toys before commencing the research training for that day. In working with preschool children the reinforcer system is best introduced to the children gradually, although with older children it can be explained in toto at the beginning. In the former case the child is first shown how to use the ten marble tube. A variety of toys of about a ten-cent value are used as back-up reinforcers. The child may simply be told, "Now we are going to play a learning game. Say jump." (In the present procedures the first part of the task is to have the child repeat words and sounds. However, any simple task would serve equally well.) After the child has made his response, E says, "You put your marble in this tube. When you have filled the tube with marbles, you will get this toy." At this point one of the toys the child has selected is hung above the tube. When the tube is filled E says, "You have filled the tube, so you have earned the toy." The toy is removed and presented to the child. Another toy is hung on the hook, the tube is emptied, and then the E produces a plastic bag, and shows the child how to put the toy in the plastic bag. All the back-up reinforcers earned are placed in the bag which removes them from the child's attention. One variation of the apparatus used a lidded box to hold the reinforcers.

After the child has participated in the training sessions for some time, has earned a number of ten-cent toys, and responds well to the basic procedures, he may be introduced to the trinket-edible mixture. Several trials where he is directed to place his marble in the hole are sufficient. Then he may be told that he can put the marble in the relevant hole and get trinkets and edibles, or he can use it to get the toys.

At a later time the child can be introduced in a like manner to the other tubes as it seems desirable to introduce more potent reinforcers. This apparatus and reinforcement procedure thus provide immediate and long-term variation, and an almost infinite variety of back-up reinforcers.

The present apparatus is constructed to have a window in front of the child in which five by eight inch cards can be placed. The stimuli to be presented to the child can be placed on the cards. The cards are simply slipped into the window which is slotted on both sides to hold the card. In addition, the stimuli can be shown directly to the child by placing them on the table in front of him. Writing and counting training have been presented to the child in this way.

ADAPTATIONS

Various degrees of mechanical and electronic sophistication can be used in adaptations of the basic apparatus and procedures. Counters can be mounted above the tubes to make the marble count precise and automatic. Furthermore, the stimuli can be presented to the child automatically. (Where it is desirable to retain the free operant characteristics of the apparatus, activation of a button by the child can be included as the event that dictates presentation of a stimulus.) Programming equipment could be used with this basic design. Memory drums could be used also. Furthermore, the response of the child can be automatically recorded in cases where the response involves the activation of a piece of equipment.

Automation of the stimulus presentation and the recording of the response (and the delivery of the toys) would make it possible to remove the experimenter from the situation. This is technically quite possible and has been approached in several of the author's studies even though complex tasks were involved (Staats *et al.*, 1964, 1964).

The simplest apparatus is depicted in the figure, however. The entire research operation can be handled by one experimenter. This only requires that the stimulus materials and presentation procedures be specified before hand, as well as the recording procedures. The E can devise data sheets for recording responses easily and well controlled experiments can then be conducted in which each stimulus presentation is recorded as well as each response. It is this simplicity that gives the basic apparatus its flexibility and generality of use.

EXPERIMENTAL APPLICATIONS

This section will be devoted to a brief mention of some of the types of research that can be conducted with this apparatus as well as some types of populations of children that can be investigated.

In the first use of the present type of apparatus the acquisition of reading responses to letters was studied as a type of discrimination learning (Staats *et al.*, 1964, 1964). It is suggested that the presently described apparatus would lend itself to the investigation of any kind of complex stimulus discrimination which requires many learning trials and long-term participation.

The author has also developed procedures for the study of the acquisition of an actual reading repertoire and has employed the apparatus and reinforcement procedure in this research (Staats, 1968). The same has been done with number concept learning and the acquisition of writing. With the apparatus it was possible to maintain the various children's voluntary participation over the long periods necessary to study the acquisition of these complex cognitive skills. For example, twelve four-year-old children participated in cognitive learning tasks over a period of eight months during which time they made thousands of responses and learned many skills. (The mean IQ of these children increased 11.6 points.)

As part of one study of letter reading discrimination learning in retarded children (Staats, in press), one mongoloid child who previously had no spontaneous language, although he would repeat a few words, was trained to name pictures. The apparatus could easily be applied to the study of speech development in pre-verbal children, or the study of further vocabulary acquisition in children who already speak. The apparatus could also be used in the study and treatment of speech problems.

The author had adapted the token-reinforcement procedure for work with children with learning problems (Staats & Butterfield, 1965; Staats, Minke, Goodwin & Landeen, 1967). This research with adolescent children has included subjects who were delinquent, retarded, or emotionally disturbed. Extensions to other deficits would be productive.

In addition, the apparatus would lend itself well to the study of more traditional areas of child learning. For example, paired associate and serial verbal learning could be studied in young children hitherto unavailable for such learning studies. Moreover, this use of the apparatus with children before they have acquired the extensive word associations of the adult, as well as various strategies of word learning, should enable verbal learning to be studied in a much more controlled manner, unconfounded by individual differences in word associations or strategies.

The same advantages would be available for investigating concept formation in children, as well as various types of complex stimulus discriminations. The author (Staats, 1966) has already studied the formation of "consonant" concepts where the consonant letter concept was presented in different consonant-vowel pairs and had to be abstracted in a manner analogous to Hull's (1920) original analysis of concept formation. In addition, the basic conditions of reinforcement may be studied through the use of this apparatus. Staats *et al.* (1964, 1964) have explored this possibility using the apparatus with various electronic adaptations. However, questions regarding the schedules best for long term learning of complex skills by young children are largely unanswered. Furthermore, interesting questions arise in the individual differences shown by the *S*s in their use of reinforcers. Rough data seems to suggest that younger children, and more retarded children, use the marbles for more immediate back-up reinforcers. This suggests that the extent to which longer term goals come to be effective is learned and this possibility could be studied using this apparatus.

Furthermore, the apparatus and procedures lend themselves to the study of various kinds of populations of children as has been implicit in some of the above examples. That is, the author has employed the apparatus and procedures with children ranging from two years of age through fourteen years of age. The learning of educable retarded children and trainable retarded children has also been investigated. It may be pointed out that the apparatus enables the study of *complex learning* with these children, such as language development, number concept learning, reading and so on. It is the long-term study of such complex skills that must be conducted to ascertain their potentialities and limitations in learning. The apparatus has also been employed with preschool culturally-deprived children, and with disturbed children who represent special learning problems.

CONCLUSIONS

The apparatus and reinforcement procedure, with adaptations in terms of type and kind of stimulus presentation and recording and type and kind of behaviors and recording, appears to enable the collection of objective data over long periods of time dealing with repertoires of varying degrees of complexity. It has the same advantages for children, and the study of complex learning, as the Skinner box has for animals and the study of simple learning.

REFERENCES

Hull, C. L. (1920) Quantitative aspects of the evolution of concepts. *Psychol. Monogr.* **123**.

Staats, A. W. (1965) A case in and a strategy for the extension of learning principles to problems of human behavior. In (Eds. Krasner, L. and Ullmann, L. P.) *Research in Behavior Modification New Developments and Implications*. Holt, Rinehart & Winston, New York.

Staats, A. W. (1966) An integrated-functional learning approach to complex human behavior. *Tech. Rep.* No. 28 between the Office of Naval Research and Arizona State University, 1965. Reprinted in large part *Problem Solving: Research, Method, and Theory* (Ed. Kleinmuntz, B). Wiley, New York.

Staats, A. W. (1968) *Learning, Language, and Cognition*. Holt, Rinehart & Winston, New York.

Staats, A. W. (1968) A general apparatus for the investigation of complex learning in children, *Behav. Res. & Therapy*, **6**, 45–50.

Staats, A. W. & Butterfield, W. (1965) Treatment of non-reading in a culturally-deprived juvenile delinquent: An application of learning principles. *Child Dev.* **36**, 925–942.

Staats, A. W., Finley, J. R., Minke, K. A. & Wolf, M. (1964) Reinforcement variables in the control of unit reading responses. *J. exp. Analysis Behav.* **7**, 139–149.

Staats, A. W., Minke, K. A., Finley, J. R., Wolf, M. & Brooks, L. O. (1964) A reinforcer system and experimental procedure for the laboratory study of reading acquisition. *Child Dev.* **35**, 209–231.

Staats, A. W., Minke, K. A., Goodwin, W. & Landeen, J. (1967) Cognitive behavior modification: 'Motivated Learning' Reading Treatment with Subprofessional Therapy—Technicians. *Behav. Res. & Therapy* **5**, Ms. 272.

Staats, A. W., Staats, C. K., Schutz, R. E. & Wolf, M. (1962) The conditioning of textual responses using "extrinsic" reinforcers. *J. exp. Analysis Behav.* **5**, 33–40.

Applying "Group" Contingencies to the Classroom Study Behavior of Preschool Children*†

DON BUSHELL, JR., PATRICIA ANN WROBEL, and MARY LOUISE MICHAELIS

University of Kansas and Webster College

Abstract: A group of twelve children were enrolled in a preschool class. During the first experimental stage they participated in special events contingent on token earning. Tokens were acquired by engaging in a variety of study behaviors. After a level of study behavior was established under this contingency, the special events were provided noncontingently. Study behavior declined throughout the noncontingent stage. Reestablishing the original contingencies produced in an immediate return to the initial level of study behavior. Noncontingent special events reduced the amount of independent study, group participation, and cooperative study. The study behavior of each child was altered in the same direction, though differences in the magnitude of effects from child to child were observed.

The experimental analysis of behavior has concentrated on the examination of responses emitted by a single subject. Recently, extensions of this research have begun to deal with groups of individuals. Behavioral research with adult psychiatric patients (Ayllon & Azrin, 1965), and retarded children (Birnbrauer, Wolf, Kidder, & Tague, 1965) has indicated that certain operant techniques can be applied effectively well beyond the "artificial" conditions of the experimentally isolated subject.

In most group situations it is not practical to programme individually special contingencies for the responses of each group member. Uniform criteria must be designed according to which a number of individuals are to be rewarded or punished. Schools, prisons, hospitals, business, and military organizations all maintain systems of response contingencies which are quite similar for all the individuals of a certain category within the organization. The objective of this research was to determine whether operant techniques may be applied to a group of individuals with effects similar to those expected when a single subject is under study. The specific behavior under analysis was the study behavior of a group of preschool children.

The dependent variables were behaviors such as attending quietly to instructions, working independently or in cooperation with others as appropriate, remaining with and attending to assigned tasks, and reciting after assignments had been completed. Counter examples are

*This study was carried out as part of the programme of the Webster College Student Behavior Laboratory, and preparation of the report was supported in part by the Institute for Sociological Research, The University of Washington. The authors gratefully acknowledge the able assistance of the observers who made this study possible: Alice Adcock, Sandra Albright, Sister Eleanor Marie Craig, S. L., Jim Felling, and Cleta Pouppart. We are particularly indebted to Donald M. Baer who encouraged us to commit this study to paper and subsequently gave thoughtful criticism to the manuscript. Reprints may be obtained from Don Bushell, Jr., Dept. of Human Development, University of Kansas, Lawrence, Kansas 66044.

†Reprinted from the *Journal of Applied Behavior Analysis*, 1968, **1**, 55–61. Copyright 1968 with permission from the Society for the Experimental Analysis of Behavior, Inc., and Don Bushell, Jr.

behaviors such as disrupting others who are at work, changing an activity before its completion, and engaging in "escape" behaviors such as trips to the bathroom or drinking fountain,
or gazing out the window. To the extent that the first constellation of behaviors is present and
the second is absent, a student might be classified as industrious, highly motivated, or conscientious; in short, he has good study habits.

METHOD

Children and Setting

The subjects were twelve children enrolled in a summer session. Three other children were
not considered in this report because they did not attend at least half of the sessions due to
illness and family vacations. Four of the twelve children were three years old, two were four
years old, five were five years old, and one was six years old. These ten girls and two boys
would be described as middle class; all had been enrolled in the preschool and preceding
spring semester, all scored above average on standardized intelligence tests, and all had
experienced some form of token system during the previous semester.

Classes were conducted from 12:45 to 3:30 p.m., five days a week for seven weeks. A large
room adjoining the classroom afforded one-way sight and sound monitoring of the class. The
programme was directed by two head teachers who were assisted for twenty-five minutes each
day by a specialist who conducted the Spanish lesson. All of the teachers were undergraduates.

Daily Programme

Data were collected in three phases during the first seventy-five minutes of each of the last
twenty class days of the summer session. During the first twenty minutes, individual activities
were made available to the children for independent study, and the amount of social interaction, student-student or student-teacher, was very slight. The next twenty-five minutes were
devoted to Spanish instruction. The interaction pattern during this period was much like that
of a typical classroom, with the teacher at the front of the assembled children sometimes
addressing a specific individual but more often talking to the entire group. The remaining
thirty minutes were given over to "study teams," with the children paired so the one more
skilled at a particular task would teach the less skilled. Composition of the groups and their
tasks varied from day to day according to the developing skills of the children.

Following this seventy-five minutes, a special event was made available to the children.
Special events included: a short movie, a trip to a nearby park, a local theater group rehearsal,
an art project, a story, or a gym class. The special event was always thirty minutes long and
was always conducted outside the regular classroom. The children were not told what the
activity would be for the day until immediately before it occurred.

Token Reinforcement

The tokens, colored plastic washers about 1.5 inches in diameter, served as a monetary
exchange unit within the classroom. As the children engaged in individual activities, Spanish,
and study teams, the teachers moved about the room giving tokens to those who appeared to
be actively working at their various tasks, but not to those who were not judged to be attending to the assignment at the moment.

To minimize unproductive talking about the tokens, the teachers avoided mentioning them.

Tokens were never given when requested. If a child presented a piece of work and then asked for a token, the request was ignored and additional work was provided if needed. Similarly, the presentation of tasks was never accompanied by any mention of tokens, such as, "If you do thus and so, I will give you a token." The tokens were simply given out as the children worked and, where possible, the presentation was accompanied by such verbal statements as "good," "you're doing fine, keep it up," "that's right," etc. The teachers avoided a set pattern in dispensing the tokens so that their approach would not become discriminative for studying. They would watch for appropriate behavior, move to that child, present a token and encouragement, then look for another instance not too nearby. During Spanish, the two teachers were able to present tokens for appropriate responding to the children who were assembled in front of the Spanish teacher. During study teams the teachers presented tokens as they circulated from group to group, and also at a checking session at the end of the period. Here, the student-learner recited what had been learned and both children were given tokens according to the performance of the learner. Each teacher distributed from 110 to 120 tokens during the seventy-five minutes.

The tokens could be used to purchase the special-event ticket. The price varied from twelve to twenty tokens around an average of fifteen each day so the children would not leave their study activities as soon as they acquired the necessary amount. Children who did not earn enough to purchase the special-event ticket remained in the classroom when the others left with the teachers. There were no recriminations or admonishments by either the teachers or the students, and the one or two children left behind typically found some toy or book to occupy themselves until the rest of the class returned. After the special event, additional activities enabled the children to earn tokens for a 3:00 p.m. snack of cookies, ice cream, milk, or lemonade, and a chair to sit on while eating. Tokens could be accumulated from day to day.

As tokens became more valuable, theft, borrowing, lending (sometimes at interest), hiring of services and a variety of other economic activities were observed. No attempt was made to control any of these except theft, which was eliminated simply by providing the children with aprons which had pockets for the tokens.

Observation and Recording Procedures

The four principal observers were seated in an observation room. Each wore earphones which enabled audio monitoring of the class and also prevented inter-observer communication. On a signal at the beginning of each five minute period, each observer looked for the first child listed on the roster and noted that child's behavior on the data sheet, then looked for the second child on the list and noted its behavior; and so on for each child. All observers were able to complete the total observational cycle in less than three minutes. During the seventy-five minutes of observation, the children's behavior was described by noting what the child was looking at, to whom he was talking, and what he was doing with his hands. Fourteen daily observations of each child by each observer produced 672 items of data each day.

Criteria were established by which each behavioral description on the data sheets could be coded as either "S," indicating study behavior, or "NS," indicating nonstudy behavior. Behaviors such as writing, putting a piece in a puzzle, reciting to a teacher, singing a Spanish song with the class, and tracing around a pattern with a pencil were classified as "S," if they were observed in the appropriate setting. Descriptions of behaviors such as counting tokens, putting away materials, walking around the room, drinking at the fountain, looking out the window, rolling on the floor and attending to another child, were classified as "NS." Singing a Spanish song was scored "S" if it occurred during the Spanish period when called for, but "NS" if it occurred during an earlier or later period. Similarly, if one child was interacting with another over instructional materials during the study teams period, the behavior was labeled "S," but the same behavior during another period was classified "NS".

If a given child's behavior was described fourteen times and eight of these descriptions were coded "S," then the amount of study time for that child was $\frac{8}{14}$ for that day. The amount of study behavior for the entire class on a given day was the sum of the twelve individual scores.

Time-Sampling Validity Check

Time-sampling assumes that, in a given situation, the behavior observed at fixed spacings in time adequately represents the behavior occurring during the total interval. To check the validity of this assumption, a fifth observer described the behavior of only three children much more frequently. At the beginning of each fifteen-second interval an automatic timing device beside the fifth observer emitted a click and flashed a small light. The observer then described the ongoing behavior of the first of the three target children of the day, noting essentially the child's looking, talking, and hand behaviors. The procedure was repeated for the second child, then the third. At the onset of the next fifteen-second interval, the sequence was repeated. The tape ran continuously. Consequently, during the same interval when the principal observers r ade fourteen observations, the fifth made slightly more than 300 observations of each of the three children. This procedure was used during nine of the twenty experimental sessions, and the three children chosen for this type of observation varied.

The data sheets completed by the four regular observers and the tapes recorded by the fifth observer were coded each day by the four principal observers who assigned either an "S" or "NS" to each description. Coding was accomplished independently by each observer without consulation. The fifth observer did not participate in classifying any of the tape descriptions.

Design

The study, a within-group design, consisted of three stages. During the first stage, participation in the special event was contingent upon the purchase of the necessary ticket with tokens. After nine days under these conditions, participation in the special event was made noncontingent. During the seven days of the noncontingent stage, the children were presented with special-event tickets and snack tickets as they arrived for school. Tokens and verbal statements of praise and encouragement were still given for the same behaviors as during the first phase, but the tokens no longer had any purchasing power. All the privileges of the classroom were available to every child regardless of how much or how little study behavior he or she displayed.

The decision to continue dispensing tokens but devalue them by providing everything free was made in order to retain all of the original procedures except the contingent special event. Had the tokens been given on a noncontingent basis at the beginning of each session, or eliminated entirely, this might have altered the behavior of the teachers toward the children throughout the remainder of the session.

After the sixteenth day of the study, the aprons containing the accumulated tokens were "sent to the cleaners" and all of the tokens were removed. As the children arrived the next day and asked where their tickets were, they were told they would have to buy them. When the children noted that they couldn't because they had no tokens, the teachers responded by saying: "Perhaps you can earn some. Your (activity – name) is over there." Thus, for the final four days, the last days of the summer session, the initial conditions were restored with

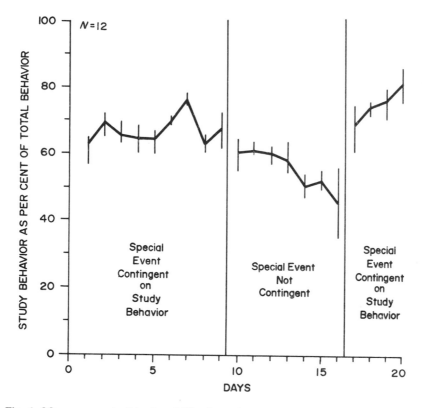

Fig. 1. Mean per cent of twelve children's study behavior over twenty school days. Vertical lines indicate the range of scores obtained by the four observers each day.

special-event and snack tickets again being made contingent upon tokens acquired by the students for study behavior.

RESULTS

Figure 1 shows that study behavior was influenced by whether or not the special event was contingent upon it. During the first nine-day stage, offering the special event contingent on study behavior resulted in an average score for the class as a whole of sixty-seven per cent. During the noncontingent stage, the observed study behavior declined twenty-five percentage points over seven days to a low of forty-two per cent. Restoring the original contingencies on Day 17 was associated with a twenty-two per cent increase in study behavior over that of the previous day.

Because the study behavior data were derived from observational measures, a number of checks were made to establish the reliability of the procedures. First, the total class score obtained by each observer for each day was compared to the scores of the other three observers. The vertical lines at each point in Fig. 1 describe the range of group scores obtained by the four observers each day. Inspection of these lines indicated that the same pattern was described even if the summary class score for any given day was drawn at random from the four available scores. Indeed, the data of any one, or any combination, of the four observers

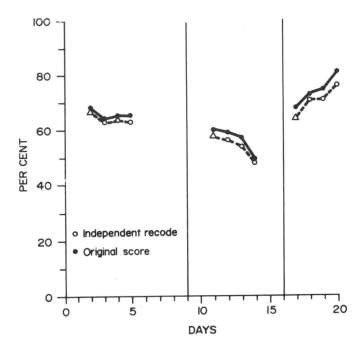

Fig. 2. Mean study behavior scores obtained by original observers compared with scores obtained by a panel of coders nine months after the completion of the study. △ indicates scores obtained by two of the original observers who recoded the original data sheets nine months after the completion of the study.

presented the same pattern with respect to the effects of contingent reinforcement upon study behavior.

The fact that the behavior descriptions of each day were coded within a few hours after they were obtained might have been an additional source of error. A description might have been coded "NS" on Day 15 and "S" on Day 19 simply because the observer expected study behavior to increase during the final contingent stage. To check for such effects, four new coders were empaneled nine months after the study was completed. These new coders had no knowledge of the details of the original investigation. They were trained to read behavioral descriptions like those appearing on the original data sheets and assign an "S" or "NS" to each according to the criteria outlined in the previous section. Once they agreed within five per cent on the independent scoring of a given data sheet, they were each given nine of the original sheets.

The data sheets given to the new coders were in scrambled order with all dates and other identifying marks obscured so they had no way of determining which stage a sheet came from even if they understood the significance of the experimental conditions. Sheets from Days 3, 4, 5, 12, 13, 14, 18, 19 and 20 (three from each stage) were recoded in this fashion. The procedure guaranteed that the expectations of the coder would not influence the scores obtained. The comparison of the original scores and those obtained by the new coders are shown in Fig. 2.

As a further check on coding bias, two of the original observers were recalled after a nine-month interval to recode one set of four data sheets from each of the three stages of the study, twelve sheets in all, also presented in random order. These two observers each recoded the

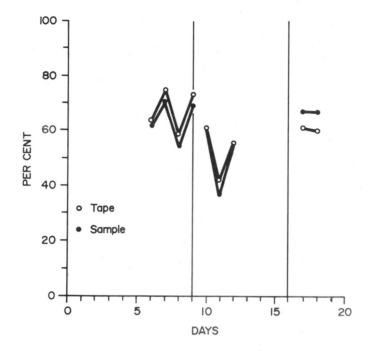

Fig. 3. Mean study behavior of various trios of children based on taped observations each day compared with written time-samples during the same period.

descriptions of one of the other observers and their own data sheets completed at the time of the original study. The results are also shown in Fig. 2 for Days 2, 11, and 17. These points, marked △, indicate that the results obtained by having the original observers recode their own and someone else's data do not differ from those obtained when newly trained coders score the original data. In all cases the scores obtained described the effects of contingent and non-contingent reinforcement in the same way.

The comparison of the total score for the three target children obtained by the regular method and the tapes is shown in Fig. 3 and supports the validity of the five-minute time-sampling technique.

The data describing the effects of the different contingencies upon each of the three instructional styles (individual activities, group instruction, teams), failed to demonstrate that this was an important dimension in the present study. Day-to-day variability was greater for these smaller periods than for the entire session, but in all cases the proportion of study behavior dropped similarly in the absence of the contingent special event and rose during the final four days.

Just as the day-to-day variability increased as the analysis moved from the whole class to periods within each day's class, individual study behavior was more variable than the aggregate data for all twelve children. It is to be expected that students of different age, sex, and educational background will perform differently in comparable settings, but all 12 records shown in Fig. 4 indicate that noncontingent reinforcement was less effective in sustaining study behavior than contingent reinforcement. There was no case in which an individual student displayed more study behavior during the second stage of the study than was displayed during the first and third stages.

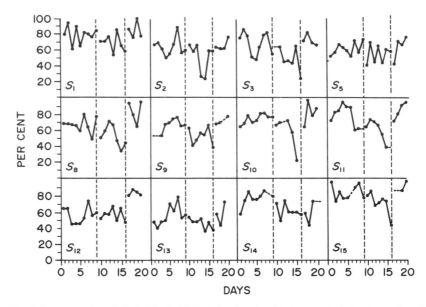

Fig. 4. Per cent of each individual child's behavior classified as study behavior under all conditions. Dotted lines without points indicate absence.

DISCUSSION

The results indicate that the contingent special event controlled much of the study behavior. In the time available it was not possible to continue the noncontingent stage until study behavior stabilized. With such an extension, study behavior might have gone lower.

A token system has much to recommend it from a practical standpoint, for there are many school activities (recess, early dismissal, extra-curricular events) which might be employed to develop and maintain higher levels of study behavior. Further, the classroom teacher responsible for the behavior of many students can manage a token system, but faces some difficulty in relying solely on verbal praise and attention as reinforcers. Behavior modification with social reinforcement requires constant monitoring of the subject's responding (Baer & Wolf, 1967). This can be done only on a very limited scale in a classroom by a single teacher.

The day-to-day variability in individual records requires further study. At first glance it would appear that the individual fluctuations could indict the smoother curve of the group as resulting from the canceling effect of numerous measurement errors at the individual level. However, the several measurement checks suggest that other factors may have been more important in explaining the variability. For example, the practice of allowing the children to accumulate tokens from day to day may have produced some variability. It allowed the children to work hard and lend one day, and loaf and borrow the next; work hard and save one day, loaf and spend their savings the next. This would tend to produce a smooth curve for the group, since not everyone could lend at the same time nor could all borrow at once. The present practice in the preschool is to remove all tokens from the children's pockets after each day's session.

The next approximation toward a useful classroom observational technique will require additional measures to determine the effects of the students' changing behavior on the attending and helping behavior of the teachers. This work is now in progress.

It may be concluded that: (1) practical reinforcement contingencies can be established in a classroom; (2) the effects of various contingencies can be ascertained by direct observational techniques where the use of automated recording equipment is not practicable.

REFERENCES

Ayllon, T. & Azrin, N. H. The measurement and reinforcement of behavior of psychotics. *Journal of the Experimental Analysis of Behavior*, 1965, **8**, 357–383.

Baer, D. M. & Wolf, M. M. The reinforcement contingency in preschool and remedial education. In Robert D. Hess and Roberta Meyer Baer (Eds.), *Early education: Current theory, research, and practice*. Chicago: Aldine, 1968, pp. 119–129.

Birnbrauer, J. S., Wolf, M. M., Kidder, J. D., & Tague, C. E. Classroom behavior of retarded pupils with token reinforcement. *Journal of Experimental Child Psychology*, 1965, **2**, 219–235.

Effects of Teacher Attention on
Study Behavior*†

R. VANCE HALL, DIANE LUND, and DELORIS JACKSON

University of Kansas

Abstract: The effects of contingent teacher attention on study behavior were investigated. Individual rates of study were recorded for one first-grade and five third-grade pupils who had high rates of disruptive or dawdling behavior. A reinforcement period (in which teacher attention followed study behavior and non-study behaviors were ignored) resulted in sharply increased study rates. A brief reversal of the contingency (attention occurred only after periods of non-study behavior) again produced low rates of study. Reinstatement of teacher attention as reinforcement for study once again markedly increased study behavior. Follow-up observations indicated that the higher study rates were maintained after the formal programme terminated.

A series of studies carried out in preschools by Harris, Wolf & Baer (1964) and their colleagues demonstrated the effectiveness of contingent teacher attention in modifying behavior problems of preschool children. In these studies inappropriate and/or undesirable rates of isolate play (Allen, Hart, Buell, Harris & Wolf, 1964), crying (Hart, Allen, Buell, Harris & Wolf, 1964), crawling (Harris, Johnston, Kelley & Wolf, 1964), and a number of other problem behaviors were modified by systematically manipulating teacher-attention consequences of the behaviors. Similarly, teacher and peer attention were manipulated by Zimmerman & Zimmerman (1962), Patterson (1966), and Hall & Broden (1967) to reduce problem behaviors and increase appropriate responses of children enrolled in special classrooms.

To date, however, there has been little systematic research in the application of social reinforcement by teachers in the regular school classroom beyond the successful case studies reported by Becker, Madsen, Arnold & Thomas (1967) in which no attempt was made to evaluate the reliability of these procedures through experimental reversals.

The present studies analyzed experimentally the reliability with which teachers could modify the study behavior of children of poverty-area classrooms by systematic manipulation of contingent attention.

*The authors wish to express appreciation to Dr. O. L. Plucker, Ted Gray, Alonzo Plough, Clarence Glasse, Carl Bruce, Natalie Barge, Lawrence Franklin, and Audrey Jackson of the Kansas City, Kansas Public Schools and Wallace Henning, University of Kansas, without whose cooperation and active participation these studies would not have been possible. Special tribute is due to Dr. Montrose M. Wolf and Dr. Todd R. Risley for their many contributions in developing research strategy and for their continuing encouragement. We are also indebted to Dr. R. L. Schiefelbusch, Director of the Bureau of Child Research, and administrative director of the project, who provided essential administrative support and counsel. Reprints may be obtained from R. Vance Hall, 2021 North Third St., Kansas City, Kansas 66101.

†Reprinted from the *Journal of Applied Behavior Analysis*, 1968, **1**, 1, 1–12. Copyright 1968 with permission from the Society for the Experimental Analysis of Behavior, Inc., and Dr. R. Vance Hall.

GENERAL PROCEDURES

Subjects and Setting

The studies were carried out in classrooms of two elementary schools located in the most economically deprived area of Kansas City, Kansas[1]. Teachers who participated were recommended by their principals. The teachers nominated pupils who were disruptive or dawdled. They were told that one or two observers would come regularly to their classrooms to record behavior rates of these pupils.

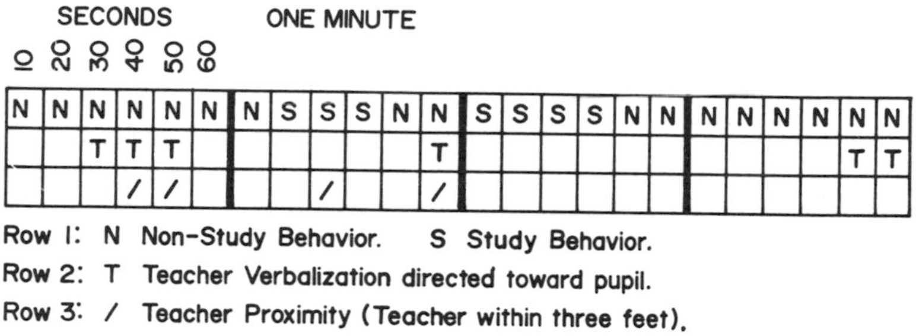

SECONDS   ONE MINUTE

10 20 30 40 50 60

N	N	N	N	N	N	N	S	S	S	N	N	S	S	S	S	N	N	N	N	N	N	N	N
	T	T	T								T											T	T
		/	/			/			/														

Row I: N   Non-Study Behavior.   S   Study Behavior.
Row 2:   T   Teacher Verbalization directed toward pupil.
Row 3:   /   Teacher Proximity (Teacher within three feet).

Fig. 1. Observer recording sheet and symbol key.

Observation

The observers used recording sheets lined with triple rows of squares, as shown in Fig. 1. Each square represented an interval of ten seconds. The first row was used to record the behavior of the student. (The definition of study behavior was somewhat different for each student and depended on the subject matter taught. Generally, study behavior was defined as orientation toward the appropriate object or person: assigned course materials, lecturing teacher, or reciting classmates, as well as class participation by the student when requested by the teacher. Since each pupil was observed during the same class period, however, the response definition was consistent for each student throughout the course of an experiment.) Teacher verbalizations to the student were recorded in the second row. The third row was used to record occasions when the teacher was within a three-foot proximity to the student.

These observations were made during each ten-second interval of each session. The observers sat at the rear or the side of the classroom, and avoided eye contact or any other interaction with pupils during observation sessions.

Inter-observer agreement was analyzed by having a second observer periodically make a simultaneous observation record. Agreement of the two records was checked interval by interval. The percentage of agreement of the records [# agreements × 100 ÷ (# agreements + # disagreements)] yielded the percentage of inter-observer agreement.

[1]The research was carried out as part of the Juniper Gardens Children's Project, a programme of research on the development of culturally deprived children and was partially supported by the Office of Economic Opportunity: (OEO KAN CAP 694/1, Bureau of Child Research, Kansas University Medical Center) and the National Institute of Child Health and Human Development: (HD-00870-(04) and HD 03144-01, Bureau of Child Research, University of Kansas).

EXPERIMENTAL CONDITIONS

Baseline

Rates of study were obtained for the selected pupils. Thirty-minute observations were scheduled at a time each day when the pupils were to be working in their seats. In most cases observations were made two to four times per week. After obtaining a minimum of two weeks of baseline, the students' study rates were presented graphically to the teachers. Then, selected studies (Hart *et al.*, 1964; Allen *et al.*, 1964; Hall & Broden, 1967) were presented to the teachers, the fundamentals of social reinforcement were discussed, and a pupil was selected for systematic study.

Reinforcement$_1$

During reinforcement sessions the observer held up a small square of colored paper in a manner not likely to be noticed by the pupil whenever the pupil was engaged in study. Upon this signal, the teacher attended to the child, moved to his desk, made some verbal comment, gave him a pat on the shoulder, or the like. During weekly after-school sessions, experimenters and teachers discussed the rate of study achieved by the pupil and the effectiveness of attention provided by the teacher, and made occasional adjustments in instructions as required.

Reversal

When a satisfactory rate of study had been achieved, the observer discontinued signaling and (as much as possible) the teacher returned to her former pattern, which typically consisted of attending to non-study behavior.

Reinforcement$_2$

When the effect of the reversal condition had been observed, social reinforcement of study was reinstituted. When high study rates were achieved again, the teacher continued reinforcement of study behavior without the observer's signals.

Post Checks

Whenever possible, periodic post-checks were made through the remainder of the year to determine whether the new levels of study were being maintained.

Correlated Behavioral Changes

Where possible, other behavioral changes, including teacher reports, grades, and other records of academic achievement were recorded. Because such data are difficult to evaluate their importance should not be unduly stressed.

INDIVIDUAL EXPERIMENTS

Robbie

Robbie was chosen because he was considered a particularly disruptive pupil who studied very little. Figure 2 presents a record of Robbie's study behavior, defined as having pencil on paper during five seconds or more of the ten-second interval. During baseline, study behavior occurred in twenty-five per cent of the intervals observed during the class spelling period. The behaviors which occupied the other seventy-five per cent of his time included snapping rubber bands, playing with toys from his pocket, talking and laughing with peers, slowly drinking the half-pint of milk served earlier in the morning, and subsequently playing with the empty carton.

During the baseline period the teacher would often urge Robbie to work, put his milk carton away, etc. In fact, fifty-five per cent of the teacher attention he received followed non-study behavior. Robbie engaged in continuous study for sixty seconds or more only two or three times during a thirty-minute observation.

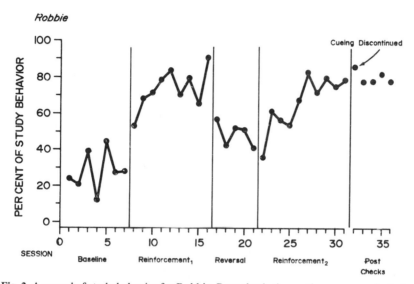

Fig. 2. A record of study behavior for Robbie. Post-check observations were made during the fourth, sixth, seventh, twelfth, and fourteenth weeks after the completion of Reinforcement₂ condition.

Following baseline determination, whenever Robbie had engaged in one minute of continuous study the observer signaled his teacher. On this cue, the teacher approached Robbie, saying, "Very good work Robbie," "I see you are studying," or some similar remark. She discontinued giving attention for non-study behaviors including those which were disruptive to the class.

Figure 2 shows an increased study rate during the first day of the first reinforcement period. The study rate continued to rise thereafter and was recorded in seventy-one per cent of the intervals during this period.

During the brief reversal period, when reinforcement of study was discontinued, the study rate dropped to a mean of fifty per cent. However, when reinforcement for study was reinstituted, Robbie's study rate again increased, stabilizing at a rate ranging between seventy per cent and eighty per cent of the observation sessions. Subsequent follow-up checks made during the fourteen weeks that followed (after signaling of the teacher was discontinued) indicated that study was being maintained at a mean rate of seventy-nine per cent. Periodic checks made during each condition of the experiment revealed that agreement of observation ranged from eighty-nine per cent to ninety-three per cent.

Robbie's teacher reported behavior changes correlated with his increased rate of study. During Baseline, she reported that Robbie did not complete written assignments. He missed two of ten, five of ten, and six of ten words on three spelling tests given during Baseline. By the final week of Reinforcement$_2$, she reported that he typically finished his initial assignment and then continued on to other assigned work without prompting. Disruptive behavior had diminished and it was noted that he continued to study while he drank his milk and did not play with the carton when finished. He missed one of ten words on his weekly spelling test.

Rose

Rose was a classmate of Robbie. Baseline observations were made during the math and/or spelling study periods. The mean rate of study during Baseline was thirty per cent, fluctuating

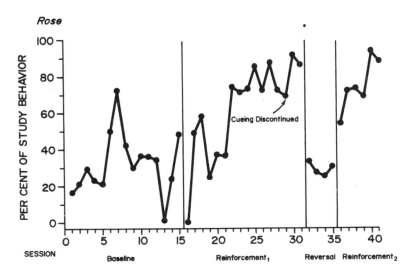

Fig. 3. A record of study behavior for Rose.

from zero to seventy-one per cent. Her non-study behaviors included laying her head on the desk, taking off her shoes, talking, and being out of her seat.

On the day her teacher was first to reinforce Rose's study behavior, Rose did not study at all, and the teacher was thus unable to provide reinforcement. Therefore, beginning with the second reinforcement session, the teacher attended to behavior that approximated study (e.g., getting out pencil or paper, or opening her book to the correct page). Once these behaviors were reinforced, study behavior quickly followed, was in turn reinforced, and had risen to fifty-seven per cent by the third reinforcement session.

During the fourth session, however, study dropped to twenty-five per cent. An analysis of the data indicated Rose had increased in out-of-seat behavior, to have her papers checked and to ask questions. Consequently her teacher thereafter ignored Rose when she approached but attended to her immediately if she raised her hand while seated. There was an immediate drop in out-of-seat behavior and a concurrent increase in study behavior. As can be seen in Fig. 3, during the last ten sessions of Reinforcement$_1$, study behavior ranged between seventy-four per cent and ninety-two per cent, the mean rate for the entire period being approximately seventy-one per cent. A high rate of study was maintained after the observer discontinued signaling after the thirteenth reinforcement session.

During the four reversal sessions, study was recorded in only twenty-nine per cent of the intervals. However, a return to attention for study immediately increased study behavior and during the second reinforcement period study was recorded in seventy-two per cent of the observed intervals. Observer agreement measured under each condition ranged from ninety per cent to ninety-five per cent.

An analysis of the attention provided Rose by her teacher demonstrated that it was not the amount of attention, but its delivery contingent on study which produced the changes in

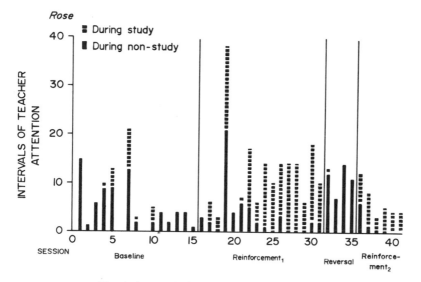

Fig. 4. A record of teacher attention for Rose.

this behavior. Figure 4 shows these amounts, and the general lack of relationship between amount of attention and experimental procedures.

In fact these data show that when teacher attention occurred primarily during non-study intervals there was a low rate of study. When teacher attention occurred primarily during study intervals there was a higher rate of study. Figure 4 also shows that the mean rate of total teacher attention remained relatively stable throughout the various experimental phases, rising somewhat in the Reinforcement₁ and Reversal phases and declining to baseline levels in the Reinforcement₂ phase.

Rose's grades at the end of the baseline phase were D in arithmetic and D in spelling. Her grades for the reinforcement phase of the experiment were C— in arithmetic and B in spelling.

Ken

Ken was one of the other forty-one pupils in Rose's class. He had a wide range of disruptive behaviors including playing with toys from his pockets, rolling pencils on the floor and desk, and jiggling and wiggling in his seat. His teacher had tried isolating him from his peers, reprimanding by the principal, and spanking to control his behavior. These efforts apparently had been ineffective. Study behavior ranged from ten per cent to sixty per cent, with a mean rate of thirty-seven per cent, as seen in Fig. 5.

Reinforcement of study behavior was begun at the same time for both Ken and Rose. The observer used different colored cards to signal when the behavior of each pupil was to be reinforced. Ken's study increased to a mean rate of seventy-one per cent under reinforcement conditions. However, during his brief reversal, Ken's rate of study was again about thirty-seven per cent. The re-introduction of the reinforcement for study recovered study behavior in seventy per cent of the observed intervals. Agreement between observers measured during each of the conditions ranged from ninety per cent to ninety-two per cent.

Ken's teacher reported several correlated behavior changes. Before the experiment she had stated that he rarely, if ever, finished an assignment. His grades for the baseline period included D in math, D in spelling and U (unsatisfactory) in conduct. After reinforcement was instituted his teacher reported a marked decrease in disruptive behavior and stated, "He's

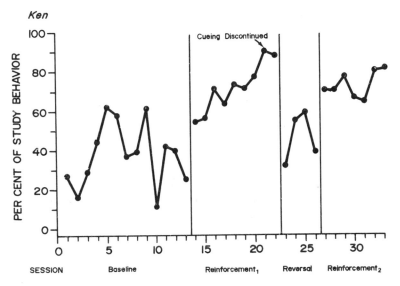

Fig. 5. A record of study behavior for Ken.

getting his work done on time now." Ken's report card grades subsequently were C in spelling, C in arithmetic and S (satisfactory) in conduct.

Gary

Gary, a third-grade boy in another classroom of thirty-nine pupils was chosen as a subject because he failed to complete assignments. The course of Gary's programme is shown in Fig. 6. Observations made during the thirty-minute morning math period indicated that Gary engaged in study during forty-three per cent of the ten-second intervals observed. Non-study behaviors included beating his desk with a pencil, chewing and licking pages of books, moving his chair back and forth in unison with a classmate, banging his chair on the floor, blowing bubbles, and making noises while drinking his milk, and punching holes in the carton so that milk flowed onto the desk. He would also gaze out the window or around the room and would say "This is too hard," "Shoot, I can't do this," and "How did you say to work it?"

Gary had been observed to engage in appropriate study for sixty seconds or more at least one to three times during most study periods. The observer thus signaled the teacher whenever

Gary had engaged in study for six consecutive ten-second intervals, and he was attended to by the teacher only on those occasions.

As shown in Fig. 6, reinforcement produced a marked increase in studying. With the rise, almost all disruptive behavior disappeared. He still talked out of turn in class but typically to say "I know how to do it," "He's wrong," "Can I do it, teacher?," "Oh, this is easy." Gary engaged in study during approximately seventy-seven per cent of the ten-second intervals observed during Reinforcement₁.

After the twentieth session a reversal was programmed, and the teacher was signaled whenever Gary engaged in non-study behavior for thirty seconds. When this occurred, the teacher gave Gary a reminder to get back to work. No attention was given for study behavior.

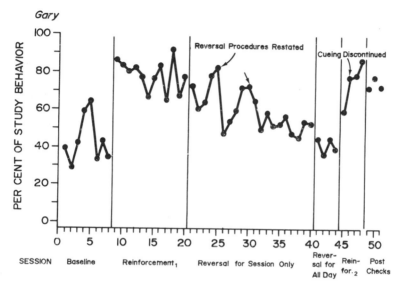

Fig. 6. A record of study behavior for Gary. Post-check observations were made during the first, fourth, and tenth weeks after completion of Reinforcement₂ condition.

As can be seen, this resulted in a fluctuating but declining rate of study during the thirty-minute math period. At this point it was noted that Gary's rate of study was again rising, and that the teacher was in fact providing intermittent reinforcement for study. Therefore, on two occasions the procedures for reversal were gone over once again in conference with the teacher and a subsequent slow but steady decline in study rate was achieved. There also appeared to be an increase in disruptive behavior. The mean rate of study at this point of Reversal was about sixty per cent.

It was then noted that a more rapid reversal effect had been brought about in the previous studies, probably because that teacher had carried out reversal procedures for the entire day whereas Gary's teacher practiced reversal only during the thirty-minute observation period. Reversal of reinforcement conditions was, therefore, extended to the entire day. The mean rate for these sessions was approximately forty-two per cent. However, resumption of reinforcement immediately recovered a study rate of sixty per cent which increased as reinforcement continued. After the first day of this reinforcement phase the teacher expressed confidence in being able to work without cues from the observer. Signaling was therefore discontinued without loss of effect. Periodic checks made during subsequent weeks indicated study behavior was being maintained at a level higher than seventy per cent. The reliability of observation measured during each condition ranged from ninety-two per cent to ninety-six per cent.

Joan

Joan, one of Gary's classmates, did not disrupt the class or bother other pupils but was selected because she dawdled. Typically, during arithmetic study period, she would lay her head on her desk and stare toward the windows or her classmates. At other times she would pull at or straighten her clothing, dig in her desk, pick or pull at her hair, nose or fingernails, draw on the desk top or play with her purse. During baseline her study rate was approximately thirty-five per cent.

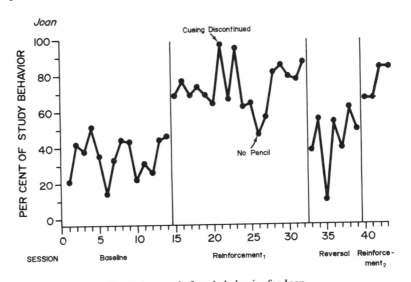

Fig. 7. A record of study behavior for Joan.

During the Reinforcement₁ phase, after the observer signaled that sixty seconds of continuous study had occurred, the teacher made comments such as, "That's a good girl," and often tugged lightly at Joan's hair or patted her shoulder. As can be seen in Fig. 7 this resulted in an immediate increase in study behavior. The observer discontinued signaling after Session 20 when the teacher stated it was no longer necessary. Though the study rate fluctuated in subsequent sessions it generally remained higher than in Baseline. The lowest rate of study came in Session 26 when Joan was without a pencil through the first part of the session. Study was observed in seventy-three per cent of the intervals of the Reinforcement₁ phase.

During the Reversal, Joan's study rate declined markedly and play with clothes, pencils, and head on desk behaviors appeared to increase. The mean study rate for the reversal sessions was approximately forty-three per cent. Reinstatement of reinforcement for study, however, resulted in a rapid return to a study rate of approximately seventy-three per cent. No post-checks were obtained because of the close of school. Observer agreement ranged from ninety-three per cent to ninety-seven per cent.

Joan's arithmetic-paper grades provided interesting correlated data. During Baseline a sampling of her arithmetic papers showed an average grade of F. During Reinforcement₁ they averaged C. All her arithmetic papers graded during Reversal were graded F. In Reinforcement₂ the average grade on arithmetic papers was C−.

Levi

Levi was a first-grade boy who was selected because of his disruptive behaviors. Although he achieved at a fairly high level, he often disturbed the class by making loud noises, by getting out of his seat, and by talking to other students. The school counselor suggested using reinforcement techniques after counselling with the pupil and teacher brought about no apparent improvement in Levi's behavior.

The counselor was trained in the observation procedures and he obtained baseline rates of Levi's study and disruptive behaviors during seatwork time. A second observer was used to supplement data gathering. During Baseline, Levi's rate of study was approximately sixty-eight per cent, ranging from thirty-four per cent to seventy-nine per cent. An analysis of

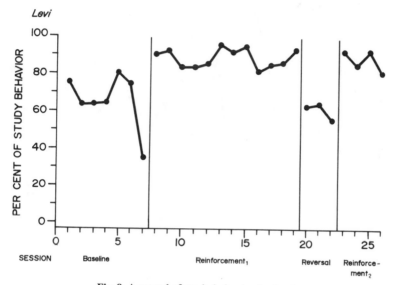

Fig. 8. A record of study behavior for Levi.

teacher attention during baseline showed that although Levi had a relatively high rate of study, he received almost no teacher attention except when he was disruptive (i.e., made noise or other behaviors which overtly disturbed his neighbors and/or the teacher).

During Reinforcement₁ the teacher provided social reinforcement for study and, as much as possible, ignored all disruptive behavior. No signals were used since Levi had a relatively high study rate and the teacher was confident she could carry out reinforcement without cues. Figure 8 shows that study occurred in approximately eighty-eight per cent of the intervals of Reinforcement₁ and at no time went below that of the highest baseline rate. A brief reversal produced a marked decrease in study to a mean rate of sixty per cent. However, when reinforcement for study was reinstated study again rose to above the baseline rate (approximately eighty-five per cent).

Figure 9 presents the disruptive behavior data for the four periods of the experiment. Disruptive behavior was defined to occur when Levi made noises, got out of his seat or talked to other students and the response appeared to be noticed by the teacher or another student. During Baseline the mean rate of disruptive behavior was seven per cent. During Reinforcement₁ the mean rate declined to 2.2 per cent. During the brief Reversal phase the mean rate rose to 3.2 per cent. In Reinforcement₂ the rate declined to an almost negligible 0.25 per cent.

No follow-up data were obtained because of the close of the school year. Observer agreement measured under each condition was consistently over eighty per cent.

The teacher and the school counselor reported at the conclusion of the experiment that in their opinion Levi was no longer a disruptive pupil.

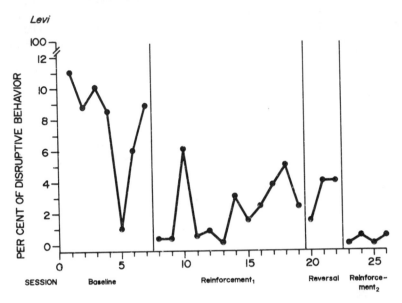

Fig. 9. A record of disruptive behavior for Levi.

DISCUSSION

These studies indicate clearly that the contingent use of teacher attention can be a quick and effective means of developing desirable classroom behavior. Effective teachers have long known that casually praising desired behaviors and generally ignoring disruptive ones can be useful procedures for helping maintain good classroom discipline. What may appear surprising to school personnel, however, is the degree to which student behavior responds to thoroughly systematic teacher attention.

One purpose of these studies was to determine whether the procedures could be carried out by teachers in public school classrooms. Although these teachers were initially unfamiliar with reinforcement principles and had had no prior experience with the procedures, they were clearly able to carry them out with important effect. The fact that they were carried out in crowded classrooms of schools of an urban poverty area underscores this point. In such areas one would expect a high incidence of disruptive behaviors and low interest in academic achievement, conditions generally conceded to make teaching and motivation for study difficult. Yet, with relatively slight adjustment of the social environment, it was possible to increase rates of study with comparative ease.

The teachers in these studies did not have poor general control of their classrooms. Most of their pupils seemed to apply themselves fairly well, although a few did not. When their baseline data were analyzed, it became clear that these pupils were in effect being motivated not to study. It became apparent that for these pupils, most teacher attention was received during non-study intervals rather than when they were studying. This was not surprising since many of the non-study behaviors were disruptive and thus seemed to the teacher to require some reprimand.

Several aspects of the teacher training programme appear worthy of mention. During baseline, as far as the teacher was concerned, the primary purpose was to determine study rates. After baseline, a simple procedure designed to increase those study rates was emphasized (rather than the fact that the teacher had in all probability been reinforcing the very behaviors which were causing concern).

The teacher was constantly informed of the results of each day's sessions and its graphed outcome. These daily contacts, plus weekly conferences in which the procedures were discussed and the teacher was praised for bringing about the desired behavioral changes, may have been central to the process of a successful study.

The teachers readily accepted the advisability of carrying out a brief reversal when it was presented as a means of testing for a causal relationship between teacher attention and pupil behavior. All, however, felt reversal sessions were aversive and were glad when they were terminated.

These procedures did not seem to interfere greatly with ongoing teaching duties. For one thing they did not necessarily result in more total teacher attention for a pupil. In fact, the teachers had more time for constructive teaching of all pupils because of the decrease in disruptive behaviors in the classroom.

Two teachers reported they were able to utilize systematic attention to increase appropriate study of other pupils in their classrooms who were not included in these studies. No corroborative data were collected to verify their reports. Investigation of the degree to which this kind of generalization occurs should be a goal of further research, however, since such a result would be highly desirable.

In the first five subjects, cueing of the teacher was initially used to make certain that the teacher could discriminate when study behavior was occurring. Later, cueing was discontinued without loss of effectiveness. In the case of Levi, cueing was never used. Further research will be needed to determine how often cueing contributes to the efficiency of the procedures.

In one classroom, a teacher was unable to carry out the procedures in spite of the fact that the same orientation and training processes were used which had previously proved successful. Although the teacher seemed sincere in her efforts to reinforce study, she observably continued to give a high rate of attention for non-study behaviors. Observations indicated that the teacher gave almost no praise or positive attention to any member of the class. Virtually her entire verbal repertoire consisted of commands, reprimands, and admonitions. Consequently, the teacher was instructed to provide positive verbal reinforcement for appropriate behavior of all class members. This did result in a measureable increase in the number of positive statements made to individuals and to the class. According to both the teacher and the observers, this greatly improved general classroom behavior. Only slight increases in study were recorded for the two pupils for whom data were available, however, and the close of the school year prevented further manipulations.

This failure prompted the authors to begin developing a system for recording appropriate behavior rates for an entire class. It also indicates that there may be certain teachers who need different or more intensive training to carry out these procedures effectively.

Finally, it should be noted that the pupils of this study did have at least a minimal level of proficiency in performing the academic tasks and thus seemed to profit from the increased time they spent in study. The teachers apparently assigned study tasks within the range of the pupils' skills, and correlated gains in academic achievement were noted. If teachers were to use the procedures but failed to provide materials within the range of the pupils' level of skill, it is unlikely that much gain in achievement would result.

REFERENCES

Allen, K. E., Hart, B. M., Buell, J. S., Harris, F. R. & Wolf, M. M. Effects of social reinforcement on isolate behavior of a nursery school child. *Child Development*, 1964, 35, 511–518.

Becker, W. C., Madsen, C. H., Jr., Arnold, R. & Thomas, D. R. The contingent use of teacher attention and praise in reducing classroom behavior problems. *Journal of Special Education*, 1967, 1, 287–307.

Hall, R. V. & Broden, M. Behavior changes in brain-injured children through social reinforcement. *Journal of Experimental Child Psychology*, 1967, 5, 463–479.

Harris, F. R., Johnston, M. K., Kelley, C. S. & Wolf, M. M. Effects of positive social reinforcement on regressed crawling of a nursery school child. *Journal of Educational Psychology*, 1964, 55, 35–41.

Harris, F. R., Wolf, M. M. & Baer, D. M. Effects of adult social reinforcement on child behavior. *Young Children*, 1964, 20, 8–17.

Hart, Betty M., Allen, K. Eileen, Buell, Joan S., Harris, Florence R. & Wolf, M. M. Effects of social reinforcement on operant crying. *Journal of Experimental Child Psychology*, 1964, 1, 145–153.

Patterson, G. R. An application of conditioning techniques to the control of a hyperactive child, Ullmann, L. P., and Krasner, L. (Eds.), *Case studies in behavior modification*, New York: Holt, Rinehart & Winston, Inc., 1966. pp. 370–375.

Zimmerman, Elaine H. & Zimmerman, J. The alteration of behavior in a special classroom situation. *Journal of the Experimental Analysis of Behavior*, 1962, 5, 59–60.

Alleviation of Reading Difficulties by a Simple Operant Conditioning Technique*

D. W. McKERRACHER

Associate Professor, Department of Psychology, University of Calgary, Calgary, Alberta

Abstract: A boy suffering from anxiety, lack of self-confidence, enuresis, and stammering, showed a marked reading disability. Three months of remedial teaching and supportive therapy in a child guidance clinic failed to make much alteration in his progress. An operant conditioning procedure was then utilized, and resulted in an almost immediate improvement in his reading age. He also reported being less upset in the classroom when asked to read. His stammer became less noticeable on those occasions. However, his general anxiety level, enuresis, and stammering during ordinary conversation, did not change appreciably. Reward conditioning alone seemed to be as effective in improving his reading age as the dual technique combining reward and avoidance conditioning.

A multiplicity of reasons lie behind the difficulties encountered by many children of average intelligence in developing the reading habit. In some, there may be minor organic anomalies, or slowness in maturation, to explain the inefficient and distorted recognition of visual symbols (Worster-Drought, 1965). In others, behavior disorders may be accompanied by general educational retardation, including reading disability (Stott, 1956). In a large number of timid, unassertive children, there are emotional components of a traumatic nature, embedded in the sentiment structures of the child, which undermine the motivation to learn, and engender feelings of anxiety, tension, and lack of self-confidence (Burt, 1937). When faced with any situation outside his previous experience, a sensitive child with emotional problems is greatly handicapped in the process of accommodation to demands made of him by the acquiring of a new skill. He may often feel distinctly threatened by his environment.

For some children the presentation of any written or printed material (however simple) may come to act as a conditional stimulus which evokes a feeling of anxiety, accompanied by intense autonomic reactivity. A child's original neurotic fear of any new experience can lead to expectation of failure upon introduction to reading material. This response set may, or may not, be confirmed, depending both upon the intelligence of the child and upon the amount of time at a teacher's disposal to ensure that easily discouraged pupils have extra grounding in the basic principles. The teacher's personality will also create a profound effect upon such children. It can well be imagined that an impatient, authoritarian attitude might make a disastrous impact. The unconditional response of fear of the teacher, or simply of the unknown, is likely to be associated with the reading material, which will then assume the quality of a conditional stimulus. Each fresh attempt to improve a child's performance will result in an actual reinforcement of his anxiety and tension. Some means of interrupting this vicious sequence is imperative. The usual therapeutic endeavors are aimed at reducing the general

*Reprinted from the *Journal of Child Psychology and Psychiatry*, 1967, **8**, 51–56. Copyright 1967 with permission from Pergamon Press Publishing Company and Dr. D. W. McKerracher.

anxiety level by invoking changes in the child's home and school environment, and by individual psychotherapy in the clinic. Remedial lessons may be introduced gradually, after a satisfactory and warm relationship of mutual trust has been established with the child.

Reports of the success of instrumental conditioning techniques with reading disabilities (Staats, 1962; Rachman, 1962) are immensely encouraging for educational psychologists. They offer the advantages of a direct attack upon the problem, combined with the expenditure of a minimal amount of the clinician's time (a precious commodity in areas where there is a staff shortage). A case is reported here of an attempt to treat a highly anxious boy of low reading ability by an operant conditioning technique employing both reward conditioning and avoidance conditioning.

CASE HISTORY

John was an eleven-year-old boy who was referred to the clinic on account of his low educational attainment, poor reading ability, stammering, and occasional enuresis. His mother reported a normal pregnancy, but a forceps delivery after medical induction. He was eight pounds at birth. He had been bowel-trained by two, but had always been inclined to wet the bed at night. He was slow to develop speech, and remained incomprehensible until three years of age. He could speak normally by the time he reached school age, but his stammer began in the first year at school. He had two younger sisters (ten and eight years of age at the time of interview). The mother claimed she had always made a special effort to handle and love her son so that he would not feel displaced. She was not a punitive person, and was not unduly perturbed about his enuresis and stammering. By contrast, his father (who was a Works Study Officer) had rather high expectations of him in his school work, and had at one time pressured him quite severely. He was especially disappointed by his son's low educational attainment. The mother commented that the boy stammered more noticeably after his father reprimanded him for something.

At interview, John was found to be highly anxious and introversive, with marked feelings of inferiority, insecurity, and lack of self-confidence. He was not overtly agitated, but stammered badly when tense. He looked frail and gawky, and appeared to be slower in comprehension than his average intelligence scores indicated. It was not felt that any psychiatric treatment was required, as the emotional problem concerned home management. The parents (in particular, his father) were encouraged to adopt a less demanding and more sympathetic attitude towards him, so that he might be allowed to gain confidence in himself. The enuresis was spasmodic, and related to stressful experiences; no medication was therefore recommended. It was noted that his stutter was scarcely perceptible once he had relaxed, but it was considered likely that it would always be present whenever he became anxious and confused.

The case was transferred to the author for remedial lessons and therapy combined. The possibility existed that improvement in his reading ability might have a chain reaction in bolstering his ego and subtracting from his environment some of its threat, thereby reducing some of the neurotic tension and anxiety he was experiencing.

TEST RESULTS

Stanford–Binet (Terman & Merrill, 1961): IQ 104.
Ravens Colored Matrices (Raven, 1963): 75th Percentile IQ approx. 110.
Burt Vernon Graded Word Reading Test (Vernon, 1938): Eight years one month.

PROCEDURES

A series of graded reading books was selected, extending from just below t᷍
patient's ascertained reading age to a nine-year plus level in vocabulary. ᷍
"Micky" series formed part of the continuum.

The first three-month period (a) was spent entirely on phonic reading methods of the "look-say" variety. Each weekly half-hour session was initiated by a ten-minute period of supportive therapy in which the boy was encouraged to discuss the difficulties he had encountered in school, or at home, during the preceding week. A fairly good relationship was formed, though the boy remained somewhat unforthcoming, and continued to stammer badly both when reading and when talking about his various experiences.

In the second three-month period (b) it was decided to introduce the dual operant conditioning techniques described below. Within two weeks the boy spontaneously confided that he felt much more relaxed in the classroom when reading, and did not dread the opening of textbooks with such marked trepidation as before.

In the third three-month period (c) the avoidance conditioning method was dropped when John became more interested in the content of what he was reading and less intent upon the mechanics of the procedure. It was felt that the employment of both techniques at this stage was slowing down his rate of reading, thus causing him to lose interest in the stories. If anything, the omission of the avoidance procedure appeared to accelerate his progress in reading, and no subjective emotional repercussions were reported. An alternative explanation might be that his motivation was improved by encouraging his concentration on the content of what he was reading, rather than the form.

A monthly check of his reading level was made by means of the Burt Vernon (1938) graded reading list.

APPARATUS

a. A wooden pencil-box was converted into a register of the pupil's success in reading words, by the simple expedient of installing within it a flat 4-V battery connected to six bulbs inserted through the lid. Each bulb was controlled by a separate switch operated manually by the psychologist. Following the dictum of Rachman (1962), correctly read words were rewarded in a fixed ratio of 1:6 by illuminating a bulb. Whenever all six lights were on together, a sweet was handed to the subject and a few words of praise and support given, whilst he masticated slowly in a relaxed position in his chair. The lights were then extinguished, and the process repeated.

The ratio of words rewarded was gradually increased, until it was felt the child was able to read complete sentences without error. Thereafter, a reward light was used progressively to signal:

1. One sentence correctly read (of varying length).
2. Two sentences correctly read (of varying length).
3. Three sentences read correctly (of varying length).
4. One paragraph correctly read (of varying lengths).

b. A loud buzzer (attached to the "bell and pad" equipment for dealing with enuresis) was used as a signal of failure for a mis-pronounced word. Again it was operated manually by the psychologist. Correct recognition and enunciation were rewarded by the non-application of the buzzer. The child was able to avoid the failure signal by slowing down his articula-

CARNEGIE LIBRARY
LIVINGSTONE COLLEGE
SALISBURY, N. C. 28144

tion and by paying closer attention to the verbal symbols he was interpreting. This was designed to reduce the number of projected wrong interpretations he had been inclined to make, based upon the initial letters of words. The avoidance conditioning was applied concurrently with the reward conditioning.

RESULTS

The treatment spanned nine months altogether, but consisted of only one half-hour session per week, excluding school holidays, illness, and other unavoidable absences. The total time involved was therefore only seventeen and a half hours. Table 1 indicates the almost total failure of attempts to increase his reading ability during the first three months, and the marked improvement which occurred after the introduction of the operant conditioning approach. It can be said that effective treatment spanned only six months (total time eleven hours), and that in that period his reading age increased by more than one year.

Table 1. Increase in reading age throughout three terms of treatment in the clinic.

	Conditions	Months	Total session time	Reading age	Reading gain
Period a =	Phonic	Sept. Oct. Nov.	6½ hours	8 years 1 month 8 years 1 month 8 years 2 months	1 month
Period b =	Reward + Avoidance conditioning	Dec. Jan. Feb.	6 hours	8 years 5 months 8 years 6 months 8 years 6 months	4 months
Period c =	Reward conditioning	Mar. Apr. May	5 hours	8 years 10 months 9 years 1 month 9 years 3 months	9 months
TOTAL =	—	9 months	17½ hours	8 years 1 month 9 years 3 months	1 year 2 months

The boy's parents moved from the area shortly after the termination of period (c), and the last few sessions prior to their removal were spent, at the boy's own request, in the reading of an enjoyable adventure story without the aid of the conditioning apparatus. Since the case had been referred partly on account of the boy's reading difficulties, it could be said that the remedial treatment had been specifically successful in reducing them. He was able to read beyond the nine-year level, and though this still left him retarded so far as his mental capacity indicated, the difference was largely one of extent of vocabulary. He was able to spell out and pronounce words like "curriculum" or "melancholy," though he did not know what they meant and claimed that he had not heard them before.

Subjectively, he had commented upon feeling better disposed towards reading after only two weeks' treatment by the conditioning method. His stammer showed some improvement when he was reading aloud, but remained very marked in ordinary conversation. His enuresis remained spasmodic, though in period (c) he reported only one instance in three months, compared with two in period (a) and three in period (b).

It is important to note that during the second week of the third period of treatment he reported a sudden speech and reading relapse. He had apparently been asked to read an extract to the class, and had been unable to do so because of a sudden return of fear of the situation, with a consequent increase in stammering. It is perhaps significant that this incident occurred a few days after the psychologist had been forced to break an appointment with John, who nevertheless waited for almost an hour in the hope that he would appear. The absence of the reassuring weekly session, plus the break in the relationship of trust with the psychologist, may have combined to reawaken his lack of self-confidence.

Interestingly, his reading progress was not affected, and he had again succeeded in increasing his reading age level at the end of the first months of period (c). The avoidance procedure was also omitted during this period, with no obvious emotional repercussions. It is therefore difficult to say whether there was much advantage in using this technique as well as the reward conditioning procedure. The boy seemed to progress rather faster with one method alone.

DISCUSSION

Perhaps the greatest advantage of this approach is that it gains the therapist an immediate foothold behind the defences of the subject. It has the qualities of a game which can be played *together*, thus destroying the "You/Me" barrier at the outset. Instead of a chore, the task of reading becomes a challenge and a pleasure. Partial reinforcement of success ensures that there is no rapid habituation to the series. The pupil receives the encouragement of (a) visible evidence of his progress (lights); (b) material reward for his efforts (sweets); and (c) the approval and support of the therapist acting as a social reinforcing agent.

It is a method which may not work with some children, and may have limited usefulness with others; but there can be little doubt that such procedures ought to be standard skills in every clinician's repertoire, to be employed whenever relevant and effective. Such techniques may work better where a subject already has some understanding of the basic mechanics of reading (a reading age of over eight years). Anxiety can then be regarded as an intervening variable. When it is successfully suppressed, a rapid improvement in reading level may occur.

Main Advantages

1. The method succeeded in improving the reading age of this boy, where more traditional methods had negligible effect.
2. There was a reduction in the amount of tension elicited by written material. His stammer was not so noticeable when he was reading aloud.
3. The rewarding of the alimentary system with sweets, after a successful reading sequence, militates against the arousal of the defensive system (sympathetic nervous system) of the body, and allows pleasure instead of fear to be associated with reading material.
4. The small amount of time spent in each session was well rewarded in terms of reading gain alone.

Main Limitations of Operant Conditioning Technique

1. The boy's stammering was not improved in ordinary conversation. This suggests that generalization did not occur. The reduction in anxiety concerning the reading situation

was not related to a corresponding reduction of anxiety about inter-personal relationships. No clear influence was exerted on his enuretic tendency, though he did report only one instance of wetting in the last period of treatment.

2. The technique is not as simple and objective as it may appear. This success was not obtained by an automated process to the exclusion of the inter-personal relationship between patient and therapist. The apparatus seemed to have a therapeutic value in helping to improve the quality of the relationship established between the therapist and the pupil. But when the relationship was threatened by the non-appearance of the psychologist for one session, the result was a severe loss of his self-confidence and a resurgence of his fear of the reading situation.

Since school holidays, and his own illness during two successive weeks, also interrupted John's weekly treatment without adverse influence, it was clearly not a simple lack of reinforcement that caused his relapse on the occasion reported. It was perhaps the weakening of his trust in the reliability of the therapist (upon whom he had become dependent) that appeared to result in an emotional crisis. When the onus for discontinuance was on an objective source (school authorities and holidays), or upon himself (illness), there was no trauma. It should be remarked that the relapse was not serious, and did not affect his actual reading progress.

In spite of the crudity of the apparatus used in this case, there was a fair measure of success. A fully automated procedure might have been more efficient and even less time-consuming in teaching reading skills, but absence of such equipment need not deter clinical therapists from attempting application of the principles of operant conditioning. It is to be noted, however, that the effects of improved reading level did not generalize to John's emotional attitudes outside of the reading situation.

Acknowledgments. I am grateful to John Wogin, the fourteen-year-old son of our Psychiatric Social Worker, for his ingenuity in constructing the reward conditioning apparatus. My thanks also include the critical appraisal of the paper by Dr. G. McK. Nicholl, Consultant Psychiatrist, Lindsey County Council.

REFERENCES

Burt, Sir Cyril (1937) *The Backward Child.* University of London Press, London.

Rachman, S. (1962) Learning theory and child psychology—therapeutic possibilities. *Child Psychol. Psychiat.* 3, 149–163.

Raven, J. C. (1963) *Guide to Coloured Progress Matrices.* H. K. Lewis, London.

Staats, A. W. & Staats, C. K. (1962) A comparison of the development of speech and reading behaviour. *Child Dev.* 33, 831–846.

Stott, D. H. (1956) *Unsettled Children and their Families.* University of London Press, London.

Stott, D. H. (1962) *Manual for the Programmed Reading Kit.* Holmes, Glasgow. (a) The "Micky" Books (7 year–9 year level).

Terman, L. M. & Merrill, M. A. (1961) *Stanford–Binet Intelligence Scale.* Manual for 3rd Revision Form L–M. Harrap, London.

Vernon, P. E. (1938) *The Standardization of a Graded Word Reading Test.* University of London Press, London.

Worster-Drought, C. (1965) Disorders of speech in childhood. In *Modern Perspectives in Child Psychiatry* (Edited by J. G. Howells). Oliver & Boyd, Edinburgh.

A Token Reinforcement Programme in a
Public School: A Replication and
Systematic Analysis*†

K. D. O'LEARY, W. C. BECKER, M. B. EVANS, and R. A. SAUDARGAS

State University of New York at Stony Brook, University of Illinois, and Florida State University

Abstract: A base rate of disruptive behavior was obtained for seven children in a second-grade class of twenty-one children. Rules, Educational Structure, and Praising Appropriate Behavior while Ignoring Disruptive Behavior were introduced successively; none of these procedures consistently reduced disruptive behavior. However, a combination of Rules, Educational Structure, and Praise and Ignoring nearly eliminated disruptive behavior of one child. When the Token Reinforcement Programme was introduced, the frequency of disruptive behavior declined in five of the six remaining children. Withdrawal of the Token Reinforcement Programme increased disruptive behavior in these five children, and reinstatement of Token Reinforcement Programme reduced disruptive behavior in four of these five. Follow-up data indicated that the teacher was able to transfer control from the token and back-up reinforcers to the reinforcers existing within the educational setting, such as stars and occasional pieces of candy. Improvements in academic achievement during the year may have been related to the Token Programme, and attendance records appeared to be enhanced during the Token phases. The Token Programme was utilized only in the afternoon, and the data did not indicate any generalization of appropriate behavior from the afternoon to the morning.

Praise and other social stimuli connected with the teacher's behavior have been established as effective controllers of children's behavior (Allen, Hart, Buell, Harris & Wolf, 1964; Becker, Madsen, Arnold & Thomas, 1967; Brown & Elliot, 1965; Hall, Lund & Jackson, 1968; Harris, Johnston, Kelley & Wolf, 1964; Harris, Wolf & Baer, 1964; Scott, Burton & Yarrow, 1967; Zimmerman & Zimmerman, 1962). When the teacher's use of praise and social censure is not effective, token reinforcement programmes are often successful in controlling

---

*Portions of this paper were presented to the American Psychological Association, September, 1968, San Francisco, California. This research was supported primarily by Research Grant HD 00881-05 to Wesley C. Becker from the National Institutes of Health and secondarily by a Biomedical Science Grant 31-8200 to K. Daniel O'Leary from the State University of New York at Stony Brook. The authors are grateful to Nancy Brown, Connie Dockterman, Pearl Dorfmann, Jeanne Kappauf, Margery Lewy, Stanley Madsen, and Darlene Zientarski who were the major observers in this study. Appreciation for support of this study is expressed to Dr. Lowell Johnson, Director of Instruction, Urbana Public Schools, and to Mr. Richard Sturgeon, elementary school principal. The greatest thanks go to Mrs. Linda Alsberg, the teacher who executed the Token Reinforcement Programme and tolerated the presence of observers both morning and afternoon for eight months. Her patience and self-control during the Praise and Withdrawal Phases of the programme were especially appreciated. Reprints may be obtained from K. Daniel O'Leary, Dept. of Psychology, State University of New York at Stony Brook, Stony Brook, N.Y. 11790.

†Reprinted from the *Journal of Applied Behavior Analysis*, 1969, **2**, 1, 3–13. Copyright 1969 with permission from the Society for the Experimental Analysis of Behavior, Inc., and Dr. K. D. O'Leary.

children (Birnbrauer, Wolf, Kidder & Tague, 1965; Kuypers, Becker & O'Leary, 1968; O'Leary & Becker, 1967; Quay, Werry, McQueen & Sprague, 1966; Wolf, Giles & Hall, 1968).

The token reinforcement programme utilized by O'Leary and Becker (1967) in a third-grade adjustment class dramatically reduced disruptive behavior. In order to maximize the possibility of reducing the disruptive behavior of the children, O'Leary and Becker used several major variables simultaneously. The first objective of the present study was to analyze the separate effects of some of the variables utilized in the former study. More specifically, the aim was to examine the separate effects of Classroom Rules, Educational Structure, Teacher Praise, and a Token Reinforcement Programme on children's disruptive behavior. Rules consisted of a list of appropriate behaviors that were reviewed daily. Educational Structure was the organization of an academic programme into specified thirty-minute lessons such as spelling and arithmetic. The second objective was to assess whether a Token Reinforcement Programme used only in the afternoon had any effect on the children's behavior in the morning. Third, the present study sought to examine the extent to which the effects of the Token Reinforcement Programme persisted when the Token Programme was discontinued.

METHOD

Subjects

Seven members of a second-grade class of twenty-one children from lower-middle class homes served. At the beginning of the school year, the class had a mean age of seven years and five months, a mean IQ score of ninety-five (range 80 to 115) on the California Test of Mental Maturity, and a mean grade level of 1.5 on the California Achievement Test. The class was very heterogeneous with regard to social behaviors. According to the teacher, three of the children were quite well behaved but at least eight exhibited a great deal of undesirable behavior. The teacher, Mrs. A., had a master's degree in counseling but had only student teaching experience. She was invited to participate in a research project involving her class and received four graduate credits for participating in the project.

Observation

Children. Mrs. A. selected seven children for observation. All seven children were observed in the afternoon and four of the seven (S_1, S_2, S_4, and S_6) were also observed in the morning. Morning observations were made by a regular observer and a reliability checker from 9:30 to 11:30 every Monday, Wednesday, and Friday. Afternoon observations were made by two regular observers and a reliability checker from 12:30 to 2:30 every Monday, Wednesday, and Friday. Observations were made by undergraduate students who were instructed never to talk to the children or to make any differential responses to them in order to minimize the effect of the observers on the children's behavior. Before Base Period data were collected, the undergraduates were trained to observe the children over a three-week period in the classroom, and attention-seeking behaviors of the children directed at the observers were effectively eliminated before the Base Period.

Each child was observed for twenty minutes each day. The observers watched the children in a random order. Observations were made on a twenty-seconds observe, ten-seconds record basis; i.e., the observer would watch the child for twenty seconds and then take ten seconds to record the disruptive behaviors which had occurred during that twenty-second period. The categories of behavior selected for observation were identical to those used by O'Leary and

Becker (1967). Briefly, the seven general categories of disruptive behavior were as follows: (1) *motor behaviors:* wandering around the room; (2) *aggressive behaviors:* hitting, kicking, striking another child with an object; (3) *disturbing another's property:* grabbing another's book, tearing up another's paper; (4) *disruptive noise:* clapping, stamping feet; (5) *turning around:* turning to the person behind or looking to the rear of the room when Mrs. A. was in the front of the class; (6) *verbalization:* talking to others when not permitted by teacher, blurting out answers, name-calling; and (7) *inappropriate tasks:* doing arithmetic during the spelling lesson.

The present study was a systematic replication of O'Leary and Becker (1967). To facilitate comparison of the two studies, the dependent measure reported is the percentage of intervals in which one or more disruptive behaviors was recorded. Percentages rather than frequencies were used because the length of the observations varied due to unavoidable circumstances such as assemblies and snow storms. Nonetheless, most observations lasted the full twenty minutes, and no observation lasting less than fifteen minutes was included.

Teacher. In order to estimate the degree to which the teacher followed the experimental instructions, Mrs. A. was observed by two undergraduates for ninety minutes on Tuesday and Thursday afternoons. Teacher behavior was not observed on Monday, Wednesday, and Friday when the children were observed because Mrs. A. understandably did not wish to have as many as five observers in the room at one time. Furthermore, because Mrs. A. was somewhat reluctant to have three regular observers and one or two graduate students in the room at most times, she was informed of the need for this observational intrusion and the mechanics thereof. This explanation made it impossible to assess the teacher's behavior without her knowledge, but it was felt that deception about teacher observation could have been harmful both to this project and future projects in the school. Nonetheless, frequent teacher observations by two graduate students who were often in the room the entire week ensured some uniformity of her behavior throughout the week. The graduate students frequently met with Mrs. A. to alert her to any deviations from the experimental instructions, and equally important, to reinforce her "appropriate" behavior. Observations of the teacher's behavior were made on a twenty-second observe, ten-second record basis. The categories of teacher behavior selected for observation were as follows:

I. Comments *preceding* responses.
   A. *Academic instruction:* "Now we will do arithmetic"; "Put everything in your desk"; "Sound out the words."
   B. *Social instruction:* "I'd like you to say 'please' and 'thank you'"; "Let me see a quiet hand"; "Let's sit up."
II. Comments *following* responses.
   A. *Praise:* "Good"; "Fine"; "You're right"; "I like the way I have your attention."
   B. *Criticism:* "Don't do that"; "Be quiet"; "Sit in your seat!"
   C. *Threats:* "If you're not quiet by the time I count three . . ."; "If you don't get to work you will stay after school"; "Do you want to stay in this group?"

The teacher's praise, criticism, and threats to individual children were differentiated from praise, criticism, and threats to the class as a whole. For example, "Johnny, be quiet!" was differentiated from "Class, be quiet!". Thus, eight different classes of teacher behavior were recorded: two classes of comments preceding responses and six classes following responses.

Procedure

The eight phases of the study were as follows: (1) Base Period, (2) Classroom Rules, (3) Educational Structure, (4) Praising Appropriate Behavior and Ignoring Disruptive Behavior,

(5) Tokens and Back-up Reinforcement, (6) Praising Appropriate Behavior and Ignoring Disruptive Behavior (Withdrawal), (7) Tokens and Back-up Reinforcement, and (8) Follow-up. Three procedures, Educational Structure and both of the Token Reinforcement Phases, were instituted for a two-hour period during the afternoon. The remainder of the procedures were in effect for the entire day. The eight procedures were in effect for all twenty-one children. The first four conditions were instituted in the order of hypothesized increasing effectiveness. For example, it was thought that Rules would have less effect on the children's behavior than the use of Praise. In addition, it was thought that the combination of Rules and Praise would have less effect than the Tokens and Back-up Reinforcers.

Base Period. After the initial three-week observer training period, the children were observed on eight days over a six-week Base Period to estimate the frequency of disruptive pupil behavior under usual classroom conditions.[1] The teacher was asked to handle the children in whatever way she felt appropriate. During the Base Period, Mrs. A. instructed all the children in subjects like science and arithmetic or took several students to small reading groups in the back of the room while the rest of the class engaged in independent work at their seats. Neither the particular type of activity nor the duration was the same each day. Stars and various forms of peer pressure were sporadically used as classroom control techniques, but they usually had little effect and were discontinued until experimentally reintroduced during the Follow-up Phase.

Classroom Rules. There were seven observations over a three-week period during the second phase of the study. The following rules or instructions were placed on the blackboard by the teacher: "We sit in our seats; we raise our hands to talk; we do not talk out of turn; we keep our desks clear; we face the front of the room; we will work very hard; we do not talk in the hall; we do not run; and, we do not disturb reading groups." Mrs. A. was asked to review the rules at least once every morning and afternoon, and frequent observations and discussions with Mrs. A. guaranteed that this was done on most occasions. The classroom activities again consisted of reading groups and independent seat work.

Educational Structure. It has been stated that a great deal of the success in token reinforcement programmes may be a function of the highly structured regimen of the programme and not a function of reinforcement contingencies. Since the Token Phase of the programme was designed to be used during structured activities that the teacher directed, Mrs. A. was asked to reorganize her programme into four thirty-minute sessions in the afternoon in which the whole class participated, e.g., spelling, reading, arithmetic, and science. Thus, the purpose of the Educational Structure Phase was to assess the importance of structure *per se.* Mrs. A. continued to review the rules twice a day during this phase and all succeeding phases. During this phase there were five observations over a two-week period.

Praise and Ignore. In addition to Rules and Educational Structure, Mrs. A. was asked to praise appropriate behavior and to ignore disruptive behavior as much as possible. For example, she was asked to ignore children who did not raise their hands before answering questions and to praise children who raised their hands before speaking. In addition, she was

---

[1]Ten of the eighteen observations during the Base Period were eliminated because movies were shown on those days, and disruptive behavior on those days was significantly less than on days when movies were not shown. Although movies were seldom used after Base Period, the seven subsequent observations when movies occurred were eliminated.

asked to discontinue her use of threats. During this phase there were five observations over a two-week period.

Token I.   Classroom Rules, Educational Structure, and Praise and Ignoring remained in effect. The experimenter told the children that they would receive points or ratings four times each afternoon. The points which the children received on these four occasions ranged from one to ten, and the children were told that the points would reflect the extent to which they followed the rules placed on the blackboard by Mrs. A. Where possible, these points also reflected the quality of the children's participation in class discussion and the accuracy of their arithmetic or spelling. The children's behavior in the morning did not influence their ratings in the afternoon. If a child was absent, he received no points. The points or tokens were placed in small booklets on each child's desk. The points were exchangeable for back-up reinforcers such as candy, pennants, dolls, comics, barrettes, and toy trucks, ranging in value from two to thirty cents. The variety of prizes made it likely that at least one of the items would be a reinforcer for each child. The prizes were on display every afternoon, and the teacher asked each child to select the prize he wished to earn before the rating period started.

During the initial four days, the children were eligible for prizes just after their fourth rating at approximately 2:30. Thereafter, all prizes were distributed at the end of the day. For the first ten school days the children could receive prizes each day. There were always two levels of prizes. During the first ten days, a child had to receive at least twenty-five points to receive a two to five cents prize (level one prize) or thirty-five points to receive a ten cents prize (level two prize). For the next six days, points were accumulated for two days and exchanged at the end of the second day. When children saved their points for two days, a child had to receive fifty-five points to receive a ten cents prize or seventy points to receive a twenty cents prize. Then, a six-day period occurred in which points were accumulated for three days and exchanged at the end of the third day. During this period, a child had to receive 85 points to receive a twenty cents prize or 105 points to receive a thirty cents prize. Whenever the prizes were distributed, the children relinquished all their points. During Token I, there were thirteen observations over a five-week period.

For the first week, the experimenter repeated the instructions to the class at the beginning of each afternoon session. Both the experimenter and Mrs. A. rated the children each day for the first week in order to teach Mrs. A. how to rate the children. The experimenter sat in the back of the room and handed his ratings to Mrs. A. in a surreptitious manner after each rating period. Mrs. A. utilized both ratings in arriving at a final rating which she put in the children's booklets at the end of each lesson period. The method of arriving at a number or rating to be placed in the child's booklet was to be based on the child's improvement in behavior. That is, if a child showed any daily improvement he could receive a rating of approximately five to seven so that he could usually earn at least a small prize. Marked improvement in behavior or repeated displays of relatively good behavior usually warranted ratings from eight to ten. Ratings from one to five were given when a child was disruptive and did not evidence any daily improvement. Although such a rating system involves much subjective judgment on the part of the teacher, it is relatively easy to implement, and a subsidiary aim of the study was to assess whether a token system could be implemented by one teacher in a class of average size. After the first week, the teacher administered the Token Programme herself, and the experimenter was never present when the children were being observed. If the experimenter had been present during the Token Phases but not during Withdrawal, any effects of the Token Programme would have been confounded by the experimenter's presence.

Withdrawal.   To demonstrate that the token and back-up reinforcers and not other factors, such as the changes that ordinarily occur during the school year, accounted for the observed reduction in disruptive behavior, the token and back-up reinforcers were withdrawn during this phase. There were seven observations over a five-week period. When the prizes and the booklets were removed from the room, Mrs. A. told the children that she still hoped that they would behave as well as they had during the Token Period and emphasized how happy she was with their recent improvement. Rules, Educational Structure, and Praise and Ignoring remained in effect.

Token II. When the tokens and back-up reinforcers were reinstated, the children obtained a prize on the first day if they received twenty-five to thirty-five points. For the next four days there was a one-day delay between token and back-up reinforcement; the remainder of the Token Reinstatement Period involved a two-day delay of reinforcement. The prize and point system was identical to that during Token I. During this phase, there were five observations over a two-week period.

Follow-up. The token and back-up reinforcers were again withdrawn in order to see if the appropriate behavior could be maintained under more normal classroom conditions. In addition to the continued use of Praise, Rules and Educational Structure, it was suggested that Mrs. A. initiate the use of a systematic star system. Children could receive from one to three stars for good behavior twice during the morning and once during the afternoon. In addition, the children received extra stars for better behavior during the morning restroom break and for displaying appropriate behavior upon entering the room at 9:15 and 12:30. At times, extra stars were given to the best behaved row of children. The children counted their stars at the end of the day; if they had ten or more stars, they received a gold star that was placed on a permanent wall chart. If a child received seven to nine stars, he received a green star that was placed on the chart. The boys' gold stars and the girls' gold stars were counted each day; and each member of the group with the greater number of gold stars at the end of the week received a piece of candy. In addition, any child who received an entire week of gold stars received a piece of candy. All children began the day without stars so that, with the exception of the stars placed on the wall charts, everyone entered the programme at the same level.

Such a procedure was a form of a token reinforcement programme, but there were important procedural differences between the experimental phases designated Token and Follow-up. The back-up reinforcers used during the Token Phases were more expensive than the two pieces of candy a child could earn each week during the Follow-up Phase. In addition, four daily ratings occurred at half-hour intervals in the afternoons during the Token Phases but not during Follow-up. On the other hand, stars, peer pressure, and a very small amount of candy were used in the Follow-up Phase. As mentioned previously, both stars and peer pressure had been used sporadically in the Base Period with little effect. Most importantly, it was felt that the procedures used in the Follow-up Phase could be implemented by any teacher. During this phase there were six observations over a four-week period.

Reliability of Observations

The reliabilities of child observations were calculated according to the following procedure: an agreement was scored if both observers recorded one or more disruptive behaviors within the same twenty-second interval; a disagreement was scored if one observer recorded a disruptive behavior and the other observer recorded none. The reliability of the measure of disruptive behavior was calculated for each child each day by dividing the number of intervals in which there was agreement that one or more disruptive behaviors occurred by the total number of agreements plus disagreements. An agreement was scored if both observers recorded the same behavior within the same twenty-second interval. A disagreement was scored if one observer recorded the behavior and the other did not. The reliability of a particular class of teacher behavior on any one day was calculated by dividing the total number of agreements for that class of behaviors by the total number of agreements plus disagreements for that class of behaviors. Reliabilities were calculated differently for child behaviors and teacher behaviors because different types of dependent measures were utilized for children and the teacher, and it was felt that reliability measures should be reported for the specific dependent measures used.

At least one reliability check was made during the afternoon on every child during the Base Period, and one child had three.[2] The average reliability of the measure of disruptive behavior during the afternoons of the Base Period for each of the seven children ranged from 88 to a 100 per cent. The following figures represent the number of reliability checks and the average of those reliability checks after the Base Period through the first Token Period for each child: S_1: 6, eighty-six per cent; S_2: 7, ninety-four per cent; S_3: 6, ninety-four per cent; S_4: 6, ninety-three per cent; S_5: 6, eighty-seven per cent; S_6: 6, eighty-four per cent; S_7: 6, ninety-seven per cent. Because of the repeated high reliabilities, reliability checks were discontinued when the token and back-up reinforcers were reinstated; i.e., no reliability checks were made during or after the Withdrawal Phase.

Adequate morning reliabilities were not obtained until the Rules Phase of the study. The following figures represent the number of reliability checks and the average of those reliability checks during the Rules Phase: S_1: 3, ninety-three per cent; S_2: 4, sixty-eight per cent; S_4: 3, ninety-one per cent; S_6: 3, eighty-eight per cent. Morning reliability checks after the Rules Phase were made approximately every three observations (approximately seven occasions) through the first Token Period. Average reliabilities of the four children during the Rules, Educational Structure, Praise and Ignore, and Token I Phases ranged from ninety-two to ninety-nine per cent.

Eleven reliability checks for the various classes of teacher behavior before the Praise and Ignore Phase was introduced yielded average reliabilities as follows: academic instruction, seventy-five per cent; social instruction, seventy-seven per cent; praise to individuals, seventy-seven per cent; praise to the class, ninety-four per cent; criticism to individuals, seventy-three per cent; criticism to the class, seventy-two per cent; threats to individuals, eighty-three per cent; and threats to the class, eighty-three per cent.

RESULTS

Child Behavior

Figures 1 and 2 present morning and afternoon data; some of the variability within conditions can be seen. Figure 3 presents data of individual children as well as an average of seven children across afternoon conditions. An analysis of variance was performed on the percentages of combined disruptive behavior, averaged within the eight afternoon experimental conditions, for the seven subjects (*see* Fig. 3). The analysis of variance for repeated measures (Winer, 1962, p. 111) indicated differences among the eight experimental conditions ($F = 7.3$; $df = 7$, 42; $p < 0.001$). On the other hand, the percentages of combined disruptive behavior of the four children observed in the morning, averaged within conditions, did not

---

[2]Before ten of the eighteen observation days during the Base Period were eliminated because movies were shown on those days, at least three reliability checks had been made during the afternoon on each child.

change during Rules, Educational Structure, Praise and Ignore, or Token I ($F = 1.0$; $df = 4$, 12). Differences among afternoon conditions were assessed by t-tests. Significant and non-significant differences are grouped individually in Table 1.[3]

It should be emphasized that comparisons between Follow-up and Praise and Ignore are more meaningful than comparisons between Follow-up and Base, Rules, or Educational Structure. Praise and Follow-up were similar procedures; both included Rules, Educational Structure, and Praise and Ignore. The Base Period did not include any of these. Furthermore, after Rules and Educational Structure were initiated, Mrs. A. stated that she required more academic work from the children than during Base Period. A statistical analysis of the group data suggests that a token reinforcement programme can reduce disruptive behavior and that

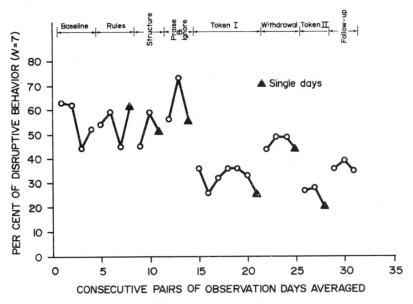

Fig. 1. Average percentage of combined disruptive behavior of seven children during the afternoon over the eight conditions: Base, Rules, Educational Structure, Praise and Ignore, Token I, Withdrawal, Token II, Follow-up.

a token reinforcement programme can be replaced with a variant of a token programme without an increase in disruptive behavior. However, a more detailed analysis of the data for individual children indicated that the Token Reinforcement Programme was more effective for some children than others.

The introduction of Rules, Educational Structure, and Praise and Ignore did not have any consistent effects on behavior (*see* Fig. 3). Praising Appropriate Behavior and Ignoring Disruptive Behavior deserve special mention. Although Mrs. A. used criticism occasionally during the Praise and Ignore Phase, she generally ignored disruptive behavior and used praise frequently. Initially, a number of children responded well to Mrs. A.'s praise, but two boys (S_2 and S_4) who had been disruptive all year became progressively more unruly during the Praise and Ignore Phase. Other children appeared to observe these boys being disruptive, with little or no aversive consequences, and soon became disruptive themselves. Relay races and hiding under a table contributed to the pandemonium. Several children were so disruptive

---

[3]Two-tailed tests.

that the academic pursuits of the rest of the class became impossible. The situation became intolerable, and the Praise and Ignore Phase had to be discontinued much earlier than had been planned.

The disruptive behavior of S_7 was reduced to a very low level of fifteen per cent by a combination of Rules, Educational Structure, and Praise and Ignore. In the previous token programme (O'Leary & Becker, 1967), in which a number of variables including rules, praise, educational structure, and a token programme were simultaneously introduced, disruptive behavior during the token period was reduced to a level of ten per cent. Thus, the present Token Reinforcement Programme probably would not be expected further to reduce disruptive behavior in this child.

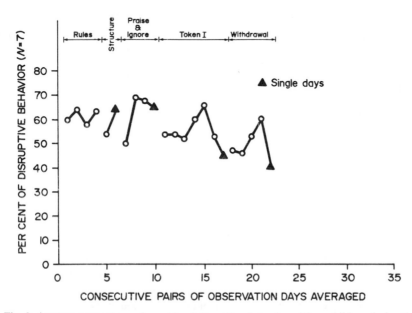

Fig. 2. Average percentage of combined disruptive behavior of four children during the morning over five conditions: Base, Rules, Educational Structure, Praise and Ignore, Token I, Withdrawal, Token II, Follow-up.

During Token I, there was a marked reduction ($\geq 18\%$) in the disruptive behavior of five children (S_1, S_2, S_3, S_4, and S_6) and a reduction of three per cent in S_5. Withdrawal of the Token Programme increased disruptive behavior from five per cent to forty-five per cent in these six children. Reinstatement of the Token Programme led to a decrease in five of these six children (S_1, S_2, S_3, S_4, S_5). The disruptive behavior of five children (S_1, S_2, S_4, S_5, and S_6) ranged from eight per cent to thirty-nine per cent lower during the Follow-up than during the Praise and Ignore Phase of the study. Since on no occasion did the Follow-up procedures precede Token I and/or Token II, this study did not demonstrate that Token I and/or Token II were necessary conditions for the success of the Follow-up procedures.

In summary, Token I and Token II were definitely associated with a reduction of disruptive behavior, *and* the Follow-up procedure was effective with three of the six children (S_1, S_2, and S_4) who had more than fifteen per cent disruptive behavior during the Praise and Ignore Phase (S_7 had fifteen per cent disruptive behavior during the Praise and Ignore Phase). Token I and Token II were associated with marked reductions of disruptive behavior of S_3, but the frequency of disruptive behavior during the Follow-up was not substantially lower than during the Praise and Ignore Phase. Definitive conclusions concerning the effects of the Token Programme cannot be drawn for S_5 and S_6, although some reduction of disruptive behavior was associated with either Token I and Token II for both of these children. In addition, the disruptive behavior of S_5 and S_6 was eight per cent and twenty per cent less respectively during Follow-up than during the Praise and Ignore Phase.

Table 1

Significant		Non-Significant	
Token I *vs.* Withdrawal	$t = 3.3**$	Rules *vs.* Educational Structure	$t = 0.8$
Token II *vs.* Withdrawal	$t = 2.9*$	Educational Structure *vs.* Praise	$t = 1.0$
Token I *vs.* Praise	$t = 3.4**$	Base *vs.* Withdrawal	$t = 1.2$
Token II *vs.* Praise	$t = 3.0*$	Token I *vs.* Follow-up	$t = 1.1$
Base *vs.* Follow-up	$t = 3.2**$	Token II *vs.* Follow-up	$t = 1.5$
Praise *vs.* Follow-up	$t = 3.3**$		
Withdrawal *vs.* Follow-up	$t = 3.2**$		

$**p < 0.02, df = 6.$ $*p < 0.05, df = 6.$

Teacher Behavior

On any one day, the percentage of each of the eight classes of teacher behavior was calculated by dividing the number of intervals in which a particular class of behavior occurred by the total number of intervals observed on that day. Percentages rather than frequencies were used because of slight variations from the usual ninety-minute time base.

The percentages of different classes of teacher behavior were averaged within two major conditions: (1) data before Praise and Ignore Phase, and (2) data in the Praise and Ignore and succeeding Phases. The data in Fig. 4 show that in the Praise and Ignore Phase, Mrs. A. increased use of praise to individual children from twelve to thirty-one per cent and decreased use of criticism to individuals from twenty-two to ten per cent. Mrs. A. also increased use of praise to the class from one to seven per cent and decreased criticism directed to the class from eleven to three per cent. Because the frequency of threats was quite low, threats to individuals and threats to the class were combined in one measure. Using this combined measure, Mrs. A.'s use of threats decreased from five to one per cent. There were no differences in Mrs. A.'s use of academic or social instruction. Consequently, the changes in the children's disruptive behavior can probably be attributed to contingencies and not to Mrs. A.'s use of cues concerning the desired behaviors.

DISCUSSION

Although a Token Reinforcement Programme was a significant variable in reducing disruptive behavior in the present study, the results are less dramatic than those obtained by O'Leary and Becker (1967). A number of factors probably contributed to the difference in effectiveness of the programmes. The average of disruptive behavior during the Base Period in the 1967 study was seventy-six per cent; in the present study it was fifty-three per cent. The gradual introduction of the various phases of the programme was probably less effective than a simultaneous introduction of all the procedures, as in the previous study. In the earlier study, the children received more frequent ratings. Five ratings were made each day at the introduction of the 1.5-hour token programme, and they were gradually reduced to three ratings per day. In the present study, the children received four ratings per day during a two-hour period. In the 1967 study, the class could earn points for popsicles by being quiet while the teacher placed ratings in the children's booklets; in the present study, group points were not incorporated into the general reinforcement programme. In the 1967 study, the teacher attended a weekly psychology seminar where teachers discussed various applications of learning principles to classroom management. An *esprit de corps* was generated from that seminar that probably increased the teacher's commitment to change the children's behavior. Although

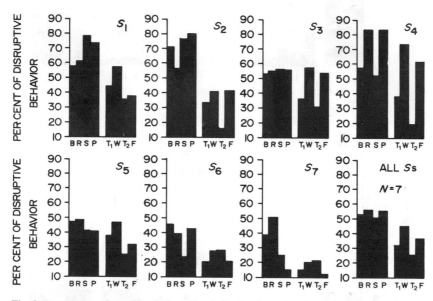

Fig. 3. Percentage of combined disruptive behavior for each of seven children during the eight conditions: Base, Rules, Educational Structure, Praise and Ignore, Token I, Withdrawal, Token II, Follow-up.

Mrs. A. received graduate credits for her extensive participation in the project, she did not attend a seminar in classroom management. A number of children in the present study had an abundance of toys at home and it was difficult to obtain inexpensive prizes which would serve as reinforcers; in the earlier study, selection of reinforcers was not a difficult problem, since the children were from disadvantaged homes.

Related Gains

Academic. The fourteen children for whom there were both pre- and post-measures on the California Achievement Test (including S_1, S_4, S_5, S_6, and S_7) gained an average of 1.5 years from October to June. The mean CAT score in October was 1.5 while the mean score in June was 3.0. Although there was no matched control group, such gains are greater than those usually obtained (Tiegs & Clark, 1963). While such gains are promising, conclusions about the effects of a token system on academic performance must await a more systematic analysis.

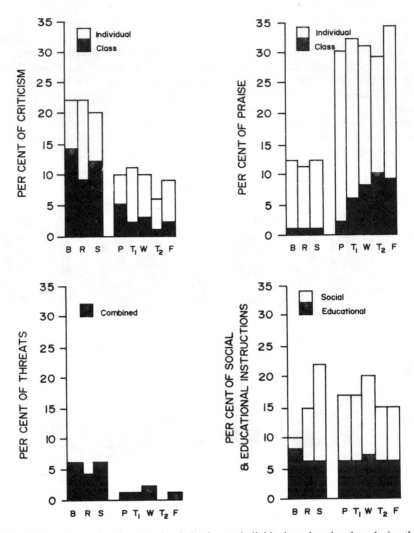

Fig. 4. Percentage of various teacher behaviors to individuals and to the class during the eight conditions: Base, Rules, Educational Structure, Praise and Ignore, Token I, Withdrawal, Token II, Follow-up.

Attendance. Comparisons of the attendance records of the seven children during the observational days of the token and non-token phases yielded the following results: the average attendance percentage during the forty-five observation days of Base, Rules, Educational Structure, Praise and Ignore, and Withdrawal was eighty-six per cent. The average attendance percentage during the twenty observation days of Token I and Token II was ninety-eight per cent; the average attendance percentage during the twenty-six observation days of Token I, Token II, and Follow-up (a variant of a token programme) was ninety-nine per cent. These attendance records are very encouraging, but because of the usual seasonal variations in attendance and the small sample of children, more definitive evidence is needed before conclusions about the effects of a token programme on attendance can be made.

Cost of Programme

The cost of the reinforcers in the present study was approximately $125.00. It is estimated that three hours of consulting time per week would be essential to operate a token reinforcement programme effectively for one class in a public school. The cost of such a programme and the amount of consulting time seem relatively small when compared to the hours psychologists spend in therapy with children, often without producing significant behavioral changes (Levitt, 1963). Furthermore, as evidenced in the present study, control of behavior may be shifted from reinforcers, such as toys, to reinforcers existing within the natural educational setting, such as stars and peer prestige.

Generalization

During the morning, the majority of the children were engaged in independent seat work, while four or five children were in a reading group with the teacher in the back of the room. Although there were rules and frequent instructions during the morning, there was little reinforcement for appropriate behavior, since Mrs. A. felt that it would be disruptive to the rest of the class to interrupt reading groups to praise children who were doing independent work at their seats. Ayllon and Azrin (1964) found that instructions without reinforcement had little effect on the behavior of mental patients. Similarly, Rules (instructions) without reinforcement did not influence the behavior of the children in this study.

Mrs. A. was instructed to praise appropriate behavior and ignore disruptive behavior in the morning as well as the afternoon. However, Mrs. A.'s criteria of appropriate behavior in the morning differed from her criteria in the afternoon. For example, in the morning she often answered questions when a child failed to raise his hand before speaking. In the afternoon, on the other hand, she generally ignored a child unless he raised his hand. In order to achieve "generalization" of appropriate behavior in a Token Programme such as this one, the teacher's response to disruptive behavior must remain constant throughout the day. The percentage of disruptive behavior was reduced during the morning of the first few days of Token I, but the children presumably learned to discriminate that their appropriate behavior was reinforced only in the afternoon. The differences in the children's behavior between the morning and the afternoon help to stress the point that "generalization" is no magical process, but rather a behavioral change which must be engineered like any other change.

REFERENCES

Allen, K. Eileen, Hart, Betty M., Buell, Joan S., Harris, Florence R. & Wolf, M. M. Effects of social reinforcement on isolate behavior of a nursery school child. *Child Development*, 1964, 35, 511–518.

Ayllon, T. & Azrin, N. H. Reinforcement and instructions with mental patients. *Journal of the Experimental Analysis of Behavior*, 1964, 7, 327–331.

Becker, W. C., Madsen, C. H., Arnold, Carole R. & Thomas, D. R. The contingent use of teacher attention and praise in reducing classroom behavior problems. *Journal of Special Education*, 1967, 1 (3), 287–307.

Birnbrauer, J. S., Wolf, M. M., Kidder, J. D. & Tague, Celia. Classroom behavior of retarded pupils with token reinforcement. *Journal of Experimental Child Psychology*, 1965, 2, 219–235.

Brown, P. & Elliot, R. Control of aggression in a nursery school class. *Journal of Experimental Child Psychology*, 1965, 2, 103–107.

Hall, R. V., Lund, Diane & Jackson, Deloris. Effects of teacher attention on study behavior. *Journal of Applied Behavior Analysis*, 1968, 1, 1–12.

Harris, Florence R., Johnston, Margaret K., Kelley, C. Susan & Wolf, M. M. Effects of positive social reinforcement on regressed crawling of a nursery school child. *Journal of Educational Psychology*, 1964, **55**, 35–41.

Harris, Florence R., Wolf, M. M. & Baer, D. M. Effects of social reinforcement on child behavior. *Young Children*, 1964, **20**, 8–17.

Kuypers, D. S., Becker, W. C. & O'Leary, K. D. How to make a token system fail. *Exceptional Children*, 1968, **35**, 101–109.

Levitt, E. E. Psychotherapy with children: A further evaluation. *Behaviour Research and Therapy*, 1963, **1**, 45–51.

O'Leary, K. D. & Becker, W. C. Behavior modification of an adjustment class: A token reinforcement program. *Exceptional Children*, 1967, **33**, 637–642.

Quay, H. C., Werry, J. S., McQueen, Marjorie & Sprague, R. L. Remediation of the conduct problem child in a special class setting. *Exceptional Children*, 1966, **32**, 509–515.

Scott, Phyllis M., Burton, R. V. & Yarrow, Marian R. Social reinforcement under natural conditions. *Child Development*, 1967, **38**, 53–63.

Tiegs, E. V. & Clark, W. W. Manual, California Achievement Tests, Complete Battery. 1963 Norms. California Test Bureau, Monterey, California.

Winer, B. J. *Statistical principles in experimental design*. New York: McGraw-Hill, 1962.

Wolf, M. M., Giles, D. K. & Hall, R. V. Experiments with token reinforcement in a remedial classroom. *Behaviour Research and Therapy*, 1968, **6**, 51–64.

Zimmerman, Elaine H. & Zimmerman, J. The alteration of behavior in a special classroom situation. *Journal of the Experimental Analysis of Behavior*, 1962, **5**, 59–60.

Developing Self-Evaluation as a Conditioned Reinforcer*†

STEPHEN M. JOHNSON and SANDER MARTIN

University of Oregon

Abstract: This study compares the effects of self-monitored and externally monitored reinforcement systems. Sixty second grade school children were presented with a visual discrimination task in a setting conducive to child play. For one group of children correct discriminations were reinforced by an externally managed token system (ER). A second group managed their own token system by evaluating the correctness of their responses and contingently reinforcing themselves (self-reinforcement of SR). A third, noncontingent reinforcement group was employed to provide a baseline control. Results showed that the two groups receiving contingent reinforcement performed at higher rates than did the control group. Self-reinforcement maintained discrimination behavior at as high a rate and accuracy level as did external reinforcement. Under one reinforcement schedule (FR-3), SR yielded significantly higher response rates than ER. The SR group also demonstrated higher response rate in the initial session of extinction as compared to the ER group. This finding replicates earlier results (Johnson, 1970) and substantiates the hypothesis that these self-reinforcement procedures can serve to establish positive self-evaluation as a conditioned reinforcer.

The development of self-regulation has consistently been viewed as one of the most important objectives of the socialization process. Recent studies have approached the self-control problem more directly than earlier work through attempts at engineering or programming behavioral self-management. The experimental investigations of self-direction and self-reinforcement have frequently adopted this "applied" methodology and provided paradigms for investigating those variables which contribute to self-generated or self-controlled behaviors.

The studies of A. R. Luria and others who have followed his lead in research on self-direction provide an example. Work in this area has forcefully demonstrated the effects of self-direction in producing verbally mediated behavior not otherwise possible in very young or "oligophrenic" children (Bem, 1967; Luria, 1961, 1963), more accurate behavior in performance tasks with hyperactive children (Palkes, Stewart & Kahana, 1968) and more "honest" behavior in settings conducive to transgression (O'Leary, 1968).

In the literature on self-reinforcement, studies have repeatedly established that self-executed reinforcement is effective in maintaining various kinds of behavior. Bandura and Perloff (1967) found that self-managed reinforcement was as effective as externally managed reinforcement in maintaining effortful motor behavior in children. Johnson (1970) demon-

*This research was supported by a grant from the Office of Scientific and Scholarly Research of the University of Oregon and made possible by the courteous cooperation of the principals and teachers of Washington, Willagelespie and Gilham Schools of Eugene, Oregon and Coburg School of Coburg, Oregon. The authors wish to thank Mrs. Lynn Craycroft who served as an experimenter in the study.

†This paper represents an original contribution to this volume. Copyright Pergamon Press, 1972.

strated that self-reinforcement procedures were as effective as external reinforcement procedures in maintaining attentive behavior in young, inattentive children. In a recent case study report, Lovitt & Curtiss (1969) found that higher academic response rates were achieved when their twelve-year-old subject managed his own contingency system as opposed to when it was managed by his teacher. Marston & Kanfer (1963) found that self-reinforcement procedures were effective in maintaining previously learned verbal discriminations. These studies have suggested that self-control skills can be trained with productive results.

The present investigation is in this more technological tradition and compares self- and external reinforcement as agents of behavioral maintenance. In a self-reinforcement system, an individual simply acts as the executor of reinforcing events to himself. As Skinner (1953, pp. 237–238) has pointed out, this process presupposes that the individual has the power to self-reinforce at any time, but that he does so only after meeting certain contingencies.

It is hypothesized that training in the self-execution of a contingent reinforcement system may have lasting effects on an individual's tendency to self-regulate his own behavior. It is suggested that such self-executed reinforcement necessitates repeated self-evaluation, and further, that this self-evaluation may, in time, be established as a conditioned reinforcer. If this occurs, the practice of self-executing a contingent reinforcement system may affect an individual's self-control capabilities. In a recent investigation (Johnson, 1970) it was found that children who had maintained their own behavior by self-reinforcement showed some greater resistance to extinction of conditioned behaviors as compared to children whose behavior had been maintained by external reinforcement. While these extinction differences were not overwhelming nor consistent throughout the entire extinction period, they were suggestive of a potentially important phenomenon. The findings were predicted and interpreted on the basis of the hypothesis that simple self-evaluation could serve as a conditioned reinforcer and maintain behavior in the absence of token rewards.

The present study involves a modified replication of this earlier experiment (Johnson, 1970) emphasizing the comparison of the effects of self- and externally monitored reinforcement systems on the maintenance and resistance to extinction of selected behaviors. In this study, second grade school children were brought to a mobile laboratory containing many attractive, age-appropriate toys and were presented with a relatively monotonous match-to-sample discrimination task. One group of children was externally reinforced (ER) on a token reward system for each correct discrimination. A second group was taught to evaluate the correctness of their own responses and to contingently self-deliver the token reward by saying "I was right" (SR). A third group was taught to self-evaluate discriminations but received non-contingent reinforcement (NCR). After four sessions of these differential treatments with gradual thinning of fixed-ratio reinforcement in the SR and ER groups, all Ss were placed on extinction. It was predicted that the contingent reinforcement groups would perform at higher rates than the non-contingent reinforcement group at all points. Secondly, it was predicted that the SR group would show greater resistance to extinction than the ER group. Previous results (Johnson, 1970) suggested that this extinction difference would be most prominent during the initial stages of extinction.

The latter hypothesis predicting differential resistance to extinction is based on assumptions concerning the development of self-evaluation as a conditioned reinforcer. In the present study, self-evaluation always occurred as part of a chain of responses which had terminated with reinforcement. Therefore, self-evaluation could be viewed as an operant response conditioned by reinforcement in the following chaining paradigm:

$$\text{Discrimination} \longrightarrow \text{Self-Evaluation} \longrightarrow \text{Token Reinforcement}$$
$$(\text{"I was right"})$$

In this paradigm, self-evaluation should be established as a secondary reinforcer due to its position in the response chain leading to reinforcement. In the external reinforcement condition, no such consistent conditioned reinforcer should be established. Extinction should be retarded in the SR group as a result of the operation of self-evaluation as a conditioned reinforcer.

Skinner (1938) was perhaps the first to hypothesize that a response could be established as a conditioned reinforcer as a result of its position in a chain of behavior terminating in reinforcement. Kelleher (1966) has presented evidence indicating that "patterns of responding were developed and maintained by scheduled presentations of stimuli that had (in conditioning) preceded primary reinforcement." These findings suggest that *stimuli* may acquire secondary reinforcing properties as a result of their position in a chain of events leading to reinforcement. The findings lend credence to the present formulation if it can be assumed that "response produced" stimuli may acquire secondary reinforcing properties in the same manner.

In summary, it was predicted that the self-management of a contingent reinforcement system would produce greater resistance to extinction of the conditioned behavior than would the same contingent reinforcement system when externally controlled. This prediction was based on the hypothesis that self-management of the reinforcement system would result in establishing self-evaluation as a conditioned reinforcer. Finally, self-evaluation should have been established as a conditioned reinforcer as a result of its position in a chain of responses which had terminated in reinforcement.

METHOD

Subjects

Sixty second grade school children of both sexes were employed as subjects. These children were recruited from four public schools in Eugene, Oregon and randomly selected from classrooms after having been given parental permission to participate. Any children who were believed to be brain damaged or who were under psychiatric treatment were excluded from the sample. Ss were randomly assigned to conditions by an alternation procedure.

Experimental Setting

The experiment was conducted in a large mobile laboratory which was brought to each cooperating school. The laboratory was divided into two rooms equipped with a one-way mirror and sound monitoring system so that Ss could be observed by E at all times. In addition to the materials necessary for the experimental task, a large number of attractive, age-appropriate toys surrounded the S.

Stimulus Material and Apparatus

A series of four-choice match-to-sample problems using pairs of symbols as stimuli were employed in the experimental task. Each problem was placed on a thirty-five-millimeter transparency and was projected on a three and a half by five inch screen encased in a small console. The sample symbols were projected on the center of the screen and the possible match symbols in each corner. A button in each corner of the screen corresponded to each of the four possible match symbols. S's task was to press the button corresponding to the correct match. A button press automatically advanced the projector after a three-second delay and the response was automatically recorded as correct or incorrect. The apparatus could be set to automatically reinforce correct responses in the external reinforcement condition. In the self-reinforcement condition, E activated the reward apparatus contingent on verbal self-evaluation ("I was right") by S.

The reward apparatus consisted of a buzzer and dial counter visible to S. The children understood that the points accumulated on the dial counter were backed by toy rewards.

Procedures

Prior to initiating differential treatment procedures, all Ss were screened on the experimental task. They were required to complete twenty or more discrimination problems in a five-minute period at a minimum accuracy level of eighty per cent. Only one S failed this requirement on the accuracy criterion and was eliminated from the sample. The experiment consisted of six repeated sessions over the period of approximately eight days. Each session was of fifteen-minutes duration and was given on consecutive days except for weekends, holidays, or days of illness for individual Ss. Each S was run at approximately the same time each day. In every sample, the screening was done on a Tuesday and subjects typically completed the experiment on Wednesday of the following week. Any subject who was absent for more than two week days was dropped from the sample.

Following the screening day, Ss were exposed to differential treatment procedures. After a standard ninety-second period in which S was encouraged to play with the available toys, E gave the following directions in the SR condition:

> Now let's go back to your place here and I'll tell you what we're going to do today. You can win toys by working on this machine. Everytime you do one of these problems, you can win a point. The points are good for any one of the toys here (pointing).
> Now I'll show you how to win points. Whenever you do one of these right, say "I was right" out loud. Then you will get a point. Let's do one. First, press the right button. Then say "I was right." Good — see, the buzzer rang and you got a point on the dial (pointing). Now do this one. Good, you got another point. Now remember, say "I was right" after each right answer to win the points and the toys. The more points you win the more toys you can win.

E remained in the room with S in this first session and when an incorrect SR was given said: "No you don't get a point this time because you were wrong. Only say, 'I was right' when you *are* right." At the end of the session, E said: "Fine, you have won many of the points you need for a toy. I'll see you tomorrow and you can earn more points toward your toy." In all groups, Ss were given toys after reinforcement Sessions 2 and 4. In the contingent reinforcement groups, this was structured as a reward based on the number of points earned; in the NCR group, it was presented as a gift.

The directions and procedures for the ER group were the same except that self-evaluative statements were not required. The reward apparatus was activated immediately upon a correct response from S. In the NCR group, the instructions and procedures were similar but there were no references to points or the winning of toys. Ss in this group were taught to say "I was right" in the same manner as Ss in the SR group, but no contingencies were mentioned in connection with this and the token reward apparatus was inoperative.

In subsequent reinforcement sessions, the schedule of token reward was gradually thinned from CRF on Day 1 to FR-2, FR-3, and FR-5 on subsequent days. On all but the first day of reinforcement, E left S alone with the discrimination problems advising him: "You can do anything you want today. You can play with the toys or work the machine." It is important to note that all Ss were asked to perform the discrimination task on the first day of the experiment with E present throughout the session. On all subsequent days, E left the S alone with the task and gave him permission to do whatever he pleased. In the SR group, incorrect SR's were not reinforced in the first session of the experiment but were reinforced in all subsequent sessions. Thus, in all but the first session, any self-reinforcement response (i.e., "I was right") was counted toward reinforcement on the appropriate schedule.

In the first session of extinction, FR-5 reinforcement was in effect in SR and ER for the first two minutes of the session followed by fifteen minutes of extinction. Extinction Session 2 consisted of fifteen minutes of non-reinforced trials.

RESULTS

A screening on the experimental task was given in order to determine the ability of each S before exposure to differential treatments. An analysis of variance of the screening scores indicated that there were no significant differences between groups in ability on the task ($F = 0.89$; $df = 2, 48$). The screening score means were: SR = 29.85, NCR = 28.30, ER = 27.60.

The experiment was divided into two periods: reinforcement (four sessions) and extinction (two sessions). The correct response (CR) scores were analyzed separately for each period by repeated measures analysis of variance. Figure 1 shows the mean number of CRs for each group in each of the six sessions. The accuracy of discrimination behavior was also assessed by computing the proportion of correct responses/total responses (CR/TR). Group comparisons on accuracy were made by use of the Kruskall-Wallis one way analysis of variance by ranks (Siegel, 1956).

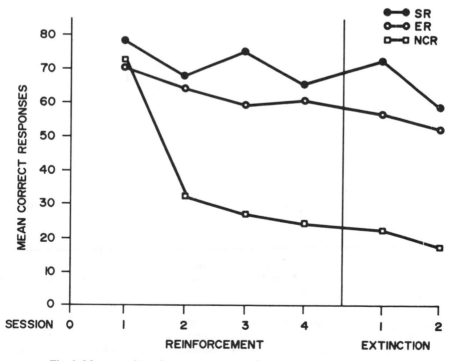

Fig. 1. Mean number of correct responses for each group in each session.

Reinforcement Period

Table 1 presents the analysis of CR data for the reinforcement period. This analysis revealed a significant treatment effect ($F = 12.84$; $df = 48$, 144; $p < 0.001$). Planned comparisons revealed that both reinforcement groups had higher response rates in this period than the NCR group ($p < 0.001$). Further analysis revealed that this difference was not present in Session 1 but was most obvious in all sessions which followed (*see* Fig. 1). The overall SR and ER group means did not differ significantly in this period and the slight superiority of the SR group during reinforcement is probably related to its slight and nonsignificant superiority in

Table 1. Analysis of variance – Reinforcement period.

Source	df	MS	F
Groups (A)	2	22744.06	12.84***
Sex of Experimenter (B)	1	4611.27	2.60
Sex of Subject (C)	1	686.82	< 1
A × B	2	5994.70	3.38*
A × C	2	2523.05	1.42
B × C	1	112.07	< 1
A × B × C	2	334.53	< 1
Error (a)	48	1770.43	—
Sessions (D)	3	6412.27	18.77***
A × D	6	2241.05	6.56***
B × D	3	293.21	< 1
C × D	3	314.41	< 1
A × B × D	6	1301.28	3.80**
A × C × D	6	616.58	1.80
B × C × D	3	166.50	< 1
A × B × C × D	6	427.53	1.25
Error (b)	144	341.62	—

$*p < 0.05.$ $**p < 0.005.$ $***p < 0.001.$

the screening period. *Post hoc* comparisons of SR and ER group means by individual session revealed a significantly higher response rate in the SR group in Session 3 (FR-3 reinforcement) at the 0.05 significance level.

The analysis of variance summary table (Table 1) also revealed other significant findings which, while not central to the main hypothesis of the study, deserve brief mention. The significant groups × sex of experimenter interaction ($F = 3.38$; $df = 1$, 48; $p < 0.05$) is simply due to the fact that while the male experimenter evoked higher response rates than the female experimenter in both reinforcement groups, he was associated with lower response rates in the NCR group. The significant trials effect ($F = 18.77$; $df = 3$, 144; $p < 0.001$) appears to have been due to the overall decline in response rate over trials. This effect was, of course, most operative in the NCR group, particularly between Sessions 1 and 2. It is important, in evaluating this result, to note that reinforcement Session 2 was the first one in which E was not present and *S*s were given the option of not attending to the task. The significant groups × trials interaction ($F = 6.56$; $df = 6$, 144; $p < 0.001$) also seems to have been due to the immediate drop in the NCR group's response rate from Sessions 1 to 2 relative to the performance of the two reinforcement groups. A separate analysis of variance on the ER and SR group data alone did not yield a significant groups × trials interaction, thus confirming the impression that the result is mainly due to NCR group performance relative to ER and SR group performance.

Computation of the CR/TR accuracy proportion yields the following group means: SR = 0.930; ER = 0.917; NCR = 0.889. There were no significant differences between groups on this accuracy measure as analyzed by the Kruskall-Wallis analysis of variance by ranks ($H = 1.59$; $df = 2$).

The accuracy of self-reinforcement was computed by the proportion SR/CR. In the four reinforcement sessions the accuracy proportions were: 1.00, 1.03, 1.06 and 1.06 respectively. These results indicate that accuracy was reasonably high throughout the reinforcement period. There were no instances of obvious cheating by Ss in dispensing SR.

Extinction Period

Table 2 presents the analysis of CR scores in the extinction period. Once again, the significant main treatment effect in this period is primarily due to the superiority of the reinforcement groups over the NCR group (*see* Fig. 1). The overall difference between the ER and SR groups is not significant for this period, but the superiority of the SR group's performance in the first session of extinction is significant ($t = 3.06$; $df = 96$; $p < 0.01$).

The data analysis also revealed a significant trials effect ($F = 7.61$; $df = 1$, 48; $p < 0.025$) reflecting the response extinction in this period. A significant groups × sex of experimenter

Table 2. Analysis of variance — Extinction period.

Source	df	MS	F
Groups (A)	2	22909.68	12.82**
Sex of Experimenter (B)	1	4118.41	2.30
Sex of Subject (C)	1	2679.08	1.49
A × B	2	10046.16	5.62*
A × C	2	250.22	< 1
B × C	1	2930.41	1.64
A × B × C	2	2131.31	1.19
Error (a)	48	1787.05	—
Sessions (D)	1	1928.01	7.61*
A × D	2	273.11	1.07
B × D	1	165.68	< 1
C × D	1	10.208	< 1
A × B × D	2	84.02	< 1
A × C × D	2	401.36	1.58
B × C × D	1	8.01	< 1
A × B × C × D	2	165.01	< 1
Error (b)	48	253.26	—

$*p < 0.025$. $**p < 0.001$.

effect replicates the earlier finding in the reinforcement period. The male experimenter was associated with higher response rates in both reinforcement groups, but lower rates in the NCR group as compared to the female experimenter.

The CR/TR accuracy proportions for this period were: SR = 0.925; ER = 0.930; NCR = 0.869. The analysis of this data revealed a significant treatment effect ($H = 15.65$; $df = 2$; $p < 0.001$). Although mean comparisons cannot be made within this analysis it is very clear in examining the data that the NCR group's lower accuracy in this period, as compared to the two reinforcement groups, accounted for the finding.

DISCUSSION

It was hypothesized that the self-management of a contingent reinforcement system could serve to establish self-evaluation as a conditioned reinforcer. It was predicted on the basis of this hypothesis, that the discrimination behaviors established in the present study would be more resistant to extinction when following self-reinforcement than when following external reinforcement. The results supported this prediction as significantly higher response rates were observed in the SR group in the first session of extinction. These findings closely replicate those of an earlier study (Johnson, 1970) in which greater initial resistance to extinction was observed in a similar self-reinforcement condition. While the magnitude of the extinction differences were not overwhelming in either study, the consistency of the results is rather persuasive. It should be noted, however, that neither of these experiments was designed to critically test the conditioned reinforcement hypothesis and rival hypotheses for the resistance to extinction findings may be quite plausible.

The superiority of the reinforcement groups over the NCR group in all sessions in which Ss were given the option of not attending to the task indicates that the token system operated to reinforce on-task behavior. These results also indicate that the high response rates observed in extinction in both reinforcement groups were a function of the conditioning programmes.

The high accuracy of the self-reinforcement responses is an encouraging finding and also replicates earlier results (Johnson, 1970). In evaluating this result, however, it should be remembered that children in the SR group were able to attain an average discrimination accuracy of ninety-three per cent and could have obtained high SR accuracy by simply reinforcing every response whether correct or not. The SR accuracy data, then, mean only that Ss did not engage in obvious "cheating" in dispensing SRs.

The superiority of the SR group's performance under the FR-3 reinforcement schedule is of interest but difficult to interpret. Of course, higher response rates under leaner reinforcement schedules for self-reinforced Ss would be consistent with the present formulation of self-evaluation as conditioned reinforcement. Within this formulation, it could be argued that the conditioned reinforcer (self-evaluation) would facilitate performance through the otherwise non-reinforced trials and thereby facilitate response rates. This line of thinking would seem, however, to predict at least equal performance facilitation on the FR-5 schedule used in the present study. It is conceivable of course, that self-execution of a reinforcement system facilitates performance on certain schedules and not on others. One may conceptualize this finding by hypothesizing that the FR-3 schedule was particularly effective in enhancing the secondary reinforcing properties of the self-evaluation response. Without replication, however, the present result cannot be clearly interpreted.

In considering the SR group's superiority in reinforcement Session 3 (FR-3) and extinction Session 1, it may be important to note that the toy rewards were delivered to all groups in the immediately preceding sessions (reinforcement Sessions 2 and 4). It is conceivable that these rewards were differentially effective in that the rewards were more powerful for the SR group. It could be suggested, for example, that the rewards were more salient for SR group *S*s due to greater self-attribution surrounding earning of the rewards. While this line of reasoning is not implausible, it represents only *post hoc* conjecture. In addition, it should be remembered that the greater initial resistance to extinction observed in the present experiment replicates the finding of an earlier study (Johnson, 1970) in which the differential effect of reward hypothesis would be less plausible. In any case, this question can be easily resolved in future research.

The unexpected findings concerning lower discrimination accuracy in the NCR group as compared to the two reinforcement groups in the extinction period are of interest. Even though the absolute mean differences were not great, the NCR group contained a large proportion of *S*s who ranked low on the accuracy dimension. In addition, the data trend was similar, though non-significant in the reinforcement period. These findings seem to suggest that when positive self-evaluation has been functional in obtaining reinforcement, it can subsequently serve to enhance the accuracy of the self-evaluated response.

In considering directions for future research in self-reinforcement, several types of questions seem relevant. For purposes of application, data on those variables which would further enhance response accuracy and resistance to extinction would seem most important. The consideration of self-evaluation as a secondary reinforcer also leads to hypotheses concerning the role of self-evaluative responses as agents of behavioral change. For example, it seems likely that the simple self-observation of one's own approved behaviors would involve positive self-evaluation. If this positive self-evaluation served as a reinforcer, one's approved behaviors could be expected to increase in frequency. The opposite results should obtain for self-observation of one's disapproved behaviors. Thus, simple self-observation of approved or disapproved behaviors might serve as a powerful clinical tool in behavior change programmes.

In a more theoretical vein, studies which more critically evaluate the conditioned reinforcement hypothesis forwarded here would seem in order. In addition, it would be of interest to compare the behavioral effects of a self-evaluative reinforcer conditioned by chaining with a non-self-evaluative reinforcer conditioned in the same manner. Studies which address these applied problems and theoretical questions are now in progress.

REFERENCES

Bandura, A. & Perloff, B. Relative efficacy of self-monitored and externally imposed reinforcement systems. *Journal of Personality and Social Psychology*, 1967, 7, 111–116.

Bem, S. T. Verbal self-control: The establishment of effective self-instruction. *Journal of Experimental Psychology*, 1967, **74**, 485–491.

Johnson, S. M. Self-reinforcement vs. external reinforcement in behavior modification with children. *Developmental Psychology*, 1970, **3**, 147–148.

Kelleher, R. T. Chaining and conditioning reinforcement. In W. K. Honig (Ed.), *Operant behavior; Areas of research and application*. New York: Appleton-Century-Crofts, 1966.

Lovitt, T. & Curtiss, K. A. Academic response rate as a function of teacher- and self-imposed contingencies. *Journal of Applied Behavior Analysis*, 1969, **2**, 49–54.

Luria, A. R. *The role of speech in the regulation of normal and abnormal behavior*. New York: Pergamon Press, 1961.

Luria, A. R. Psychological studies of mental deficiency in the Soviet Union. In N. R. Ellis (Ed.), *Handbook of mental deficiency*. New York: McGraw-Hill, 1963, pp. 353–387.

Marston, A. R. & Kanfer, F. H. Human reinforcement; experimenter and subject controlled. *Journal of Experimental Psychology*, 1963, **66**, 91–94.

O'Leary, K. D. The effects of verbal and non-verbal training on learning and immoral behavior. Unpublished manuscript, University of Illinois, 1968.

Palkes, H., Stewart, M. & Kahana, B. Effects of self-directed verbal commands or porteus maze qualitative scores of hyperactive boys. Unpublished manuscript, University of Illinois, 1968.

Siegel, S. *Nonparametric statistics for the behavioral sciences*. New York: McGraw-Hill, 1956.

Skinner, B. F. *The behavior of organisms: An experimental analysis*. New York: Appleton-Century, 1938.

Skinner, B. F. *Science and human behavior*. New York: MacMillan, 1953.

Control of Fear Responses

Vicarious Extinction of Avoidance Behavior*†

ALBERT BANDURA, JOAN E. GRUSEC, and FRANCES L. MENLOVE

Stanford University

Abstract: This experiment was designed to investigate the extinction of avoidance responses through observation of modelled approach behavior directed toward a feared stimulus without any adverse consequences accruing to the model. Children who displayed fearful and avoidant behavior toward dogs were assigned to one of the following treatment conditions: one group of children participated in a series of brief modelling sessions in which they observed, within a highly positive context, a fearless peer model exhibit progressively stronger approach responses toward a dog; a second group of Ss observed the same graduated modelling stimuli, but in a neutral context; a third group merely observed the dog in the positive context, with the model absent; while a fourth group of Ss participated in the positive activities without any exposure to either the dog or the modelled displays. The two groups of children who had observed the model interact nonanxiously with the dog displayed stable and generalized reduction in avoidance behavior and differed significantly in this respect from children in the dog-exposure and the positive-context conditions. However, the positive context, which was designed to induce anxiety-competing responses, did not enhance the extinction effects produced through modelling.

Recent investigations have shown that behavioral inhibitions (Bandura, 1965a; Bandura, Ross & Ross, 1963; Walters & Parke, 1964) and conditioned emotional responses (Bandura & Rosenthal, 1966; Berger, 1962) can be acquired by observers as a function of witnessing aversive stimuli administered to performing subjects. The present experiment was primarily designed to determine whether pre-existing avoidance behavior can similarly be extinguished on a vicarious basis. The latter phenomenon requires exposing observers to modelled stimulus events in which a performing subject repeatedly exhibits approach responses toward the feared object without incurring any aversive consequences.

Some suggestive evidence that avoidance responses can be extinguished vicariously is furnished by Masserman (1943) and Jones (1942) in exploratory studies of the relative efficacy of various psychotherapeutic procedures. Masserman produced strong feeding inhibitions in cats, following which the inhibited animals observed a cage mate, that had never been negatively conditioned, exhibit prompt approach and feeding responses. The observing subjects initially cowered at the presentation of the conditioned stimulus, but with continued exposure to their fearless companion they advanced, at first hesitantly and then more boldly, to the goal box and consumed the food. Some of the animals, however, showed little reduction in avoidance behavior despite prolonged food deprivation and numerous modelling trials. Moreover,

*This research was supported by Public Health Research Grant M-5162 from the National Institute of Mental Health.

The authors are indebted to Janet Brewer, Edith Dowley, Doris Grant, and Mary Lewis for their generous assistance in various phases of this research.

†Reprinted from the *Journal of Personality and Social Psychology*, 1967, **5**, 1, 16–23. Copyright 1967 with permission from the American Psychological Association and Dr. Albert Bandura.

avoidance responses reappeared in a few of the animals after the normal cat was removed, suggesting that in the latter cases the modelling stimuli served merely as temporary external inhibitors of avoidance responses. Jones (1924) similarly obtained variable results in extinguishing children's phobic responses by having them observe their peers behave in a non-anxious manner in the presence of the avoided objects.

If a person is to be influenced by modelling stimuli and the accompanying consequences, then the necessary observing responses must be elicited and maintained. In the foregoing case studies, the models responded to the most feared stimulus situation at the outset, a modelling procedure that is likely to generate high levels of emotional arousal in observers. Under these conditions any avoidance responses designed to reduce vicariously instigated aversive stimulation, such as subjects withdrawing or looking away, would impede vicarious extinction. Therefore, the manner in which modelling stimuli are presented may be an important determinant of the course of vicarious extinction.

Results from psychotherapeutic studies (Bandura[1]) and experiments with infrahuman subjects (Kimble & Kendall, 1953) reveal that avoidance responses can be rapidly extinguished if subjects are exposed to a graduated series of aversive stimuli that progressively approximate the original intensity of the conditioned fear stimulus. For the above reasons it would seem advisable to conduct vicarious extinction by exposing observers to a graduated sequence of modelling activities beginning with presentations that can be easily tolerated; as observers' emotional reactions to displays of attenuated approach responses are extinguished, the fear-provoking properties of the modelled displays might be gradually increased, concluding with interactions capable of arousing relatively strong emotional responses.

If emotion-eliciting stimuli occur in association with positively reinforcing events, the former cues are likely to lose their conditioned aversive properties more rapidly (Farber, 1948) than through mere repeated nonreinforced presentation. It might therefore be supposed that vicarious extinction would likewise be hastened and more adequately controlled by presenting the modelled stimuli within a favorable context designed to evoke simultaneously competing positive responses.

The principles discussed above were applied in the present experiment, which explored the vicarious extinction of children's fearful and avoidant responses toward dogs. One group of children participated in a series of modelling sessions in which they observed a fearless peer model exhibit progressively longer, closer, and more active interactions with a dog. For these subjects, the modelled approach behavior was presented within a highly positive context. A second group of children was presented the same modelling stimuli, but in a neutral context.

Exposure to the behavior of the model contains two important stimulus events, that is, the occurrence of approach responses without any adverse consequences to the performer, and repeated observation of the feared animal. Therefore, in order to control for the effects of exposure to the dog *per se*, children assigned to a third group observed the dog in the positive context but with the model absent. A fourth group of children participated in the positive activities, but they were never exposed to either the dog or the model.

In order to assess both the generality and the stability of vicarious extinction effects, the children were readministered tests for avoidance behavior toward different dogs following completion of the treatment series, and approximately one month later. It was predicted that children who had observed the peer model interact nonanxiously with the dog would display significantly less avoidance behavior than subjects who had no exposure to the modelling stimuli. The largest decrements were expected to occur among children in the modelling-

---

[1]A. Bandura, "Principles of Behavioral Modification," unpublished manuscript, Stanford University, 1966.

positive context condition. It was also expected that repeated behavioral assessments and the general disinhibitory effects of participation in a series of highly positive activities might in themselves produce some decrease in avoidance behavior.

METHOD

Subject

The subjects were twenty-four boys and twenty-four girls selected from three nursery schools. The children ranged in age from three to five years.

Pre-treatment Assessment of Avoidance Behavior

As a preliminary step in the selection procedure, parents were asked to rate the magnitude of their children's fearful and avoidant behavior toward dogs. Children who received high fear ratings were administered a standardized performance test on the basis of which the final selection was made.

The strength of avoidance responses was measured by means of a graded sequence of fourteen performance tasks in which the children were required to engage in increasingly intimate interactions with a dog. A female experimenter brought the children individually to the test room, which contained a brown cocker spaniel confined in a modified playpen. In the initial tasks the children were asked, in the following order, to walk up to the playpen and look down at the dog, to touch her fur, and to pet her. Following the assessment of avoidance responses to the dog in the protective enclosure, the children were instructed to open a hinged door on the side of the playpen, to walk the dog on a leash to a throw rug, to remove the leash, and to turn the dog over and scratch her stomach. Although a number of the subjects were unable to perform all of the latter tasks, they were nevertheless administered the remaining test items to avoid any assumption of a perfectly ordered scale for all cases. In subsequent items the children were asked to remain alone in the room with the animal and to feed her dog biscuits. The final and most difficult set of tasks required the children to climb into the playpen with the dog, to pet her, to scratch her stomach, and to remain alone in the room with the dog under the exceedingly confining and fear-provoking conditions.

The strength of the children's avoidant tendencies was reflected not only in the items completed, but also in the degree of vacillation, reluctance, and fearfulness that preceded and accompanied each approach response. Consequently, children were credited two points if they executed a given task either spontaneously or willingly, and one point when they carried out the task minimally after considerable hesitancy and reluctance. Thus, for example, children who promptly stroked the dog's fur repeatedly when requested to do so received two points, whereas subjects who held back but then touched the dog's fur briefly obtained one point. In the item requiring the children to remain alone in the room with the dog, they received two points if they approached the animal and played with her, and one point if they were willing to remain in the room but avoided any contact with the dog. Similarly, in the feeding situation children were credited two points if they fed the dog by hand, but a single point if they tossed the biscuits on the floor and thereby avoided close contact with the animal. The maximum approach score that a subject could attain was twenty-eight points.

On the basis of the pre-treatment assessment, the children in each nursery school were grouped into three levels of avoidance behavior, with the corresponding scores ranging from 0 to 7, 8 to 17, and 18 to 20 points. There were approximately the same number of children, equally divided between boys and girls, at each of the three avoidance levels. The subjects from each of these groups were then assigned randomly to one of four conditions.

Treatment Conditions

Children who participated in the *modelling-positive context* condition observed a fearless peer model display approach responses toward a cocker spaniel within the context of a highly enjoyable party atmosphere.

There were eight ten-minute treatment sessions conducted on four consecutive days. Each session, which was attended by a group of four children, commenced with a jovial party. The children were furnished brightly colored hats, cookie treats, and given small prizes. In addition, the experimenter read stories, blew large plastic balloons for the children to play with, and engaged in other party activities designed to produce strong positive affective responses.

After the party was well under way, a second experimenter entered the room carrying the dog, followed by a four-year-old male model who was unknown to most of the children. The dog was placed in a playpen located across the room from a large table at which the children were seated. The model, who had been chosen because of his complete lack of fear of dogs, then performed prearranged sequences of interactions with the dog for approximately three minutes during each session. One boy served as the model for children drawn from two of the nursery schools, and a second boy functioned in the same role at the third school.

The fear-provoking properties of the modelled displays were gradually increased from session to session by varying simultaneously the physical restraints on the dog, the directness and intimacy of the modelled approach responses, and the duration of interaction between the model and his canine companion. Initially, the experimenter carried the dog into the room and confined her to the playpen, and the model's behavior was limited to friendly verbal responses ("Hi, Chloe") and occasional petting. During the following three sessions the dog remained confined to the playpen, but the model exhibited progressively longer and more active interactions in the form of petting the dog with his hands and feet, and feeding her wieners and milk from a baby bottle. Beginning with the fifth session, the dog was walked into the room on a leash, and the modelled tasks were mainly performed outside the playpen. For example, in addition to repeating the feeding routines, the model walked the dog around the room, petted her, and scratched her stomach while the leash was removed. In the last two sessions the model climbed into the playpen with the dog where he petted her, hugged her, and fed her wieners and milk from the baby bottle.

It would have been of interest to compare the relative efficacy of the graduated modelling technique with bold displays of approach behavior from the outset. However, pretest findings showed that when modelled displays are too fear provoking, children actively avoid looking at the performances and are reluctant to participate in subsequent sessions. The latter approach would therefore require additional procedures designed to maintain strong attending behavior to highly aversive modelling stimuli.

Children assigned to the *modelling-neutral context* condition observed the same sequence of approach responses performed by the same peer model except that the parties were omitted. In each of the eight sessions the subjects were merely seated at the table and observed the modelled performances.

In order to control for the influence of repeated exposure to the positive atmosphere and to the dog *per se*, children in the *exposure-positive context* group attended the series of parties in the presence of the dog with the model absent. As in the two modelling conditions, the dog was introduced into the room in the same manner for the identical length of time; similarly, the dog was confined in the playpen during the first four sessions and placed on a leash outside the enclosure in the remaining sessions.

Children in the *positive-context* group participated in the parties, but they were never exposed to either the dog or the model. The main purpose of this condition was to determine whether the mere presence of a dog had an adverse or a beneficial effect on the children. Like the third condition, it also provided a control for the possible therapeutic effects of positive experiences and increased familiarity with amiable experimenters, which may be particularly influential in reducing inhibitions in very young children. In addition, repeated behavioral assessments in which subjects perform a graded series of approach responses toward a feared object without any aversive consequences would be expected to produce some direct extinction of avoidance behavior. The inclusion of the latter two control groups thus makes it possible to evaluate the changes effected by exposure to modelling stimuli over and above those resulting from general disinhibition, direct extinction, and repeated observation of the feared object.

Post-treatment Assessment of Avoidance Behavior

On the day following completion of the treatment series, the children were readministered the performance test consisting of the graded sequence of interaction tasks with the dog. In order to determine the generality of vicarious extinction effects, half the children in each of the four groups were tested initially with the experimental animal and then with an unfamiliar dog; the remaining children were presented with the two dogs in the reverse order.[2] The testing sessions were separated by an interval of one and a half hours so as to minimize any transfer of emotional reactions generated by one animal to the other.

The unfamiliar animal was a white mongrel, predominantly terrier, and of approximately the same size and activity level as the cocker spaniel. Two groups of fifteen children, drawn from the same nursery-school population, were tested with either the mongrel or the spaniel in order to determine the aversiveness of the two animals. The mean approach scores with the spaniel ($M = 16.47$) and the mongrel ($M = 15.80$) were virtually identical ($t = 0.21$).

Follow-up Assessment

A follow-up evaluation was conducted approximately one month after the post-treatment assessment in order to determine the stability of modelling-induced changes in approach behavior. The children's responses were tested with the same performance tasks toward both animals, presented in the identical order.

After the experiment was completed, the children were told that, while most dogs are friendly, before petting an unfamiliar dog they should ask the owner. This precautionary instruction was designed to reduce indiscriminate approach behavior by children who were in the modelling conditions toward strange dogs which they would undoubtedly encounter.

Measurement Procedure

The same female experimenter administered the pre-treatment, post-treatment, and follow-up behavioral tests. To prevent any possible bias, the experimenter was given minimal information about the details of the study and had no knowledge of the conditions to which the children were assigned. The treatment and assessment procedures were further separated by the use of different rooms for each activity.

In order to provide an estimate of interscorer reliability, the performances of twenty-five per cent of the children, randomly selected from pre-treatment, post-treatment, and follow-up phases of the experiment, were scored simultaneously but independently by another rater

---

[2] The authors are especially indebted to Chloe and Jenny for their invaluable and steadfast assistance with a task that, at times, must have been most perplexing to them.

who observed the test sessions through a one-way mirror from an adjoining observation room. The two raters were in perfect agreement on ninety-seven per cent of the specific approach responses that were scored.

A dog's activity level may partly determine the degree of fear and avoidance exhibited by the children; conversely, timorous or unrestrained approach responses might differentially affect the animals' reactivity. Therefore, during the administration of each test item, the animals' behavior was rated as either passive, moderately active, or vigorous. The raters were in perfect agreement in categorizing the dogs' activity levels on eighty-one per cent of the performance tests.

Changes in children's approach-response scores across the different phases of the experiment, and the number of subjects in each treatment condition who were able to carry out the terminal performance task served as the dependent measures.

RESULTS

The percentages of test items in which the animals behaved in a passive, moderately active, or vigorous manner were fifty-five, forty-three, and two, respectively, for the model-positive context group; fifty-three, forty-four, and two for the children in the model-neutral context condition; fifty-two, forty-five, and three for the exposure-positive context group; and fifty-seven, forty-one and two for the positive-context subjects. Thus, the test animals did not differ in their behavior during the administration of performance tasks to children in the various treatment conditions.

Approach Responses

Table 1 presents the mean increases in approach behavior achieved by children in each of the treatment conditions in different phases of the experiment with each of the test animals.

The children's approach responses toward the two dogs did not differ either in the post-treatment assessment ($t = 1.35$) or in the follow-up phase ($t = 0.91$) of the study. Nor were

Table 1. Mean increases in approach responses as a function of treatment conditions, assessment phases, and test animals.

Phases	Treatment conditions			
	Modelling– positive context	Modelling– neutral context	Exposure– positive context	Positive context
Post-treatment				
Spaniel	10.83	9.83	2.67	6.08
Mongrel	5.83	10.25	3.17	4.17
Follow-up				
Spaniel	10.83	9.33	4.67	5.83
Mongrel	12.59	9.67	4.75	6.67
Combined data	10.02	9.77	3.81	5.69

there any significant effects ($t = 1.68$) due to the order in which the test animals were presented following completion of the treatment series. A t-test analysis also disclosed no significant change ($t = 1.50$) in mean approach scores between measurements conducted in the post-treatment and the follow-up phases of the experiment. Moreover, analysis of variance of the post-treatment scores revealed no significant Treatment $\times$ Dogs ($F = 2.15$) or Treatment $\times$ Order ($F = 0.30$) interaction effects. The data were therefore combined across phases and test animals in evaluating the major hypotheses.

An analysis of covariance, in which adjustments were made for differences in initial level of avoidance, was computed for mean responses approach performed by children in the various groups. The results reveal that the treatment conditions had a highly significant effect on the children's behavior ($F = 5.09$; $p < 0.01$). Tests of the differences between the various pairs of treatments indicate that subjects in the modelling-positive context condition displayed significantly more approach behavior than subjects in either the exposure ($F = 9.32$; $p < 0.01$) or the positive-context ($F = 8.96$; $p < 0.01$) groups. Similarly, children who had observed the model within the neutral setting exceeded both the exposure ($F = 6.57$; $p < 0.05$) and positive-context groups ($F = 4.91$; $p < 0.05$) in approach behavior. However, the data yielded no significant differences between either the two modelling conditions ($F = 0.04$) or the two control groups ($F = 0.76$).

Within-Group Analysis of Approach Responses

The approach scores obtained by the different groups of children in pre-experimental and subsequent tests are summarized graphically in Fig. 1. Within-group analyses of changes between initial performance and mean level of approach behavior following treatment disclose significant increases in approach behavior for children in the modelling-positive context

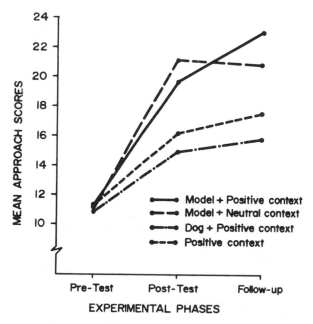

Fig. 1. Mean approach scores achieved by children in each of the treatment conditions on the three different periods of assessment.

group ($t = 7.71$; $p < 0.001$) and for those who observed the modelling performance within the neutral setting ($t = 5.80$; $p < 0.001$). Although the positive-context group showed an increment in approach behavior ($t = 5.78$; $p < 0.001$), children who were merely exposed to the dog in the positive context achieved a small, but nonsignificant ($t = 1.98$), reduction in avoidance responses.

Terminal Performances

Another measure of the efficacy of modelling procedures is provided by comparisons of the number of children in each condition who performed the terminal approach behavior at least once during the post-treatment assessment. Since the frequencies within the two modelling conditions did not differ, and the two control groups were essentially the same, the data for each of the two sets of subgroups were combined. The findings show that sixty-seven per cent of the children in the modelling treatment were able to remain alone in the room confined with the dog in the playpen, whereas the corresponding figure for the control subjects is thirty-three per cent. The χ^2 value for these data is 4.08, which is significant beyond the 0.025 level.

Within the control groups, the terminal performances were attained primarily by subjects who initially showed the weakest level of avoidance behavior. The differences between the two groups are, therefore, even more pronounced if the analysis is conducted on the subjects whose pre-treatment performances reflected extreme or moderately high levels of avoidance behavior. Of the most avoidant subjects in each of the two pooled groups, fifty-five per cent of the children in the modelling conditions were able to perform the terminal approach behavior following the experimental sessions, while only thirteen per cent of the control subjects successfully completed the final task. The one-tailed probability for the obtained $\chi^2 = 4.74$ is slightly below the 0.01 level of significance.

The relative superiority of the modelling groups is also evident in the follow-up phase of the experiment. Based on the stringent criterion in which the most fearful task is successfully performed with *both* animals, a significantly larger number of children in the modelling conditions (forty-two per cent) than in the control groups (twelve per cent) exhibited generalized extinction ($\chi^2 = 4.22$; $p < 0.025$). Moreover, not a single control subject from the two highest levels of avoidance behavior was able to remain alone in the room confined in the playpen with each of the dogs, whereas thirty-three per cent of the most avoidant children in the modelling conditions successfully passed both terminal approach tasks ($\chi^2 = 4.02$; $p < 0.025$).

DISCUSSION

The findings of the present experiment provide considerable evidence that avoidance responses can be successfully extinguished on a vicarious basis. This is shown in the fact that children who experienced a gradual exposure to progressively more fearful modelled responses displayed extensive and stable reduction in avoidance behavior. Moreover, most of these subjects were able to engage in extremely intimate and potentially fearful interactions with test animals following the treatment series. The considerable degree of generalization of extinction effects obtained to the unfamiliar dog is most likely due to similar stimulus properties of the test animals. Under conditions where observers' avoidance responses are extinguished to a single animal, one would expect a progressive decrement in approach behavior toward animals of increasing size and fearfulness.

The prediction that vicarious extinction would be augmented by presenting the modelling stimuli within a highly positive context was not confirmed, although subjects in the latter condition differed more significantly from the controls than children who observed approach behavior under neutral conditions. It is entirely possible that a different temporal ordering of emotion-provoking modelling stimuli and events designed to induce anxiety-inhibiting responses would facilitate the vicarious extinction process. On the basis of evidence from conditioning studies (Melvin & Brown, 1964) the optimal treatment procedure might require repeated observational trials, in each of which aversive modelling stimuli are immediately followed by positively reinforcing experiences for the observers. These temporal prerequisites depend upon the abrupt presentation and termination of the two sets of stimulus events that cannot be readily achieved with live demonstrations. It would be possible, however, to study the effects of systematic variations in the temporal spacing of critical variables if modelling stimuli were presented pictorially. Apart from issues of economy and control, if pictorial stimulus material proved equally as efficacious as live modelling, then skillfully designed therapeutic films could be developed and employed in preventive programmes for eliminating common fears and anxieties before they become well established and widely generalized.

Although children in both the exposure and the positive-context groups showed some increment in approach behavior, only the changes in the latter group were of statistically significant magnitude. Apparently the mere presence of a dog had some mild negative consequences that counteracted the facilitative effects resulting from highly rewarding interactions with amiable experimenters, increased familiarity with the person conducting the numerous tests of avoidance behavior, and any inevitable direct extinction produced by the repeated performance of some approach responses toward the test animals without any adverse consequences. As might be expected, the general disinhibitory effects arising from these multiple sources occurred only in the early phase of the experiment, and no significant increases in approach behavior appeared between the post-treatment and follow-up assessments.

The data obtained in this experiment demonstrate that the fearless behavior of a model can substantially reduce avoidance responses in observers, but the findings do not establish the nature of the mechanism by which vicarious extinction occurs. There are several possible explanations of vicariously produced effects (Bandura, 1965b; Kanfer, 1965). One interpretation is in terms of the informative value of modelling stimuli. That is, the repeated evocation of approach responses without any adverse consequences to another person undoubtedly conveys information to the observer about the probable outcomes of close interactions with dogs. In the present study, however, an attempt was made to minimize the contribution of purely cognitive factors by informing children in all groups beforehand that the test animals were harmless.

The nonoccurrence of anticipated aversive consequences to a model accompanied by positive affective reactions on his part can also extinguish in observers previously established emotional responses that are vicariously aroused by the modelled displays (Bandura & Rosenthal, 1966). It is therefore possible that reduction in avoidance behavior is partly mediated by the elimination of conditioned emotionality.

Further research is needed to separate the relative contribution of cognitive, emotional, and other factors governing vicarious processes. It would also be of interest to study the effects upon vicarious extinction exercised by such variables as number of modelling trials, distribution of extinction sessions, mode of model presentation, and variations in the characteristics of the models and the feared stimuli. For example, with extensive sampling in the modelled displays of both girls and boys exhibiting approach responses to dogs ranging from diminutive breeds to larger specimens, it may be possible to achieve widely generalized extinction effects. Once approach behaviors have been restored through modelling, their maintenance and further generalization can be effectively controlled by response-contingent reinforcement administered directly to the subject. The combined use of modelling and reinforcement procedures may thus serve as a highly efficacious mode of therapy for eliminating severe behavioral inhibitions.

REFERENCES

Bandura, A. Influence of models' reinforcement contingencies on the acquisition of imitative responses. *Journal of Personality and Social Psychology*, 1965, **1**, 589–595. (a)

Bandura, A. Vicarious processes: A case of no-trial learning. In L. Berkowitz (Ed.), *Advances in experimental social psychology*. Vol. 2. New York: Academic Press, 1965. pp. 1–55. (b)

Bandura, A. & Rosenthal, T. L. Vicarious classical conditioning as a function of arousal level. *Journal of Personality and Social Psychology*, 1966, **3**, 54–62.

Bandura, A., Ross, D. & Ross, S. A. Vicarious reinforcement and imitative learning. *Journal of Abnormal and Social Psychology*, 1963, **67**, 601–607.

Berger, S. M. Conditioning through vicarious instigation. *Psychological Review*, 1962, **69**, 450–466.

Farber, I. E. Response fixation under anxiety and non-anxiety conditions. *Journal of Experimental Psychology*, 1948, **38**, 111–131.

Jones, M. C. The elimination of children's fear. *Journal of Experimental Psychology*, 1924, **7**, 383–390.

Kanfer, F. H. Vicarious human reinforcement: A glimpse into the black box. In L. Krasner & L. P. Ullmann (Eds.), *Research in behavior modification*. New York: Holt, Rinehart & Winston, 1965, pp. 244–267.

Kimble, G. A. & Kendall, J. W., Jr. A comparison of two methods of producing experimental extinction. *Journal of Experimental Psychology*, 1953, **45**, 87–90.

Masserman, J. H. *Behavior and neurosis*. Chicago: University of Chicago Press, 1943.

Melvin, K. B. & Brown, J. S. Neutralization of an aversive light stimulus as a function of number of paired presentations with food. *Journal of Comparative and Physiological Psychology*, 1964, **58**, 350–353.

Walters, R. H. & Parke, R. D. Influence of response consequences to a social model on resistance to deviation. *Journal of Experimental Child Psychology*, 1964, **1**, 269–280.

The Group Desensitization of Children's Snake Phobias using Vicarious and Contact Desensitization Procedures*

BRUNHILDE RITTER

Stanford University, Stanford, California

Abstract: The effectiveness of vicarious and contact desensitization procedures for the group treatment of snake-avoidant children was investigated. Forty-four pre-adolescent boys and girls served as Ss. Vicarious desensitization children observed E and five peer models engage in gradually bolder interactions with a tame four-foot Gopher snake. Contact desensitization subjects not only observed E and peers perform as in the foregoing conditions but also had opportunities for physical contact with model-therapists and the phobic object. Treatment consisted of two thirty-five-minute sessions for both conditions. Performance on a behavioral avoidance test was used to measure treatment effects. The following predicted results were obtained: (a) contact desensitization yielded significantly greater reductions in avoidance than did vicarious desensitization; (b) both desensitization groups demonstrated significantly larger avoidance decrements than did non-treated controls. During post-testing, eighty per cent of the children receiving contact desensitization, 53.3 per cent of those in the vicarious desensitization condition and none of the control children successfully completed the stringent terminal task of the avoidance test.

Extensive investigations (Jersild & Holmes, 1935; Jersild, Markey & Jersild, 1933) indicate that one of the most frequent childhood fears, and often the most intense, is that of animals. A survey of 303 adults (Jersild & Holmes, 1935) revealed that these phobic reactions were also by far the most persistent. Since animal phobias do not appear to have a high probability of being outgrown spontaneously, the development and experimental test of techniques designed specifically to eliminate these avoidance responses in children seems indicated. While behavior therapy procedures suitable for treating adult animal phobics have frequently been tested experimentally (e.g. Cooke, 1966; Davison, 1965; Lang & Lazovik, 1963; Lang, Lazovik & Reynolds, 1965; Lomont & Edwards, 1967; and Schubot, 1966), reports on treatments used to eliminate children's animal fears have largely been limited to case histories (e.g., Jones, 1924; Lazarus, 1960; and Lazarus & Abramovitz, 1962). Two very interesting exceptions, Bandura, Grusec and Menlove (1967) and Bandura and Menlove (1967), investigated the use of vicarious desensitization procedures in treating children who were fearful of dogs.

In the present study, vicarious desensitization (in which children observed the experimenter and several peer models fearlessly participate in increasingly bolder interactions with the phobic object) was contrasted with contact desensitization. The latter procedure had been used previously by the experimenter in treating a female college student who had an extreme fear of performing dissections. The student had made several attempts to overcome this inhibition "with reason and will" in a biology course which required each student to

---

*Reprinted from *Behavior Research and Therapy*, 1968, **6**, 1–6. Copyright 1968 with permission from Pergamon Press Publishing Company and Brunhilde Ritter.

dissect his "personal" foetal pig. Failure made dropping the course seem inevitable though this action would have had serious consequences for the student's graduate study plans. The following therapy was initiated. During one class session the student merely observed three enthusiastic fellow students (who shared a laboratory table with her engaging in dissection activity. She then enlisted the cooperation of one of her sympathetic tablemates and was permitted to rest her hand on the performing student's as dissection procedures were being conducted. When this contact no longer evoked anxiety, the dissection implement was held independently while the model-therapist watched. Within a few sessions the erstwhile fearful student was performing dissections unaided and with considerable anxiety-free interest. The course was successfully completed.

Preliminary investigation indicated that this technique was also suited for group use with children and was therefore tested in the present study. It is being referred to as contact desensitization because not only physical contact with the phobic object is involved, but also with the model-therapist(s). Vicarious desensitization, using multiple models, was selected as the comparison treatment method for the following reasons: (a) investigations by Bandura and colleagues (1967) suggest it is a powerful procedure; (b) it serves as a control for the effects due solely to model observation which is intrinsic to the contact desensitization procedure.

The relative efficacy of the treatment methods were tested with children who exhibited phobic behavior toward snakes. The children's performance on a snake avoidance test (Schubot, 1966) prior to and following treatment served as the dependent measures. In order to control for effects due to the testing procedure itself, one group of children was exposed to preliminary and post assessment only. It was predicted that treated children would show significantly greater approach behavior than non-treated controls. Contact desensitization, which provides a strong counter response to anxiety (physical contact with models) and a greater sampling of graduated aversive stimuli (physical contact with the phobic object in addition to visual stimulation), was expected to yield larger decrements in avoidance than vicarious desensitization.

METHOD

Subjects

Twenty-eight girls and sixteen boys ranging in ages from five to eleven years served as subjects.

Preliminary Assessment of Snake Avoidance

A twenty-nine-item performance test devised by Schubot (1966) was used to measure strength of snake avoidance. This test required increasingly more direct interactions with a harmless four-foot snake. The children were tested individually by a female research assistant. Each child was told the following: (1) there was a harmless caged Gopher snake at the far end of the room he was about to enter with the assistant; (2) he would be asked to do various things with the snake and (3) he was to inform the assistant if at any time he became too afraid to continue and she would stop the testing immediately. Children were additionally asked to rate their fear while performing each task according to whether they were: (a) "not afraid at all," (b) "a little afraid," or (c) "very afraid — afraid a lot."

Initial tasks of the avoidance test required the *S* to move from a point fifteen feet away from the caged snake to a point one foot away (Items 1 through 4). Tasks 5 through 12 involved the following: standing directly in front of the cage, looking down at the snake, touching the cage with gloved and bare hands, and inserting gloved then bare hand into the cage up to the wrist. Tasks 13 and 14 required the S to briefly touch the snake with one gloved and bare hand respectively. Items 15 through 20 required the S to lift the snake within the cage with one bare or gloved hand for periods ranging from five to thirty seconds. Ss were subsequently requested to lift the snake out of the cage with two gloved or two bare hands until told to put him back within five to thirty seconds (Tasks 21 through 26). Task 27 involved taking the snake out of the cage with bare hands, placing it on the floor, lifting it after a few seconds then holding it until told to put it back in thirty seconds. Task 28 required holding the snake approximately five inches from the face for thirty seconds. Finally the S was asked to sit in a chair with his arms at his sides while the snake was in his lap for thirty seconds (terminal behavior, Item 29).

Only Ss who could not perform Task 15, i.e. holding the snake within the cage with one gloved hand for five seconds, were included in the study. The total number of tasks successfully completed (Ss received one point for each task) served as the Ss approach scores. Using these scores, children were divided into two levels of avoidance and assigned to one of the three conditions on a random stratified basis while balancing for sex.

Treatment Procedures

In both experimental conditions children participated in two thirty-five-minute treatment sessions spaced a week apart. Treatment was conducted in groups made up of seven to eight children (the ratio of boys and girls and level I and II avoiders was similar in each). The experimental room was equipped with chairs arranged in a circle. A glass cage containing Posie, the experimental snake, and a large towel were placed toward the center of the circle.

During the first session, the children were assembled outside the experimental room, told that they would again be seeing the snake they were tested with and assured they would not be forced to do anything they did not want to do. They were then led into the room by E and invited to sit. One extremely fearful girl (contact desensitization condition) was told she could remain at the door and not even watch.[1] E was generally warm and approving throughout treatment. At the close of each session children were reminded that snakes should never be handled unless one were certain that they were harmless.

In the *vicarious desensitization condition* the models, who were referred to as demonstrators during treatment, were already seated at the far corner of the room when the Ss entered. (There were five peer models at each session. These were selected from a pool of "fearless" boys and girls.) E told the Ss that on this occasion they could not touch Posie but were to watch the demonstrators. E added that they would have a chance to touch Posie some other time. E then took the snake out of her cage, sat next to two of the demonstrators, and began petting her. She invited the demonstrators to pet Posie also. Soon most of Posie's four feet were covered by stroking hands, some gloved and some bare. E subsequently had a few of the models perform tasks included in the avoidance test, e.g., stroking Posie with one gloved then one bare hand, lifting her with gloved and bare hands, placing her on towel with bare hands, lifting her and sitting with her, holding her head approximately five inches from face, leaving hands at side while Posie remained on lap, placing Posie back in cage. Subsequently Ss took turns being "teacher." The "teacher's" activities follow: (a) he sent a selected demonstrator out of the room; (b) called him back within a few seconds; (c) instructed him to perform the foregoing tasks (with prompting from E as required). During the "Posie on

---

[1]She originally cowered at the exit but soon, voluntarily and eagerly, joined in the activities.

lap with hands at side" task all the children occasionally counted to ten with E to time the performance. Both "teachers" and "demonstrators" rotated during this phase of the procedure. Ss, of course, only were permitted to serve as teachers. At the end of the session E reminded the children that what had happened was to be a secret for a couple of weeks. They were then thanked, told that E would see them again, and sent back to their classrooms. During the second session the teacher and demonstrator rotations were continued.

E began the *contact desensitization* treatment by having Ss observe E taking Posie out of the cage, sitting with her and petting her. E continued playing with Posie until interest had been generated and one of the bolder subjects looked like he or she wished to participate. E then had this child put on a glove and place his hand on hers while she was stroking Posie. Gradually the child was eased into stroking with his gloved hand unaided. This was repeated with bare hands. E sat in various places in the room to give all the children a chance to sit close and participate. (E and demonstrators also changed their "sitting locations" during vicarious desensitization.) Some children readily engaged in handling Posie, with gloved or bare hands, after having observed others perform. The experimenter used the *S*-on-*E*'s hand prompt with the more hesitant Ss. Following this, E had a few of the bolder children carry out avoidance test items as in the preceding condition. Subsequently subjects took turns being teacher and demonstrator. From this point on the procedure was the same as in the vicarious desensitization treatment, however, children who were having difficulties were allowed to perform with the assistance of bolder demonstrators.

Controls were not contacted between assessment tests.

Post-treatment Behavioral Assessment

The avoidance test used for preliminary assessment was readministered to subjects the day following the final treatment session. Whenever a *S* failed to perform a test item, testing was discontinued. Treatment success was operationally defined as performance of the terminal behavior (Task 29).

Assessment Procedure

In order to determine whether modification of a specific avoidance behavior would produce generalized changes in reported anxiety, Ss were administered a twenty-five-item fear inventory prior to and following the treatment phase of the experiment. E administered this survey which listed animal, social (e.g., being ridiculed by peers), and inanimate (e.g. thunder) stimuli to the children individually. The children were asked to rate each item as evoking no fear, "a little" fear, or "a lot" of fear. Ss received one point for each rating of "a little," and two points for each rating of "a lot." The total number of points obtained comprised the fear inventory score. The self-ratings of fear were also included to explore the feasibility of using this procedure with pre-adolescent children.

All avoidance tests were administered by the same female assistant who participated in no other phase of the experiment. In order to prevent assessment bias she was given no information regarding the treatments to be administered or *S* assignment. The modelling of fearless behavior during testing was minimized by having the assistant stand behind the *S* at all times except when it was necessary for her to remove the cage top or assist the *S* (e.g. prevent the snake from leaving *S*'s lap during the performance of Task 29 if necessary). The activity level of the snake was rated throughout testing in order to determine whether activity fluctuations contributed to any differential treatment results.

RESULTS

Preliminary analysis of avoidance-test change scores (pretest minus post-test) indicated that there were no significant sex differences, nor significant effects due to initial avoidance level. Data were therefore pooled with respect to these two variables for subsequent evaluation of treatments. An analysis of variance was performed on the change scores obtained in the three conditions. A highly significant treatment effect was obtained. As shown in Table 1, additional one tail *t*-tests revealed that both treatment conditions yielded significantly greater changes in behavior than did the control groups. Furthermore, contact desensitization (CD) was superior to vicarious desensitization (VD). Differences in the approach scores obtained during the pretest and post-test within each condition were also analyzed. These were found to be significant for the contact desensitization and vicarious desensitization subjects only ($p < 0.01$). The experimental hypotheses were confirmed.

Table 1. Analysis of mean avoidance test change scores.

Treatments	N	Mean change scores	Contrasts	t	p
Contact Desensitization	15	17.13	VD vs. CD	2.61	< 0.025
Vicarious Desensitization	15	10.93	VD vs. Controls	3.88	< 0.005
Controls	14*	2.14	CD vs. Controls	8.38	< 0.005

*One *S* moved from state prior to post-testing.

All items in the avoidance test were successfully performed by eighty per cent of the children receiving contact desensitization, by 53.3 per cent of the children in the vicarious desensitization condition and by none of the control children. Chi-square analyses indicated that though differences in frequency of terminal-behavior-achievement between each of the treatment conditions and the control condition are significant ($p < 0.01$), the difference between the treatment groups themselves is not.

The fear rating on the final task *S*s completed during preliminary avoidance testing was compared with the rating given during the performance of the same item at post-avoidance-test assessment. There was an overall reduction in reported fear. Though the ratings of treated *S*s had decreased more than those of controls, this difference was not significant. There was also a nonsignificant overall decrease in fear inventory scores during post-testing of both subjects who were able to complete the terminal task and those who were not. "Successes" and "failures" did not differ in amount of change beyond chance. Fluctuations in snake activity did not differ significantly during the testing of *S*s in the three conditions or during preliminary and post assessment.

DISCUSSION

The effectiveness of vicarious desensitization procedures for reducing avoidance behavior was confirmed by the results of the present study. Moreover, it was demonstrated that physical contact with the phobic object and/or physical contact with fearless models yielded therapeutic results over and above those obtained by vicarious desensitization alone. Additional studies are planned to investigate the role of these two variables. The combination both of social approval and of material rewards with vicarious and contact desensitization procedures will also be systematically explored. Reports by Bandura, Grusec & Menlove (1967) and Lazarus (1960) suggest that such techniques may be highly effective. Since all the children included in the study attended the same elementary school, it is possible that familiarity with peer models and co-subjects contributed to treatment effects.[2] The procedures should be studied using Ss and models who have had no contact prior to participation in the investigation.

Though significant effects were not obtained using self-reports of fear on either the avoidance test or the fear inventory, it is interesting that overall reductions were noted in the second assessment phase and that treated Ss tended to report greater decreases in fear than controls during post avoidance testing. Further study is needed to determine the reliability and validity of these ratings. Though validity of the self-reported fear ratings of adults have been investigated (Lanyon & Manosevitz, 1966), those of children have not been as yet.

In conclusion, it appears that group contact desensitization is a powerful and economical therapeutic procedure for eliminating children's animal phobias. Using this method twelve children were successfully treated with a total expenditure of 140 minutes of the T's time. Vicarious desensitization was also found to be effective. Research is planned to extend the use of variations of both these treatments for the modification of children's fears.

REFERENCES

Bandura, A., Grusec, Joan E. & Menlove, Frances L. (1967) Vicarious extinction of avoidance behavior. *J. pers. soc. Psychol.* 5, 16–23.

Bandura, A. & Menlove, Frances L. (1967) Factors determining vicarious extinction of avoidance behavior through symbolic modeling. Unpublished manuscript, Stanford University.

Cooke, G. (1966) The efficacy of two desensitization procedures: An analogue study. *Behav. Res. & Therapy* 4, 17–24.

Davison, G. C. (1965) The influence of systematic desensitization, relaxation, and graded exposure to imaginal aversive stimuli on the modification of phobiac behavior. Unpublished doctoral dissertation, Stanford University.

Jersild, A. T. & Holmes, F. B. (1935) Children's fears. *Child Dev. Mong.* Bureau of publications, Teachers College, Columbia University, New York.

Jersild, A. T., Markey, Frances V. & Jersild, Catherine L. (1933) Children's fears, dreams, wishes, daydreams, likes, dislikes, pleasant and unpleasant memories. *Child Dev. Mong.* Bureau of publications, Teachers College, Columbia University, New York.

Jones, M. C. (1924) The elimination of children's fears. *J. exp. Psychol.* 7, 383–390.

Lang, P. J. & Lazovik, A. D. (1963) Experimental desensitization of a phobia. *J. abnorm. soc. Psychol.* 66, 519–525.

---

[2]Subjects promised not to discuss any of the treatment procedures until the study was over. This was to eliminate any contamination resulting from knowledge of the different treatment conditions. Teachers and children indicated that the "oath of secrecy" was maintained.

Lang, P. J., Lazovik, A. D. & Reynolds, D. J. (1965) Desensitization, suggestibility and pseudotherapy. *J. abnorm. Psychol.* **70**, 395–402.

Lanyon, R. I. & Manosevitz, M. (1966) Validity of self-reported fear. *Behav. Res. & Therapy* **4**, 17–24.

Lazarus, A. A. (1960) The elimination of children's phobias by deconditioning. In *Behaviour Therapy and the Neuroses*. (Ed. H. J. Eysenck). Pergamon Press, Oxford.

Lazarus, A. A. & Abramovitz, A. (1962) The use of "emotive imagery" in the treatment of children's phobias. *J. ment. Sci.* **108**, 191–195.

Lomont, J. F. & Edwards, J. E. (1967) The role of relaxation in systematic desensitization. *Behav. Res. & Therapy* **5**, 11–25.

Schubot, E. D. (1966) The influence of hypnotic and muscular relaxation in systematic desensitizations of phobias. Unpublished doctoral dissertation, Stanford University.

Reduction of Examination Anxiety and "Stage-Fright" by Group Desensitization and Relaxation*

O. KONDAŠ†

Department of Psychology, Comenius University, Bratislava, Czechoslovakia

Abstract: The results of the experiment in group desensitization, relaxation and imagination of exam situations in groups of children ($N = 23$) and students ($N = 13$) show that systematic desensitization is an efficient method for reducing stage-fright. Some transient positive effects were also achieved with a modification of the Schultz method of relaxation. Interviews, a Fear Survey Schedule and a test of palmar perspiration were used in the assessment of effects. The main conclusions are concordant with previous studies in desensitization (e.g. Lang & Lazovik, 1963; Rachman, 1965, 1966a and b; Lazarus, 1961; Paul & Shannon, 1966) and the present results provide interesting comparisons.

INTRODUCTION

Fear of failing in examinations and of giving reports in class are relatively common worries of pupils. They appear in forty-four to ninety per cent of sixth-grade pupils, and twenty per cent of school children experience fear of school examinations (Eysenck & Rachman, 1965). In relation to school examinations, pedagogical psychology uses the term "pre-examination" state which is characterized by excessive tension (Přihoda, 1924; Ďurič, 1965). This state of excitement generally has a positive influence on performance, and Přihoda found that only in 13.3 per cent of pupils did their school performance deteriorate. This deterioration can be included in the term "stage-fright" which represents a state of higher emotive tension and fear in personally important situations such as examinations or facing an audience. The teachers found 18.1 per cent of pupils suffering from stage-fright ($N = 414$), and psychological examination showed that for 9.9 per cent of them stage-fright was a serious personal problem (Kondaš, 1966b). Since stage-fright is characterized by learned fear and increased tension, one may assume that desensitization treatment and relaxation might reduce it.

In 1965 and 1966 Rachman published studies concerning the separate effects of relaxation and desensitization in treating spider phobias. The present paper investigates similar problems under group treatment procedures while the Schultz method of autogenic training was used to induce relaxation. It also allows us to compare group desensitization in children and in adults. Further it appears to give a support to Paul and Shannon's (1966) finding on the efficiency of group desensitization in treating social-evaluative anxiety. In comparison with Paul and Shannon's work with students, our research was centred mainly on sixth to ninth-grade children.

---

*Reprinted from *Behaviour Research and Therapy*, 1967, **5**, 275–281. Copyright 1967 with permission from Pergamon Press Publishing Company and Dr. O. Kondaš.
†Now at: Bratislava, Exnárova 17, Czechoslovakia.

METHOD

Subject Selection and Samples

In October 1965, the teachers of a large school were requested to select all fifth to ninth-grade pupils who appeared to experience stage-fright and then to describe their symptoms and degree on a standard schedule (Kondaš, 1966b). Sixty-nine of the children concerned were examined by Raven's PM, Eysenck's MPI adapted for children, and adapted Fear Survey Schedule (Wolpe & Lang, 1964) and by interview. The examinations were conducted by two psychologists with randomized order of the methods used in five or seven-member groups.

The pupils of this sample with stage-fright (according to their teachers' description, own data, and FSS score) were selected and divided into four six-member groups. They comprised the first sample, consisting finally of twenty-three children (age range eleven to fifteen years; average age thirteen years).

The second sample consisted of thirteen psychology students in the fifth to seventh semester of their studies (average age 21.9 years). These were divided into three groups. Each potential subject was interviewed and completed an examination questionnaire and the FSS. The final sample was selected from a larger group of thirty students.

Procedure

Group sessions were conducted as follows. In the first (schoolchildren) sample one group ($N = 6$) was given only relaxation by autogenic training (AT), the second group ($N = 6$) was given systematic desensitization (SD), the third group ($N = 5$) presentation of hierarchy items without relaxation and the fourth group ($N = 6$) served as a control group. The control Ss were examined and re-examined at the same time as experimental groups. The procedure in the second (student) sample was analogous to the first one; six subjects received SD, four received relaxation by AT, and three subjects formed a control group.

For relaxation, Schultz's autogenic training was used. The children sat in comfortable armchairs and the following exercises of relaxed breathing, relaxation of right hand, left hand, muscles of legs, and relaxation of abdomen and breast muscles were provided in single sessions. The AT exercises were led by two psychologists, and there were ten sessions given at weekly intervals. The children were also asked to practice the same AT exercises at home, once a day. After the seventh session, the AT group was requested to do two to three minutes of relaxation while in the classroom, at the beginning of a lesson and while the teacher was writing in the classbook.

The SD group began desensitization after the seventh AT session. Five desensitization sessions were conducted at five to seven day intervals. Systematic desensitization was conducted by a psychologist with experience in individual desensitization treatment.

The third group was required to shut their eyes and to imagine two to three hierarchy items in each session with two presentations of each item. There were four sessions altogether.

Examination Fear Hierarchy
A. For sixth to ninth grade children
   1. Going to school in the morning—you think that you may be asked to give reports.
   2. The lesson begins—the teacher begins to examine.
   3. Writing a written exam.
   4. Examination begins—you think that you will be asked to give a report.
   5. As above—the teacher pronounces your name.

    6. You stand up and answer questions while in your place.

    7. Answering questions at a map.

    8. Calculating an arithmetic example on the blackboard.

    9. Answering questions in front of the class.

   10. As above — while the school director is present.

B. For university students

    1. One week before an important examination.

    2. Two days before the examination.

    3. You are to sit an exam tomorrow.

    4. It is the morning of the exam day — it is one to two hours before the time of the exam.

    5. Sitting for the examination.

    6. Reading the questions and preparing answers.

    7. Selecting questions (i.e. from written questions in envelopes).

    8. Entering the exam room.

    9. Waiting for exam in front of an examination work-room.

Measures

In addition to the interview data, two parallel series of FSS were used as the main indicator of effects. The adapted FSS consists of thirty-one items, eleven of which referred to stage-fright situations, each being estimated in five degrees. In the first sample, a test of palmar perspiration with Boymond's mixture (Král, 1964; Barlogová, 1965) was conducted under school examination conditions before and after treatment. Perspiration turns the treated filter paper blue; the resultant colors have different intensities and extent. Its evaluation was done qualitatively by two judges. An advantage of this assessment is its technical easiness, and it can be used directly in the classroom; a disadvantage lies in its qualitative character.

The follow-up evaluation was done by FSS in the children's group five months after the termination of treatment. (The follow-up N is smaller as some children had left the school.)

After the publication of Rachman's data (1965) where he gives an account of the absence of changes in the MPI after desensitization, this inventory was not repeated.

RESULTS

Both autogenic training and systematic desensitization can be provided in group conditions. In all six members of children's SD group, agreement was reached in the sequence of hierarchy items. This criterion could not be wholly fulfilled in the SD group of psychology students. The differences in hierarchy item sequences demanded a division of the six-member group into two, three-member subgroups. As a consequence of differences in item sequences there were more frequent disturbances of relaxation when presenting "dissequenced" items, and therefore the presentations times of each such item had to be abbreviated. In the children's SD group, however, two presentations of all items except Items 5, 9 and 10 were sufficient. The possibilities and limitations of group desensitization have already been discussed (Kondaš, 1966a).

The results of the experiment are given in Table 1.

The greatest decrease of FSS score appears in both groups with systematic desensitization. The decrease is twenty-eight points in children and fourteen points in university students. Statistical comparison with non-treated control groups shows, according to the Mann–Whitney test, that this difference is significant ($p = 0.001$).

The results in groups with relaxation by means of the Schultz method are interesting.

Table 1. Main results of experiment.

Group	Full FSS score		The sum of cases with decrease of 10 or more points in FSS	Decrease of palmar perspiration ($N = 5$)
	Before	After		
	Treatment			
A. Children				
AT relaxation	87.6	81.6	2	1
Desensitization	81.7	53.0	3	3
Imagination of hierarchy items	78.8	73.0	2	0
Control group	84.2	88.5	0	0
B. University students				
AT relaxation ($N = 4$)	75.5	73.0	2	—
Desensitization ($N = 6$)	82.5	68.6	4	—
Controls ($N = 3$)	62.0	64.3	0	—

The difference in FSS score in the student group is slight and insignificant, while in the children's group it reaches the three per cent level of significance ($p = 0.03$). There was, however, an important difference in doing AT relaxation. The children also carried out the relaxation before the beginning of a lesson (in the classroom), that is, right before the examination. This was not done by the students who had three AT sessions less than the children's AT group.

In the palmar perspiration test, there were distinct decreases in perspiration during the examination. In the AT group only one *S* showed a decrease, while after systematic desensitization all but two *S*s showed a decrement of perspiration in the examination condition.

Regarding the interview data, it may be mentioned that all students reported a reduction or elimination of stage-fright after desensitization. Two students described a feeling of calmness similar to indifference, and a further two ate breakfast prior to the last examination period in the eighth semester—something they had never done until undergoing desensitization. The children of SD group said that examination no longer disturbed their calmness (four cases) and two cases reported a reduction of examination fear. The mother of a pupil spontaneously reported that her daughter now speaks calmly about her course of school examinations where she had never done so before. Previously her sleep had been disturbed and she complained of diarrhoea.

In the group receiving AT relaxation, one student reported being more relaxed at interview, and three of the AT children said that they were calmer during examinations than they had been before the treatment.

The follow-up data in mean FSS score is presented in Table 2 (children's group).

Table 2. Differences of three treatment procedures at follow-up.

Procedure	Mean FSS score		
	Before	After	At Follow-
	Treatment		up
AT relaxation ($N = 4$)	2.89	2.63	2.94
Desensitization ($N = 5$)	2.73	2.34	2.30
Imagination of hierarchy items ($N = 3$)	2.20	2.03	2.17

The follow-up evaluation shows the stable effect of systematic desensitization. The effect of AT was only transient and after five months, the pre-treatment level had been restored. The changes of main FSS scores after the simple imagination of hierarchy items were very slight.

DISCUSSION AND CONCLUSIONS

The results show that the method of systematic desensitization is efficient in reducing "stage-fright." The present outcome is similar to Lazarus's work (1961) on the method of group SD in adults; group desensitization it appears is also possible with children. Moreover, the comparison between our first sample (children) and the second sample (students) shows even better performance of group SD in children. This may be attributable to the difficulty in achieving uniformity in the hierarchy item sequence with the students. The more frequent disturbances of relaxation occurred precisely in those subjects where the group-presented situation did not correspond with their individual hierarchy. This observation is further evidence that it is essential in the SD method to order the sequence of hierarchy items correctly (Wolpe, 1963) and of the importance of a graduated approach to desensitization (Rachman, 1966a). This fact requires that the therapist has some experience in the construction of a hierarchy.

The limitation of group desensitization which arises from the difference between individually-constructed but group-presented hierarchy items was minimized by Paul and Shannon (1966). They constructed hierarchy lists by group discussion. The hierarchy thus included common elements from all Ss with some broadening of the items by elements from the most anxious group-member. At the beginning of each desensitization session, they provided further discussion of social-evaluative anxiety situations which resulted in changes of the anxiety hierarchies or the construction of a new hierarchy. In this way the combination of group desensitization with group discussion overcomes the problem of how to achieve uniformity of hierarchy items.

Paul and Shannon (1966) found combined group desensitization superior to both insight-oriented psychotherapy and an attention-placebo programme in the treatment of social-evaluative anxiety (public speaking situations). Snake phobias (Lang & Lazovik, 1963) or spider phobias (Rachman, 1965; 1966a and b), like social-evaluative anxiety, examination-anxiety or stage-fright are suitable problems for experiments in desensitization (also from the standpoint of the ethics of therapeutic research).

The reduction of stage-fright by systematic desensitization may be accounted for by the fact that its main feature is that it is a learned fear in which punishment, feeling ashamed, criticism, decrease of prestige and similar effects work as negative reinforcing factors. Stage-fright symptoms like tremor, excitement, muscle rigidity or a feeling of stomach spasm indicate the presence of tension in this state (Kondaš, 1966b). Since the relaxation in itself does not seem to be efficient (Rachman, 1965; Franks, 1966), our better results in the children's group might be ascribed to the effect of another form of relaxation (Schultz's method which is supposed to reduce tension — Kleinsorge & Klumbies, 1961). A more probable explanation is, of course, that owing to the relaxation given in the classroom situation just before the examination, some fear-reduction was obtained as a consequence of the connection of the real examination-fear situation with a reaction incompatible with fear (i.e., AT relaxation). This conclusion is supported by the absence of any effect in the student's AT group in which the connection of relaxation and examination did not take place. The reciprocal inhibition effect is a probable explanation of some of the positive results (Kleinsorge & Klumbies, 1961) achieved by autogenic training. The effect of AT in our children's group was, however, only transient, while the effect achieved by group desensitization was stable for at least five months after treatment.

The imagination of examination-fear situations without inducing a state incompatible with fear does not produce fear-reduction. This supports the notion of reciprocal inhibition as the main basis of therapeutic effects in systematic desensitization (Wolpe, 1954). It may be mentioned that according to the data collected from students (Kondaš, 1966b), as well as common observation, that stage-fright seems to be considerably resistent to extinction by natural events. Despite the fact that students for example, have a large number of opportunities for public-speaking as well as examinations, the stage-fright reaction had not been eliminated in many cases — even though some of them had tried to be calm before exams, and had tried deep breathing or to think about pleasant things when stage-fright had arisen. Contrary to the inefficient extinction occurring in natural circumstances, immediate reduction of fear occurs by SD, and "the desensitization of imaginal stimuli does indeed generalize to real-life situations" (Rachman, 1966b).

Acknowledgments. Thanks are due to colleague E. Borzová from Psychiatric Hospital V. Leváre for her assistance with this research and to the school director V. Hudzovič for arranging good conditions for the research. Appreciation is further expressed to Dr. S. Rachman for his kind critical reading of the manuscript.

REFERENCES

Barlogová, D. (1965) Stupeň potivosti kože. CSc. Dissertation, Bratislava.

Ďurič, L. (1965) Práceschopnosť žiakov vo vynučovacom procese. *Slov. pedag. naklad.*, Bratislava.

Eysenck, H. J. & Rachman, S. (1965) *The Causes and Cures of Neurosis.* Routledge & Kegan Paul, London.

Eysenck, H. J. (Ed.) (1960) *Behaviour Therapy and the Neuroses.* Pergamon Press, Oxford.

Eysenck, H. J. (Ed.) (1964) *Experiments in Behaviour Therapy.* Pergamon Press, Oxford.

Franks, C. M. (1966) Clinical application of conditioning and other behavioral techniques. *Conditioned Reflex* 1, 36–50.

Kleinsorge, H. & Klumbies, G. (1961) *Technik der Relaxation — Selbstentspannung.* VEB G. Fisher, Jena.

Kondaš, O. (1966a) Experiences with Wolpe's method of systematic desensitization. Paper read at *Third Czsl. Psychiat. Conf.* Included in the book O. Kondaš: Discentná psychoterapia, pp. 109–111. *Vydav. Slov. akadémie vied,* Bratislava, 1969.

Kondaš, O. (1966b) Tréma ako forma naučeného strachu. *Psychol. a Patopsychol. dieťaťa,* 1967, **2**, 67–77.

Král, J. (1964) Fyziologie a biochemie potu. *Štát. zdrav. naklad.*, Praha.

Lang, P. J. & Lazovik, A. D. (1963) The experimental desensitization of phobia. *J. abnorm. Soc. Psychol.* **66**, 519–525. Cited in Eysenck (1964), pp. 40–50.

Lazarus, A. A. (1961) Group therapy of phobic disorders by systematic desensitization. *J. abnorm. Soc. Psychol.* **63**, 504–510. Cited in Eysenck (1964), pp. 87–98.

Paul, G. L. & Shannon, D. T. (1966) Treatment of anxiety through systematic desensitization in therapy groups. *J. abnorm. Soc. Psychol.* **71**, 124–135.

Přihoda, V. (1924) *Psychologie a Hygiena Skoušky,* Praha.

Rachman, S. (1965) Studies in desensitization — I. The separate effect of relaxation and desensitization. *Behav. Res. & Therapy* 3, 245–251.

Rachman, S. (1966a) Studies in desensitization — II. Flooding. *Behav. Res. & Therapy* 4, 1–6.

Rachman, S. (1966b) Studies in desensitization — III. Speed of generalization. *Behav. Res. & Therapy* 4, 7–15.

Wolpe, J. (1954) Reciprocal inhibition as the main basis of psychotherapeutic effects. *A.M.A. Archs Neurol. Psychiat.* **72**, 205–226. Cited in Eysenck (1960), pp. 88–113.

Wolpe, J. (1963) Quantitative relationships in the systematic desensitization of phobias. *Am. J. Psychiat.* **119**, 1062–1068.
Wolpe, J. & Lang, P. J. (1964) A Fear Survey Schedule for use in behaviour therapy. *Behav. Res. & Therapy* **2**, 27–30.

SECTION II

Emotionally Disturbed Children

INTRODUCTION

The papers in this chapter present a variety of treatments for emotionally disturbed children. Systematic desensitization of fear responses and covert sensitization of socially unacceptable behaviors are introduced; operant conditioning to modify maladaptive behaviors continue to be used successfully.

Unfortunately, most studies, with the exception of that by Meichenbaum *et al.*, are descriptions of single case studies. They are included primarily to indicate the differences in behavior disorder that can be treated, to provide a description of methodology and to delineate specific problems which remain to be resolved in doing behavior therapy with children.

Systematic desensitization with children is fairly new. These selected studies reveal that chronological age may be a factor in determining the subject's ability to visualize. Tasto and Montenegro found that very young children (six years and under) could not visualize situations. However, as there are data from only three patients, no generalizations can be made. We have found that with adults there are individual differences in ability to visualize images; these may well hold for children, irrespective of age, as well.

The study by Kolvin on covert sensitization of socially unacceptable behaviors is included as a description of a method which may prove useful with children. Again research with young patients is required to determine whether the treatment has validity.

As would be expected operant conditioning can be effective in modifying the behaviors of emotionally disturbed children. Included here are papers dealing with a variety of situations in which this treatment has been carried out.

The question confronting the therapist is how to choose the best method for the alleviation of specific symptoms. Generally speaking, if a particular phobic-like fear is found to maintain the response, then the treatment of choice is desensitization. An interesting result of systematic desensitization, reported in these papers, is that other symptoms (untreated) have remitted as well. This is not usual with adults.

Control of Anxiety Responses

The Use of "Emotive Imagery" in the Treatment of Children's Phobias*

ARNOLD A. LAZARUS

Department of Psychology, Yale University, New Haven, Conn.

and

ARNOLD ABRAMOVITZ

Abstract: A Reciprocal Inhibition (Wolpe, 1958) technique for the treatment of children's phobias is presented which consists essentially of an adaptation of Wolpe's method of "systematic desensitization" (Wolpe, 1961). Instead of inducing muscular relaxation as the anxiety-inhibiting response, certain emotion-arousing situations are presented to the child's imagination. The emotions induced are assumed, like relaxation, to have autonomic effects which are incompatible with anxiety. This technique, which the authors have provisionally labelled "emotive imagery," was applied to nine phobic children whose ages ranged from seven to fourteen years. Seven children recovered in a mean of 3.3 sessions and follow-up enquiries up to twelve months later revealed no relapses or symptom substitution. An outstanding feature of this pediatric technique is the extraordinary rapidity with which remission occurs.

Some of the earliest objective approaches to the removal of specific anxieties and fears in children were based on the fact that neurotic (learned, unadaptive) responses can be eliminated by the repeated and simultaneous evocation of stronger incompatible responses. An early and well-known example of this approach was the experiment of Jones (1924) in which a child's fear of rabbits was gradually eliminated by introducing a "pleasant stimulus" i.e., *food* (thus evoking the anxiety-inhibiting response of eating) in the presence of the rabbit. The general method of "gradual habituation" was advocated by Jersild and Holmes (1935) as being superior to all others in the elimination of children's fears. This rationale was crystallized in Wolpe's (1958) formulation of the Reciprocal Inhibition Principle, which deserves the closest possible study:

> If a response antagonistic to anxiety can be made to occur in the presence of anxiety-evoking stimuli so that it is accompanied by a complete or partial suppression of the anxiety responses, the bond between these stimuli and the anxiety responses will be weakened.

A crucial issue in the application of this principle is the choice of a clinically suitable anxiety-inhibiting response. The most widely-used method has been that of "systematic desensitization" (Wolpe, 1961) which may be described as gradual habituation to the imagined stimulus through the anxiety-inhibiting response of *relaxation*. Lazarus (1960) reported several successful pediatric applications of this procedure, using both feeding and relaxation. It was subsequently found, however, that neither feeding nor relaxation was feasible in certain cases. Feeding has obvious disadvantages in routine therapy, while training in relaxation is often both time-consuming and difficult or impossible to achieve with certain children. The

---

*Reprinted from the *Journal of Mental Science*, 1962, **108**, 191–195. Copyright 1962, with permission from The British Journal of Psychiatry and Dr. A. A. Lazarus.

possibility of inducing anxiety-inhibiting *emotive* images, without specific training in relaxation, was then explored, and the results of our preliminary investigation form the subject of this paper.

Our use of the term "emotive imagery" requires clarification. In the present clinical context, it refers to those classes of imagery which are assumed to arouse feelings of self-assertion, pride, affection, mirth, and similar anxiety-inhibiting responses.

The technique which was finally evolved can be described in the following steps:

  a. As in the usual method of systematic desensitization, the range, intensity, and circumstances of the patient's fears are ascertained, and a graduated hierarchy is drawn up, from the most feared to the least feared situation.
  b. By sympathetic conversation and enquiry, the clinician establishes the nature of the child's hero-images — usually derived from radio, cinema, fiction, or his own imagination — and the wish-fulfilments and identifications which accompany them.
  c. The child is then asked to close his eyes and told to imagine a sequence of events which is close enough to his everyday life to be credible, but within which is woven a story concerning his favourite hero or *alter ego*.
  d. If this is done with reasonable skill and empathy, it is possible to arouse to the necessary pitch the child's affective reactions. (In some cases this may be recognized by small changes in the facial expression, breathing, muscle tension, etc.)
  e. When the clinician judges that these emotions have been maximally aroused, he introduces, as a natural part of the narrative, the lowest item in the hierarchy. Immediately afterwards he says: "if you feel afraid (or unhappy, or uncomfortable) just raise your finger." If anxiety is indicated, the phobic stimulus is "withdrawn" from the narrative and the child's anxiety-inhibiting emotions are again aroused. The procedure is then repeated as in ordinary systematic desensitization, until the highest item in the hierarchy is tolerated without distress.

The use of this procedure is illustrated in the following cases:

Case 1

Stanley M., aged fourteen, suffered from an intense fear of dogs, two and a half to three years duration. He would take two buses on a roundabout route to school rather than risk exposure to dogs on a direct 300-yard walk. He was a rather dull (IQ 93), sluggish person, very large for his age, trying to be cooperative, but sadly unresponsive — especially to attempts at training in relaxation. In his desire to please, he would state that he had been perfectly relaxed even though he had betrayed himself by his intense fidgetiness. Training in relaxation was eventually abandoned, and an attempt was made to establish the nature of his aspirations and goals. By dint of much questioning and after following many false trails because of his inarticulateness, a topic was eventually tracked down that was absorbing enough to form the subject of his fantasies, namely racing motor-cars. He had a burning ambition to own a certain Alfa Romeo sports car and race it at the Indianapolis "500" event. Emotive imagery was induced as follows: "Close your eyes. I want you to imagine, clearly and vividly, that your wish has come true. The Alfa Romeo is now in your possession. It is your car. It is standing in the street outside your block. You are looking at it now. Notice the beautiful sleek lines. You decide to go for a drive with some friends of yours. You sit down at the wheel, and you feel a thrill of pride as you realize that you own this magnificent machine. You start up and listen to the wonderful roar of the exhaust. You let the clutch in and the car streaks off . . . . You are out in a clear open road now; the car is performing like a pedigree; the speedometer is climbing into the nineties; you have a wonderful feeling of being in perfect control; you look at the trees whizzing by and you see a little dog standing next to one of them — if you feel any anxiety, just raise your finger. Etc., etc." An item fairly high up on the hierarchy: "You stop at a café in a little town and dozens of people crowd around to look enviously at this magnificent car and its lucky owner; you swell with pride; and at this moment a larger boxer comes up and sniffs at your heels — If you feel any anxiety, etc., etc."

After three sessions using this method he reported a marked improvement in his reaction to dogs. He was given a few field assignments during the next two sessions, after which therapy was terminated. Twelve months later, reports both from the patient and his relatives indicated that there was no longer any trace of his former phobia.

Case 2

A ten-year-old boy was referred for treatment because his excessive fear of the dark exposed him to ridicule from his twelve-year-old brother and imposed severe restrictions on his parents' social activities. The lad became acutely anxious whenever his parents went visiting at night and even when they remained at home he refused to enter any darkened room unaccompanied. He insisted on sharing a room with his brother and made constant use of a nightlight next to his bed. He was especially afraid of remaining alone in the bathroom and only used it if a member of the household stayed there with him. On questioning, the child stated that he was not anxious during the day but that he invariably became tense and afraid toward sunset.

His fears seemed to have originated a year or so previously when he saw a frightening film and shortly thereafter was warned by his maternal grandmother (who lived with the family) to keep away from all doors and windows at night as burglars and kidnappers were on the prowl.

A previous therapist had embarked on a programme of counselling with the parents and play-therapy with the child. While some important areas of interpersonal friction were apparently ameliorated, the child's phobic responses remained unchanged. Training in "emotive imagery" eliminated his reperoire of fears in three sessions.

The initial interview (ninety minutes) was devoted to psychometric testing and the development of rapport. The test revealed a superior level of intelligence (IQ 135) with definite evidence of anxiety and insecurity. He responded well to praise and encouragement throughout the test situation. Approximately thirty minutes were devoted to a general discussion of the child's interests and activities, which was also calculated to win his confidence. Towards the end of this interview, the child's passion for two radio serials, "Superman" and "Captain Silver" had emerged.

A week later, the child was seen again. In addition to his usual fears he had been troubled by nightmares. Also, a quarterly school report had commented on a deterioration in his school-work. Emotive imagery was then introduced. The child was asked to imagine that Superman and Captain Silver had joined forces and had appointed him their agent. After a brief discussion concerning the topography of his house he was given his first assignment. The therapist said, "Now I want you to close your eyes and imagine that you are sitting in the dining-room with your mother and father. It is night time. Suddenly, you receive a signal on the wrist radio that Superman has given you. You quickly run into the lounge because your mission must be kept a secret. There is only a little light coming into the lounge from the passage. Now pretend that you are all alone in the lounge waiting for Superman and Captain Silver to visit you. Think about this very clearly. If the idea makes you feel afraid, lift up your right hand."

An ongoing scene was terminated as soon as any anxiety was indicated. When an image aroused anxiety, it would either be represented in a more challengingly assertive manner, or it would be altered slightly so as to prove less objectively threatening.

At the end of the third session, the child was able to picture himself alone in his bathroom with all the lights turned off, awaiting a communication from Superman.

Apart from ridding the child of his specific phobia, the effect of this treatment appeared to have diverse and positive implications on many facets of his personality. His school-work improved immeasurably and many former manifestations of insecurity were no longer apparent. A follow-up after eleven months revealed that he had maintained his gains and was, to quote his mother, "a completely different child."

Case 3

An eight-year-old girl was referred for treatment because of persistent nocturnal enuresis and a fear of going to school. Her fear of the school situation was apparently engendered by a series of emotional upsets in class. In order to avoid going to school, the child resorted to a variety of devices including temper tantrums, alleged pains and illnesses, and on one occasion she was caught playing truant and intemperately upbraided by her father. Professional assistance was finally sought when it was found that her younger sister was evincing the same behavior.

When the routine psychological investigations had been completed, emotive imagery was introduced with the aid of an Enid Blyton character, Noddy, who provided a hierarchy of assertive challenges centred around the school situation. The essence of this procedure was to create imagined situations where Noddy played the role of a truant and responded fearfully to the school setting. The patient would then protect him, either by active reassurance or by "setting a good example."

Only four sessions were required to eliminate her school-going phobia. Her enuresis, which had received no specific therapeutic attention, was far less frequent and disappeared entirely within two months. The child has continued to improve despite some additional upsets at the hands of an unsympathetic teacher.

DISCUSSION

The technique of "emotive imagery" has been applied to nine phobic children whose ages ranged from seven to fourteen years. Seven children recovered in a mean of only 3.3 sessions. The method failed with one child who refused to cooperate and later revealed widespread areas of disturbance, which required broader therapeutic handling. The other failure was a phobic child with a history of encephalitis. He was unable to concentrate on the emotive images and could not enter into the spirit of the "game."

Of the seven patients who recovered, two had previously undergone treatment at the hands of different therapists. Two others had been treated by the same therapist (A.A.L.) using reassurance, relaxation and "environmental manipulation." In none of these four cases was there any appreciable remission of the phobic symptoms until the present methods were applied. In every instance where the method was used, improvement occurred contemporaneously with treatment.

Follow-up enquiries were usually conducted by means of home-visits, interviews and telephone conversations both with the child and his immediate associates. These revealed that in no case was there symptom substitution of any obvious kind and that in fact, favourable response generalization had occurred in some instances.

It has been suggested that these results may be due to the therapist's enthusiasm for the method. (Does this imply that other therapists are unenthusiastic about *their* methods?) Certainly, the nature of the procedure is such that it cannot be coldly and dispassionately applied. A warm rapport with the child and a close understanding of his wish-fulfilments and identifications are essential. But our claim is that although warmth and acceptance are necessary in any psychotherapeutic undertaking, they are usually not *sufficient*. Over and above such non-specific anxiety-inhibiting factors, this technique, in common with other reciprocal inhibition methods, provides a clearly defined therapeutic tool which is claimed to have *specific* effects.

Encouraging as these preliminary experiences have been, it is not claimed that they are, as yet, anything more than suggestive evidence of the efficacy of the method. Until properly controlled studies are performed, no general inference can be drawn. It is evident, too, that our loose *ad hoc* term "emotive imagery," reflects a basic lack of theoretical systematization in the field of the emotions. In her review of experimental data on autonomic functions, Martin (1960) deplores the paucity of replicated studies, the unreliability of the measures used, and the lack of operational definitions of qualitatively labelled emotions. The varieties of emotion we have included under the blanket term "emotive imagery" and our simple conjecture of anxiety-inhibiting properties for all of them is an example of the *a priori* assumptions one is forced to make in view of the absence of firm empirical data and adequately formulated theory. It is hoped that our demonstration of the clinical value of these techniques will help to focus attention on an unaccountably neglected area of study, but one which lies at the core of experimental clinical psychology.

REFERENCES

Jersild, A. T. & Holmes, F. B. Methods of overcoming children's fears. *J. Psychol.,* 1935, 1, 75–104.

Jones, M. C. Elimination of children's fears. *J. Exp. Psychol.,* 1924, 7, 382–390.

Lazarus, A. A. The elimination of children's phobias by deconditioning. In H. J. Eysenck (Ed.), *Behaviour Therapy and the Neuroses.* Oxford: Pergamon Press, 1960.

Martin, I. Somatic reactivity. In H. J. Eysenck (Ed.), *Handbook of abnormal psychology.* London: Pitman Medical Publishing Co. Ltd., 1960.

Wolpe, J. *Psychotherapy by reciprocal inhibition.* Stanford Univ. Press and Witwatersrand Univ. Press, 1958.

Wolpe, J. The systematic desensitization treatment of neuroses. *J. Nerv. and Mental Disease,* 1961, 132, 189–203.

Systematic Desensitization, Muscle Relaxation and Visual Imagery in the Counterconditioning of Four-year-old Phobic Child*

DONALD L. TASTO

Department of Psychology, Colorado State University, Fort Collins, Colorado 80521

Abstract: A four-year-old boy with a severe phobia for loud sudden noises was successfully treated with behavior modification utilizing muscle relaxation and *in vivo* conditioning in six sessions. The question of theoretical importance was whether muscle relaxation and systematic desensitization by imagining feared stimuli could successfully be employed to treat a phobia in a child this young. The literature does not, to the author's knowledge, contain any reports of the combined use of muscle relaxation and imagination of fear-producing stimuli for treating phobic children of such a young age.

BACKGROUND

R.S. was a four-year-old boy (IQ = 131) who had developed extreme psychophysiological and motor reactions to loud sounds, and these reactions were generalizing to other stimuli that typically occurred in contiguity with loud noises such as rain with thunder. The parents reported that his typical reaction to a loud sound was to become hyperexcited and begin uncontrolled running in unpredictable directions. He sometimes ran toward the source of the sound and sometimes away from it. They were quite concerned that if he were not watched very closely he might, for example, run into the street with the unexpected onset of a loud noise.

Both of his parents were college teachers on leave of absence to pursue their doctorates, and after interviewing and working with both of them, there seemed to be no evidence of pathological conditions in the home environment. The phobia appeared to be quite an isolated and specific phenomenon which did, however, greatly inhibit certain social activities such as going to parties where there were balloons, attending sports events with loud crowds, playing games with other children that involved loud sudden noises, etc.

METHOD OF TREATMENT

Since the literature was rather insufficient for offering specific recommendations based on empirical research, it was decided to follow the Wolpe & Lazarus (1966) technique of relaxation and systematic desensitization until some part of the procedure should prove ineffective.

*Reprinted from *Behaviour Research and Therapy*, 1969, **7**, 409–411. Copyright 1969 with permission from Pergamon Press Publishing Company and Dr. D. L. Tasto.

Therefore, the first part of the first session was devoted to muscle relaxation training which apparently seemed to work quite well. The directions for muscle relaxation were derived from Wolpe & Lazarus (1966; p. 177) in which the author explained the process and systematically instructed R.S. to tense and relax various muscles throughout his body. After this (while no longer in a position of relaxation) R.S. named thirteen noise stimuli that evoked fear.[1] By a paired comparison technique he indicated which of the two pairs was more fear producing until all stimuli became arranged in a rank order. It was with relative ease that specific hierarchies for each of these stimuli could be built, namely on the basis of sound intensity.

Since the relaxation process seemed to work quite well the first time, one of the fear producing stimuli (the sound of wood dropping) was verbally presented in hierarchial fashion for R.S. to imagine. (For a more detailed explanation, see Wolpe & Lazarus, 1966.) A low item on this hierarchy would be imagining the therapist dropping a piece of wood from a quarter of an inch above the floor while an item high on the hierarchy was dropping from a height of five feet. The rather curious phenomenon that occurred, however, was that in moving up the hierarchy R.S. never signalled anxiety by raising his finger. Throughout the first three sessions various hierarchies were attempted with the same result that the child never signalled anxiety, and when his fear of an item was subsequently tested *in vivo*, it had not diminished. It was also of interest to note that prior to the desensitization sessions utilizing stimuli presented to the imagination, R.S. specifically asked whether he would only have to imagine the stimuli in question or whether the therapist would actually produce the stimuli such as popping a balloon or dropping a piece of wood, and, as long as he was told that he would only have to imagine these stimuli, he did not display any noticeable signs of anxiety.

Since this process of imagining the fear provoking stimuli was not having a beneficial generalized effect toward the actual feared stimuli, it was decided to use *in vivo* conditioning both in the therapy sessions and at home via the parents. From the first session R.S. was trained in, and instructed to practice each night, muscle relaxation. The therapist began the second session by having him relax and then presented actual stimuli on the hierarchies such as dropping a board, popping a balloon, etc. The therapist would move up a hierarchy by letting R.S. determine, for example, how big a balloon could be before the therapist would pop it or from what height the therapist could drop a board. The process worked quite well for those stimuli that could be handled in therapy. For other stimuli that were common in his life his parents were taught the importance of his relaxation and the gradual increase in the intensity of noise stimuli as a prerequisite for success. One example of cooperative parental involvement was to have R.S. go target practicing with his father. R.S. would go quite a distance from his father, get relaxed, and signal his father to shoot. He gradually moved closer until he was shooting the gun himself. Another example illustrating the implementation of counterconditioning by parental cooperation was that the father would place a dime inside a balloon and the only way R.S. could get the dime was to pop the balloon, thus producing the noise himself. R.S. reported that to accomplish this, he would go through a brief muscle relaxation procedure and then pop the slightly inflated balloon. The balloons were gradually inflated more until the popping of a full size balloon reportedly produced no signs of fear. (Prior to this time, he would become extremely frightened at just the sight of a balloon.)

During the first three weeks of therapy the parents reported that they practiced with R.S. each day on various items in the hierarchies. It was shortly after this time they began to report that relaxation was now very easy for R.S. and he could handle most anticipated noises by

---

[1]The fear provoking stimuli were ranked ordered from high to low as follows: gun, balloon breaking, cannon, siren, thunder, crowds, heavy piece of steel falling, board falling on floor, trash can falling, mother saying "boo," air plane noise, glass breaking, piece of paper being crunched.

relaxing himself. Therapy was terminated after six sessions by request of the parents because they reported that R.S. was having no problems with noises and that he even seemed more relaxed living a normal day than was the case prior to therapy. One month and four months after the termination of therapy, the parents reported that he had no relapses and that he was actually becoming more sociable with other children as well as being more relaxed in general.

DISCUSSION

Typically, the use of counterconditioning in the treatment of phobias for children (Jones, 1924a, 1924b; Lazarus, 1960) has utilized some pleasant behavior, such as eating, as the response antagonistic to anxiety for conditioning to occur. Other studies (*see* Gelfand and Hartman's review, 1968) have used "suggestion, hypnosis, or drugs" to induce feelings of relaxation. This particular case, however, suggests that the ability to effectively employ *muscle* relaxation as a response antagonistic to anxiety, which will allow for counterconditioning, probably begins at a relatively early age. The capacity for imagined stimuli, however, evoke anxiety is probably somewhat a function of development and more research is needed to determine when, developmentally, imagined stimuli have sufficient capacity to evoke anxiety so that counterconditioning might be effective. Also the success in this case of having parents work with relaxation and the items on the hierarchy suggests that, if *in vivo* conditioning is necessary for young children, agents besides the therapist might be efficiently utilized to implement counterconditioning in the treatment of phobic children.

Regarding the effectiveness of muscle relaxation and the ineffectiveness of imagined stimuli to evoke anxiety, this case suggests a verbal mediation hypothesis. Following the directions involved with the muscle relaxation primarily involves CNS mediated responses (tensing and relaxing the muscles). Children of this age have no trouble following directions that involve simple overt muscular movements. However, it is possible that for verbal mediators to evoke autonomically mediated emotional responses, it is necessary to have many pairings of words with the stimuli that evoke such responses. If this is the case, adults would have much more opportunity than children for experiencing words paired with actual stimuli that evoke emotional responses. This could account for adults reporting anxiety to imagined stimuli and the failure of children to do so if indeed this is a general phenomenon to be found in children.

REFERENCES

Gelfand, D. M. & Hartman, D. P. Behavior therapy with children: A review and evaluation of research methodology. *Psychol. Bull.*, 1968, 204–215.

Jones, M. C. The elimination of children's fears. *J. exp. Psychol.*, 1924, **7**, 382. a

Jones, M. C. A laboratory study of fear. The case of Peter. *Pedagogical Seminar*, 1924, **31**, 308. b

Lazarus, A. A. (1959) The elimination of children's phobias by deconditioning. In H. J. Eysenck (Ed.), *Behaviour therapy and the neuroses*. Oxford: Pergamon Press, 1960.

Wolpe, J. & Lazarus, A. A. *Behaviour therapy techniques*. Oxford: Pergamon Press, 1966.

Severe Separation Anxiety in Two Preschool Children: Successfully Treated by Reciprocal Inhibition*†

HERNAN MONTENEGRO‡

Children's Psychiatric Service, The Johns Hopkins University School of Medicine and Hospital, Baltimore, Maryland

Abstract: Separation anxiety of pathological degree in two preschool children was successfully and expeditiously treated (in 15 and 16 sessions, respectively) by structuring a real-life systematic desensitization based on reciprocal inhibition, using the feeding responses as the physiological state to counteract the anxiety. As part of the symptomatology, one of the children showed a refusal to speak, which was successfully treated using operant conditioning techniques.

A full description of the treatment procedure and results is given, and the rationale of the method is discussed. Emphasis is placed on counteracting and resolving the current circumstances that are maintaining and reinforcing the undesirable behavior, rather than on a detailed analysis of origins of the difficulty.

INTRODUCTION

This paper describes two children with separation anxiety of pathological degree, who were successfully treated using the behavior therapy technique of reciprocal inhibition, employing the feeding responses as a physiological state antagonistic to anxiety. One child (Case 2) showed a refusal to speak which was successfully treated using operant conditioning.

The therapy used in both cases was a modification of Wolpe's (1954, 1958, 1966) desensitization procedure. Wolpe's method characteristically employs muscular relaxation (following Jacobson's technique, 1938) and hypnosis as the anxiety-inhibiting state, during which the patient is asked to imagine himself in selected anxiety-generating situations, previously graded by the therapist into a hierarchy. In the present cases, three modifications of Wolpe's technique were introduced: (1) Hypnosis was not used. (2) Instead of the relaxation method, which is difficult to use with non-cooperating young children, the feeding responses were employed as the physiological state to oppose anxiety. (3) Instead of asking the patient to imagine the anxiety-producing conditions, he was gradually exposed to a graded series of situations involving the actual stimulus — in this case, separation from the mother — as described later. (This use of the actual stimulus has been called *direct* or *real-life* or *in vivo* desensitization.)

---

*This work was carried out while the author was a recipient of a World Health Organization (WHO) Fellowship.

†Reprinted from the *Journal of Child Psychology and Psychiatry*, 1968, **9**, 93–103. Copyright 1968 with permission from Pergamon Press Publishing Company and Dr. H. Montenegro.

‡Author's present address: Children's Psychiatric Unit, Department of Pediatrics, Hospital Roberto del Rio, Santiago, Chile.

Successful use of the feeding responses in a desensitization procedure was reported as early as 1924 by Mary Cover Jones (1924a, b), including her classical treatment of a three-year-old patient, Peter, to eliminate a rabbit phobia. Despite her successful results, and the proven validity of the therapeutic technique of reciprocal inhibition, the literature apparently contains no subsequent reports that duplicate her clinical findings with the feeding responses, until the work of Lazarus (1959). Lazarus treated an eight-year-old boy who had developed a fear of moving vehicles.

Although there has been an increasing volume of literature in recent years on behavior therapy in children, many of these deal with the treatment of phobic or psychotic children (e.g., Eysenck, 1960, 1964; Rachman, 1962, 1963; Lazarus & Abramovitz, 1962; Russo, 1964; and Wolpe *et al.*, 1964). The procedure described in the present two cases provides a highly successful technique for treatment of problems of separation anxiety also.

Wolpe (1958) describes experimental observations made by him on cats "in which lasting neurotic states had been induced by the administration of several punishing but non-damaging" doses of electrical shock in a small cage. In every case, the neurotic anxiety and other reactions were later "entirely removed by getting the animals to eat in the presence of small, and at later sessions progressively larger, 'doses' of anxiety-evoking stimuli." These findings revealed a useful "antagonism between feeding responses and anxiety responses."

Jones in 1924 had provided clinical evidence for the same principle when she succeeded in overcoming phobias in young children by giving them "attractive food to eat in association with the presentation of a feared object, first at a distance and then progressively closer at hand." Jones called this technique the method of *direct conditioning*, meaning by this:

> ... attempts to associate with the fear-object a definite stimulus, capable of arousing a positive (pleasant) reaction. The hunger motive appears to be the most effective for use in this connection. During a period of craving for food, the child is placed in a high chair and given something to eat. The fear-object is brought in, starting a negative response; it is then moved away gradually until it is at a sufficient distance not to interfere with the child's eating. The relative strength of the fear impulse and the hunger impulse may be gauged by the distance to which it is necessary to remove the fear-object. While the child is eating, the object is slowly brought nearer to the table, then placed upon the table, and finally as the tolerance increases it is brought close enough to be touched. Since we could not interfere with the regular schedule of meals, we chose the time of the mid-morning lunch for the experiment. This usually assured some degree of interest in the food, and corresponding success in our treatment. The effectiveness of this method increases greatly as the hunger grows, at least up to a certain point. ... This method obviously requires delicate handling. Two response systems are being dealt with: food leading to a positive reaction, and fear-object leading to a negative reaction. The desired conditioning should result in transforming the fear-object into a source of positive response (substitute stimulus). But a careless manipulator could readily produce the reverse result, attaching a fear reaction to the sight of food. (Jones, 1924a, p. 389f.)

These observations by Jones, were clinical antecedents of the later elaboration of the principle of reciprocal inhibition by Wolpe (1948, 1952, 1954, 1958).

Wolpe states the essence of his technique in the following terms:

> *If a response antagonistic to anxiety can be made to occur in the presence of anxiety-evoking stimuli so that it is accompanied by a complete or partial suppression of the anxiety responses, the bond between these stimuli and the anxiety responses will be weakened.* (Wolpe, 1958, p. 71; italics added.)

In the two cases described in the present paper, the tendency to respond pathologically to the anxiety-producing stimulus (separation from the mother) is suppressed by the counter-vailing feeding-responses. Repeated clinical use of this reciprocal inhibition — which is, in a given instance, temporary in effect — steadily builds up a permanent "conditioning" that tends to inhibit the neurotic behavior.

Besides feeding responses, other responses have also been used to counter the effects of anxiety-evoking stimuli in adults. The most useful of these have been relaxation responses, assertive responses, and sexual responses (Wolpe, 1958, pp. 114–138).

CASE REPORTS

Case 1

Romeo, a six-year-old Caucasian boy, was referred to our psychiatric clinic by his pediatrician. On the first visit, his mother said at the start, "He's terrified of doctors. Every time he must go for a check-up he doesn't want to be touched. You have to hold him to keep him from running away." Three months before this, the boy had been taken to the doctor because of a scalp wound; he became so agitated that the doctor had to strap him down in order to examine him.

The child could not accept being separated from his mother, even for a few minutes. When he was five years old the parents tried to enrol him in a kindergarten, but it was impossible for the school to tolerate his behavior when his mother left him. She was allowed to stay with him the first few days, but as soon as she left the school he began to cry and shout desperately. After ten days the school gave up the attempt to manage him, and the boy was not allowed to continue.

Romeo is an only child; and he was born after his parents had been married for twenty years, although they had never used contraceptive measures. Both parents agreed that the child's behavior problems were due largely to the fact that "we love him too much."

The behavior of both parents has done much to reinforce Romeo's inadequate behavior. For instance, they have never left him at home with a baby-sitter; consequently, the parents have seldom gone out by themselves since Romeo's birth. Occasionally, when they must go to something important, they leave him with the maternal grandmother. The boy always "gets his way." If there is any sign of parental restriction, he goes into a temper tantrum and finally gets what he wants. When he dislikes a given food item, for example, the mother does not hesitate to prepare something different for him. Although six years old, both his parents referred to him as "the baby." The mother is the only one who has dared to punish him and she said, "When I do spank him, I go to my room and cry."

Romeo's mother had an operation when he was four years old. She was hospitalized a month, and during this time the child saw her only twice. She thinks his inability to bear separation from her dates from that experience. The boy sleeps with his father. He sleeps well, but it is hard to get him to bed. He still wets the bed occasionally, and rocks during his sleep. He has a poor appetite. He bites his nails and sucks his thumb, and he tries to put everything into his mouth. It is extremely difficult for him to tolerate frustration; he has developed "a terrible temper," and he refuses to heed when being corrected. He simply says, "Don't beat me!" His mother still helps him to dress; she also bathes him, and sometimes still gives him his food.

Having taken the foregoing history from the parents at the first session, I saw the child at the next. As expected, he did not want to leave his mother. As soon as I asked him to come with me to my office, he started sobbing and shaking while clinging to her. He kept crying to her, "Come with me, come with me; I want to stay with you!" . . . etc. After all efforts failed to convince him that nothing would happen to him, I invited his mother to come along with him.

In my office, he continued to cling to her and refused to sit down. He was constantly either kissing her or sucking his thumb or a plastic toy. The only time he said anything was to tell his mother, "You stay here; you stay with me." When I asked him his name, he asked his mother to answer me. The same thing happened regarding his age and address; he was willing only to repeat his age. During the rest of the interview, he continued to refuse to sit down.

When I asked his mother to leave the office for a while, he immediately started shaking and sobbing again; and he tried to get out. When she did leave the office he became extremely anxious. He stayed with me five minutes but then went to join his mother. Since I needed to complete some aspects of the family history, I used the rest of the session to interview the mother while Romeo stayed in the waiting room. The mother said her main concern was Romeo's behavior. It had been especially frustrating to her when he could not cope with the school situation the previous September. Then, after fifteen minutes of the interview, we got a call from the secretary's office saying the child was crying in the waiting room; and so we had to stop.

Case 2

Donna, a Negro girl of three and a half years, was referred to our clinic from another department of this hospital. The mother stated that they had noticed the child's behavior problem when she enrolled the child in a private nursery school. She had planned to work outside the home. She said the girl had not had any opportunity to play with other children before, and could not adjust to the school. The teacher had reported that Donna did not conform to the group and displayed withdrawn behavior. Although she would occasionally obey an instruction, she would not converse at all. She refused to stay with the other children, and when she was invited to play with them she would begin crying. During the first months of school she cried every time she had to leave her mother, and she could continue crying for hours.

The child's behavior pattern also changed at home. Although she had been able to talk in sentences by the age of two, she stopped talking four months prior to her coming to the clinic, coinciding with her going to nursery school. When she wanted something, she would show it by pointing with her index finger. Occasionally, but only at home, she would speak to herself in such sentences as: "Stop crying, Donna" or "Don't touch it, Donna." She stopped calling her parents "Mommy" or "Daddy." She also began displaying a bad temper at that time. She resented any interference with her pursuits, and she could not tolerate frustrations.

Donna has always been extremely attached to her mother, and was accustomed to spending the whole day with her until her mother decided to take outside work four months ago. The mother now works for a government agency. She is thirty-eight years old and completed the second year of college. She had a job before, until she was six months' pregnant with this child. Donna has one brother; he is eleven years old and is doing well. When the boy was an infant, the father took care of him most of the time because his work (as a clerk with a government agency) has always been at night. The father is also thirty-eight, and he also had two years of college. He is a quiet but pleasant person.

Both parents agreed that they get along well together, and that they do not have financial problems. The mother said she started working again because she "wanted to give the child a better education." Two years ago the family moved into a neighborhood in which most of the people are "white," and they do not have friends there. When I asked the mother why Donna lacked opportunity to play with other children, she said, "Because there are no children around home to play with." When I expressed some surprise at that, she said there were "two white boys" across the street but that she considered it "very dangerous" to let Donna play there. Although the mother did not acknowledge the fact, it seemed quite apparent that she was afraid to allow her children to play in the neighborhood because of the possibility of racial discrimination. It was also obvious that she had an ardent desire to improve the social status of her family. The mother is a pleasant woman who speaks well, and one gets the impression that her education is better than average.

Donna's mother was twenty years old when she got married. With Donna, she had a normal pregnancy and delivery. The child's developmental milestones have been unremarkable, except that she still wets the bed occasionally. She started speaking when she was one-and-a-half years old, and her first words were "Mama" and "Daddy." By two years of age she was speaking in simple sentences, such as "Want some bread," and she had a normal vocabulary for that age. She has always been quite healthy.

I made two attempts to see Donna alone prior to using reciprocal inhibition therapy, but other sessions were quite unsatisfactory. On the first visit she started crying desperately as soon as her mother left my office. It was impossible to establish any kind of communication with her, and after fifteen minutes I discontinued the attempt. I called the parents, and the father took Donna to the waiting room while I talked to the mother. The child continued crying, even though she was then sitting on her father's lap in the waiting room. Finally, however, she went to sleep.

On the second visit, a week later, I saw her with her mother in my office. She was able at this time to take a pencil I offered her. She very reluctantly copied a circle, but she then began to scribble and continued very briefly. After that she spent most of the time staring at various objects on the walls, and she did not pay any attention when I talked to her. As expected, she did not speak at all. When I asked her mother to leave the office, Donna immediately began crying, as she had on the first visit; and again it was impossible to achieve any useful relationship with her.

THERAPEUTIC METHOD AND RESULT

Treatment Procedure

Case 1. After explaining to the boy's parents briefly the theoretical basis of the technique to be used, I instructed them on how to prepare him for each session. The child was told that these were the doctor's plans, and that the child would receive a good breakfast as soon as he got into the doctor's office. Each time, Romeo's mother would bring some of his favorite goodies — such as chocolates, potato chips, ice cream, pop, banana, etc.

In preparation for the desensitization sessions, I prepared the following *anxiety hierarchy* in relation to Romeo:

1. Patient and his mother in my office. Duration of the first session: fifteen minutes.
2. Patient with me in office, with the door open so that he can see his mother standing in corridor outside my office. Duration, thirty minutes.
3. Patient with me in office, with door closed. Mother still available in corridor with patient allowed to check on his mother's presence whenever he wishes. Duration, thirty minutes.
4. Patient with me in office, and mother in waiting room. Patient allowed to see mother whenever he wishes. Duration, thirty minutes.
5. Mother again in waiting room, but child not allowed to see mother until end of session. Duration, forty-five minutes.
6. Patient goes with therapist to hospital cafeteria (downstairs on first floor) for fifteen minutes, after being allowed to tell his mother where he is going.

7. Patient goes with therapist to cafeteria for thirty minutes to have some ice cream. This time child is not permitted to notify his mother.
8. Patient goes with therapist to drug store, across the street from the hospital, for fifteen minutes. Child is allowed to tell his mother before he goes; the therapist has already asked her permission in advance.
9. Same situation as in Session 8.
10. Patient and therapist go to hospital cafeteria for forty-five minutes, and then tour other parts of the hospital for remainder of the hour. (A more detailed report of results of individual therapeutic sessions is given with Case 2.)

After this hierarchy was successfully completed in ten consecutive sessions, during two and a half weeks, the parents were instructed to leave the child at home with a competent baby-sitter, for an hour the first time and then increasingly longer. Also, specific recommendations were made to the parents regarding suitable ways of loosening the almost symbiotic parent–child relationship, to decrease the excessive mutual dependence. The child was to sleep by himself and wash and dress and feed himself. Both parents were instructed to be firm and consistent in setting limits.

After the child could tolerate, without difficulty, being left at home with a baby-sitter, I instructed the mother to place him in a nursery school. Since it was summer, he was placed in a "Bible School" (vacation church school) at one of the neighborhood churches. He attended two hours a day for one month; and when the church school ended, Romeo was quite disappointed. One month later he entered the first grade at public school, and he showed no adjustment problems at all.

Case 2. It was evident from the beginning that the first objective must be to counteract the separation anxiety sufficiently to be able at least to communicate with the child. This and other therapeutic goals were to be pursued using the direct conditioning procedures, adapted primarily from Jones (1924a, b) and Wolpe (1958). First, I briefly explained the technique to the parents and asked them to leave the child without dinner the night before and without breakfast the day of the session. The appointments were always arranged for 9 a.m. I also asked the parents to bring each time some of the child's favorite candies and cookies, and to report to me each time whether they had noticed any changes in Donna's eating habits and appetite. The rationale of these procedures is based on the well-documented operation of primary appetitive drives in conditioning: the relevant stimuli (such as food or water) acquire maximum effect of reinforcement or reciprocal inhibition only after a period of deprivation of those stimuli. Similarly, the effectiveness of social reinforcers can be enhanced by the operation of deprivation (Gerwirtz & Baer, 1958).

First session using reciprocal inhibition.   Donna's mother came with her into my office. When the session began I gave Donna some of the cookies and candy her mother had brought; the child accepted them quickly and eagerly. After a few minutes, I asked her mother to leave the office but to stay in the corridor near the door, so that Donna could see her. The child started sobbing and continued sobbing for five minutes; then I closed the door. She began to suck her thumb, and continued during the interview; but each time I offered her something to eat, she accepted it willingly. I drew pictures for her, and by the end of the session (which lasted only thirty minutes) she had become somewhat interested.

Second session (Day 4).   Donna's mother left her in my office. Again, when her mother left the room the child did not cry outright but just sobbed, for two minutes this time. She was now able to tolerate sitting on my lap while eating the sandwiches and cookies her mother had brought. Later, while we were drawing pictures, she obeyed for the first time some simple directions, such as to take a pencil or to put it down. At the end of the session, which lasted forty-five minutes, she started sobbing again when her mother came into my office to get her.

Third session (Day 8).   This session, for the first time, Donna did not even sob when her mother left her in my office. It was also the first time the child smiled, while playing on my revolving office chair. Also, her mother reported that after the last session Donna had asked to ride on the back seat of the car on the way home; before that, she had always ridden on her mother's lap.

Fourth session (Day 12).   This time I met Donna at the waiting room, so that neither of her parents came with her to my office. She did not cry or sob at all. When the interview started, I sat her on my lap and she ate with good appetite. Her appetite at home has also been good since the initiation of this therapy. I then made some designs on paper, and she was willing to copy them – but only after much insistence from me. Her father reported that she has been definitely improving at home; she has started talking a little, although only when she wants something: e.g. "Want some milk; want some bread."

Fifth session (Day 16).   I met Donna at the waiting room again; she accepted holding my hand, and came with me to the office without apparent anxiety. While she was playing with some dolls this time, she smiled again. However, she still was not expressing herself verbally. However, her father reports that she has been talking more and more each time; but this is only at home, She shows her parents various objects now and identifies them by name. The nursery teacher has reported to her parents that Donna is doing better at school. To confirm the accuracy of the parents' report, I telephoned the teacher, who stated: "Donna is able to stay in the group now; she is not so withdrawn, and she doesn't cry out as she did before; but there is no communication yet. When she becomes frustrated, she just cries." The teacher told me that they are not sure how to handle Donna in a school setting. At lunchtime the teacher tries to anticipate Donna's wishes (such as by offering more soup), because the child does not talk. "I usually have to guess what she wants."

At this stage of treatment I judged that the problem of separation anxiety had greatly improved, not only in the therapeutic setting but also generally. Therefore, I focused next on her refusal to speak. The method of handling this problem was based on operant conditioning.

I talked with the parents and the teacher to explain to them briefly how to handle Donna's behavior regarding her not talking. I requested that they did not ask her to talk; but that every time she did try to communicate spontaneously, they should reward her immediately (e.g., candy) and accompany this with an affectionate remark. For my part, I started doing the same – and not only for language behavior but for any kind of social or cooperative behavior in the play situation. Both parents and the teacher have proven to be highly cooperative in this connection, and I think it accounts for much of Donna's improvement.

Up to that point, I had not insisted that Donna play any active role during the therapeutic sessions – except in the fourth, when I asked her to take a pencil and copy some simple geometric designs. She finally complied, but much insistence was required before she would even take a pencil. Before that, her role was simply to eat – usually on my lap while I entertained her in one way or another. Her active cooperation was almost nil. Each time I had encouraged her to imitate something I had done, she had not responded at all. And she had not demonstrated any positive affect that I could detect, except for one or two smiles in some of the interviews. But she was showing some progress.

From the sixth session on, she was permitted to have dinner the night before; and thus she lacked only breakfast before the sessions. My practice was to give her part of the food as soon as the session started, but to reserve the rest of it (mainly cookies and chocolate candies) to reward any kind of desired behavior. If she merely followed the simplest request — to take a pencil, to come closer to me, to catch a ball, etc. — she was rewarded. These activities occupied the sixth and seventh sessions (Days 20 and 25); but she still would not speak, and her affect was equally neutral.

Eighth session (Day 32). We started out playing with the ball, and each time that she caught the ball and handed it back to me I gave her candy or cookie. Then, suddenly, she started laughing — for the first time. Later on, the ball was under a chair and she had to crawl to get it. While she was doing this she started muttering some words. This was the first time I had heard her voice. I could not understand the words, because she was only mumbling. But she was immediately given a suitable reward.

After a while she stopped playing and again started saying something unintelligible; but she was trying to tell me something. Finally, I realized that she wanted to ask me to help her pull up her trousers; she had had to bend down several times to get the ball, and her trousers had slipped half-way down her belly. As soon as I helped her pull the trousers up she started playing again. Then I showed her a tape recorder and explained how it works. She was quite interested, and after hearing my voice played back she began to mumble again.

After the session was over and her father and I were sitting in the office talking, Donna said to her father: "Come on. Come on — Wanna stand up," as she pulled on his hand to get him to stand up. Finally she asked him to take her to the bathroom.

Ninth session (Day 39). We played with the ball and she was doing very well, catching it and giving it back to me. I asked her then to throw the ball back, instead of handing it to me; but she refused to do it this new way. So I picked up a book and for ten minutes pretended I was reading. During this time she stood still, with the ball in her hand. Then I explained to her again the new way of playing, but she kept the same attitude — looking at the chocolate candy. So I lit a cigarette and continued the reading for ten more minutes without making any comment. She stayed where she was, looking at her hand or the ball or the candy. Finally I closed the book and said, "Well, let's play now." I showed her again the way of throwing the ball back, and this time she did it. I gave her two candies; and at my request she again threw back the ball.

At the end of the session I showed her the tape recorder again, and I invited her to hear her own voice on it; but she did not speak during the entire session. However, her father reported that she was talking more and more, but still only at home where she greets people by saying "hi" or "how are you?" She is also starting to say "thank you" when she receives something.

Tenth session (Day 46). Again I introduced modifications in the play routine, but she would not cooperate. I employed the same technique of withholding my attention and rewards. This succeeded twice; but it failed once when, after ten minutes of silence, she started crying. I let her cry several minutes, and then I went back to the former way of playing — catching and handing the ball. But she did not speak during the entire time.

Eleventh session (Day 53). For the first time, she was willing to converse. I had noticed that she had a scar from a scratch on her forehead, and when I asked her about it she was willing to tell me that she had fallen down while playing at school. She also told me later that she was wearing a new dress.

Donna's mother had come with her at this time, and she wanted to talk with me. She was quite happy with Donna's improvement. She said that, starting two weeks before, she had noticed that Donna was now using the pronoun "I." Also, she is greeting people; and her appetite is still good. When she wants something she will say "please." She is calling her "Mommy" again, and she is talking much more. The mother also reported an interview she had with Donna's teacher a week before; the teacher said she thought Donna had received "medication" recently, because of the sudden improvement in her whole behavior pattern at school.

Twelfth session (Day 60).   This time she was willing to sing with me, and she was very enthusiastic when she heard her own voice on the tape recorder. She was obviously quite relaxed and she spoke quite a bit when she played. During most of the time, Donna named various objects in the play situation.

Thirteenth session (Day 67).   After she had played for almost a half-hour with me — with balls, cubes, crawling, singing — she sat down close to the play table, looking very interested in the dolls and the little toys. Then she spontaneously began naming the various objects with the appropriate names, and taking for the first time a really active role in the play situation. Until then, she had been cooperative only if I started some kind of play; then she would follow my lead. But now she assumed my role, in a sense; and she began to make a distribution of the various toys, saying: "This one is yours . . . this one is mine . . . these checkers are yours." When I asked for the names of the dolls, she answered appropriately: "baby, mommy, daddy, girl," etc. Then she asked me for some more candy, and this time I asked her to say "please" and "thank you," which she did.

Curiously enough, this time (because her father misunderstood the time of the appointment) the family had had to wait an hour before the session could begin; this was the only time I was scheduled to see her at 10 a.m. instead of 9 a.m. During most of the hour before I could see her, Donna had been running and playing in the corridors; and contrary to my expectation that she would be bored or tired, the relaxation had left her more talkative and cooperative than usual.

There were three more therapeutic sessions after the thirteenth, and in them she continued the pattern of active cooperation and increasing spontaneity and talkativeness.

Follow-up of Patients

Case 1. During treatment of Romeo, I initially saw him two or three times a week for one month. By the end of that time, he was able to attend a summer church school nearby; it lasted two and a half hours each day. Romeo did not demand that his mother stay with him at the school, either the first day or thereafter. He not only adjusted well to the school environment, he enjoyed it. The second month of therapy I saw him once a week and only twice after that. Just before we decided to discontinue therapy (after 15 sessions), he had begun attending the first grade of a public school without any difficulty.

After a ten-month follow-up, Romeo was still doing well in school; and his parents told me that his behavior at home was "much more mature." During this interval Romeo had to go to his pediatrician three or four times; and not only did he not cry as he always had before, he cooperated well during the physical examination. The same type of favorable report was received after Romeo visited the dentist.

Case 2. Following the thirteenth session, two and a half months after treatment was begun, we received the following report from Donna's teacher. "She is trying to converse with me. Sometimes it is not clear, but it is in sentence form. Donna's outbursts of temper are now infrequent, and she has learned how to defend herself and can yell out 'stop that!' and 'no'. She moves along with the group and enjoys being mischievous now."

After an eighteen-month follow-up, Donna was continuing this pattern of increased socialization and talkativeness. She is doing well, both at home and in school

DISCUSSION

Although most of the cases in the literature that were treated with reciprocal inhibition have been phobias, the use of this technique in the present two cases seemed a valid extension of principle because the common element in all of them is anxiety. Thus the method of deconditioning with reciprocal inhibition was judged to be applicable to the treatment of separation anxiety, and in practice this proved correct; the patients received effective, speedy, and continuing relief of symptoms.

The logic of this extrapolation has been well stated by Lazarus and Rachman (1957, p. 937), as follows:

> What conditions indicate systematic desensitization therapy? On theoretical and experimental grounds (*see* Gantt . . . and Jones . . . for example) it may be expected that phobic states, where concrete and definable stimuli produce the neurotic reaction, would be most amenable to this technique. In fact, wherever clinical symptomatology permits the ready construction of appropriate hierarchies, and where specific rather than "free floating" anxiety is present, systematic desensitization is strongly indicated (Cited: Gantt, 1944 and Jones, 1924a).

Most of the dynamic-oriented psychotherapists are much more concerned with the patient's past history than with the present conditions that are maintaining and reinforcing the patient's symptomatology. In contrast, the behavior-therapy approach in general (and the technique used to treat these two cases in particular) is directed primarily to removing or counteracting the circumstances that are perpetuating the given behavior problem. With some psychiatric problems, this latter approach appears to be not only useful but, at times, essential to achieving any therapeutic goal. This was particularly true in Case 1, in which the extent of emotional disturbance in both parents made it highly important to produce a convincing symptomatic change in the child, as a prerequisite to a change of attitude in the parents. It was essential to demonstrate to them in the real-life situation that a separation between them and the child could be successfully achieved; only then could they carry out the specific practical recommendations that were then made for handling the child's immature behavior. These environmental changes in the parental attitudes clearly had much to do with the boy's definite and rapid improvement, but the parents' attitudes could not have been improved as effectively unless the child's separation anxiety had been lessened first. The basic principle of the importance of symptomatic relief applies also to Case 2 in which the immediate separation-anxiety was hampering any therapeutic effort. Regarding the specific refusal to speak in Case 2, it is interesting to note that the parents and the teacher, in an effort to "help the child" by incessantly urging her to talk, were reinforcing the undesired behavior by attempting to deal with symptoms in the wrong way.

It is also important to emphasize that in neither of these two cases did the therapy produce the slightest disturbance in the children's eating habits. Thus it seems that the possible danger (Jones, 1924a, p. 389) of reversing the conditioning process (thus attaching the anxiety to the sight of food) is rather remote when therapy is properly conducted. In any event, if one wishes or needs to reduce this possibility to a minimum, one can construct a closely graded hierarchy of anxiety-producing stimuli, with a large number of easy transitional steps. Then, if a patient becomes too anxious at any point during the desensitization procedure, the therapist can immediately stop and return to a much less difficult situation; or one can repeat the immediately preceding situation several times.

Finally, the way in which such factors as time, place, and distance (between the patient and sources of anxiety or reassurance) are arranged and managed is a crucial aspect of any systematic desensitization. And the opportunity to make creative use of such factors challenges the ingenuity of the therapist as he seeks to combine sound theory with constructive care and invention.

Acknowledgments. I would like to thank Professor Leon Eisenberg for reading the manuscript and offering valuable suggestions.

REFERENCES

Bowlby, J. (1961) Separation Anxiety: A critical review of the literature. *J. Child Psychol. Psychiat.* 1, 251–269.

Eysenck, H. J. (Ed.) (1960) *Behaviour Therapy and the Neuroses.* Pergamon Press, Oxford.

Eysenck, H. J. (Ed.) (1964) *Experiments in Behaviour Therapy.* Pergamon Press, Oxford.

Gantt, W. H. (1944) *Experimental Basis for Neurotic Behaviour.* Hoeber, New York.

Gantt, W. H. (1964) *Autonomic Conditioning,* pp. 115–126 in Wolpe, J. *et al.*

Gewirtz, J. L. & Baer, D. M. (1958) The effects of brief social deprivation on behaviors for a social reinforcer. *J. Abnorm. Soc. Psychol.* 56, 49–56.

Jacobson, E. (1938) *Progressive Relaxation.* University of Chicago Press, Chicago.

Jones, M. C. (1924a) Elimination of children's fears. *J. Exp. Psychol.* 7, 382–390.

Jones, M. C. (1924b) A laboratory study of fear. The case of Peter. *J. Genet. Psychol.* 31. 308–315.

Lazarus, A. A. (1959) The elimination of children's phobias by deconditioning. *Med. Proc.* (South Africa) 5, 261, 265. (Also in Eysenck, 1960.)

Lazarus, A. A. & Rachman, S. (1957) The use of systematic desensitization in psychotherapy. *South African Medical Journal,* 31, 334–337.

Lazarus, A. A. & Abramovitz, A. (1962) The use of "emotive imagery" in the treatment of children's phobias. *J. Ment. Sci.* 108, 191–195. (Also in Eysenck, 1964.)

Rachman, S. (1962) Child psychology and learning theory. *J. Child Psychol. Psychiat.* 3, 149–163.

Rachman, S. (1963) Introduction to behavior therapy. *Behav. Res. Ther.* 1, 3–15.

Russo, S. (1964) Adaptations in behavior therapy with children. *Behav. Res. Ther.* 2, 43–47.

Wolpe, J. (1948) An approach to the problem of neurosis based on the conditioned response. M.D. thesis, University of the Witwatersrand, S. Africa.

Wolpe, J. (1952) Experimental neurosis as learned behaviour. *Br. J. Psychol.* 43, 243–268.

Wolpe, J. (1954) Reciprocal inhibition as the main basis of psychotherapeutic effects. *Arch. Neurol. Psychiat.* 72, 205–226.

Wolpe, J. (1958) *Psychotherapy by Reciprocal Inhibition.* Stanford University Press, Stanford, Calif.

Wolpe, J. & Lazarus, A. A. (1966) *Behaviour Therapy Techniques.* Pergamon Press, Oxford.

Wolpe, J., Salter, A. L. & Reyna, L. J. (1964) *The conditioning therapies.* Holt, Rinehart & Winston, New York.

Restoration of Eating Behavior in Anorexia Nervosa through Operant Conditioning and Environmental Manipulation*

JACOB AZERRAD† and RICHARD L. STAFFORD‡

Children's Rehabilitation Center, Department of Pediatrics, University of Virginia Medical School

Abstract: A token system of reinforcement was employed to increase the rate of eating in a girl with anorexia nervosa. This token system increased eating rate when it was superimposed on the existing reinforcement-laden environment of a residential treatment center for children. In addition, during the entire course of the experiment (baseline R-1 R-2 R-3 R-4), the patient was receiving noncontingent reinforcement in the form of supportive therapy with a psychologist who allowed her to speak about current problems. No attempt was made to explore "dynamics" nor to perform what is often termed probing or depth therapy. In addition, a re-educational programme for the parents assisted them in learning the methods being used at the Center and assisted them with the transition between Center and Community.

INTRODUCTION

Operant methodology has only been infrequently employed to restore eating behavior in anorexia nervosa. Bachrach, Erwin & Mohr (1965) restored eating in a woman which chronic anorexia whose weight had fallen from 120 to 47 pounds. All possible reinforcers were removed from her hospital environment (radio, T.V., books, magazines, social contacts) and, subsequently, returned to her contingent on the eating of increasingly larger amounts of food. Barlow, Agras & Leitenberg (1967) also employed positive reinforcement to restore the eating behavior in two teen-age girls. A therapist was with the patients at the dinner meal at which time the patients were asked to count mouthfuls of food eaten. In addition, social reinforcers were given (T.V. and trips downtown) for weight gain. Both Bachrach *et al.* (1965) and Barlow *et al.* (1967) removed all potential reinforcers from their patients' environments during the experimental procedures. The present research employs similar procedures in a residential treatment center for children where it was not possible to remove all potential reinforcers from the patient's environment prior to initiating the experimental procedures.

The patient, a thirteen-year-old girl, was admitted to the University of Virginia Hospital

*Reprinted from *Behaviour Research and Therapy*, 1969, **7**, 165–171. Copyright 1969 with permission from Pergamon Press Publishing Company and Dr. J. Azerrad.

†Director of Psychological Research, Community Evaluation and Rehabilitation Center, Walter E. Fernald State School, Waverly, Massachusetts.

‡Associate Professor of Psychology, Department of Psychology, University of South Alabama, Mobile, Alabama.

Children's Rehabilitation Center on November 6, 1967. A physical examination revealed "...a markedly emaciated, white female who appeared to be in no distress. When asked how she was feeling, she said, 'I guess I'm sick because I was brought here'... Extremities were markedly thin." A psychiatric evaluation four days after admission described her as a "...very emaciated looking young girl...extremely lethargic, sitting in her chair with her head leaning against the back of the chair, speaking in a very soft, slow fashion. My feeling was that this girl was quite disturbed, that she had great difficulties with separation and that she was concerned about growing up and the sexual maturation which was taking place." Her only previous hospitalization was at age six for appendicitis.

Her loss of weight began as a self-imposed diet during the summer of 1967. She attributed this dieting to her peers teasing her about her weight. It was at about this time that her mother recalled overhearing the patient and a girlfriend discussing dieting. It was only after the family had returned from a vacation trip during the latter part of August that they noticed her loss of weight. In addition, mother also recalls diet magazines, and brochures about dieting in the patient's room. On August 25, she was taken to her local physician. He did not consider her weight loss excessive and attributed it to puberty and adolescence. A tranquilizer and appetite stimulant were prescribed; however, she refused to take them.

In mid-October, she was examined by a physician in a neighboring town. His impression was that she "...presents the classical instance of anorexia nervosa and...her illness is serious enough to demand immediate psychiatric care." It was at this point that the parents contacted the senior author. The initial interview with the parents revealed the existence of extreme manipulation within the home environment. The family's anxiety about the patient's failure to eat resulted in their allowing her to dictate grocery purchases, meal planning, and the foods which the individual members of the family were, and were not, permitted to eat. Her younger brother would often sneak ice-cream treats late at night when the patient was not looking, because this was one of the foods which was on his sister's prohibited list. The patient also saved her lunch money since she did not wish to eat lunch. She also hoarded sizeable quantities of food in her room. At mealtime, she was apt to throw away food when she believed the other members of her family were not looking, in order to give the impression that she was eating more than she actually was.

During the next three weeks, recommendations were made to help the family eliminate manipulative behaviors and reduced rate of eating. An attempt was made to establish mealtime as a discriminative stimulus, Ferster *et al.* (1962); socialization at mealtime was made contingent on eating, and pleasurable activities were postponed until after improved eating behaviors had occurred. Discussions of her failure to eat were to be avoided, and all manipulative behaviors were to be handled by not allowing them to control the activities of the other members of the family. Within a week, manipulative behaviors within the home were totally eliminated; however, her weight continued to fall. Two weeks later, her weight had dropped seven-and-one-half pounds. She was then admitted to the Children's Rehabilitation Center.

Hoarding was the most conspicuous behavior during the patient's first week at the Center. Among the items hoarded were food, ball pens, scissors, paper cups, napkins, and a syringe which had been disregarded in a waste paper basket. Though she was observed stealing on only one occasion, several items which were missing were found among her belongings. Subsequently, if something was missing, she was the first one to be accused and, often, was unjustly blamed for stealing. On one occasion, a nurse who had become angered by her behavior called her a "thief," and later told her that she had given up on her. A consulting psychologist diagnosed her as "obviously psychotic," and many members of the medical staff put considerable pressure on the authors to transfer her to another treatment center where they were more familiar with children who had "psychiatric problems."

METHOD

During the first week after admission, the patient was seen daily in a supportive counselling relationship. No attempt was made to explore "dynamics" and "depth therapy." She was simply allowed to talk about current problems. Sessions took place every day for the first week, and then twice weekly until she was discharged. At the beginning of the second week, the reinforcement programme was initiated.

Instructions to the Staff

1. The patient should be weighed each morning at 6:30, just prior to the breakfast meal.
2. If the patient is observed taking food from the dining area, the nurse assigned to observe her should tell her what she had observed, and ask her to return the food with a minimum of social interaction.
3. Discussions about the patient's failure to eat are to be avoided. If she initiates a conversation about her eating difficulties, the topic of conversation should be politely changed.
4. The patient's parents will be allowed a one-hour visit with her each week. No telephone calls may be made by the patient.

Initial Reward System (R-1)

1. Reward points (three by four inch white index cards with the denomination 1, 2, 3, 5, or 10 and the words "reward points" handwritten across the face of the card) were established as a token of exchange redeemable for items often used, but unavailable to the patient at the Center (hair curlers, writing paper, stamps). Special events (movies, trips) were also made contingent on the patient trading in a specified number of reward points. Later, these same reward points could be used to purchase items from local department stores or from the Sears and Roebuck catalogue.
2. Reward points were earned by the patient each morning immediately after she had been weighed at the rate of:
   a. One reward point for maintaining her weight of the morning before.
   b. One reward point for each 0.1 kg of weight gain thereafter.
   c. If weight loss occurred, reward points were withheld until weight lost had been regained.

Intermediate Reward System (R-2)

The initial reward system was terminated on day twelve. Subsequently, reward points were made contingent on amount of food eaten during the three previous meals. Kitchen personnel recorded food eaten at each meal and were advised to observe her during mealtime rather than record food eaten on the basis of food remaining on her tray. This was to insure the recording of food actually consumed rather than food hoarded or put on another child's plate.

Final Reward System (R-3) (R-4)

On day thirty-five, each food was assigned a specific reward point value as noted in Table 1. Reward points were administered immediately after the completion of each meal rather

Table 1. Mealtime point schedule.

Liquids		Main dishes		Desserts	
Milk (8 oz)	2	Bun	1	Cookie	1
Orange juice (6 oz)	2	Cereal	2	Ice cream	2
Soup (bowl)	2	Egg (one)	2	Pudding	2
Tomato juice (6 oz)	2	Hamburg	4	Toast and jelly	2
		Meat or fish (full portion)	4		
		Potatoes or rice	2		
		Salad	2		
		Sandwich	4		
		Serving bacon	2		
		Slice of bread	1		

than after each three meals. A nurse, assigned to observe the patient at the specific meal, recorded foods consumed on a small white pad. At the completion of the meal, she showed the patient what had been recorded, and then gave her the reward points earned at that meal. Reward points were redeemable for items at local department stores or for items in the Sears and Roebuck catalogue (R-3).

On day fifty-eight, the final reward system was modified (R-4). In addition to reward points being capable of purchasing material objects, they could also be used to purchase extra days of home visit on the sliding scale noted in Table 2. Home visit was available in the following manner. The patient was allowed to go home every week on Saturday evening at 6 p.m., and return the following Tuesday at 9:30 a.m., regardless of the number of reward points earned. However, reward points earned at mealtime could be traded in for extra days of home visit (whole days only) which would allow her to leave on Friday evening, Thursday

Table 2. Earned home visit schedule.

Weight (kg.)	Number of hours required to earn one day of home visit*
29.0	14
29.5	12
30.0	10
30.5	9
31.0	8
31.5	7
32.0	5
35.0	3
39.0	2

*Points earned at mealtime will be converted into extra hours of home visit at the rate of one hour for each fifteen points earned. All points earned during any given week must be converted into extra hours of home visit. Hours not used because they could only be converted into a part-day of home visit can be carried over until the next week.

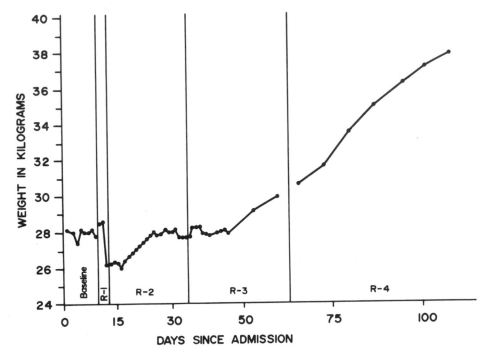

Fig. 1. Effect of reinforcement on weight in a case of anorexia nervosa.

evening, and so on, according to the number of extra days of home visit earned. She would always return to the Center on Tuesday morning, because this was more convenient for her parents. The patient was given a copy of the schedule and the system was explained to her in detail.

Discussions with the Parents

After the patient was admitted, her parents were seen for one hour a week to provide them with the information necessary to modify their behavior. The discussions had a two-fold purpose: (1) To teach the parents the behavior modification programme being employed at the Center; (2) To instruct them in the methods which would be most effective in making the transition between treatment center and community.

During home visits, the patient was gradually introduced to individuals and activities within the community. Initially, she made short trips to the local shopping center, and visits to relatives were of short duration. Later, visits were lengthened, and she gradually was permitted to meet with more of her friends and relatives. At a later date, she went to church with her parents, to Sunday school, and finally made visits to her public school just prior to discharge.

RESULTS

Figure 1 shows the effect of the reinforcement programme on the patient's weight. Within one day after the implementation of the Initial Reward System (R-1), the patient's weight

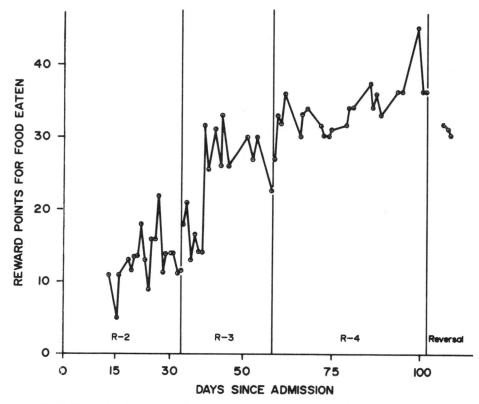

Fig. 2. Reward points earned for food eaten (approximate caloric intake) in a case of anorexia nervosa.

began to increase. However, it was soon noted that this weight gain was due to the patient stuffing heavy objects in her clothing, and the fact that she was wearing more and heavier articles of clothing. All future weighings were in the nude.

Figure 2 indicates the number of reward points earned for food eaten, a measure which roughly parallels the caloric value of the food eaten each day. The Intermediate Reward System (R-2) began on day twelve. After an initial plateau, both amount of food eaten (Fig. 2) and weight (Fig. 1) increased significantly. After ten days of steady weight gain, the patient's weight plateaued once again.

Thirty-four days after admission, the Final Reward System was put into effect (R-3). All foods were assigned reward point values on the basis of their approximate caloric value (Table 1), and reward points were made contingent on specific foods eaten at each meal. Within one week, there was a marked increase in amount of food eaten, followed by an increase in weight several days later. This Final Reward System was modified on day fifty-eight, at which time extra days of home visit were made contingent on reward points earned at mealtime, in addition to the material items which had been available since the beginning (Table 2). A significant increase in amount of food eaten was noted within two days, and this was followed by an increase in rate of subsequent weight gain. Amount of food eaten remained at this new level until day 108, at which time the patient was told that she would be discharged on the following weekend. Amount of food eaten during the next three days declined. Five months after discharge she was continuing to gain weight at the rate of one pound per month.

DISCUSSION

The results suggest that a token system of positive reinforcement (in the form of reward points redeemable for material items and home visit) contingent on amount of food eaten is an effective method of increasing eating rate in anorexia nervosa. The initial failure to increase eating rate through the administration of reward points contingent on very small units of weight gain was due to the fact that weight gain, no matter how small, is too far removed from the behavior of eating. When reward points were subsequently administered, contingent on amount of food eaten, both food eaten and weight increased. There were three distinct levels of eating rate, each significantly higher than the preceding one; and each increase followed interventions which increased the immediacy or amount of reinforcement which followed eating behavior. Initially, amount of food eaten increased when reward points (redeemable for material items and special privileges) were administered contingent on amount of food eaten per day. Eating rate increased once again when the reward points were administered immediately after each meal, each food being assigned a specific reward point value. Finally, a significant increase in food intake was noted after reward points were given added value in that they were redeemable for extra days of home visit in addition to the material items. Though no attempt was made to reverse procedures, it was noted that eating rate did, in fact, drop immediately after the patient was told that discharge was scheduled for the following week-end (reward points would no longer be needed to earn home visit).

This study demonstrates the use of positive reinforcement to increase eating rate in anorexia nervosa when a token system of reinforcement is superimposed on existing reinforcers within the environment. Bachrach *et al.* (1965) and Leitenberg (1968) employed positive reinforcement to increase eating rate; however, both removed all existing reinforcers from the patient's environment prior to the onset of experimental procedures. In the present study, the bulk of potentially reinforcing events at the Center were present during the course of the experiment (occupational therapy, parties, school, girl scout activities, supportive therapy, etc.).

REFERENCES

Bachrach, A. J., Erwin, W. J. & Mohr, P. J. (1965) The control of eating behavior in an anorexic by operant conditioning techniques. In *Case Studies in Behavior Modification* (Eds. L. P. Ullmann and L. Krasner). Holt, Rinehart & Winston, New York.

Barlow, D. H., Agras, W. S. & Leitenberg, H. (1967) Control of classic neurotic "symptoms" through reinforcement and non-reinforcement. (September, 1967). Association for Advancement of Behavioral Therapies, Washington, D.C.

Ferster, C. B., Nurnberger, J. I. & Levitt, E. B. (1962) The control of eating. *J. Mathetic*, **1**, 87–110.

Leitenberg, H., Agras, W. S. & Thomson, L. E. (1968) A sequential analysis of the effects of selective positive reinforcement in modifying anorexia nervosa. *Behaviour Research and Therapy*, **6**, 211–218.

Adolescent Anorexia Nervosa Treated by Desensitization*

EDWIN A. HALLSTEN, Jr.†

Galesburg State Research Hospital, Galesburg, Illinois, U.S.A.‡

Abstract: A case of pathological food avoidance in a twelve-year-old female is described in terms of learning theory principles. A relevant behavioral treatment was immediately successful in resolving the disorder and re-establishing normal eating habits. Follow-up five months after termination of treatment indicated that neither relapse nor symptom substitution had occurred.

Anorexia nervosa is a maladaptive behavior pattern which has been variously formulated and treated. Noyes & Kolb (1958) place it among the psychophysiological disorders and note that, "The presenting symptom of this reaction is persistent lack of appetite, or rather disgust for food, with vomiting if it is forced." Fenichel (1945) notes, "It may be a hysterical symptom expressing the fear of an orally perceived pregnancy or of unconscious sadistic wishes. It may be a part of an ascetic reaction formation in a compulsion neurosis. It may be an affect equivalent in a depression...." Gardner (1959), speaking specifically about anorexia in adolescents says, "All intensive psychotherapeutic and psychoanalytic work with such adolescents would seem to indicate that the central and most powerful motivating force resulting in dieting to the degree that extreme emaciation supervenes is the desire on the part of these adolescents to stalemate physiological growth in the sexual sphere, and thereby to continue a denial of their identification with members of their own sex."

Treatments as extreme as prefrontal lobotomy (Carmody & Vibber, 1952) have been reported in the literature. More typically, however, treatment tends to follow the regimen suggested by Noyes and Kolb (1958): "Treatment consists of psychotherapy with an associated effort to improve the total adjustment of the personality. During treatment, reference to the anorexia should usually be avoided. Intimate personal attention at meals, including spoon feeding, may be effective in getting the patient to eat normally. Small doses of insulin are advisable."

An alternative view of chronic anorexia derives from clinical extensions of psychological learning theories. Successful treatment of the symptom by behavioral techniques has been reported by Lang (1965), Bachrach, Erwin and Mohr (1965), and White (1959). Ullmann & Krasner (1965) articulate the central thesis of this approach concisely, pointing out that all behavior, adaptive as well as maladaptive, is acquired and maintained or changed following essentially the same rules. This acquisition, maintenance and change lawfully follows the principles which have been formulated and experimentally established in the laboratories of experimental psychology.

---

*Reprinted from *Behaviour Research and Therapy*, 1965, **3**, 87–91. Copyright 1965 with permission from Pergamon Press Publishing Company and Edwin A. Hallsten, Jr.

†Appreciation is expressed to Dr. Leonard P. Ullmann of the University of Illinois for his wise and considerable assistance in the preparation of this manuscript.

‡This report was prepared while the author was a student at the University of Illinois completing a clinical internship at Galesburg State Research Hospital.

The case of anorexia nervosa to be reported here has at least three facets of interest. First, it demonstrates the central behavior-therapy assumption that the laws governing maladaptive behavior are the same as those which govern adaptive behavior. Secondly, it is, as far as the author knows, the first case in which anorexia nervosa has been successfully treated by the desensitization technique developed and popularized by Wolpe (1958). Third, it is of interest in that the patient is a child of twelve whereas most work with this technique has been done with adults.

PROBLEM

Ann was a twelve-year-old girl admitted to Galesburg State Research Hospital on September 2, 1964, at a weight of fifty-seven pounds and height of fifty-seven inches. This is approximately twenty-five pounds below the normal weight for her age and height. Although the patient was ambulatory, her energy resources were severely limited and she appeared emaciated. Three years prior to admission she had weighed ninety pounds and was called "Fatty" by her peers at school. An excellent student, she undertook a study of nutrition and prepared a diet of a thousand calories per day which was approved, with supplementary vitamins, by the family pediatrician. The patient followed the diet and began to lose weight, continuing, in spite of all that her parents could do by pleading, persuasion, and punishment, until it compelled her hospitalization. In April, 1964, she was given an extensive physical examination with essentially negative results (except for her below normal weight). During the summer she entered a general hospital twice for treatment of this anorexia. Treatment on these occasions consisted mainly of forced feedings, actual or threatened. On returning to her home the former highly selective pattern of eating was re-established almost immediately. Finally, she was taken to a neurologist who recommended her placement in a psychiatric hospital.

Ann was known to have two unrealistic fears. One was a storm phobia of sufficient magnitude to be quite disruptive to family life on stormy or dark days. This began after a visit to an area that had been rather thoroughly and recently devastated by a tornado. The second was the fear of gaining weight or becoming fat which had led to the stringent dieting. There was no fear of food itself, only of foods which were associated with gains in weight. She would eat lean meats, leafy vegetables, etc. Occasionally in the hospital and at home Ann would eat and then force the regurgitation of the food later to prevent it from having its feared effect. Nor was Ann's fear one of growing up, for she often indicated that what she wanted was to be tall and slender. It appeared that this was specifically a fear of growing fat. The assumption involved in the counterconditioning treatment was that this fear of growing fat had developed when the patient was obese. Dieting and the rewards that followed it reduced this fear and were therefore rewarding. At first, as she began to lose weight, there were many positive rewards from family and friends which strengthened this bond further. After a time, however, the behavior which had been acquired as an adaptive response to weight-inducing foods became maladaptive when her weight began to drop below normal levels. The patient now began to encounter punishment and loss of affection as the concern of family and friends increased. This rejection and censure generated anxiety for Ann. She then apparently failed to make the important discrimination between the different contingencies which had given rise to the same kind of subjective experience. She generalized from the former situation (censure for being too fat) to the latter (censure for being too thin) and responded to the latter with the means of fear reduction which had been most effective in dealing with earlier fear. This "anxiety reducing" response was food-avoidance and the felt need to become even thinner. The ineffectiveness of this response in the new contingency situation was not effectively earned. The most probable reason for this blocking is the increase of anxiety and fear, amplified to pathological proportions by her inability to deal effectively with it. The treatment reported here assumed that associating the eating of fattening foods with a situation incompatible with fear or anxiety would weaken the anxiety association sufficiently to permit the desired discrimination. The linking of relaxation with the eating of fattening foods would be such an incompatible association.

TREATMENT AND RESULTS

At the staff conference on the twenty-third day following her admission, two main recommendations were made for treatment. The first was to restrict visits by relatives and to make them contingent upon weight gains – one visit for every two pounds gained in weight. This programme was to be implemented by the unit staff as a whole. The second recommendation was to employ a reciprocal inhibition or counterconditioning technique to attack the fear associated with gaining weight and becoming fat. This dual recommendation was, from the research point of view, unfortunate, since it confounded two methods, although both recommendations involved essentially behavioral approaches to treatment that were quite different from the traditional methods. However, the actual implementation and the pattern of effects on the eating behavior mitigated the confounding to a very large degree. Five days after the staff decision (Day 28) the patient was informed that visits were to be restricted and would henceforth be contingent on her gaining weight. Reference to Fig. 1 illustrates that no weight change of any significance followed this information, Ann's weight remaining quite stable at fifty-nine pounds until Day 37.

Treatment of Ann's fears by means of counterconditioning began on the twenty-seventh day after her admission. The first session consisted of simply explaining the treatment strategy and then training the patient in the use of Paul's (1964) modification of Jacobsen's relaxation technique (1938). The basic strategy was described by Wolpe as systematic desensitization (1958).

It was decided that the first of Ann's two fears to be dealt with would be the fear of storms. It was perceived to be the less difficult and more likely to yield a success which would provide

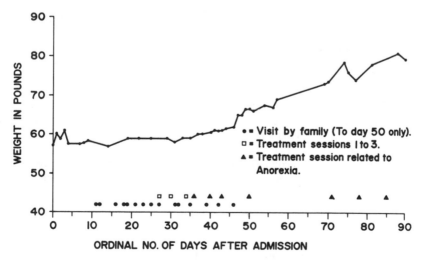

Fig. 1. Weight chart showing the relationship between changes in weight, visits by members of the family, and the desensitization treatment.

additional confidence in the treatment. Accordingly, a hierarchy of the situations relevant to the fear of storms was developed following Wolpe's procedure. This hierarchy was completely mastered by the end of the third session on Day 34 of her hospitalization. There had been no change in her eating behavior or her weight up to this time.

Meanwhile the programme of restricting family visits had never actually been implemented as threatened. Members of the family continued to visit as indicated by the solid circles in Fig. 1. The patient was given her first off-grounds pass on Days 31 and 32 with no observable change in weight or in eating behavior. On Day 35 the mother was informed that members of the family were to visit only with the hospital's permission and that this would depend upon the patient's gaining weight. Nonetheless, another visit took place on Day 39 without the required increase in weight and without any invitation or special permission being granted.

At therapy session four, on Day 36, work was begun on the fear of gaining weight. The patient was instructed to relax as she had been trained to do in previous sessions. She did this readily. Then she was told to imagine a particularly comfortable situation at home. In carefully monitored steps she was then instructed to feel (visualize) herself being called to the table, at the table, eating, eating specifically fattening foods, enjoying them, having eaten, and then going to stand before a mirror in her mother's bedroom and perceiving that she was gaining weight. In none of these steps, as they were undertaken, was there any sign of anxiety or any observable change in the relaxed state of the body.

That evening, according to nursing personnel, she ate her entire evening meal. The following day (Day 37) the charge nurse noted a remarkable change in appetite and in eating behavior at all meals. That afternoon Ann weighed an additional pound, and gained weight more or less steadily both in the hospital and at home, until she is now at a weight normal for her age and height.

In subsequent treatment sessions, the hierarchy was repeated, intensified, and extended to include a situation where she was being teased by her peers for becoming fat again. After Session 6, treatment was reduced from twice weekly to once weekly and continued to a total of twelve sessions, none of which exceeded one hour in length.

Changes in personality began to appear slowly but spontaneously within a few weeks, and communication with her parents and family members was greatly improved. No attention was given to the development of any dynamic insight into how the eating problem had arisen, and none was ever indicated. Ann, as she left the hospital, could talk rather freely about her not eating but was still mildly puzzled about why she had allowed it to become such a disruptive issue in the home.

Long-term effects are confounded by a later staff decision to involve the family in family group therapy. However, there is good reason to believe that the eating habits would have remained normal at home even without this therapy. First, all imagery in treatment was centered on the home situation rather than on the hospital situation. Secondly, eating and weight gains persisted without reduction or interference on several weekend home visits and on a ten-day home visit which included Ann having an attack of influenza and experiencing the death of a close relative. This was prior to the introduction of family group therapy. Follow-up five months after termination indicated that the eating patterns continued to be normal and that Ann had made a good readjustment to her home and school situation.

REFERENCES

Bachrach, A. J., Erwin, W. J. & Mohr, J. P. (1965) The control of eating behavior in an anorexic by operant conditioning techniques. In *Case Studies in Behavior Modification* (Editors, L. P. Ullmann and L. Krasner). Holt, Rinehart & Winston, New York.

Carmody, J. T. & Vibber, F. M. (1952) Anorexia nervosa treated by prefrontal lobotomy. *Ann. intern. Med.* **36,** 647.

Fenichel, O. (1945) *The Psychoanalytic Theory of Neurosis,* p. 176. W. W. Norton, New York.

Gardner, G. E. (1959) Psychiatric problems of adolescence. In *American Handbook of Psychiatry* (Editors S. Arieti), p. 878. Vol. 1. Basic Books, New York.

Jacobsen, E. (1938) *Progressive Relaxation.* University of Chicago Press, Chicago.

Lang, P. J. (1965) Behavior therapy with a case of nervous anorexia. In *Case Studies in Behavior Modification,* (Editors, L. P. Ullmann and L. Krasner). Holt, Rinehart & Winston, New York.

Noyes, A. P. & Kolb, L. C. (1958) *Modern Clinical Psychiatry,* pp. 464 and 465. W. B. Saunders, Philadelphia.

Paul, G. L. (1964) Effects of insight, desensitization, and attention-placebo treatment of anxiety: An approach to outcome research in psychotherapy. Unpublished doctoral dissertation, University of Illinois.

Ullmann, L. P. & Krasner, L. (1965) Introduction. In *Case Studies in Behavior Modification,* (Editors L. P. Ullmann and L. Krasner). Holt, Rinehart & Winston, New York.

White, J. G. (1959) The use of learning theory in the psychological treatment of children. *J. clin. Psychol.* **15,** 227–229.

Wolpe, J. (1958) *Psychotherapy by reciprocal inhibition.* Stanford University Press, Stanford, Calif.

Classical and Operant Factors in the
Treatment of a School Phobia*†

ARNOLD A. LAZARUS,‡ GERALD C. DAVISON, and DAVID A. POLEFKA

Stanford University

Abstract: To the best of our knowledge, this report is the first to recognize the advantages of employing both classical and operant conditioning procedures in the treatment of a neurotic case. A model which appeared to have heuristic value was developed. When avoidance behavior is motivated by high levels of anxiety, classical counterconditioning techniques are called for; when anxiety is minimal, and avoidance behavior is seemingly maintained by various secondary reinforcers, operant strategies should be applied. Furthermore, this paper indicates that the practice of interchanging therapists not only failed to disrupt or impede therapeutic progress but had certain distinct advantages.

Although the formal application of "learning theory" to clinical problems is widespread, the literature on this topic reflects a basic cleavage. Wolpe (1958) and Eysenck (1960) typify the use of the classical conditioning paradigm in the treatment of neurotic disorders, while Lindsley & Skinner (1954), King, Merrell, Lovinger & Denny (1957), and Ferster (1961) exemplify the use of operant conditioning in the treatment of psychotic behavior. On the assumption that both "operants" and "respondents" enter into all therapeutic processes, the writers hypothesized that the deliberate and strategic use of both classical and operant conditioning procedures would have greater therapeutic effect than exclusive reliance on techniques derived from either procedure alone. The therapeutic utility of this rationale became obvious in the treatment of a severely disturbed (nonpsychotic) school-phobic child.

Strategy in "behavior therapy" consists essentially of introducing reinforcement contingencies that encourage the emergence of nondeviant response patterns. This may be achieved by pairing the reinforcer with a *stimulus* (as is the case in classical conditioning) and/or by making the reinforcer contingent upon a *response* (as is the case in operant conditioning). Apart from Patterson's (1965) successful application of predominantly operant techniques to a school-phobic child, the treatment of children's phobias by conditioning methods has hitherto relied almost exclusively on the classical paradigm (Bentler, 1962; Jones, 1924; Lazarus, 1960; Lazarus & Abramovitz, 1962; Lazarus & Rachman, 1957; Wolpe, 1958). It could be argued, however, that some of the above-named investigators made inadvertent use of the operant rubric. In a case alluded to by Lazarus and Abramovitz (1962) for instance, a child with "widespread areas of disturbance" failed to benefit from counterconditioning therapy but required "broader therapeutic handling." The therapeutic mainstay in this instance actually amounted to persuading the parents to alter certain of their actions which were sustaining their child's deviant responses (i.e., an operant strategy). The reapplication of counterconditioning techniques then effected a rapid recovery. The present paper is an

---

*Reprinted from the *Journal of Abnormal Psychology*, June, 1965, **70**, 3, 225–229. Copyright 1965, with permission from the American Psychological Association, Inc., and Dr. A. A. Lazarus.

†Reprints may be obtained by writing to the second author at Stanford University.

‡Now at the Department of Psychology, Yale University, New Haven, Conn.

endeavor to illustrate how the deliberate (rather than inadvertent) use of these two theoretical models at crucial phases throughout treatment proved therapeutically expeditious.

CASE STUDY

History of the Problem

When he was referred for therapy Paul, age nine, had been absent from school for three weeks. The summer vacation had ended six weeks previously, and on entering the fourth grade, Paul avoided the classroom situation. He was often found hiding in the cloakroom, and subsequently began spending less time at school each day. Thereafter, neither threats, bribes, nor punishments could induce him to re-enter school.

Paul's history revealed a series of similar episodes. During his first day of kindergarten he succeeded in climbing over an extremely high wall and fled home. His first-grade teacher considered him to be "disturbed." Serious difficulties regarding school attendance were first exhibited when Paul entered the second grade of a parochial school. It was alleged that the second-grade teacher who, according to Paul, "looked like a witch," generally intimidated the children and was very free with physical punishment.[1] Paul retrospectively informed his parents that he felt as though "the devil was in the classroom." At this stage he became progressively more reluctant to enter the school and finally refused entirely. A psychiatrist was consulted and is reported to have advised the parents to use coercion, whereupon Paul was literally dragged screaming to school by a truant officer. Paul was especially bitter about his experience with the psychiatrist. "All we did was talk and then the truant officer came." In the third grade Paul was transferred to the neighborhood public school where he spent a trouble-free year at the hands of an exceedingly kind teacher.

Family History

Paul was the fourth of eight children, the first boy in a devout, orthodox Roman Catholic family. His sisters were aged fourteen, thirteen, eleven, seven and six years, respectively; his two brothers were eight and two and a half years old. The father was a moody, anxiously ambitious electronics engineer who had insight into the fact that his subjective occupational insecurities intruded into the home. A harsh disciplinarian—"I run a tight ship"—he impulsively meted out punishment for any act which deviated even slightly from his perfectionistic standards. He found it significant that Paul, of all the children, was particularly sensitive to his moods, and described himself as being "especially close to Paul" while commenting that "he rarely tells me things." In his desire to protect his family from everyday hazards he was inclined to emphasize extreme consequences: "Don't touch that fluorescent bulb, son; there's poison in it and it will kill you!"

The mother, although openly affectionate and less rigid and demanding than her husband, took pains to respond towards her eight children in an unbiased fashion. She stressed, however, that "Paul touches my nerve center," and stated that they frequently quarrelled in the father's absence. She had always found Paul "less cuddlesome" than his siblings. When he was two years old, she would lock him out of the house, "so as to develop his independence." It is significant to note that this occurred immediately following the birth of his first brother. In general, she was inclined to be inconsistent when administering rewards and punishment. Psychometric testing suggested that Paul was uncertain whether a given response would meet with criticism and rejection or kind attention from his mother. It was nevertheless

---

[1]Vehement complaints from many parents finally led to the dismissal of this teacher.

evident that Paul was eager to receive a greater share of his mother's highly-rationed time.

The lad himself was somewhat small and frail-looking. Although reticent, essentially aloof and somewhat withdrawn, he was capable of unexpected vigor and self-assertion when he chose to participate in sporting activities. From the outset, the therapists noted his labile and expressive reactions to all stressful stimuli. The extent of his subjective discomfort was easily gauged by clearly discernible responses. As the magnitude of anxiety increased, there was a concomitant progression of overt signs — increased reticence, a postural stoop, a general constriction of movement, tearfilled eyes, mild trembling, pronounced blanching, culminating in sobbing and immobility. As will be shown below, these emotional indices were crucial in selecting appropriate therapeutic strategies.

A series of specific traumatic events commenced with his near-drowning when five years old. Towards the end of his third grade, he underwent a serious appendectomy with critical complications, which was followed by painful post-operative experiences in a doctor's consulting room. During one of these examinations, as Paul bitterly recounted, he had been left alone by his parents. Shortly after his recovery from surgery, he witnessed a drowning which upset him considerably. Following his entry into the fourth grade, the sudden death of a twelve-year-old girl, who had been a close friend of his elder sister, profoundly affected the entire family. It is also noteworthy that Paul's father experienced personal stress in his work situation during the child's turbulent second grade, as well as immediately preceding fourth grade. Finally, Paul seemed to have been intimidated by a warning from his eldest sister that fourth grade school work was particularly difficult.

Therapeutic Procedure

After the initial interview, it was evident that Paul's school phobia was the most disruptive response pattern of a generally bewildered and intimidated child. Although subsequent interviews revealed the plethora of familial tensions, situational crises, and specific traumatic events outlined above, the initial therapeutic objective was to reinstate normal school attendance. Nevertheless it was clearly apparent that the home situation in general, and more particularly, specific examples of parental mishandling would ultimately require therapeutic intervention.

The application of numerous techniques in the consulting room (e.g., systematic desensitization[2]) was abandoned because of the child's inarticulateness and acquiescent response tendency. It was obvious that his verbal reports were aimed at eliciting approval rather than describing his true feelings. Desensitization *in vivo* was therefore employed as the principal therapeutic strategy.

The school was situated two and one half blocks away from the home. The routine was for Paul to leave for school at 8:30 a.m. in order to arrive by 8:40. The first recess was from 10:00–10:30; lunch break from 12:00–1:00; and classes ended at 3:30 p.m. At the time when therapy was initiated, the boy was extremely surly and dejected in the mornings (as reported by the parents), refused breakfast, rarely dressed himself, and became noticeably more fearful toward 8:30. Parental attempts at reassurance, coaxing, or coercion elicited only sobbing and further withdrawal.

Accordingly, the boy was exposed to the following increasingly difficult steps along the main dimensions of his school phobia:

---

[2]Systematic desensitization entails the presentation of carefully graded situations, which are subjectively noxious, to the imagination of a deeply relaxed patient until the most personally distressing events no longer evoke any anxiety (*see* Wolpe, 1961).

1. On a Sunday afternoon, accompanied by the therapists, he walked from his house to the school. The therapists were able to allay Paul's anxiety by means of distraction and humor, so that his initial exposure was relatively pleasant.
2. On the next two days at 8:30 a.m., accompanied by one of the therapists, he walked from his house into the schoolyard. Again, Paul's feelings of anxiety were reduced by means of coaxing, encouragement, relaxation, and the use of "emotive imagery" (i.e., the deliberate picturing of subjectively pleasant images such as Christmas and a visit to Disneyland, while relating them to the school situation; *see* Lazarus & Abramovitz, 1962). Approximately fifteen minutes were spent roaming around the school grounds, after which Paul returned home.
3. After school was over for the day, the therapist was able to persuade the boy to enter the classroom and sit down at his desk. Part of the normal school routine was then playfully enacted.
4. On the following three mornings, the therapist accompanied the boy into the classroom with the other children. They chatted with the teacher, and left immediately after the opening exercises.
5. A week after beginning this programme, Paul spent the entire morning in class. The therapist sat in the classroom and smiled approvingly at Paul whenever he interacted with his classmates or the teacher. After eating his lunch he participated in an active ball game, and returned to his house with the therapist at 12:30. (Since parent-teacher conferences were held during the entire week, afternoon classes were discontinued.)
6. Two days later when Paul and the therapist arrived at school, the boy lined up with the other children and allowed the therapist to wait for him inside the classroom. This was the first time that Paul had not insisted on having the therapist in constant view.
7. Thereafter, the therapist sat in the school library adjoining the classroom.
8. It was then agreed that the therapist would leave at 2:30 p.m. while Paul remained for the last hour of school.
9. On the following day, Paul remained alone at school from 1:45 p.m. until 2:45 p.m. (Earlier that day, the therapist had unsuccessfully attempted to leave the boy alone from 10 until noon.)
10. Instead of fetching the boy at his home, the therapist arranged to meet him at the school gate at 8:30 a.m. Paul also agreed to remain alone at school from 10:45 a.m. until noon provided that the therapist return to eat lunch with him. At 1:45 p.m. the therapist left again with the promise that if the boy remained until school ended (3:30 p.m.) he would visit Paul that evening and play the guitar for him.
11. Occasional setbacks made it necessary to instruct the lad's mother not to allow the boy into the house during school hours. In addition, the teacher was asked to provide special jobs for the boy so as to increase his active participation and make school more attractive.
12. The family doctor was asked to prescribe a mild tranquilizer for the boy to take on awakening so as to reduce his anticipatory anxieties.
13. After meeting the boy in the mornings, the therapist gradually left him alone at school for progressively longer periods of time. After six days of this procedure, the therapist was able to leave at 10 a.m.
14. The boy was assured that the therapist would be in the faculty room until 10 a.m., if needed. Thus, he came to school knowing the therapist was present, but not actually seeing him.
15. With Paul's consent the therapist arrived at school shortly *after* the boy entered the classroom at 8:40 a.m.

16. School attendance independent of the therapist's presence was achieved by means of specific rewards (a comic book, and variously colored tokens which would eventually procure a baseball glove) contingent upon his entering school and remaining there alone. He was at liberty to telephone the therapist in the morning if he wanted him at school, in which event he would forfeit his rewards for that day.

17. Since the therapist's presence seemed to have at least as much reward value as the comic books and tokens, it was necessary to enlist the mother's cooperation to effect the therapist's final withdrawal. The overall diminution of the boy's anxieties, together with general gains which had accrued to his home situation, made it therapeutically feasible for the mother to emphasize the fact that school attendance was compulsory, and that social agencies beyond the control of both therapists and parents would enforce this requirement eventually.

18. Approximately three weeks later, Paul had accumulated enough tokens to procure his baseball glove. He then agreed with his parents that rewards of this kind were no longer necessary.

THEORETICAL IMPLICATIONS

It should not be inferred that Paul's improvement followed a smooth monotonic progression. Numerous setbacks of varying degrees of severity occurred throughout the entire treatment programme, which extended over four and a half months. These episodes were differentially handled depending upon the therapist's assessment of the child's anxiety at that time, and his judgment of the degree to which the boy had mastered the preceding therapeutic steps.

It became apparent that the school phobia was comprised of two separate factors: (a) avoidance behavior motivated by intense fear of the school situation, and (b) avoidance behavior maintained by various secondary reinforcers, mainly attention from parents, siblings, and therapists. During the initial phases of therapy, the boy's high level of anxiety dictated the use of reciprocal inhibition methods (Wolpe, 1958). The therapists actively inhibited the boy's anxiety elicited by various aspects of the school setting (as in Step 2 above). The later stages of therapy were characterized by a decrease in Paul's overall anxiety without a concomitant decrease in avoidance behavior. After Step 15 the boy appeared to be minimally anxious. An operant strategy which made various rewards contingent on school attendance was therefore selected.

A Proposed Model

Although the division between classical and operant procedures became clearly discernible towards the terminal phases of treatment, many situations arose which necessitated the deliberate choice of one or other paradigm. A model was developed for determining when each was likely to prove maximally effective. On several occasions for instance, Paul left the classroom, entered the library and told the therapist, "I'm scared." At this point the choice of strategy became crucial. In strict operant terms, active attempts to reduce anxiety by means of attention and reassurance would reinforce classroom-leaving behavior. On the other hand, the classical paradigm would predict that to withhold immediate attention and make it contingent upon returning to the classroom would augment the child's anxiety and thus reinforce avoidance behavior. The critical factor in determining the appropriate procedure was the degree of anxiety as judged by the therapist.

An inappropriate use of the operant model could prove anti-therapeutic. If the level of anxiety is very high, a premature re-exposure to the feared situation will probably lead to increased sensitivity. Moreover, if this heightened level of anxiety leads to another escape response, the resultant anxiety-reduction will strengthen the avoidance responses (classroom-leaving behavior in this instance). It was also reasoned that when highly anxious, the boy would be unable to attend to the teacher, interact with his peers, or make any other responses which ordinarily reduced his anxiety.

An inappropriate use of the classical model would also impede therapeutic progress. The very acts of inducing relaxation, employing "emotive imagery," and giving reassurance may provide positive reinforcement for dependent behavior. The afore-mentioned difficulties in "phasing out" may be attributed to this possible side effect of *in vivo* desensitization. The gains which accrue when high levels of anxiety are thus decreased, however, temporarily out-weigh the disadvantages of increased dependency.

DISCUSSION

It may be argued that a disproportionate amount of time and effort was expended in attaining the principal therapeutic objective, *viz.*, normal school attendance. Urgent cases, however, who are neurotically incapacitated and unamenable to interview techniques, would seem to require therapeutic intervention beyond the confines of the consulting room. It should be emphasized that school phobia in a child is almost as pressing and disruptive a problem as occupational fears in an adult.

Since therapy *in vivo* makes heavy demands on the therapist's time, the senior author decided to enlist the assistance of two graduate students in clinical psychology (the co-authors). During the first exposure to school (*see* Step 1) Paul rapidly developed an attachment to one of the cotherapists (G.C.D.). As the application of reciprocal inhibition methods is conceivably facilitated by the nonspecific anxiety-inhibiting effects of a "good relationship" (Lazarus, 1961), this therapist carried out the first eight steps. Thereafter, the choice of therapist was partly determined by the academic and clinical commitments of the respective authors. Significantly, very little disturbance was occasioned by the constant change of therapists. There was often a distinct advantage in being able to alternate therapists; it was found, following a setback, that it was helpful to change therapists in order to offset the negative effects of being associated with sensitizing experiences.

The adjunctive use of a tranquilizer seemed to be of limited therapeutic value. Initially, it appeared to reduce the boy's anticipatory anxieties, but the absence of negative effects whenever it was forgotten, suggests that a placebo would have been as effective.

The therapists kept in close communication with the parents, who were encouraged to telephone whenever situational crises arose. As soon as normal school attendance had been more or less reinstated (Step 14), the therapists held a "family conference." In the main, the implications of the father's harsh and restrictive tendencies, along with the mother's inconsistent and ambivalent attitudes, were made clear to them. A long list of specific "do's" and "dont's" was drawn up and discussed. Apart from minor points of disagreement, the parents responded in an intelligent and receptive manner and subsequently implemented many of the recommendations.

According to the mother's reports, Paul's behavior also improved in areas outside of the school situation. She referred to his marked decrease in moodiness, his increased willingness to participate in household chores, more congenial relationships with his peers, and general gains in self-sufficiency.

Ten months after the termination of therapy, a follow-up inquiry revealed that Paul had not only maintained his gains, but had made further progress.

REFERENCES

Bentler, P. M. An infant's phobia treated with reciprocal inhibition therapy. *Journal of Child Psychology and Psychiatry*, 1962, **3**, 185–189.

Eysenck, H. J. (Ed.) *Behaviour therapy and the neuroses*. New York: Pergamon Press, 1960.

Ferster, C. B. Positive reinforcement and behavioral deficits in autistic children. *Child Development*, 1961, **32**, 437–456.

Jones, Mary C. Elimination of children's fears. *Journal of Experimental Psychology*, 1924, **7**, 383–390.

King, G. F., Merrell, D., Lovinger, E. & Denny, M. Operant motor behavior in acute schizophrenics. *Journal of Personality*, 1957, **25**, 317–326.

Lazarus, A. A. The elimination of children's phobias by deconditioning. In H. J. Eysenck (Ed.), *Behaviour therapy and the neuroses*. New York: Pergamon Press, 1960.

Lazarus, A. A. Group therapy of phobic disorders by systematic desensitization. *Journal of Abnormal and Social Psychology*, 1961, **63**, 504–510.

Lazarus, A. A. & Abramovitz, A. The use of "emotive imagery" in the treatment of children's phobias. *Journal of Mental Science*, 1962, **108**, 191–195.

Lazarus, A. A. & Rachman, S. The use of systematic desensitization in psychotherapy. *South African Medical Journal*, 1957, **31**, 334–337.

Lindsley, O. R. & Skinner, B. F. A method for the experimental analysis of the behavior of psychotic patients. *American Psychologist*, 1954, **9**, 419–420.

Patterson, G. R. A learning theory approach to the treatment of the school phobic child. In L. P. Ullmann & L. Krasner (Eds.), *Case Studies in Behavior Modification*. New York: Holt, Rinehart & Winston, 1965.

Wolpe, J. *Psychotherapy by reciprocal inhibition*. Stanford: Stanford University Press, 1958.

Wolpe. J. The systematic desensitization treatment of neuroses. *Journal of Nervous and Mental Disease*, 1961, **132**, 189–203.

Control of Other Maladaptive Responses

Elimination by the Parents of Fire Setting Behavior in a Seven-year-old Boy*

CORNELIUS J. HOLLAND

University of Windsor, Windsor, Ontario, Canada

Abstract: This article reports on a method which proved effective in treating a persistent and serious behavior problem in a short time. The method utilized positive reinforcement and the threat of punishment by loss effectively to eliminate in a child a fire setting habit of two years standing.

CASE REPORT

Robert was a seven-year-old boy, the oldest of three children, whose parents were referred to a psychiatric clinic by a private physician in order to receive counseling for family difficulties, the most distressing of which was Robert's habit of setting fires in the home. Since no child therapists were available at the time, Robert was placed on a waiting list but his parents, both high school graduates, were placed in a married couples group for the discussion of marital and family difficulties. The author was the group therapist and saw the couple for approximately a year, once weekly. The child was not seen by the author.

It soon became apparent that the fire setting problem was reaching increasingly serious proportions in terms of frequency and possibility of disaster for the family. Three months after the parents started the group, Robert was setting fires once or twice weekly. Usually the opportunities occurred on mornings of weekends whenever matches were available and the parents were still in bed or out of the house. Matches were either carelessly left around the home or Robert would find them in the street and hide them until an opportunity arose. Punishments such as being slapped, locked in his room or touched with a smouldering object were successful for only short periods. Both parents, but the mother especially, by this time felt helpless and enraged so that she and Robert exchanged very little affection, and apparently avoided each other as much as possible. The mother saw the child as an oppressive duty and her feelings of impotence and anger made it difficult for her to express anything positive toward him. Her attempts to control his behavior were almost exclusively through aversion. The father was able to be affectionate but his feelings of helplessness in coping with the problem often erupted into anger and physical punishment. The author at this time decided to attempt a more active intervention and saw the parents five times alone following the group session.

The problem was conceptualized as follows:

1. Some reinforcer obviously was maintaining the behavior. The reinforcer was never determined although many possibilities came to mind, some through the psychological and social history reports and were available for speculation.

---

*Reprinted from *Behaviour Research and Therapy*, 1969, 7, 135–137. Copyright 1969 with permission from Pergamon Press Publishing Company and Dr. Cornelius J. Holland.

2. The behavior occurred only under discriminative conditions of presence of matches and absence of parents.
3. One goal was to make fire setting behavior a discriminative situation for effective punishment, thus suppressing the behavior.
4. A second goal was to strengthen the operant of bringing matches into the presence of the parents when the parents were available. This of course would prevent fire setting.
5. A third goal was to strengthen non-striking behavior when matches were available but the parents were not present to dispense reinforcers. This goal was designed to control Robert's fire setting behavior in the neighborhood, or in the home when the parents were away.

PROCEDURES

Since the mother saw little hope in changing Robert and was not willing to participate initially, the following programme was carried out by the father.

1. Robert had just been given a new baseball glove which he valued highly. The father told Robert that if he set any more fires he would lose the glove irrevocably. The father said he would either give it away or destroy it in Robert's presence. It was hoped that this rather drastic threat, to Robert, would induce a strong suppression of the behavior long enough for adaptive behavior to be instituted. This hope was realized. The tactic was also used to help make fire setting a discriminative situation for a significant loss.

2. At the same time the father told Robert that if matches or match covers were found around the house they were to be brought to the father immediately. That same evening the father conspicuously placed on a table an empty packet. It was assumed this was of little value to Robert so that compliance with the father's commands would be readily emitted. When Robert brought the empty packet he was immediately given five cents and told he could now go to the store and spend it if he wished, which he did. These instructions were given to enhance the reinforcing properties of any money Robert was to receive during the programme. During the same evening and for the next few evenings, the father placed around the house packets containing matches which Robert promptly brought to him. Robert was put on a continuous reinforcement schedule for about eight trials with varying magnitudes of rein-forcers, from one to ten cents. He was told also during this phase of the programme that he was not to expect money every time. Very shortly the desired behavior was occurring at a high frequency so that matches or covers found outside during the day were saved and brought to the father when he returned from work. By this time the mother became interested in the programme and began to reinforce Robert when he brought matches to her, although she said she found it somewhat difficult to reward the child for behavior incompatible with what "he should not have been doing in the first place."

3. The possibility remained that Robert would find matches outside the home when either parent was not available for dispensing reinforcers. A procedure to strengthen non-striking behavior (or anything but striking) was started after the match-bringing behavior was believed to be strongly established. The procedure used was an approach-approach conflict. One even-ing about a week after the start of the programme the father told Robert he could strike a full packet of matches if he wished under the father's supervision. The father also placed twenty pennies beside the pack and told Robert that for every match unstruck he would receive one penny. Conversely one penny was removed for every match used. The first trial resulted in Robert striking ten matches and receiving ten pennies. The second trial the follow-ing evening earned Robert seventeen pennies, and the third trial, twenty pennies. Thereafter Robert systematically refrained from striking matches. The father then told Robert he was

not going to know what he would receive if he did not strike a match and varied the reward for the next few trials from no money to ten cents.

4. Throughout this programme the father was instructed (it is likely he would have done so nevertheless) to give social reinforcers with the monetary rewards, so that desired behavior was brought under control of a more relevant reinforcer.

RESULTS

The first three weeks of the programme were spent in developing the procedures while the remaining two were spent in making minor modifications and discussing progress. The programme was begun by the father at the end of the second week, and by the fifth week the habit was eliminated. The parents remained in the group until the author left the city eight months later. During this period the behavior did not recur, neither in the home nor from all evidence in the neighborhood. It was observed during the remaining months that without further guidance the father applied a variable ratio schedule for the money reinforcer.

Secondary results developed which were unexpected but gratifying. The mother was surprised with the changes she was observing and participated to some extent in the procedures described above. In addition, she began to apply some of the principles on her own to some problems involving Robert's disobedience. Although a programme was not developed for this problem the mother proved to be effective in applying the principles with desired results. Also by this time the procedures were a topic for group discussion and created much interest, and support for the mother. With her increased sense of adequacy in dealing with problem behavior, she began to relax her aversive control and was able to express affection for Robert, something which rarely occurred prior to this time.

DISCUSSION

The growing evidence of the possibility of replicating the results obtained in this case history is too impressive to dismiss lightly (*see* Russo, 1964; Wahler, Winkel, Peterson & Morrison, 1965). Shortly after the above case for example, the author had an opportunity to work with another group of parents (four couples) all of which came to the clinic for problems involving their children, such as "pathological" lying, disobedience, hyperactivity, aggression against siblings. Following the success with Robert and other cases, he defined the latter group as one employing directive parental counseling, applied operant principles systematically to analyses of the problems, taught the parents procedures for remediation, and achieved similar success. At times it was embarrassing to discuss with the rest of the staff changes in a child brought about by the parents. After much preliminary preparation by social workers, the psychological workup, the psychiatric evaluation, the ensuing staffings, the speculations and interpretations, and the often immense resulting gap between diagnosis and treatment, the problem was amenable to control within a relatively short period of time, within weeks or a few months. Although much research is needed in this area, such as a study of those personality variables of the parents which best predict success with this method, it promises to contribute at least to the amelioration of the manpower shortage in an important treatment area.

REFERENCES

Russo, S. Adaptations in behavioural therapy with children. *Behav. Res. & Therapy*, 1964, **2**, 43–47.

Wahler, R. G., Winkel, G. H., Peterson, R. F. & Morrison, D. C. Mothers as behaviour therapists for their own children. *Behav. Res. & Therapy*, 1965, **3**, 113–124.

A Marathon Behavior Modification of a Selectively Mute Child*

JOHN B. REID, NANCY HAWKINS, CAROLIN KEUTZER, SHIRLEY A. McNEAL, RICHARD E. PHELPS, KATHLEEN M. REID, and HAYDEN L. MEES†

Psychology Clinic, University of Oregon, Oregon, U.S.A.

Abstract: A technique for using reinforcement and stimulus fading for generalization of speech in a selectively mute child is described. Seven therapists, two children, and the child's mother all worked in various sequential and group combinations in a one-day treatment programme.

CASE HISTORY

Sally, aged six, would speak to no one but her immediate family, and not even to a family member when a stranger was present. Just the sight of an outsider changed her manner from fluent activity to quiet preoccupation. Her family physician referred her to the Psychology Clinic for evaluation and treatment. Although her mutism and withdrawal had caused innumerable inconveniences (e.g., when going to the doctor, or fitting her with shoes), it became a major problem as she approached elementary school age. The many attempts to get her to talk by parents, nursery school and kindergarten teachers, and playmates, had failed. Neither embarrassment, coercion, nor incentives affected her speech behavior.

Physically, Sally was frail and appeared extremely fearful and tense in the presence of others. She had a long history of medical problems, stemming from a congenital heart defect, which necessitated regular physical examinations and tests, some of which were quite painful. This physical limitation probably inhibited the development of normal social and verbal interactive skills. Though she entered into most types of play, she tired easily, and consequently spent most of her time in the home with her mother.

PRE-TREATMENT INTERVIEWS

Prior to the treatment programme, three interviews were held with Sally's mother. She met twice with one therapist to discuss Sally's history and development, and once with the entire treatment team to establish a comfortable working relationship and to discuss plans for her participation in the treatment programme. Sally's mother was cooperative and seemed quite concerned about her daughter's welfare. No systematic attempt was made to assess family dynamics nor the psychological state of the parents.

Sally was seen with her mother on two occasions in a typical playroom situation. These

---

*Reprinted from the *Journal of Child Psychology and Psychiatry*, 1967, **8**, 27–30. Copyright 1967 with permission from Pergamon Press Publishing Company and Dr. J. B. Reid.

†J. B. Reid is now at the University of Wisconsin, Madison, Wisconsin, and H. L. Mees at Seattle University, Seattle, Washington.

meetings were held to determine if she would speak to a male therapist in her mother's presence, and if she could be persuaded to speak using common clinical procedures, such as puppets or free play. She did not speak either to the therapist or to her mother in his presence; nor could she be persuaded to speak through the use of typical clinical techniques.

TREATMENT PROGRAMME

Treatment was carried out in a playroom, containing only a table and chairs. An adjoining observation room was equipped with a one-way window, a tape recorder and an intercom for monitoring the sessions.

The treatment plan was based on the assumption that the presence of strangers aroused responses incompatible with speaking. The behaviors resembled fearfulness, anxiety responses, withdrawal, and quiescence. Desensitization, or fading-in techniques, similar to those used by Jones (1924), Wolpe (1958), and Wolf *et al.* (1964) were considered appropriate for modifying these behaviors.

Sally was brought to the Clinic without breakfast at 8 a.m. Her mother put breakfast on the playroom table, cutting a slice of toast and a banana into small pieces. The goal at this point was for her mother to establish a constant rate of speech by having Sally ask for bites of food. Sally and her mother were alone in the playroom at this time. Every thirty seconds a tap on the observation window signalled her mother to ask Sally if she wanted a bite of food. An appropriate verbal request for food, including its identification, was required for receiving a bite. If no response occurred, the mother was to wait until the next tap and ask again. This stage of the programme lasted five and a half minutes or eleven trials, during which Sally responded appropriately on every trial with verbalizations ranging from "orange juice" to "I'd like some cereal please, Mummie."

The second step of the programme involved fading another person (E_1) into the playroom while Sally continued to ask for food. E_1, a male, moved from a point in the hall to one of the chairs at the table by steps of three to four feet. There were ten positions through which E_1 moved, while pretending to read a magazine. The criterion for him to move to each closer position was at least four consecutive appropriate responses from Sally. A total of forty-three responses was required for E_1 to move from the hall to his seat by the table. Sally failed only one trial at this stage, and her verbal responses expanded from an average of 1.7 words for the first ten trials to 2.6 words for the last ten. Thus, she actually became more verbal as E_1 was faded into the room. A short break was then taken for rest and planning.

After the break, Sally, her mother, and E_1 returned to their seats at the table. It was not necessary to go through the fading-in procedure to reinstate Sally's speaking to her mother in the presence of E_1. However, she did not talk to E_1. The mother continued asking her if she wanted food at thirty-second intervals.

The third stage involved shaping Sally to look at, attend and respond to E_1. This was accomplished by fading E_1 into the mother-child interaction in the following manner. At the thirty second signal, E_1 asked mother, "Why don't you ask Sally if she would like another bite to eat?" The mother asked, and Sally responded. After two trials, E_1 directly asked Sally, "Would you like something more?" Sally responded appropriately. From this point on, E_1 asked Sally, at each thirty-second interval, if she wanted another bite to eat. It was noted that although Sally was responding to E_1, she was not looking at him. After ten trials, E_1 moved his chair directly opposite Sally, so that she would have to look at him while requesting food. Within fifteen trials from the beginning of this stage, E_1 was carrying on a limited, highly structured, conversation with Sally. The procedure was continued for twenty-five more trials.

She failed to answer on two occasions, but when her mother repeated the questions, Sally responded appropriately. This stage accomplished the goals set for this day as Sally was, for the first time, talking with a stranger.[1] Another rest period was taken to plan a generalization programme.

Mother and E_1 returned to the situation and E_1 continued feeding and talking with Sally. At this point, E_2, a woman therapist, was faded into the room in stages twice as large as E_1 had used. Within seven minutes or fourteen trials, E_2 was seated at the table and Sally continued to respond to E_1.

After another break, during which breakfast was removed, a test situation was contrived to see if verbal responding would generalize to a stranger who was not faded in, and who did not use food as an incentive. A male therapist (E_3) was seated at the table when Sally and her mother re-entered the room. Mother introduced him as "the Doctor." Immediately E_3 asked Sally about herself and about a puzzle that interested her. She played with the puzzle, putting in pieces, but avoided responding to, or making eye contact with, E_3. Finally, after approximately three minutes, Sally responded to a question about a puzzle piece. Another response occurred fifteen seconds later, then responses continued at a fairly rapid rate. E_3 made increasingly difficult demands on her, asking her to name parts and describe pieces of the puzzle. A story book was then used and Sally described Peter Rabbit. Finally the subject of food came up and several responses were made about food preferences. The rate of responding was never high, but Sally did answer numerous questions and went willingly from the room with E_3 to find a playmate. The test was considered a successful demonstration of generalization to a stranger without the use of the fading-in technique.

At noon Sally went to the house of another team member for lunch. She was accompanied by two female E's and two small girls, aged one and three and a half. There was no hesitation to leave her mother behind, but some apprehension appeared as Sally entered the automobile. She had not met either woman before this time, but the presence of the other children probably helped her to enter the situation willingly. Soon she talked freely with the three and a half-year-old child and sporadic conversation continued throughout lunch.

On her return to the Clinic, Sally went to her mother in the playroom and all seven therapists entered, together with Sally's playmate. A game was established between the children and E_3, naming colors, asking questions and offering M & M candies. Another child, a boy, was then brought into the game, but Sally did not interact with him. Since the boy was also somewhat reluctant to interact, no communication was established between them, and Sally became tense until the session ended. Evidently, the candies were not powerful reinforcers so soon after lunch.

FOLLOW-UP

Two weeks later, Sally returned to the Clinic in order to test the durability of her progress in speech. In the playroom with mother and E_1, Sally conversed easily for about fifteen minutes. At this point another E entered the room and Sally immediately became tense and withdrawn but continued to speak to E_1. Food was brought in and the new E fed her some breakfast; within seven minutes she was talking freely to him. Another E entered, but Sally did not stop responding. This E then took over the feeding and Sally continued to respond.

---

[1] The efficacy of the programme, in getting Sally to speak to E_1, appeared to be a function of gradually associating E_1 (a previously ineffective stimulus, in terms of eliciting speech from Sally) with mother and food reinforcers (historically effective elicitors of Sally's speech). As this association was strengthened, E_1 became effective in eliciting speech from Sally.

On this second visit, Sally's behavior was qualitatively different. She was free and spontaneous, initiating topics and showing almost none of her typical fearfulness. The E's she had talked and played with this time were two that she would not respond to previously.

A third meeting occurred the following week. Again, several E's talked and played with her, but no food was used. Mother reported that Sally had begun to talk to people outside the family, e.g., to her Sunday school teacher and to friends of the family. Thus, it appeared that verbal responding was generalizing beyond the Clinic.

FUTURE PLANS

In order to extend this experimental programme into a continuing treatment programme, it is planned that her social environment be reprogrammed along the lines of Straughan's (1965) adaptation of Patterson's (1965) technique. This will consist of setting up natural contingencies for the reinforcement of verbal initiations and responsiveness to her neighbors and peers.

REFERENCES

Jones, M. C. A laboratory study of fear: The case of Peter. *Ped. Semin.*, 1924, **31**, 308–315.

Patterson, G. R. An application of conditioning techniques to the control of a hyperactive child. In L. P. Ullmann and L. Krasner (Eds.), *Case Studies in Behavior Modification*. New York: Holt, Rinehart & Winston, 1965.

Straughan, J. Conditioning techniques with elective mutism and autism. Paper presented at a symposium, *Outpatient and Environmental Conditioning Techniques with Children*, biennial meeting of the Society for Research in Child Development, 1965, Minneapolis, Minnesota.

Wolf, M., Risley, T. & Mees, H. Application of operant conditioning procedures to the behavior problems of an autistic child. *Behav. Res. & Therapy*, 1964, **1**, 305–312.

Wolpe, J. (1958) *Psychotherapy by Reciprocal Inhibition*. Oxford University Press, London.

Modification of Classroom Behavior of Institutionalized Female Adolescent Offenders*

DONALD H. MEICHENBAUM, KENNETH S. BOWERS and ROBERT R. ROSS

University of Waterloo and Ontario Reception and Diagnostic Center, Galt, Ontario

Abstract: A highly reliable time sampling assessment technique, which dichotomized classroom behavior into appropriate and inappropriate categories, was used to assess classroom behavior of institutionalized female adolescent offenders. Following a two-week baseline period, an operant procedure was implemented in which money was used as a reinforcer. Prior to treatment the institutionalized girls, compared with non-institutionalized peers, performed significantly less appropriately in class. Following three weeks of treatment the institutionalized girls' classroom behavior was comparable to non-institutionalized peers. Particular problems and possible solutions of establishing an operant programme with institutionalized adolescents were examined.

The effectiveness of operant procedures in establishing and maintaining appropriate classroom behavior has been demonstrated with conduct problem children (O'Leary & Becker, 1967; Quay, Werry, McQueen & Sprague, 1966), and retarded children (Birnbrauer, Bijou, Wolf & Kidder, 1965; Birnbrauer, Wolf, Kidder & Tague, 1965; Birnbrauer & Lawler, 1964). The goal of establishing appropriate classroom behavior is a major concern with institutionalized adolescent offenders who have a long history and high incidence of inappropriate classroom behavior. Generalized social reinforcers such as praise, teacher attention, and positive feedback, often have minimal effects or negative effects upon their classroom behavior. The marked disruptive behavior of institutionalized adolescents in many cases precludes the possibility of the teacher administering an academic programme.

Institutionalized adolescents differ markedly in many aspects from the school age children who have been used in classroom reinforcement programmes. The girls used in the present programme were much more responsive to immediate peer reinforcement of inappropriate behavior than immediate negative reinforcement by the teacher, or more severe delayed negative reinforcement administered by staff supervisors. The high frequency and potent value of peer reinforcement is consistent with the ward observations of institutionalized adolescent girls made by Buehler, Patterson and Furness (1966).

Another characteristic of the institutionalized delinquent's undesirable classroom behavior is that the nature of her classroom misbehavior is quite varied topographically. Despite the manifest variety of undesirable classroom responses, however, apparently diverse misbehaviors do seem to have a certain functional equivalence. A student can try to gain the teacher's attention by walking out of the classroom, by throwing pencils or chalk, or by swearing. One consequence of the marked variety of misbehavior which results in the same reinforcement (e.g., teacher's attention) is that extinction or punishment of one particular response (e.g., swearing) results in an immediate decrease in the frequency of that response and

*Reprinted from *Behaviour Research and Therapy*, 1968, **6**, 343–353. Copyright 1968 with permission from Pergamon Press Publishing Company and Dr. D. H. Meichenbaum.

a subsequent increase in other inappropriate responses (e.g., throwing objects) which lead to the same reinforcement. Adolescent delinquents thus pose a problem for operant procedures not encountered in work with populations which manifest highly stereotyped response units (e.g., schizophrenics, autistic children, retardates). The present study attempts to deal with this problem by dichotomously categorizing classroom behavior as either appropriate or inappropriate. The hope was that appropriateness of behavior could be defined and reliably identified in the context of a classroom situation. An advantage of the dichotomous, appropriate-inappropriate classification scheme, is that the delinquents have little opportunity to manipulate the observers by shifting from one kind of misbehavior to another when they discern the pertinent response-reinforcement contingencies. By making all inappropriate behavior functionally equivalent insofar as it leads to the postponement or elimination of desired consequences, we utilize to advantage the principle of the functional equivalence of behavior that otherwise threatens to undermine treatment efficacy. Moreover, in light of the inverse relationship between number of diagnostic categories and reliability, it was reasonable to expect fairly high inter-observer reliability (Miller & Bieri, 1963).

Preliminary observations of the classroom behavior of these adolescents revealed that, in most instances, appropriate classroom behavior was available in their behavioral repertoires but was emitted sporadically. Thus, the goal of treatment was to maintain appropriate classroom behavior at a high level rather than to shape new responses. The relative effectiveness of different schedules of reinforcement on maintaining appropriate classroom behavior was examined. The behavioral consequence of operant treatment in one classroom on behavior in other non-treated classrooms was also examined.

Attempts to modify classroom behavior with operant procedures have been characterized by careful and intensive training of the teachers. The present study attempted to modify classroom behavior by means of a strong reinforcer (money) without staff training.

In order to assess the overall effectiveness of the operant treatment programme, a group of non-institutionalized peers in a nearby community school was assessed for comparative purposes.

In summary, the present investigation proposed (1) to establish the reliability and efficacy of a dichotomous behavior classification in the assessment of classroom behavior; (2) to establish the effectiveness of monetary reinforcement upon the appropriateness of classroom behavior for institutionalized female adolescent offenders; (3) to determine the differential effectiveness of various schedules of reinforcement on behavior change; (4) to compare the classroom behavior of adolescent female offenders with that of normal age peers before and after treatment.

METHOD

Subjects

*S*s were ten adolescent female offenders institutionalized in a special unit in a training school complex. Each girl had been selected from the total population of girls in training schools in Ontario on the basis of their apparent inability to profit from a training school programme. The girls had been found to be completely unmanageable in their home setting, in foster home placements, in institutional settings and in training schools. They were described as manipulative, rebellious, uncontrollable, hostile, aggressive, and the term adolescent psychopath was often used as the diagnostic label for them. Most had previously had a considerable amount of involvement with psychologists and psychiatrists prior to their committal to training school. They evidenced a heterogeneous variety of behavior problems such as assault, truancy, promiscuity, absconding from institutions, suicidal gestures, and vandalism. All presented major management problems in the classroom. They were inattentive, disobedient, insolent, and frequently disrupted the class by fighting, swearing, incessant talking, threatening the teachers, or simply walking out of class. All were academically retarded by at least one grade, although intellectually the majority fell within the normal range. Their mean age was fifteen years four months (S.D. = 1.18), and mean length of present institutionalization 240 days (S.D. = 76.32).

The girls were divided into two classes. Class I ($N = 4$) worked at the remedial eighth grade level and devoted most of its time to academic course-work. Class II ($N = 6$) also worked at the eighth grade level, but devoted twenty per cent of its time to commercial courses such as typing and clerical skills. Each class of girls had two teachers, one in the morning and the other in the afternoon. Two observations, of approximately sixty minutes each, were made in morning classes and two in afternoon classes at varying times in order that all classroom behavior was sampled. The study began in the middle of May when five male psychology interns were available to begin classroom observation, and lasted until the end of June when school terminated. The fact that the modification programme was implemented so late in the school year means that a considerable history of habitual misbehavior had to be overcome in a very short period of time.

The girls were in school six hours per day on each weekday except for one afternoon and one morning per week, when they were involved in group therapy sessions or sewing instruction groups. The group therapy meetings had been going on for several months before the onset of the present study.

A control group of twelve non-institutionalized girls from a nearby community school were also assessed on the observational measure. Teachers at this school were instructed to submit names of twelve girls (four with average classroom behavior, four above average, and four below average). They were observed daily for two hours for a period of two weeks.

Observations

A major objective of this study was to develop a highly reliable observation technique which would be sensitive to the varied types of inappropriate behavior manifested. A time sampling observational technique was used. Observations were made on a ten-second-observe, ten-second-record basis. During the record-period the observer indicated whether the behavior during the prior observe-period was appropriate or inappropriate, and briefly described any inappropriate behavior. This procedure was continued until all girls in the classroom were observed and was then repeated throughout the period of observations which averaged sixty minutes. Within a one-hour observation period in a classroom of six girls approximately thirty observations were made on any particular girl.

Inappropriate classroom behavior was defined as any behavior which was not consistent with the tasks set forth by the teacher, i.e. behavior which was not task-specific. If a girl during her ten-second observational period manifested any single instance of behavior which was not conducive to academic performance she was marked "inappropriate." A single instance of inappropriate behavior resulted in the entire ten-second period being marked inappropriate. This stringent criteria facilitated reliability and provided a rigorous test of the effectiveness of the present treatment programme.

The time sampling observational measure did produce certain problems initially. The girls quickly determined the time sequence of observations, and the O's looking at a particular girl became a discriminative stimulus to behave appropriately only during her ten-second period. In fact, one girl who sought to sabotage the programme learned to anticipate the sequence of observations and attempted to get other girls in trouble during their respective ten-second observational periods. Fortunately, during the treatment phase, the other girls extinguished this *S*'s attempt to get them in trouble. The use of multiple observers and randomizing the sequence of observations constitute two means by which this problem was eventually overcome.

Procedure

The project involved four phases. Phase I was the baseline period during which the observers secured operant rates of the girls' classroom behavior. The observers were in the classrooms for two weeks during the operant period. The first week was spent becoming familiar with the classroom routine, and training raters on the observational measure. The second week's observations provided the baseline measures. At first, the girls repeatedly attempted to interact with the Os and the teachers reported that the girls' classroom behavior deteriorated when the Os were present. The Os persistently ignored the girls and the girls' interactions with them diminished.

The teachers were instructed to continue teaching in their typical fashion throughout the research programme. No attempt was made to have them modify their teaching methods or their methods of controlling the girls.

The treatment procedure was initiated in Phase II. The girls were instructed that they could earn money (reinforcement) if they behaved appropriately in the afternoon classroom. They were told the definition of appropriate and inappropriate classroom behavior and given several examples of both. They were told that they would be observed in the morning classes as well, but that their behavior in the morning class would not affect how much money they would receive. The general importance of developing appropriate classroom behavior and good work habits was also mentioned. Every ten minutes in the afternoon classes the girl received a slip of paper from one of the Os indicating the percentage of appropriate behavior (frequency of appropriate behavior over total number of observations made within a ten-minute period, times 100). Throughout the treatment programme each girl met daily with one of the psychology interns for banking hours. During this period each girl was told the amount of money she had earned and the frequency of her inappropriate classroom behavior. The girls received no feedback concerning morning classroom behavior. During Phase II of the study, a girl could earn $2.00 a day if she obtained 100 per cent appropriate behavior for the observations during the afternoon class. A differentially weighted payment scale (logarithmically derived) was used such that a given high percentage of appropriate behavior (e.g., 100 per cent) was reinforced by considerably more than twice the amount of money paid to only fifty per cent appropriate behavior. During this phase of treatment a girl could not lose money already earned, and zero per cent appropriate behavior resulted in nothing earned. Money was placed in the girl's account at the end of each week. The girls had access to the money on week-ends. For almost all girls the possibility of earning $8.00 a week was a very strong incentive.

The treatment approach in Phase III was modified slightly. The afternoon class was treated in Phase III in exactly the same manner as in Phase II. During Phase III, appropriate classroom behavior in the previously untreated morning class was also reinforced. However, because of the girls' requests for immediate feedback in terms of money earned, a change in the nature of feedback was made in Phase III. Secondary reinforcers such as tokens have been used in many operant programmes. Nevertheless, care must be taken to avoid making the secondary reinforcement too distant from the primary reinforcement. Prior to Phase III, the feedback of percentage appropriate behavior had to be later translated into money values. Finally the money receipts could be traded in for cash each week-end. The feedback modification in Phase III shortcircuited this process. The girls were told that instead of receiving slips of paper indicating percentage of appropriate behavior, the slips would indicate the amount of money (denominations of 25, 20, 15, 10, 5 or 0 cents) they had earned. During the two hours of morning observation, six slips of paper would be dispensed to each girl, permitting a girl to earn $1.50 a morning if she manifested 100 per cent appropriate behavior. If the girl manifested no inappropriate behavior during a specified period of observations she received a slip reading 25c: if one inappropriate behavior, 20c; two, 15c; three, 10c; four, 5c; five or more, 0c. In the afternoon class during Phases II and III, the feedback slips indicating the percentage of appropriate behavior were dispensed on a fixed interval (FI) schedule (every ten minutes). In the morning class during Phase III, they were dispensed on a variable interval (VI) schedule for each girl with the constraint that a minimum of five ten-second observations was made for a particular girl before dispensing feedback. Thus, the time when reinforcement was dispensed varied on a random basis and was unpredictable.

The girls' classroom behavior during Phases I and II was marked by daily and hourly fluctuations from appropriate to inappropriate behavior. The inclusion of feedback on a VI schedule in the morning class was designed to foster maintenance of appropriate behavior at a high level.

Phase IV introduced a further modification designed to increase the maintenance of appropriate classroom behavior. Reinforcement in both the morning and afternoon class during Phase IV was dispensed in the same manner as in the morning class of Phase III, *viz.* VI schedule of reinforcement with feedback consisting of money values. However, during Phase IV the girls were instructed for the first time in the treatment programme that if their classroom behavior was inappropriate they could lose money they had earned the previous day. For every percentage point of inappropriate classroom behavior they obtained on a certain day, they would lose one and a half cents of what they had earned the previous day. For example, if a girl earned eighty cents one day and received an average of seventy per cent appropriate on the following day, she would lose forty-five cents from the previous day's earnings (thirty per cent inappropriate times one and half cents). A girl could not lose more money than she had earned the previous day and go into debt, which might result in a loss of incentive. This modification was included in order to attempt to gain control of daily fluctuations in percentage appropriate behavior. Also during this phase (for reasons of diminished funds) the amount of money available for reinforcement was cut from a potential of $3.50 a day to $1.50 if the girl behaved at a 100 per cent appropriate level during all classroom observations.

In summary, the treatment programme included four phases: Phase I — operant period; Phase II — feedback on FI schedule only in the afternoon class; Phase III — FI feedback afternoon class and VI feedback morning class; and Phase IV — VI feedback both morning and afternoon classes tied with possible loss of previously earned reinforcement.

RESULTS

An exceptionally high reliability between raters was found which reflects the sensitivity of the observational measure in classifying the behaviors into appropriate or inappropriate categories. During the operant period, 3194 pairs of observations were made of the institutionalized adolescents' classroom behavior. The raters disagreed on the appropriateness or inappropriateness of behavior on only 190 of these pairs of observations, yielding agreement of ninety-four per cent. Similarly, in the classroom with non-institutionalized girls, 1569 pairs of observations were made on which two independent raters disagreed on only eighteen observations, yielding agreement of ninety-eight per cent. Most of the disagreements occurred in discriminating between daydreaming behavior and paying attention. Often a girl would have her head on her desk, from the vantage point of the observer it was difficult to assess if the girl was daydreaming or listening to the teacher. Similarly, if a girl was staring at her book it was sometimes difficult to determine if she was in fact reading or merely passing time. Future research should include academic performance measures such as amount of material recalled as the criterion of appropriate behavior.

One additional reliability check was made. Since the same Os were making observations during the operant phase and the treatment phase, it was deemed necessary to check their reliability against raters who were naive to the study in order to insure against a subtle shift in criterion of inappropriate behavior or experimenter bias (Rosenthal, 1966). During the treatment phase, 685 observations were made by two naive observers and psychology interns who had participated in the study throughout. They disagreed on only fifty-five observations, yielding agreement of ninety-two per cent. This result indicated that there was no shift in criteria of what constituted inappropriate behavior between the operant and the treatment phase of the study.

The time sampling measure was sensitive in discriminating between appropriate and inappropriate classroom behavior of adolescent non-institutionalized females. The mean percentage appropriate behavior for normal girls classified by their teachers as above average was ninety-four (S.D. = 6.86); average eighty-four (S.D. = 13.51); and below average sixty-nine (S.D. = 12.87). The difference between the above and below average girls was significant at less than the 0.05 level. The teachers' average rank ordering of the twelve girls on the basis of their estimation of appropriate classroom behavior correlated 0.85 with mean percentage appropriate classroom behavior. These results indicate the discriminant validity of the observational measure in a normal classroom setting.

The inclusion of the non-institutionalized girls provided a comparison group for the treated institutionalized girls. The mean percentage appropriate classroom behavior for the non-institutionalized girls was eighty-three (S.D. = 17.38), with a range from forty to ninety-nine per cent. The mean percentage appropriate classroom behavior for institutionalized girls during the operant period was forty-five (S.D. = 30.15), with a range from zero to 100 per cent. The difference in percentage appropriate classroom behavior between non-institutionalized girls and institutionalized girls during the operant period was significant at the 0.01 level. The inappropriate behavior of the institutionalized girls during the operant period was not only more frequent but more intense. For example, inappropriate verbalizations during operant period for institutionalized girls was characterized by swearing and insolence; whereas for non-institutionalized girls it consisted of quietly talking to one's neighbor. Future research should attempt to assess the intensity of inappropriate behavior as well as its frequency.

The pre-treatment behavior for the institutionalized girls also indicated that appropriate classroom behavior was in their repertoires since nine of the ten girls obtained at least eighty per cent appropriate classroom behavior for two observational periods, and two girls secured above ninety per cent appropriate classroom behavior. As noted previously, the task for the treatment programme was clearly to foster prolonged maintenance of appropriate classroom behavior, and to reduce frequency of inappropriate behavior.

The effectiveness of the treatment programme in modifying the girls' inappropriate classroom behavior is reflected in (a) the mean percentage of appropriate classroom behavior for baseline vs. treatment phases for the ten institutionalized girls (Table 1); (b) the group performance curves for the two separate classes (Figs. 1 and 2); and (c) the individual performance curves (Table 2). A consistent pattern of results was obtained. The operant period was marked by a generally high level of inappropriate classroom behavior. The introduction of reinforcement in the afternoon class had a sudden and dramatic effect. The girls' behavior in the afternoon class quickly improved while their initial behavior in the morning class remained

Table 1. Mean percentage appropriate classroom behavior for ten institutionalized girls during operant and treatment periods.

	Phase I	Phase II		Phase III	Phase IV
	Operant Period	First Week	Second Week		
Morning class	54.20	52.13	36.29	84.50	78.17
Afternoon class	46.00	65.25	82.86	92.00	80.00

the same as in the operant period. It is important to note that the girls had their first opportunity to spend the money they had earned between days nine and ten. Following the occasion
of this initial, direct reinforcement, classroom behavior in the afternoon class improved quite
substantially in Class II, while appropriate classroom behavior in the morning decreased below
the operant level. A similar pattern was apparent in Class I. One girl reported: "If you don't
pay us, we won't shape up." Clearly, the girls were manipulating the psychologists into
initiating payment in the morning class and were offering appropriate behavior in the morning
class as the possible reward. The girls proved to be effective modifiers of behavior. During the
remainder of the treatment, the girls received reinforcement in both the morning and afternoon
classes.

During Phase III the girls were given feedback on a VI schedule in the morning and continued on FI schedule in the afternoon. The introduction of reinforcement in the morning class
was dramatically effective in fostering appropriate classroom behavior. Percentage appropriate behavior jumped from twenty-nine to 100 per cent in Class I, and from forty-four to ninety-
five per cent in Class II. In order to achieve a score of 100 per cent appropriate behavior, each
of the girls had to behave perfectly in all of her ten-second time samples for two complete
hours. This sudden rise in appropriate behavior was attributable to the introduction of reinforcement and also to the fact that the girls had developed a discriminated repertoire of appropriate
classroom behavior during the previous phase of treatment. The previous training increased
response availability, or response strength of appropriate classroom behavior which was
quickly transferred to a situation in which it was rewarded. The mean percentage appropriate
classroom behavior in the afternoon class was ninety-two (S.D. = 9.50) where feedback was
dispensed on FI schedule and eighty-four (S.D. = 8.45) in the morning class where feedback
was dispensed on a VI schedule (nonsignificant). However, Figs. 1 and 2 indicate a decreasing trend in classroom performance under the VI schedule. Even though the VI schedule
led to a precipitous rise in appropriate classroom behavior, the girls perceived the reinforcements as unpredictable. The unpredictableness of reinforcement on the VI schedule seems to
have caused the drop in the appropriateness of classroom behavior.

Thus far, the treatment programme had significantly increased the mean level of appropriate classroom behavior. However, there remained the problem of some girls who occasionally regressed in their classroom performance to their former pre-treatment level. Although
these behavioral reverses were becoming less frequent, a reinforcement schedule was selected
which would make the girl pay for such drops in behavior. During the final phase of treatment,
feedback was dispensed on VI schedule in all classes and in addition, the girls lost money
from previous days' earnings if they behaved inappropriately. The introduction of this regime
also resulted in a slight drop in appropriate classroom behavior from the high level obtained
in Phase III. This appeared to be related to the girls' negative reactions to the possibility of
the loss of money previously earned and a decrease in the amount of money they could earn.
Furthermore, those girls most directly affected instigated and reinforced misbehavior on
the part of their peers. With the end of the school year approaching, the effectiveness of the
treatment programme to attenuate peer reinforcement of inappropriate behavior diminished.

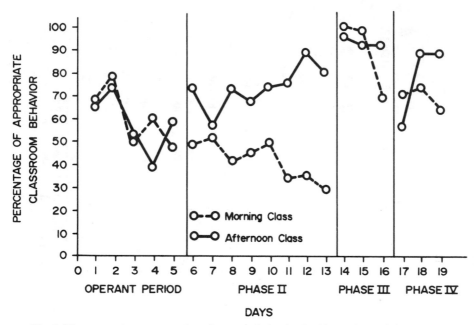

Fig. 1. Mean percentage appropriate classroom behavior for Class I ($N = 4$) for operant and treatment periods.

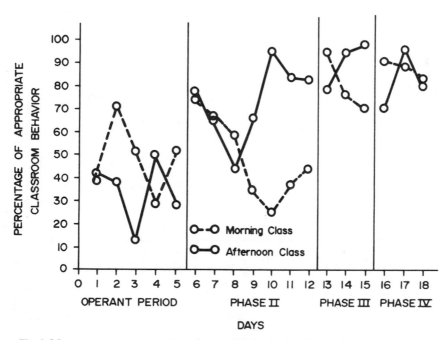

Fig. 2. Mean percentage appropriate classroom behavior for Class II ($N = 6$) for operant and treatment periods.

Table 2. Individual classroom behavior for ten institutionalized girls during operant and treatment phases.

	Phase I*					Phase II								Phase III			Phase IV		
Days	1	2	3	4	5	6	7	8	9	10	11	12	13	14	15	16	17	18	19
Ss Class I																			
S_1 Morning	54	64	60	53	20	18	28	36	0	80	10	49	32	100	100	99	38	abs	64
Afternoon	20	85	57	12	38	30	10	11	12	88	40	92	97	97	100	93	28	73	90
S_2 Morning	62	70	33	63	abs†	43	56	32	59	41	50	45	24	100	94	92	96	84	97
Afternoon	76	80	40	29	88	81	63	90	85	92	90	78	70	100	88	73	93	100	88
S_3 Morning	84	94	54	72	46	62	48	32	66	31	abs	12	13	100	98	26	63	64	39
Afternoon	75	50	58	56	10	93	83	100	87	37	abs	96	75	93	80	100	44	80	86
S_4 Morning	71	84	55	55	72	72	75	66	57	45	42	abs	48	100	98	51	85	71	53
Afternoon	89	80	52	58	96	90	71	87	87	77	95	abs	78	90	100	100	61	100	abs
Ss Class II																			
S_5 Morning	56	45	27	15	abs	20	46	64	0	3	21	9	*‡	100	50	50	79	100	52
Afternoon	0	0	0	0	abs	79	41	27	75	97	95	99	*	95	99	abs	45	100	100
S_6 Morning	15	74	35	0	abs	97	62	32	87	abs	66	97		96	98	99	abs	88	100
Afternoon	58	50	0	84	27	74	38	0	94	abs	95	91		95	97	100	89	100	100
S_7 Morning	45	60	74	10	44	76	71	81	18	17	14	abs		100	88	66	abs	100	97
Afternoon	0	10	48	15	27	90	96	89	65	100	100	100		73	100	100	100	100	abs
S_8 Morning	20	76	66	40	31	77	69	45	13	13	43	0		90	33	22	87	abs	53
Afternoon	53	40	22	20	39	65	32	22	40	90	26	87		32	97	abs	40	100	70
S_9 Morning	75	92	73	70	75	91	91	86	87	70	68	84		96	93	97	100	100	99
Afternoon	80	51	13	30	62	91	96	82	81	96	95	97		95	100	100	53	99	100
S_{10} Morning	27	79	31	35	54	83	54	41	0	abs	13	31		85	92	88	98	50	100
Afternoon	55	65	12	20	4	64	90	47	45	92	98	29		89	80	95	100	79	37

*Phase I = Operant period, Days 1–5; Phase II = FI feedback morning class, Days 6–13; Phase III = FI feedback afternoon class, VI feedback morning class, Days 14–16; Phase IV = VI feedback both morning and afternoon class tied with possible loss of previously earned reinforcement.

†abs = absent, girl was absent from class due to illness, or medical examination.

‡Ss in Class II were absent from school on Day 13.

Even with these factors, the institutionalized girls' mean level of appropriate behavior (seventy-nine per cent) did not approach their mean pre-treatment level (forty-five per cent) and was not significantly different from the mean level of non-institutionalized girls (eighty-three per cent). An analysis of the descriptions of inappropriate classroom behavior for institutionalized girls revealed that not only the frequency of inappropriate behavior decreased, but also its nature and form changed as a function of the treatment programme. Both the teachers and Os reported that the topography of the girls' inappropriate classroom behavior more closely approximated that observed in non-institutionalized classrooms.

DISCUSSION

The present investigation demonstrated that high frequency inappropriate classroom behavior of female institutionalized adolescent offenders is readily modifiable by means of an operant procedure. Prior to treatment, the institutionalized girls manifested almost twice as much intense inappropriate classroom behavior as non-institutionalized peers. Even though the teachers were not trained in operant procedures, the treatment programme showed that with monetary reinforcement, disruptive classroom behavior of such girls can be reduced to the level of non-institutionalized adolescents, and peer reinforcement of inappropriate classroom behavior is attenuated.

It is difficult to assess the relative merits of the two schedules of feedback used in the present study (FI and VI) because of: (a) the short period of time available; (b) the contamination of order and time effects; and (c) varying amount of money dispensed under the two schedules. Further research is needed to assess the relative effectiveness of such schedules in modifying behavior in such situations. However, the results suggest that factors of complexity, perceived unpredictability, and temporally remote secondary reinforcement undermine the effectiveness of an operant approach. The limited time available for the treatment programme did not permit phasing out of monetary reinforcement or transferring to the teachers the control of reinforcement.

The present study indicated that institutionalized female adolescent offenders present particular problems for behavior modification programmes based on operant techniques and suggested some solutions to these problems. Most of the problems were related to the girls' skills in manipulation, the potency of peer reinforcement, and the wide range and variability of their inappropriate behavior. The latter problem precluded preselection of behavioral categories and definition of specific response classes. The use of a reliable dichotomous recording technique which treated the variety of classroom misbehavior as functionally equivalent, dealt adequately with the problem of behavioral complexity and variety. The attenuation of peer reinforcement of misbehavior in the present study was accomplished by means of a potent reinforcer (*viz.* money). Further research along the lines of making reinforcement contingent upon group performance, or reinforcement of the group contingent upon an individual's behavior, may lead to even better control of peer reinforcement. The behavior to be reinforced was largely present in the girls repertoire during the operant period and the goal of treatment was to maintain it at a high level rather than to shape new responses. The use of intermittent schedules of reinforcement, and withholding reinforcement as a function of fluctuations in appropriate behavior are two techniques to handle this problem. The need to phase out reinforcement and to pair potent reinforcers with social reinforcement is also indicated.

The possibility of applying operant procedures to the modification of other inappropriate behavior of institutionalized adolescents is clearly indicated.

Acknowledgments.   The authors gratefully acknowledge the cooperation of the administrators, teachers and staff of the Ontario Reception and Diagnostic Center, Galt, Ontario, and the Lincoln Heights School, Waterloo, Ontario. The authors are indebted to the following students whose careful observations made this research possible: A. Fedoravicius, J. Johnson, J. Knox, V. Koop, R. Morris, S. Notar, B. Palmer and B. Taub.

REFERENCES

Birnbrauer, J. S., Bijou, S. W., Wolf, M. M. & Kidder, J. D. (1965) Programmed instruction in the classroom. In *Case Studies in Behavior Modification* (Eds. Ullmann, L. and Krasner, L.). Holt, Rinehart & Winston, New York.

Birnbrauer, J. S. & Lawler, Julia (1964). Token reinforcement for learning. *Ment. Retard.,* **2,** 275–279.

Birnbrauer, J. S., Wolf, M. M., Kidder, J. D. & Tague, Cecilia E. (1965) Classroom behavior of retarded pupils with token reinforcement. *J. exp. Child Psychol.,* **2,** 219–235.

Buehler, R. E., Patterson, G. R. & Furness, J. M. (1966) The reinforcement of behavior in institutional settings. *Behav. Res. & Therapy,* **4,** 157–167.

Miller, H. & Bieri, J. (1963) An informational analysis of clinical judgment. *J. abnorm. soc. Psychol.,* **67,** 317–325.

O'Leary, K. D. & Becker, W. C. (1967) Behavior modification of an adjustment class: A token reinforcement program. Unpublished manuscript, University of Illinois.

Quay, H. C., Werry, J. S., McQueen, Marjorie & Sprague, R. L. (1966) Remediation of the conduct problem child in the special class setting. *Except. Child.,* **32,** 509–515.

Rosenthal, R. (1967) Covert communication in the psychological experiment. *Psychol. Bull.,* **67,** 356–367.

"Aversive Imagery" Treatment in Adolescents*

ISRAEL KOLVIN

Nuffield Child Psychiatry Unit, Fleming Memorial Hospital in association with the University of Newcastle-upon-Tyne

Abstract: A technique of "Aversive Imagery" in the treatment of intellectually dull and verbally unforthcoming adolescents is described. Two cases are discussed, namely a fetishist and a petrol addict. With the fetishist the treatment was supplemented by psychosexual instruction, education and reassurance about acceptable heterosexual relationships. The fetishist recovered in eight sessions, the petrol addict in twenty sessions. Later enquiries revealed no relapses but the fetishist merits prolonged follow-up.

INTRODUCTION

Adolescents with persistent compulsive disorders or disorders with a compulsive component have always constituted a major psychotherapeutic problem. Generally, the response to traditional psychotherapy has not been impressive, but it is especially poor in the intellectually dull and verbally unforthcoming. The author knows of no published work which claims any measure of success with this latter group.

In these circumstances he was led to an *exploration* of a variation of behavior therapy. Both chemical and electrical physical aversion techniques have now been widely used for such conditions as alcoholism and sexual perversions (Rachman, 1965). However, due to a reluctance to use physical methods with adolescents, the author considered possible ways of deconditioning the unwanted behavior by the use of noxious aversive stimuli at an imagery level.

The inspiration for the technique derives from three major sources—firstly Wolpe (1958) in his description of psychotherapy by reciprocal inhibition indicated it was not necessary to present actual objects; Franks (1958) pointed out that it was not essential to use a nausea-inducing agent to produce conditioned aversion; and finally Lazarus and Abramovitz (1962) used "emotive imagery" in the treatment of children's phobias.

"Aversive Imagery Therapy" essentially consists of the evocation, in the imagination, of the specific erotogenic or compulsive stimulus and the immediate disruption of it by the evocation of a noxious aversive stimulus.

An account is given here of a fetishist and a petrol addict.

METHOD

The patient's help was enlisted in drawing up a list of "dislikes" which consisted of situations or experiences which were for him unpleasant. The only use made of this list was to

---

*Reprinted from *Behaviour Research and Therapy*, 1967, **5**, 245–248. Copyright 1967 with permission from Pergamon Press Publishing Company and Israel Kolvin.

ascertain for the particular patient the maximum noxious stimuli. In addition, an attempt was made to ascertain the precise fetishist situation.

Thereafter, the patient was taken into a darkened consulting room where he reclined on a couch and closed his eyes. He was encouraged to conjure up imagery according to a story related by the therapist. Empirically it was found that vivid imagery was more easily produced when the adolescent was in a relaxed state. A colorful story of the crucial event was now presented and the patient was asked to visualize accordingly. By careful observation it became apparent when the patient was just becoming affectively excited, i.e. motor tension, breathing, expression, etc. At this stage the aversive image was introduced, in a suggestive and vividly descriptive manner. The response was immediate and in the main reflected in the patient's expression of distaste. In this way the full erotically toned course of events was truncated and the sequence of events unpleasantly anticlimaxed.

With the fetishist, outpatient sessions were conducted twice weekly; this was determined by geographical considerations. With the petrol addict, the sessions were undertaken daily for five days a week. Each session consisted of two to four trials. In the case of the fetishist, the treatment was supplemented by an exposition of the biology and psychology of normal sexual behavior, and simple explanations and reassurance and indications of how to advance towards achieving socially acceptable heterosexual relationships.

THE PATIENTS

Case X. Fetishist aged Fourteen Years

The parents separated following an unhappy and argumentative marriage. The father is reported to be an irresponsible, unstable and inadequate psychopath. Mother is an intelligent, warm and insightful person who has managed to maintain reasonable standards in the face of considerable economic adversity.

X was the fourth child. His early development was normal. The first discordant note was the presence of severe shyness in the immediate preschool period followed by some excessive anxiety on first attending school. At school his progress was poor and he was described as academically slow. Then at the local secondary school he was considered educationally backward and found his way into the lowest stream. At this latter school he stole a sum of money from one of the teachers and was placed on probation for one year; he apparently complied satisfactorily with the terms of the probation order.

At the age of fourteen he was charged with indecent assault on three women. It was suspected that he had committed a further series of similar offences which the victims had not reported. X's description of the acts suggests that they were essentially unplanned. On certain occasions when he saw a young woman wearing a skirt, he would be overcome by a kind of trembling and other emotions which he did not have the language to describe; he would feel compelled to run after her and put his hand up under her clothes. He would then run away trembling with exhilaration, excitement and fear.

His mother described him as a quiet, shy, solitary boy who is prone to be solemn and sulky. She added that he erected barriers around himself and it was difficult to get through to him.

At the clinic he revealed himself as a serious-minded person, pleasant but shy, timid, reserved and verbally unforthcoming. He reluctantly admitted to anxiety and guilt about his frequent masturbation and also reported a number of frightening dreams. On the Mill Hill

Vocabulary Scale (1948) he was rated as grade V and on the Progressive Matrices (1938) he was rated as grade IV. During the course of the early interviews the boy denied any psychosexual knowledge. His problems were explored with him during a psychotherapeutic approach but progress was limited. This was thought to be due to the boy's dullness and inaccessibility. He remained plagued by the urge to commit the above-mentioned acts. At this stage it was decided to decondition him with an aversive technique.

His list of unpleasant experiences included some food-fads and other minor dislikes, but the only major distressful situation for him was falling in his dreams and looking down from a precarious situation or from a great height. It was decided to use this unpleasant falling experience from his dreams as the noxious stimulus. Seven half-hour sessions were undertaken over a period of three weeks. One month later some reinforcement was administered. Towards the end of therapy the mother reported that the boy was more approachable, less difficult and less inclined to sulk. The probation officer who had known him for some time claimed that there was some evidence of "a growing maturity." The boy denied experiencing any further compulsive urges.

Case Y. Petrol Addict aged Fifteen Years

At the time of referral Y was at a residential school for the educationally subnormal. There he was described as a sensible, even-tempered youth, hardworking to the extent of being obsessional and extremely stable except in the area of his addiction. On occasions, after sniffing the petrol, he would pass out completely; and it was these attacks of unconsciousness which eventually after some seven years, brought the addiction to light. Y had even gone to the length of breaking into a shed in order to obtain petrol.

At interview, the school's description was confirmed. He was a sturdily-built youth who proved to be intense but friendly, forthcoming to a limited extent, and intellectually dull. He denied sipping the petrol though he did admit to having once tasted it. He said he enjoyed the smell of it. In addition, it both made him feel "smashing" and also resulted in what can be described as expansive visual hallucinatory experiences in the form of cowboy pictures. He preferred being on his own because this provided him with the opportunity of seeking out petrol. His main interests were television, work and snooker.

The background history is as follows — Y's milestones, except for late speech development, were apparently normally achieved. The school psychologist reported that in the early school years he was stubborn and difficult but these remitted on his admission to the residential E.S.N. school. His IQ (Terman–Merrill) was sixty-three. His EEG was slightly immature.

The family is an intellectually dull one — both parents are dull and two other siblings are educationally subnormal. The parents are described as reliable and conscientious farm-workers.

There were grave doubts about whether any form of treatment would be efficacious because of Y's intelligence and his persistence. It was eventually decided to try a form of aversion therapy. A list of unpleasant experiences was obtained, but, as in the first case, his main aversion concerned heights and falling. Again, this was used as a noxious stimulus. Twenty half-hour sessions were undertaken on consecutive days except for weekends.

Thirteen months after the completion of treatment the patient is well and has not returned to his petrol-sniffing habits. This is indeed satisfactory in view of Ackerly & Gibson's (1964) statement in their review of a dozen cases of lighter-fluid sniffing; "Up to the present time the social agencies' and Juvenile Courts' methods of controlling the long-standing 'sniffers' who can be considered addicted have not been successful."

PROGRESS

Soon after the initiation of treatment both patients became mildly distressed. They then asserted that they were no longer experiencing the unwanted urges and claimed that they would no longer act in the undesirable manner. (This closely parallels Raymond's experience with adult fetishists.) They were persuaded to remain in therapy and completed the course of treatment without any further untoward reactions.

When there was evidence that a distaste or an aversion had developed (at the imagery level) for the compulsive and sexually provocative situation, the close supervision of the boys was relaxed. Both reported that the previous urges and desires had completely disappeared.

FOLLOW-UP

The length of follow-up is indicated below
Petrol Addict: thirteen months, no relapse reported.
Fetishist: Eleven months quite well. Thirteen months after the completion of treatment he accused a neighbor's wife of an illicit affair. When confronted, he claimed that he had been misled by a friend and that he had behaved "stupidly." That this may not be the reflection of a highly moral attitude but a different expression of a sexual problem has to be borne in mind. Seventeen months afterwards, X working and apparently quite well.

DISCUSSION

Adolescents suffering from perversion or addictions are nearly always a major treatment problem. Though many drop this behavior once it comes to light, or alternatively, rapidly respond to probationary supervision or simple measures instituted at a psychiatric clinic, there is a small percentage who do not respond. Unfortunately, up to the present, in this latter group the repertoire of treatments available has been small and their efficacy dubious. The aversive drug and shock therapies available for older perverts and addicts are, in relation to children and adolescents, still regarded with disfavor ethically and aesthetically by psychiatrists.

However, the writer considered these disorders so gravely handicapping and of such serious consequence to the adolescent, that any method that may be beneficial could not be lightly discarded. The benefits accruing from the removal of the symptoms in certain cases would far outweigh the moral and ethical objections, especially if more acceptable aversive techniques could be evolved. The use of aversive imagery was examined from this point of view; and in the case of this particular group of boys was considered worthy of exploration.

Some major criticisms of aversion techniques with sexual perversions is that they fail to remove the underlying psychopathology and in addition, could result in the patient developing an aversion to all sexual relations — even normal ones. The writer has tried to minimize this risk by supplementary explanations and reassurances about normal heterosexual relationships. He therefore combined both "aversive therapy" and psychotherapy in the case of the fetishist. These are unusual but not unique bedfellows as a number of behavior therapists have recently expressed the view that it is "practical to submit some cases to both" concurrently (Meyer & Crisp, 1966; Gelder, 1964).

It must be admitted that aversive images are not ideal aversive stimuli. They have the disadvantage that the timing of the noxious stimulus is difficult; in this respect they can however be considered to be at least more accurate than aversive drug techniques. The technique also depends on the capacity of the patient for visual imagery and for life-equivalent autonomic responses to pleasant and unpleasant imagery. Then there are the inevitable questions about the propriety of using drug and faradic shocks with adolescents. In the writer's experience most parents of adolescents and the adolescents themselves are reluctant to consider any treatment which incorporates a form of punishment; in this respect faradic shocks are viewed more antipathetically. In the few cases, completed and current, there have been no serious objections to aversive imagery therapy. More problematic is the choice of the noxious stimuli—neither of the two boys had any major dislikes and the only important noxious situation for both was falling in their sleep and looking down from great heights. So far there has been no substitution of the disorder by any other specific type of behavioral or sexual abnormality.

It must be pointed out that in both cases the home, in spite of previous unsettlement, was at the time of referral to the clinic reasonably stable and supportive. It is impossible to say what part this has played in the apparent sustained improvement.

A method bearing some resemblance to the above was previously described by Gold & Neufeld (1965). The main difference and similarities of the two methods are delineated in the following table.

The Gold & Neufeld Technique	The Kolvin Technique

A. 4 components
  1. Relaxation.
  2. Desensitization technique to overcome fears of failure.
  3. Imaginary aversive therapy.
  4. Discrimination learning technique which teaches the patient to actively reject and choose the two alternatives presented in the same session.
	A. 3 components
	  1. Relaxation.
	  2. Aversive imagery.
	  3. Psychotherapy.

B. Imaginary therapy consists of a gradual deconditioning process	B. Aversive Imagery consists of the evocation of the compulsive or erotogenic stimulus and the immediate disruption of it by a noxious one.
C. More elaborate technique.	C. Less elaborate technique.

Acknowledgment. I should like to thank Dr. V. Pillai for his help in one of the above cases, and Miss L. J. Wright of the Newcastle Child Psychiatry Unit for her secretarial assistance. I am also grateful to Dr. A. W. Drummond and Dr. P. Leyburn for referring the above cases. Also Mr. I. Mottahedin for advice on certain theoretical aspects.

REFERENCES

Ackerly, W. C. & Gibson, G. (1964) Lighter fluid "sniffing". *Am. J. Psychiat.*, **120**, 1056–1061.

Franks, C. M. (1958) Alcohol, alcoholics and conditioning. *J. ment. Sci.*, **104**, 14–33.

Gelder, M. G. (1964) Behaviour therapy and psychotherapy for phobic disorders. Paper read at *Sixth int. Congr. Psychother.*, London.

Gold, S. & Neufeld, I. L. (1965) A learning approach to the treatment of homosexuality. *Behav. Res. & Therapy*, **2**, 201–204.

Lazarus, A. & Abramovitz, A. (1962) The use of "emotive imagery" in the treatment of children's phobias. *J. ment. Sci.,* **108,** 191–195.

Meyer, V. & Crisp, A. H. (1966) Some problems in behaviour therapy. *Br. J. Psychiat.,* **112,** 367–381.

Rachman, S. (1965) Aversion therapy: Chemical or electrical? *Behav. Res. & Therapy,* **2,** 289–300.

Raymond, M. J. (1956) Case of fetishism treated by aversion therapy. *Br. med. J.,* **2,** 854–856.

Wolpe, J. (1958) *Psychotherapy by Reciprocal Inhibition.* University Press, Stanford.

Symptom Treatment and Symptom Substitution in Enuresis*†

BRUCE L. BAKER‡

Yale University

Abstract: This study explored the hypotheses that (a) aspects of the therapist-patient relationship are responsible for successful behavior therapy; and (b) substitute problems will arise following remission of symptoms. Thirty enuretic children were treated either by a conditioning method or by methods devised to duplicate its motivational aspects. Adjustment measures on the enuretic *S*s and control children were obtained independent of treatment. Conditioning was superior to other methods, suggesting that successful treatment was not based solely on the therapist-patient relationship. Subsequent to treatment, test measures did not indicate a decline in adjustment; on several measures, significant improvement was found.

Two questions are frequently posed to the behavior therapist. First, what are the total effects of treatment on the individual? Traditional psychiatry (e.g., Freud, 1959) views maladjustive behavior as a sign that there is an underlying disorder, and warns that even if a problem can be removed by a nondynamic therapy a relapse or another new problem will follow, since the basic causes have not been treated. This "symptom substitution" hypothesis is probably the principal theoretical reason why many clinicians hesitate to use behavior therapy. Yet while the vast majority of behavior-therapy follow-up reports indicate that no new problems have arisen following successful treatment (e.g., Kahn, Baker & Weiss, 1968; Lang & Lazovik, 1963; Lazarus, 1961, 1963; Wolpe, 1961), there has been no well-controlled study of this hypothesis.

Second, why does behavior therapy work when it does? Although behavior therapists stress the role of the learning paradigm in treatment, the learning theory upon which some of these methods are based has been criticized as outmoded (Breger & McGaugh, 1965). It seems possible that behavior therapy's success might be attributed to other aspects of the treatment, such as the therapist's enthusiasm, the kind of therapist-patient relationship which behavior-therapy methods establish, and the demands implicit in a "scientific" treatment.

The present study was concerned with both of the above questions. Behavior-therapy methods were employed to treat enuresis in children, and special attention was directed toward the efficiency of conditioning relative to other methods, and the changes in adjustment immediately following cure.

---

*Based on a dissertation submitted to the faculty of the Graduate School of Yale University in partial fulfillment of the requirements for the Ph.D. degree. The author wishes to thank Michael Kahn, his major advisor, and Fred D. Sheffield and Sidney J. Blatt, who served on his Advisory Committee. The author also wishes to thank Gilda Hymer for obtaining the schoolroom measures, and Irving H. Frank, Phillip Morse, and Ragaa Mazen for judging drawings. The conditioning devices were generously provided by Sears, Roebuck and Co.

†Reprinted from the *Journal of Abnormal Psychology*, 1969, **74**, 1, 42–49. Copyright 1969 with permission from the American Psychological Association and B. L. Baker.

‡Now at the Department of Social Relations, Harvard University.

Bed-wetting seems a particularly appropriate disorder for research into the questions posed. Improvement can be accurately assessed, and the point of complete symptomatic relief is attainable and well defined. Also, traditional psychiatric conceptions of enuresis as a symptom of emotional disturbance (summarized in Mowrer, 1950) are quite different from the behavior therapist's view of enuresis as an isolated habit deficiency in the great majority of cases (e.g., Lovibond, 1964). Although the conditioning treatment of enuresis has been reported to be quite effective by many investigators (summarized in Lovibond, 1964), it is still not widely used, in part because of the symptom-substitution concern. For example, Sperling (1965) has recently written: "The removal of the symptom of enuresis, without providing other outlets for the child, leads to a replacement by other symptoms . . . [p. 30]." The few studies which have investigated this question of adjustment following cure (Baller & Schalock, 1965; Behrle, Elkin & Laybourne, 1956; Biering & Jespersen, 1959; Lovibond, 1964) are inconclusive, however, because they were poorly (or not at all) controlled, for the most part lacked quantified measures, and did not assess change independent of the therapy.

The present study separated the treatment of enuresis and measurements of adjustment, so as to avoid the subtle forms of experimenter bias (Rosenthal, 1966) and demand characteristics (Orne, 1962) which continue to haunt practically all therapy-outcome studies. Measures of adjustment were taken by another E in the enuretic child's school, and these measures were taken under the guise of an entirely different research project.

METHOD

Subjects

The Ss were ninety elementary school children—thirty enuretics and sixty controls. Two control Ss of the same sex as the enuretic S were selected randomly from each enuretic S's classroom.

The enuretic Ss were obtained primarily in response to a newspaper article describing the project and inviting participation. A preliminary phone interview obtained the child's name, address, age, school and grade, and information about the enuresis. Also, the parent's report that in the family physician's opinion there was no organic problem was a prerequisite for being included. The enuretic sample consisted of ten girls and twenty boys, with a median age of eight years and a range from six to twelve years. All but four of the children had been wetting since birth, and more than half were wet seven nights a week.

Apparatus

The conditioning units used two foil pads, with holes in the top pad, separated by an absorbent sheet, and placed under S's lower bed sheet. The pads were connected to a white plastic box which contained two six-volt batteries, a sensitive relay, and a buzzer. Within seconds after the child began to wet, a circuit was completed and the buzzer sounded. The buzzer continued to sound until S got out of bed and shut it off.

The "gadgetry" device, used in the subsequent treatment of four waiting-list Ss, consisted of a bulletin board for a star chart, a container for stars, and a wind-up alarm clock, all mounted on a white wooden stand.

Procedure

The thirty enuretic Ss were arranged in triads according to the data obtained in the phone interviews, and one S was randomly assigned to each of three experimental conditions. Ter children were placed immediately in behavior therapy with a conditioning device (Group C). Ten children were concurrently given a wake-up treatment designed to duplicate all features of the conditioning treatment except the conditioning procedure (Group WU). Ten children were placed on a waiting list to begin treatment in the near future (Group WL). The Group WL families were scheduled for a brief home interview, in which E obtained further information about the child's enuresis.

Treatment

All treatment was carried out in the child's home. In the first visit, E told S's parents that he was investigating both the process of cure and the changes which follow a child's becoming dry. Parents were asked to be particularly attentive to any changes in their child — especially new problems — both during and after treatment.

Group C. The E explained the operation of the conditioning device and encouraged the child to practice setting it up himself. The S was kept on the device until he had fourteen consecutive days dry; the device was then taken off the bed but left in the house for an additional fourteen days, after which S was designated as dry. If a child was not dry (or much improved) after fifty reinforcements (buzzer sounds), he was designated a failure. If a child later relapsed, he was begun again on the device when possible.

Group WU. The wake-up treatment was similar to the routine prescribed by many pediatricians, but with emphasis on regularity and thorough awakening (adapted from Smith, 1948). A fixed time was chosen before S usually wet, and the parents were told to awaken S every night at this time; the best time evolved during treatment. It was stressed that the child must be wide awake before going to the bathroom. When S had been dry for a week, he was not awakened for several nights during the next week. If he was dry on these nights, he was put on a new schedule whereby he would only be awakened the two nights following a wet night.

Otherwise, treatment was the same for conditioning and wake-up children. All parents aided the child in getting up at night and kept daily records of progress; all children kept progress records with star charts. Every child was visited at home once a week and phoned once a week by the author to review progress and offer suggestions. Parents in both groups were generally very cooperative in keeping records and appeared to be adequately following the treatment routine.

Group WL. Approximately ten weeks after the original interview, E phoned the ten waiting-list families. One S in Group WL had become dry and another S had not been examined medically after repeated requests; consequently, these two Ss were not begun in treatment. To explore some peripheral hypotheses, the remaining eight waiting-list Ss were now treated in the following way.

It seemed possible that the conditioning method might be effective because E brings a "gadget" into the home, thus in some way increasing the child's motivation. To obtain pilot data on this question, four Ss were placed in wake-up treatment, but were also brought the gadget described above, with instructions to place it beside the bed and to set the alarm clock at the time designated for awakening. The other four Ss received the same conditioning treatment as the original Group C.

Also, as an exploratory means of assessing the importance of the therapist's presence, there were two levels of contact with E, full and partial. Two Ss in each group received the same amount of contact with E as Group C and Group WU Ss had received (full contact: one visit and one phone call each week). The remaining Ss received only half as much contact with E (partial contact: a visit one week, a call the next week, etc.).

Measures of Adjustment

Parent measures. Parents were periodically asked whether they had observed any changes in their child, and they completed two rating scales, both before treatment began and several weeks after treatment was terminated. The Adjective Check List (ACL) was adapted from a scale used by Sarason, Davidson, Lighthall, Waite, and Ruebush (1960) and included twenty items designed to assess personality attributes such as confidence, anxiety, and responsibility. The scale included the twelve Sarason items which could readily be scored for adjustment and eight new items. Items were presented in the form (Sad 321 123 Cheerful), and parents were asked to select the word which better typified *S* and to indicate the extent (a little, definitely, very much) by circling one number. The Behavior Problem Record (BPR) was a checklist of twenty-six specific childhood problems; the first fifteen items were a scale devised by Lovibond (1964) in his work with enuresis, and the last eleven were added by the author. Many of the problems in the BPR have been associated with enuresis in the psychiatric literature or have been suggested as possible new symptoms if enuresis is removed without treating an underlying cause (e.g., fire-setting, thumbsucking, temper outbursts).

Teacher ratings. The enuretic *S*s in the study were distributed throughout twenty-three public schools and two parochial schools; since no two enuretic *S*s happened to be in the same classroom, thirty teachers were involved in the ratings. From each enuretic *S*'s class list, two other children of the same sex were randomly selected as controls.

Although E initially contacted the superintendents and principals, all contacts with the teachers and all testing of the children were performed by another E (E_2). The research was presented to the teachers as a study of creativity. No mention ever was made of bed-wetting. Teachers were told that their class and these children had been selected at random. The E_2 explained that many of the hypotheses in the project would be biased if the teachers were made aware of them, but that after the data were all gathered she would welcome the chance to meet with the teachers and explain more fully the project and how their work fit into it. Thus, only when the study was completed did teachers learn of the enuresis treatment and their relation to it.

The teachers were given a sixty-seven-item rating form for each of the three children. Each item was to be rated on a scale of either one to five or one to seven. Most of the items were taken from the Devereux Elementary School Rating Scale (Spivack & Swift, 1966) and the Devereux Child Behavior Rating Scales (Spivack & Levine, 1964). Both scales had been factor analyzed, and in devising the teachers' ratings form items were drawn from each of the factors. These factors represented either aspects of school behavior (e.g., academic anxiety, dependence on the teacher for learning) or personal maladjustment (e.g., social aggression, fears, inability to delay). Since most of the items were stated negatively and measured "problems," new items were added exploring such things as creativity, happiness, confidence, responsibility, maturity, and capacity for play. Items were stated in terms of overt behavior, and teachers were asked to compare *S*'s current behavior with that of other children his age.

Teachers were asked to complete these questionnaires three times throughout the year. Test I was just before treatment began for the enuretic *S*, Test II was about ten weeks later, and Test III about twelve weeks after Test II.

Child measures. At these same times, the enuretic child and one of the two control children in each class were tested by E_2, who was not aware of the specific hypotheses being investigated and did not know which child was enuretic. It was announced to the class that E_2 wanted to find out some things about elementary school children and that two names had been picked "out of a hat." The test battery began with the Draw-A-Person and Draw-Your-

Family Tests and included four TAT cards (not to be reported here) and a self-report questionnaire in two parts: (a) the Self-Image Questionnaire, a sixteen-item scale designed by the author to measure feelings which might arise from being enuretic and including positively and negatively stated items such as, "My parents are very happy with me," and "I often do things I wish I had never done"; and (b) the Neurotic Inventory, a twenty-item scale measuring neurotic problems devised and employed with enuretics by Lovibond (1964) and including items such as, "I worry quite a bit about things which might happen," and "Most of the time I feel down in the dumps." Items in both scales were presented verbally to *S* as "things which boys [girls] I know have said," and *S* was asked if he was like that child. (E.g., "Bob said: I get a lot of headaches. Are you exactly like Bob? Somewhat? Not at all?")[1]

Neither the parents of tested *S*s nor *S*s themselves had any knowledge of the relationship between this school testing and treatment; if parents inquired at school about the testing, they too were told that their child was in a creativity study of randomly selected children.

After the final testing it was necessary to determine which of the control *S*s happened to be enuretic. The E phoned the parents of the control *S*s requesting that they complete a questionnaire about their child. Parents were sent the same questionnaire which the parents of enuretic *S*s had filled out, except that two additional items were added to the BPR: bed-wetting and daytime wetting.

RESULTS

Reliability and Intercorrelation of the Scales

Table 1 shows the Spearman-Brown corrected split-half reliabilities of the questionnaire measures for Test I and the test-retest coefficients. These reliabilities are satisfactory for questionnaires of this type. Drawing variables requiring subjective judgment were scored independently by the author and another judge, with Test I interjudge reliabilities ranging from 0.43 to 0.95. For analyses of drawing variables, an average of the two judges' ratings was used.

Comparison of Enuretics and Controls on Pre-treatment Measures

Enuretics and controls did not differ significantly on any item in the self-report scales, any factor in the teachers' ratings, or either total score. None of the specific drawing variables in either the Draw-A-Person or Draw-Your-Family Tests differentiated enuretics from controls. Also, two clinical psychologists making blind judgments of enuretic-control pairs of drawings were unable to identify the enuretics' drawings any better than chance expectation.

Treatment

Figure 1 summarizes the results of the first ten weeks of treatment. There was a sizable initial drop in wetting frequency from the pre-level to the first two weeks of treatment for both treatment groups. Following this, the conditioning group frequency decreased over the ten-week period, while the frequency of wetting in wake-up *S*s remained essentially unchanged. This Conditions × Weeks interaction was significant at $p < 0.05$ ($F = 2.54$; $df = 4/72$) by

---

[1]After the first testing, it seemed that some *S*s might be responding defensively to the questionnaire scales, and the need for a defensiveness measure was realized. Hence, the D scale employed by Sarason *et al.* (1960) was administered to most *S*s in Test II and to all *S*s in Test III.

Table 1. Spearman-Brown corrected split-half reliabilities of the questionnaire for Test I and test-retest reliabilities.

Scale	Corrected *r*	Tests I–II*	Tests I–III
Children's Neurotic Inventory	0.94	0.80	0.70
Children's Self-Image Questionnaire			
Negative items†	0.79	0.74	0.67
Teachers' rating form	0.85	0.86	0.83
Adjective Check List			
Mother	0.89	0.87	—
Father	0.83	0.92	—
Behavior Problem Record			
Mother	0.89	0.62	—
Father	0.93	0.71	—

*For the child and teacher measures, there was an average of ten weeks between Tests I and II and an average of twenty-two weeks between Tests I and III. For the parent measures, the questionnaire completed just before treatment was correlated with the measure following treatment, yielding only one coefficient.

†The positive self-image items were unreliable and did not correlate with the negative items or other measures; consequently, only the negative items were considered.

a Lindquist (1956) Type I analysis of variance of the treatment data (excluding the prelevel). Comparing the number of wet nights in Weeks 1–2 and Weeks 9–10, a second-order t test found the improvement in Group C to have been significantly greater than in Group WU ($t = 2.89$; $df = 18$; $p < 0.01$). These results indicate that the two conditions produced differential effects over time. By Weeks 9–10, the conditioning group was wetting significantly less than the wake-up group ($t = 1.70$; $df = 18$; $p = 0.05$).[2]

An interview with waiting-list families an average of 10.6 weeks after E's first visit found the reported mean frequency of wet nights unchanged. During this period, one Group WL S had become dry, but his previous frequency had been only two wet nights a week, the lowest in the study, and his decrease was offset by two Ss whose frequency increased. Contrasting the number of wet nights in the previous three weeks with the comparable three weeks for Group C and Group WU (Weeks eight to ten of treatment), the mean number of wet nights for Group WL ($\bar{X} = 17.7$) was significantly greater than either the mean for Group C ($\bar{X} = 5.5$; $t = 4.30$; $df = 18$; $p < 0.001$) or the mean for Group WU ($\bar{X} = 9.3$; $t = 3.21$; $df = 18$; $p < 0.01$).

The improvement during the first eight weeks of subsequent conditioning or "gadgetry" treatment for the waiting-list children was analyzed by an analysis of variance. While the conditioning treatment was more effective than the gadgetry control, this difference was not statistically significant. (The Ss with the gadget did no better than previous wake-up Ss, but Ss on conditioning did not do as well as previous conditioning Ss.) Children who had been

---

[2]In evaluating treatment differences, it is important to note that Group WU Ss had the aid of being awakened during the night until they had progressed sufficiently to be left on their own, whereas Group C Ss did not. The implication is that Group WU Ss appear to be more improved than was actually the case. For example, six Group WU Ss had improved sufficiently to be left on their own some nights. The mean percentage of wetting was 22.5 on nights when they were awakened and 38.5 on nights when they were not awakened ($t = 2.51$; $df = 5$; $p < 0.03$).

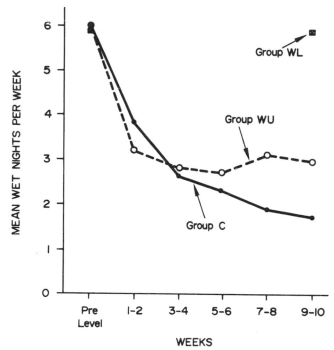

Fig. 1. Mean number of wet nights a week over the first 10 weeks of treatment for Groups C, WU, and WL.

seen less frequently (partial contact) showed more improvement than Ss who received full contact, though this difference was not statistically significant.

Treatment summary. In all, fourteen Ss were begun on the conditioning device; of these, eleven attained initial arrest. Fourteen Ss were begun in wake-up conditions; of these, two attained initial arrest. Ten Ss who had shown little improvement were switched to conditioning, and seven subsequently became dry.

Of the thirty enuretic Ss, then, one became dry without treatment, one was not begun in treatment, and one was terminated before treatment could be completed. Of the remaining twenty-seven Ss, seventy-four per cent were "cured" (dry for at least a period of 1 month), and an additional fifteen per cent were "very much improved" (dry for at least a two-week period and wetting less than one night a week). During the follow-up, which averaged six months, four cured Ss relapsed, although two of these who were retreated became dry again.

Changes Following Treatment

Parents' interviews and questionnaires. It is important to note in assessing the results of parents' measures that changes similar to those reported for enuretic Ss might also have been reported for control Ss if such comparable measures were available. In addition, parents' measures may reflect a desire to please E. It was for these reasons, of course, that independent school measures were taken on both enuretic and control Ss.

The most frequently reported observation of parents was the child's happiness at becoming dry. Many children were able for the first time to sleep overnight with friends or relatives or to go to summer camp; three boys immediately joined the Boy Scouts. Children were reported to be venturing into new activities, taking more responsibility, and becoming more autonomous. For instance, parents made such statements as, "She seems able to do things for herself"; "He started a paper route"; "Now she's cooking, sewing, reading."

While most parents reported that they had observed no new problems, several parents did report a new problem at some time. One boy defecated in his pants several times immediately following treatment. Another began to depend more on his mother to make decisions for him. A third boy developed an "eyeblink." None of these proved to be lasting, and each seemed to arise from specific new stresses, although it is not possible to say if they had any relation to the treatment.

Both mothers and fathers of cured Ss indicated improvement in adjustment on the ACL and the BPR. Combined parents' scores on the ACL showed a mean improvement of 3.5, significant at $p = 0.002$. Combined parents' scores on the BPR showed a mean improvement (decrease in reported problems) of -2.8, significant at $p = 0.05$.

School measures. Test II afforded a measure of changes which occurred either during treatment or immediately thereafter. There was an average of ten weeks from Test I to Test II, at which time seventeen Ss were judged improved (wetting less than half their original frequency). There was an average of twenty-two weeks from Test I to Test III. By Test III, thirteen Ss were cured, and another eight Ss were very much improved (wetting once a week or less). Children designated as cured had not been wetting for an average of almost three months.

Teacher ratings. Change scores were determined for total teachers' ratings from Test I to Test II; enuretics were divided into "improved" and "unimproved" and compared with each other and with their controls. For Test I to Test III comparisons, enuretics were classified as cured, very much improved, or slightly improved and compared with their respective controls. None of the mean change scores, nor the differences between them, approached statistical significance; teachers showed a high degree of consistency in their ratings, and mean change scores were small. Change scores on only three of the twenty-four factors significantly differentiated cured enuretics from their controls, with cured enuretics increasing significantly more ($p < 0.05$) in academic anxiety, drive for academic success, and unethical behavior.[3]

Children's self-report questionnaires. There was a general downward trend (fewer reported problems) on the questionnaires from Test I to Test II. The direction of changes for enuretics and controls is shown in Table 2. While treatment was in progress or only recently terminated, enuretic Ss who had shown improvement in bed-wetting reported fewer problems than previously. This improvement compared favorably with changes shown in questionnaire scores for both unimproved enuretic Ss and control Ss.

In analyzing changes from Test I to Test III, special attention was given to Ss designated as cured,[4] as these Ss would be most likely to evidence adverse changes according to the symptom-substitution hypothesis. On the Neurotic Inventory, no cured S reported more problems, and on the Self-Image Questionnaire only one S increased in score. The mean improvement for cured enuretics was greater than the mean improvement for their controls on both the Neurotic Inventory ($t = 1.49$; $df = 20$; $p = 0.08$) and the Self-Image Question-

---

[3]Actually, cured enuretics only increased somewhat in drive for academic success and unethical behavior, but controls decreased in score on these variables, resulting in the significant difference. However, there was a large Test I difference for these Ss on these factors, and even after the above changes the control Ss still scored higher than enuretics.

[4]One cured S and his control could not be tested a third time due to lack of cooperation from the school. The control of another cured S had moved away, so this pair was not included. In all, then, there were eleven cured-control pairs.

Table 2. Direction of change in questionnaire scores from Test I to Test II.

Questionnaire	Improved enuretics	Unimproved enuretics	Controls
Neurotic Inventory*			
Increase	0	3	10
Same	0	3	1
Decrease	17	7	19
Self-Image Questionnaire†			
Increase	2	4	6
Same	1	1	1
Decrease	14	8	23

Note. – Decrease indicates improvement (fewer reported problems).
$*\chi^2 = 15.19, p < 0.01.$ $\dagger\chi^2 = 2.14, p > 0.10.$

naire ($t = 1.79$; $df = 20$; $p < 0.05$). Combining the questionnaires, the mean improvement from Test I to Test III for cured enuretics ($\bar{X} = -15.6$) was significantly greater than for their controls ($\bar{X} = -6.4$) at $p = 0.03$ ($t = 1.93$; $df = 20$).[5]

There were no questionnaire items on which cured and very much improved enuretics showed a significant change for the worse or their controls improved more than the enuretic Ss. Cured and very much improved enuretics improved significantly more than did the controls ($p < 0.05$) on the following items: "I'm always being scolded or punished by someone"; "I've often been punished for nothing"; "I often feel sick in the stomach"; "Most of the time I feel down in the dumps."

Drawings. Scoring of specific variables on the Draw-A-Person and Draw-Your-Family Tests failed to reveal significant changes. A total score was derived for each S on the former, based on conceptions in the drawing literature (e.g., Machover, 1951; Mazen, 1963) of what constitutes an improvement in adjustment. To weigh each variable equally, only the sign of change was considered. Signs of a shift toward better adjustment were an increase in number of body parts, size of the person, number of colors used, appropriateness of colors, amount of clothing, smile and movement, and a decrease in erasures, pressure, distortion, bizarreness, paper chopping, transparency, stick figures, drawing side views, drawing the opposite sex, and negative affect. Cured enuretics showed a mean improvement ($\bar{X} = 1.36$; $p = 0.06$) and differed significantly from their controls who showed a slight worsening ($\bar{X} = -1.45$; t, second-order difference $= 2.29$; $df = 20$; $p = 0.02$).

Also, two clinical psychologists with the diplomate and fifteen and thirty years of experience in therapy and diagnosis were asked to evaluate the Draw-a-Person Test drawings for expressions of maladjustment. Each of the thirty enuretic and thirty control Ss was randomly assigned a number between one and sixty, and each S's three drawings (Tests I, II and III) were randomly ordered in one of the six possible permutations. Judges were told the age, race, and sex of each child and were to rank order the three drawings with respect to overall adjustment. In assessing the drawings, then, a judge knew neither which drawings had been done by enuretic and nonenuretic Ss nor the order in which they had been drawn.

In this type of analysis, differences between groups are reflected in the slope of the curves connecting mean ranks across testings. As seen in Fig. 2, for each judge the mean ranks for the cured enuretics decrease across the three tests, whereas the control slope is essentially flat.

---

[5]One explanation for this decrease would be increased defensiveness. Since no D-scale scores were available for Test I, the only change which could be analyzed was from Test II to Test III. The defensiveness scores were fairly stable, and the changes did not differentiate cured enuretics and controls.

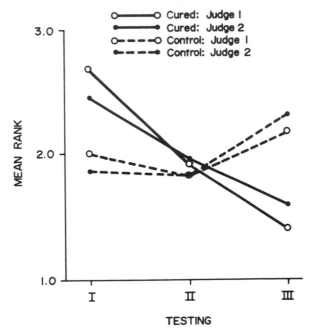

Fig. 2. Judges' ranks of overall adjustment in Draw-A-Person Test drawings; mean ranks for each judge are plotted over the three testings for cured enuretic Ss and their control Ss. (Lower ranks indicate better adjustment.)

The improvement in adjustment rank from Test I to Test III for cured enuretics was significant for both Judge 1 ($t = 3.81$; $df = 10$; $p = 0.002$) and Judge 2 ($t = 2.36$; $df = 10$; $p = 0.02$). When this Test I–Test III change score for cured enuretics was compared with a similar score for their controls, the second-order t test showed that improvement in adjustment for cured enuretics was significantly greater than for controls—for Judge 1, $p = 0.007$ ($t = 2.72$; $df = 20$) and for Judge 2, $p = 0.004$ ($t = 2.88$; $df = 20$).

DISCUSSION

The present study suggests, then, that it is extremely doubtful that the successful conditioning treatment of bed-wetting can be explained as some kind of "transference cure," based on only the therapist-patient relationship and the motivation which it engenders. The wake-up procedure was not as effective as the total behavior-therapy treatment, despite an equal amount of therapist contact. These findings are similar to those of Lang and Lazovik (1963), Lazarus (1961), Paul (1966), and Davison (1968) who contrasted systematic desensitization to other methods with equal therapist contact.

Another approach to this question of the relative importance of the therapist and his technique is to withdraw the therapist to some extent and to see if treatment becomes less effective. The exploratory findings indicated that treatment is just as effective with less therapist contact, a result consonant with the fact that many parents buy conditioning devices and cure their child's enuresis with no professional help at all.

The measures of adjustment did not show a worsening in adjustment subsequent to treatment; rather, other improvements were found. Children were reported to be happier, less anxious, and more grown-up, assuming responsibility and venturing into new activities. The changes on childrens' self-report items about punishment suggest that the cure may have had beneficial effects on the parent-child relationship or at least the child's perception of it. Finally, the drawings showed a dramatic improvement in what might be termed "self-image."

Whereas enuresis is considered to be a symptom of emotional disturbance by many clinicians, traditional predictions about treatment and subsequent adjustment for such symptoms were not upheld. This might suggest that the symptom-substitution hypothesis is untenable and that neurotic symptoms, in the traditional dynamic sense, can be removed with equanimity despite the psychological gains they afford. Perhaps in those cases where treatment succeeds, the benefits derived from being dry outweigh such "primary gains." On the other hand, it is possible that new symptoms did not arise because bed-wetting is simply a habit deficiency rather than an expression of, and outlet for, internal conflict. In any case, the dangers of a direct treatment of enuresis seem to have been overstated, and similar research on other classical disorders might be of considerable value in further understanding the symptom-substitution issue and the more basic question of symptom formation.

REFERENCES

Baller, W. & Schalock, H. Conditioned response treatment of enuresis. *Exceptional Child*, 1956, **22**, 233–236.

Behrle, F. C., Elkin, M. T. & Laybourne, P. C. Evaluation of a conditioning device in the treatment of nocturnal enuresis. *Pediatrics*, 1956, **17**, 849–855.

Biering, A. & Jespersen, I. The treatment of enuresis nocturna with conditioning devices. *Acta Paediatrica*, 1959, **48** (Monogr. Suppl. No. 118), 152–153.

Breger, L. & McGaugh, J. L. Critique and reformulation of "learning-theory" approaches to psychotherapy and neurosis. *Psychological Bulletin*, 1965, **63**, 338–358.

Davison, G. C. Systematic desensitization as a counterconditioning process. *Journal of Abnormal Psychology*, 1968, **73**, 91–99.

Freud, S. On psychotherapy. (Orig. publ. 1904) In, *Collected papers of Sigmund Freud*. Vol. 1. New York: Basic Books, 1959.

Kahn, M., Baker, B. L. & Weiss, J. M. Treatment of insomnia by relaxation. *Journal of Abnormal Psychology*, 1968, **73**, 556–558.

Lang, P. J. & Lazovik, A. D. Experimental desensitization of a phobia. *Journal of Abnormal and Social Psychology*, 1963, **66**, 519–525.

Lazarus, A. A. Group therapy of phobic disorders by systematic desensitization. *Journal of Abnormal and Social Psychology*, 1961, **63**, 504–510.

Lazarus, A. A. The results of behaviour therapy in 126 cases of severe neurosis. *Behaviour Research and Therapy*, 1963, **1**, 69–80.

Lindquist, E. F. *Design and analysis of experiments in psychology and education*. Boston: Houghton Mifflin, 1956.

Lovibond, S. H. *Conditioning and enuresis*. Oxford: Pergamon Press, 1964.

Machover, K. Drawings of the human figure. In H. Anderson & G. Anderson (Eds.), *An introduction to projective techniques*. Englewood Cliffs, N.J.: Prentice-Hall, 1951.

Mazen, R. Comparative study of the drawings of normal and disturbed children. Unpublished manuscript, Yale University, 1963.

Mowrer, O. H. *Learning theory and personality dynamics*. New York: Ronald Press, 1950.

Orne, M. T. On the social psychology of the psychological experiment with particular reference to demand characteristics and their implications. *American Psychologist*, 1962, **17**, 776–783.

Paul, G. L. *Insight versus desensitization in psychotherapy*. Stanford: Stanford University Press, 1966.

Rosenthal, R. *Experimenter effects in behavioral research*. New York: Appleton-Century-Crofts, 1966.

Sarason, S. B., Davidson, K. S., Lighthall, F. F., Waite, R. R. & Ruebush, B. K. *Anxiety in elementary school children*. New York: Wiley, 1960.

Smith, S. *The psychological origin and treatment of enuresis.* Seattle: University of Washington Press, 1948.

Sperling, M. Dynamic considerations and treatment of enuresis. *Journal of the American Academy of Child Psychiatry*, 1965, **4,** 19–31.

Spivack, G. & Levine, M. The Devereux Child Behavior Rating Scales: A study of symptom behaviors in latency age atypical children. *American Journal of Mental Deficiency*, 1964, **68,** 700–717.

Spivack, G. & Swift, M. The Devereux Elementary School Rating Scale: A study of the nature and origin of achievement related to disturbed classroom behavior. *Journal of Special Education*, 1966, **1,** 71–90.

Wolpe, J. The systematic desensitization treatment of neuroses. *Journal of Nervous and Mental Disease*, 1961, **132,** 189–203.

Behavior Therapy and Encopresis in Children*

D. H. NEALE†

St. Andrew's Hospital, Thorpe, Norwich

Abstract: A method of treating encopresis based on learning theory is described. It entails the following steps:

1. Accurate diagnosis of the physiological derangement by abdominal and rectal examination and inspection of stools as is normal in medical practice.

2. Correction of the physiological derangement if required by such measures as prescription of a bulk laxative such as Isogel.

3. Accurate diagnosis of the behavioral aetiology of the encopresis.

4. If the conditioned avoidance drive is not excessive (as in Cases 1, 2 and 3) then instrumental conditioning will be adequate and the regime as described may be instituted. The child is taken to the lavatory four times a day, to sit until a motion is passed or five minutes has elapsed whichever is shorter. If a motion is passed he is congratulated and given a sweet (or other appropriate reward). If his pants are soiled he is given clean ones. No punishments or rebukes of any sort are given for dirty pants and no rewards for clean ones. Once the child is clean he should still be rewarded intermittently for successful bowel actions for several months.

If the conditioned avoidance reaction is excessive as in Case 4 (and this could have been discovered before commencing the training regime) then a programme to reduce this must be devised. It may still be necessary to use the training regime at a later date.

This method has been applied to four cases of longstanding psychogenic encopresis resistant to other methods. There was rapid success in three cases and in the case which failed this is attributable to faulty application of learning theory rather than defects in the approach. Comparisons are made with paediatric and psychotherapeutic approaches and a wide area of agreement in practice with the principles of learning theory is found.

It is concluded that learning theory can usefully be applied to encopresis but methods can be further refined.

This paper records experience in treating four boys with encopresis. The selection of cases was fortuitous in that of a group of about twenty-five children who were in-patients in the unit to which the author was assigned for a six-month period, these four were the only encopretic children. It is hoped to illustrate an approach to the problem which is therapeutically useful, which is open to theoretical development in a way in which analytic formulations are not, and at the same time avoids the false dichotomy between psychogenic and organic diseases.

The method involves utilization of physiological and neuro-anatomical knowledge of bowel function, as well as learning theory. This paper abstracts a particular aspect of the children's treatment but they were of course receiving all the benefits of a children's psychiatric

---

*Reprinted from *Behaviour Research and Therapy*, 1963, **1**, 139–149. Copyright 1963 with permission from Pergamon Press Publishing Company and Dr. D. H. Neale.

†Now at Matsqui Institution, Abbotsford, B.C., Canada.

unit. What is reported here leans heavily on learning theory. In particular the method of operant conditioning, which has a long history of study in laboratory conditions (Skinner, 1959; Ferster, 1958) is used to bring about the desired response. The concept of desensitization to phobic situations as described by Wolpe (1958) was a guide to making possible the decay of the conditioned phobic response to defaecation although in these particular children it was not necessary to use relaxation techniques. The work of Mowrer & Mowrer (1938) and others on conditioning treatment of enuresis is of great importance inasmuch as it has encouraged other applications of learning theory to clinical problems. It is not however directly applicable to the forms of encopresis described here. The two conditions of incontinence of urine and incontinence of faeces are physiologically and behaviorally different. The former requires encouragement of a conditioned inhibition of bladder emptying and the development of the ability to store urine, while the latter requires encouragement of the act of defaecation and restoration of the physiologically normal state of emptiness of the rectum.

Using the division of neurotic behavior into the conditioned avoidance drive (C.A.D.) and the instrumental responses by which C.A.D. is reduced (H. Gwynne-Jones, 1960) it may be seen that in this study treatment was directed at the instrumental response and in three cases this was sufficient. In the fourth case it was insufficient and cure was not achieved; probably an attack on the C.A.D. itself was required.

Encopresis is considered in terms of stimulus and response and the formation of an S–R connection by appropriate reinforcement.

THE STIMULUS

In health the rectum is empty. When a faecal mass is moved into the rectum a sensation of fullness is experienced which normally calls forth the response of proceeding to a lavatory and defaecating there. If defaecation does not occur then the sensation of fullness passes off. The subject then becomes unaware of his full rectum. If the rectum is distended the anus may also become dilated without the subject being aware of it and overflow incontinence can occur (Gaston, 1948). If there is impairment of the sensory path of the reflex then S–R training will be impaired or prevented. This is clearly demonstrated in cases of anatomical interruption by Goligher and Hughes (1951). It seems reasonable to suppose a similar effect where the interruption is functional. All the subjects of this study reported absence of the sensation of rectal fullness.

THE RESPONSE

This consists of an expulsive act emptying the rectum and descending colon and requiring only a few moments for completion in healthy subjects. This act is itself a series of co-ordinated reflexes which can be disorganized by a failure of any one member of the series. In all four subjects discussed, this act was severely disorganized at the commencement of training. The syndrome of dyschezia (Keele & Neil, 1961) was fully developed with a constantly filled rectum from which small quantities of faeces would be expelled at short intervals without ever producing complete evacuation.

THE S–R LINK

Anthony (1957) has drawn attention to the subtleties of the mother-child relationship in the training situation which he terms "the potting couple." Factors which appear relevant will be detailed in each case study. Prominent in these cases is inhibition of R by fear. Pinkerton (1958) in his study of psychogenic megacolon gives details of this process. Once constipation with resulting impairment of S and encopresis has developed, the child draws down upon himself extreme parental wrath which adds to the fear and further inhibits R. This is particularly the case in that the usual parental injunction is to "control yourself" and "hold it in" in order to avoid soiling.

METHOD OF TREATMENT

The aim of treatment was to encourage a normal R by instrumental conditioning while creating circumstances in which the conditioned anxiety response could decay. This latter was encouraged by the method of reciprocal inhibition. The children were taken to the lavatory after each main meal and at bedtime (four times daily). This was done in a kindly manner by a nurse known to the child. The child was permitted to shut the lavatory door if he wished and in one case (W.S.) provided with a sweet to suck and a comic book to read, both measures designed to inhibit the anxiety reaction associated in this child with sitting on the lavatory. The procedure was fully explained to the child and every effort made to ensure that it was not unpleasant nor received by him as punitive.

In two cases (R.C. and W.S.) Isogel (Allen & Hanbury) (which is dried mucilage of tropical seeds) was given to provide additional bulk for the colon to work on and to render the stools soft and not painful to pass. The child found that success in passing faeces in the lavatory was rewarded. The most powerful reinforcement was probably the approval of the nurse and the knowledge on the part of the child that he was making progress towards losing a hated symptom. In addition he received a reward consisting of either sweets, chocolate bars, peanuts, stars in a book or pennies, these varying with the interests of the child and being changed as the child grew bored with them.

Once the child had become accustomed to using the lavatory and was free from soiling, the four times daily routine was abandoned. The child was now instructed to go whenever he felt the sensation of rectal fullness (which had returned by this stage). After reporting a successful result, he received his reward. This constituted a period of overlearning. An attempt was made to provide partial reinforcement but this ran into procedural difficulties and was abandoned as an inessential refinement of the method.

A record was kept of acts of defaecation. A score of two points was assigned to a normal bowel action. In the early stages it frequently happened that two or three pellets of faeces each the size of a pea, would be produced. A score of one was assigned to such a bowel action. If pants were soiled this was similarly scored one or two and clean pants were provided. Enquiry as to the state of pants was made tactfully and no form of rebuke was administered. All these children had previously had excessive punishment for soiling and it was considered that the fear engendered had actively interfered with learning the desired response. The records are displayed graphically as a pair of curves, one representing decay of the undesired response (involuntary and uncontrolled defaecation) and the other the growth of the desired response (defaecation in the lavatory). During treatment there was not other change in the boys' life in the ward and milieu therapy, occupational therapy and play therapy continued as before.

Case 1. R.C., Age Seven and a Half Years IQ 80 (W.I.S.C.)

Reported to have been continent of urine and faeces by day and night at one year. Age three began attending day nursery where the lavatory was inconveniently situated. Faecal incontinence occurred about twice weekly. This was treated by smacking and forced sitting on the pot for long periods after the act of incontinence. This was followed, as would be predicted from learning theory, by refusal to defaecate in the pot and by the age of five he would not enter a toilet unless accompanied and if he did so he would not defaecate there. He was constantly defaecating in his trousers by day or pyjamas by night and nowhere else. His father died when he was four. On commencing primary school (age five) he showed so much aggressive behavior that the head teacher feared for the safety of other children. We have no data by which to determine if his hostility to other children was in part determined by their dislike and scorn of his dirty conditions.

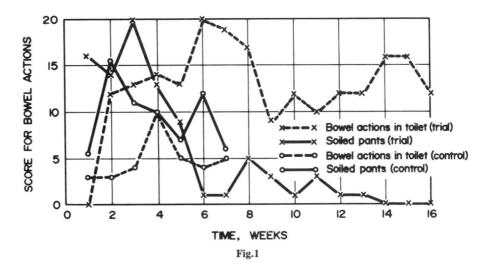

Fig.1

He began attending the psychiatric children's out-patients clinic weekly, aged five and a half but neither encopresis nor behavior improved. He became an in-patient at six years and three months. For the first two months a record was kept, solely for diagnostic purposes, which showed that he was incontinent two or three times daily and by night often passing large, formed stools involuntarily. He reported that he never felt the urge to defaecate and was unaware of the occurrence of defaecation. This record was scored in a similar manner to the present study and serves in some degree as a control. It is not quite satisfactory as a control because it is not known to what extent the child may have been rewarded by nurses' approval of bowel actions in the lavatory. The graphic record does not show unequivocally that learning did or did not take place, but if learning took place at all it did not do so at the rate achieved in the planned treatment.

At seven years and three months, after a year in hospital, his general demeanor had improved but the encopresis was worse. He never defaecated in the lavatory at all and on examination multiple faecal masses were palpable in the lower abdomen. Rectal examination was not performed but the abdominal examination indicated extreme constipation. The training procedure was instituted and within a few days he began using the lavatory and after five weeks was having only occasional accidents (Fig. 1).

After three months he was considered cured by the nurses responsible for him in so far as he was never noticeably soiled. However, close inspection of his underpants showed that two or three times a week they were stained to a slight extent, as if he had been careless in wiping himself. This situation has persisted unchanged on his transfer to a boarding school for educationally subnormal children. It seems that bowel physiology has not yet returned completely to normal, but all the social disabilities previously associated with this boy's state have gone. There has been no relapse in his behavior at the boarding school.

Comment

Normal bowel control broke down under unfavorable environmental stress and the damage was compounded by punishment. The boy's situation at the commencement of treatment was constipation with loss of rectal sensation and reflex emptying of the bowel occurring without the boy being aware of it. It seems unnecessary to relate encopresis to loss of his father one year after commencement or to postulate that encopresis and the aggressive behavior occurring from five to six were both manifestations of the same aggressive instinct.

Case 2. J.E., Age Ten W.I.S.C. IQ Full Scale 117; Verbal 124 Performance 108

Clean and dry from age two. Encopretic but not enuretic from age four. There had been pot phobia aged one year but this subsided. Aged four, he had an attack of diarrhoea after eating fruit and soiled himself. Father was outraged and smacked him severely; mother sympathized and a major parental quarrel ensued. He was then encopretic until father, a violent man frequently drunk, left home, eighteen months later. For six months he was clean but then father returned and had a violent quarrel with mother, striking her in front of the child. Encopresis returned and persisted. Mother threatened him, bribed him and beat him with a strap, all these measures being associated with instructions to hold in his faeces. He attended as an out-patient weekly for a year for play therapy, while his mother was the subject of social casework, but without improvement. He was admitted to the ward and after a month there was no change. At the end of this month when the training programme was commenced, faecal masses were palpable per abdomen and on rectal examination a mass of faeces was present just inside the sphincter. He never used the lavatory to defaecate and would pass bulky faeces into his trousers on average once daily. He could report brief periods, up to a week of cleanliness but in these periods he did not defaecate at all. This behavior indicates that the only approach to continence the boy knew was to inhibit defaecation. He reported that he could not voluntarily expel faeces and that when involuntary expulsion occurred he had no conscious awareness of it.

For the training programme no purgatives were used and sweets were given as a reward. It was intended to use the first week as a control period without sweets, but as the graph shows, use of the lavatory began at once so that the sweets played only a minor part in this. It was two months before full continence was obtained and after four months the descending colon was palpable and faeces were found on rectal examination so that the colon and rectum were not functioning with complete normality. He remained in hospital a further three months because of a legal wrangle between his parents over his custody, neither being able to provide a satisfactory home. He was discharged to a boarding school where he remains a happy and well integrated member of the community, fully contingent six months after cessation of treatment (Fig. 2).

Comment

The aetiology of encopresis in this case could well be formulated in terms of the Oedipus complex, and much evidence not quoted here, emerged which was consistent with such a formulation. However from the point of view of treatment it seems more profitable to see this in terms of a conditioned inhibition of defaecation by a prepotent anxiety response established by an intolerant and punitive father and maintained by a bewildered and desperate mother. The rapidity with which this boy used the lavatory in hospital when the training regime began may be explained in several ways. The anxiety response may have been conditioned to the lavatory in his own home, and so would not necessarily and completely generalize to a different lavatory. In addition the month in hospital prior to commencing training may have been essential in lowering his overall anxiety by providing a tolerant non-punitive atmosphere. Finally this intelligent ten-year-old may have benefitted from the full explanations of what was been done, given on several occasions in a friendly and supportive manner.

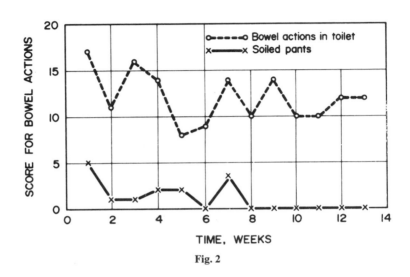

Fig. 2

Case 3. G.M., Age 9 10/12 Years, W.I.S.C. IQ, Verbal factor 112 Performance factor 69

Constipation had been a great problem to mother as a girl and she was very frightened of it developing in her son. It did. He was clean and dry by two and a half but had colic and constipation requiring enemata from three to four, again at seven and again at eight and a half. Defaecation appeared painful and in retrospect he said he was frightened to defaecate because of the pain. In arguments with his mother one of the threats the boy made was, "If I don't get my way, I won't go to the bloody lavatory."

He was first brought to a Child Guidance Clinic at the age of six because of aggressive behavior, phobias and sex play, but defaulted after a few visits. He was again referred at age eight for the same troubles to which scholastic retardation was now added. He received weekly play therapy but after four months, encopresis commenced. Its onset was not associated with improvement or change in any other respect, and its occurrence at this point rather than say a year earlier or later seems fortuitous. He continued weekly attendance with his mother for six months but was then admitted largely because his mother was worn out by the encopresis. Six months after admission his general behavior was somewhat improved but the encopresis persisted. There was a continuous flow of liquid faeces and he wore napkins and plastic pants. He did not use the lavatory for defaecation at all. On examination faecal masses were palpable per abdomen. He was too nervous to permit rectal examination but on gently retracting the buttocks the anal sphincter could be seen open to half an inch diameter with bulging faeces behind it. The response to treatment was rapid and complete in that he became fully continent of faeces day and night. After three months of training the colon was still palpable per abdomen but not loaded as before. The anal sphincter was firmly closed as in normal children. The slow improvement in other aspects of his behavior continued unchecked and he was discharged home three months after completion of bowel training, a year after first admission. After three months back in his own home there has been no relapse in bowel habit or in general behavior (Fig. 3).

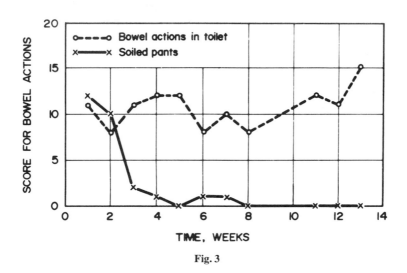

Fig. 3

Comment

Parent and child both had bowel problems. Transmission may have been genetic but very probably it was mother's over-anxiety about the boy's use of the pot which led to mishandling of the training situation. Judicious use of bland laxatives in the early years might have avoided encopresis but later the boy was refusing to enter the lavatory as one way of exerting his will against his mother with whom he was continuously in conflict. Constipation with overflow incontinence was the result of refusal to defaecate in the lavatory. Removal to hospital created a new situation, cutting short the conflict with his mother and providing alternative authority figures more skilled in avoiding conflict. In this setting his encopresis did not spontaneously cease but rapidly improved when the training programme commenced. At the time of his return home the total situation has been considerably improved so that parental anxiety has subsided below the point at which the whole vicious circle would start again.

Case 4. W.S., Age 10 9/12. W.I.S.C. IQ 108

As a baby he required weekly milk of magnesia for constipation but there were no battles over the pot and he was clean and dry by age two years. Encopresis began at age seven and a half with daily incontinence of formed stools and a great deal of play with the stools, which were deposited, sometimes wrapped in paper, in various parts of the house, and smeared on walls and furniture. He would spend long periods in the lavatory without successful defaecation. He freely inserted his fingers in his rectum to obtain faeces for smearing and as a means of assisting defaecation. He was a quiet, overly good boy with a compulsion to swear, but he dealt with this by limiting himself to the initial letters F . . , S . . , S . . , C . . .

He began attending as an out-patient in May 1960 and received psychotherapy on fifty occasions. Simultaneously his mother saw P.S.W. The encopresis, smearing and swearing continued but in addition there was open rebellion and disobedience to his parents.

He was admitted as an in-patient and six months later his condition was unchanged. Examination showed hard coils of faeces-packed colon in the abdomen and hard faeces in the rectum. After an initial purge using Dulcolax suppositories, the training programme was instituted. There was no sustained improvement. Subsequently a course of rectal washouts followed by neostigmine has produced no benefit. Great difficulty exists in getting this boy to talk about his condition but he has said that at night he keeps his fingers in his rectum for long periods because he likes the sensation (Fig. 4).

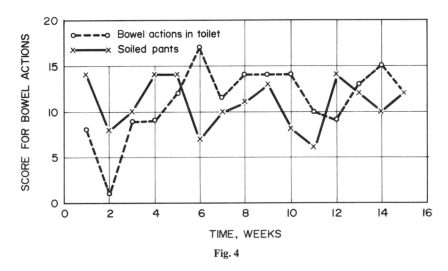

Fig. 4

Comment

This case represents a failure by a psychotherapeutic approach and by the orthodox medical approach of purgation. The method of operant training failed. However, theoretically the S–R analysis could have been pushed further although for practical reasons this was not possible for the present author. It appears that in this case, some stimulus connected with a distended rectum was a source of considerable gratification which was not outweighed by the reward we were able to offer for emptying the rectum. We never knew what the significant stimulus was, nor precisely what gratification resulted. Had we known it might have been possible to link the stimulus to an unpleasant response or to offer an alternative, socially acceptable gratification. Alternatively on a wider plane this boy appeared to delight in faeces, and an aversion reaction to faeces, real or imaginary in a variety of contexts might have been built up.

DISCUSSION

The four in-patients here are a small series to report, but their importance lies in part in that they were considered sufficiently disturbed on grounds other than encopresis to merit admission to a children's psychiatric in-patient unit. Probably none could have been treated in their homes, but on the other hand admissions to the therapeutic environment of the hospital and individual psychotherapy had not of itself cured the encopresis.

In interpreting the shape of the graphs here presented, note must be made of technical imperfections in the method of scoring. In the graph of "bowel actions" occurring other than in the lavatory, what is really scored is the number of occasions on which pants or pyjamas were seen to be soiled. This has a maximum score of ten points per day because only four inspections were made of day wear and one inspection of nightwear. Case 3, with a constant trickle of faeces, scored higher than Case 2 who passed large, formed motions although they were both invariably encopretic at the start of training. As Case 3 improved, the sphincter regained its competence and the trickle stopped. This is reflected by an abrupt early fall in the curve. However after the first few weeks no boy was incontinent of a full-sized formed stool, but only of small quantities. In Case 1 the faecal soiling was so slight that there was doubt as to whether he had been incontinent or merely careless in wiping himself after bowel action. However a score of one was made each time soiled pants were found.

In the case of bowel actions in the lavatory there is a peak early in treatment followed by a falling off. This is misleading. Early in treatment these boys passed frequent small formed stools. Later they were passing less frequent but larger stools. The latter condition more closely resembles normality, but the size of stool could not be adequately represented in the scoring method. This alteration in the size and frequency of bowel action presumably represents a recovery of tone and co-ordination of colonic activity which is not under voluntary control, consequent on correct action of the anal sphincter which is under voluntary control. In one boy cessation of medication with Isogel reduced the total faecal material to be passed. At the time of first follow-up, approximately four months after onset of treatment and one to two months after clinical continence, it was noted that none of the three continent boys were normal, if the criteria of normality is taken as an empty rectum.

Bearing these considerations in mind the scores plotted could well represent on the one hand an exponential curve representing learning to perform the act in a particular situation and on the other hand decay of a learned response to perform in another situation, which response is related to several different factors, all of which are being affected by decay of learned responses.

To obtain learning curves which would be capable of accurate and rigid interpretation in terms of learning theory would require very detailed and numerous physiological measurements on each boy to ascertain precisely what physiological responses were contributing to the final clinical score of pants soiled or "normal" bowel actions.

The attempt to investigate them however would have caused so much discomfort to the boys as to interfere with the training programme.

In the three cases in which success was achieved it was postulated that an aversion reaction to voluntary defaecation had been built up by earlier experiences. In Case 1, the inconvenience and unpleasantness of the lavatory may have been the initiating factor. In Case 2, violent punishment for the initial acts of incontinence and in Case 3 chronic constipation with the frequent experience of pain during passage of hard faecal masses may have started the process.

Aversion reactions tend to decay unless persistently reinforced (Eysenck, 1963). If a child is punished for any act of defaecation, then the experience tends to generalize to all acts of defaecation unless other factors are at work to produce a situation in which discrimination can be learned. In the present cases a situation was reached in which every act of defaecation was punished, because they always defaecated in the wrong place. In Case 1 we know that he was repeatedly punished for defaecation and the smacking was immediately followed by the further punishment of a long period of enforced sitting on a pot – when his rectum must have been empty. The consequence of emptying the rectum was punishment, whereas it should have been a manifestly gratified mother or mother-substitute.

In Case 2 there were violent beatings following bowel actions, without any maternal congratulation or reward for bowel action in the lavatory. It is not surprising that discrimination failed and the boy became constipated.

The normal mother training her child expresses pleasure when he uses the pot. In Case 3, the mother's anxiety about faeces may well have prevented her from feeling or expressing this pleasure. The boy was subjected to a great many unpleasant procedures affecting his rectum and recollects the passage of faeces as painful and frightening. Lavatory refusal also became a satisfying piece of behavior because it annoyed and alarmed his mother.

In each case the conditions for reinforcing an aversion reaction were maintained prior to admission to hospital. After admission, reinforcement largely ceased. During the treatment period scrupulous care was taken to avoid associating defaecation with pain or unpleasantness. Simultaneously during the treatment period, discrimination training occurred by rewarding defaecation in the right place, but not in the wrong place. Once this process began it tended to be self-reinforcing because the children could appreciate the significance of their success.

There is a considerable degree of agreement between authors of different view-points that learning is an essential factor in development of normal faecal continence. Thus Anthony (1957) draws attention to cues given by the child to the mother and the mother to the child but goes on to reach the conclusion that the discontinuous type of encopretic, which includes all four cases mentioned here needs prolonged psychotherapy, which is at variance with the experience reported here. Pinkerton (1958) describes the same factors as were present in the cases described here, but proceeds to make a false dichotomy when he states that treatment was "first directed to convincing the parents that what they had formerly regarded as a physical disorder was in fact of emotional origin." He ascribes his success to the disinhibitions of aggressive impulses which were finding expression symbolically in defaecation, but it may well have been that the success was equally due to his having enlightened the parents about the factors in training, of which he was himself acutely aware and his play therapy was in fact a variation of the method of reciprocal inhibition of anxiety by self-assertive behavior.

The same false dichotomy is made by Coekin & Gairdner (1960) who successfully treated children complaining of constipation and incontinence with laxatives. They postulated a constitutional colonic inertia, although this is as yet without supporting evidence, but offered no reason as to why the use of laxatives should produce normal bowel action after the administration of laxatives has ceased. It is suggested that the use of laxatives, together with the advice offered to the parents and child when prescribing the laxatives created conditions for the decay of the aversion reaction and learning of the new pattern of bowel action. The present author's experience with successful treatment of encopresis in adolescents by laxatives in a general medical clinic is consistent with this explanation. The thesis that the child, his parents and their medical advisors should tolerate this sort of unpleasant symptom (Winnicot, 1953) in the interests of the child's overall mental health requires a very powerful defence when relatively simple measures, with a sound basis in theory can be applied. Finally there seems no reason why a psychiatrist should not prescribe a laxative to assist his behavior therapy, nor a paediatrician give advice on training based on learning theory to complete the action of his pills.

Acknowledgments.   The major part of the treatment of these children was carried out by the nursing staff of the Children's Unit, Maudsley Hospital. It would not have been possible without the sustained efforts and enthusiasm and careful record keeping of the charge nurse, Mr. I. Dimmick, R.M.N., S.R.N. and his deputy Mrs. V. Verrell, R.M.N. Thanks are due also

adaptive learning: behavior modification with children

beatrice a. ashem

ernest poser

to Dr. K. Cameron, Physician in charge of the Children's Dept., Maudsley Hospital for permission to study and report on the children in his care. I also wish to thank Dr. S. Rachman of the Institute of Psychiatry for his suggestions on the psychological aspects of this study.

REFERENCES

Anthony, A. (1957) An experimental approach to the psychopathology of childhood: Encopresis. *Brit. J. med. Psychol.* **30**, 146–175.

Coekin, M. & Gairdner, D. (1960) Faecal Incontinence in Children: The physical factor. *Brit. med. J.*, **2**, 1175–1180.

Eysenck, H. J. (1963) Behaviour therapy, extinction and relapse in neurosis. *Brit. J. Psychiat.*, **109**, 12–18.

Ferster, C. B. (1958) Reinforcement and punishment in the control of human behaviour by social agencies. *Psychiat. Res. Rep.*, **10**, 101–118.

Gaston, E. A. (1948) The physiology of faecal continence. *Surg. Gynec. Obstet.*, **87**, 280–290 and 669–678.

Goligher, J. C. & Hughes, E. S. R. (1951) Sensibility of the rectum and colon. Its role in the mechanism of anal continence. *Lancet*, **1**, 543–548.

Gwynne-Jones, H. (1960) Learning and abnormal behaviour, in *Handbook of Abnormal Psychology* (Ed. H. J. Eysenck). Pitman, London.

Keele, C. A. & Neil, E. (1961) Samson Wright's *Applied Physiology*. 3rd Edn. London.

Mowrer, O. H. & Mowrer, W. (1938) Enuresis a method for its study and treatment. *Amer. J. Orthopsychiat.*, **8**, 436–459.

Pinkerton, P. (1958) Psychogenic megacolon in children: The implications of bowel negativism. *Arch. Dis. Childh.*, **33**, 371–380.

Skinner, B. F. (1959) *Cumulative Record*. Appleton-Century-Crofts, New York.

Winnicot, D. W. (1953) Symptom tolerance in paediatrics. *Proc. roy. Soc. Med.*, **46**, 675–684.

Wolpe, J. (1958) *Psychotherapy by Reciprocal Inhibition*. Stanford University Press, Stanford.

Infantile Autism, Childhood Schizophrenia, Organic Dysfunction and Mental Retardation

INTRODUCTION

Severe forms of psychopathology typically manifest themselves in the form of multiple behavior disorders. In these cases it is often difficult to distinguish between primary and secondary deviations and to decide in what order they should be treated. Selection of the most appropriate corrective techniques also presents problems. Resolution of these difficulties depends to a large extent on the adequacy of pre-treatment behavior analyses and subsequent recording of baseline data.

The first three papers in this section describe methods of behavioral analysis whereby the deviant behavior of children with communication deficits can be quantified. While the papers by Lovaas *et al.* and Risley deal with individual cases, that by Martin *et al.* describes a technique applicable in the classroom. An interesting methodological point is made by Risley who takes issue with Lovaas' management of inattentive behavior.

All of these contributions deal with multiple problem behaviors. Frequently, however, the most prominent behavior to be modified concerns some form of speech deficiency. In such instances, baseline observations are more easily obtained and generally focus upon the quantity and level of speech. That is, articulate versus non-articulate sounds, words versus sentences, etc.

Many papers in this section deal with the conditioning of speech because communication disorders are a frequent source of behavior problems in psychotic children. Articles are ordered by level of pathology. Thus studies concerned with the conditioning of imitative responses, motor and verbal, precede the conditioning of normal speech in an echolalic child.

The papers by Metz and McConnell deal with the crucial matter of response generalization in children trained on specific tasks. Timeout from positive reinforcement is discussed by McReynolds who successfully decreased maladaptive vocalizations in a five-year-old brain damaged child in whom other attempts at experimental extinction of non-communicative speech had failed.

An alternative to timeout procedures for the elimination of undesirable behaviors is offered by Sailor *et al.* who used contingent alternation of low and high difficulty verbal tasks to control temper tantrums during experimental sessions. Other papers in this sub-section concern the modification of attentional deficits, speech and repetitive motor responses. The study by Pascal exemplifies the degree of specificity behavior therapists can achieve in making their treatment goals explicit.

The section ends with two papers describing the control of self-destructive behaviors. In one study positive reinforcement is used contingent upon non-destructive responses and in the other self-injurious behavior is counterconditioned by the elicitation of incompatible responses.

Analysis of Behavioral Problems

Experimental Studies in Childhood Schizophrenia: Analysis of Self-Destructive Behavior*†

O. IVAR LOVAAS, GILBERT FREITAG,‡ VIVIAN J. GOLD,

and IRENE C. KASSORLA

University of California, Los Angeles

Abstract: This paper reports on three studies concerned with investigating variables which controlled self-destructive behaviors in a schizophrenic child. The self-destructive behaviors included head- and arm-banging which was usually so intense that the child's skin was discolored, bruised, and swollen.

Methodologically, the experimental procedure followed an intrasubject replication design which involved repeated presentations of the same experimental variables in order to insure reliability.

The results illustrate the lawfulness and regularity which characterized the self-destructive behavior. The data clearly show the functional relationships between very specific environmental operations and the self-destruction: reinforcement and extinction of other behaviors in a given setting controlled the frequency and magnitude of self-destructive behavior, and delivery of sympathetic comments, contingent upon the occurrence of self-destructive behavior, increased its frequency and magnitude.

Conceptually, the system which best fit the observed relationships involves a consideration of self-destructive behavior as learned, operant, or instrumental social behavior.

This paper reports on three studies concerned with investigating variables which controlled the self-destructive behavior of a schizophrenic child. The self-destructive behavior included head- and arm-banging against sharp corners of the furniture. This behavior was usually so intense that the child's skin was discolored, bruised, and swollen.

The self-destructive behavior of this child will be viewed as learned (operant or instrumental) behavior; the strength of self-destructive behavior will be considered functionally related to the presentation and the withdrawal of social reinforcement.

In considering self-destructive behavior as similar to other learned social behaviors, one probably is working with the simplest and most easily testable notion designed to account for such behavior. Most alternative conceptual systems (to be presented subsequently) appear based on mechanisms other than social reinforcement as the explanation of self-destructive behavior. These other mechanisms might center on the assumption that the negatively reinforcing pain-inducing consequences of the behavior outweighs the positively reinforcing consequences from such sources as the social environment might provide, such as sympathy

---

*This study was supported by a grant from the National Institute of Health (M-6241).

†Reprinted from the *Journal of Experimental Child Psychology*, 1965, **2**, 67–84. Copyright 1965 with permission from Academic Press, Inc., and Dr. O. I. Lovaas.

‡Now at Yale University.

or attention. This is not to say that such an assumption excludes the possibility of positively reinforcing consequences, but that such consequences are de-emphasized and subordinated to the role of "secondary"gains.

Conceptualizations involving guilt, and the reduction of guilt consequent upon self-inflicted pain, have become familiar through psychoanalytic writings. Equally familiar notions center on self-destructive behavior as a form of aggression. This aggression, instigated by frustration, is turned against the self, insofar as punishment had previously been associated with outward expression of aggression (Dollard *et al.*, 1939). Somewhat more circumscribed conceptualizations, formulated primarily with young children in mind, consider destructive behavior toward one's own person as serving to establish a "bodily reality" (Freud, 1954) and a "solidification" of the body image (Greenacre, 1954). Similarly, Bychowski (1954), in comparing the head-banging of adult schizophrenics with that of infants, maintains such behaviors are attempts to delimit the "self" from external reality. It has also been argued that aggression might be directed toward one's own person because of a *failure* to distinguish one's self from the external world (Hartmann, Kris & Loewenstein, 1949). Some writers (Levy & Patrick, 1928) have considered head-banging to be autoerotic, hence self-reinforcing. Others (Goldfarb, 1945) consider it to provide compensatory stimulation in otherwise non-stimulated (e.g., institutionalized) children.

Cain (1961) has brought together several observational reports regarding self-destructive behavior in animals and young children. As far as the authors of this study are aware, there appears to be no study in print in which self-destructive behavior has been investigated systematically, i.e., where the investigator has attempted control over self-destruction by systematically manipulating the variables of which it might be a function.

There were three studies in which self-destructive behavior was investigated. Two concerned observation of self-destructive behavior which occurred while appropriate social behaviors were reinforced and subsequently extinguished. The third concerned changes in self-destructive behavior under a variety of conditions.

In all studies, observation centered on one *S*, a nine-year-old schizophrenic girl.[1] It is relevant to know that her history of self-destructive behavior dates back to her third year of life. This behavior was primarily "head-banging" (against walls and furniture, at times with great force), "arm-banging" (against sharp corners), pinching and slapping herself, setting her hair on fire by sticking her head into the electric wall heater, etc. It is also relevant that social approval (smiles, verbal praise, etc.) was a positively reinforcing event to her, a fact which was experimentally established in our laboratory. Her "appropriate" social behaviors were minimal (e.g., her speech was largely echolalic), and she engaged in considerable self-stimulatory behavior (fondling herself, and moving her arms and hands in repetitive, stereotyped manners). Similarly, her interaction with physical objects (play with toys, etc.) was stereotyped and restricted.

All experiments were conducted in sparsely furnished rooms which contained only tables and chairs. Adjoining observation rooms were connected by one-way mirrors and sound equipment which permitted observation and recording of the child's behavior. The *S*'s behavior was recorded on an Esterline Angus pen recorder by equipment and procedures which have been more fully described in an earlier paper (Lovaas *et al.*, 1963). In short, the observer could, with a panel of button-switches, reliably record both the frequency and duration of several behaviors simultaneously.

---

[1]The *S* was diagnosed as schizophrenic, with autistic and symbiotic features, at the Neuropsychiatric Institute and the Psychology Clinic, U.C.L.A., 1962, and had been so diagnosed previously at other clinics in the Los Angeles area.

STUDY 1

The first acquisition.   During this phase of the study, S acquired a repertoire of appropriate behavior to music. The repertoire consisted of clapping her hands and rocking in rhythm with the music, making correct gestures to the songs as were indicated by the words (e.g., "clap your hands"), and saying or singing some words of the songs at appropriate times. Es reinforced this behavior with approval. Smiles and comments such as "that's a good girl" were used. The acquisition was carried out somewhat informally over a two-month interval. No accurate recording was made of the first acquisition.

The first extinction.   The only difference between the extinction and acquisition sessions was that *the reinforcement, social approval, was not given contingent upon any behavior of S.* The S's appropriate musical behavior now ceased to have an effect on Es. However, Es maintained the same amount of friendly behavior, i.e., they smiled continuously and looked pleasant. Each session lasted for ten minutes and occurred once a day, five days a week, for forty-one days. The songs and dance were the same as in the acquisition; the order and duration of their presentation was held constant.

During the music sessions S's behavior in general had been unusually appropriate compared with sessions with S in other settings such as the playroom. The importance of the effect of music per se, relating to the appropriateness of S's behavior, was assessed by omitting the guitar from the music sessions on alternate days. During these sessions the words of the songs were not sung, but spoken. Otherwise conditions were the same as on the days when the guitar was included. Although this operation appears to be irrelevant in understanding the variables involved in this study, mention is made of it since it accounts for certain fluctuations in her behavior. These alternations, of music and no music, occurred only during the first extinction of Study 1.

The second acquisition.   The second acquisition started forty-eight days after termination of the first extinction and lasted for twenty-seven sessions. A new set of three songs and a dance were employed. Singing with the guitar (i.e., music) was present on every session. Whenever S emitted appropriate music behavior, she was again socially reinforced with verbal comments and smiles.

In other respects the sessions were the same as during the extinction; they lasted for ten minutes and occurred once a day, five days a week. The Es were pleasant and smiling, etc.

The second extinction.   The second extinction lasted for five sessions and was identical to the first extinction except that music was present each time.

In short, the first step consisted of reinforcing S for appropriate behaviors in the music sessions with social approval. The second step consisted of withholding social approval for these behaviors. The third and fourth steps were replications of the first and second, respectively.

Starting with the first extinction, an observer in the adjoining room recorded the following behaviors of S:

1. *Appropriate Music Behavior* was defined as clapping hands or rocking in time to the music; singing or saying the words to the songs at the correct time (as they appeared in the lyrics and were sung or spoken by the Es); making suitable gestures in conjunction with parts of the songs (such as wiggling the body during the phrase, "the children in the bus go 'wiggle-wiggle-wiggle'").

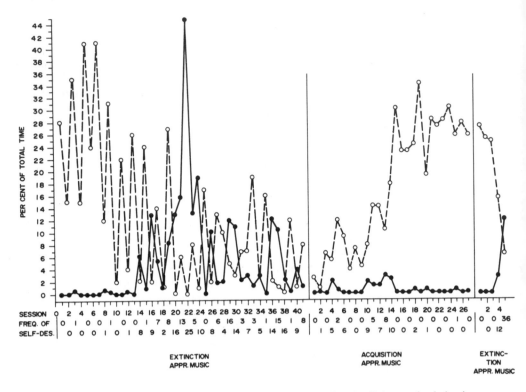

Fig. 1. Percentage of appropriate music behavior (O---O) and self-destructive behavior (●———●) over sessions where attention and approval were removed (Extinction 1 and 2) and presented (Acquisition 2) for appropriate music behavior. Frequency of self-destructive behaviors in the various sessions are given immediately below session numbers on the abscissa. Music was present on even numbered sessions (Extinction 1).

2. *Self-Destructive Behavior* was defined as hitting head, elbows, wrists, or other parts of the body against the wall, sharp corners of the furniture, the light switch, etc.

When *S* initiated any one of the defined behaviors, the observer pressed the button on the operating panel assigned to that behavior. The button was pressed at the time the behavior occurred and was kept down until the behavior terminated. If more than two seconds separated two responses (e.g., two words, or two-head-bangs) these were recorded as separate responses. In this way, the apparatus kept a running account of both frequency and duration of each behavior.

Results of Study 1

The data from Study 1 are presented in Fig. 1. The abscissa gives the sessions, numbered from the first extinction; the ordinate gives the percentage of total session time *S* engaged in the two behaviors, self-destructive and appropriate music behavior. The frequencies of self-destructive behaviors over the various sessions are given directly below the session numbers on the abscissa.

The percentage of appropriate music behavior alternated from high to low from one session to the next, the alternations becoming less marked by the twenty-eighth session. These alternations correlate with and probably are a function of the presence and absence of music (music was present on even-numbered sessions). These noticeable alternations in the record, if considered a function of music per se, are irrelevant in understanding the main variables involved in this study.

The first extinction (reinforcement withheld for appropriate music behavior) is accompanied by an initial increase in appropriate music behavior. By the seventh session, however, this behavior decreased. On the other hand, self-destructive behavior, which stayed at almost zero level during the first part of the extinction, increased. By the twentieth session the percentage of self-destructive behavior exceeded that of appropriate music behavior, and by the twenty-second session reached the level previously attained by appropriate music behavior. Self-destructive behavior then decreased. From the twenty-fifth session on, very systematic alternations of the relative magnitude of the two behaviors occurred. On days when self-destructive behavior was high, appropriate music behavior was low, and vice versa. It is to be noted that there was no correlation between the amount of self-destructive behavior in the music room and other places such as the playroom or home. In fact, on the day of the twenty-second session, when she peaked on self-destructive behavior, S had no self-destructive behavior in any other setting. So far as Es know, S was not treated differently, in the clinic or the home, on the days when she was self-destructive in the music room as compared with other days. It is concluded, therefore, that variations in her self-destructive behavior were due to the experimental manipulations.

The second acquisition (reinforcement delivered for appropriate music behavior) showed a gradual increase in appropriate music behavior over the twenty-seven sessions, while self-destructive behavior decreased to a near-zero level. The sudden drop in self-destructive behavior during the second acquisition was probably due to the introduction of a new set of songs and dances (which had not been associated with reinforcement withdrawal). A further discussion of this point will be presented in Study 3, when a similar reduction was observed.

The second extinction (reinforcement withheld for appropriate music behavior) showed a relatively rapid decrease in appropriate music behaviors, accompanied by a similarly rapid increase in self-destructive behaviors. By the fifth session the percentage of self-destructive behaviors exceeded appropriate music behavior. The study was terminated at that point so as to prevent S from further self-inflicted damage.

In summary, then, the data indicate that the occurrence and magnitude of self-destructive behavior is a function of the reinforcement and subsequent extinction of another behavior in that same situation. The data also show that when one of these behaviors is high, the other is low, the behaviors systematically alternating in relative magnitude. The inference that the two behaviors are members of the same response class, i.e., that they are both social responses or responses controlled by social stimuli, will be discussed after additional data are examined.

STUDY 2

A replication of Study 1, involving acquisition and extinction of another social response, was made with the same S in another experimental setting. The S was brought into another room, similar to the one in Study 1. Study 2 was initiated immediately after the completion of Study 3, but is presented here because of its similarity to Study 1. On a table was a bar-pressing apparatus which consisted of a wooden box, about one foot on a side, with a six-inch

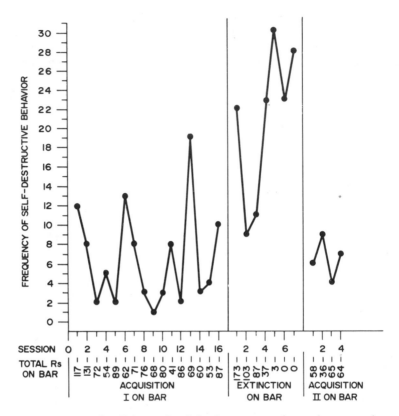

Fig. 2. Frequency of self-destructive behavior over sessions where attention and approval were presented (Acquisition 1 and 2) and removed (Extinction 1) for bar-pressing behavior. Frequency of bar-pressing in the various sessions is given immediately below session numbers on the abscissa.

bar extending in front. The bar-pressing apparatus was placed on a table between E and S, who were both seated on opposite sides of the table facing each other.

When S first entered the room, she was told by E to press the bar, and praised when she did so. After this initial prompted response, E maintained an inattentive position, i.e., looking down in her lap and not conversing, unless S pressed the bar. When S did press the bar, E would look up at S, smile, and provide five seconds of "pleasant talk": "That's a good girl; I love you very much; you are a sweetheart"; etc. The E would then resume her original inattentive position until S again pressed the bar. With a stable and high rate of bar-pressing, it was possible for S to keep E delivering attention and approval at a continuous, almost non-interrupted level. The sessions had lasted for ten minutes daily, five days a week, for thirty days. Since S reached a relatively stable rate of responding by the fourteenth day, only the last sixteen days of this training will be presented (in Fig. 2).

Once a steady rate of bar-pressing had been acquired, extinction began. The E no longer attended to S contingent upon bar-press responses, but remained in an inattentive position throughout the sessions. The extinction for bar-pressing behavior lasted for seven days. The end of these seven extinction sessions was followed by a second acquisition period, with E reintroducing attention and approval contingent upon S's bar-press for another four days.

Each response on the bar activated a cumulative recorder located in an adjacent observation room. The observer in this room kept recordings of S's self-destructive behavior in the same manner as in Study 1.

Results of Study 2

The data of Study 2 are presented in Fig. 2. The abscissa gives the acquisition and extinction sessions. The ordinate gives the frequency of self-destructive behaviors during the ten-minute session. (Since there was a high correlation between frequency and duration of self-destructive behaviors (*see* Study 1, Fig. 1), and in order to avoid the time-consuming task of deriving the duration measures, only frequency of self-destructive behavior will be presented in Studies 2 and 3.) Total numbers of bar-pressings for the social reinforcer over the various sessions are presented on the abscissa, immediately below the session numbers.

As can be observed, extinction of the bar-pressing response shows an immediate increase in frequency of that response which is accompanied by an increase in self-destructive behavior over the level maintained while the bar-press was reinforced. The figure also shows a decrease in self-destructive behavior and reinstatement of the bar-pressing response upon reintroduction of reinforcement for bar-pressing (the second acquisition).

The E considered it unnecessary to repeat the extinction operations for the bar-press in lieu of the similarity of these data to Study 1. A further consideration for termination of the study at this time was based on protecting S from additional self-inflicted injury.

In summary, Study 2 supports the findings of Study 1. Frequency of self-destructive behavior appears to be a function of the presentation and withdrawal of reinforcement for other behaviors in the same situation. The behaviors alternate in relative magnitude with the alternation of conditions of reinforcement for the other response.

STUDY 3

This study was undertaken to investigate the effect of three variables involved in self-destructive behavior. First, an attempt was made to investigate the effect of verbal comments made contingent upon S's self-destructive behavior. The question asked was whether or not this kind of social consequence would change the frequency of that behavior. To test this effect, the comment "I don't think you are bad" was expressed by E in an emphatic and reassuring manner after S engaged in self-destructive behavior. The rationale underlying the choice of this comment rather than any other comment will be discussed later. Second, an attempt was made to investigate the effect upon S's self-destructive behavior of E's "ignoring" her. To test the effect of ignoring, Es would not smile and attend to S for the duration of entire sessions. Third, an attempt was made to investigate the effect upon self-destruction of a change in the particular stimulus events which had been associated with reinforcement withdrawal. The concern here was the extent to which the songs with which withdrawal of reinforcement had been associated in the recent past (within the last month) had acquired stimulus control over the occurrence of self-destructive behavior in the music situation. In order to accomplish this test, a set of new songs with which S had had no previous reinforcement history (hence no history of reinforcement withdrawal) was introduced.

The experimental design consisted of introducing these experimental variables, i.e., comments, "ignoring," and new songs, during certain sessions (experimental sessions), interspersed with sessions when no experimental variables were introduced (control sessions). The criterion for alternations of these sessions was that S's self-destructive behavior in control sessions should fall within the level of the pre-experimental sessions before the experimental variables were introduced. Essentially, then, the pattern follows a single subject, "baseline" design.

Study 3 took place in the same room as Study 1. Study 3 was started immediately after the completion of Study 1 and before the initiation of Study 2. Except for the experimental variables the procedure was identical to that of the *second extinction* of Study 1: *S* was not reinforced for appropriate music behavior, Es maintained friendly and attentive behavior throughout, the sessions lasted for ten minutes, *S*'s behavior was recorded in the same manner, etc.

The experimental variables became distributed over the sessions in the following manner: (1) The comment "I don't think you're bad" followed every self-destructive response during Sessions 16 through 19 (FR:1). During Sessions 20, 24, 25, 26, 33, and 38 a comment was made on the average of every 5th self-destructive response (VR:5). No comments were given during the remaining sessions. (2) During Sessions 30–38, Es, who had been smiling and attentive to *S* throughout the sessions, did not smile and became inattentive. During Sessions 33 and 38, E smiled and attended to *S* only while commenting, and continued to "ignore" when not commenting. (3) On Sessions 44, 46, and 48, Es introduced a set of new nursery school songs with which *S* had had no prior experience and therefore no history of reinforcement withdrawal. All other sessions (1–15, 21–23, 27–29, 39–43, 45, 47) were control, or "baseline" sessions. The experimental operations are given in Fig. 3 to facilitate their presentation.

Results of Study 3

The data are presented in Fig. 3. The abscissa indicates the various experimental manipulations in abbreviated form below their respective sessions. The ordinate gives the frequency of self-destructive behaviors in the ten-minute music session.

Effect of the comment.   Examination of the frequency of self-destructive behaviors on the sessions where E commented upon that behavior (Sessions 16–20, 24–26, 33, 38) shows a definite increase in the behavior over the frequency of self-destruction on control days. This increase is attributed to the comments, i.e., the comments served to increase the frequency of *S*'s self-destructive behavior. No attempt was made to separately evaluate the effect of the two schedules of comment delivery.

Effect of attention and smile withdrawal.   There was no change in self-destructive behavior when E's smiles and attention were withdrawn from the sessions (Sessions 30–37). Self-destructive behavior was not effected by a change in E's smiles and attention per se: "ignoring" when presented continuously during a session did not increase self-destructive behavior. However, these same social stimuli presented and withdrawn *in relationship to S's behavior* did effect self-destruction, i.e., the presentation and removal of smiles and attention, contingent upon appropriate music behavior, effected her self-destructive behavior (*see* Studies 1 and 2). Similarly, the comment, which involved attention and smiles, when delivered contingent upon her self-destructive behavior, altered that behavior. It is possible that the withdrawal of smiles and attention functioned as a deprivation operation, thereby increasing the effectiveness of such stimuli as reinforcers. This operation might account for the peak in self-destructive behaviors in Session 33 when they are again presented contingent upon that behavior.

Effect of the new songs.   During Sessions 44, 46, and 48, when new songs were introduced, the level of self-destructive behavior fell to zero or near-zero level. A similar drop in self-destructive behavior with the introduction of new songs was observed during the second

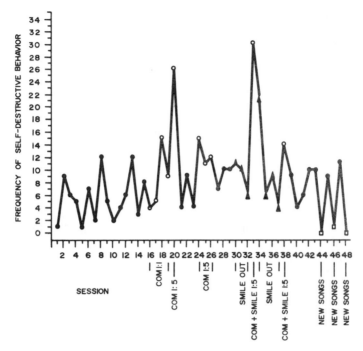

Fig. 3. Frequency of self-destructive behavior over sessions when E commented (○) upon that behavior (16–19, 20, 24–26, 33, 38), when Es withdrew smiles and attention (▲) from entire sessions (30–38), and when new songs were introduced (□) (44, 46, 48). All other sessions were control sessions (●).

acquisition in Study 1. In the case of the new songs *S* does not have a history of reinforcement-withdrawal since reinforcement had not been delivered previously. Thus, *S*'s self-destructive behavior appears to be functionally related to the kinds of history she has had with the stimulus situation presented to her.

The data of Study 3 can be summarized by saying that (1) the effect of verbal comments contingent upon self-destruction served to increase the frequency of that behavior, (2) the effect of ignoring per se was not enough to produce any changes in self-destructive behavior (although the same operation, in specific behavioral contingencies, was effective), and (3) the removal of a stimulus previously associated with reinforcement withdrawal decreases the frequency of self-destructive behavior.

DISCUSSION

The results illustrate the lawfulness and regularity which characterize the self-destructive behavior of this child. The data show the functional relationships between very specific environmental operations and the self-destruction: reinforcement and extinction of other behaviors in a given setting controls the frequency and magnitude of self-destructive behavior; delivery of social reinforcement contingent upon the occurrence of self-destructive behavior increases its frequency and magnitude. The data also show a systematic reversal of self-destructive responses with appropriate social behaviors which argues for their membership in the same response class, as social behaviors. Conceptually, the system which best fits these functional relationships involves a consideration of self-destructive behavior as learned, operant, or instrumental behavior. An attempt will be made to relate the behavioral observations as evidenced in this study to this system.

The occurrence of operant behavior is controlled by two kinds of stimuli, discriminative and reinforcing. We shall label those stimuli discriminative which "set the occasion" for self-destructive behavior because they signalled reinforcement for such behavior. In other words, they "cued" the self-destructive behavior. A stimulus is called a reinforcing stimulus when, produced by self-destructive behavior, it strengthens that behavior. In a sense, it served as a "reward" or "pay-off" for that behavior. Since both of these kinds of stimuli were social (i.e., provided by another person), the self-destructive behavior will be labelled as social behavior. The two kinds of control (reinforcing and discriminative) over the self-destructive behavior will be discussed separately.

Reinforcement control.   The effect of social reinforcement upon self-destructive behavior is shown in Study 3. A social event ("I don't think you are bad"), when delivered contingent upon self-destructive behavior, increases the frequency of that behavior. By definition, then, the comment serves as a social reinforcer, and the behavior follows the laws of operant behavior. No attempt was made to analyze the particular stimulus aspect which was reinforcing in this comment, but Es consider it reasonable to expect that almost any comment, delivering attention, would have had a similar effect.

The reinforcement control is also apparent when reinforcement is withheld for the self-destructive behavior, in which case the self-destructive behavior should decrease in strength, as did appropriate music behavior. The first extinction of Study 1 shows this effect – the self-destructive behavior was "cued off" by the reinforcement withdrawal, but since self-destructive behavior is not reinforced, it decreases in strength and thereby has the form of operant behavior. In the last part of the first extinction the two behaviors (appropriate music and self-destruction) alternate in relative magnitude from one session to another. In a sense, the two behaviors compete for social reinforcement. They have the same history of nonreinforcement in this particular setting, hence they have about equal (and low) probability of occurrence, or strength. The self-destructive behavior appears, then, to have the same relationships to consequential environmental events as does appropriate music behavior.

Discriminative stimulus control.   The discriminative stimulus control over self-destructive behavior is evident in the sudden reduction of this behavior to zero level when the new stimuli (songs) were introduced. Conceptually, the new songs were not discriminative for self-destruction. The argument supporting this statement would be based on the different reinforcement history S has had with the two sets of songs. The old songs have been associated with withdrawal of reinforcement for appropriate musical behavior. The new songs have not been associated with reinforcement withdrawal, since no reinforcement had been given for music behavior appropriate to these songs. Thus, introduction of new songs reduced self-destructive behavior rather than maintaining it at the level at which it occurred in the presence of the old songs. It is considered, therefore, that withdrawal of reinforcement *from a previously reinforced response* is the discriminative stimulus for self-destructive behavior. The establishment of this event as discriminative for self-destruction would indicate that in the past this event has signalled reinstatement of reinforcement, should S behave self-destructively. In popular terms, it can be said that, whenever reinforcement was withheld (as in a demand situation), S could obtain reinforcement (the demand would be withdrawn and reinforcement produced) provided she hurt herself. This self-destruction, therefore, had an immediate "pay-off," the reinstatement of the desired reinforcement.

The same kind of discriminative stimulus control is present in Studies 1 and 2, the effects shown particularly well in Study 2. When a response (appropriate music behavior) fails to bring reinforcement during extinction as it has previously during acquisition, this marks the occasion for S to engage in self-destructive behavior, i.e., the self-destructive behaviors in Studies 1 and 2 were controlled by reinforcement withdrawal for another response, namely the appropriate music behavior to the songs.

Theoretically, the operation of withholding reinforcement should be discriminative for any response which could serve to "reinstate" the reinforcement, and not only for self-destructive behavior. Both in Studies 1 (first extinction) and 2 (extinction), the withdrawal of reinforcement is accompanied by an increase in the magnitude of the response being extinguished (music behavior and bar-press) before the increase of self-destructive behavior occurs. We also observed, but were unable to replicate, an increase in appropriate and acceptable verbal behavior during the first seven days of Study 1 (first extinction). From a reinforcement theory point of view, the withholding of reinforcement is discriminative for a number of behaviors, some more socially acceptable than others. One might state that when a response, previously effective in bringing about reinforcement, ceases to bring on these effects, this signals the person to either increase the magnitude of this same behavior or to switch to some other behavior, however acceptable, which in the past has been operative in obtaining reinforcement. Predicting what specific responses will be emitted, and at what times, involves a detailed knowledge of the person's past reinforcement history, which most often is unavailable. It can be considered that S exhausted her repertoire of social behavior in a hierarchal manner during the extinction sessions: the first behaviors to appear and the first to extinguish were those most recently acquired in the laboratory (e.g., appropriate music behavior, bar-pressing, appropriate verbal behavior), and the last behaviors to appear and the last to extinguish were those brought into the laboratory from home and other situations (e.g., self-destructive behaviors).

Further support for discriminative stimulus control is given by two additional considerations which show how highly discriminating S was in the very specific times and explicit circumstances during which she was self-destructive. A physically rather gross operation, such as Es' removal of smiles and attention from entire Sessions 30–37 of Study 3, did not alter S's behavior. Yet the removal of attention and smiles *for responding* in Study 1, an operation which was physically so small that a casual observer would not have been able to discern it in Es' behavior, did produce major changes in S's behavior.

A second observation, this time in another setting, supports the notion of S's ability to discriminate the highly specific circumstances in which to be self-destructive. The day of Session 22 of the first extinction in Study 1, when she peaked on self-destruction in the music room, was her "best" day in another setting, the preschool room. Concurrent recordings of her acceptable social behaviors in the preschool room, to which she returned immediately following the music sessions, show a steady rise in these behaviors, completely unrelated to her self-destructive behavior in the music room.

The data, then, support the notion of very specific environmental control over her self-destruction rather than control from internal "states" (such as guilt and "hostile introjects"). A discussion of the effects of the comment "I do not think you are bad" is particularly related to this point. The choice of the comment was made after consulting several professional people, who in agreement, concluded S's self-destructive behavior to be a function of internal states, predominantly guilt. The comment, they hypothesized, might reduce her self-destruction by reducing her guilt-level (or the magnitude of the "hostile introject"). It was shown in Study 3 that, on the contrary, this comment, when made contingent upon self-destructive behavior, increased such behavior. According to the considerations already mentioned in this paper, *any* verbal response by E delivering attention contingent upon self-destructive behavior would serve to positively reinforce that behavior. An implication of this finding is that when one responds to a patient — even with a minor comment to a "socially insulated" (i.e., autistic) child — one may cause considerable harm rather than good, unless one is aware of several possible stimulus aspects of one's response and their *temporal relationships* to the patient's behavior.

Although the findings in these studies indicate that social stimuli controlled the self-destructive behavior, we have no evidence that *only* social stimuli control self-destruction. Furthermore, the authors do not intend the data, presented here on a single child, to be explanatory of self-destructive behavior in children in general. Rather, the findings demonstrate a phenomenon (certain reliable relationships between self-destructive behavior and social stimuli), but its generality over Ss have not been established. However, the findings we have presented are consistent with those obtained by other investigators. In Cain's descriptions (1961, pp. 183–185) of self-destructive behaviors in children, almost every instigation to self-destruction appears to involve reinforcement withdrawal: "... when things 'went wrong' ... whenever he was cross ... when isolated ... put in crib against her wishes ... thwarted in any way ... touch a toy in her possession ... not get his own way ... not allowed to go out ..." etc. Although there are no studies in which self-destructive behavior has been systematically reinforced, several studies report extinction of self-destructive behavior when social stimuli have been withheld contingent upon such behavior. For example, Wolf *et al.* (1963) extinguished self-destructive behavior in a six-year-old autistic boy by isolating him from interpersonal contact whenever he was self-destructive. In a similar manner, Ball *et al.* (1964) reduced self-destructive behavior in a twelve-year-old psychotic retarded boy. His self-destruction had been so severe and prolonged that it had necessitated physical restraints (both arms and feet) for twenty-four hours a day, for most of the seven years he had been hospitalized. Williams (1959) also reports extinction in the case of children's tantrum behavior.

Although self-destructive behavior will extinguish, or at least reach very low magnitudes when not reinforced, this is a slow procedure requiring several sessions or days. Furthermore, in placing the child on extinction, E temporarily exposes the child to danger because of the apparent increase in self-destruction immediately accompanying the onset of extinction. To overcome these problems of the slow extinction and the temporary danger to the child, Lovaas *et al.* (1964) delivered painful electric shock contingent upon such behaviors with two children who engaged in self-destructive (and tantrum) behaviors. The behaviors were suppressed within minutes, and remained suppressed for eleven months. One noncontingent shock re-suppressed the behavior for the remainder of the study (several months).

The beneficial effect of suppressing and/or extinguishing self-destructive behavior is probably obvious — when one is attempting to educate these children one invariably places demands on the child, i.e., reinforcement is withheld until the desired response is emitted. Ensuing tantrum and self-destructive behaviors of the child not only retard educational efforts of others, but interferes with the likelihood that the desired response would be emitted.

REFERENCES

Ball, T. S., Dameron, L. E. & Lovaas, O. I. Control of self-destructive behaviors in mentally retarded children. (Unpublished manuscript, 1964.)

Bychowski, G. Problems of infantile neurosis: a discussion. In: *The psychoanalytic study of the child.* Vol. IX. New York: International Universities Press, Inc., 1954.

Cain, A. C. The presuperego turning inward of aggression. *Psychoanal. Quart.* 1961, **30**, 171–208.

Dollard, J., Doob, L. W., Miller, N. E., Mowrer, O. H. & Sears, R. R. *Frustration and aggression.* New Haven: Yale University Press, 1939.

Freud, A. Problems of infantile neurosis: a discussion. In: *The psychoanalytic study of the child.* Vol. IX. New York: International Universities Press, Inc., 1954.

Goldfarb, W. Psychological privation in infancy. *Amer. J. Orthopsychiat.*, 1945, **15,** 247–255.

Greenacre, P. Problems of infantile neurosis: a discussion. In *The psychoanalytic study of the child.* Vol. IX. New York: International Universities Press, Inc., 1954.

Hartmann, H., Kris, E. & Loewenstein, R. M. Notes on the theory of aggression. In *The psychoanalytic study of the child.* Vol. III–IV. New York: International Universities Press, Inc., 1949.

Levy, D. M. & Patrick, H. T. Relations of infantile convulsions and head-banging to fainting and headache in parents. *Arch. Neurol. Psychiat.*, 1928, **19,** 864–887.

Lovaas, O. I., Freitag, G., Gold, V. J. & Kassorla, I. C. A recording method and observations of behaviors of normal and autistic children in free play settings. Paper delivered to Society for Research in Child Development, Berkeley, California, April, 1963.

Lovaas, O. I., Freitag, G., Kinder, M. I., Rubenstein, D. B., Schaeffer, B. & Simmons, J. B. Experimental studies in childhood schizophrenia. Developing social behavior using electric shock. Paper read at American Psychological Association meetings, Los Angeles, September, 1964.

Williams, C. D. The elimination of tantrum behaviors by extinction procedures. *J. abnorm. soc. Psychol.*, 1959, **59,** 269.

Wolf, M., Mees, H. & Risley, T. Application of operant conditioning procedures to the behavior problems of an autistic child. Paper delivered to Western Psychological Association. Santa Monica, California, May, 1963.

Operant Conditioning of Kindergarten-Class Behavior in Autistic Children*†

G. L. MARTIN, G. ENGLAND, E. KAPROWY, K. KILGOUR and V. PILEK

St. Paul's College, University of Manitoba, Winnipeg, Manitoba, Canada

Abstract: This paper describes the procedures used to condition classroom behavior in autistic children. Beginning with a one-to-one S: E(S:E) ratio, in a small barren room, tokens were established as reinforcers, tantrum behavior was extinguished, Ss were conditioned to mimic words when prompted, and to identify several objects. During the next three months: (1) the location for daily sessions was changed to a typical elementary-school classroom; (2) new tasks were introduced; and (3) the S:E ratio was increased to 7:1 for some of the tasks.

A departure in procedure from that of Dr. Lovaas (as described in the film, Reinforcement Therapy, 1966) is discussed.

INTRODUCTION

It has become increasingly clear that the application of operant conditioning techniques can lead to dramatic improvement in the behavior of autistic children (Wolf *et al.*, 1964; Lovaas & Simmons, 1965; Metz, 1965; Marshall, 1966; Lovaas *et al.*, 1967; Risley & Wolf, 1967; Wolf & Risley, 1967). In these experiments, techniques were utilized when the S:E ratio was 1:1. The present research explores procedures whereby the S:E ratio can be increased beyond 1:1. More specifically, the initial goal of the research reported here was to train ten autistic children to function as a group in a kindergarten class under the supervision of one teacher.

To achieve this goal, college students, schooled in operant conditioning, worked with the students for three hours a day, five days a week, for a total of sixty sessions. Desired behavior from the students was reinforced with tokens (poker chips) that were backed up with reinforcing events on a 5:1 ratio. The back-up reinforcers consisted of the S's breakfast or noon meal dispensed in small amounts, candy, salty items like potato chips or pretzels, and small amounts of soft drink.

The plan was to develop the desired behavior of sitting quietly in a desk, echoing sounds and words when prompted, emitting appropriate words to objects, tracing and copying, and identifying objects that are alike (match-to-sample). After this behavior was developed in a one-to-one situation, the pupil-teacher ratio was to be slowly increased.

This plan was followed and the procedures proved to be effective in varying degrees for seven of the ten Ss. The procedures employed and the results obtained with these seven Ss

*The research reported here was part of a summer research project conducted at The Manitoba Training School, Portage la Prairie, Manitoba. Grateful acknowledgment is due to Dr. Lowther, Medical Superintendent, Mr W. Bembridge, Director of Education, and the staff at this institution for their excellent cooperation.

†Reprinted from *Behaviour Research and Therapy*, 1968, **6**, 281–294. Copyright 1968 with permission from Pergamon Press Publishing Company and Garry L. Martin.

are described in more detail in the following pages. The remaining three *S*s emitted virtually no recognizable words to objects and would not mimic any word presented to them, rather they emitted only a few sounds and grunts. Consequently, the sessions with these *S*s were spent entirely on language training and the results obtained with these *S*s will be reported in a separate paper.

SUBJECTS

The *S*s were chosen primarily because of their availability and their diagnosis of "Infantile Autism." They varied in age from eight to thirteen. According to hospital records, all subjects were considered untestable regarding IQ, and were observed to display typical defining features of autism, namely, withdrawal, self-stimulation (such as constant rocking back and forth), and little or no verbal behavior. In order to facilitate presentation, the progress of one subject, Peter, will be described in detail. Reference will occasionally be made to other *S*s where their progress deviated greatly from Peter's.

Peter was ten years old when the project began. He is the son of middle, socio-economic class parents and has three normal siblings. He was reportedly delayed in such areas of development as walking and toilet training. Peter attended speech therapy, play therapy, and occupational therapy at the Saskatchewan Training School, with no success. His hospital records indicate that in 1963, 1964 and 1966, no estimate of his IQ or level of functioning could be obtained due to extreme withdrawal.

In addition to the information from the hospital records, direct observation of Peter in a variety of situations over a five-day period revealed the following: regarding verbal behavior, Peter had an extensive echoic or mimicking repertoire, and would mimic the name of most clothing, toys, and food items. Peter would often reply to a question by mimicking the last word in the question. For example, to the question, "What is your name?", Peter replied "Name." However, his verbal behavior was not under object or stimulus control. The subject was presented with a large number of objects and for each item asked, "What's this?". Peter emitted the correct response *only* to a toy ball.

Regarding social behavior, Peter did not interact with the other children on the ward. When approached by an adult, he often initiated a tantrum (varying from mild to severe) which was invariably accompanied by his pointing to his arm or some other part of his anatomy, and saying, "cut," "needle," "Doctor," in varying combinations. Our initial observations and later manipulations indicated that his bizarre tantrum behavior was maintained by the attention given it by the nurses and other adults.

GENERAL PROCEDURE

The sessions were conducted in rooms of the school department of The Manitoba Training School. Sessions for each *S* were conducted for one and a half hours in the morning and one and a half hours in the afternoon, each period having a fifteen-minute recess. The reinforcers consisted primarily of the *S*'s breakfast (a cereal such as Sugar Pops) in the morning, and the *S*'s lunch (a cold plate) in the afternoon, each dispensed in small amounts. If these were depleted, other edibles were used.

The *S*:E ratios and the room location progressed through three major stages.

1. Week 1: Sessions were conducted in a small room (12 × 8ft) in which were located three tablet-arm chair desks, and three chairs. Two or three Es, at the same time, worked with *S*s on a 1:1 *S*:E ratio. Each chair desk was pushed against a wall in such a

fashion as to make it difficult for the S to leave the desk. Sessions were concerned with eliminating tantrums, token training, conditioning the S to sit quietly, and verbal training.

2. Weeks 2–6: For each S, the morning sessions were conducted in the small room and the afternoon sessions were conducted in the regular Grade One classroom.

   a. During Week 2, the S:E ratio in both the small room and the classroom remained at 1:1, and the number of Ss dealt with at any one time in the classroom, as well as the small room, was never more than three. Since the Ss had adapted to the presence of each other during the first week in the small room, and since the desks in the classroom were initially arranged so as to prevent Ss from getting up, the transition from the small room to the classroom for the afternoon sessions was accomplished with a minimum of disturbance to the Ss.

   b. From Weeks 3–6 in the classroom, the desks were gradually shifted to positions approximating the normal classroom, and the number of Ss in the classroom at any one time was gradually increased to seven.

   During this period the S:E ratio was gradually increased for some tasks in the classroom. The S:E ratios are presented in Table 1.

3. Weeks 7–12: Beginning the seventh week, each session began with all Ss sitting quietly in the Grade One classroom. For the first thirty minutes, the Ss received verbal training on a 7:1 ratio. Some of the Ss were then sent to an adjoining classroom for thirty-minute sessions on either matching, tracing or copying training. In the adjoining room,

Table 1. Subject: Experimenter $(S:E)$ ratios.*

		Types of training	
Weeks	Verbal tracing	Copying	Matching
1	1:1		
2	2:1		
3	2:1	1:1	
4	3:1	1:1	Peter:1	1:1
5	3:1	Peter and Kenny:1	Peter:1	1:1
6	5:1	Peter and Kenny:1	Peter:1	1:1
7	7:1	Peter, Kenny and Grant:1	Peter:1; Grant:1	Peter and Grant:1
8	7:1	Peter, Kenny and Grant:1	Peter:1; Grant:1	Peter and Grant:1
9	7:1	Peter, Kenny, Grant and Roger:1	Peter and Grant:1	Peter, Grant and Kenny:1
10	7:1	Peter, Kenny, Grant and Roger:1	Peter and Grant:1	Peter, Grant, Kenny and Roger:1
11	7:1	Peter, Kenny, Grant and Roger:1	Peter and Grant:1	Peter, Grant, Kenny and Roger:1
12	7:1	Peter, Kenny, Grant and Roger:1	Peter and Grant:1	Peter, Grant, Kenny and Roger:1

*A number as numerator in the $S:E$ ratio indicates that all Ss participated at that ratio. Where S's names are cited, the ratio applies only for the Ss cited, and the other Ss remained on a 1:1 ratio. No entry in the table means that the training had not yet begun.

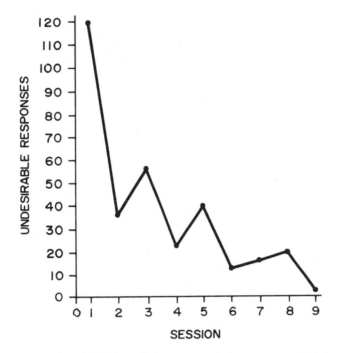

Fig. 1. Extinction of undesirable verbal responses during tantrums. Each instance of Peter's "cut," "needle," or "doctor" was counted as an undesirable response. Each dot represents the number of undesirable responses in a session.

the S:E ratio for these sessions varied with individual subjects as described in Table 1. Subjects remaining in the classroom were instructed as a group by one E on verbal tasks and commands.

SPECIFIC PROCEDURES AND RESULTS

Initial Behavior Problems

The main problem encountered was the frequent occurrence of tantrums. With Peter, these tantrums were consistently accompanied by his saying, "Cut, needle, doctor," and pointing to some part of his anatomy. When such a tantrum occurred, Peter was completely ignored until the tantrum ceased and a brief period of sitting quietly occurred, at which time Peter was reinforced with a "Good boy!" and a token. Figure 1 shows the gradual reduction of the undesirable verbal responses over the first nine sessions, as a consequence of the extinction procedure. The occurrence of either "cut," "needle," or "doctor," was counted as one response. A tantrum consisted of several such responses as well as crying, whining, and face-slapping. The frequency of tantrums during the first nine sessions would therefore be somewhat less than the frequency of the verbal responses as described in Fig. 1.

After the ninth session, this behavior dwindled to around zero. Peter still emitted the occasional "cut" or "doctor," but not more often than once every three or four sessions. The nurses reported that the behavior also decreased on the ward, although not to zero.

The persistence of this behavior on the ward appeared to be a function of the occasional reinforcement given it by visitors and nurses who were not familiar with the programme.

Three of the remaining Ss also emitted frequent tantrums and instances of whining and crying. These were handled by extinction and the extinction curves were comparable to Peter's.

Occasionally, undesired responses by the S necessitated the use of punishment. One such example was the severe tantrum behavior of a subject named Kenny. On nine different occasions during the initial five-day observation period, Kenny emitted severe tantrum behavior, a part of which was biting his own hand and/or beating his head against that of another child. In either case, a consistent consequence was the attention of a nurse, either to prevent Kenny from biting his hand or to stop him beating the other child.

In order to prevent injury to the other children, the head-beating was consistently punished by the experimenter by a sharp slap and the removal of Kenny from the vicinity of the other child. If Kenny bit his hands, the E simply held Kenny's hands behind his (Kenny's) back. After four weeks of these procedures, the head-beating tantrums had decreased to approximately one a week, but the hand-biting had decreased only slightly. Therefore, the E continued to punish the head-beating, but proceeded to ignore the hand-biting tantrums, even though Kenny occasionally drew blood. By the third week of this procedure (the 7th week in all), the hand-biting had also decreased to approximately once a week. Both types of tantrums persisted at this low level in the classroom for the duration of the programme. As with Peter's "cut," "needle," "doctor," however, Kenny's tantrums continued to occur on the ward, where they were frequently followed by much attention and concern from the nurses.

Token Training

Token reinforcers are tangible objects which, in and of themselves, have no reinforcing power. They acquire their reinforcing efficacy via appropriate pairings with other reinforcing events. The effectiveness of token systems was demonstrated in laboratory studies by Staats *et al.* (1962); and by Heid (1964); and their efficacy with retarded children was demonstrated by Birnbrauer *et al.* (1965); and by Birnbrauer, Wolf, Kidder & Tague (1965). Therefore, the direct investigation of the relative importance of the use of tokens (vs. no tokens) was not a feature of this programme.

Procedure

In order to develop the tokens as reinforcers for the children, the student experimenters were given the following instructions:

Require the child to sit in the desk, placing the desk against the wall so that the child cannot get up and walk around.

Set a token on the desk in front of the child, hold out your hand, and say, "Give me the chip."

  a. If the child places the chip in your hand, then smile, say, "Good Boy!", and give him a bite of food.
  b. If the child retains the chip, repeat the instructions, and hold out your hand for five seconds. Then take the chip, ignore the child for fifteen seconds, and repeat (a).
  c. If the child throws the chip, say, "No!" sharply, slap his fingers, and ignore him for two minutes. Then repeat the procedure.
  d. If the child cries or whines or emits other tantrum behavior, ignore him until the undesirable behavior ceases and a brief period of sitting quietly occurs. Then repeat the procedure.

After five successive successful trials, place two chips on the desk top and require the child to hand over both chips for *one* piece of food.

Continue in this fashion until the ratio of chips to back-up reinforcers is 5:1.

Results

By the end of the first session, Peter would quickly pick up the tokens as they were placed in front of him and hand them back to the E for a piece of food. The number of reinforced trials that occurred at each token:reinforcer ratio during the first session was as follows:

	Token:reinforcer ratio				
	1:1	2:1	3:1	4:1	5:1
Number of food-reinforced trials at each ratio	7	14	11	6	18

During the subsequent sessions the tokens were presented to Peter contingent upon some desirable response, rather than merely placed in front of him.

Four of the remaining six *S*s showed a rate of progress during token training that appeared comparable to Peter's progress. That is, these *S*s returned the tokens at a 5:1 token:reinforcer ratio by the end of the first session, and would respond to earn the tokens during the second and subsequent sessions. The remaining two *S*s progressed more slowly, and did not respond for a 5:1 ratio until the fourth and fifth sessions respectively.

At the fourteenth session, each child was given a token "bank," a small wooden block with five slots in it, each slot capable of holding one chip. When the token bank was full, the five chips were "cashed in" for a piece of food. The main reason for using the bank was to prevent the *S* from playing with and dropping the tokens. The introduction of the token bank did not disrupt any *S*'s performance beyond the session in which the bank was introduced.

Conditioning Subjects to Sit Quietly

As sitting quietly is a prerequisite to any successful classroom activities, this behavior was the first to be developed.

Procedure

During the second session of token training, the tokens were presented contingent upon a brief period of sitting quietly, rather than merely placed in front of the *S*s. This brief period was determined by observations taken during the first session regarding the length of time a child would sit quietly to the instruction, "Sit still." If the child had been observed to sit still for fifteen seconds, for example, then a token was presented during the first part of the second session, contingent upon fifteen seconds of sitting quietly. After several reinforced trials, the requirement for reinforcement was increased to twenty seconds, then thirty seconds, then one minute, then one and a half minutes, and so on. If the child attempted to get out of his desk, he was forced to sit down by the E, and that particular interval of time-of-quiet-sitting required for reinforcement was retimed. If the child was noisy while sitting in the desk, he was ignored and the time interval for reinforcement began as soon as the noise ceased.

Once the child was conditioned to sit quietly, the reinforcers were then presented contingent upon other desirable behavior, such as emitting desirable verbal responses. However, for the duration of the programme, each child was occasionally reinforced just for sitting still. That is, if an E was working with child A, and child B was sitting quietly, the E might reinforce child B by saying, "Good boy for sitting quietly," and by giving child B a token.

Results

All Ss were conditioned, within two sessions, to sit quietly for a minimum of five minutes. The results of the first session of this procedure (the second session of token training) with one particular S, Terry, are reported here, since Terry was one of the worst offenders for making noise and getting out of his desk.

After a total of sixty reinforced trials with tokens (exchanged for back-up reinforcers at a 5:1 ratio) at intervals of five seconds, fifteen seconds, thirty seconds, one minute, and two minutes, and seven occasions of being punished with a sharp "No!" and a slap on the fingers for attempting to leave the desk, Terry sat quietly for four consecutive two-minute periods. At this point, the E instructed Terry to sit still, placed Coke and cake on a nearby desk, then left the room. Upon return five minutes later, Terry was still sitting quietly with the food untouched. Since Terry continued to respond and consume the reinforcers for an additional hour, his failure to eat the cake and drink the Coke could not have been due to satiation.

By the end of the third week, the Ss would typically sit quietly and respond to the E for the entire session. Occasionally, however, exceptions were observed. These exceptional outbursts or fits of restlessness may have been at least partially due to the inattentiveness of the E. On several occasions an E inadvertently reinforced a S with social attention following a Ss jumping up to go to the washroom, to grab a toy that had dropped, or the like. These instances were invariably followed by bursts of restlessness on the part of the S.

Verbal Training I (Object and Picture Naming)

The procedures to be described in this and the remaining sections make use of a technique referred to as "fading." The term refers to the gradual alteration of the stimuli controlling a response, so that the response eventually occurs to a completely different set of stimuli. Fading was experimentally demonstrated by Terrace (1963a, b) on pigeons, and was utilized by Wolf *et al.* (1964) and Risley and Wolf (1967) to train autistic children to name various objects.

Procedure

Since Peter and other Ss would mimic some words and sounds, mimicking served as the starting point for verbal training. The Es initially had the Ss mimic the names of clothing items and parts of their anatomy. The initial instructions to the E were as follows:

Point to your shirt and say, "Shirt." Repeat this sequence until the S correctly mimics "Shirt," each time reinforcing the S for the correct response.

When the S correctly mimics "Shirt," then gradually fade in new verbal prompts. That is, say, "What's this? Shirt," while pointing to the shirt. To this, the S usually mimics, "Shirt." Then, over a period of several trials gradually decrease the intensity of "Shirt" to zero, so that the S eventually responds to the question, "What's this?" with the answer, "Shirt." Again, each appropriate response is to be reinforced.

If the name of the item is faded out too fast, so that the question, "What's this?" brings the wrong reply or none at all, wait for five seconds and repeat the last step to which the S did respond correctly.

When the S:E ratio was increased from 1:1 to 7:1, the procedure was identical to that described above with the following additions:

a. Each S was given a variable three trials (range of from 1–6) in succession before proceeding to the next child.

b. If the E was interacting with Child I, Child II would not be given a trial unless Child II was attending closely to the E.

c. The occurrence of an undesirable response immediately led to the E switching to the other child, providing the other child was attending to the E.

d. If both or all the Ss emitted undesirable behavior, they were ignored until one of the Ss sat quietly and attended to the E for five seconds. This S was then given the opportunity to earn a reinforcer.

These rules were followed for tracing and matching training, as well as for verbal training.

Results

For Peter, five trials were required to fade the cue "Shirt." Thereafter, when the E pointed to a shirt and asked, "What's this?", Peter replied, "Shirt." For most objects or pictures, the name of the object in the sequence, "What's this? (Name of the object)", was faded within ten trials or less. By the end of the programme, Peter was able to identify clothing items, parts of his anatomy (such as eyes, ears, and finger), most objects in a typical classroom, and most pictures in a typical kindergarten book of the "Dick and Jane" variety. In short, Peter had acquired an extensive naming vocabulary during the sixty sessions in which the programme was in effect. Three other Ss showed progress comparable to that of Peter. The remaining three Ss progressed less rapidly.

In order to provide an indication of the summer's progress, the results of the median pupil, Terry, are reported. The initial five-day observation period prior to the onset of the programme revealed that Terry, like Peter, had an extensive echoic repertoire, but verbal responses were under exclusive echoic and not stimulus control. After sixty sessions (approximately 65 hours), Terry was exposed to a series of items, pictures, and objects and asked the question, "What's this?". Terry correctly named 136 of the 200 items to which he was exposed. Some examples of items named: parts of the anatomy such as eyes, ears, arm; toys such as football, whistle, skipping rope; clothing items such as mitts, shirt, zipper; food items such as corn, meat, lettuce; animal pictures such as bear, monkey, cow; pictures of household items such as window, T.V., scissors.

The increase in the $S:E$ ratio did not produce any observable disrupting effects on either the latency of the response or the error rate. The overall rate of response was decreased at higher $S:E$ ratios, since there was less opportunity to ask questions of each individual. By the seventh week, all seven Ss would sit quietly in the classroom and, in turn, answer questions or follow commands directed to them by a single E.

Verbal Training II (Listening Training)

This refers to the technique used to train the Ss to respond to questions about various items, pictures, or events. Some questions: "What do you write with?", "What is your name?", "Where do you live?". This training was initiated after the S learned to identify and name the object about which the question was concerned. The procedure followed and the results obtained for increasing the $S:E$ ratios were similar to the procedure and results for object naming and, therefore, are not discussed here.

Procedure

As the procedure is essentially the same for most questions, the procedure for one question will be described, namely, "Where does milk come from?". The Es began by pointing to some milk and asking, "Where does milk come from? Milk comes from a cow.", to which the S usually mimicked, "Cow." The E then faded out the words of the required response over several trials. That is, the E would ask, "Where does milk come from? Milk comes from a

————.", to which the *S* would respond, "Cow." The prompts, "Milk comes from————.", "Milk comes ——————.", "Milk ———————————.", were faded until the *S* would respond to a glass of milk and the question, "Where does milk come from?", with the statement "Milk comes from a cow."

Results

Following this procedure, the last two or three words in a statement (such as ". . . from a cow." in the last example) were typically faded out within twenty trials or less. However, it was exceedingly difficult to develop and maintain a complete answer (often requiring as many as seventy-five additional trials). After thirty hours of training, the median pupil, Terry, responded to the following questions with the following answers:

Question	Answer
What do you clean your teeth with?	Toothbrush.
What do you read?	Read book.
What do you eat with?	Eat with fork.
Where does a bird live?	Bird cage.
What do you ride in?	Ride in car.
What do you drink from?	From cup.
What do you wear on your head?	Wear hat.
What says meow?	Pussycat.
What says bow wow?	Doggie bow wow.
What says moo?	Cow.
What says quack?	Duck.
What do you eat lunch with?	Eat with fork.
What do you see in the sky?	Sun.
Where do you swim?	Swimming pool.
What do you dry your hands with?	Towel.
What do you do when you get up?	Get dressed.
Where does the garbage go?	Garbage can.
What do you sit on?	Sit on chair.
What do you play with?	Play with toys.

Tracing and Copying

The purpose of these procedures was to teach a child to trace lines and figures and eventually to copy from a sample.

Procedure

The tracing began with a sheet on which was a heavily dotted circle and square separated by a dotted line. The E placed a pencil in the *S*'s hand, instructed the *S* to "Trace the circle.", and then proceeded to guide the *S*'s hand, so that the pencil actually traced the circle, following which the *S* received a "Good boy," and a token. This procedure was repeated with the line and the square. After several such trials, the E faded out the pressure of his hand, as a cue controlling the subject's tracing, by:

Holding the *S*'s hand lightly for several trials.
Touching the back of the *S*'s hand with his (the E's) fingertips for several trials.
Pointing to the item to be traced.
And finally, simply giving the instructions, "Trace the . . . . ."

Each trial was accompanied by verbal instructions and if the *S*'s response was appropriate, followed by reinforcement.

When the *S* traced the circle, line, and square adequately, he was exposed to a second type of sheet on which were several dotted "1's." Beginning with the most heavily dotted "1" on the left side of the sheet, the frequency of dots in each successive "1" was decreased to the point where the right side of the sheet contained a blank space. Thus, once the *S* had been taught to trace, he could be taught to copy via the technique of fading out the dotted cues that guided the tracing. The E pointed to the most heavily dotted "1" and instructed the *S*, "Trace number 1 here." The desired response was reinforced and the procedure was repeated for each of the more lightly dotted "1's" until the *S* drew a "1" in the absence of cues. It was then a simple matter to fade in the instructions "Draw a 1" or "Copy a 1" to this newly acquired response. After this, the E had the *S* do several practice sheets of the number he had just learned before going on to the next number. In a similar fashion, the *S*s were taught to copy letters of the alphabet and simple figures.

The *S*:E ratio was increased as described in Table 1. The criterion for increasing the ratio was that *S*s trace at least one sheet of a number or letter for one token. At ratios greater than 1:1, the *S*s were placed in desks in front of the E and, in turn, told to trace the "1's", or whatever number they happened to be working on. The E followed the rules cited in the section on Verbal Training for increasing the ratio.

Results

After thirty hours of training, Peter and one other *S* would trace any sequence of dotted lines and would copy several simple geometrical figures and designs. Some sample designs and a *S*'s copying performance are shown in Fig. 2b. Two other *S*s acquired a tracing repertoire within thirty hours. However, neither of these *S*s will yet copy in the absence of dotted lines. The *S*:E ratio for these four *S*s was increased to 4:1. The higher ratios for these *S*s did not produce any obvious disrupting effects on the tracing performance.

The remaining three *S*s exhibited a very short attention span, that is, they would not look at the paper except for very brief glances. Consistent with the operant conditioning analysis of attention span proposed by Martin and Powers (1966), the following procedure was adopted. The E began with a sheet of paper, on which were several columns of dots, each successive dot being approximately one inch apart. The E placed the *S*'s hand on the pencil and then moved the pencil from dot to dot. The *S* was reinforced if he watched the pencil while it moved from one to the next. The initial distance between the dots was short enough so that the length of time required to move the pencil coincided with the duration of the *S*'s glance. The *S*, therefore, frequently received reinforcement. After a number of such trials, the distance between the dots was gradually increased until, finally, the successive dots were on opposite sides of the paper.

To ensure that the *S* was in fact attending to the successive dots to which the pencil was being guided, a second sheet was introduced. This sheet had a dot in the center and a number of dots around the periphery. The *S* was required to observe the pencil as it was guided from the center dot to a dot on the periphery that was randomly pointed to by the E. After several sheets of this procedure, the E gradually faded out his hand, until the *S*, without guidance, drew lines from the center dot to the dots on the periphery. The regular tracing sheets and procedures were then introduced.

The final performance of one of these *S*s, Mike, after a total of thirty hours tracing training, is shown in Fig. 2a. Since these three *S*s did not progress to the point where they would trace a row of items for one token, they remained at a 1:1 ratio.

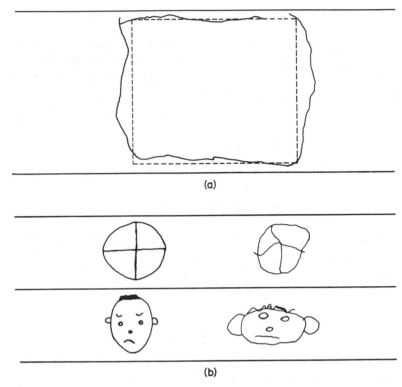

Fig. 2. Samples of sheets used in tracing and copying training. (a) The continuous line was made by Mike in his final attempt to trace the dotted lines. (b) The drawings on the left served as samples which the subject was required to copy. The right-hand drawings were made by Peter.

Matching Training

The purpose of this part of the training programme was to teach the Ss to identify, from a group of items, examples that matched, by marking the items which were alike with an X.

Procedure

Matching training was initiated with the sheet shown in Fig. 3(a). Using the fading techniques described in the section on Object and Picture Naming, the S was conditioned to respond to "Show me the shoe." The E then asked, "Show me two shoes" and proceeded to guide the S's hands to the two shoes. As in tracing training, the E then faded out his hands until the S eventually responded to the statement, "Show me the two shoes," by pointing to the two shoes. In similar fashion the S was taught to point to each of the pairs of items on the matching sheets.

The next step was similar to the listening training in that the E stated, "Show me the objects that are alike, show me the two shoes," and then proceeded to fade out the phrase, "Show me the two shoes" in appropriate steps, so that eventually the S responded to the statement, "Show me the objects that are alike," by pointing to the two shoes. The S was likewise taught to respond to the phrase, "Show me the items that are the same."

The S was then taught to mark an "X" when told to do so via the previously described

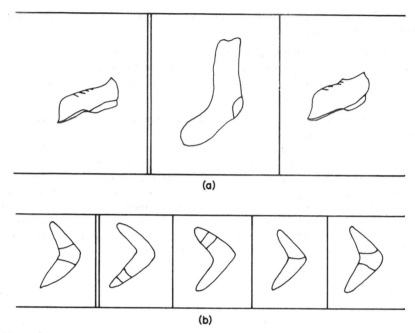

Fig. 3. Samples of sheets used in matching training. (a) Matching training was initiated with the objects shown drawn on eight and a half by eleven inch paper. (b) Training progressed to an eight and a half by eleven inch sheet containing four rows of objects comparable to the matching task shown.

tracing and copying procedures for the letter X. The final step involved conditioning the *S* to respond to the statement, "Mark an X on the items that are the same." Although each response was initially reinforced, the E eventually progressed to an intermittent schedule, so that the *S* would correctly match a page of items for a single token.

The *S* : E ratio was increased as described in Table 1. The criterion for increasing the ratio was that each *S* match at least one page of items, three matches per page, for one token. At ratios greater than 1 : 1, each *S* was placed in a desk and, in turn, told to "Draw an X on the ones that are the same."

Results

Peter and one other *S* progressed rapidly, and after thirty hours would correctly match a wide variety of items ranging in difficulty from the items in Fig. 3a to those shown in Fig. 3b. The remaining *S*s, however, did not acquire a copying repertoire and consequently did not draw an X when told to do so. These *S*s progressed only to the point where they would point to like items on some of the matching sheets, when told to do so.

As was observed on the other tasks, increasing the *S* : E ratio did not produce any noticeable disrupting effects.

DISCUSSION

A surprising finding of this research was the apparent absence of any disrupting effect of increasing the *S* : E ratio. This may have been due to features of the initial sessions. That is, since the initial sessions involved three Es and three Ss all working in the same small room, a S experienced many instances of:

a. Being reinforced for appropriate behavior while another S was throwing a tantrum.
b. Observing other Ss being reinforced while going unreinforced himself.
c. In general, adapting to the presence of other Ss and Es in the context of a conditioning situation.

Thus, possible disrupting effects from the presence of other active Ss may have been adapted to during the first two weeks.

Some of the procedures utilized here have extensive overlap with those of Risley & Wolf (1967) and Lovaas *et al.* (1967). However, an obvious difference between our procedures and those utilized by Dr. Lovaas and his colleagues was made apparent from viewing a film, Reinforcement Therapy (1966), which presented some of the procedures utilized by Dr. Lovaas. Specifically, one of the rules that our Es adhere to: If the child is not paying attention, the E does *not* tell the S to pay attention and does *not* provide the S with an opportunity to earn a reinforcer, rather the E ignores the S until the S is sitting quietly and attending to the E. The only permissible alternative to ignoring undesirable behavior is to punish it with a slap on the fingers. In contrast to this rule, the film portraying Dr. Lovaas' procedures indicated that a child frequently received the E's attention, contingent upon inattentiveness. More specifically, in a twenty-minute film, we counted fifteen instances where the E said something like, "Look at me," contingent upon a child's inattentiveness. In the same film, while one of the Ss engaged in a mild tantrum involving facial contortions and hand waving, the E, eight times in succession, asked, "What color is it?" in regard to a colored object. In this instance, the tantrum persisted until Dr. Lovaas physically punished the S. It cannot be concluded, on the basis of the data reported here, that our procedure was more effective than that utilized by Dr. Lovaas. However, the research on social reinforcers (Greenspoon, 1955; Gewirtz & Baer, 1958; Zimmerman & Zimmerman, 1962; Harris *et al.*, 1966; Gelfand *et al.*, 1967) strongly suggests that a contingent relationship between a S's undesirable behavior and the E's attention would maintain that S's undesirable behavior. At any rate, this would seem to be a fruitful area for further research.

Another variable that may have contributed greatly to the success of the programme reported here was the reinforcement system. Since the E had control over the S's total food intake prior to the evening meal, poor performance meant little or no food for the greater part of the day. This, undoubtedly, added to the efficacy of the breakfast, lunch and edibles as back-up reinforcers for the tokens.

After the results in this report were obtained, the programme underwent the following changes:

a. The S's breakfast and noon meal were gradually eliminated as back-up reinforcers for the tokens, leaving such edibles as candies, potato chips, and popcorn as the back-up reinforcers.
b. A star system (similar to the star system described by Birnbrauer *et al.*, 1965) was substituted for the poker chips.
c. The autistic children began meeting daily as a group with the kindergarten teacher at the Manitoba Training School for one and a half hours a day.

The effect of these changes has not yet been thoroughly assessed. However, superficially at least, the changes do not appear to have disrupted the progress and daily performance of the Ss, except in two instances. Two of the Ss described in Part F, who would not initially attend to the paper during tracing training, have regressed in their tracing behavior since the above changes were instituted. Although both Ss had progressed previously to the point of tracing a circle and a square, on a one-month follow-up test neither *S* would attend to the paper while moving the pencil.

It should be emphasized that, at the end of this study, the group was far from comparable to a normal kindergarten class. However, they would sit quietly in a classroom, respond to many commands and questions, and some of the *S*s would trace, copy, and match with a minimum of supervision from one teacher.

REFERENCES

Birnbrauer, T., Bijou, S., Wolf, M. & Kidder, J. (1965) In *Case Studies in Behavior Modification* (Eds. Ullmann and Krasner). Holt, Rinehart & Winston, New York.

Birnbrauer, T., Wolf, M., Kidder, J. & Tague, C. (1965) Classroom behavior of retarded pupils with token reinforcement. *J. exp. child Psychol.*, **2**, 219–235.

Gelfand, D. M., Gelfand, S. & Dobson, W. R. (1967) Unprogrammed reinforcement of patient's behavior in a mental hospital. *Behav. Res. & Therapy*, **5**, 201–207.

Gewirtz, J. L. & Baer, D. M. (1958) Deprivation and satiation of social reinforcers as drive conditions. *J. abnorm. soc. Psychol.*, **57**, 165–172.

Greenspoon, J. (1955) The reinforcing effect of two spoken words on the frequency of two responses. *Am. J. Psychol.*, **68**, 409–416.

Harris, F. R., Wolf, M. & Baer, D. M. (1966) Effects of adult social reinforcement on child behavior. In *Control of Human Behavior* (Eds. Ulrich, Stachnik and Mabry). Scott, Foresman & Co., Glenview, Illinois.

Heid, W. (1964) Nonverbal conceptual behavior of young children with programmed instruction. Unpublished Doctoral Thesis, University of Washington.

Lovaas, O. I. & Simmons, J. Q. (September, 1965) A reinforcement-theory approach to childhood schizophrenia: An overview of the treatment program. Paper presented to Am. Psychol. Ass., Chicago.

Lovaas, O. I., Freitas, L., Nelson, K. & Whalen, C. (1967) The establishment of imitation and its use for the development of complex behavior in schizophrenic children. *Behav. Res. & Therapy*, **5**, 171–181.

Marshall, G. R. (1966) Toilet training of an autistic 8-yr-old through conditioning therapy: A case report. *Behav. Res. & Therapy*, **4**, 242–245.

Martin, G. L. & Powers, R. B. (1966) Attention span: An operant conditioning analysis. *Exceptional Children*, 565–570.

Metz, R. J. (1965) Conditioning generalized imitation in autistic children. *J. exp. child Psychol.*, **2**, 389–399.

Reinforcement Therapy (1966) A film by Smith, Kline & French Laboratories.

Risley, T. & Wolf, M. (1967) Establishing functional speech in echolalic children. *Behav. Res. & Therapy*, **5**, 73–88.

Staats, A. W., Staats, C. K., Schutz, R. E. & Wolf, M. (1962) The conditioning of textual responses using "extrinsic" reinforcers. *J. exp. anal. Behav.*, **6**, 223–232.

Terrace, H. S. (1963a) Discrimination learning with and without "errors". *J. exp. anal. Behav.*, **6**, 1–27.

Terrace, H. S. (1963b) Errorless transfer of a discrimination across two continua. *J. exp. anal. Behav.*, **6**, 223–232.

Wolf, M. & Risley, T. (1967) Application of operant conditioning procedures to the behavior problems of an autistic child: A follow-up and extension. *Behav. Res. & Therapy*, **5**, 103–111.

Wolf, M., Risley, T. & Mees, H. L. (1964) Application of operant conditioning procedures to the behavior problems of an autistic child. *Behav. Res. & Therapy*, **1**, 305–312.

Zimmermann, E. H. & Zimmerman, J. (1962) The alteration of behavior in a special classroom situation. *J. exp. anal. Behav.*, **5**, 59–60.

The Effects and Side Effects of Punishing
the Autistic Behaviors of a
Deviant Child*†

TODD R. RISLEY

University of Kansas

Abstract: Timeout procedures in the home and extinction and reinforcement of incompatible behaviors in the laboratory failed to eliminate the disruptive and dangerous climbing behavior of a deviant child. Punishment with electric shock was used to eliminate this behavior in the laboratory and then in the home. The effects were reversible and were restricted to specific stimulus conditions. A less severe form of punishment was used to eliminate the child's autistic rocking. Other behaviors of the subject were continuously measured in the laboratory to determine the side effects of punishment. No suppression of other behaviors correlated with punishment was noted. However, the rate of some behaviors increased when punishment was used to eliminate deviant behaviors, but these increases were, primarily, desirable.

A prime agrument against punishment has been that it allegedly produces undesirable side effects. Traditionally, the evidence supporting this argument has been based on clinical anecdotes describing cases of "symptom substitution." More recently, the results of experimental research have similarly suggested that punishment procedures are likely to produce undesirable side effects.

For example, the conditioned suppression literature suggests that aversive stimulation may suppress other behaviors, including desired behaviors, in addition to suppressing the behavior being punished. The negative reinforcement literature suggests that aversive stimuli may produce and maintain escape and avoidance behaviors which may be undesirable, such as leaving, avoiding, or removing the punishing situation, or the person dispensing the punishment. The literature on pain-elicited aggression (or "reflexive fighting") suggests that aversive stimuli may elicit aggression toward the person dispensing punishment and toward other organisms and objects as well. A corollary is that punishment procedures may, in fact, increase rather than eliminate aggressive behaviors. And finally, the stimulus properties of the person dispensing punishment may become altered by being paired with aversive stimulation such

*Preparation of this paper was partially supported by National Institute of Child Health and Human Development grant HD-03144-01 to the Bureau of Child Research and The Department of Human Development at the University of Kansas. This work was done in 1963–64 while the author was a research assistant at the Developmental Psychology Laboratory of the University of Washington. Financial and moral support was provided by Donald M. Baer, early suggestions by Montrose M. Wolf, later suggestions by Ivar Lovaas and technical assistance by Gary Millar, Betty Hart, Nancy Reynolds, and Cordelia McIntosh. This investigation was possible only through the constancy and cooperation of the child's mother. Reprints may be obtained from the author, Juniper Gardens Children's Project, 2021 N. Third St., Kansas City, Kansas 66101.

†Reprinted from the *Journal of Applied Behaviour Analysis*, 1968, 1, 1, 21–34. Copyright 1968 with permission from the Society for the Experimental Analysis of Behavior and Dr. Todd R. Risley.

that his presence and attention become more aversive and less reinforcing. Virtually every summary account of punishment research in recent literature (excepting Solomon, 1964) has appended a warning statement to the effect that, for these reasons, the use of punishment is contraindicated when dealing with applied problems of human behavior. (See Azrin and Holz, 1966 for a recent example, as well as for a thorough and clear review of punishment research.)

The present study describes the application of a series of procedures designed to reduce the highly dangerous and disruptive climbing behavior of a severely deviant child. After other methods had failed, electric shock punishment was applied under several conditions. Another punishing stimulus, shouting at, and shaking the child, was applied to the child's autistic rocking. Other behaviors of the child were recorded to assess possible side effects of these punishment procedures.

Antecedent to this study in both time and function was the initial work on the use of shock punishment with autistic children by Lovaas, Schaeffer & Simmons (1965). A verbal report of that work provided the instigation and some of the techniques to investigate further the effects of punishment.

METHOD

Subject

The subject, S, was a six-year-old girl who was hyperactive and exhibited bizarre behaviors. She had been consistently diagnosed as having diffuse brain damage caused by pneumococcal meningitis at age seven months, although recent diagnoses included an "overlay" of emotional disturbance and autism. She had occasional seizures and was taking anticonvulsant medication. She exhibited no verbal behavior but almost continuously emitted howls, moans, and clicks. These vocalizations did not correspond in length, inflection or topography to normal speech. She exhibited no imitative behavior, either verbal or non-verbal. Her predominant behaviors in all situations were climbing in high places (on furniture, window sills, trees, houses, etc.), alternating with sitting and rocking rhythmically. Her climbing was a constant source of concern to her parents due to the threat to her life and limb (her body bore multiple scars from past falls; her front teeth were missing, having been left embedded in a two by four inch molding from which she had fallen while climbing outside the second story of her house), and the attendant destruction of furniture in the house. She had attended several schools for special children but had been dropped from each because of these disruptive behaviors and her lack of progress.

S's parents, who both possessed advanced academic degrees, had resisted placing her in an institution, as they predicted that her climbing would result in her being kept in continuous physical restraint on a custodial ward. However, as she had become larger and more skillful, her climbing and her aggression toward her younger brother at home were causing them to consider institutionalization seriously.

Reinforcer

S was brought to the laboratory four times a week around noon after having had only three ounces of milk at breakfast time. Milk, which was the only food she would reliably consume, was used as a reinforcer. Even under this amount of food deprivation, she exhibited long latencies of drinking the milk when it was presented. Each reinforcer was about one tablespoon of milk in a paper cup placed on the table in front of S, accompanied by the statement, "Good girl!"

Setting

The experimental sessions were either twenty or thirty minutes long, and were conducted in an eight by twelve-foot experimental room with an eleven-foot ceiling. At one end of the room, next to the door, a ventilator frame formed a five-inch deep ledge, six feet above the floor. Directly across from the door a large one-way mirror permitted observation from an adjacent room. The experimenter and the child sat in chairs, facing each other across a small table in the center of the room (*see* Risley & Wolf, 1967). Initially the room also contained several extra chairs and a canvas cot. At the experimenter's request, *S*'s mother observed all sessions through the one-way mirror.

Recording

Frequency and duration of the child's behaviors were recorded on a six-pen event recorder located in an adjacent room, via a bank of microswitches placed on the table. On occasional sessions an observer behind a one-way mirror would independently record those behaviors for which reliability was considered to be a problem. However, most of the behaviors were so highly distinctive that reliability checks were not considered necessary.

The data presented on *S*'s behaviors at home were collected by the mother throughout each day. Periodically, the experimenter would observe in the home for several hours. During these periods there was always complete agreement between the experimenter's and the mother's recording. Since there were no systematic differences in the mother's data on those days, as compared to the prior and succeeding days, the mother's data were considered to be reliable.

PROCEDURES AND RESULTS

Timeout for climbing in the home. The mother's response to *S*'s climbing was originally considered to be the most likely variable maintaining that climbing. Since the climbing usually endangered the child and/or destroyed the home furnishings, the mother's contingent attention and interaction was consistent and predictable. A simple extinction procedure (ignoring the behavior) did not appear feasible. Therefore, physical isolation (timeout) from social interaction was made contingent upon climbing behavior. Accordingly, her mother was instructed to say "No!", lift *S* to the floor, and lead her to her bedroom (with minimal physical contact and no further verbalization) contingent upon each instance of inappropriate climbing. The bedroom door was reopened after ten minutes (timed on a kitchen timer). The mother was also instructed to attend to and to interact with her as frequently as possible when *S* was not climbing. Inappropriate climbing was defined as standing, sitting or hanging on anything not specifically designed for such, with neither foot touching the floor.

After seventeen days, no reduction in the rate of climbing was observed. The timeout contingency was then applied to climbing in only one location (the bathroom) and the mother was instructed to do whatever she had previously been doing for all other climbing. It seemed likely that a concurrent schedule of social interaction for climbing in other places and the timeout procedure for climbing in the bathroom would provide a more sensitive measure of the effects of the timeout procedure. However, no reduction in the rate of climbing in the bathroom was obtained during forty-six days of this procedure (average daily rate of climbing was 5.5 per day over the first twenty-three days and 5.7 over the last twenty-three). The time-out procedure was therefore discontinued.

Fig. 1. Tracings from photographs showing the subject's climbing behavior (a and b), eye contact topography (c), and consummatory response (d). Note the bookcase, door, and ventilator frame in a and b and the micro-switch recording panel beside the experimenter's hand in c and d. Original photographs were taken through the one-way observation window.

Reinforcement for incompatible behaviors and extinction for climbing in the laboratory. Concurrent with these attempts to eliminate climbing at home, procedures for establishing imitative behaviors were initiated in the laboratory.

In a preliminary session, S moved about the room almost continually standing on the chairs and table, moving furniture to the door and climbing from it to the door knob, then to the ventilator frame next to the door, and then to the door lintel (a and b, Fig. 1). Alternately she would sit on the floor or in the chair, rhythmically rocking and humming with closed eyes. Throughout this period she frequently struck the side of her head with her palm or fist, sometimes resoundingly. She occasionally would approach and grab for the food reinforcer, but she never looked directly at the experimenter, and actively averted her gaze whenever the experimenter stood in front of her.

In order to establish attending to the experimenter's face, which was a necessary prerequisite for vocal imitation training, systematic shaping of eye contacts (S's gaze focusing

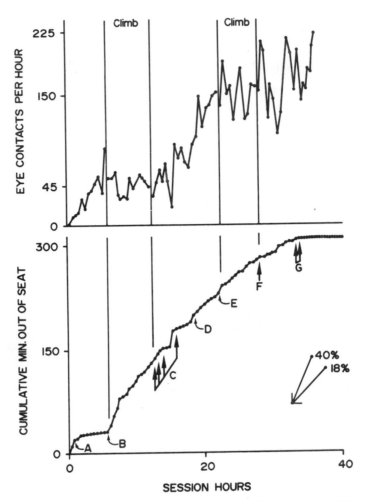

Fig. 2. Graphs showing the relationship between the rate of eye contacts and the amount of time *S* spent out of her chair. Each dot represents one session. The portions of the graphs between the dotted lines labelled "CLIMB" indicate blocks of sessions during which *S* was climbing on the bookcase. At A all furniture was removed from the room, precluding climbing. At B the bookcase was placed in the room. At C climbing on the bookcase was punished with electric shock. Beginning at D the shock device was not brought into the experimental room. At E a footstool was placed in the room in front of the bookcase and climbing resumed. At F climbing on the bookcase was again punished with shock. At G standing on the chair was punished with shock.

on the experimenter's eyes) was begun. During the preliminary session, the experimenter periodically said "Sit down" and patted the chair. Initially, standing by the chair, and then only sitting in the chair was reinforced.

The original plan was to work with the mother to control climbing behavior at home, while concentrating on developing imitative behavior in the laboratory. Therefore, climbing was eliminated in the laboratory by removing the opportunity to climb. Between Sessions 2 and 3 (Point A, Fig. 2) all furniture was removed from the room except a table and two chairs which were fastened to the floor in the middle of the room. After several unsuccessful attempts to step up onto the doorknob without a chair in the next two sessions, all climbing activity ceased. Time spent out of the chair decreased from thirty-eight per cent of Sessions 1 and 2, to less than two per cent of Sessions 5 through 12.

Once S was sitting in the chair during most of the session, reinforcers were delivered only when she looked at the milk cup. As looking at the cup became more frequent, the experimenter gradually moved the cup toward his face, thereby increasing the probability of eye contacts. A few fleeting glances at the experimenter's face occurred and were reinforced. These gradually became more frequent. After eye contacts had reached a rate of six per minute, reinforcement for looking at the cup was discontinued. At this point S was first looking at the cup and then looking at the experimenter; successively longer eye contacts were reinforced until the topography of this behavior was a focused stare at the experimenter's eyes of one second or longer (*see* c, Fig. 1). Concurrently, the experimenter gradually moved the cup away from his face, finally holding the cup out of sight under the table. The frequency of eye contacts systematically increased during these procedures from zero per minute in the first session to 1.5 per minute in Session 12 (Point B, Fig. 2).

Meanwhile, the timeout procedure had failed to reduce the climbing behavior at home. Now that sitting in the chair and looking at the experimenter (behaviors incompatible with climbing) had been established in the laboratory it was decided to see if climbing would re-occur there if the opportunity were again presented. A small bookcase was placed under the ventilator next to the door (*see* a and b, Fig. 1) before Session 13. As can be seen in Fig. 2 at Point B, time out of the chair immediately increased from less than two per cent of the previous eight sessions to forty-two per cent of the first four sessions with the bookcase present, as S again began to climb. In the fourteen sessions (totalling 6.4 hours) after the bookcase was introduced, S climbed on the bookcase, and the ventilator and door above the bookcase, and average of 6.7 times per hour (from Point B to first arrow, Fig. 3), occupying eighteen per cent of the time in the sessions. During these sessions the experimenter did not look at her or respond in any way when she was out of the chair, but sat staring down at the table. When S resumed her seat, the experimenter would look up and wait for S to meet his gaze. Eye contacts of one second or longer were reinforced with milk.

Thus it did not appear that the climbing behavior was maintained by consequences which the experimenter could manipulate. Attempts to supplant climbing by establishing competing behaviors, coupled with the removal of all experimenter-controlled consequences for this behavior had had no apparent effect in reducing its frequency or duration. Therefore, it was decided to attempt to eliminate the climbing behavior by the contingent application of shock.

Punishment with shock for climbing in the laboratory. A hand-held inductorium was constructed which operated on a series of seven 1.5 volt flashlight batteries. When a button was pressed this device, delivered shock across two contacts three-quarters of an inch apart. The coil, interrupter, and shock contacts were obtained from a commercially available device for shocking livestock (Hot Shot Products, Minneapolis 16, Minnesota). From oscilloscope readings it was estimated that the average voltage output was in the range of 300 to 400 volts, with occasional spikes exceeding 1000 volts. Subjectively, the shock produced a sharp, extremely painful sting, localized in the area of the body to which the contacts were touched, much like being struck with a vigorously applied willow switch. The pain terminated with the removal of the shock, with no after effects such as redness, swelling of the skin, tingling, or aching. (Observers of the session in which shock was applied reported that, on the basis of observable autonomic responses such as flushing, trembling, etc., the subject recovered from the shock episodes much faster than the experimenter.)

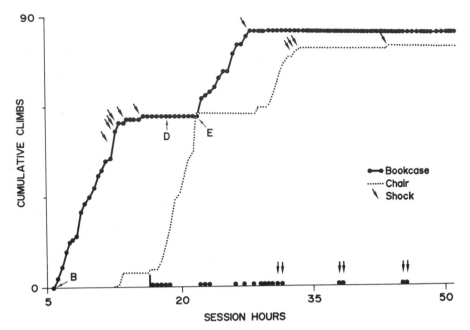

Fig. 3. A cumulative graph of the rates of *S*'s climbing on the bookcase and standing on her chair. Each dot on the top line represents one session. Heavy arrows indicate where each behavior was punished with electric shock. At B the bookcase was placed in the experimental room. Beginning at D the shock device was not brought into the experimental room. At E a small stool was placed in front of the bookcase. Beginning at the short vertical line above the X-axis *S* was placed in the room alone for five minutes before each session. The dots above the X-axis indicate instances of climbing on the bookcase in these periods.

In the twenty-seventh experimental session (first and second arrows, Fig. 3) when the bookcase had been present for fourteen sessions (6.4 session-hours), shock was applied contingent upon climbing. When the child climbed on the bookcase, the experimenter would shout "No!", run to her, take hold of one leg, touch the shock contacts to the calf or lower thigh and depress the switch for approximately one second. The experimenter then returned to his chair, looked down at the table until *S* returned to her chair, and then looked up and resumed reinforcing eye contacts.

In Session 27, *S* climbed nine times, but only two shocks were delivered. On the first four climbing episodes the experimenter began the punishment sequence (shouting "No!" etc.) immediately contingent upon the initial stages of climbing, when *S* was still on the lower shelf of the bookcase. On these occasions, when the experimenter shouted "No!" and approached, *S* stepped down from the bookcase to the floor. As the shock was to be made immediately contingent only upon climbing, no shocks were delivered. On the fifth climbing episode, the experimenter waited until *S* had climbed from the top of the bookcase to the ventilator frame; he then shouted "No!" and approached, *S* stepped down to the top of the bookcase, where she was standing when the shock was applied (first arrow, Fig. 3). When shocked, *S* abruptly sat down on the top of the bookcase. The experimenter took her arm and assisted her down to the floor, then returned to his chair. *S* returned to her chair twenty-three seconds after the shock, looked at the experimenter and consumed the consequent milk reinforcer within seventy seconds after the shock. On the sixth, seventh, and eight climbing episodes, when "No!" was shouted, *S* jumped to the floor before the experimenter reached her, and no shock was delivered. On the ninth climbing episode in Session 27, *S* was still climbing when reached and the shock was applied.

In Session 28 (third and fourth arrows, Fig. 3), the first climbing episode was terminated without shock when, upon the shouted "No!", *S* jumped six feet from the ventilator frame to the floor. It was apparent that although the procedure had not eliminated the climbing, it had quickly produced behaviors which avoided the shock. Therefore, on succeeding climbing episodes the experimenter shouted "No!" and then, irrespective of *S*'s behavior when reached, shock was applied. On the second climbing episode, *S* had jumped to the floor when shock was applied (third arrow, Fig. 3). On the next climbing episode *S* got up from her chair, pushed the bookcase across the room to the other side of the door and climbed there. Shock was again applied after *S* had jumped to the floor (fourth arrow, Fig. 3). Approximately five minutes later *S* got up, pushed the bookcase back to its original position, looked at the experimenter, and then returned to her chair. No further climbing occurred in the remainder of Session 28 or in Session 29. One climbing episode, followed by shock, occurred in Session 30 (fifth arrow, Fig. 3). Four sessions (1.5 hours) later (Session 34) one additional climbing episode occurred and was followed by shock (sixth arrow, Fig. 3). No further climbing occurred in the subsequent twelve sessions (6.5 hours).

When climbing had been eliminated, correlated with the contingent application of shock, the generality and reversibility of the effect were investigated.

The mother reported no noticeable decrease in climbing at home correlated with the elimination of climbing in the laboratory. Thus, the effects of the shock punishment appeared to be specific to the laboratory situation. From Session 36, *S* was placed in the experimental room alone for five minutes before the session started to see if climbing would occur when the experimenter was absent. Climbing occurred during each of the first five pre-session periods and during intermittent periods thereafter (dots above X-axis, Fig. 3) but did not occur in the regular sessions when the experimenter was present with the shock apparatus. From Session 40 (Point D, Fig. 3) the shock apparatus was not present during the regular sessions, with no recurrence of climbing. Clearly, the reduction in climbing was primarily under the discriminative control of the presence of the experimenter.

Before Session 47, after no climbing had occurred in the experimenter's presence for twelve sessions (six hours), a one-foot high metal stool was placed in front of the bookcase (Point E, Fig. 3). During this session, *S* approached the stool, placed one foot on it, looked at the experimenter, and then returned to her chair. A few minutes later she again approached the stool, stood on it, and again looked at the experimenter. She then placed one foot on the bookcase, looked back, paused, and climbed on the bookcase. The experimenter did not respond. After this, climbing occurred at an average of 4.9 times per hour during the subsequent eleven sessions (5.5 hours) (Point E to seventh arrow, Fig. 3), occupying twelve per cent of the time in the sessions. At Session 50, the shock apparatus was again brought to the sessions, with no discernible effect on the frequency of climbing. Clearly, the effects of the shock punishment were reversible (not permanent).

In Session 58 one shock was applied contingent upon the second instance of climbing in the session. No further climbing occurred during the next fifty-nine sessions (twenty-three hours). However, climbing still occurred during the pre-session periods when the experimenter was not in the room. From the period preceding Session 65, whenever *S* climbed, the experimenter would enter the room shouting "No," apply the shock, and leave again. This procedure reduced the proportion of pre-session periods in which climbing occurred from fifty-two to ten per cent (dots above X-axis, Fig. 3).

The side effects of punishing climbing with shock.   As climbing on the bookcase decreased, another, topographically similar, behavior increased. S began to stand and climb on the seat and back of her chair. She would sit on the back of the chair, stand on the chair seat, and often stand on the back of the chair with her hands braced against the wall. Climbing on the chair was defined as S being on the chair with neither foot on the floor except when she was either sitting or kneeling on the chair seat. This behavior first occurred in Session 28, when climbing on the bookcase was nearly eliminated. During Sessions 35 to 46, when climbing on the bookcase had been reduced to zero, climbing on the chair occurred at an average rate of 8.8 per hour occupying 8.4 per cent of the session time (dotted line, Fig. 3). When the foot stool was introduced (Point E, Fig. 3) and climbing on the bookcase again occurred at its previous high rate, climbing on the chair immediately ceased. When climbing on the bookcase was again eliminated by contingent shock (seventh arrow, Fig. 3), climbing on the chair again occurred, at a rate of four per hour occupying 3.1 per cent of the session time. After ten sessions, during which the frequency of climbing on the chair was relatively stable, shock was then applied contingent upon this behavior. After three applications of shock contingent upon each instance of climbing on the chair during two sessions, no chair climbing occurred during the subsequent twenty-eight sessions (9.6 hours). During Session 99 another instance of chair climbing occurred, shock was applied, and no further chair climbing occurred in the subsequent eighteen sessions (7.7 hours).

Another side effect was observed in a second, topographically dissimilar behavior, eye contact. Throughout the procedures to eliminate climbing, sitting in the chair and meeting the experimenter's gaze for one second had been continuously reinforced with milk. During Sessions 3 to 12 (4.7 hours), when climbing was made physically impossible by the absence of furniture, the frequency of eye contacts had steadily increased from 5.5 to a peak of eighty-eight per hour (A to B, Fig. 2). During Sessions 13 to 26 (6.4 hours) when the bookcase was introduced and climbing reoccurred, the frequency of eye contacts remained relatively stable at an average of forty-two per hour (B to C, Fig. 2). During Sessions 27 to 46 (9.7 hours) when climbing was eliminated by the contingent application of shock, the frequency of eye contacts steadily increased from forty-two to a peak of 152 per hour (C to E, Fig. 2). During Sessions 47 to 57 (5.5 hours), when climbing again occurred, the frequency of eye contacts remained relatively stable at an average of 151 per hour (E to F, Fig. 2). During Sessions 58 to 77 (8.8 hours), after climbing was again eliminated by the contingent application of shock, the frequency of eye contacts, though variable, again slowly increased to a peak of 222 per hour (F to end, Fig. 2).

From behind the one-way mirror, another observer recorded the duration of S looking at the experimenter's face during six sessions between Sessions 13 to 26 and six sessions between Sessions 27 to 46. During these sessions the observer started a stopwatch whenever S looked at the experimenter's face (when S was sitting in her chair) and stopped it whenever S looked away. Although this measure included other instances of S looking at the experimenter in addition to the eye contacts recorded (S often looked at the experimenter when he was pouring the milk, looking at the microswitch recording panel, etc.; or during the reinforcement "cycles" while S was holding the cup), the changes in magnitude of both were closely correlated. The close correspondence between the relative levels of this measure and the relative levels of eye contacts recorded during both of the experimental conditions, as shown in Table 1, substantiates the magnitude of the changes in eye contacts between these two conditions recorded by the experimenter.

Eye contacts could occur only when S was seated in her chair: the experimenter did not look at her when she was out of her chair. Eliminating climbing with contingent shock did not noticeably affect the amount of time S spent sitting in her chair. Except when climbing was physically impossible, due to the absence of furniture, the amount of time S spent out of her chair gradually declined across all conditions, from forty-two per cent during Sessions 13 to 16 (when the bookcase was first introduced) to zero per cent during Sessions 107 to 117. The periods in which eye contacts remained constant or systematically increased were not correlated with the amount of time S was in or out of her chair. The systematic increases in eye contacts during periods when climbing was not occurring were not due to S spending a greater proportion of time in the chair, but to S looking at the experimenter more frequently when she was in her chair.

Table 1

	Session	Eye Contacts Per Hour (Experimenter's Record)	Min. of Looking at Experimenter Per Hour (Observer Record)
S Climbing	14	54	3.1
	16	34	2.6
	17	30	1.9
	18	32	2.1
	20	54	3.0
	25	50	2.7
S Not Climbing	36	88	4.5
	37	70	3.7
	39	92	4.6
	41	140	7.6
	44	138	7.8
	46	152	8.1

Punishment with shock for climbing in the home. After these effects and side effects of shock were evaluated in the laboratory, climbing in the home was punished with shock. The mother was again instructed to record each instance of inappropriate climbing in the home. After sixteen days of recording, during which inappropriate climbing occurred on the average of twenty-nine times per day, the mother began to punish climbing with shock. On the seventeenth day, when the shock was first applied, the experimenter was present in the home instructing the mother in the use of the shock apparatus. The mother carried the shock apparatus in the pocket of her apron. When the child climbed, the mother was instructed to shout "No!", and to continue to scold the child in a loud voice while approaching, apply the shock, and then, with no further interaction, resume her previous activity. The mother continued to attend to, and interact with the child intermittently when she was not climbing. Shock reduced the inappropriate climbing from an average of twenty-nine per day to two per day within four days (Fig. 4). The mother reported that the shock device had been malfunctioning on Day 29 through Day 32, delivering shock only on intermittent trials (dotted lines, Fig. 4). On Day 33 the shock device was repaired (arrow, Fig. 4). Subsequently, inappropriate climbing decreased quickly to zero (from arrow to Day 50, Fig. 4).

Another problem of long standing had been that S would occasionally strike her three-year-old brother with an object, push him down the stairs, etc. As the mother was extremely concerned for the safety of the young child, shock was also applied contingent upon aggressive behavior toward her brother. Although no baseline was taken on the frequency of this behavior before shock was applied, the mother had estimated that the behavior occurred three or four times a day. S was shocked contingent upon seventeen instances of hitting her brother over twenty days. During this time the behavior decreased from 2.3 per day on the first three days of shock contingencies to zero (upper graph, Fig. 4) with no further instances of this behavior reported during the subsequent seventy days.

On the fifty-first day, when no climbing had occurred on fourteen of the last fifteen days, the shock device was removed from the home. The mother was instructed to try to control the climbing by spanking the child whenever she climbed. During twenty-five days of this, the climbing averaged 2.0 per day, and showed a slightly increasing trend (Fig. 4). Furthermore,

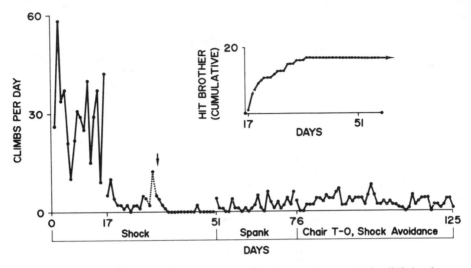

Fig. 4. Graphs of the frequencies of *S*'s climbing and aggressions against her little brother at home. Each dot represents one day. Beginning on Day 17 each occurrence of either behavior was punished with electric shock. The dotted lines during the shock condition represent days when the shock device was malfunctioning. The device was repaired at the arrow. Beginning on Day 51 the shock device was removed from the home and the mother was instructed to spank the child for climbing. Beginning on Day 76 the child was given a ten-minute timeout in a chair for climbing. Sitting quietly on the chair avoided shock.

the mother complained that spanking the child was more unpleasant and "brutalizing" for both herself and the child than the shock had been. Therefore, further procedures were sought to maintain a low, tolerable frequency of climbing without the direct use of shock.

After the daily sessions in the laboratory, the child was taken to a large nursery school playroom. A chair was placed in the middle of the room. As *S* was wandering around the room, periodically she would be told to sit in the chair. The experimenter would point to the chair and say loudly, "(Name), go sit in the chair." If the child moved in any direction but toward the chair or did not move at all for five seconds the experimenter would slowly approach the child with the shock device until she sat in the chair. After *S* had been sitting in the chair for a variable length of time, she would be helped up from the chair, and told, "O.K., you can go now." If *S* attempted to get up before this occurred, the experimenter would shout "No!" and approach her with the shock apparatus. Under these conditions, *S*'s compliance with the instructions to sit in the chair improved only slightly. Her first move was never in the direction of the chair. Her latency of getting to the chair remained long (averaging twenty-six seconds) and it was necessary to approach her with the shock apparatus on sixty-three per cent of the first thirty trials. On the thirty-first trial the child was shocked when she had to be approached with the shock apparatus. On the next six trials the child went directly to the chair, arriving there within six to fifteen seconds without being approached with the shock device. During the next forty-four trials shock was applied five times. By Trials 84 to 101, *S* was going directly to the chair when instructed, arriving within seven to twelve seconds, with the shock apparatus never being presented. After the first shock, *S*, once seated, never attempted to get up until instructed to do so.

This procedure was then used as a basis for controlling climbing behavior in the home. From Day 76 (Fig. 4) the mother no longer spanked *S*, instead, *S* was made to sit in a chair for a ten-minute timeout contingent upon each instance of climbing. If *S* did not go to the chair when instructed, got up from the chair before the mother instructed her to leave, or did not sit quietly in the chair, shock was applied. Under this procedure inappropriate climbing in the home occurred at an average rate of 2.9 times per day during the next fifty days (Days 76–125, Fig. 4). Sitting in the chair was "backed up" with shock on nineteen per cent of the occasions when *S* was sent to the chair for climbing (approximately one shock every other day), although the mother's records indicate that "shockable offenses" occurred on thirty-six per cent of the occasions.

This procedure was not as effective as the direct use of shock punishment in controlling climbing and, in fact, resulted in a greater frequency of shocks. However, this timeout procedure was continued because it approximated normal child-rearing procedures and, as such, was also used by the mother to control *S*'s less severe disruptive behaviors, such as opening the refrigerator, pulling clothes off of the closet hangers, throwing the pots and pans out of the kitchen cupboards, etc.

Imitation training in the laboratory. After the effects and side effects of shock in eliminating disruptive climbing were analyzed, the original programme of establishing imitative behavior was resumed.

S had occasionally exhibited two discrete responses in the previous sessions, clapping her hands, and pounding on the table with the palms of one or both hands. Whenever *S* looked at (made eye contact with) the experimenter, he would model one of these two behaviors for *S* to imitate. Whenever *S* emitted these behaviors within five seconds after the model behavior had been presented, a reinforcer was delivered. Initially, models for both clapping and pounding were alternated randomly. When no improvement in the frequency of imitation was noted after eight sessions, only one of the models, clapping, was presented. The experimenter began clapping his hands repeatedly and reinforcing *S*'s clapping behavior. *S* exhibited such a low rate of clapping (two or three per session) that no discernible progress was made in two sessions. The experimenter then began holding *S*'s arms and bringing her hands together. Reinforcers were first delivered contingent upon not struggling and then contingent upon slight cooperative movements while the experimenter was moving her hands. Successively greater force produced by *S* was then reinforced while fading out the force supplied by the experimenter in bringing her hands together, until the experimenter would clap his hands and then just touch *S*'s arms and *S* would clap her hands. The experimenter then faded out touching *S*'s arms, first to a gesture which was made smaller and finally eliminated until, after two sessions, *S* would respond to the model stimulus of the clap alone. (These procedures are modifications of those developed by Sherman (1965) to reinstate verbal behavior in adult psychotics and further developed by Metz (1965) and Baer, Peterson & Sherman (1965) to establish verbal behavior in autistic and retarded children.) While the rate of clapping systematically increased from an average of two to an average of twenty-five per ten-minute period, no improvement in imitative clapping occurred over five sessions. Imitative claps occurred at an average frequency of 5.3 per ten-minute period (first fourteen ten-minute periods, bottom graph, Fig. 5) and to only twelve per cent of the models presented.

Punishment for autistic rocking.   Two other deviant behaviors were recorded. *S* would frequently strike the side of her head with the palm of her hand, sometimes resoundingly, and she spent a significant portion of the time in the sessions engaged in autistic rocking behavior. No contingencies were applied to the self-striking behavior, but their frequency was recorded. A contact of a hand with the side of her head which resulted in an audible sound was the criterion for recording a self-hit. The frequency of self-hitting gradually declined from an average of seventy-seven per hour in the first fifteen sessions to thirteen per hour in Sessions 105 through 117.

Rhythmic twisting of the head was the criterion for recording a period of autistic rocking. This rocking usually included movement of the shoulders and upper trunk and was always accompanied by a monotonic humming. *S*'s eyes were either closed or focused on her hand, which was held out in front of her face. Autistic rocking occupied an average of twenty-five per cent of the time in the session and did not systematically change over 107, twenty- to thirty-minute sessions.

Midway through Session 108 (arrow, Fig. 5) the following procedure was introduced. The experimenter shouted "Stop that!", seized *S* by the upper arms, and shook her whenever she began rocking. He would wait until her eyes were closed or fixed on her hand before abruptly shouting and shaking her. This event invariably produced a "startle reflex" and flushing in *S*. This contingency, which terminated each rocking episode, of course, decreased the time spent rocking from twenty-five per cent to less than one per cent of the session (top graph, Fig. 5). More important, the frequency of rocking episodes also decreased steadily from 0.94 per minute in the first session where this contingency was applied, to 0.03 per minute in the tenth session. This indicated that shouting and shaking *S* was a punishing stimulus which decreased the probability of the behaviors, in addition to terminating each occurrence of the behavior.

The side effects of punishing autistic rocking.   When autistic rocking was eliminated by this punishment procedure imitative claps immediately increased to sixty-four per cent of the models presented and to an average rate of sixteen per ten-minute period in the first session (fifteenth to seventeenth ten-minute periods, Fig. 5), and continued to increase to seventy-six per cent of the models presented and to a rate of twenty-five per ten-minute period by the fourth session of this procedure (twenty-second and twenty-third ten-minute periods, Fig. 5).

In the fifth session after autistic rocking had been eliminated, the experimenter began to establish imitative pounding of the table. He pounded on the table contingent upon eye contact and reinforced any pounds which occurred within approximately five seconds after this model. Imitative pounds systematically increased from an average of thirteen per cent of the models presented and a rate of three per ten-minute period to ninety-three per cent of the models presented and a rate of twenty-six per ten-minute period in five sessions (twenty-fourth to thirty-eighth ten-minute periods, Fig. 5). Models for both pounds and claps were presented in a random order in the final session. Accurate imitation of pounds and claps occurred to eighty-seven per cent of the models presented and at a rate of twenty-three per ten-minute period in this session (thirty-ninth to forty-first ten-minute period, Fig. 5). Thus, punishing autistic rocking not only immediately increased imitative clapping but also permitted the rapid establishment of a new imitative response.

Imitation training in the home.   After the procedures to control *S*'s disruptive behaviors had been developed and employed in the home, the mother was able to devote her time to the training of appropriate behaviors.

The mother had observed the establishment of the two imitative behaviors in the laboratory. After one session in which the mother worked with *S* under the experimenter's supervision, the mother began conducting imitation training sessions at home. Due to extra-experimental factors, the experimenter no longer worked with *S*, and communicated with *S*'s

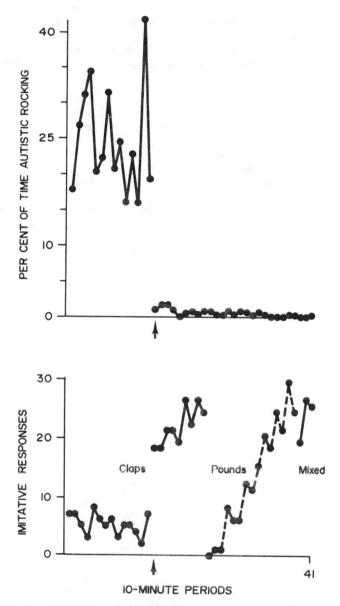

Fig. 5. Graphs showing the relationship between autistic rocking and frequency of imitative responses. At the arrows, autistic rocking was punished by the experimenter shouting at and shaking *S*. Following the increase in frequency of imitative clapping, imitative pounding was trained, and then clapping and pounding were both randomly presented.

mother via letter and telephone. The mother reported that in 115 sessions (a total of 41 hours) she had established five new imitative responses (pounding on wall, stamping feet, standing up, raising arms, and placing a hat on head) in addition to the two already established, and all seven imitative responses would reliably occur when their models were presented in random order. From data sheets which the mother kept, it appeared that the last of these five imitative responses was established in less than 1.5 hours of session time. At last report the mother was working on imitative mouth movements in a mirror and imitative behaviors which produce noises (blowing a whistle and a harmonica, squeezing a horn, etc.) as a step toward establishing verbal imitation.

DISCUSSION

The failure of the initial attempts to eliminate climbing (in the home with contingent timeout from social interaction and in the laboratory with extinction procedures coupled with the establishment of incompatible behaviors) obviates even a tentative statement about the variables which maintained this behavior. It appears that social interaction was not functional in maintaining this behavior (although even this statement must be tentative, since the initial procedures were applied for a short period of time, relative to the lengthy history of the behavior).

Although the electric shock was applied contingent upon several behaviors, it was seldom applied concurrent with those behaviors. The actual behavior ongoing when the shock was applied was usually vigorous struggling. Nevertheless, the shock (preceded by "No!") functioned as a punishing stimulus, decreasing the future probability of the behaviors. Climbing on the bookcase and standing on her chair in the laboratory, and hitting her brother and climbing at home were all quickly eliminated by the contingent application of shock. Shouting and shaking S contingent upon and concurrent with autistic rocking also functioned as a punishing stimulus for that behavior. (However, this consequence was apparently not a punishing stimulus for climbing behavior, as the parents reportedly had been applying it for several years without success.)

The original direct effect of the punishment was restricted to the specific stimulus conditions of the presence of the experimenter in the laboratory room. After punishment, climbing occurred in the laboratory when the experimenter was absent, at home when he was present, but not in the laboratory in his presence, even when the shock device was absent. Identical stimulus control was noted, but not measured, following punishment of autistic rocking. In light of the continued climbing at home and in the laboratory in the absence of the experimenter, the stimulus control exerted by his presence in the laboratory room was remarkable. Only by evoking approximations to climbing by placing a new piece of furniture in front of the bookcase, did climbing recur in the experimenter's presence. The continued, intermittent occurrences of climbing when S was alone in the room during the pre-session periods, even when this climbing was punished, was perhaps due to the specificity of the punishment effect to the experimenter's presence.

A prime argument against the use of punishment procedures is that these procedures will generate undesirable side effects. Most of the behaviors of S were continuously recorded in the laboratory sessions to evaluate the side effects of punishment of other behaviors. Several marked side effects were, in fact, observed.

When climbing on the bookcase was punished S began to stand and climb on the seat and back of her chair. This behavior subsequently varied inversely with climbing on the bookcase. When the punished behavior was allowed to recover, standing on the chair immediately ceased. When climbing was again punished, standing on the chair again resumed. This side effect corresponds to the clinical model of "symptom substitution" in that the substituted behavior was topographically similar and similarly undesirable to the punished behavior. This "contrast effect" may have been related specifically to the punishment procedure since standing on the chair did not increase during the nine sessions when climbing was eliminated by removing the furniture. However, when this "symptom" was also punished, no other undesirable behaviors appeared.

No suppression of other behaviors was noted, either through generalization of the punishment effect or through conditioned "emotional" suppression, correlated with the punishment of the target behaviors. On the contrary, all changes noted in other behaviors were increases. The brevity of the general suppression directly produced by the shock, if any, is indicated by S obtaining and consuming food within seventy seconds after the first shock.

S quickly learned to jump down from the bookcase in the laboratory, and to sit in the timeout chair at home, to avoid shock. Although strong escape and avoidance behaviors were produced with the shock, both intentionally and inadvertently, no general avoidance of or attempts to escape from the room or the experimenter were seen.

No aggressive behavior toward any person or object occurred in the laboratory. When the aggressive behavior toward her little brother (which antedated this study) was punished with shock, no evidence of pain-elicited aggression was noted, only a systematic decrease in the behavior.

The experimenter was closely paired with the shock presentations in the laboratory. The effects of the punishment were specific to his presence in the laboratory, attesting to the fact that he was discriminative for shock. However, the only observed alteration in S's behavior toward the experimenter following punishment was an increased frequency of attending to (making eye contact with) him. This increase in frequency of eye contacts after a behavior was eliminated by shock is in marked contrast to the theoretical discussion by Hutt and Ounsted (1966) predicting that increasing the level of arousal and anxiety of a child would result in a decrease in eye contacts.

The most significant side effect was the fact that eliminating climbing and autistic rocking with punishment facilitated the acquisition of new desirable behaviors. When climbing was occurring, the reinforcement procedures were ineffective in increasing the rate of eye contacts. When climbing was punished the reinforcement procedures produced a steady increase in the rate of eye contacts, which ceased when climbing resumed. Whereas the absolute level of the rate of eye contacts could be maintained when climbing was occurring, systematic increases in rate were produced only when climbing was suppressed. An almost identical relationship was observed between autistic rocking and rate of imitation.

This effect did not appear to be related to the punishment procedures *per se*, but only to the presence or absence of the climbing behavior, as a systematic increase in the rate of eye contacts also occurred when climbing was simply precluded by the absence of furniture. However, the relationship between climbing and eye contacts, or autistic rocking and imitation, was not simply a function of the physical incompatibility between the behaviors. Subtracting the total time spent climbing or rocking from each session and recomputing the rate of eye contacts or imitations does not alter the relationships depicted in Figs. 2 and 5. The physical incompatibility does not account for those relationships. However, the necessity of eliminating climbing or rocking before increases could be obtained in eye contacts or imitations demonstrates a relationship between the behaviors. This relationship might be termed "functional incompatibility." The possibility that the stereotyped behaviors of deviant children are functionally incompatible with the establishment of new, socially productive behaviors could play an important role in remediating the deficits of deviant children.

In summary, this study found that when punishment was used to eliminate a child's deviant behavior, side effects in the form of behavioral contrast or "symptom substitution" did occur, but that these side effects were primarily desirable. Some deviant behaviors, maintained by unknown variables, interfered with the establishment of new behaviors. This interference was not primarily due to a physical incompatibility between the behaviors. This interference, which might be termed "functional incompatibility," suggests that the elimination of such deviant behaviors may be a necessary prerequisite to the establishment of new behaviors.

This paper should not be interpreted as a blanket endorsement of punishment with children. In the opinion of the author, the punishment procedures were therapeutically justified for this child. Shock punishment was employed only after other procedures to control disruptive and dangerous behaviors had been extensively but unsuccessfully employed. The possibility of deleterious effects and side effects were thoroughly considered before shock was used. The effects and side effects were carefully assessed in the laboratory before shock was employed in the home. The benefits to the child, in fact, far exceeded the author's expectations. Of course, no statement about the generality of these findings to other children can yet be made. However, these findings do serve to limit the generality of extrapolations from past research which contraindicates the use of punishment.

REFERENCES

Azrin, N. H. & Holz, W. C. Punishment. In W. K. Honig (Ed.) *Operant behavior: Areas of research and application.* New York: Appleton-Century-Crofts, 1966, pp. 213–270.

Baer, D. M., Peterson, R. F. & Sherman, J. A. Building a generalized imitative repertoire be reinforcing similarity to a model. Paper presented at annual meeting of the Society for Research in Child Development, Minneapolis, 1965.

Baer, D. M., Peterson, R. F. & Sherman, J. A. The development of imitation by reinforcing behavioral similarity to a model. *Journal of the Experimental Analysis of Behavior,* 1967, **10**, 405–416.

Catania, A. C. Concurrent operants. In W. K. Honig (Ed.) *Operant behavior: Areas of research and application.* New York: Appleton-Century-Crofts, 1966, pp. 213–270.

Hutt, Corinne & Ounsted, C. The biological significance of gaze aversion with particular reference to the syndrome of infantile autism. *Behavioral Science.* 1966, **11**, 346–356.

Lovaas, O. I., Schaeffer, B. & Simmons, J. Q. Building social behavior in autistic children by use of electric shock. *Journal of Experimental Research in Personality.* 1965, **1**, 99–109.

Metz, J. R. Conditioning generalized imitation in autistic children. *Journal of Experimental Child Psychology.* 1965, **2**, 389–399.

Risley, T. R. & Wolf, M. M. Establishing functional speech in echolalic children. *Behavior Research and Therapy.* 1967, **5**, 73–88.

Sherman, J. A. Use of reinforcement and imitation to reinstate verbal behavior in mute psychotics. *Journal of Abnormal Psychology,* 1965, **70**, 155–164.

Solomon, R. L. Punishment. *American Psychologist.* 1964, **19**, 239–253.

Development of Imitative Responses

Conditioning Generalized
Imitation in Autistic Children*†

J. RICHARD METZ‡

Children's Division, Camarillo State Hospital

Abstract: Generalized imitative behavior, commonly found in normal children but reduced or absent in autistic children, was studied in two autistic children. Operant conditioning methods were applied to teach the children generalized imitative behavior in a laboratory setting. The children learned to imitate on specifically trained tasks. More important, this learning generalized to similar but new tasks where specific training and specific rewards were not given.

The value of imitation for learning and socialization in early childhood has long been recognized. As Bandura (1962) has pointed out, the learning of complex acts would be extremely difficult if each small detail of behavior had to be acquired separately. It would be very difficult to conceive of a child learning language, for example, without his first having developed the ability to imitate sounds. In experiments with normal nursery school children Bandura (1964) has shown that modelling is a powerful force in determining the behavior of children who have imitative skills.

It has been recognized that autistic children typically do not imitate other people (Ritvo & Provence, 1953). This apparently essential ingredient of normal social development seems to be considerably reduced or lacking in autistic children. This paper reports an application of operant conditioning methods to teach two autistic children generalized imitative behavior, or imitation of relatively new behavior on which training has not specifically been given. This study was designed to show that (1) the subjects learned to imitate, (2) imitation generalized to similar, but relatively new tasks on which no training was given, and (3) generalized imitation persisted even when unrewarded.

METHOD

Subjects

The Ss were a seven-year-old boy (S_1) and girl (S_2), hospitalized one year and two and a half years, respectively, who had responded little, if at all, to conventional therapeutic programmes. They were diagnosed by the psychiatric team, "Schizophrenic reaction, childhood type." Their records indicated long histories of autistic behavior, including mutism, social isolation, stereotyped behavior or mannerisms, primitive interests, and resistance to change.

---

*The cooperation and encouragement of Norbert I. Rieger, M.D., Assistant Superintendent, Children's Division, and the assistance of Rodney Freeborg, Howard Hammerman, Barry Singer, and the hospital staff are gratefully acknowledged.

†Reprinted from the *Journal of Experimental Child Psychology*, December 1965, 2, 4, 389–399. Copyright 1965 with permission from Academic Press Inc., and Dr. J. Richard Metz.

‡Now at Permanente Medical Group, 2200 O'Farrell St., San Francisco, California 94115.

247

General Procedures

The breakfast-deprived S was seen (individually) at lunch time for one half to three quarter hour sessions, six days a week. For convenience, two adults worked with each S. The E gave a standard demonstration without verbal instruction, of the behavior that S was to follow. The E also provided the conditioned rewards ("good" and tokens) for correct responses. An assistant provided food rewards as required (delivered in small portions from a lazy Susan-type dispenser) and recorded the data. The position of assistant was filled by whoever was available to help, but E remained the same for all testing sessions. During experimental periods in which behavior was rewarded by food, S received his entire lunch in this manner and was not fed upon returning to the ward.

Experimental Design

The experiment was divided into six periods as follows: (1) pre-testing, (2) preliminary training, (3) early testing. (4) intensive training, (5) later testing, and (6) post-testing. (Table 1.) Essentially, the experimental design consisted of a within-S comparison of the number of imitative responses occurring in each of the four testing periods listed above. The first (pre-testing) was a baseline observation made prior to any training whatsoever. The number of imitative responses elicited during this period was compared with the number elicited during 'the last (post-testing) period, under identical test conditions. The number of imitative responses elicited during the early testing period, as against the later testing period were similarly compared. These comparisons were made to observe the increase, after training, of generalized imitative behavior. The experiment was then replicated with the second S.

Imitation Defined

For the purpose of this experiment, generalized imitation is defined in terms of three necessary conditions. First, the behavior must be similar to, and occur upon the occasion of the specific example demonstrated by a model. This is a necessary but not sufficient condition of imitation. An observer may simply perform a response which he has previously learned, using the model's example only as a cue for *when* to perform it. For example, a child may be

Table 1. Summary of experimental periods.

Period	Tasks used	Rewards*	Test criterion†
Pre-testing	List I; 1 session.	G	1
Preliminary training	List V-A, as required for training to criterion.	G T F	—
Early testing	Ten tasks per session from List I, mixed with tasks from Lists IV and V-A, presented over several sessions.	G T F	2
Intensive training	Tasks from List V (B or C) as required for training.	G T F	—
Later testing	Ten tasks per session from List II, mixed with tasks from Lists IV and V-A, presented over several sessions.	G T F	2
Post-testing	List III; 1 session.	G	1

*G = "Good"; T = tokens; F = food.

†1 = Response on first trial; 2 = Response on first trial, confirmed by response on one of next two trials.

taught to touch his toes, with E touching his own toes as an S^d. Each time E gives the example (S^d), S performs by touching his toes. The behavior sequence of E followed by S touching toes appears to be imitation. However, its limitation is easily shown when E touches his head instead. If S nevertheless responds by touching toes (as commonly occurred during training in this study) it shows the E's S^d is used by S only to indicate the occasion of responding.

A second necessary condition for imitation, then, is that S respond differentially, by using E's S^d discriminatively. For example, S touches head or toes depending upon which of the two actions E demonstrates. Such discriminative imitation was explored by Miller and Dollard (1941). However, the imitative behavior demonstrated in their experiments seems to represent only the special case of discrimination learning (Bandura & Walters, 1964, pp. 54, 55). The discriminative imitative behavior demonstrated during the preliminary training period of the present experiment appears to be of the same type. For example, in place of the model's demonstration, a red and green light could probably have served equally well as S^ds for head or toe touching. A higher form of imitative response has, in this study, been called generalized imitation.

In addition to the necessary conditions listed above, such imitation requires as a third condition that the behavior in question be relatively novel as an item under S^d control. The action itself may not be novel, but S has not been specifically taught to perform it upon presentation of the S^d. This immediately raises the problem of relevant dimensions along which such generalization can be described. This problem was met only indirectly in this study by the procedure of random selection of imitative tasks from a large pool of apparently different tasks.

Imitation Tasks

All of the simple, nonverbal tasks used in this experiment are listed in Table 2. Lists I, II, and III were drawn at random from a pool of 100 such tasks. List I was used in the pre-testing period, and again in the early testing period. Lists II and III were used in the later testing and post-testing periods, respectively. Definitions of acceptable responses were written for all tasks. Also displayed in Table 2 are all training tasks and a special list of four nonrewarded tasks to be explained later.

Table 2. Tasks used in testing and training for generalized imitation.

List I – Test items	List II – Test items
Insert peg in peg board	Put doll into crib
Run across room	Mark with crayon on paper
Stamp foot	Slide block across floor
Throw softball	Turn crank on music box
Operate busy box	Roll small ball
Clap hands	Bang hand on table top
Open paint box	Bang hand on tambourine
Kick bean bag	Kick block
Line up kindergarten blocks	Squat
Kick large ball	Put blanket on doll
Hug doll	Put large box over block
Pile up books	Wiggle fingers
Knock over large block tower	Insert one shape into form board
Hop on one foot	Wave arms
Blow horn	Climb onto first step of stepstool
Push buggy	Blow cotton off hand

Table 2 (*Continued*)

List III — Test items	
Slap thigh	Squeeze horn
Stamp foot on paper	Spin top
Clasp self	Pile up wood blocks
Knock block off box	Pile up wood cubes
Punch Bobo clown	Line up large cardboard blocks
Ride hobby horse	Sound triangle
Roll rolling pin	Sound symbols
Open lid of card file	Mark with chalk on slate

List IV — Nonreward items	
Shake bell	Bang stick against musical block
Place doughnut over post	Hammer pegs on toy workbench

List V — Training items	
A. *Preliminary training*	Place block on chair, table, floor, etc.
Sit on box	Position block
Stand on box	Arrange configuration of blocks
Place block into box	Rotate fists
Place block onto box	Interlock clothspins
Touch head	Drop bean bag
Touch toes	Blow whistle
B. *Intensive training.* S_1	Open purse
Play xylophone	Bounce ball
Put clothspin into box	Place bean bag on various parts of body
Push toy box	Pat bean bag
Open paint box	C. *Intensive training.* S_2
Blow party favor	Kneel
Throw bean bag	Place block onto table
Place eraser onto cube	Place bean bag into box
Turn egg beater	Ring cash register
Place cube onto block	Blow whistle
Touch nose, cheeks, etc.	Open purse
Place chalk into box	Place cloth over block
Stretch rubber band	Jump over block
Select object from group	

Description of Experimental Periods

In the *pre-testing period*, the tasks of List I were presented to *S*. The E demonstrated each task. If *S* responded correctly within approximately ten seconds E said "Good," and went on to the next task. If *S* gave no response or an incorrect response, E went on to the next task without comment. There were no tokens or food rewards available during this period. This period lasted one session, for both *S*s.

In the *preliminary training period*, the first step was to orient *S* to the procedure and establish "Good" and tokens as rewards. Regardless of *S*'s behavior, E said "Good," handed *S* a token, then demonstrated how the token could be inserted into a formboard to receive food. At first, only one token was required for a food reward. Gradually, the required number was increased to three (FR-3 schedule). The verbal stimulus, "Good" was intended to make it possible to reinforce a desired response instantly, from any point in the room, regardless of

S's position. This was particularly valuable for shaping new behavior, where it was necessary to capitalize immediately upon fleeting variations of behavior. The use of tokens was intended to make more concrete the FR-3 schedule and serve as a bridge between "good" and food rewards. The first step of the preliminary training period was accomplished for both *S*s in one session.

The next step of the preliminary training period was to teach *S* by using passive demonstration and shaping procedures, a repertoire of three pairs of tasks: sitting or standing upon a box; placing a block into or onto a box; and touching head or toes. Pairs of tasks, in which the same materials were used, were devised so that *S* would be forced to attend to E's demonstration as a discriminative stimulus (S^d) in order to respond correctly. Shaping procedures were similar to those described by Sidman (1962). Passive demonstration consisted of "putting the child through" the desired action by physically guiding him and then rewarding the action thus produced. Then the external guidance of the behavior provided by E was gradually withdrawn or "faded" until *S* produced the behavior spontaneously. Each instance of behavior leading to reward in this way was considered a trial, during the training period. A task was considered learned if *S* imitated it correctly (i.e., performed it after E's demonstration), without any other help, six times in a row when it was presented in a series with the other five tasks. This discriminative (and therefore more truly imitative) behavior was more difficult to achieve than the simple performance of one task after massed practice. The S_1 learned the three pairs of imitative tasks to this criterion in ten sessions, or a total of about 300 trials. The S_2 took five sessions or approximately 150 trials.

The second purpose of this experiment was to teach *generalized* imitative behavior. To test for generalized responses, the three lists of sixteen tasks were administered during the remaining testing periods. Thus, in the *early testing period*, the tasks of List I were used, no more than ten being administered during any one session. During this period the model gave a standard demonstration. Imitative responses were followed by "Good," tokens and food as described earlier. Interspersed among these ten tasks were the six familiar tasks from the preliminary training period. They were included to guarantee some success and at least a minimum of lunch. Also interspersed were four nonrewarded tasks (List IV, Table 2) which were presented every test session to determine if nonreward would lead to extinction of the generalized imitative response. The list used in a given test session, which thus contained a total of twenty tasks, was presented to *S* twice during that session. An example of such a list is given in Table 3. When a task was imitated in two out of three trials, it was credited and then dropped from the list to be replaced by another. A maximum of ten presentations were allowed per task. The early testing period lasted ten sessions for S_1, nine sessions for S_2.

In the *intensive training period*, *S* was trained on those tasks which he had failed during early testing, and on the additional tasks of List V, Table 2. The S_2 learned sixteen such tasks (including eight failed from early testing and eight new ones) in five sessions. The S_1, however, learned more slowly. In his training, therefore, the imitative response was broken down into several component parts, with training given in each. For example, in the first part, selection from among a group of objects, the task was to select the same object E selected, from a group consisting of several pairs of objects. At first, two pencils and two erasers were displayed on the table. If E selected a pencil, *S* was required to select the other pencil. The S_1's usual response was to select the object which was last rewarded, rather than follow E's example. After six training sessions devoted exclusively to this kind of task, S_1 was able to select imitatively, with virtually no errors, the correct object of a pair from among a dozen pairs scattered at random on the table. The objects were paper clips, thumb tacks, cubes, beads, rubber bands, etc. Additional training was given on location of placement (e.g., on a table vs. the floor, the chair, etc.); position (e.g., upright vs. flat, on edge, etc.); and configuration of objects (arrangement of two blocks in relation to each other). The purpose of this kind of

Table 3. Tasks used in first session of early test period.

Task	Function
Insert peg in pegboard	Test item
Sit on box	Trained item
Run across room	Test item
Shake bell	Nonrewarded item
Stamp foot	Test item
Stand on box	Trained item
Throw softball	Test item
Place doughnut over post	Nonrewarded item
Operate busy box	Test item
Touch head	Trained item
Clap hands	Test item
Bang stick against musical block	Nonrewarded item
Open paint box	Test item
Touch toes	Trained item
Kick bean bag	Test item
Hammer pegs on workbench	Nonrewarded item
Line up kindergarten blocks	Test item
Place block onto box	Trained item
Kick large ball	Test item
Place block into box	Trained item

training was to develop in S a set to attend to the S^d provided by E. Altogether, the intensive training period for S_1 lasted twenty-five sessions.

In the *later testing period*, the tasks from List II were administered in exactly the same manner as were List I tasks in the earlier testing period. This period lasted six sessions for S_1, four sessions for S_2.

Finally, in the *post-testing period*, List III tasks were administered under exactly the same conditions as were List I tasks in the pre-testing period (correct responses followed by "Good," but no tokens or food available). This period lasted one session for each S.

RESULTS AND DISCUSSION

Figure 1 compares the number of generalized imitative responses occurring (A) at the pre- and post-testing periods and (B) at the early and later testing periods. The graph shows, for each S, the number of tasks out of sixteen imitated on the first trial. Comparisons A and B are presented separately, since the testing conditions of the pre- and post-testing periods were not identical with the testing conditions of the early and later testing periods. In the early and later testing periods an imitative response was not credited unless it was repeated again on one of the next two trials. Thus the criterion of success for the B comparison was more stringent than for the A comparison. On the other hand, tokens and food rewards were available in the early and later testing periods, while they were absent in the pre- and post-testing periods. The results, as shown in the graph, suggest an increase in generalized imitative responses for both Ss, in both comparisons.

Figure 2 shows the course of responses to nonrewarded tasks (List IV, Table 2). Along the ordinate is represented the number of nonrewarded tasks (out of four) which were imitated during each presentation of a testing list. Along the abscissa is represented the repeated presentations of the set of four nonrewarded tasks. Since the performance of S_2 was better

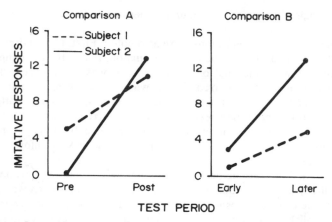

Fig. 1. Generalized imitative responses occurring in each of four test periods.

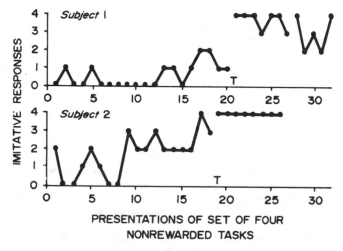

PRESENTATIONS OF SET OF FOUR
NONREWARDED TASKS

Fig. 2. Generalized imitative responses occurring in repeated presentations of the set of four nonrewarded tasks. Break for intensive training is indicated by T.

than that of S_1, she required fewer test trials. Hence the abscissa in her case is shorter. The graph shows an increase of imitative responses to these tasks over the course of the experiment. With intensive training (on the training tasks) the number of imitative responses per group of four nonrewarded test tasks increased sharply. These data suggest that the generalized imitative response to these tasks persisted and increased, in a context of reward for imitation, without specifically being rewarded.

The results suggest that (a) autistic children can learn to imitate, (b) the learning can generalize to similar but new behaviors without specific training, and (c) the generalized imitative response can persist, in a context of reinforcement of *other* imitative behavior, without specifically being reinforced. Findings (a) and (b) are consistent with those reported by Lovaas (1964) and Hewett (1964) for autistic children, and by Baer, Peterson & Sherman (1965) for profoundly retarded children. The later authors also imbedded nonreinforced imitative tasks among reinforced tasks as was done in this study, with results similar to (c).

This effect was originally reported by Baer & Sherman (1964) for normal nursery school children.

The following subjective observations were also noted. First, the children appeared to be reasonably well motivated in the experimental situation, but at the beginning the behavior apparently directed toward the goal of receiving food was inappropriate and ineffective. Temper tantrums occasionally occurred. There was a very strong tendency to form what Skinner (1948) has called "superstitious" responses, i.e., responses adventitiously rewarded in the course of rewarding appropriate responses. Moreover, responses which were appropriate and rewarded in a particular situation often were repeated by S inappropriately in new, unfamiliar situations. To the outside observer, unfamiliar with S's reinforcement history, an impression of bizarreness was thus created by such inappropriate responses.

Second, as appropriate learning occurred, "inappropriate" motor and emotional behavior spontaneously disappeared. Not only did the children learn to do what was required by the task, but appropriate emotional responses also seemed to appear. For example, the children expressed joy or delight upon "solving" a problem, an affect rarely seen in these children in other situations. The children eventually appeared to enjoy the whole procedure, sought E out whenever he appeared on the ward, ran eagerly to the experimental room, etc. Temper tantrums and "rituals" disappeared even though food and tokens were sometimes withheld for long periods of time (as in the post-testing session, where none were available at all).

Finally, although generalized imitative behavior increased in both Ss concomitant with application of the conditioning procedures described above, one is limited in drawing conclusions with respect to causation. No control was provided that would allow one to infer that the increase of generalized imitative behavior was specifically the result of the training procedures employed. Experiments intended to clarify such ambiguities are now under way.

REFERENCES

Baer, D., Peterson, R. & Sherman, J. Building an imitative repertoire by programming similarity between child and model as discriminative for reinforcement. Read at biennial meeting of the Soc. Res. Child Developm., Minneapolis, Minnesota, 1965.

Baer, D. & Sherman, J. Reinforcement control of generalized imitation in young children. *J. exp. child psychol.*, 1964, **1**, 37–49.

Bandura, A. Social learning through imitation. In M. R. Jones (Ed.), *Nebraska symposium on motivation*. Lincoln, Nebraska: Univer. of Nebraska Press, 1962. pp. 211–269.

Bandura, A. & Walters, R. *Social learning and personality development*. New York: Holt, Rinehart & Winston, 1964.

Hewett, F. M. Teaching speech to autistic children through operant conditioning. Unpublished manuscript, Neuropsychiatric Institute, Univer. of California, Los Angeles, 1964.

Lovaas, O. I. Experimental studies in childhood schizophrenia. Paper read at meetings of California State Psychological Assoc., Los Angeles, Dec. 1964.

Miller, N. E. & Dollard, J. *Social learning and imitation*. New Haven: Yale Univer. Press, 1941.

Ritvo, S. & Provence, Sally. Form perception and imitation in some autistic children: Diagnostic findings and their contextual interpretation. *Psychoanal. Stud. Child.* 1953, **8**, 155–161.

Sidman, M. Operant techniques. In A. Bachrach (Ed.), *Experimental foundations of clinical psychology*. New York: Basic Books, 1962. pp. 170–210.

Skinner, B. F. "Superstition" in the pigeon. *J. exp. Psychol.*, 1948, **38**, 168–172.

Control of Eye Contact in an Autistic Child*

OWEN L. McCONNELL

University of North Carolina at Chapel Hill, and Murdoch Center, Butner, North Carolina, U.S.A.

Abstract: This study demonstrates the use of operant conditioning techniques in overcoming the visual avoidance of a five and a half year-old Negro boy with infantile autism. The research included thirty-three sessions, each lasting forty-five minutes. The paradigm involved baseline rates, conditioning, extinction, and reconditioning sessions. Stimulus control was demonstrated by alternating S^ds and S^Δs. Finally eye contact was chained to the subject's emerging verbal responses. Related changes in approach, exploratory, and emotional behaviors were observed. Discussion focuses of problems of generalization and on the therapeutic effects of acquiring eye contact.

INTRODUCTION

In their investigation of the phenomenology of autism, Wolff & Chess (1964) found abnormal eye contact in every case and concluded that "it was difficult to define behavior indicative of autism except for abnormalities of eye-to-eye contact from which a clinical impression of emotional withdrawal appears to be derived." Norman (1955) also emphasized that the impression of being in touch with another person is conveyed by the other person's looking into one's face so that gaze meets gaze. Wolff & Chess (1964) differentiated two forms of abnormal eye behavior: (a) visual avoidance and (b) unusual staring. Visual avoidance was associated with the more severe cases of autism.

The autistic child's "anxiously obsessive desire for the preservation of sameness" (Kanner, 1965) has presented an obstacle to modifying his behavior through traditional therapeutic methods (Rimland, 1964). Operant conditioning, however, has been used to reduce the stereotypy of the autistic child and expand his repertoire of behavior toward the physical and social environment (Ferster & DeMeyer, 1962; Hingtgen, Sanders & DeMeyer, 1965; Lovaas *et al.*, 1964; and Wetzel *et al.*, 1966). The primary purpose of the present study was to determine if the visual avoidance of an autistic child could be overcome with operant conditioning techniques.

SUBJECT

Tom was a five and a half-year-old Negro who had no primary motor or sensory handicaps, but showed many features of the psychotic child with underdeveloped abilities. After a week's in-patient evaluation in the Diagnostic Clinic of Murdoch Center by a team consisting of a pediatrician, child psychiatrist, psychologist, social worker and nurse, the director (child psychiatrist) concluded that Tom's "reaction falls fairly clearly into the general category

*Reprinted from the *Journal of Child Psychology and Psychiatry*, 1967, **8**, 249–255. Copyright 1967 with permission from Pergamon Press Publishing Company and Dr. Owen L. McConnell.

of Infantile Autism." In addition, Rimland's (1964) diagnostic check list was used to differentiate infantile autism from childhood schizophrenia. Fifty-eight per cent of the autism items and eighteen per cent of the schizophrenic ones applied to Tom. Tom's behavior was atavistic and asocial. He ate with his fingers, played with his feces and had no self-care behavior. He not only avoided eye contact but also resisted physical contact and control, dropping to the floor when one tried to lead him. Destructive with plastic human figures, he pulled off their appendages and chewed on their heads. Unusual abilities, such as skillful manipulation of toys, humming of complex tunes, and reading city names on licence tags and advertising phrases appearing on television, suggested potential for a higher level of behavior. His frequent vocalizations were "expressive jargon," except for a few clearly articulated words and phrases emitted out of context without apparent communicative intent.

METHOD

During the research period Tom resided in the medical infirmary of Murdoch Center, a state institute for the mentally retarded. The infirmary was not a very therapeutic milieu, being crowded with infirm and malfunctioning retardates of varied ages. Due to shortage of nursing staff and Tom's danger to other patients (e.g., by pulling off their bandages or tubes), he was frequently restrained with cloth straps.

The research was conducted in a private office in the basement of the infirmary for a forty-five-minute session each weekday at approximately 10 a.m. During each of thirty-three sessions, E sat in a chair beside a desk at one side of the room, allowing Tom to play in front of him in a ten by ten foot area equipped with a cabinet filled with numerous toys. In a drawer of the desk was a silent button switch which E held down as long as Tom was making eye contact. The switch was wired to a Gerbrands cumulative recorder (in another room) which stepped one response for every 0.5 seconds of eye contact and to counters which totalled the number and duration of eye contacts.

PROCEDURE AND RESULTS

Operant Level

During four baseline sessions E assumed a silent, impassive role, controlling for a possible "attention" effect by observing Tom continuously. Figure 1 shows a graph of the number of eye contacts during each session (mean = 11 eye contacts per session).

Stable low rates of eye contact occurred and the mean duration of a single eye contact was 0.7 seconds. Cumulative eye contact for the last baseline session is shown in Fig. 2 (a photograph of the original record).

Initial Conditioning

In Sessions 5 through 13 E reinforced every eye contact by warmly saying, "That's good." or "Very nice," immediately after the onset of eye contact and by smiling for the remaining duration of eye contact. To determine the ease of conditioning eye contact, E planned to start with presumed ineffective or weak reinforcers and proceed toward stronger ones as necessary. Tom's avoidance of contact with his parents and other persons suggested that social reinforcers would be ineffective for him. However, to E's surprise, they were strong enough to condition eye contact. Figure 1 shows the increase in number of eye contacts during the reinforcement sessions. During the last conditioning session (Fig. 2), seventy-five eye contacts

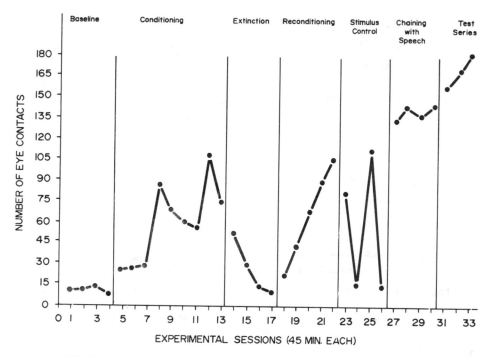

Fig. 1. Number of eye contacts as a function of environmental manipulations.

occurred for a total duration of 2.14 minutes. The number of eye contacts increased approximately sevenfold while the duration of a single eye contact merely doubled. Because praise and smiling occurred at the onset of a response and praise was not contingent on duration, the greater effect on number of responses is understandable. The smaller increase in duration probably resulted from the few seconds it took to deliver praise, and from the smiling which continued during eye contact, but no doubt lost some of its lustre after a few seconds.

Extinction

To show that eye contacts were controlled by the reinforcing stimuli and not by extraneous variables, the reinforcement was delivered on a non-contingent basis. During Sessions 14–17, E gave reinforcement (praise and smile) sixty times per session, i.e. as frequently as reinforcements were given on the average during the conditioning sessions. Reinforcements were dispensed on a variable-interval schedule with an average interval of forty-five seconds and a range from six to eighty-four seconds. As Fig. 1 shows, number of eye contacts progressively declined. On the fourth and last session on non-contingent reinforcement, the rate (Fig. 2) was approximately the same as during the baseline period. Only twelve eye contacts were made for a total duration of 9.6 seconds.

Reconditioning

Conditions were the same during Sessions 18–22 as they were during initial conditioning. Figure 1 shows the smooth recovery of eye contact which was achieved in five sessions of conditioning. Figure 2 presents the cumulative curve for the last reconditioning session.

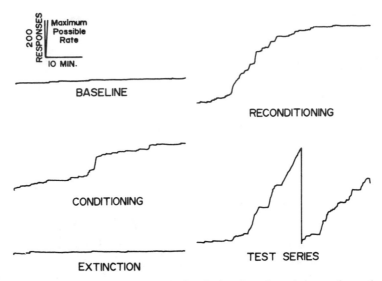

Fig. 2. Cumulative eye contact curves during the last forty-five minute session under five experimental conditions: baseline, conditioning, extinction, reconditioning and test series. Each 0.5 second of eye contact produced one vertical step of the pen.

Stimulus Control

Observations made during reconditioning sessions suggested that certain toys had become discriminative stimuli (S^ds) for eye contact and other toys had become S^Δs. The majority of eye contacts appeared to be made while Tom played with musical toys (specifically a musical jack-in-the-box, a humming top and a drum). Play with these objects had occurred most frequently during the conditioning periods and had apparently become the occasions on which eye contact was followed by reinforcement. Play with marbles (called "footballs"), and with a baseball and bat, had occurred frequently during extinction sessions and had become the occasions upon which eye contact would not be followed by reinforcement. These five toys were practically the only ones Tom played with by this time, as he was showing the stereotypy typical of the autistic child.

Sessions 23–26 were designed to demonstrate the strong stimulus control over Tom's eye contacts. During Sessions 23 and 25 the S^ds (musical toys) were present, but the S^Δs (marbles and baseball equipment) were removed from the room. During Sessions 24 and 26 the conditions were reversed: S^Δs were present and S^ds were absent. Reinforcement of eye contact continued. The pronounced alternations in number of eye contacts (Fig. 1) under these two conditions demonstrated the marked stimulus control. When S^Δs were present, eye contact rates were as low as baseline rates; when S^ds were present, rates were as high as during the last conditioning sessions.

Chaining Eye Contact with Speech

The narrowness of the range of stimuli controlling eye contact was undesirable for at least two reasons. First, observing or play responses to the musical toys (S^ds) were not emitted at a high rate, thus limiting the occasions for eye contact. Secondly, the S^ds were uncommon objects, i.e., ones which are not found in most social situations where eye contact is appropriate. Hence, the generalization of eye contact responses was likely to be restricted.

It seemed more therapeutic to have eye contacts controlled by stimuli which would be available in many diverse physical surroundings and which would be frequently attended to. Tom's own vocal responses seemed to meet these requirements.

Tom vocalized continually and a number of his utterances were recognizable words. If recognizable words could be established as S^ds for eye contact, the effect would be socially natural, since normal children usually make eye contact while speaking. It might also allow reinforcement to strengthen both eye and speech responses simultaneously. Since Tom did not utter as many recognizable words as was needed to carry out this plan, a research assistant was assigned the task of reinforcing intelligible words (with social and consumable reinforcers) for one hour a day in another building.

During Sessions 27–30 E attempted to chain eye contact to speech. The research assistant discovered that repetition of Tom's speech was quite reinforcing; therefore, when eye contact followed intelligible speech, E not only smiled and praised Tom but also repeated the word or phrases which he had just said. E would not repeat a word until eye contact was made. Eye contacts not preceded by speech were reinforced in the usual manner.

As shown in Fig. 1, the number of eye contacts during the chaining-with-speech sessions rose to a new high. This increase may be attributed to the increase in S^ds for eye contact (since Tom's words were also becoming S^ds) and/or the strengthening of reinforcement by word repetition.

Test Series

The purpose of the test series was to show how much stimulus control Tom's speech had acquired over his eye contacts. During Sessions 27–30 eye contacts controlled by the musical toys were not differentiated from those controlled by speech. During the test Sessions 31–33, the musical toys were removed from the room but the S^Δs (marbles, baseball, and bat) remained. The physical conditions were, therefore, similar to those in Sessions 24 and 26 (*see* Fig. 1) when low baseline rates were obtained. Reinforcement continued to be given for all eye contacts.

In the test series the highest number of eye contacts were obtained (Fig. 1). Figure 2 shows the high rate of eye contact during the last test session. Because all eye contacts were recorded, regardless of whether or not they followed recognizable speech, a tape recording was made of the last session in order to differentiate eye contacts following speech from other eye contacts. The recording indicated that 129 out of 180 eye contacts (seventy-two per cent) were immediately preceded by words spoken by Tom which E repeated. This provides further evidence of the stimulus control Tom's speech had acquired over his eye contact responses. The fifty-one eye contacts which apparently were not controlled by Tom's speech or the musical toys, because they were absent, suggest that some desirable generalization of eye contact was occurring.

OTHER BEHAVIORAL CHANGES

Behavior notes were written by E during the sessions and supplemented from memory immediately afterward. Because their objectivity and reliability were not demonstrated, they are reported merely as clinical evidence requiring further investigation. In the baseline sessions, Tom made many attempts to leave the play area. He stood with his back to E much of the time; several times, however, he made momentary physical contact by backing into E.

When reinforcement of eye contacts began, Tom became excited, laughed and clapped his hands. He backed into E's lap almost immediately, but the physical contact seemed to evoke aggression. He bit E's shirt, pulled his tie and rubbed his feet on E. Once, after eye contact, he tilted E's head upward, preventing E from gazing into his eyes. Aggression toward E subsided; but, after climbing on E's lap, Tom would then run around the room, screaming and sometimes flinging himself on the floor. In Session 9, Tom made his first prolonged eye contact. With his eyes riveted to E's, Tom approached until his face was almost touching E's and stared for about thirty seconds. In Session 10, he explored E's face manually, sticking his finger into E's nose and mouth. He also gave E an affectionate hug and tried to take his belongings, e.g., pen and watch. In the next session he offered E some toys. In Session 13, he spontaneously gave E a kiss on the forehead, and explored E's eyes with his fingers. He solicited E's help in turning the crank of the music box.

When extinction began Tom prolonged his gaze at E, watching expectantly; finally he asked, "That's good?" When no reinforcement followed, he twisted E's nose. Then he offered E toys. This offering was followed by his trying to eat clay. Non-contingent rein- forcements did not seem to reassure him. After several non-reinforced eye contacts, Tom began screaming and throwing the football. He repeated, "That good," to himself. Finally he flung himself at E in head-on assault, rubbed his feet on E and tried to chew his tie. In the next extinction session, less aggression occurred. In the third and fourth extinction sessions, there was long, isolated, but apparently happy play with marbles.

In response to the first reinforcement during reconditioning, Tom frowned. However, he crawled directly into E's lap and played with his pen. Approach behavior, without aggression or emotional upset, followed many eye contacts. At the end of the first reconditioning session, Tom resisted leaving. In Session 22, Tom explored E's face and kissed him on the cheek. During the remaining sessions there was much physical contact and continued displays of affection.

DISCUSSION

The results indicate that eye contact responses in an autistic child were controlled by both reinforcing and discriminative stimuli. No claim is made as to the generality of the findings to other children or to situations beyond the experimental one. A problem characteristic of autistic children — a narrow generalization gradient (Rimland, 1964) — arose even within the experimental situation. The problem was dealt with by chaining the desired response (eye contact) to another socially desirable but more frequent and generalized response (speech). This method may have potential for developing other behaviors which are difficult to genera- lize. It also has the advantage of efficiency in that two desirable responses can be simultan- eously increased.

It is not suggested that the present method of establishing eye contact is similar to condi- tions which determined the normal child's eye contact. However, there are suggestions that development of eye contact by operant conditioning techniques may have considerable therapeutic value. First, increased eye contact in the autistic child creates a sense of relation- ship and affects the reactions of others to him. Secondly, changes in other behavior suggest that positive side effects may accompany conditioning of eye contact responses. The effects, of course, need to be more objectively recorded before definite conclusions can be drawn. The experimenter was nevertheless impressed with the increase in approach, exploratory and affective behavior which accompanied the development of eye contact. This may be because of accidental reinforcement stemming from the natural tendency of eye contact and approach behavior to occur together, or through a chain of mediating stimuli and responses. The behavior notes indicate that while the approach and exploratory behavior increased syste- matically with reinforcement of eye contact, the pattern of affective responses was more complicated. The emotional response to the reinforcement was probably slightly positive. The reaction to eye contact *per se* seemed ambivalent (note that at first Tom tried to prevent E from gazing into his eyes). Actual bodily contact issuing from the approach tendencies evoked considerable aggression at first and generalized excitement later. Only after the aggression and excitement adapted, did affectionate responses appear. Further research giving attention to past reinforcement patterns and associations is needed to clarify these diverse emotional reactions.

REFERENCES

Ferster, C. B. & DeMeyer, M. K. (1962) A method for the experimental analysis of the behavior of autistic children. *Am. J. Orthopsychiat.* **32**, 89–98.

Hingtgen, J. N., Sanders, B. J. & DeMeyer, M. K. (1965) Shaping cooperative responses in early childhood schizophrenics. In (Eds.: L. P. Ullmann and L. Krasner) *Case Studies in Behaviour Modification.* Holt, Rinehart and Winston, New York.

Kanner, L. (1965) Infantile autism and the schizophrenias. *Behav. Sci.* **10**, 412–420.

Lovaas, O. I., Freitag, G., Kinder, M. I., Rubenstein, D. B., Schaeffer, B. & Simmons, J. B. (1964) *Experimental Studies in Childhood Schizophrenia: Building Social Behaviors Using Electric Shock.* Paper read at American Psychological Association Annual Convention, Los Angeles, California.

Norman, E. (1955) Affect and withdrawal in schizophrenic children. *Br. J. Med. Psychol.* **28**, 1–18.

Rimland, B. (1964) *Infantile Autism.* Appleton-Century-Crofts, New York.

Wetzel, R. J., Baker, J., Roney, M. & Martin, M. (1966) Out-patient treatment of autistic behaviour. *Behav. Res. & Therapy,* **4**, 169–177.

Wolff, S. & Chess, S. (1964) A behavioural study of schizophrenic children. *Acta psychiat. scand.* **40**, 438–466.

Application of Timeout from Positive Reinforcement for Increasing the Efficiency of Speech Training*†

LEIJA V. McREYNOLDS

University of Kansas

Abstract: Language training procedures, which involved positive reinforcement for verbal imitation, were applied to increase the appropriate verbal behavior of an almost non-verbal, brain damaged, five-year-old boy. Two experiments assessed the effectiveness of timeout from positive reinforcement as a training procedure viewed as having potential punishing and negatively reinforcing functions. In both experiments, timein, termination of timeout and resumption of training, was arranged to have reinforcing properties in that it presented an opportunity to receive positive reinforcers. In Exp. I, the procedure consisted of temporarily halting language training (timeout) following verbal jargon and resuming it (timein) contingent upon the boy sitting quietly in his chair for approximately thirty seconds. The jargon declined to almost zero for an extended period each time the procedure was employed. In Exp. II, the procedure consisted of halting language training (timeout) after emission of undesired verbal responses which previously had been reinforced as the desired approximation to the target verbal behavior. Resumption of training (timein) was made contingent upon the emission of the then-desired approximation of the target verbal behavior. In each experiment, the contingent timeout and timein of the language training that involved positive reinforcement effectively reduced the undesired and increased the desired responses.

One procedure that can be used for training a child to acquire topographically appropriate speech is imitation: the child is presented with a unit of speech as a verbal model. The child's response is reinforced each time he responds with a vocalization that approximates the model presented. At each successive approximation, the criteria for an appropriate response become more stringent and responses that do not meet the criteria are placed on extinction (ignored) while appropriate approximations are reinforced. Although speech can be trained by using positive reinforcement and extinction, it sometimes requires a rather extended training period, due to some of the behaviors in the child's repertoire. Not only does the child come to therapy with a low rate of emission of appropriate speech, but he frequently comes with a repertoire of inappropriate vocalizations (jargon), which he emits spontaneously during each session. Furthermore, as the training progresses and more precise articulation is required, or the phoneme to be acquired is a difficult one to produce, the formerly appropriate approximations may take a considerable amount of time to be extinguished.

*The research was supported by Research Grant HD 00870-04 from the National Institute of Child Health and Human Development to the Bureau of Child Research at the University of Kansas. Reprints may be obtained from the author, Bureau of Child Research Laboratory, Children's Rehabilitation Unit, University of Kansas Medical Center, 39th and Rainbow Blvd., Kansas City, Kansas 66103.

†Reprinted from the *Journal of Applied Behavior Analysis*, 1969, **2**, 3, 199–205. Copyright 1969 with permission from the Society for the Experimental Analysis of Behavior, Inc., and Dr. L. V. McReynolds.

As long as these inappropriate vocalizations continue to be emitted in speech sessions, progress in training appropriate speech is hampered. Usually a procedure in which appropriate responses are reinforced while inappropriate behavior is placed under extinction is successful in training speech. Sometimes, however, the inappropriate behaviors are not readily modified by these procedures. It is possible that a more efficient programme might result if a consequent event, rather than extinction, were used to modify the jargon and inappropriate responses.

A consequent event that has been used successfully to decelerate incompatible behavior in children is timeout from positive reinforcement (Baer, 1962; Wolf, Risley & Mees, 1964). Timeout has been used also during speech training with echolalic children to decrease the frequency of emission of inappropriate verbal statements and shrieks (Risley & Wolf, 1967), and to decelerate incorrect responses (Sloane, Johnston & Harris, 1968). The results indicate that in situations in which positive reinforcers have been established, timeout can be an effective consequence for quickly decelerating inappropriate behavior. It is possible that in attempting to modify jargon and inappropriate responses, timeout as a consequent event will function more effectively than extinction, thereby increasing the efficiency of speech training.

The present study sought to explore whether timeout from positive reinforcement within and across sessions would function (1) as a punishing event to decrease the frequency of jargon vocalizations, and (2) as a negatively reinforcing event to increase the probability that a specific speech unit would be emitted, rather than a previously correct (but currently incorrect) speech response.

METHOD

Subject

A five-year-old boy, who had been diagnosed as brain-damaged, served. Although his parents had attempted to enroll him in a special class, he had not been accepted due to his severely limited behavioral repertoire. No evaluation results were available because no responses had been obtained from the child during diagnostic procedures. During baseline observations the child emitted no speech and did not respond appropriately to verbal directions. In three observation periods he emitted no vocalizations. He was accepted in our experimental speech training programme after he had been excluded from other special programmes.

Operant procedures were used for speech training. In the initial phases of training, emphasis was placed on shaping vocal behavior. The child's vocalizations were reinforced and by the time the study began, he was imitating isolated speech sounds. The imitation training consisted of presenting the child with a model of the phoneme. Vocalizations that approximated the model were reinforced with ice cream. No consequences were presented for incorrect responses. The present study was initiated during imitative word training.

Experimental Setting

The imitative speech training was conducted in a two-room experimental suite. The experimental and control room were separated by a wall containing a one-way vision window. A microphone was mounted in the ceiling of the experimental room and led to a Roberts Tape Recorder, Model 770, and a speaker located in the control room. The training took place in the experimental room while an observer recorded the data in the control room.

Three pens of a Gerbrands four-pen event recorder were used to record the events in the experimental room. The pens were activated by foot switches placed on the floor of the control room. The first pen was used to record the experimenter's presentation of the model, the second recorded the subject's response, and the third recorded the consequent event if one occurred. The observer, a speech pathologist, transcribed in phonetic symbols on the event recorder tape his own observations regarding the subject's responses. Each notation was written directly beside the response as it occurred and was recorded with the pen. In this manner, agreement or disagreement on each response between the observer and experimenter was recorded. Because of the continuously running tape, occurrences of events within any specified time interval for each session could be counted. To check reliability, a second observer was introduced periodically and both would make simultaneous observation records of a session.

For the jargon behavior, percentage of agreement between the observers was obtained by dividing the smaller number of observed occurrences by the larger number when the frequency scores of the observers were not identical. In this case, interest was centered on obtaining a reliability index of frequency *per se*, and the amount of agreement over the total number of jargon occurrences.

For the subject's imitative responses, reliability was assessed between the experimenter and observer as well as the two observers. The percentage of agreement was obtained by dividing the total number of agreements by the number of agreements plus the number of disagreements. The percentage of agreement in all reliability calculations ranged from eighty-one to eighty-six per cent.

Preliminary Procedures

The procedure for word training followed the imitation paradigm. Instead of using a gradual fading of phoneme prompts (Risley, 1966) for word training, the procedure consisted of backward chaining. Each word was taught by first presenting the child with the final phoneme in the word; when he had acquired imitation of this phoneme, the next to the final phoneme was introduced. Chaining continued until the child had acquired all the phonemes in the chain and was imitating the complete word. When the child's imitation was appropriate, the experimenter said, "Good," and immediately followed this with a bite of ice cream. It was observed, however, that as responses with more precise topographies were required, i.e., correct articulation of all phonemes in a sequence, the rate of acquisition of the chain of phonemes was considerably slower than it had been in the earlier isolated phoneme training. The slow acquisition was partly attributable to the fact that the child, after correctly imitating the new response chain for some time, would then revert to the previously learned shorter chain.

At this time the child also began to jargon; i.e., after he had responded, and before the experimenter presented another stimulus, the child began to emit a number of irrelevant vocalizations. Originally, any inappropriate response or jargon was placed on extinction; no consequence was applied. The experimenter waited until he had stopped vocalizing before presenting a new stimulus, but the jargon increased. It was evident that, whereas reinforcement and extinction had been sufficient for training the speech response thus far, they were less efficient for training correct articulation of several phonemes in the context of a word. At this point, the study was initiated to explore the efficiency of using a combination of consequent events other than reinforcement and extinction for word training. An attempt was made to determine if timeout from positive reinforcement would function more effectively to decrease the jargon and increase the probability that the correct response would be emitted.

Procedures

Jargon was defined as unintelligible vocalizations consisting of one or more spoken sounds resembling English phonemes. When these vocalizations occurred after a response had been emitted and before a new model was presented, they were scored as jargon. When timeout was used as a punishing event for jargon, the procedure consisted of the following sequence of events: after jargon was emitted the experimenter took the ice cream, turned in her chair, and sat with her back to the child. Turning to face the child again was contingent on his ceasing the jargon and remaining quietly in his chair for approximately thirty seconds. If the child had been sitting quietly for thirty seconds, the experimenter turned to face him, smiled, and presented the verbal model. If the child imitated the model, the experimenter reinforced the behavior by presenting the child with a bite of ice cream and a verbal "Good."

Timeout was instituted for jargon during training of the words "pop" and "boat." In both instances, timeout was contingent upon the emission of jargon after it had increased in extinction.

When timeout was used in a negative reinforcement paradigm for emission of a specific speech response, the procedure was somewhat different. Timeout for incorrect responses was applied only after (1) the subject had previously demonstrated that he could imitate the new response, (2) the subject showed no increase in the correct responses within at least a five-minute period in a training session, and (3) his responses consisted of the previous response that had been appropriate before a new phoneme or word was added to the chain.

Timeout as a negative reinforcer was applied for incorrect responses four times. It was presented twice in the second session of training for the chain "cream," once during the second session of training for the word "dog," and once during the second session of training for the sentence "I want pop." On all four occasions, timeout was contingent upon continued emission of a formerly correct, but presently incorrect response in imitation of the experimenter's model. Timeout was terminated contingent upon the emission of the correct response. In training for "cream," timeout was contingent upon emission of "eam," and terminated contingent on emission of "ream." In training for "dog," timeout was contingent upon emission of "og," and terminated contingent upon emission of "dog." Timeout was instituted when the subject emitted, "want pop," and terminated when the child emitted, "I want pop."

RESULTS

Timeout contingent on jargon usually resulted in a decrease in the number of vocalizations within five minutes after its application. In both cases of timeout for jargon, the rate of vocalizations decreased from an average of four vocalizations per minute before application of timeout, to nearly zero per minute after termination of timeout. Figure 1 presents the results of applying timeout for jargon during training for the word "pop."

In the first session of training for the word "pop," the jargon vocalizations averaged one every two minutes. No consequences were presented after these vocalizations were emitted. In the second session, the jargon vocalizations increased to a rate of approximately three per minute by the fourteenth minute. At this time, timeout was applied, contingent on the emission of the next jargon vocalization. During the first two minutes of timeout, the subject emitted eight vocalizations, and then gradually the vocalizations decreased to three within the last two minutes. After thirty seconds of silence, the experimenter turned to face the subject and presented the model. A correct response was reinforced. No jargon occurred during the rest of Session 2. Except for three vocalizations in the next session, jargon remained at a zero rate.

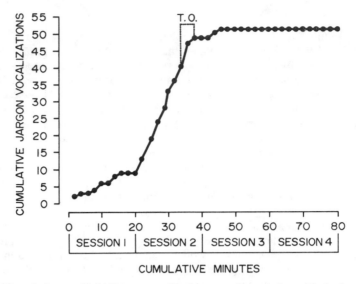

Fig. 1. Cumulative number of jargon vocalizations over four sessions of imitative speech training before and after timeout (T.O.) from positive reinforcement for jargon. Each dot represents two minutes.

Figure 2 presents the data on application of timeout for jargon during training of the word "boat."

On the second occasion, timeout functioned to decelerate jargon in much the same manner as it did in the first situation. Jargon was emitted at a rate of approximately one vocalization per minute during the first session of training. In the first ten minutes of the second session, the child emitted approximately three jargon vocalizations per minute. Contingent timeout was in effect for the emission of jargon after the first ten minutes. During timeout, five jargon vocalizations occurred within the first two minutes and then ceased. After a silence of thirty seconds, the experimenter terminated timeout and presented the model. Correct responses increased and jargon decreased to a zero level for the remainder of the session. Although some jargon was emitted in the next session, it did not increase to the former high level.

Timeout for incorrect responses was applied on four occasions, one during training for the word "cream." The results are presented in Fig. 3.

The chain for "cream" consisted of a sequence of four training phases: imitation of /m/, then /im/, /rim/ and finally /krim/. Timeout from positive reinforcement was introduced during the addition of the third phoneme to the chain. Before timeout, the subject had reached an eighty per cent level of correct imitations of /im/. Therefore, the /r/, a somewhat difficult phoneme to learn to articulate, was added to the chain.

As shown in the first session of /rim/ training, the subject had imitated /rim/ twenty-eight times during the first fifteen minutes of training. He was also emitting some /im/ responses, but as long as he continued to increase the number of /rim/ responses no consequences were applied for the /im/. The child reverted to the /im/ response in the final two minutes of Session 1. In the initial six minutes of the next session, his emission rate of /rim/ was zero. His response consisted of the two phonemes /im/. Timeout was applied after the next /im/ response and remained in effect until the child emitted /rim/. When he said /rim/ the experimenter turned to face him, presented the model, and reinforced /rim/ with ice cream and verbal approval. As shown in Fig. 3, the child correctly imitated five /rim/ presentations, and then reverted once more to the /im/ response. Therefore, a second timeout period was instituted after five

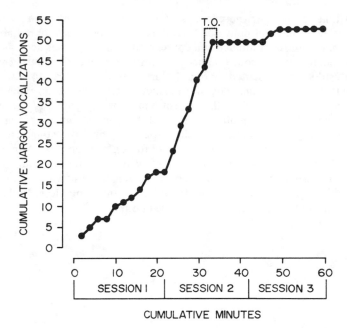

Fig. 2. Cumulative number of jargon vocalizations over three sessions of imitative speech training before and after timeout (T.O.) from positive reinforcement for jargon. Each dot represents two minutes.

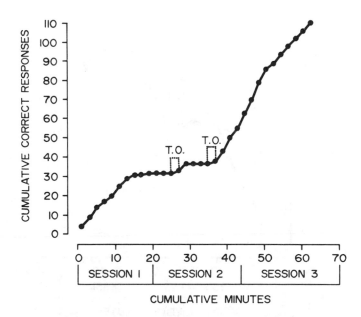

Fig. 3. Cumulative number of correct responses over three sessions when timeout (T.O.) was used to increase the probability of emission of "cream." Each dot represents two minutes.

minutes. After timeout had been in effect for 2.5 minutes, the child said /rim/. The experimenter turned to face him and delivered a reinforcement for correctly imitating /rim/. The frequency of /rim/ responses continued to increase while /im/ responses decreased.

Another application of timeout for incorrect responses occurred during training of the word "dog." Results are presented in Fig. 4. Timeout in this situation was contingent on emission of the response /og/ when /dog/ was the model presented by the experimenter. In the first ten minutes of the first session, the subject had correctly emitted /dog/ approximately thirty times. After the first ten minutes of Session 1, he stopped imitating /dog/. At this time, he reverted to emitting the two-phoneme chain /og/ each time the stimulus was presented. After eight minutes of incorrect responses, timeout for /og/ was applied. After approximately three minutes of timeout, the subject said, /dog/ and the experimenter turned to face him. The experimenter presented the word /dog/ and a correct response was reinforced. As shown in Fig. 4, the subject quickly increased the frequency of imitating /dog/. In the next session, he reached criterion and progressed to a new phase of training.

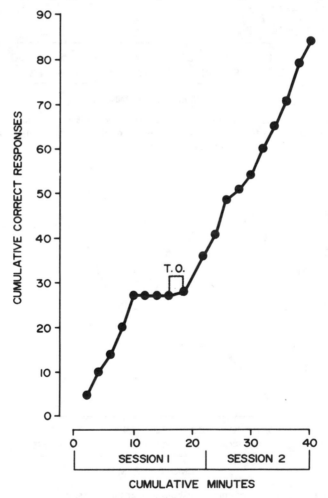

Fig. 4. Cumulative number of correct responses over two sessions when timeout (T.O.) was used to increase the probability of "dog." Each dot represents two minutes.

Timeout contingent on inappropriate responses also was used in training the subject to emit a three-word chain. The subject had learned to emit "want pop" and the third item in the chain, "I," was added to the response. The model presented by the experimenter consisted of "I want pop." Results of the fourth application of timeout for incorrect responses are presented in Fig. 5.

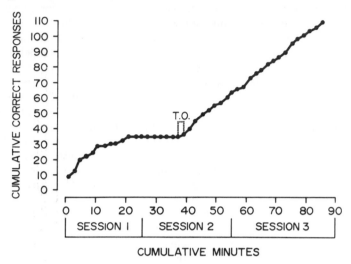

Fig. 5. Cumulative number of correct responses over three sessions when timeout (T.O.) was used to increase the probability of emission of "I want pop." Each dot represents two minutes.

In the initial eighteen minutes of Session 1, the subject had correctly emitted the three-item chain approximately thirty times, but the responses alternated between "I want pop," and "want pop." At the end of the session, all his responses consisted of the two-word chain. The same response, "want pop," continued to be emitted in the initial ten minutes of Session 2, so timeout was applied. After two minutes had elapsed, the subject said, "I want pop." The experimenter turned in her chair and presented the model "I want pop." The two-word chain decreased in frequency and emission of the three-word chain increased. By the end of the third session, he was emitting the three-word chain at criterion level and training for that phase was terminated.

In general, timeout contingent on emission of incorrect responses resulted in a rapid increase in emission of the complete chain of phonemes or words with more precise articulation on each phoneme. Timeout for incorrect responses was applied on four occasions. On each occasion after timeout was terminated contingent on the emission of a correct response, the number of correct responses increased rapidly. Conversely, the number of incorrect responses rapidly decreased and were gradually eliminated from the child's repertoire. Usually the child reached criterion in that phase of training within the next two sessions and progressed to the next step in training.

DISCUSSION

Timeout contingent on emission of jargon successfully decreased vocalizations when extinction (ignoring the jargon) was ineffective for this purpose. Although timeout did not eliminate the jargon for the remainder of the programme, it reduced vocalizations across several sessions to a point at which the jargon no longer interfered with training. Subsequently, when jargon again increased in frequency, timeout effectively reduced it within a short time.

The present results are similar to those obtained by Risley & Wolf (1967) in a training programme in which timeout functioned to decelerate crying, temper tantrums, and inappropriate imitative vocalizations. The imitative vocalizations were somewhat similar to the jargon vocalizations emitted by the child in the present study. In both studies, timeout consisted of the experimenter remaining in the room and turning away from the child. Termination of timeout was contingent on the child's ceasing the inappropriate behavior. Vocalizations for the children in the two studies decreased in frequency within the session in which timeout was applied, and remained close to zero throughout the following sessions.

In the present study, the probability that a specific phoneme chain would be emitted was increased when timeout was used as negative reinforcement in situations in which positive reinforcement and extinction had been ineffective. Timeout, however, was used for this purpose only when the child had demonstrated that the response was in his repertoire, and when the problem was one of increasing the frequency of emission, rather than shaping the topography of the response. When the child had emitted the correct response at approximately a thirty to forty per cent level during a session, it was concluded that the response was present and available to the child.

Timeout has been successfully used to decelerate emission of incorrect responses by Sloane, Johnston & Harris (1968). They did not, however, use timeout as a negative reinforcer. That is, their procedure consisted of the teacher dropping her head on the chest, remaining mute, and averting her eyes for sixty seconds if the child made two consecutive incorrect responses or unsatisfactory approximations. Termination of timeout, however, was contingent on passage of time in their study, not on the emission of a particular correct response by the child.

The procedures used in the two studies increased the frequency of correct responses. In the Sloane *et al.* (1968) study, timeout functioned as a punishing event to decelerate incorrect responses. As the incorrect responses decreased, the frequency of the correct response increased, but emission of the correct response was not required to terminate timeout.

In the present study, the behavior that terminated the aversive stimulus was specified as the emission of the correct response. In this capacity, timeout functioned as a negative reinforcer to increase the emission of the correct response as well as a punisher to decrease incorrect responses. Once the required response had occurred, timein was instituted. With the resumption of training, emission of the correct response was maintained by positive reinforcers.

CONCLUSIONS

Timeout from positive reinforcement in speech training has been used primarily as a decelerating consequence for inappropriate behavior, not directly to increase emission of the appropriate speech response. As a punishing event, it functions to eliminate behaviors that are incompatible with, or interfere with training. Elimination of inappropriate behaviors indirectly results in an increase in correct responses because they have a greater probability of emission when other behaviors are not occurring.

The present study replicated the findings of other studies in which timeout functioned to reduce inappropriate behavior during speech training. In addition, it demonstrated that the specific speech response being trained could be required to terminate timeout in speech training. In some phases of training, timeout would appear to have greater value for functioning as negative reinforcement to increase directly the frequency of the correct response, rather than as a punishing event that "clears the way" for correct responses to occur.

REFERENCES

Baer, D. M. Laboratory control of thumbsucking by withdrawal and representation of reinforcement. *Journal of the Experimental Analysis of Behavior*, 1962, **5**, 525–528.

Risley, T. *The establishment of verbal behavior in deviant children*. Ph.D. dissertation, University of Washington, 1966.

Risley, T. & Wolf, M. M. Establishing functional speech in echolalic children. *Behavior Research and Therapy*, 1967, **5**, 73–88.

Sloane, H., Johnston, Margaret & Harris, Florence. Remedial procedures for teaching verbal behavior to speech deficient or defective young children. In H. N. Sloane and B. D. MacAulay (Eds.), *Operant procedures in remedial speech and language training*. Boston: Houghton Mifflin Co., 1968, pp. 77–101.

Wolf, M. M., Risley, T. & Mees, H. Application of operant conditioning procedures to the behavior problems of an autistic child. *Behavior Research and Therapy*, 1964, **1**, 305–312.

Speech and Social Development

Control of Tantrum Behavior by Operant Techniques During Experimental Verbal Training*

WAYNE SAILOR,† DOUG GUESS, GORIN RUTHERFORD, and DONALD M. BAER

University of Kansas and Kansas Neurological Institute

Abstract: A technique of controlling undesirable or disruptive behavior during an ongoing programme of verbal training with a retardate is described. The technique required that the stimulus materials of the verbal training programme be graded according to difficulty, i.e., in terms of the length and complexity of the stimulus materials. (This resulted in an initial grading of the stimulus materials into different levels of probability of reinforcement.) Changes by the experimenter from high-difficulty to low-difficulty stimuli for two trials contingent upon disruptive behavior increased the rate of that behavior; changes from low-difficulty to high-difficulty stimuli for two trials contingent upon disruptive behavior decreased its rate. Thus, contingent alternation of the stimulus materials of the ongoing training programme controlled the frequency of undesirable behaviors within the experimental sessions. This technique may comprise an alternative to other procedures which require punishment or timeout from the ongoing programme.

The application of operant conditioning procedures to language training with speech-deficient children is a relatively recent development. Research has typically focused on language modification and acquisition techniques. A frequent problem with studies of this kind has been the treatment of undesirable competing responses which emerge in the experimental setting. So far, the most common procedure for controlling undesirable behavior has been timeout from positive reinforcement. The exact function of this procedure, whether it is a form of simple extinction or a punishing event, remains in doubt pending further experimental analysis (Leitenberg, 1965).

Risley & Wolf (1967), developing speech in echolalic children, found that the most frequent competing responses were chanting, singing, inappropriate imitation of the experimenter, and temper tantrums. These authors successfully eliminated disruptive behaviors with a timeout procedure applied over as many as twenty-six hourly sessions. The authors caution that this procedure is effective only to the extent that the positive reinforcer being withheld is potent. Lovaas (1967) taught verbal skills to children with severe behavior disorders (schizophrenic) who had no history of verbal behavior. Disruptive competing behaviors were treated by a short timeout: a turning away from the child for five seconds in the case of mildly disruptive behaviors such as echolalia and temper tantrums. For more severe disruptions, a long-term timeout was applied by isolating the subject. In still other cases, punishment by application of an aversive consequence was used. These procedures apparently succeeded, although details of their cost in programme time were not provided.

*Reprinted from the *Journal of Applied Behavior Analysis*, 1968, **1**, 3, 237–243. Copyright 1968 with permission from the Society for the Experimental Analysis of Behavior, Inc., and Dr. W. Sailor.

†This study was conducted while the senior author was a member of the research staff of the psychology division of the Kansas Neurological Institute in the summer of 1967. Reprints may be obtained from Wayne Sailor, Clarke Institute, 250 College St., Toronto 2B, Ontario.

The control of undesirable competing responses in experimental language-training settings involves several considerations. If the objective is to accomplish speech training rapidly in alingual children, the most efficient procedures should be those which least disrupt the training process. The timeout procedure may have the disadvantage of subtracting from the time available for training. This is especially true of restraint and long-term isolation procedures. Other aversive controls such as shock may in fact punish the desired verbal responses when they occur simultaneously with the undesirable behaviors.

The purpose of the present study was to investigate a technique for controlling competing temper tantrums that would mitigate the possible disadvantages of timeout or punishment by rearranging, rather than interrupting, the ongoing language-training procedures. The tantrum control procedure was instituted with one subject as part of a programme of training verbal skills in speech-deficient children.

METHOD

Subject

Janet was a 9.5-year-old girl, institutionalized at the Kansas Neurological Institute for the past four years, and diagnosed as retarded. She reportedly had developed a meager verbal repertoire by the age of 2.5 years, but then acquired a new home and stepmother, whereupon she became completely mute and began to develop chronic tantrum behaviors. The tantrums reportedly increased in frequency and severity and eventually led to her hospitalization. Janet's case-record described her as an extremely unhappy girl who "suffers a great deal of pain." Her tantrums were described by various psychiatric observers as "extreme pain," "excessive anger," and "masturbating excessively to orgasm." The present investigators' observations of Janet's ward behavior suggested that the tantrums, which occurred at the average rate of two or three per hour, were highly functional. They seemed to produce the effect of terminating contact with other individuals who usually were making some demand of her. The topography of the behavior was such that it strongly suggested pain simulation. She would lash out with one arm, clutching at her groin with the other. Her legs jerked wildly, sometimes hurling her to the floor or into objects. Her face and neck flushed deep red, and tears would flow, accompanied by loud screams. These tantrums, usually of ten- to fifteen-seconds duration, were occasionally repeated several times in succession. Other than cries and screams, no vocal or verbal behavior had been reported for Janet since her arrival at the institution (four years before).

Procedure

Verbal acquisition. The initial phase of the study consisted of a programme for imitation of words. Janet came easily under vocal imitative control, which eliminated the need to introduce imitation as a generalized response class through shaping motor behavior, etc. The basic unit of speech selected for acquisition was the word or phrase, graded into levels of ascending difficulty, i.e., into levels of increasing numbers of words and syllables in each unit of the stimulus material. The stimulus units for this study consisted of four lists of words and phrases, beginning with one- and two-syllable words in List 1 and concluding with four-word phrases, some of them containing four and some containing eight syllables, in List 4. The four lists are presented in Table 1.

Each stimulus unit was presented by the experimenter, preceded by "Janet, say...." Each imitated response was reinforced with a bite of food selected from an assortment of ice cream, Kool-aid, or dry cereal. Experimental sessions were conducted twice daily, and were

Table 1. Four word and phrase lists used as stimulus materials for the verbal acquisition procedure and alternated for the tantrum control experiment.

List 1	List 2	List 3	List 4
Dog	Red ball	How are you	I brush my teeth
Cat	A box	Go to bed	I tie my shoes
Cup	One boy	Cup of milk	Wash hands with soap
Book	Big house	Set the clock	Drink with a glass
Girl	Two feet	My right arm	Ice cream is good
Chair	Hot soup	Feet and legs	I comb my hair
Juice	Ice cream	A green bush	Feed the brown dog
Spoon	Blue sky	In the house	Walk to the store
House	Cold snow	Wind the watch	Eat with a spoon
Five	The door	Ring the bell	A piece of toast
Table	Little flower	Tiny yellow flower	Stepping over cardboard boxes
Cookie	Broken window	Little baby rabbit	Jumping into running water
Button	Pretty picture	Pretty orange candle	Pretty little yellow flower
Hammer	Lettuce salad	Drinking apple cider	Pouring water into glasses
Apple	Cherry Kool-aid	Painting nurse's picture	
Chicken	Birthday party	Peanut butter sandwich	
Window	Yellow napkin	Drinking cherry Kool-aid	
Napkin	Kitchen cupboard	Eating lettuce salad	
Sleeping	Eating candy	Swimming under water	
Running	Watermelon	Jumping over boxes	

fifteen minutes in length. Janet's initial verbal attempts were simply mouthed silently and subsequently whispered. These were reinforced at first; then intensity was differentially reinforced over the first ten sessions until an audible response was emitted to each stimulus (from the first ten words on List 1). The experimenter then established a criterion of response which required a clearly audible and well-articulated imitation of the stimulus unit. Responses were clearly audible by the beginning of the study and presented no difficulty for accurate recording. Apart from the tantrum-control procedure, Janet's responses were reinforced when acceptable to the experimenter, or followed by re-presentation of the stimulus unit when an unacceptable response was made. If no response was forthcoming, the stimulus unit was re-presented after a five-second pause. Progress along the stimulus unit list was dictated by the experimenters' judgment of Janet's satisfactory imitation of the currently presented units. All of Janet's attempts, as well as her successes which resulted in reinforcement, were recorded by an observer using a check list.

The observer was positioned behind a one-way mirror with two-way sound transmission connecting the observation and experimental rooms. His task was to record tantrum and verbal frequencies[1] and to signal the experimenter when an experimental operation was to be applied. This was accomplished by transmitting an audible click over the intercom to the experimenter whenever a tantrum was recorded. A total of sixteen sessions of verbal training were conducted before the tantrum-control procedure was initiated.

---

[1]In a later part of this subject's language training programme, following the tantrum-control procedures, reliability of this system of recording such selected aspects of her speech was formally assessed. In this assessment, the observer in the adjoining room, listening to the subject over an intercom, recorded each utterance as correct or incorrect (reinforceable or not reinforceable), trying always to make this judgment before the experimenter could reinforce the response (if reinforceable). The experimenter kept similar records. Comparison of their judgments of correctness (reinforceability) showed a percentage of agreement in excess of ninety-nine per cent for over 1000 judgments.

Tantrum control. The procedure alternated difficulty of stimulus unit in either of two possible contingencies. Each contingency was applied twice over a series of four successive conditions. In Conditions I and III, the occurrence of a tantrum produced two consecutive presentations of new stimulus units of decreased difficulty (shorter length), relative to the stimulus units currently being presented. In Conditions II and IV, the procedure was reversed: a tantrum resulted in two consecutive presentations of new stimulus units of increased difficulty (greater length). For example, in Condition I, Janet was initially presented with units from List 3, beginning with the first phrase. When tantrums occurred, two successive stimulus units were presented from List 1. The first of these units was presented when the tantrum ceased. Each additional tantrum during these words from List 1 caused two additional units from List 1 to be presented. Under Condition II the procedure was reversed. Initially, units from List 1 were presented. Contingent upon tantrum, two units from List 3 would be presented. Conditions III and IV paralleled Conditions I and II, except that Janet had progressed further along the word lists. Thus, in Condition III the initial stimulus unit was the seventeenth phrase in List 3. A tantrum at this point would then produce a switch to the seventeenth word in List 1. Thus, with the word lists arranged so that the stimulus material increased progressively in length, a switch from a later list to an earlier list should have increased the probability of immediate reinforcement. The reverse should have been true for a switch from an earlier list to a later list.

Before onset of the tantrum-control procedure, Janet was successfully imitating stimulus units of comparable length and complexity to those presented in all lists of Table 1, the probability of reinforcement ranging between 60 and 100 per cent.

RESULTS

Figure 1 displays the rate of tantrums and the average level of stimulus difficulty (number of syllables) during the four tantrum-control conditions. These data show that during Conditions I and III, Janet's tantrums served an operant function of reducing the difficulty of the stimulus units presented to her, and were maintained at a high level; but during Conditions II and IV, her tantrums served only to increase that difficulty level, and were greatly reduced.

Figure 2 illustrates the effect of tantrum control on Janet's verbal performance. These data represent the total number of attempts by Janet on all words per session, and the total number for each session that met the criterion and were reinforced. (These curves do not include the two responses following any stimulus switch in any of the conditions.) Figure 3 presents the same data as Fig. 2, expressing reinforced responses as a percentage of the total number of attempts. As can be seen from these figures the effects of the tantrum-control procedures were multiple. When a high rate of tantrums was maintained, relatively few words could be presented or reinforced; when a low rate of tantrums was effected, far more words could be presented and reinforced. The relative quality of Janet's imitation (the percent of words acceptable for reinforcement) was more stable, however; it was markedly reduced only under Condition III (the second tantrum-acceleration condition).

DISCUSSION

The differences in tantrum rate shown over the two sets of experimental conditions were produced by operations involving contingencies between tantrums and consequent stimulus difficulty (defined as number of syllables in each stimulus item). However, those operations

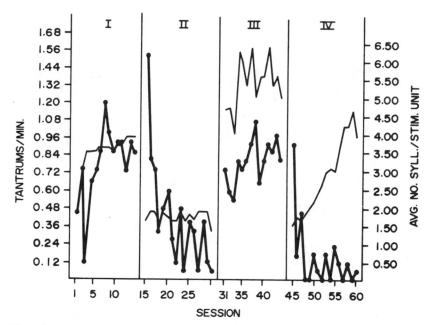

Fig. 1. Tantrum rate (heavy line) for the four conditions is shown on the left ordinate while stimulus difficulty (thin line), depicted as the average number of syllables in the stimulus material for each session, is shown on the right ordinate. In Condition I, stimulus units from List 3 are alternated with units from List 1 contingent upon tantrums. In Condition II, stimulus units from List 1 are alternated with units from List 3 contingent upon tantrums. In Condition III, stimulus units from Lists 3 and 4 are alternated with units from Lists 1 and 2 contingent upon tantrums. In Condition IV, stimulus units from Lists 1 and 2 are alternated with units from Lists 3 and 4 contingent upon tantrums.

involved other factors as well. One was the average difficulty of the stimuli prevailing for the experimental condition. Figure 1 shows a rough correlation between experimental condition and item difficulty: in general, Conditions I and III involved more difficult items than Conditions II and IV. It might be argued that the corresponding differences in tantrum rates were simply results of the prevailing item difficulty, with difficult items producing many tantrums and easy items producing few, and that the contingency between tantrums and item difficulty was irrelevant. However, close examination of the data of Fig. 1 shows that in Condition IV, item difficulty was deliberately manipulated into a steadily increasing level. In fact, Sessions 45 to 48 began with the first unit on List 1; Sessions 49 to 52 began with the tenth unit of List 1; Sessions 53 to 56 with the first unit of List 2; and Sessions 57 to 60 with the tenth unit of List 2. Yet this increase in item difficulty produced no corresponding increase in tantrum rate. Furthermore, the difficulty level of Condition III, although substantially higher than that of Condition I, was not associated with a higher average rate of tantrums than had been the case in Condition I. Spearman rank correlation coefficients were calculated for each of the conditions, between tantrum rate and level of stimulus difficulty. The correlations were: Condition I, 0.62 ($p < 0.02$; $df = 12$); Condition II, 0.38 (n.s., $df = 14$); Condition III, 0.50 (n.s., $df = 12$); Condition IV, -0.45 (n.s., $df = 14$). With the exception of a significant positive relationship for the first tantrum-acceleration condition between number of tantrums per session and level of stimulus difficulty, this factor did not, of itself, significantly contribute

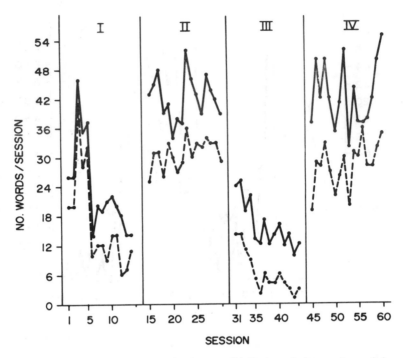

Fig. 2. The total number of verbalizations (solid line), and the number reinforced (broken line) per session are shown on the ordinate. The manipulations which define the four conditions are the same as those specified in Fig. 1.

to the tantrum management data. In fact, the fourth condition (tantrum deceleration) reveals a strong but non-significant negative relationship between tantrums and difficulty. Coupled with such internal data, there remains a fact of procedure: in Conditions II and IV, tantrums were followed by two items of increased difficulty each time they occurred. If difficulty in fact did evoke tantrums, then the tantrum rate should have been increased locally by these two trials, thus requiring an additional two trials of increased difficulty for each such tantrum evoked, and implying a run-away condition for tantrums, if such control were powerful. But in fact, the need to programme additional two-item contingencies for tantrums occurred only three times during these two conditions (II and IV).

Figure 2 shows that the number of reinforcers given the subject per session also was generally correlated negatively with her tantrum rate, over the two sets of experimental conditions. It might be argued that a low density of reinforcers over each fifteen-minute session could evoke tantrums, and a high density reduce them, apart from the contingency holding between tantrums and stimulus difficulty. However, it must be remembered that those conditions which increased tantrum rate necessarily reduced the number of reinforcers given, in that the tantrums took up considerable amounts of time during these sessions. The Spearman rank correlation coefficients between tantrum rate and number of reinforcers earned, within each of the four experimental conditions, were: Condition I, -0.50 (n.s., $df = 12$); Condition II, 0.02 (n.s., $df = 14$); Condition III, -0.58 ($p < 0.05$; $df = 12$) and Condition IV, -0.39 (n.s., $df = 14$). Significance levels were computed for two-tail tests. With the exception of the second tantrum-acceleration condition, Condition III, wherein the high rate of tantrums produced would be expected to be associated with a lower probability of reinforcement, the density of reinforcers within each condition was not significantly correlated

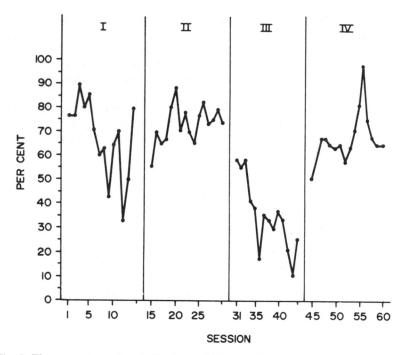

Fig. 3. The percentage of verbalizations which met the criterion of acceptability and were reinforced are shown on the ordinate. Data are not included for verbalizations to the two items following a stimulus switch contingent upon a tantrum emission. The manipulations which define the four conditions are the same as those specified in Fig. 1.

with tantrum rate. It is therefore unlikely that reinforcer density was responsible for the increase and decrease in tantrum rate across the four conditions.

In general, then, it is argued that the contingency between tantrums and consequent stimulus difficulty was the factor responsible for the control of tantrum rate achieved in this study, rather than prevailing conditions of stimulus difficulty or reinforcement density.

There are typically three important aspects of the paradigm for language training with speech-deficient children, all of which need experimental refinement. These are the sequential programming of training phases, the basic response units suitable for training, and the management of competing responses during training. This study addressed itself to the third consideration, and attempted to demonstrate an advantageous technique of extraneous behavior control. Earlier procedures for modifying undesirable competing responses have involved either timeout from positive reinforcement or the application of a contingent noxious consequence. In the present study, tantrum control was accomplished by manipulating the stimulus characteristics as a consequence of emission of tantrums. The disadvantages of timeout and aversive consequences have already been noted. One advantage of the present procedure is that virtually no experimental time is sacrificed, and no extinction or punishment of the response to be strengthened occurs.

Although the general topography of the tantrums remained constant throughout the study, several changes in detail had taken place by the beginning of the fourth experimental condition. While the duration of the response and its extensiveness in space remained constant, its intensity decreased substantially. These tantrums originally involved violent muscle jerks, immediate profuse tearing, and deep flushing of the face and neck. By Condition IV, these presumably respondent components had almost disappeared. The intensity of the screams had also decreased considerably. The tantrums of Condition IV appeared to be almost a sham. In some instances during that condition the tantrums seemed to occur in alternation with laughter, a behavior seldom evidenced by Janet before this experiment. These changes in tantrum intensity were not sufficient to alter the definition of the response during the experiment.

The present study may have some implications for programmed educational instruction. Many teachers currently employ the practice of returning to easier material when a child makes errors. This procedure conceivably may strengthen error-prone behaviors incompatible with the goals of instruction.

REFERENCES

Leitenberg, H. Is time-out from positive reinforcement an aversive event? *Psychological Bulletin*, 1965, **64**, 428–441.
Lovaas, I. I. A behavior therapy approach to the treatment of childhood schizophrenia. J. P. Hill (Ed.), *Minnesota symposium on child psychology*. Vol. 1; Minneapolis, Minn.: University of Minnesota Press, 1967, pp. 108–159.
Risley, T. & Wolf, M. Establishing functional speech in echolalic children. *Behavior Research and Therapy*, 1967, **5**, 73–88.

Differential Effects of Token Reinforcement on Instruction-following Behavior in Retarded Students Instructed as a Group*†

ELAINE H. ZIMMERMAN, J. ZIMMERMAN, and C. D. RUSSELL

Butler University School of Education and Indiana University School of Medicine

Abstract: This study was addressed to the problem of applying behavior modification techniques on a group basis to a class of retarded students with "attentional deficits." Seven boys, age eight to fifteen years, characterized as showing severe "attentional" problems or disruptive behavior in their respective classrooms, participated daily for thirty-minute sessions in a special class over a 1.5-month period. In each session, verbal instructions were given to the class as a whole. In control sessions, each appropriate instruction-following response by a child produced praise for that child. In experimental sessions, appropriate responses also produced tokens exchangeable for tangible reinforcers after the session. Token reinforcement differentially maintained instruction-following behavior in four children while one responded appropriately to most instructions and a second improved continuously during the study. While the data suggest that the present approach can be successfully applied to the alteration of instruction-following behavior in retarded children, its major contribution may be that of providing objective quantitative information about such behavior.

Many behavior modification studies have been conducted in the classroom setting (i.e., Hall, Lund & Jackson, 1968; Harris, Wolf & Baer, 1964; Zimmerman & Zimmerman, 1962). Most such studies have focused upon the objective assessment of treatments applied to individual class members. In contrast, several classroom studies have involved (a) the concurrent, systematic treatment of each student participating in the class, and (b) the application of a set of common treatments to all members of the class (i.e., Birnbrauer, Wolf, Kidder & Tague, 1965; Burchard, 1967). These and similar studies have involved individually groomed classroom assignments, but have placed greater emphasis upon treating the class as a whole in that every member of the class is exposed to similar sets of differential token-reinforcement contingencies.

A related set of classroom procedures was applied recently by Bushell, Wrobel & Michaelis (1968). Their procedures placed less emphasis upon the idiosyncratic treatment of individual class members and more emphasis upon the use of a set of common treatments. Classroom assignments were not explicitly groomed to specific individuals. Under conditions

*Reprints may be obtained from Elaine H. Zimmerman, The Institute of Psychiatric Research, Indiana University School of Medicine, 1100 West Michigan Street, Indianapolis, Indiana 46202. The authors wish to thank Mr. David Shearer, Principal, and the faculty of Noble School for their cooperation and interest. Special thanks go to Mrs. Marcia Yaver, the teacher next door, who volunteered her time and assistance whenever she was able.

†Reprinted from the *Journal of Applied Behavior Analysis*, 1969, **2**, 2, 101–112. Copyright 1969 with permission from the Society for the Experimental Analysis of Behavior, Inc., and Elaine H. Zimmerman.

in which class members engaged in several different activities, all were exposed to one generally defined set of differential token reinforcement contingencies.

To our knowledge, no published study has employed a procedure that exclusively involved the concurrent exposure of all class members to a single, specific set of differential-reinforcement contingencies. Although Burchard (1967, Exp. 1) applied such a set of contingencies to the sitting-at-desk behavior of each member of his class, this common treatment was employed in the context of the concurrent application of separate, individually groomed reinforcement contingencies.

The obvious need to develop techniques to facilitate the efficient instruction of an entire group of students under conditions in which behavior in each member can be monitored and examined as a function of common instructional procedures and common treatments, gave impetus to the present study. The general purpose of this study was that of experimentally examining a classroom procedure designed for use with a group of retarded students characterized by their teachers as having "severe attentional deficits" and/or frequently displaying behaviors disruptive to ongoing classroom activities. The specific purpose was to examine behavior in each class member under conditions in which the class was addressed as a whole and as a function of the application of two sets of common response-contingent consequences.

Before implementing and conducting the study the experimenters informally observed the tentatively selected subjects in their classroom settings and interacted with their teachers in informal conferences. The latter interactions suggested that the teachers tended to attribute disruptive behavior and other undesirable classroom performances to the students' "attentional deficits." The only generalization which could be made after informally observing the students' classroom performances was that each frequently failed to follow instructions. As a consequence, we designed a list of simple classroom instructions and used instruction-following behavior as the dependent variable. In line with the specific purposes of this investigation, instructions were presented to the group at large and as a whole and appropriate behavior was examined as a function of response-contingent praise and response-contingent token reinforcement.

METHOD

Subjects and Setting

Seven retarded boys with "attentional problems," selected by teacher recommendation from three classes at the Noble School in Indianapolis, served as the members of the experimental class. A brief clinical description of each is provided in Table 1.

The study was conducted in a ten- by fifteen-foot room that contained a teacher's desk and chair, a round table around which were placed seven student chairs, and the materials and props that were utilized in conjunction with the instruction list and token reinforcement system. The seven students participated as a class in daily thirty-minute sessions over a period of seven weeks. A dimly lighted, empty classroom immediately adjacent to the experimental room was used for timeout purposes, and occasionally served as an observation room for interested faculty. This observation was facilitated by a one-way vision mirror mounted in the door between the two rooms.

The Instruction List

Five initial sessions were devoted to observing the students in the experimental room and to constructing an instruction list that could be used to measure objectively the instruction-following behavior. The list was constructed on the basis of several considerations and criteria.

Table 1. Age, IQ, and diagnosis of each subject.

Subject	Age (years)	IQ	Diagnosis
S_1	8	46	Moderately retarded
S_2	11	40	Moderately retarded, brain-damaged
S_3	9	70	Mildly retarded, educable but deaf
S_4	10	41	Brain-damaged, autistic, hyperactive
S_5	11.5	48	Moderately retarded
S_6	9.5	25 or below	Severely retarded, atoxic spinal deformity
S_7	15	30	Cerebral dysgenesis

First, items on the list were to call for many behaviors already within the repertoires of the subjects. Prior informal observations of the subjects in their classroom settings and interactions with their teachers permitted the listing of behaviors that were either observed to be or alleged to be in the subjects' repertoire. Second, and this was considered of paramount importance, items were to call for behaviors that could be easily and objectively monitored; observers would not be called upon to make judgments based on ambiguously defined behaviors. Finally, it was considered important to construct a list that would call for a broad spectrum of observable behaviors, since a functional repertoire generally accepted as being prerequisite for any student if he is to benefit from a classroom experience would include many different kinds of instruction-following responses. Classes of behavior called for by the instruction list included: motor performance, imitation, recognition, verbalization, and other social behavior.

An initial list was constructed and tested. This was revised several times in order to improve the continuity and logical sequencing of the items and to replace ambiguous items with items that called for more readily and reliably monitored behaviors. In addition, to further emphasize the importance of "paying attention" on the part of the students, while at the same time maintaining the systematic and highly structured nature of the classroom procedures to be employed, the order of items on the final list was fixed, but equivalent choices of instructions were installed within more than half of the items. For example, Item 21 always followed Item 20 but the instruction: "Point to the picture of the *dog*," could be substituted for by "Point to the picture of the *rabbit* (*lion*)." In the subsequent formal application of the instruction list, choices within such items were varied randomly from session to session.

The final version of the thirty-item instruction list is presented in Table 2. The first twenty-five items were group items presented to the class as a whole. The five final items were directed to specific individuals. Their inclusion permitted examination of behaviors that could not be reliably monitored in individuals under conditions in which two or more children responded concurrently.

Specific Experimental Procedures

The subjects, as a group, were exposed to a successive series of control and experimental conditions, designed to assess the effects of token reinforcement delivered contingent upon the behavior of following instructions. In each of eleven control and eight experimental (token-reinforcement) sessions, the following standard operating procedures were employed:

1. Each of three adults followed a copy of the thirty-item instruction list. One adult served as instructor and the other two acted as independent observers. The instructor read items from the instruction list one at a time, and praised any subject who responded appropriately. The praise was simply the statement: "Very good, (name of subject who responded correctly)." Concurrently, and independently, each observer recorded correct responses. The roles of instructor and observers were alternated across sessions.

1a. The first twenty-five items were exclusively directed to the group at large. Each was repeated once before the next item was read in order to provide two opportunities for appropriate responding. The final five items were each first directed to the group at large and then

Table 2. The final instruction list.

Items are listed in the order that they were presented on the instruction list sheets. Underlined words were read to the class at large. Words not underlined served merely as information to the teacher. Alternatives within items appear in parentheses.

1. Sit down at the table and raise your hand. Reinforce and check only if seated for all "sitting" items.
2. Sit down at the table and do what I do. (clap hands   tap head   salute)
3. Get on the line. (point at the line on floor).
4. Sit down at the table and point at your (nose   mouth   eyes   ears).
5. Stand behind desk. Come to me.
6. Take out some clean sheets of paper from desk and place on desk. Take one piece of paper. Paper is now always available.
7. Take out crayons. Take one crayon. Spare crayons now always available.
8. Sit down at the table and draw what I draw. Draw (A   B   C   D   E).
9. Sit down at the table and draw what I draw. Draw a (diamond   square   triangle).
10. Sit down at the table and give your paper to another child.
11. Sit down at the table and draw a (circle   face   round clock).
12. Stand behind desk. Come up and show your paper to me.
13. Take out and hold scissors. Take one scissors. Put them on desk.
14. Sit down at the table and cut out the (circle   face   round clock) that you drew. Must approximate circle.
15. Stand behind desk. Bring me what you cut out. Acceptable to bring anything he just cut out providing it approximates circle.
16. There is a picture of a triangle on the wall. Point to the picture of the triangle.
17. Stand against one of the walls. Back to wall.
18. There are pieces of colored paper on the walls. Point to the (green   blue   pink) paper.
19. Sit down at the table and do what I do. (Tap table with one hand. Tap table with two hands. Place both hands in the middle of the table.)
20. Sit down at the table and touch another child's (hand   chest   arm).
21. There are animal pictures on the walls. Point to the picture of the (dog   lion   rabbit).
22. Sit down at the table and hold up (1   2   3   4   5) fingers.
23. There are pictures of numbers on the walls. Point to the number (1   2   3   4).
24. Sit down at the table and do what I do. Hold up (1   2   3   4   5) fingers.
25. Stand behind desk. Pick up one scissors and bring it to me.

Individual Items

26. Sit down at the table. Individually to each child who is seated Get up and point to your name.
27. Sit down at the table. Individually to each child who is seated Say what I say (Good morning teacher. How are you? I am fine).
28. Sit down at the table. Individually to each child who is seated Tell me your name.
29. Sit down at the table. Individually to each child who is seated Count to (2   3   4   5).
30. Sit down at the table. Individually to each child who is seated Say what I say (A, B, C, D   1, 2, 3, 4   Red, white and blue).

individually to each eligible (*see* below) child. As in the case of the other items, in order to provide two opportunities for appropriate responding, each individually directed item was repeated once to the same individual before the next individual was instructed.

1b. The pacing of the instructions and repetitions was based upon the behavior of the subjects, rather than upon an arbitrarily prearranged set of temporal criteria. A subject's behavior-based pacing procedure was chosen because we wished to employ an instructional procedure that could not only be systematically employed and objectively defined, but which would also be practical in the sense that it could be employed by a teacher working alone. While a time-based pacing procedure could probably be devised to meet all these criteria, the procedure employed (described immediately below) would probably be more readily negotiable by a teacher without props or outside aid.

In the case of each of the twenty-five group items, the instructor presented an instruction, monitored the group, and praised any child immediately after he correctly followed an instruction, provided that the child was eligible for such praise. Eligibility was determined on the basis of a set of rules which involved among other things the differential pacing of given instructions. More specifically, in the case of twenty-three of the twenty-five items, praise was given to each child who responded to the instruction immediately after it was presented. If a child who did not immediately respond correctly did so while or immediately after another child was being praised, he too was praised. No child was praised twice for responding to the same item. As soon as the instructor failed to observe a single eligible child responding correctly, he immediately repeated the instruction. Praise was given to any remaining eligible child who immediately followed the repeated instruction. As soon as the instructor failed to observe any eligible child responding correctly, he proceeded to read the next instruction.

In contrast with most of the instructions, in the case of two of the alternative choices of Item 11, and in the case of Item 14, the instruction could not readily and/or immediately be negotiated by a subject with a single movement or set of movements. Thus, after Items 11 or 14 were presented, the instructor paused as long as at least one child was in the process of correctly following the instruction. As soon as a correct instruction-following sequence was completed by a given subject, the latter was praised. This procedure obtained until no eligible child was observed to be in the process of correctly following the instruction. At that time the item was repeated. The rule for going on to the next instruction was the same as the rule for repeating the item.

In the case of each of the five individually directed items, the instructor first presented the item to the group at large and then to a specific eligible individual. If the individual did not immediately respond correctly, the item was repeated to that same individual. If the individual did not immediately respond correctly to the repetition, the item was then presented to a different individual. If and when the item was correctly responded to by the individual to whom it was directed, the latter was immediately praised and the item was then immediately presented to the next individual. This procedure continued until all eligible children were given the opportunity to respond and then the next numbered item was presented with the entire process repeated.

1c. For each of the first twenty-five items each observer independently monitored all members of the class, while for each of the final five items each observer focused upon the specific individual to whom an instruction was directed. Each observer placed a check in the appropriate space on the instruction list when he observed a subject responding appropriately to a given instruction. A subject was checked for a correct response even if the instructor failed to praise the child. Similarly, a subject was not checked for a correct response if it was not observed, even if the instructor praised the child. Finally, a child could be checked for a maximum of only one correct response per item, even if he responded correctly to it on each repetition.

2. Behaviors incompatible with following instructions (for example, running around the room or shouting) were generally ignored. Exceptions to ignoring inappropriate behavior took place when one subject aggressed physically against another, or if a subject tampered with exchange items present in a compartmentalized box during token-training and token-reinforcement sessions. When the latter behaviors occurred, they produced a timeout for the offending subject. He was placed alone in a dimly lighted adjacent room by the instructor for a period of ten to twenty seconds (the instructor counted silently to 15). No timeout termination delay contingency was applied because offenders neither kicked nor screamed when placed in the timeout room.

All other procedures employed were idiosyncratic to particular control and experimental conditions and will be specified under the description of those specific conditions.

Table 3 lists the order of presentation of the control and experimental conditions, together with the associated consequences of attending to instructions. The associated number of successive daily sessions is also given.

Table 3. Order and nature of the conditions to which the group was exposed.

Condition	Consequence of Following an Instruction	Number of Sessions Exposed
Pre-Control (Pre-C_1)	Verbal praise only. Instructor says, "Very good, (*name*)"	2
Initial Control (C_1)	Same as Pre-C_1	3
Token Training	See text	4
Second Control (C_2)	Same as Pre-C_1	3
Initial Token (T_1)	Verbal praise as above plus token dropped into tumbler. Tokens exchanged for tangible reward at end of session.	3
Second Token (T_2)	Same as T_1 except that the words, "that's a token" are added to the verbal praise	2
Final Control (C_3)	Same as Pre-C_1	3
Final Token (T_3)	Same as T_2	3

Pre-control (Pre-C_1) condition. This was the first condition in which the standard operating procedures described above were employed. Subjects were exposed to each of two sessions in which a thirty-item instruction list was used. A subject was praised by the instructor for each appropriate response, regardless of his physical place in the room.

Initial control (C_1) condition. In this condition, subjects were exposed to three sessions conducted exactly like the Pre-C_1 sessions with one exception. At this point and thereafter, the final version of the instruction list was used. In this list the words "Sit down at the table and ..." were added to seventeen of the items. Now praise was contingent upon both being seated at the table and responding appropriately to the given instruction.

Token training. During the subsequent four sessions, standard operating procedures were employed. In these sessions, the subjects were given a step-wise exposure to materials and procedures which would later form the basis of the token reinforcement system. During the first session, poker chips (referred to as tokens) were dispensed to each subject on a response-independent basis. That is, each token was delivered to a subject regardless of what he was doing. Each time a token was handed to a subject, it was immediately accompanied by an edible, such as candy. The token was taken back upon the receipt of the edible. During the first few such exchanges, subjects were assisted manually. Later, subjects had independently to return the token to receive the edible. These initial steps were scheduled simply first to pair tokens with tangible reinforcers, and second to teach them to trade tokens for a reinforcer. During the initial part of the second session, similar exchanges were made but each exchange involved a choice of three edibles. As this session progressed, the subjects were exposed to a series of exchanges in which gradually increasing delays between token delivery and token exchange were systematically scheduled.

Before the third session, additional materials were introduced into the room. These included a wooden block which contained seven colored transparent tumblers and a sixteen-compartment box (called "the store") which was filled with tangible rewards. The tumbler block was placed on the teacher's desk. Each subject was assigned a particular tumbler which could be distinguished from every other tumbler on the basis of several independent stimulus dimensions such as color, position in the wooden block, and a geometric symbol painted directly under it on the block. To aid a fourth adult, who was to drop tokens into appropriate tumblers at appropriate times, each child's name appeared on the back of the block, beneath the appropriate tumbler. The "store" was placed on a chair in a corner of the room so that it was away from all other props. Articles "for sale" included small edibles, balloons, candy bars, whistles, toy cars, trucks and planes, and a variety of trinkets and other toys. They were arranged according to size and "price." The largest ("costliest") articles were placed in the two upper rows of four compartments each, while the smallest ("least expensive") articles were placed in the bottom row.

In the third and fourth token training sessions, the class was visually and functionally exposed to the tumblers and the store. Tokens were delivered into tumblers instead of directly to the children. In the first ten minutes of the third session, tokens were delivered on a response-independent basis and subjects were called up one at a time to the teacher's desk after each delivery for the purpose of immediate exchange. Each removed his token from his tumbler, handed it to the teacher, and proceeded immediately to the store. Selection of a reward was permitted from the bottom row only at this point. Before one of these exchanges, and in an effort further to facilitate discrimination between the tumblers, each subject was asked to select and paste an animal sticker on his tumbler. During the remainder of this third session, tokens were delivered on a response-contingent basis. Instructions different from those on the instruction list were given to the group at large and praise, together with token reinforcement, was given to each individual who responded appropriately. After several sets of immediate exchange transpired, exchange delays were increased by going through three and then more instructions before calling any subjects up to the desk. The final delay involved a period of no exchange for seven to ten minutes.

The last token-training session was conducted in a manner similar to that which would be employed during subsequent experimental sessions; i.e., throughout the session, appropriate responses produced praise and token reinforcement. As in the previous session, instructions were different from those on the instruction list, but, in contrast, only a single token exchange was scheduled at the end of the session. Each given subject had to be seated at the table in order to be eligible for his exchange. A subject who had earned nine or fewer tokens could choose and item only from the bottom row of the store. A subject who had earned from ten to nineteen tokens could choose an item from the two bottom rows. Only twenty or more tokens allowed a child *carte blanche* at the store.

Second control (C₂) condition.   To assess the effects of the token-training procedures, *per se*, on performance previously generated, the behavior of the subjects was again examined under control conditions. Data obtained after token training might reflect changes in behavior attributable to rapport and to the pleasant interactions implicit in the token-training procedure. Therefore, in an effort to avoid ambiguity of interpretation, the group was exposed to three additional control sessions immediately after token training terminated and before being exposed to the experimental conditions.

Initial token (T₁) and second token (T₂) conditions.   The subjects were subsequently exposed to three sessions in which the behavioral effects of adding token reinforcement were examined. These sessions were conducted with the tumbler for tokens and the "store" present in the room. A fourth adult was available to drop tokens into appropriate tumblers when a subject was praised by the instructor. Tokens were exchanged for an article in the "store" at the end of the session.

During the initial two sessions under the T_1 condition, subjects were required to earn twenty tokens to gain free choice at the "store." Range of selection was restricted on the basis of the number of tokens less than twenty that were earned. In the third T_1 session, and in all subsequent token-reinforcement sessions, choices and restrictions placed upon choices were determined on an individual basis. A subject was given free choice of anything in the "store" if he earned more tokens than in the previous session. Subjects whose earnings equalled those of the previous session, were restricted to articles that appeared in the bottom two rows; those accumulating fewer tokens than in the previous session could select only from the bottom row.

Because of the possibility that some subjects may have failed to associate the verbal praise with the delivery of a token during the T_1 sessions, two additional token-reinforcement (T_2) sessions were conducted which differed from the T_1 sessions only in that the words, "that's a token" were added to the teacher's statement of praise.

Final control (C_3) and final token (T_3) conditions.   To determine whether the differential effects of token reinforcement previously obtained could be reliably reproduced, the group was re-exposed to three additional control sessions and then to three additional token sessions. The C_3 sessions were conducted in the same fashion as the C_2 sessions and the T_3 sessions duplicated the T_2 sessions.

In each C and T session, two observers equipped with the instruction list placed a check mark in the appropriate space on that list whenever a given subject responded correctly. At the end of each session, the number of items responded to by each subject was independently totalled by each of the observers. When there was disagreement between the two totals for a given subject, the average of the two was taken as the subject's score for that session.

RESULTS AND DISCUSSION

Overview

For four of the seven subjects (Student 1 through Student 4), token reinforcement generated and maintained higher frequencies of instruction-following behavior compared to that behavior maintained under control (praise only) conditions. The behavior of Student 5 and Student 6 did not appear to be differentially influenced by the token-reinforcement procedure, but the data did provide important quantitative information about their instruction-following behavior over the course of the study. Finally, one subject (Student 7) failed to follow any instruction throughout the study.

Specific Results

Figures 1 through 6 present the daily results obtained from Student 1 through Student 6, respectively. In each figure, the total number of items responded to appropriately, per session, is plotted as a function of the successive control and experimental conditions.

Figure 1 presents the data obtained with Student 1. This subject responded appropriately to approximately twenty-five of the items during the first two sessions in which the standard operating procedures were employed. During these two pre-control condition (Pre-C_1)

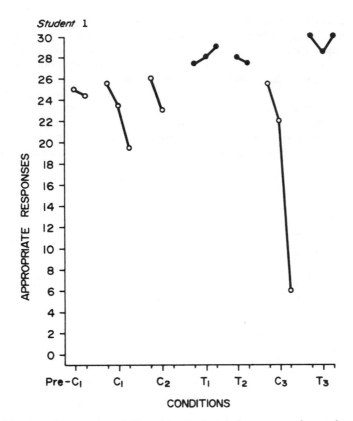

Fig. 1. Number of instructions followed by Student 1. In every session each such response produced praise ("Very nice, *name of student*"). In Pre-control (Pre-C$_1$) sessions praise was never contingent upon being seated at the table. In Initial Control (C$_1$) sessions and *all* sessions thereafter, praise was also contingent upon being seated at the table in the case of seventeen instructions. In Initial Token (T$_1$) sessions appropriate responses also produced a token. In the remaining Token (T$_2$ and T$_3$) sessions, the words, "that's a token" were added to the praise.

sessions, he was out of his seat and moving about the room much of the time. The instruction list used at this time did not require that he be seated in order to be praised by the instructor. As a consequence of the observation of this subject's concurrent appropriate and disorderly behaviors (as well as similar observations with other subjects), the final revision of the instruction list was made. This revision was designed to maximize the incompatibility of obtaining reinforcement while at the same time engaging in disorderly conduct. In the first control (C$_1$) session, the number of correct responses for Student 1 did not change, but it was apparent that he spent more time sitting at the table. In each of the two subsequent C$_1$ sessions, his total number of appropriate responses decreased. During the token-training sessions he was orderly and attentive. During the C$_2$ session that immediately followed token training, his appropriate response total was identical to that obtained in the first C$_1$ session. In his next C$_2$ session this total decreased. This subject was not present for the final C$_2$ session.

In each of the first five (T$_1$ and T$_2$) token-reinforcement sessions, Student 1 responded correctly to between twenty-seven and twenty-nine items on the thirty-item instruction list. Thus, each daily T$_1$ and T$_2$ total exceeded any obtained previously. In the first C$_3$ session, his response total decreased to twenty-five. In the two subsequent C_3 sessions, his totals decreased markedly, and his disruptive behavior appeared to increase and subjectively resembled his behavior in his regular classroom. The total of only six correct responses which he obtained in the third C_3 session clearly indicates the extent to which his instruction-following behavior deteriorated. Finally, with the reinstatement of the token-reinforcement procedures in the T_3 sessions, appropriate responding on the part of S_1 increased markedly. He actually followed each of thirty instructions in two of the three T_3 sessions. The beneficial effect of token reinforcement was, thus, clearly established for this subject.

The results obtained with Student 1 were representative of results obtained with Students 2, 3, and 4. These results are shown in Figs. 2, 3, and 4 respectively. In the case of each of these

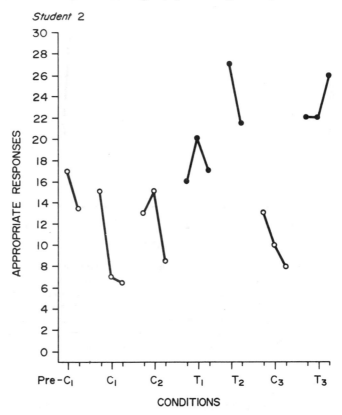

Fig. 2. Number of instructions followed by Student 2.

subjects, the highest totals of correct responding were obtained in token-reinforcement sessions. Each of these three subjects differed from Student 1 in one respect. Their response totals increased, when the words, "that's a token," were added to the verbal reinforcement in the T_2 sessions. This suggests that the use of this specific verbal bridge may have added to the effectiveness of the token-reinforcement system. This possibility must remain speculative, however, because this verbal factor was not systematically manipulated and because it is also quite possible that either (a) the changes in the token-exchange criteria introduced at the end of the third T_1 session and/or (b) continued exposure to token reinforcement, *per se*, could have accounted for the increases in appropriate response totals observed with these subjects after the third token-reinforcement session.

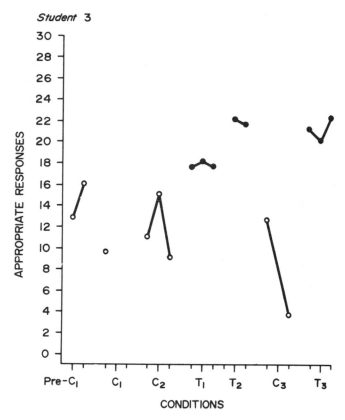

Fig. 3. Number of instructions followed by Student 3.

Two subjects did not appear to be differentially influenced by the application of token reinforcement over the study. Figure 5 presents the daily results for Student 5. Between the initial Pre-C_1 session and the final C_3 session, his totals of correct responding varied between sixteen and twenty-three. This range of values was obtained under both token-reinforcement and control conditions. That Student 5 may have been influenced by tokens is suggested only by the results obtained in the T_3 sessions. His highest totals in the study (26 and 25) were obtained in the first and third T_3 sessions. In general, however, it would be more appropriate to summarize his results by indicating that he responded appropriately to the majority of items throughout the investigation. We would point out that while Student 5's teacher reported that he "paid poor attention" in her class, the data obtained for him in the experimental class demonstrated that he was certainly capable of following simple instructions. In contrast, these data are not compatible with statements often made about this student which suggest that he has "severe attentional deficits." These data, when considered in combination with his reported classroom history and with the subjective interpretations of his regular classroom performance suggest that a systematic approach, *per se*, which is necessary to obtain objective behavioral measurements, may be critically important to the future successful education of this subject.

Figure 6 presents the results for Student 6. An examination of his results suggests that he continuously improved with respect to following instructions during the study and independent of specific conditions. This subject was assigned the lowest IQ of all subjects in this study.

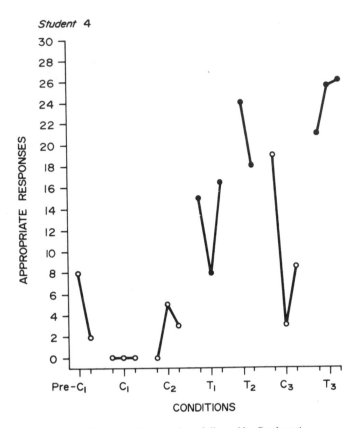

Fig. 4. Number of instructions followed by Student 4.

While on the one hand it might be argued that his results are certainly compatible with this evaluation (he followed fewer total instructions over the study than all but one subject) they are not compatible with several subjective reports which indicated that he was "incapable of paying attention and learning much of anything." The data obtained for Student 6 demonstrate that under repeated systematic exposure to at least one general set of classroom conditions, this child's instruction-following behavior can be accelerated. It is quite probable that this acceleration, observed over the course of the study, would not have been detected had we either subjectively observed his performance or exposed him to fewer sessions. Thus, as in the case of Student 5, the data obtained with Student 6 suggest that a systematic approach, *per se*, may also be critically important to his future education.

Student 7 failed to respond to any item on the instruction list throughout the study. He was, thus, a poor selection for the present approach. Informal efforts with this subject, in isolation, did indicate, however, that he might benefit from a reinforcement programme applied on an individual basis.

Reliability of the Instruction List

In an experimental study such as the present one, the reliability of the data-gathering instrument depends upon the extent to which responses called for can be objectively monitored. On the basis of a comparison of the pairs of individual session totals obtained for each subject

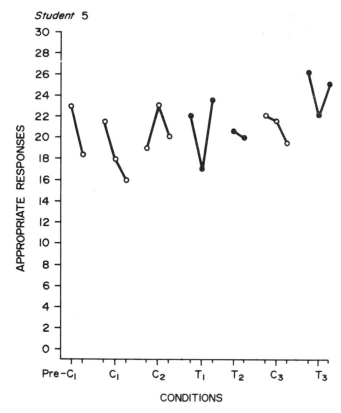

Fig. 5. Number of instructions followed by Student 5.

between the two independent observers across the study, the final list appeared to call for behaviors that were well defined and readily observable. In fifty-five per cent of the daily individual subject totals compared, no disagreement was found between observers. Furthermore, a difference of only one response was obtained in the two totals in thirty-three per cent of these comparisons. Finally, no difference greater than three responses was ever obtained in any comparison and this occurred in no more than five per cent of the comparisons.

Associated Results and Further Discussion

Three additional sets of observations remain to be described. They involve (a) some comments about the effectiveness of the timeout procedure, (b) some speculations about a possible relationship between the potency of the present token-reinforcement procedures and the nature of the subjects' "attentional" problems, and (c) some impressions and speculations about the apparent development and differential maintenance of some social emergents.

Timeout.   Timeout was primarily instituted to deal with occasions on which one subject aggressed physically against another. It was also used to discourage tampering with the store. Basically, this procedure involved the teacher's removal of an offending child from the experimental room. The offender was placed in the dimly lighted adjacent classroom. He was returned to the classroom after the teacher had completed a silent count of fifteen. Had an offender emitted tantrum-like behavior while in isolation, termination of such behavior

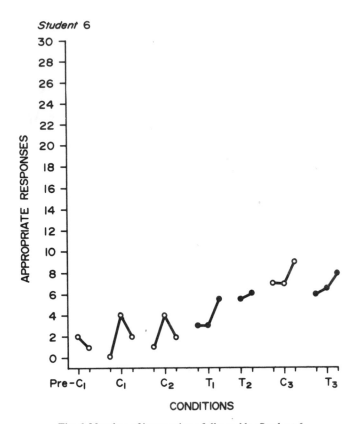

Fig. 6. Number of instructions followed by Student 6.

would have been required before permitting him to return; no such delay contingency was necessary. The use of timeout appeared to discourage repeated offending within any given session. It never had to be used more than twice in a given session and was used twice in only two sessions. Generally, when a subject was placed in timeout, no further timeout-producing behavior on the part of any of the subjects was observed over the remainder of that session. No definitive conclusions can be drawn with respect to the effects of timeout over sessions. Timeout was used after Student 5 tampered with the store on two occasions. These were both delivered during the first token-reinforcement session. The fact that this procedure never required repetition for this subject, suggests (but does not prove) its effectiveness. Timeouts were employed eighteen times following aggressive behavior over the course of the study. Student 4 produced thirteen of these. The fact that he received eleven timeouts during the initial twelve sessions and only two over the final eleven sessions might suggest that this procedure was effective across sessions. It should be pointed out, however, that he tended differentially to produce timeouts during control sessions, and that these comprised the majority of the initial sessions, while only three of the final eleven sessions were control sessions.

Potency of treatment and "attentional" problems. In first proposing this study to the principal and faculty of Noble School, we emphasized an interest in wording with children whose disruptive behavior in and out of the classroom often led to their being characterized, among other things, as being "hyperactive." Over the course of the investigation, it was the impression of all observers that behavior that might be "attributed" to "hyperactivity" occurred less frequently during token sessions than during control sessions. The data obtained with some subjects over the investigation are certainly in logical agreement with these subjective impressions. What appears to be most significant about this observation is the fact that those four subjects who were reported to be "extremely hyperactive" and/or extremely disruptive in their regular classrooms were the same four subjects who showed dramatic improvement in instruction-following behavior under the token-reinforcement situation. To the extent that our subjective impressions were valid, these findings support the notion that a major observable contributor to "attentional deficit" type inferences drawn to teachers about students may be the frequent failure of the latter to follow instructions.

The apparent emergence of "helping" behavior. Perhaps of greatest relevance to the potential benefits that might be derived from the present and similar approaches, above and beyond those of economy and objective information, is the description of what subjectively appeared to be the emergence of potentially significant and unexpected social behavior. During the Pre-C_1, C_1 and C_2 sessions, although the class was treated as a group with respect to instructions, there appeared to be little, if any, group cohesiveness. The only interaction between members of the group involved "playful" and "not so playful" fighting between pairs of subjects. There did not appear to be any instance of "cooperation" between subjects or "assistance of one by another." In contrast, after the initial token session and in all subsequent token sessions, we frequently observed behaviors on the part of each of five subjects (Student 1 through Student 5) which (subjectively) appeared to be socially directed toward another subject, and which we inferred to be designed to help the latter subject earn reinforcement. On one occasion, for example, Student 1 brought scissors to Student 6 when scissors were needed to fulfill the requirement of an item on the instruction list. Various subjects were seen to raise Student 7's hand for him when an instruction called for that behavior. Other dramatic examples of similar social behaviors included Student 2 leading Student 4 to the table, thereby making the latter eligible for reinforcement, and Student 4 pointing to the appropriate card with the name of a fellow subject on it, seeming to encourage imitation.

We can, at best, only speculate about these alleged cases of "helping" behavior, because no objective measurement procedures were utilized to monitor their occurrence, and because no explicit contingencies were scheduled with respect to their occurrence. Tokens were not delivered to a subject as a consequence of "assisting another subject." The emergence of this behavior could have crucially depended upon one or more of the characteristics of the programme. This behavior may have been controlled, in part, by the presence or absence of the props and cues associated with token reinforcement, since it was apparently not observed during control sessions. This behavior could have emerged as a consequence of addressing the group as a whole and/or of the fact that all children could equally obtain tangible goods (competition was not involved).

Since the instructor and observers focused their attention upon appropriate instruction-following behavior throughout this investigation, the observations reported above, while provocative, must be regarded as generally anecdotal in nature. Time limits set upon the present study did not permit a more systematic examination of these phenomena and excluded the possibility of further appropriate experimental manipulations.

A final comment. We have no special investment in token reinforcement, *per se*, as a method of generating and improving classroom behavior. A token-reinforcement system involves a complex set of procedures which demands much attention and includes vast numbers of stimulus elements and environmental variables. From an experimental point of view, those invested in the effects of token reinforcement would have carefully to isolate the numerous variables involved in order to determine objectively the factors necessary and sufficient to the generation of observed reliable behavioral changes. Instead, our bias is in the direction of a systematic arrangement of an environment and the systematic application of any given treatment in such way as to facilitate objective and reliable measurements. Quantitative data alone reveal whether a specific treatment (be it the use of token reinforcement, electric shock, M and M's, threats, or instructions) is therapeutic, ineffective, or noxious with respect to a chosen target behavior. In the case of the "treatment" applied and treatment effects assessed in the present study, the data suggest that the approach taken can be successfully applied to the problem of altering behavior of individuals treated as a group in a group setting. We would here reiterate that not every member of the group was differentially influenced by token reinforcement under the conditions which obtained. However, in the case of two of the three subjects who were not differentially influenced, the use of the present procedures provided objective information about their behavior which could be as valuable with respect to their further education as that provided for the subjects whose performances were differentially influenced by token reinforcement!

REFERENCES

Birnbrauer, J. S., Wolf, M. M., Kidder, J. D. & Tague, C. E. Classroom behavior of retarded pupils with token reinforcement. *Journal of Experimental Child Psychology*, 1965, **2**, 219–235.

Burchard, J. D. "Systematic socialization: A programmed environment of the habilitation of anti-social retardates," *Psychological Record*, 1967, **17**, 461–476.

Bushell, D., Wrobel, P. A. & Michaelis, M. L. Applying "group" contingencies to the classroom study behavior of preschool children. *Journal of Applied Behavior Analysis*, 1968, **1**, 55–61.

Hall, R. V., Lund, D. & Jackson, D. Effects of teacher attention on study behavior. *Journal of Applied Behavior Analysis*, 1968, **1**, 1–12.

Harris, F. R., Wolf, M. M. & Baer, D. M. Effects of adult social reinforcement on child behavior. *Young Children*, 1964, **20**, 8–17.

Zimmerman, E. H. & Zimmerman, J. The alteration of behavior in a special classroom situation. *Journal of the Experimental Analysis of Behavior*. 1962, **5**, 59–60.

Application of Behavior Modification by Parents for Treatment of a Brain Damaged Child*

CHARLES E. PASCAL

McGill University

Abstract: The present paper discusses the use of behavior modification for the treatment of a brain damaged nine-year-old male. The three basic therapeutic goals were: (1) to eliminate the maladaptive behaviors of handslapping and emission of bizarre noises, (2) to develop intelligible speech, and (3) to have the child's mother become responsible for maintenance of the treatment programme. A treatment plan, based mainly on the token system, was carried out by the experimenter, an assistant, and two relatives who spend the most amount of time with the child. Preliminary results after two months of the programme indicate achievement of goal one and significant progress toward goals two and three.

INTRODUCTION

Brief Case History

This case study is concerned with a nine-year-old male, Steven, who was diagnosed as "brain damaged" at six months of age. The diagnosis was made by a neurologist who concluded that partial motor difficulties on the right side suggested damage to the left temporal lobe. Further consultation one year later with another neurologist confirmed the earlier diagnosis with the additional information that the child exhibited speech difficulties.

The child lives with his mother who is currently finishing her degree while the child attends a local school for the mentally retarded. Reports from the school indicate that the child is considered unmanageable and unable to interact properly with the other children in his class (all retarded children). The director of the school, like other psychologists, psychiatrists, and neurologists, has suggested institutionalization for the child.

Steven is presently on probation pending improvement of his behavior. Also, the speech therapist at the school, as three other speech therapists in the past have found, is unable to get Steven to pay attention to the task at hand and to produce intelligible sounds.

Statement of the Problem

The problems in this case fall into two general categories. First, the child exhibits two maladaptive behaviors: (a) he is unable to produce intelligible speech. Intelligible speech is, in this case, defined as speech which can be understood by someone who is interacting with Steven for the first time or infrequently; (b) he constantly emits bizarre sounds and exhibits an autistic handslapping behavior (i.e., slaps his hands together). Both behaviors are quite annoying to those people around him and prevent other people, including other children at his school, from wanting to interact with him.

---

*This paper represents an original contribution to this volume. Copyright Pergamon Press, 1971.

Secondly, the child is unable to interact "properly" with other people. Obviously the previous problematic behaviors must be dealt with before adequate social interaction can be developed.

In addition to these two broad problem areas, Steven also limps and has trouble using his right hand due to partial paralysis. Since these motor problems are considered to be tangential to the primary problem, they will not be discussed in this paper.

Ullmann & Krasner (1965) suggest a simple but useful strategy for cases for which behavior therapy seems most appropriate:

> The working behavior therapist is likely to ask three questions: (a) what behavior is maladaptive, that is, what subject behaviors should be increased or decreased, (b) what environmental contingencies currently support the subject's behavior (either to maintain his undesirable behavior or to reduce the likelihood of his performing a more adaptive response), and (c) what environmental changes, usually reinforcing stimuli, may be manipulated to alter the subject's behavior?

An application of this strategy to the present case is in order. Part (a) of this approach has been mentioned: the maladaptive behaviors are the bizarre sounds and handslapping; the desired adaptive behavior is intelligible speech.

Next, it is important that the supporting nature of Steven's maladaptive behaviors is discussed. It is believed that this sound represents a pleasurable reaction on Steven's part. His attention to children playing (Steven plays *beside, not with* other children), lawn mowers, cars and any machine which makes noise is quite sustained and is always accompanied by this sound.

The handslapping behavior, the experimenter believes, is not a reaction to something pleasurable, but is in itself stimulating and therefore is quite frequently emitted. The baseline rates of both of these behaviors are indicated in Figs. 1 and 2.

Perhaps the most critical problem is Steven's lack of intelligible speech. As the previous definition of "intelligible" implies, communication between Steven and those who spend the most time with him is adequate. In other words, his speech, though unintelligible to an infrequent or novel visitor, is adequate to communicate basic needs such as for food, etc. There is no reason for him to speak in any other way since he is consistent in his associations of objects of need and the nonsense syllables which he uses to label these objects. He and his mother are able to interact quite well since they both know Steven's "language." His short and long memory, therefore, appear to be quite adequate. Every time Steven gets water by saying "wakee" this symbol is strengthened. In this way Steven developed a "nonsense syllable" vocabulary which serves his basic needs quite well. Initial interaction with Steven for two weeks yielded a baseline measurement of one "intelligible" word—"mama." This was confirmed by a relative who had infrequent visits with the boy for over a year and by the experimenter's assistant who also spent several days "talking with" Steven.

Apart from the specific reinforcing contingencies responsible for sustaining all of the above-mentioned maladaptive behaviors, there exists a more general, but nonetheless valid, reason for the maintenance and nurturing of these behaviors. Bijou (1968) points out that there are several reasons why maladaptive behavior is caused and maintained. First, he discusses abnormal physiological functioning: Steven's source of stimulation (experience) necessary for development may be inhibited because (1) physiological impairment makes certain stimuli forever inaccessible to the child and (2) his *appearance* may result in other people avoiding interacting with him, resulting in social deprivation.

Finally, and perhaps most significant, is the influence of the expectations of those around the child. If those people who interact with the child treat him as though he were abnormal or chronically ill, as is often the case, then this will in itself have a retarding effect on the child.

Studies concerning the effect of expectations of behavior on the resulting behavior have been done with normal students (Rosenthal, 1964) as well as with retarded children. In all cases, if someone is labelled "bright" or "brain damaged" the result is that the therapist, the parent, the teacher, etc. reinforce those behaviors of the child consistent with the label. Normal behavior is not expected of brain damaged or mongoloid children, etc. and behavior compatible with their diagnosis is reinforced. This is not to imply that there are no limits to a brain damaged child's potential. This is probably true, but in most cases, this potential is not significantly approached.

It is apparent that Steven's problems go beyond those dictated by this "brain damaged" label. "Many retarded children are also behaviorally disturbed and practically all severely maladjusted children are also developmentally retarded" (Bijou, 1968).

A summary of the cause and maintenance of Steven's present problems is in order. His problems — social, verbal, and emotional — are due to three basic conditions. First, physiological damage to the left temporal lobe has resulted in motor difficulties and lack of coordination necessary for proper speech. The effect of this damage on the development of intelligible speech is believed to be a retarding rather than a preventative influence on achieving this goal. Secondly, it is believed that his physical and verbal problems have resulted in a lack of experiential stimulation and, therefore, emotional difficulties.

Finally, it is felt the maintenance of these problems is largely due to the effect of expectations of what Steven's behavior should be according to his diagnosis. This has resulted in reinforcement contingent on maladaptive behaviors.

It is thus the conclusion of this observer that his behavior is maintained by reinforcements in the environment and that behavior modification is the most appropriate therapy since its methods deal directly with reinforcement contingencies. It is important to note that while some of his emotional problems may be aided, this therapist is concerned with establishing verbal ability which will then allow a more precise analysis of these other problems to take place. At some future point in time another method of therapy may be quite appropriate.

Therapeutic Goals

With these preliminary statements concerning the practical implications of using behavior modification for treating Steven in mind, a precise statement of the terminal objectives of the present programme is in order.

1. Elimination of bizarre sounds and handslapping behavior. (*Criterion:* Zero instances for one week.)
2. Development of intelligible and functional speech, which is self-initiated and responsive. (*Criterion:* Ability to speak in full sentences which he either initiates or uses in response to other relatively novel and familiar social objects and in so doing achieving functional communication with these objects.)
3. Management of the programme to be maintained predominantly by the child's mother. (*Criterion:* Significant improvement towards criteria of objectives one and two when therapist is no longer involved in interacting directly with patient; consultation between mother and therapist will be continued.)

The last of these objectives seems to be an *ideal* goal of many therapy programmes with children but with the use of behavior modification techniques it is felt to be a most *realistic* objective as well.

METHOD

General Programme

The initial stages of the programme involve the cooperation of the child's relatives (those who spend more than ten hours weekly — mother, grandmother, and an aunt) and two therapists. This cooperation involves a consistent execution of the principles of the programme.

The following "memo" is presented to all of those involved. This statement of principles and theory is the essential strategy of the programme.

To: Friends of Steven
From: C. E. Pascal
Re: Speech and Behavior Training Programme

As you are aware, I've been interacting with Steven for several weeks and I am convinced that he is capable of intelligible speech and socially acceptable behavior. It doesn't matter whether you label his behavior "retarded," "brain damaged," or "abnormal" for as far as Steven is concerned, his behavior serves him quite well; that is to say that he has no immediate need to speak or act differently since his basic needs are satisfied. Very seldom is any other kind of behavior expected from a "brain damaged" child. Since language is merely symbolic, the communication that takes place between Steven and those around him is as richly productive as those verbal interactions between "normal" people.

I have found that Steven is capable of making almost every sound necessary for speech; some combinations of these sounds are more difficult than others but nonetheless, he has the potential. What I am proposing is to employ a Reinforcement Therapy programme demanding the participation and cooperation of all of Steven's frequent companions. The success of this programme depends completely upon adherence to a few basic principles and rules. Success in this venture will mean intelligible speech and socially acceptable behavior for Steven.

REINFORCEMENT THEORY AND STEVEN

1. Anytime Steven says or does something and he receives some reward such as an object, a smile, acknowledgment, etc. — that word or behavior is strengthened. If the behavior is a desirable one, then rewarding it is beneficial. But if the behavior is not acceptable, e.g., he says "Beebeh" for his name, then acknowledging this word has strengthened an undesirable response.

2. Steven's behavior is "retarded" mainly because this label has given him and millions of other people an excuse for not being called upon for more adept behavior, i.e., he can't be expected to do more than those around him demand. E.g., if he is expected to get dressed by himself then eventually through trial and error, he will, if he is *consistently expected* to do so; he may suffer some negative consequences at first, like his mother leaving him in the house for a few hours while she goes outside, but he will dress himself (I do not know if this is a *real* example but let it suffice as an illustration).

3. "Punishment" used to extinguish an unwanted behavior does not have to be aggressive on your part or painful to Steven. I prefer to think of this concept in two ways:

   a. Withholding Steven's *expected consequences* of an action will weaken the behavior preceding these consequences. E.g., when coming home after a ride, he often begins crying or whining because the ride is over; quite often those with him have sat there arguing with him or at least calling attention to his whining, etc. This has served his purpose since it usually results in getting you mad or perhaps in making a "deal" with Steven to do something else. By getting out of the car and ignoring this whining, it will extinguish within one week *if everybody is consistent* in enforcing this rule. Any time Steven does something which is for the express purpose of getting you angry (whining, pushing you away, etc.) then getting mad reinforces this behavior, but ignoring it weakens it.

b. The other way of weakening behavior is to deprive him of something of value following a negative behavior; this may be food or a privilege. If possible, the "fine" should relate to the crime, e.g., if he throws food, he will not be allowed to eat any more. It is not possible though to always relate the "fine" to the act. For instance, he may throw a neighbor's toy and break it. It would be difficult to *enforce* a rule like "you can't play with Johnny's toys any more." And any rule which can't be consistently enforced is a bad one. In this case, then, we will deprive him of what is known as a "generalized reinforcer" which is a symbol for many other things of value to him. E.g., money is something we all work for because it pays rent, buys food, etc. *We will "fine" Steven tokens* (pennies) *for behaviors we wish to extinguish and reward him with tokens for those behaviors we wish to strengthen.* These pennies already have meaning for Steven since he has been earning them by doing positive behaviors (e.g., saying words properly) and he exchanges these pennies for cokes, rides, candy, toys, and eventually he will be required to pay for everything including dinner at home. In this way, he will place much value (as we do) in these tokens since they "buy" so many things of value. Taking a penny away will eventually weaken any behavior preceding this "fine" and likewise giving Steven a penny for doing something will strengthen the preceding behavior. Eventually, Steven will be doing chores, etc. to earn his tokens.

RULES

1. Once you have shaped a desirable word or behavior, be sure to write it on the chart. In this way, we can be *consistent in expecting* that behavior and demanding that, for instance, he say "ride" in order to get a ride.
2. As you may have gathered, CONSISTENCY is the key concept. Any behavior or rule of conduct that has been consistently reinforced will soon become a common unit in Steven's behavioral repertoire. But if Steven can have a coke by saying "coke" sometimes and "coh" at other times, then the proper word cannot be expected to be a stable part of his vocabulary.
3. Steven should be able to learn between three and five words a day when we begin this programme. Choose words that come up during the day, e.g., today he wanted me to open the curtains in my house; I began shaping the word "open" using actual opening of the curtain as reinforcement. *If he wants something, then teach him to say it properly and make him say it to receive the desired object or act.*
4. There is no need for yelling or aggression when you "fine" Steven, since this may be reinforcing to him. Simply walk over, take a penny (from his changer) and *state the reason for the fine in a normal tone of voice.*
5. When Steven is to be rewarded for a behavior, be sure to *state the reason for the reward.*

In addition, each of these people are exposed to sessions in which the therapist applies these principles to the patient's behavior and then in turn the therapist observed these procedures as practiced by the other therapist and the child's relatives. Finally, they are shown the movie "Reinforcement Therapy" (Lovaas) which provides them with some very positive longitudinal findings of a behavior modification programme.

Shaping Procedures

Shaping words or successively approximating proper pronunciation of words is the first step towards achieving objective two. Any word which is too difficult for Steven to say is broken down into its syllables. If these syllables are too difficult then each syllable is broken down into its component sounds. Gradually, the word is put together until he is able to "echo" the model.

Phrases and then sentences are shaped in this manner. Throughout this process "meaning" is conditioned to the words by associating each word and phrase with the object or act being labelled (use of pictures, slides, etc. and especially interacting with the environment).

Breaking down individual words also aids the learning of new words based on these smaller units. As Staats & Staats (1963) point out, "syllabic units come under 'echoic' control so that entirely new words may be quickly produced by the child when he 'echoes' the syllables pronounced by the adult training him. The learning task which remains in this case only involves establishing a chain between the syllable responses the child already has in his repertoire."

Eventually, the amount of cueing is reduced. At first the cue is a model which must be echoed. Gradually proper pronunciation is elicited to a picture or object. Finally, when the trainers are certain that Steven is capable of saying the word, he must produce the word properly if he is allowed to interact with the object (e.g., have a glass of water). If he says the word improperly than a quizzical glance or a "what did you say" response is in order. This postpones reinforcement (obtaining the water), weakens the improper response and forces the child to make another response. This is done until the child reaches the approximation appropriate for that particular word or phrase and then he is reinforced by the object (e.g., given a glass of water). Appropriateness of a response depends on the strength of the criterion response exhibited in training sessions. Some words are more difficult at first and approximations to the criterion pronunciation may be acceptable at first. It is this use of differential reinforcement of speech responses by the trainers which is the basis of shaping verbal behavior.

Reinforcers

As the programme indicates, it is always best to use the natural reinforcers in the environment to shape words. This is for two reasons. First, it maximizes the use of the child's motivation. If he *wants* a glass of water, or he *wants* to open the door, ride in a car, etc., obtaining his desired object (reinforcement) then should be contingent on verbalizing properly what he wants ("water," "ride," "open door"). Secondly, using the environment is more *meaningful* since the occurrence of the response (word) and reinforcement (object) are real and contiguous.

In shaping words initially, however, especially those words which are not immediately necessary for *him* to say, the use of a primary reinforcer should be used. The use of M & M's and other food is used for shaping at the outset for two reasons: (1) to introduce him to the shaping procedure, and (2) to keep his attention since at first he has no motivational reason for participating.

Gradually, social reinforcement (which is a conditioned stimulus presented along with the primary reward) "takes over," and this secondary reinforcer along with the natural environmental reinforcers mentioned previously are the basic rewards used in the verbal aspect of the programme.

Elimination of the maladaptive behaviors—the bizzare sounds and the handslapping—required a different type of reinforcing scheme: the use of tokens as generalized secondary reinforcers. As described previously these tokens have value since he needs to have them for meals and privileges. He is initially taught the concept of tokens by first giving him a token and then replacing it with food, etc. Then latency of exchanging tokens for primary reinforcer is gradually increased. The reason for the use of tokens is that performing a maladaptive behavior which is in itself pleasurable, must have more than neutral consequences. Making a bizarre sound or slapping his hands must be followed by negative consequences. The use of aversive stimulation has already been dismissed and this implies that he must be deprived of something of value. Removal of a token from his changer (e.g., conductor's changer is worn by child, making token removal easy and immediate) following a maladaptive behavior then should extinguish these responses. Likewise, Steven is given tokens following desirable and adaptive behaviors.

Consistency

Finally, it is important to again stress that consistency is essential. Communication (e.g., a chart indicating new words, etc. is kept by all those involved in the programme) among the trainers regarding newly acquired words facilitates strengthening these responses since he is *expected* by *everyone* to *produce* them.

Further, Steven will no doubt "test the rule" and not be able to "afford" dinner, for instance. Depriving him of dinner in this case is essential in maintaining the value of tokens and thus the ability to negatively reinforce the maladaptive behaviors.

RESULTS

The data reported in this section are a result of two months of the programme. Figures 1 and 2 illustrate a comparison between the pre-programme operant levels of the bizarre sounds and handslapping and a current measure of these behaviors (after two months of the pro-gramme being in effect). These data indicate a marked decrease in both behaviors.

It must be noted that before the later measurement was taken, intermittent occurrences or "spontaneous recoveries" of handslapping were recorded. The experimenter then asked all of the trainers to observe and record when these instances occurred and to describe the environment at that time. Analysis of the possible supporting conditions of the handslapping behavior revealed that Steven did this whenever there were at least two other people present, especially when these people were interacting with one another rather than with Steven.

Thus, the recurrence of this behavior was believed to be an attention-getting device since slapping his hands brought one trainer over to him immediately to ask him to state the rule, etc. This constituted interaction with Steven for about thirty seconds to a minute, which appeared pleasing to him rather than unpleasing (since a token was removed).

The reason for this lack of concern for loss of a token became obvious at this point. Since Steven was able to earn tokens any time he needed them by saying words or exhibiting an adaptive behavior, he could always earn "dinner money," etc. Thus, losing a token for hand-slapping had no negative consequences (e.g., losing dinner) and it *did* have immediate positive consequences – interaction with another person.

The experimenter thus altered the contingencies of reinforcement. Since social reinforce-ment and the natural environmental reinforcers were quite effective for rewarding and shaping verbal and social behavior, the trainers no longer give Steven tokens for these behaviors. Rather, Steven's mother currently gives Steven a fixed number of tokens every morning. This number is based on the amount of tokens needed for meals and basic privileges (e.g., going for rides). In this way, removal of tokens are still contingent on exhibition of a maladaptive behavior but Steven is no longer able to earn tokens. Thus, eating dinner, etc. is *directly* contingent on *not* exhibiting these behaviors. In addition, the trainer no longer asks Steven to state the rule. He was stating it before the trainer was able to ask for it in some cases. In other words, he was getting social reinforcement for stating the proper rule. Therefore, the trainers currently remove a token immediately following one of these acts and ignore his statement of the rule.

In order to negatively reinforce these behaviors when he no longer has tokens, the trainers use a "timeout" procedure which places Steven on a seat removed from the social interaction

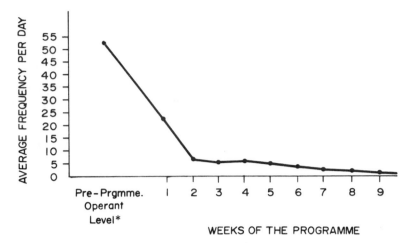

Fig. 1. Bizarre sounds.

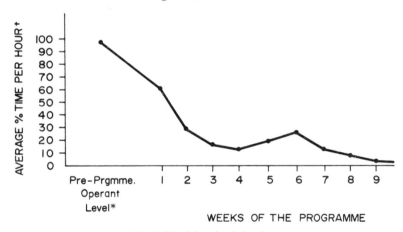

Fig. 2. Handslapping behavior.

*Pre-Programme operant level figured over period of one week.

†Average percentage figured on randomly selected two-hour period each day.

in the environment. It is important to note that this seat is placed in a relatively neutral setting (e.g., the hallway) in order to avoid conditioning negative cues to his bedroom (or bathroom). The length of the "timeout" depends on Steven's behavior during the period. He is never removed while exhibiting crying, yelling, etc.

The result of this change in the programme was quickly apparent. Steven could not "afford" dinner on two successive evenings (the first two dinners following the change) and since then the maladaptive behaviors have returned to criterion level.

The effect of the programme on Steven's verbal behavior is recorded in Table 1 which lists the frequency of words, phrases, and sentences which Steven currently uses with and without a model. This list includes some verbalizations which require some cueing (e.g., a quizzical look, a "what did you say"). With these minimal cues Steven is able to reach criterion and will eventually be able to produce them without cues due to the effect of this differential reinforcement.

Table 1. Verbal repertoire (After nine weeks).

	Self-Initiated*	"Cued"**	Modelled***	Totals
Words	149	22	12	183
Phrases	13	2	4	19
Sentences	8	4	3	15
Totals	170	28	19	217

*Intelligible words produced without cue or model.

**Intelligible words produced with minimal cue (e.g., quizzical look, or "what"?).

***Intelligible words produced with model (e.g., word, syllable, sound) provided.

Note: The pre-programme baseline was one intelligible word recorded over a one-week period by each of two "novel" visitors who interacted with Steven for two hours per day. This baseline was also verified by several relatives who spent considerable time with Steven. This table reports only those words, phrases, and sentences recorded during the eighth and ninth weeks. These words were recorded by the experimenter's wife who rarely interacted with Steven. This is in keeping with the present definition of "intelligible speech." Due to generalization, the number of words, phrases, and sentences, which the child can potentially produce with a model, is much greater.

It is also important to note that initially it was necessary to use reinforcers other than food to maintain Steven's attention. In interacting with Steven it became apparent that anything which produced noise was pleasing (e.g., lawn mower, vacuum cleaner, running water, etc.).

With this in mind, the trainers used a tape recorder to produce the models for his speech. In some cases, however, it was necessary to help him physically with some sounds. An example of this is holding his lips together to help him say "P." Eventually all help was removed and he was able to produce the sound unaided.

In addition, he had some difficulty with pronunciation of the final sound of a syllable within a word. For instance, at first in shaping the word "coffee" he could say "cau" and "fee" but in putting them together would say "cau-ee." In order to aid him in coordinating these syllables, a candle (which is extremely reinforcing for him) was placed before his mouth; he was shown that saying the model, "coffee" (with emphasis on the final syllable) would blow out the candle (also, very reinforcing); and that "cau-ee" would not. After three attempts, Steven produced "co-feeee."

Since most of Steven's speech problems stem from lack of verbal *coordination*, developing coordination in these ways has been quite helpful. In addition, a particular coordination (e.g., saying coffee) generalizes and results in the ability to say an entirely new class of words (e.g., puppy instead of "pu-ee").

SUMMARY AND DISCUSSION

The results of the programme indicate the achievement of objective one: Steven's production of bizarre noises and handslapping has practically extinguished. Complete extinction is dependent upon increased consistency on the part of all those people who interact with Steven. It is important to note that the data reported in this paper were recorded in the home setting and other settings (restaurants, other homes) with the exception of the school. Visits to the classroom by this observer have revealed an interesting but anticipated outcome.

Steven's behavior at school may be labelled as "environmental regression." The operant level of his maladaptive behaviors at school is significantly higher than reported in this paper.

Enforcing the programme at school is inconsistent (the experimenter attempted to bridge this "environmental gap" by giving Steven's teachers the programme) due to the fact that Steven is in a classroom with fifteen other children being treated quite differently. Because of this, it is most difficult for the teachers to maintain a different set of rules for one child. In addition, the teachers are still quite convinced that Steven is untrainable. The influence of these *expectations* is quite profound. It is believed that Steven is discriminating between two sets of expectations and his behavior is differentially conforming to both environments (school, and out of school).

The probability of achieving objective two is evident. Approach toward the criterion is consistent as evidenced by the data reported in the previous section.

Finally, the progress toward achieving objective three represents the most promising and generalizable finding of this study. The role of the "chief" therapist has been taken over by the mother who is responsible for most of the programme's success. The maintenance of the value of the tokens depends upon consistent enforcement of "costs" of activities and "payment" by Steven. In addition, the mother is quite adept at shaping words and phrases.

In addition, the mother has applied the programme's principles to shaping other adaptive behaviors (e.g., answering the phone, getting dressed, etc.).

It is important to mention that the other therapist is an undergraduate with an interest in working with children but had no previous experience in behavior modification.

The simplicity of both theory and application of behavior therapy together with a high level of intrinsic motivation on the part of the parent suggests the practical and feasible implications of such an approach. The self-satisfaction gained by the parents' awareness that *they* are responsible for the success of their child's progress cannot be underestimated. This has been the case in this study.

REFERENCES

Bandura, A. Behavioral psychotherapy. *Scientific American*, 1967, **216**, 78–86.

Bijou, S. The mentally retarded child. *Psychology Today*, 1968, Vol. 2, No. 1.

Cook, C. & Adams, H. E. Modification of verbal behavior in speech deficient children. *Behaviour Research and Therapy*, 1966, **4**, 265–271.

Eysenck, H. J. Learning theory and behavior therapy. *Journal of Mental Science*, 1959, **105**, 61–75.

Gelfand, Donna M. & Hartmann, D. P. Behavior therapy with children: A review and evaluation of research methodology. *Psychological Bulletin*, 1968, **69**, 204–215.

Honig, Werner K. *Operant behavior: Areas of research and application*. New York: Appleton-Century-Crofts, 1966.

Kimble, G. *Hilgard and Marquis' conditioning and learning*. New York: Appleton-Century-Crofts, 1961.

Krasner, L. & Ullmann, L. *Research in behavior modification*. New York: Holt, Rinehart & Winston, Inc., 1966.

Lovaas, O. I., Berberich, J. P., Perloff, B. F. & Schaeffer, B. Acquisition of imitative speech by schizophrenic children. *Science*, 1966, **161**, 705–707.

Lovaas, O. I., Schaeffer, B. & Simmons, J. B. Building social behavior in autistic children by use of electric shock. *Journal of Experimental Research in Personality*, 1965, **1**, 99–109.

Metz, J. R. Conditioning generalized imitation in autistic children. *Journal of Experimental Child Psychology*, 1965, **2**, 389–399.

Rosenthal, R. Experimenter outcome orientation and the results of the psychological experiment. *Psychological Bulletin*, 1964, **61**, 405–412.

Russo, S. Adaptations in behavioral therapy with children. *Behaviour Research and Therapy*, 1964, **2**, 43–47.

Staats, A. (Ed.) *Human learning: Studies extending conditioning principles to complex behavior*. New York: Holt, Rinehart & Winston, Inc., 1964.

Staats, A. W. & Staats, C. K. *Complex human behavior*. New York: Holt, Rinehart & Winston, 1963.

Ullmann, L. & Krasner, L. *Case studies in behavior modification*. New York: Holt, Rinehart & Winston, Inc., 1965.

Establishing Functional Speech
in Echolalic Children*†

TODD RISLEY and MONTROSE WOLF

University of Kansas, U.S.A.

Abstract: This paper is a summary of research by the authors in the development of speech in echolalic children. The procedures are based on operant behavior-modification techniques such as: (1) *shaping* and *imitation training* for the development of speech; (2) *fading in* of new stimuli and *fading out* of verbal prompts to transfer the speech from imitative control to control by appropriate stimulus conditions; and (3) *extinction* and *time-out from reinforcement* for the reduction of inappropriate behavior in conjunction with the *differential reinforcement* of appropriate responses which are incompatible with the inappropriate behavior.

INTRODUCTION

Echolalia

" . . . autistic children usually do learn to talk, sometimes very well, but their speech fails to follow the normal patterns. Often prominent in their speech is a compulsive parroting of what they hear called echolalia. They pick up a phrase, a name, a snatch of song, or even a long verse, and repeat it endlessly" (Stone & Church, 1957).

The sporadic and usually inappropriate imitation of words, phrases and snatches of song, is observed in many deviant children. Although this behavior pattern is generally associated with the diagnosis of emotional disturbance or autism, it is also a frequently observed behavior pattern of children diagnosed as retarded or brain-damaged. The procedures described in this paper have been developed from work with echolalic children with almost every conceivable diagnosis. Indeed, the records of each of these children usually contained diagnoses of retardation and brain-damage as well as autism, each label applied to the same child by a different diagnostician. For our procedures, the diagnostic classification of the child is largely irrelevant. The presence or absence of echolalia is the important predictor of the ease of establishing more normal speech in a deviant child.

In alleviating any deficit in behavior, the most time-consuming task is the teaching of new topographies of behavior. When a child's repertoire does not include a particular behavior and the child cannot be taught by conventional means, training can be carried out by the behavior modification technique called *shaping*. This procedure involves the long and intricate process of reinforcing behaviors which resemble (although, perhaps only remotely) the desired terminal behavior, and then, in successive steps, shifting the reinforcement to behaviors which more and more closely resemble the terminal behavior. When the terminal response is obtained, the response can then be shifted to imitative control by *imitation training*.

*This work was partially supported by PHS grant HD00870-04 and OEO contract KAN CAP 670694/1 to the Bureau of Child Research, University of Kansas.

†Reprinted from *Behavior Research and Therapy*, 1967, **5**, 73–88. Copyright 1967 with permission from Pergamon Press Publishing Company and Dr. Todd Risley.

Imitation training involves reinforcing a response made by the child only when it immediately follows the same response made by the therapist. The child's response may already have existed in his echolalic repertoire or it may have been shaped into a high probability response. The therapist can shift the response to imitative control by reinforcing it when it occurs after the presentation of an identical modelled stimulus or *prompt*. In this manner large units of previously randomly occurring behavior can be brought under imitative control. Once a child accurately imitates most words, phrases, and sentences, then any topography of verbal behavior (i.e. any word, phrase, or sentence) can be produced when desired by presenting the child with the prompt to be imitated.

Echolalia, then, is of significance to the therapist, for, since the echolalic child already has verbal responses, the arduous task of shaping them is unnecessary. Once the child's responses are brought under imitative control, so that, for example, he says "that's a cow" when the therapist has just said "that's a cow," the only remaining step is to shift the control of his responses to the appropriate stimuli, so that, for example, he says "that's a cow" to a picture of a cow. This shift to naming is made by *fading out* the imitative prompt in gradual steps as described in detail below. In this manner the responses acquire their appropriate "meanings." Thus, the procedures for establishing functional speech in echolalic children are relatively simple and produce appropriate speech rapidly, in contrast to the procedures which have been used in establishing speech in non-echolalic, speech-deficient children (e.g., Lovaas, 1966; Risley, 1966).

GENERAL PROCEDURES

The authors developed the procedures summarized in this paper while working with children with echolalic speech. The general methodology was initially developed in the course of dealing with the behavior problems of an autistic child named Dicky (Wolf, Risley & Mees, 1964). We will review his case before describing the more refined procedures which evolved from it.

Our contact with Dicky began four years ago when he was three and a half years old. He had been diagnosed as autistic and had been institutionalized previously for a three-month period. Prior to this he had been diagnosed variously as psychotic, mentally retarded, and brain-damaged. Dicky had a variety of severe problem behaviors, and lacked almost all normal social and verbal behavior. His verbal repertoire was quite bizarre though not atypical of children diagnosed as autistic. He was echolalic, occasionally exactly mimicking in form and intonation bits of conversation of the staff. He sang songs, "Chicago," for example. He emitted a variety of phrases during tantrums, such as "Want a spanking," and "Want to go bye-bye" but none of his verbal behavior was socially appropriate. He never made requests, asked questions, or made comments. Although he mimicked occasionally, he would not mimic when asked to do so.

Our training began with the attendant presenting, one at a time, five pictures, approximately three by four inches in size, of a Santa Claus, a cat, etc. The attendant would prompt, for example, "This is a cat. Now say cat." After she had gone through all five pictures, she would mix their order and go through them again. Just as Dicky occasionally mimicked the speech of other people, he would occasionally mimic the attendant by saying "This is a cat," "Now say cat." On those occasions the attendant would say, "Good boy" or "That's right," and give him a bite of his meal. As a result Dicky began mimicking more frequently, until after about a week he was mimicking practically every prompt in addition to almost everything else the attendant said during the session.

However, during this time Dicky was not looking particularly closely at the pictures. Instead, he twisted and turned in his seat. So an *anticipation procedure* was introduced, where anticipating the correct response would result in a reinforcer sooner than if he waited for the prompt. The attendant would present the picture for a period of several seconds before giving the prompt.

Gradually, Dicky began looking at the pictures and saying the phrases in the presence of the pictures without the prompts. In three weeks he did this in the presence of about ten pictures. We then introduced picture books and common household objects which he learned with increasing ease. At the same time temporally remote events were taught in the following manner. Dicky would be taken outside and swung or allowed to slide and then brought back inside and asked: "What did you do outside?" and then after a few seconds given a prompt. Imitations and finally the correct answers were followed by a reinforcer.

He was taught the answers to other questions such as, "What is your name?" and, "Where do you live?". The question would be asked and, if after a pause he had not answered, the prompt would be given and the correct response reinforced.

After several weeks of training, Dicky's verbal repertoire was markedly expanded, although he still had several verbal anomalies, such as imitating the question before answering and reversing his pronouns, e.g. he would ask for a drink by saying, "You want some water." Dicky was released from hospital seven months after our contact began. The training was continued by his parents, and after about six months he was using pronouns appropriately and was initiating many requests and comments, although he still was making frequent inappropriate imitating responses. After attending the Laboratory Preschool at the University of Washington for two years, his verbal skills had developed to the point that he was ready for special education in the public school.

Dicky's verbal behavior now resembles that of a skilled five-year-old. This means that since his operant training his rate of language development has been approximately normal. This probably has been the result of the diligent efforts of his parents and teachers to provide an environment which reinforced his verbal behavior. However, now the naturally occurring rewards of verbal behavior (*see* Skinner, 1957, for a discussion of these) appear to be the most important factors in maintaining and expanding his verbal repertoire.

These procedures for developing speech were subsequently refined in the course of working with the following echolalic children.

Pat was a blind twelve-year-old boy who has been recently institutionalized with the diagnosis of childhood autism. He had previously been enrolled in a school for the blind, but had been dropped from the programme due to his disruptive behavior and general lack of progress.

Billy was a ten-year-old boy who had been institutionalized for several years with the diagnosis of childhood autism.

Carey was a seven-year-old boy who lived at home although he had been diagnosed variously as autistic, retarded, and brain-damaged, and institutionalization had been recommended. He had attended a day-school for special children during the previous two years, but had been dropped due to a general lack of progress.

Will was an eight-year-old boy who had been institutionalized for two years with the diagnosis of severe retardation and brain-damage. He was not considered to be trainable and had been placed on a custodial ward.

The Physical Arrangement

To work most efficiently with a deviant child, particularly one with disruptive behaviors, the speech training should be carried out in a room containing as few distractions as possible. In our training room, we usually have only chairs for the child and teacher, a desk or table between them, and a small table or chair next to the teacher on which to place the food tray. Such an arrangement is shown in Fig. 1.

In a room where the child may reach for, throw, or destroy many items, turn on and off light switches and climb on furniture, the therapist may inadvertently train the child to engage in these behaviors, since they must be attended to by the therapist. For some children with high rates of tantrums and disruptive behavior, the rooms have been entirely cleared except for the chairs and tables which have been secured to the floor.

The Reinforcer

Certain consequences of a behavior will increase the frequency of that behavior. Those consequences, which are technically termed reinforcers, are usually events which are commonly described as important, significant, or meaningful for the particular child. With normal children, attention and praise can be used as consequences to strengthen behavior (Harris *et al.*, 1964). Such sophisticated social consequences often are only weak positive reinforcers for a severely abnormal child. For this reason food must often be relied upon as a reinforcing consequence for modifying speech and other behaviors of deviant children.

The ideal food reinforcer is one which the child particularly "likes," many bites of which can be eaten, and which cannot be readily "played with." We have found that the food reinforcer which best satisfies these criteria is ice cream or sherbet. It is generally a favorite food of children, it can be eaten in quantity, and it disappears rapidly from the mouth. Many other foods have been used, such as sugar coated cereals (Captain Crunch, Fruit Loops), T.V. dinners, peanut butter sandwiches, and regular meals. Bites of food are given to a child on a spoon or fork. Each bite is small, which allows large numbers of responses to be reinforced before the child becomes satiated.

A small portion of food (e.g., $\frac{1}{4}$ teaspoon of ice cream) is placed on the spoon (Fig. 1a). The spoon is held directly in front of the therapist's face. As a child will tend to look at the food, this procedure ensures that he will be looking toward the therapist's face. The therapist then waits until the child's glance shifts from the spoon to his face and reinforces this by quickly presenting the stimulus for the child to imitate (Fig. 1b). As the sessions progress, a child will tend to look at the food less and at the therapist's face more, and the position of the spoon can then gradually be varied to suit the convenience of the therapist. The same procedure is used later in the programme to train a child to attend to pictures or objects, except that, in that case, the spoon is held behind the items.

When the child responds appropriately, the therapist *immediately* says "Good" or "That's right," while extending the spoon of food to the child. This verbal statement serves to bridge the time between the appropriate response and the presentation of the food, and makes the reinforcement contingencies more precise. To save time, the food on the spoon is placed directly in the child's mouth by the therapist (Fig. 1c).

The effectiveness of the food reinforcer can be increased by mild food deprivation of about half a day. For example, when training sessions are held around noon, the mother or institutional staff are told to provide the child with only a very light breakfast, such as a glass of juice and a vitamin pill. Similar instructions involving lunch are given to caretakers of children for sessions later in the day.

For the most rapid and significant changes in deviant children the necessity of using powerful extrinsic reinforcers, made more effective by sufficient deprivation, *cannot be overemphasized.* (Examples showing the importance of the food reinforcers in the treatment of two children will be presented later.)

The Elimination of Disruptive Behavior

Most deviant children exhibit behavior which is incompatible with the behavior involved in speech training. With echolalic children the most usual disruptive behavior is repetitive chanting of songs or T.V. commercials, inappropriate imitation of the experimenters,

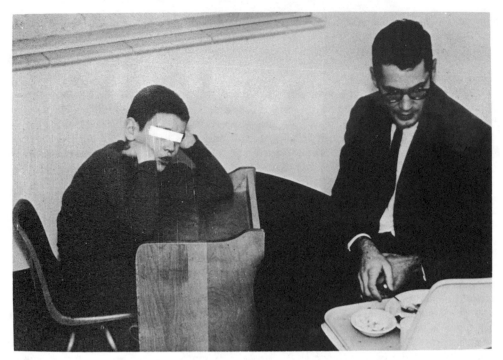

Fig. 1 (a).

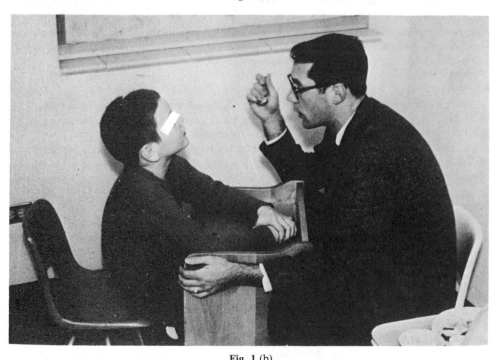

Fig. 1 (b).
Fig. 1 (a–c). These three pictures illustrate the physical arrangement of the therapy room, and the method of presenting the food reinforcers.

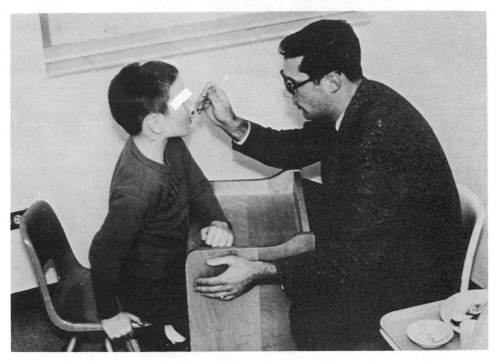

Fig. 1 (c).

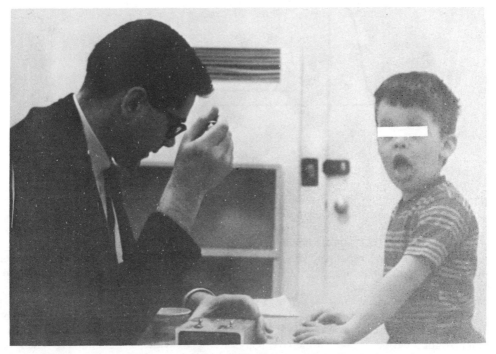

Fig. 2. An illustration of a therapist extinguishing disruptive behavior by looking away from a child contingent upon disruptive behavior.

comments, and, frequently, temper tantrums whenever the reinforcer is withheld. The frequency of this behavior must be reduced before notable progress can be made in establishing functional speech. Systematic extinction procedures, in conjunction with reinforcement of appropriate responses incompatible with the disruptive behaviors, have usually been sufficient to eliminate these behaviors.

Mild disruptive behavior in the therapy situation (such as leaving the chair, autistic mannerisms, mild temper tantrums, repetitive chanting, or inappropriate imitation) can usually be eliminated by removing all possible positive reinforcers for these behaviors. Once the child spends at least some of the session sitting quietly in the chair and has come into contact with the reinforcers, the experimenter should simply look away from the child whenever mild disruptive behavior occurs (Fig. 2). When the child is again sitting silently in his chair, the experimenter reinforces this by attending to him and proceeding with the session. (This procedure is technically termed *time-out from positive reinforcement*.)

The temper tantrums of a child (Carey) were eliminated as a consequence of these procedures (Fig. 3). The duration of crying systematically declined from an average of sixteen

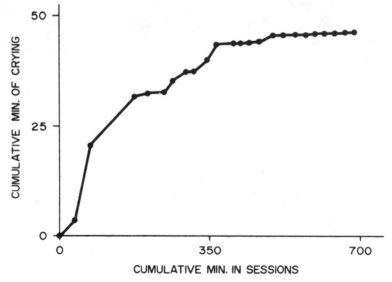

Fig. 3. The elimination of temper tantrums (crying) of Carey. (Each dot represents the end of a session.)

minutes/hour in the first three sessions to an average of twenty seconds/hour in the twenty-fourth to twenty-sixth sessions of these conditions.

The procedures were also effective in reducing the frequency with which a child (Carey) inappropriately imitated and repeatedly chanted the verbal statement "Very good" which accompanied the food reinforcer (Fig. 4). During the four sessions in which this behavior was recorded, the rate declined from 3.4 to 0.12 per minute. By the eight session this behavior was almost totally absent.

Where disruptive behaviors are at high strength or experimental conditions are such that these behaviors are inadvertently reinforced, a more rigorous time-out procedure may be necessary. This procedure involves both extinction of the undesirable behavior and the removal, for a period of time, of the possibility of *any* behavior being reinforced. Whenever an instance of disruptive behavior occurs, either the therapist leaves the room (with the

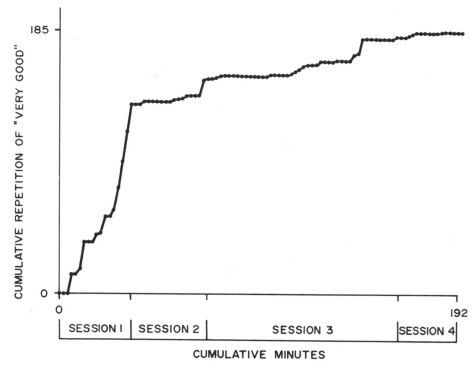

Fig. 4. The elimination of Carey's inappropriate repeating the statement "very good," which accompanied the food reinforcer. Whenever the child would say "very good" the therapist would look away for approximately five seconds. Each dot corresponds to the two minutes of session time.

food tray), or the child is removed to an adjacent room. The therapist re-enters or the child is allowed back in the therapy room only after both (1) a set time period had elapsed (e.g., ten minutes) and (2) the child had not engaged in the disruptive behavior for a short period of time (e.g., thirty seconds).

Dicky's severe temper tantrums accompanied by self-destructive behavior were eliminated by this procedure (Fig. 5). The severity of the tantrums, which necessitated their rapid elimination, also made the tantrums difficult for observers to ignore. It appeared highly likely that the attendants who were working with the child, while attempting to simply ignore (extinguish) the tantrums, would feel compelled to "stop the child from hurting himself" whenever the self-destructive behavior became severe. If this had occurred, they would have been, in effect, differentially reinforcing the more extreme forms of self-destructive behavior thereby increasing the problem.

To avoid this, the child was isolated in a room whenever temper tantrums occurred. This *time-out* procedure resulted in a gradual decline in the severity of the tantrums (which is not reflected in Fig. 5, as only the frequency of tantrums was recorded) and finally a complete cessation of tantrums.

The effectiveness of either of these procedures is dependent upon the strength of the positive reinforcer which is being withheld. This is another important reason for using the strongest reinforcers possible. When only weak positive reinforcers (such as M&M's with a non-food-deprived child) are used, not only will the progress in speech be slow, but disruptive behavior will be persistent.

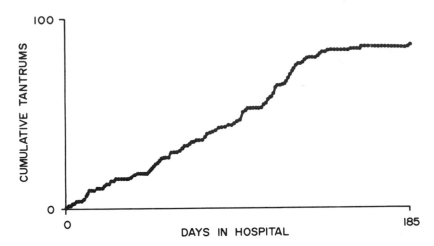

Fig. 5. The elimination of Dicky's temper tantrums. This child was isolated in his room for ten minutes contingent upon each tantrum, after which time he was allowed to leave the room following thirty seconds of silence, each dot represents one day.

The Establishment of Control over Imitation

Although echolalic children do imitate words and phrases, usually this imitation is sporadic and cannot be consistently evoked. Imitation must reliably occur immediately after a word or phrase prompt is presented before significant advances in speech can be made.

Reliable and immediate imitation can be obtained by systematic reinforcement of imitation. The therapist presents a given word every four to five seconds. Whenever the child says this word he is reinforced. Initially the probability of imitation can be somewhat increased by varying the intonation, pitch level and loudness of the word presented; however, this procedure should be deleted as soon as the child is reliably repeating the word.

Systematically reinforcing an imitated word will increase the frequency with which the child imitates that word, but it may also increase the frequency of non-imitative repetitions of the word. Other verbal utterances such as phrases or snatches of song may also increase and should be extinguished. The therapist should wait until the child is silent before again presenting the word to be imitated. In this manner only *imitation* is being reinforced.

When the child is frequently imitating the word (five to six times/minute), extraneous behavior should be extinguished and attending to the therapist reinforced by presenting the word to be imitated only when the child is sitting quietly, looking at the therapist. As the probability of immediate imitation is greater when the child is looking at the therapist, this procedure, which increases the proportion of attending, increases the number of immediate imitations.

When the child is reliably and immediately imitating the first word, a new word is introduced, and the above procedure is repeated. The two words are then alternately presented. When the child is reliably imitating both words, new words are presented interspersed with the two original words. Usually by the second or third word, a general imitative response class will have been established, i.e. the child will then reliably and immediately imitate any new word.

Figure 6 shows the establishment of control over a child's (Carey) imitation. From the start of Session 2 the word "train" was repeated by the experimenter. The child imitated this word once early in the session, and was reinforced. Sixteen minutes later, during which

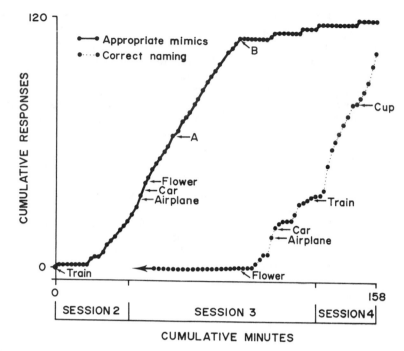

Fig. 6. A record of the initial rate of appropriate imitations (mimics) and correct naming of objects by Carey (*see* text). Each dot represents two minutes of session time.

time he was intermittently having tantrums, he again imitated "train" and was reinforced. After this the rate of imitating the word rapidly increased. Three other words, "flower," "car" and "airplane," were then introduced, and the child imitated each of them on the *first* presentation as well as on each subsequent presentation. Thus, in approximately thirty minutes, control was established over the child's imitative speech.

The Transition from Imitation to Naming

Naming involves the emission of the appropriate verbal response in the presence of some stimulus object. After imitative responses occur with high probability and short latency following each verbal prompt, stimulus control is shifted from the verbal prompts (imitation) to appropriate objects and pictures (naming).

Once reinforcement for imitation has produced a high probability of successful imitation of the verbal prompt alone, a picture or object is presented together with the verbal prompt, and the child is reinforced for imitating the name. Then the imitative prompt is faded out, while the child continues to receive reinforcement for saying the object's name.

The therapist holds up an object (if necessary holding the spoonful of food behind it) and says, "What is this?" When the child looks at it, the therapist immediately prompts with the object's name. The child is reinforced for imitating the prompt. When the child is reliably looking at the object without the food being held behind it, the time between the question "What is this?" and the prompt is gradually lengthened to more than five seconds. If after several trials the child continues to wait for the presentation of the verbal prompt, a *partial prompt* is given, for example, "Trr" for train. If the correct response does not occur within about five seconds more, the complete prompt is then presented. A correct response is followed by a social consequence such as "right" or "good," and the partial prompt is immediately repeated. A correct response to the partial prompt results in a bite of food.

When the child begins saying the name when only the partial prompt is presented, the therapist continues the above procedure but begins to say the partial prompt more softly. The loudness of the partial prompt is varied according to the child's behavior. When the child fails to respond to a partial prompt and the complete prompt is presented, the next partial prompt is given more loudly. When the child correctly responds to the partial prompt, the next partial prompt is given more softly. This continues until the therapist only "mouths" the partial prompt and then, finally, discontinues it altogether as the child responds to the object and the question "What is this?" with the name of the object.

Throughout this procedure, whenever the child inappropriately imitates the question "What is this?", a timeout is programmed, i.e. the object is withdrawn and the therapist looks down at the table. After two or three seconds of silence by the child, the therapist looks up and continues the procedure.

The transition from imitation to naming with one child (Carey) is illustrated in Fig. 6. From point A in Fig. 6, the pictures of the four objects were held out one at a time, and the child was required to look at them before the therapist said the name. The child quickly began attending to the pictures. The therapist's presentation of the words had been discriminative for the child to imitate and be reinforced. The increased proportion of attending indicated that the word presentations themselves had become reinforcers.

Just before B in Fig. 6, the therapist began delaying naming the picture, requiring a longer period of attending by the child, so that he would be more likely to name the picture instead of imitating the therapist. At B the child began to tantrum during an especially long delay. The therapist merely sat quietly looking down at the table. The tantrum gradually subsided and the therapist again held up the picture (the flower). The child attended to the picture and promptly named it. After this he named the picture with increasing speed with each presentation.

The picture of the airplane was re-introduced. The child immediately said "Car." The therapist said, "No, airplane." The child mimicked this and correctly named the picture when it was immediately re-presented. The remaining two pictures were then re-introduced, and the child correctly named each after a single prompt. After this he correctly named the four pictures when each was presented. Next, a new object, a cup, was presented. After imitating only two prompts, the child correctly named it and continued to name it correctly when it was presented interspersed with the original four pictures. Thus, by the end of the third session a small naming vocabulary had been established.

The following two examples demonstrate the role of food reinforcers in the maintenance of appropriate naming behavior. During the first five training sessions with Will, reliable imitation and then appropriate naming had been developed. The reinforcer involved a variety of edibles, such as ice cream, Coke, and M&M's.

The contribution of the food reinforcer was investigated by reversing the relationship between the naming behavior and the reinforcer. About a third of the way through the sixth session, the procedure was changed so that the child was reinforced only when he *did not* correctly name a picture for ten seconds. This procedure is technically termed *differential reinforcement of other behavior* (DRO) because any behavior except one particular response, in this case naming, is reinforced. As can be seen in Fig. 7, the naming responses dropped from about eight per minute to zero. After forty-five minutes, when no naming responses were being made, the procedure was changed back so that naming responses were again the only responses being reinforced. The rate of naming quickly increased to approximately the same rate as during the first part of the session. These results show the power of the reinforcer over the occurrence and accuracy of Will's naming behavior.

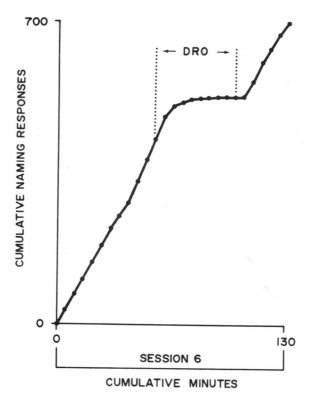

Fig. 7. A cumulative record showing the results of changing the food reinforcement contingency on Will's rate of correct naming. During the sixth session a DRO contingency (*see* text) was introduced for nine minutes and Will's rate of naming decreased to zero. When the original food reinforcement contingency was reinstated the behavior increased to its pre-DRO rate.

Once a reliable rate of naming had been developed with Carey the procedure was changed in that ice cream was given on a non-contingent basis. Instead of giving him bites of ice cream after each correct response, he was given the spoon and bowl of ice cream and allowed to eat at his own rate. Pictures continued to be presented, he was still asked to name them, and when he named them correctly he was praised. The rate of correct naming dropped immediately from approximately eight to three per minute and then stabilized at about two per minute (Fig. 8). When the ice cream was again presented only after correct naming responses, the rate immediately increased to approximately ten responses per minute.

To summarize, Carey's results show that after naming responses have been acquired, it may be possible to maintain them (although at a lower rate) with a weak reinforcer such as praise alone, but, as shown in the case of both the children the more powerful food reinforcer maintained a much higher and more steady rate of appropriate behavior.

The Expansion of the Naming Vocabulary

After the child has been taught to name several pictures or objects, naming any new picture or object can be quickly established. However, the child often will not correctly name an item at the beginning of the next daily session or subsequent to learning other new items

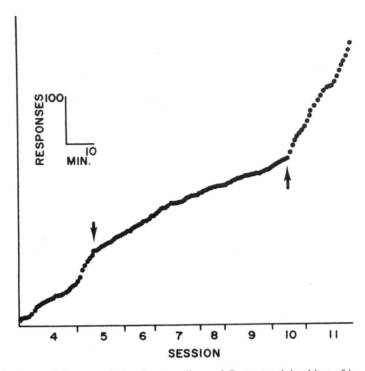

Fig. 8. A cumulative record showing the effects of Carey receiving bites of ice cream independent of his picture naming responses. For the first session and a half in Fig. 8 Carey was fed a bite of ice cream after each correct response. At the first arrow Carey was allowed to feed himself ice cream independent of his naming responses. At the second arrow the food reinforcers were again made contingent upon correctly naming the pictures. Each dot represents a one-minute period.

in the same session. A new response cannot be considered to be added to a child's naming vocabulary until he can name an item when it is presented again after other items have been learned, and following a passage of time. This is accomplished by gradually changing the context in which the item is presented. After a child is consistently naming new items on repeated presentations, a previously learned item is presented. When the child names the old item he is reinforced and the new item is presented again. When the child is reliably naming a new item when it follows one presentation of any of several previously taught items, two, then three, then four old items are presented between each presentation of the new item. (The well-established naming of old items need be reinforced only intermittently with food to maintain accuracy and short latencies.) When the child is reliably naming a new item under these conditions, another new item is introduced. When an item is reliably named the first time it is presented in several subsequent sessions, it can be considered to be a member of the child's naming vocabulary; only occasional reviews in subsequent sessions are needed to maintain it.

Figure 9 shows the increasing naming vocabulary of Pat, a blind echolalic boy, who was taught to name common household objects which were placed in his hands. An item was considered to be "learned" when the child correctly named it on its first presentation in three successive sessions.

Carey's naming vocabulary was expanded under two reinforcement conditions. The items

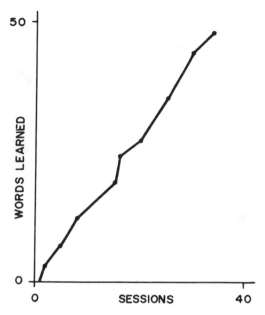

Fig. 9. A cumulative record of Pat's learning to name objects correctly. The name of an object was recorded as "learned" when Pat named it correctly the first time it was presented in three successive sessions.

to be named were pictures (line drawings) of various objects. Two ten-minute sessions a day were held, with separate pictures for each session. In one of the sessions each day, the reinforcer was praise ("That's right, very good") and a bite of ice cream, whereas praise alone was used in the other session. Several pictures were repeatedly presented in a random order during each session. New pictures were added when the child was consistently naming all the pictures used during a session. A picture was considered to be learned when the child correctly named it the first time it was presented, three sessions in a row. It would then be retired until ten subsequent pictures had been learned, at which time it would be presented again to test for recall.

While the child learned to name fifty per cent more pictures when both praise and ice cream were used as reinforcers (———, Fig. 10), his naming vocabulary was significantly expanded when praise was the only reinforcer (----, Fig. 10). Furthermore, items were recalled equally well whether they had been reinforced with praise only or with both praise and ice cream (histogram, Fig. 10). However, following this evaluation, since only one session per day could be held, the more effective reinforcer, a combination of ice cream and praise, was used throughout the remaining sessions. Approximately one new word per session was established with this reinforcer (. . . . ., Fig. 10).

Just as Fig. 8 demonstrates that established naming can be maintained (although at a lower rate) with praise as the only reinforcer, Fig. 10 shows that when a child can readily be taught to name new items with food reinforcers his naming vocabulary can then be significantly expanded (although at a lower rate) when only social reinforcers of the type available in a "normal" environment are used.

The authors consider it necessary to use strong reinforcers such as food to establish the initial instances of appropriate mimicking and naming behavior and to eliminate disruptive behavior in a reasonable period of time. However, it appears that once disruptive behaviors

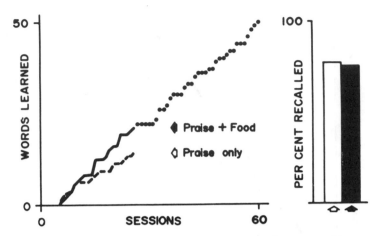

Fig. 10. Records of the number of pictures which Carey learned to name and later recalled in daily sessions under two reinforcement conditions, praise alone ("that's right" or "very good") and both praise and food (bites of ice cream). A picture was considered to be learned when the child named it when it was first presented in three successive sessions. A picture was considered to be recalled when the child correctly named it when it was re-presented after ten subsequent pictures had been learned.

have been eliminated and some appropriate mimicking and naming have been established, these appropriate behaviors can be maintained and expanded by the systematic use of social reinforcers. This does *not* imply that food deprivation and food reinforcers should then be discontinued. The magnitude of a child's speech deficits and the value of a therapist's and of a child's time require the utilization of those procedures which will produce the greatest gains in the shortest time. The strongest reinforcers or combination of reinforcers available should be used in the therapy sessions so long as large behavioral deficits exist. However, social re-inforcers outside the therapy sessions can generally be relied upon to maintain and expand the behaviors established in the sessions.

The Establishment of Phrases

Once naming is established, the response units can be expanded to phrases and sentences. In most cases this expansion occurs without explicit training. In those instances where multiple word units have to be taught, the procedure is the same as in teaching individual words, i.e. mimics of the phrases are reinforced until the phrases are consistently imitated. Then the control is shifted to the appropriate circumstance itself, by introducing partial prompts which are gradually faded out. In this case, the partial prompts are the first word or words of the phrase.

At first, phrases such as "That's a———," or "I want———" are taught, using the child's newly acquired naming vocabulary. Then more varied phrases are taught, such as answering the appropriate questions with "My name is———," "I live at———." "I am———years old," "My sisters' names are———and———."

Food reinforcers are used to build the initial responses, but, once established, the opportunity to obtain some natural consequence can usually maintain the behavior. For example, for Carey the comment, "Out (or in) the door," was maintained by opening the doors to and from the therapy room. The therapist would say, "Out the door," and when the child would mimic this, the door would be opened.

After several trials on succeeding days, the therapist began introducing a partial prompt, saying only, "Out," and the child continued to say, "Out the door." The partial prompt was then gradually faded out until the therapist put his hand on the door knob and looked at the child, and the child said, "Out the door." The therapist gradually faded in the appropriate controlling stimulus – the question, "Where are you going?" This was presented by at first mumbling it softly as they approached the door and then increasing the volume on succeeding trials. Whenever the child inappropriately imitated the question "Where are you going?" the therapist repeated the question at a lower volume and followed it with a loud partial prompt: "Where are you going? OUT." On succeeding trials the partial prompt, "Out," was then decreased in volume until the child responded to the closed door and the question, "Where are you going?" with the response "Out the door."

The same procedure was used to establish appropriate answers to the question, "Where are you going?," such as "Up the stairs," "Down the hall" or "In the car." In each case, the reinforcer which maintained appropriate answering was simply being allowed to proceed up the stairs, down the hall, and so on. In this manner the child came to make appropriate verbal comments about his environment. Once such simple comments have been learned, the child tends to generalize the grammatical form with appropriate substitutions. One example of such establishment and generalization, which could be termed "generative speech," resulted from a procedure used with Carey. On many occasions at home, this child would chant a word or short phrase over and over, with gradually increasing volume which terminated in piercing shrieks and crying. For example, while standing by the couch, he would repeat "Sit down, sit down." His parents could terminate this by responding in any way, e.g., "Yes, Carey," "O.K., sit down," "You can sit down if you want to," "Be quiet." The parents were requested to record these instances of stereotyped chanting, and also to send him to his room for five minutes whenever the chanting developed into shrieking and crying. This decreased the occurrences of the shrieking (———, Fig. 11), but did not decrease the frequency of the stereotyped chanting episodes (....., Fig. 11). The therapist decided to change the form of this behavior, rather than attempt to eliminate it, as it contained elements of appropriate social behavior.

The parents were instructed to turn away from the child when he chanted. One parent (e.g. the father) would then call out the name of the other parent ("Mommy"), and when the child would mimic this the mother would attend to him and say "Yes, Carey." The first parent would then say a complete sentence ("I want to sit down, please."). When the child would mimic this, the other parent would respond accordingly ("Oh, you want to sit down. Well, you can sit down right here."). On subsequent occasions the verbal prompts were faded out. Finally, the parents withheld reinforcement by looking away until the child called their names, and they would wait while looking at him until he gave the complete sentence before responding to his request. This procedure was begun at the arrow in Fig. 11. The stereotyped chanting soon decreased to zero as the child began to indicate more appropriate requests such as "Mommy, I want to sit down, please," or "Daddy, I want a drink of water, please."

The grammatical structure of "(name), I want———, please," after being established with several people's names and many different requests in the home began to generalize to new people and new requests. One recorded instance of this occurred in the therapy sessions. Prior to the start of each session, when Carey was seated in the room, the therapist would spend some time setting up the tape recorder. During this time the child would usually start chanting "Ice cream, ice cream" softly. When the therapist was ready, he would turn to the child and say, "What do you want?" to which the child had been taught to answer "I want some ice cream." Prior to one session, after the grammatical form of requests mentioned above had been established at home, the child was, as usual, chanting "Ice cream, ice cream"

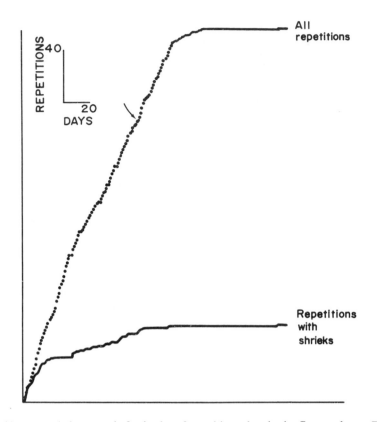

Fig. 11. A cumulative record of episodes of repetitious chanting by Carey at home. From the onset, he was sent to his room for five minutes whenever he began shrieking during one of those episodes. At the arrow his parents began establishing appropriate speech behavior which was incompatible with chanting. Each dot represents one day.

while the therapist threaded the tape recorder. He suddenly stopped and after a pause, said "Mr. (therapist's name), I want some ice cream, please." Most of the elements of this sentence had been established in the therapy sessions, e.g., "Hello, Mr. (therapist's name)," and "I want some ice cream," but they had always been given as responses to specific stimuli, (e.g. "Hello, Carey" and "What do you want?"). However, the particular grammatical structure of "(Name), I want——, please," had only been taught in the home.

Carey's extension of his home training exemplifies our general observation that once rudimentary generative speech and grammatical structure have been established they will tend to generalize broadly, often with appropriate substitutions.

OTHER CONSIDERATIONS

The Generalization of Appropriate Speech

The term "generalization" can refer to the *phenomenon* of the occurrence of appropriate behavior under other than the original training conditions or it can refer to the *procedure* used to establish this occurrence.

While newly acquired appropriate speech often will "spontaneously" generalize widely, the therapist need not passively rely on this phenomenon. He can, instead, set out to extend the occurrence of the behavior to other situations by systematically reinforcing appropriate speech under a variety of conditions. The child can be systematically trained to respond appropriately to a variety of individuals, including members of his family and other caretakers, and in a variety of situations, such as at home, in the family car, and in the therapist's office. Once appropriate speech has been established in the therapy sessions, the child's parents can be present during occasional sessions and the child reinforced for responding appropriately to their questions. Whenever a new word has been established in a therapy session, the therapist can continue to ask for, and reinforce the appropriate use of this word after the formal session, for instance, while walking around the building. The therapist can also conduct therapy sessions in the child's home, teaching the child to name household objects.

Generalization training can be facilitated by initially selecting words and phrases to be taught which can be appropriately asked for frequently during the day, e.g., "car" is better than "zebra," and which are immediately functional in the child's environment, e.g., "I want a cookie."

Perhaps the most effective means of generalizing the appropriate use of speech is to train the parents or caretakers to use the therapeutic procedures. They can then take advantage of naturally-occurring events during the day to generalize appropriate speech to a wide variety of situations, as well as to establish new speech in appropriate contexts.

The Usefulness of Data in Therapy

The gathering of continuous data throughout the course of therapy can be valuable in many ways. For example, it can provide objective information about the long term course of therapy. Behaviors followed over a long period of time, as described in this paper, often reveal an orderliness which is not clear from the day-by-day observations. Gradual changes can be discerned in spite of large daily fluctuations, as in the instance of the rate of Carey's shreiking (Fig. 11). The frequency of the shrieks decreased in a manner which was orderly overall even though some of the individual days (sometimes several consecutive days) showed considerable variability.

A second use of data is in the analysis of the functions of therapeutic procedures. An *experimental probe* is usually necessary if the therapist wants to isolate the variables responsible for a behavioral change. Isolation is accomplished by keeping all of the therapeutic conditions the same except one. If varying this condition produces a reliable change in the data, which disappears when the condition is reversed to its pre-experimental value, then the importance of the variable has been established. Sidman (1960) has discussed in detail strategies and considerations for research with individual subjects. Probe experiments of the above type were described in this paper. For example, the role of the food reinforcement contingency in Will's progress in naming was evaluated (Fig. 7). Its importance was dramatically demonstrated when the DRO procedure was interjected into a session. A similar probe experiment, in a slightly different manner and over a longer period of time, demonstrated the function of the food reinforcement in Carey's rate of naming pictures (Fig. 8).

The easiest of data-gathering methods is to use a tape recorder to record all of the sessions. The therapist or an assistant can replay tapes from previous sessions and count the frequencies of various responses (e.g., correct imitations) or the duration of certain behaviors (e.g., temper tantrums, inappropriate chanting). Tapes of earlier sessions are particularly useful for gathering data about behavior that was not originally thought to be of interest.

A multi-pen event recorder can be used if the therapist is certain in advance of the classes of behavior that he will want to record. A bank of push-button switches can be wired from the therapist's table to the recorder so that durations and frequencies of responses can be recorded by the therapist and/or by an independent observer.

A pencil and paper can always be used to take simple frequencies. Duration of a specific behavior can be recorded during each session with a stop watch.

Such data and probe experiments enable the therapist to give a more complete and objective description of his procedures and their effects to others, including colleagues who are also interested in developing a more effective technology of speech modification through a systematic analysis of speech modification procedures.

CONCLUSIONS

This paper indicates that functional verbal behavior can be developed from rudimentary imitative behavior by established behavioral techniques. We have outlined procedures which were effective in establishing functional speech in echolalic children. However, the procedures as they are described here should not be taken as fixed and unchanging. The developing strength of behavioral technology lies in the continued refinement of its procedures.

Acknowledgments. The teachers who played particularly important roles in Dicky's speech development were Florence Harris, Margaret Johnston, Eileen Allen, Nancy Reynolds and Thelma Turbitt. Will's data was collected by Jacqulyn Raulerson and Thomas Dillon under the senior author's supervision. We are indebted to Stephanie Stolz, Nancy Reynolds and Betty Hart for critical readings of the manuscript.

REFERENCES

Harris, F. R., Wolf, M. M. & Baer, D. M. (1964) Effects of adult social reinforcement on child behavior. *Young Child*, **20**, 8–17.

Lovaas, O. I. (1966) A program for the establishment of speech in psychotic children. In J. K. Wing (Ed.), *Childhood Autism*. Pergamon Press, Oxford.

Risley, T. R. (1966) The establishment of verbal behavior in deviant children. Unpublished dissertation, University of Washington.

Sidman, M. (1960) *Tactics of Scientific Research*. Basic Books, New York.

Skinner, B. F. (1957) *Verbal Behavior*. Appleton-Century-Crofts, New York.

Stone, J. L. & Church, J. (1957) *Childhood and Adolescence*. Random House, New York.

Wolf, M. M., Risley, T. R. & Mees, H. I. (1964) Application of operant conditioning procedures to the behavior problems of an autistic child. *Behav. Res. & Therapy*, **1**, 305–312.

Control of Self-Injurious Behavior

The Use of Positive Reinforcement in the Control of Self-Destructive Behavior in a Retarded Boy*†‡§

ROBERT F. PETERSON

University of Illinois

and

LINDA R. PETERSON

Illinois State Department of Mental Health

Abstract: Severe self-destructive behaviors in an eight-year-old boy were observed to change as a function of treatment procedures which included both primary and secondary reinforcers and a brief walk across the room. The presentation and withdrawal of a blanket also appeared to exert considerable control over the frequency of self-destructive behaviors. The results were discussed in terms of environmental control through self-injurious behaviors and the development of the blanket as a reinforcing stimulus.

One of the most severe problems observed in young children involves self-inflicted physical injury. Disturbed children have been observed to strike various parts of their body against hard surfaces or hit themselves until tissue injury results. Recently, investigators have become interested in studying self-destructive behaviors from a general behavior theory point of view, and have suggested techniques which may control them. For example, Allen and Harris (1966) investigated severe scratching in a five-year-old girl. They found that by teaching the child's parents to attend to incompatible behaviors they were able to eliminate the scratching. Similarly, Lovaas, Freitag, Gold, and Kassorla (1965) analyzed self-abusive behaviors in a schizophrenic girl and likewise found the behavior to be influenced by social reinforcement. Using a brief period of isolation as a "timeout" from reinforcement, Wolf, Risley & Mees (1964) reduced tantrum behaviors which involved self-slapping, hair pulling, and head banging.

Aversive stimulation has also been used to control self-injurious behaviors. Both Tate & Baroff (1966) and Lovaas, Freitag, Kinder, Rubenstein, Schaeffer & Simmons (1964) suppressed self-destructive responses in psychotic children for several months by employing contingent electric shock.

---

*The present paper is based on a report delivered to the Society for Research in Child Development, New York, March 30, 1967.

†This research was supported in part by grants from the Children's Bureau (Training for Nursing in Mental Retardation, 306) and the National Institute of Mental Health (MH 12067) and was carried out while both of the authors were at the University of Washington.

‡The authors acknowledge their debt to Mr. Frank Junkin, Superintendent, and the staff of Fircrest School whose cooperation made this study possible, and would like to thank Dr. Sidney Bijou for his helpful criticism of this manuscript.

§Reprinted from the *Journal of Experimental Child Psychology*, September 1968, **6**, 3, 351–360. Copyright 1968 with permission from Academic Press Inc., and Dr. Robert F. Peterson.

Despite their effectiveness in controlling some undesirable behaviors, techniques involving the application of aversive stimuli (punishment) have certain disadvantages. As Azrin and Holz (1966) have pointed out, social relationships may be disrupted. The punished individual may avoid the person administering the aversive stimuli and may also aggress against him or others nearby. Furthermore, for social and ethical reasons, many professionals have been extremely reluctant to use punishment as a form of educational or clinical treatment.

The present study was designed to explore the use of positive reinforcement in the control of self-destructive behavior. A second concern involved an assessment of the functional properties of a blanket that seemed to play a significant role in the behavior of the S.

SUBJECT

The S was an eight-year-old boy who had been admitted to a state institution at the age of six because he was unmanageable at home. At the time of the study, S was not toilet trained, had no speech, but was ambulatory. He would respond to a variety of commands such as "come here," and could feed himself. Due to his behavioral problems it was not possible to assess his skills with conventional psychological procedures. Most of the day S lay or rocked on his bed, wrapped in a small quilt. Often he carried a blanket with him when not on his bed. When not so engaged, S displayed violent self-injurious responses, slapping the side of his head or leg with either hand, hitting his hand against his teeth, or banging his forehead against his forearm. He also struck his head and hands against chairs, tables, and walls. The S cried loudly but tearlessly when behaving in this fashion. These responses were so forceful that his face, arms, and legs were covered with bruises, scabs, abrasions, and on occasion, open wounds.

PROCEDURE

The study was conducted in a small room which contained three tables and a few chairs. S was seen from one to eleven times a week with a typical session lasting fifteen minutes. Sessions coincided with mealtime (lunch and/or supper) and portions of food were used as reinforcers. The S sat on one side of a table, the E on the other, with a tray of food between them.

The study was divided into five stages: the baseline period, the first and second experimental periods, the reversal period, and a third experimental period.

Baseline Period

The baseline period consisted of twelve observations on the ward and five in the experimental room, both with and without the blanket. Because of the severity of the child's behavior the observation periods were limited to five minutes each. Self-destructive behavior was defined as those responses which involved striking one part of the body with another. Behaviors which involved striking objects were excluded.

Observer reliability in recording these behaviors was assessed by the E and a second O in Sessions 7, 17, and 18. It was obtained by comparing the respective scores of two observers during each thirty-second interval of recording. For any given interval where a difference in scoring occurred, the smaller score was subtracted from the larger to obtain a difference score. These difference scores were summed over all intervals. The smaller scores in each interval were also summed over all intervals. Reliability was computed by dividing the sum of the smaller scores by the sum of the difference scores plus the sum of the smaller scores. The result was multiplied by 100. The average reliability for all three sessions exceeded ninety-five per cent. A slightly higher reliability figure was obtained when reliability was computed over the total session without regard for differences within thirty-second intervals.

First Experimental Period

During this part of the study, reinforcement in the form of food (one-quarter teaspoon) and the word "good" were given contingent upon a three- to five-second interval of no self-injurious responses. Whenever a self-injurious response did occur, the E took the food from the table, turned away from the child, and began counting silently. If no self-destructive behavior occurred during the next ten seconds, E then turned back to the child, said "good," and gave him a bit of food. Attempts were made to lengthen the interval between self-injurious responses. This procedure continued for ten sessions (Sessions 18–27 inclusive).

Second Experimental Period

In order to reduce further the rate of self-destructive responses, the previous procedure was altered. Reinforcement was still given following a brief interval of any behavior other than self-destructive (excluding the striking of objects) but the time between responses was not increased nor was the food removed. Instead, S was given verbal and gestural instructions, contingent upon a self-destructive response, to walk across the room (a distance of twelve feet) and sit in a chair. If no self-injurious responses occurred while walking to the chair, the E immediately went to the child and reinforced his behavior with "good" and food. If self-destructive behaviors did occur, S was again instructed to walk across the room. This procedure was continued until he had walked from one chair to another without a self-injurious response. (It should be noted that the S was free to engage in self-destructive behavior at all times. Walking in no way hindered him from doing so.) In addition, S was taught to indicate which particular part of his meal (potatoes, meat, beans, etc.) he would like to eat by pointing to it. Thus, after a brief interval of no self-injurious behavior, the E said, "Show me what you want," waited until S pointed or gave some indication, and fed it to him.

Reversal Period

Following the second experimental period, the reinforcement operations were again modified beginning in Session 64. The S was now instructed to walk from one chair to another not as a consequence of a self-injurious response, but until such a response occurred. When this happened the E immediately reinforced the behavior. These operations then, are exactly the reverse of those in the previous Experimental Period. Because these procedures were in effect for only a brief period (3 sessions), they might be more accurately viewed as a behavioral "probe," which was designed to study the effects of the changed contingency on self-injurious behaviors.

Third Experimental Period

During this part of the study, reinforcement contingencies were identical to those in the Second Experimental Period. S was instructed to walk across the room, following a self-destructive response. If further responses did not occur, the E said "good," and gave him a bit of food. If self-injurious behaviors were displayed during the walk, S continued walking until he had crossed the room without injuring himself.

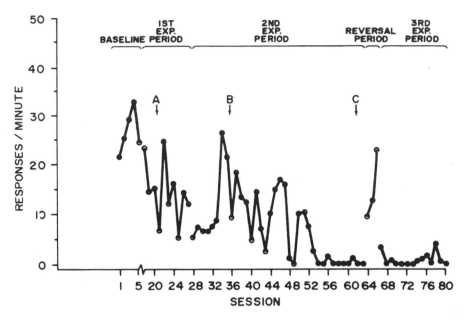

Fig. 1. Rate of self-injurious behavior during successive sessions.

RESULTS

Reduction in Self-Destructive Behavior

The overall changes in self-destructive behavior can be seen in Fig. 1 which shows the rate of behavior while the child was in the experimental room without his blanket. During the basline period the behaviors ranged between 21.6 and 32.8 responses per minute. Although there was a drop in self-injurious behaviors following the introduction of the treatment procedures, there was also considerable variability. The response rate ranged from 5.3 to 24.6 responses per minute. The mean number of responses per minute during the first experimental period was 14.2. This contrasts with a mean rate of 26.6 responses per minute during the baseline.

The Second Experimental Period began with Session 28, and the introduction of new procedures. Response rate dropped from the previous session and after remaining relatively stable for six sessions became extremely variable. There was a gradual reduction in the rate of self-destructive behaviors over the next twenty sessions. Ultimately, the responses disappeared.

Two sessions prior to the beginning of the Reversal Period (point C on Fig. 1) the E was changed. A second E was needed because the first E was no longer available. The new E did not appear to affect the rate of self-destructive behavior.

During the Reversal (probe) Period all experimental contingencies were altered. The S was instructed to walk across the room; however, the instruction was not contingent upon self-injurious behavior. The results may be seen in Fig. 2 which shows the child's responses during successive minutes of the three reversal sessions. Seven minutes elapsed before a self-destructive response occurred. This response was reinforced while subsequent self-injurious responses were only occasionally reinforced. This intermittent reinforcement resulted from

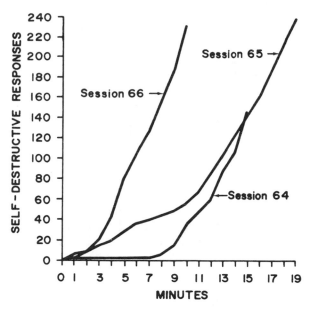

Fig. 2. Frequency of self-destructive behavior in three reversal sessions.

the E's attempts to reinforce those behaviors which appeared to be least harmful to the child, e.g., slapping his leg. The response rate rose to a high level amost immediately. A comparison of all three reversal sessions shows an increase in the acceleration of self-injurious behaviors from the first through the third sessions. Figure 1 shows that the average response rate rose to 9.5 in Session 64, increased to 12.6 in Session 65 and reached 23.2 responses per minute in Session 66.

When the contingencies were returned to those of the previous experimental period, the rate of self-destructive behavior dropped to 3.2 responses per minute in Session 67 and remained at or near zero thereafter.

Subsequently, attendants reported that S engaged in fewer self-destructive behaviors while on the ward and spent more time with other children. Such reports should be viewed skeptically, however.

Effect of Manipulating the Blanket

Figure 3 shows how closely the blanket controlled S's behavior. During the base line, the blanket was presented and taken from S according to a series of thirty-second intervals. The intervals were programmed in such a way that S held the blanket for a minimum of thirty seconds on some occasions and a maximum of sixty seconds on others. He was allowed to keep the blanket a total of two and a half minutes out of each five minute observation period. Typically, the loss of the blanket produced self-destructive responses while repossession of the blanket caused a fairly abrupt cessation of responding.

Figure 4 shows the effect of the blanket over the entire baseline period. In the experimental room, S's rate of self-destructive behavior ranged from twenty-two to thirty-two responses per minute without the blanket and nine to nineteen responses per minute with the blanket. Stimulus control was even greater when S was lying or sitting on his bed in the ward. Here, when deprived of the blanket, self-destructive behaviors occurred at a rate of twenty to forty-two per minute; when allowed to keep the blanket, the range of injurious responses was from

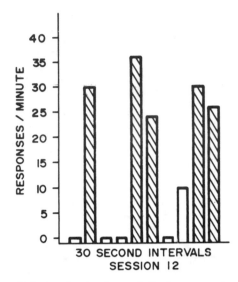

Fig. 3. The effects of blanket deprivation and blanket possession on self-destructive behaviors within a single session. Striped columns = without blanket; white columns = with blanket.

zero to twenty-four responses per minute. During seven of the twelve sessions on the ward, no self-destructive behavior was observed while *S* was in possession of the blanket.

The *S* also cried when engaging in self-destructive behaviors. Figure 5 shows the rate of crying from Sessions 9 through 17. (Data on this behavior was not obtained before Session 9.) Crying was defined as a loud high-pitched sound of more than a two-second duration. Figure 5 shows a high rate of crying (measured in ten-second intervals) when deprived of the blanket. Over all nine sessions the rate of crying was some fifty-six per cent lower when *S* kept his blanket. However, crying was not as closely controlled by the blanket as was self-injurious behavior.

DISCUSSION

Although it is clear that the term "good" coupled with food did function as a positive reinforcer for *S*, the interpretation of the walking procedure is open to discussion. Since it was possible to expand the interval between injurious responses from a few seconds to as long as the entire session after instituting the walking response, it may be that the use of this procedure gave the child a behavior which functioned to mediate the minimal period between self-abusive behaviors needed for reinforcement to occur (Ferster & Skinner, 1957). It is also possible that walking functioned as a punishing stimulus which delayed reinforcement (Azrin & Holz, 1966). The effects of the walking procedure cannot, however, be separated from the effects of reinforcement. Further analysis is needed to estimate just how much and in what way this operation contributed to the reduction in self-destructive behavior.

In contrast, the role of the blanket seems somewhat clearer in that it appeared to function as a powerful reinforcer. When deprived of it, *S* would reach for it or attempt to retrieve it. Sometimes he would accept a second blanket while on other occasions only the original would do. The loss of the blanket did produce an immediate display of self-injurious behavior.

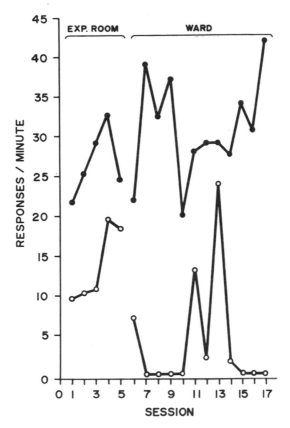

Fig. 4. Rate of self-injurious responses during periods of blanket possession and blanket deprivation. Open circles = with blanket; solid circles = without blanket.

The *S*'s behavior in this situation is similar to that of the child reported by Lovaas *et al.* (1965). These investigators found that the withdrawal of reinforcement from a previously reinforced response was the discriminative stimulus for self-destructive behavior. In *S*'s case it was not obvious just what response the blanket was reinforcing. Holding the blanket did *not* prevent *S* from engaging in self-destructive behavior. He would occasionally hit himself while under the blanket or even through the blanket. Bijou & Baer (1965) have noted that a blanket may develop the properties of a generalized reinforcer. This may result from the blanket being discriminative for skin temperature changes, for rest and sleep, and being a source of tactual stimulation, all of which may be reinforcing. For *S*, the blanket may also have been discriminative for periods of time where few stimulus events produced self-destructive behaviors. Such a condition may have given the blanket additional reinforcing properties.

Although the blanket exerted strong control over *S*'s behavior early in the study, this control was reduced by the end of treatment. Unfortunately, no data which would allow quantitative comparisons were obtained. However, it was possible to remove the child's blanket without producing immediate self-destructive behaviors as before. Nevertheless, *S*, like the comic strip character, Linus, preferred to keep his blanket with him much of the time, perhaps for the "security" it provided.

Both prior to and during most of the present study, *S* received drugs (thioridazine and

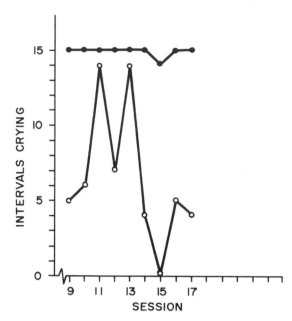

Fig. 5. Intervals crying during periods of blanket availability and unavailability. Open circles = with blanket; solid circles = without blanket.

chlorpromazine) except for the period covered by Sessions 21 through 36 inclusive (*see* points A and B in Fig. 1). Despite this complication no relationship between the presence or absence of medication and the rate of self-destructive behavior was observed. In addition, the results of the reversal period clearly show that the medications were not responsible for the changes in self-destructive behavior.

It should be apparent that by engaging in self-destructive behavior a child may exert considerable control over his environment. It is possible therefore, that the development and strength of self-injurious responses may be at least partially dependent upon the presence and effectiveness of alternative behaviors which can also be used to influence the environment. If so, maximum therapeutic gain might be achieved by integrating procedures designed to expand the child's behavioral repertoire along with procedures for the control of self-destructive behavior.

REFERENCES

Allen, K. Eileen & Harris, F. R. Elimination of a child's excessive scratching by training the mother in reinforcement procedures. *Behaviour Research and Therapy*, 1966, **4**, 79–84.

Azrin, N. H. & Holz, W. C. Punishment. In W. K. Honig (Ed.), *Operant behavior: Areas of research and application.* New York: Appleton, 1966.

Bijou, S. W. & Baer, D. M. *Child development: The universal stage of infancy.* Vol. II. New York: Appleton, 1965.

Ferster, C. B. & Skinner, B. F. *Schedules of reinforcement.* New York: Appleton, 1957.

Lovaas, O. I., Freitag, G., Kinder, M. I., Rubenstein, D. B., Schaeffer, B. & Simmons, J. B. Experimental studies in childhood schizophrenia: Developing social behavior using electric shock. Paper read at American Psychological Assoc., 1964.

Lovaas, O. I., Freitag, G., Gold, Vivian J. & Kassorla, Irene C. Experimental studies in childhood schizophrenia: Analysis of self-destructive behavior. *Journal of Experimental Child Psychology*, 1965, 2, 67–84.

Tate, B. G. & Baroff, G. S. Aversive control of self-injurious behavior in a psychotic boy. *Behavior Research and Therapy*, 1966, 4, 281–287.

Wolf, M. M., Risley, T. & Mees, H. Application of operant conditioning procedures to the behavior problems of an autistic child. *Behavior Research and Therapy*, 1964, 1, 305–312.

Effect of Vibratory Stimulation on a Retardate's Self-Injurious Behavior*†

JON BAILEY‡ and LEE MEYERSON

University of Kansas and Arizona State University

Abstract: Brief response-contingent and continuous, non-contingent vibration conditions were presented to a profoundly retarded, crib-bound child who exhibited several persistent self-injurious behaviors. Lever pressing (for six seconds of vibration) proved to be incompatible with these self-injurious behaviors and reduced them from baseline levels. Free continuous vibration, however, was found to be even more effective in reducing self-injurious behavior in this subject.

A continuing problem in institutions for the retarded are children who engage in self-injurious behavior (SIB). The generic term covers a long list of topographies including, among others, head-banging, face-slapping, hair-pulling, biting or sucking skin off the extremities, scratching and tearing flesh.

Prescription of sedatives or tranquilizers appears to be a common treatment for SIB but, unlike the mental hospital where the forced immobilization of patients has virtually disappeared, chemical restraints have not replaced the straitjacket, the strangulation cord, and other forms of physical restraint common in the institution for the retarded. If drug therapy fails to reduce SIB, and alternative treatments are not readily available, the self-injurious retardate may be placed in restraints for long periods—possibly for a lifetime.

An obvious, behavioral approach to the control of SIB is the positive reinforcement of an incompatible response. It is difficult, however, to find convenient, effective and durable reinforcers for such a behavior, and perhaps, for this reason no previous studies using such an approach have been found in the literature.

The present investigation was stimulated by a demonstration that contingent, vibratory reinforcement maintained consistent, long-term lever pressing in a seven-year-old, crib-bound, self-injurious retardate (Bailey & Meyerson, 1969). In this report, the effects on SIB of contingent and non-contingent vibratory stimulation are presented.

METHOD

Subject

The subject, whose descriptive characteristics were reported previously (Meyerson, Kerr & Michael, 1967; Bailey & Meyerson, 1969) engaged almost constantly during his waking

*This paper is based on a thesis submitted by the senior author in partial fulfillment of the M.A. degree at Arizona State University. This investigation was supported in part by Office of Education Grant No. 5-0415. Preparation of this manuscript was partially supported by NICHHD grant HD-00183-03 to the Bureau of Child Research, University of Kansas. The authors are indebted to Brian Jacobson whose technical assistance was invaluable for this study.

†Reprinted from *Psychological Aspects of Disability.* 1970, **17**, No. 3. Copyright 1969 with permission from the Editor and Mr. Jon Bailey.

‡Jon Bailey is now Assistant Professor, Department of Psychology, The Florida State University, Tallahassee.

hours in self-stimulatory and self-injurious behavior unless he was physically restrained. The SIBs which resulted in visible tissue damage were the following: chewing on his fingers and hands, hitting his head on the bars of his crib, and hitting a foot against the bars of his crib. A hand chewing response was marked when the subject placed either hand (at least up to the knuckle) in his mouth and lateral jaw movements could be observed. Head and foot-to-bars were counted when these extremities were struck against the bars with such intensity as to be heard at least five feet away.

The subject had previously been conditioned to press a lever for vibration and was not restrained, receiving medication or involved in any other therapy during this study.

Apparatus

An industrial vibrator (Model DVE-10, Martin Engineering Company, Salt Lake City) which was mounted on the underside of the springs of the subject's crib and wired to appropriate electro-mechanical programming equipment provided vibratory stimulation under two conditions: (a) Contingent: six seconds of vibration each time the subject activated his lever if the vibrator was not already operating. (b) Non-contingent: ten minutes of free, continuous vibration. Lever presses under either condition were counted and recorded on a Gerbrands cumulative recorder. A hand-held microswitch connected to a second Gerbrands recorder allowed an observer to simultaneously record each SIB as it occurred.

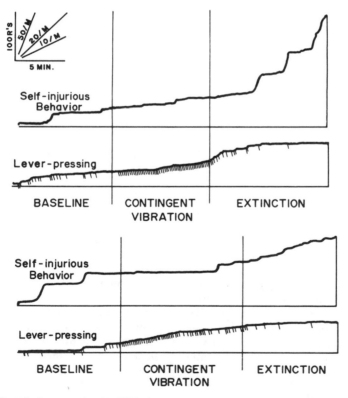

Fig. 1. Cumulative records of self-injurious behavior and lever pressing for two sessions showing the effect of vibratory reinforcement of lever pressing on concomitant self-injurious behavior.

Procedure

During seven sessions of thirty to sixty minutes each, the following procedures were in effect: a leather-padded oval lever, 8.5 by 5.5 inches in size was attached to the subject's crib. An observer stood beside the crib and recorded the SIBs via the hand-held switch connected to a cumulative recorder. Operant levels of SIB and unreinforced lever pressing were obtained in the first ten minutes of each session. In subsequent ten-minute periods, one of three conditions was in effect: (a) response contingent vibration; (b) non-contingent, free vibration; and (c) extinction.

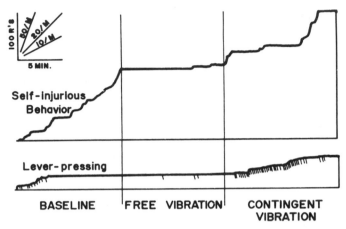

Fig. 2. Cumulative records of self-injurious behavior and lever pressing showing the effects of free continuous vibration and vibratory reinforcement of lever pressing on self-injurious behavior.

A reliability check on the recording of SIBs was made by having two observers stand on either side of the crib and record the SIBs independently by activating hand-held microswitches connected to a Gerbrands six-pen event recorder. An agreement was counted if both observers activated their pens within a one-second interval. Reliability was calculated by dividing the number of such agreements by the agreements plus disagreements.

RESULTS

Three reliability checks with two observers were made on two separate days. Reliability ranged from seventy-five to ninety-one per cent and averaged eighty-six per cent.

Figure 1 shows the typical relationships between total SIBs and lever pressing during operant level, response contingent vibration and extinction. It can be seen that SIB varied inversely with lever pressing. When vibratory stimulation was contingent on lever pressing, the rate of lever pressing was high and SIB was low. In comparison with operant levels and extinction conditions, the functional incompatibility of lever pressing and SIB is evident.

Figure 2 displays the results of a typical session when response contingent vibration followed a ten-minute period of free vibration. It is apparent from this comparison that free vibration was much more effective in reducing the frequency of SIB than was response contingent vibration.

Figure 3, a record of one of the longer experimental sessions, shows that regardless whether response-contingent vibration preceded or followed a period of free vibration, non-contingent vibration resulted in fewer SIBs. Response contingent vibration reduced SIB

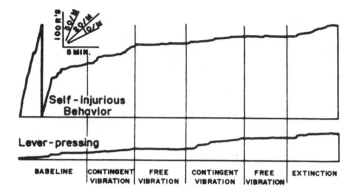

Fig. 3. Cumulative records of self-injurious behavior and lever pressing showing a within session comparison of response contingent vibration and free, continuous vibration on self-injurious behavior.

below the initial operant level, but free vibration had the effect of almost completely eliminating SIB.

DISCUSSION

The results supported the expectation that the frequency of SIB would be reduced if the presentation of a reinforcing stimulus was made contingent upon a response temporally and functionally incompatible with a self-injurious response. What was surprising, however, was the strikingly greater control over SIB that was obtained by the presentation of free, non-contingent vibratory stimuli.

The data lend support to some speculations in the literature that self-injurious responses in some retardates represent attempts to obtain sensory input under extremely restrictive environmental conditions such as exist in some institutions (McKinney, 1962; Provence & Ritvo, 1961); attempts to overcome some physiological barrier to perceiving stimulus input such as may exist in some organically defective organisms (DeLissovoy, 1963; Kravitz, Rosenthal, Teplitz, Murphy & Lesser, 1960); or some combination of the two. These speculations are compatible with the experimental literature on sensory deprivation in man (Bexton, Heron & Scott, 1954) and animals (Butler, 1953; Butler & Alexander, 1955) which suggest that sensory input may function as a primary reinforcer. (See also Kish, 1966 for a review of this literature.)

From a practical standpoint, further research to determine the long-term durability of non-contingent, sensory stimulation in reducing the SIBs of retardates would be desirable.

REFERENCES

Bailey, J. & Meyerson, L. Vibration as a reinforcer with a profoundly retarded child. *Journal of Applied Behavior Analysis*, 1969, **2**, 135–137.

Bexton, W. H., Heron, W. & Scott, T. H. Effects of decreased variation in the sensory environment. *Canadian Journal of Psychology*, 1954, **8**, 70–76.

Butler, R. A. Discrimination learning by rhesus monkeys to visual-exploration motivation. *Journal of Comparative and Physiological Psychology*. 1953, **46**, 95–98.

Butler, R. A. & Alexander, H. M. Daily patterns of visual exploratory behavior in the monkey. *Journal of Comparative and Physiological Psychology*. 1955, **48**, 247–249.

DeLissovoy, V. Head-banging in early childhood, a suggested cause. *Journal of Genetic Psychology,* 1963, **102**, 109–114.

Kish, G. Studies of sensory reinforcement. In W. K. Honig (Ed.), *Operant behavior: Areas of research and application.* New York: Appleton-Century-Crofts, 1966, 109–159.

Kravitz, M., Rosenthal, V., Teplitz, Z., Murphy, J. & Lesser, R. A study of head-banging in infants and children. *Diseases of the Nervous System,* 1960, **21**, 203–208.

McKinney, J. A multidimensional study of the behavior of severely retarded boys. *Child Development,* 1962, **33**, 923–938.

Meyerson, L., Kerr, N. & Michael, J. L. Behavior modification in rehabilitation. In S. Bijou and D. Baer (Eds.), *Child development: Readings in experimental analysis.* New York: Appleton-Century-Crofts, 1967, 214–239.

Provence, S. & Ritvo, S. Effects of deprivation on institutionalized infants. In *The psychoanalytic study of the child.* Vol. XVI. New York: International University Press, Inc., 1961.

The Training of Professional and Non-Professional Change Agents

INTRODUCTION

It has long been recognized that the implementation of behavior modification programmes calls for two levels of personnel. The experimental behavior analysis which precedes treatment certainly requires a level of psychological sophistication generally associated with professional training. Such training is also required of those whose responsibility it is to select the most appropriate treatment strategy, to evaluate it and to decide when it should be changed or terminated. But these are very different functions from the day-to-day application of certain management techniques derived from learning theory. These operations such as contingent reinforcement, modelling, and the implementation of token systems have been successfully carried out by parents, student volunteers and inexperienced professionals. It is one of the great advantages of these newer methods that they do not depend upon highly trained professionals for their widespread application. In view of the present manpower shortage in the mental health professions, this is an invaluable asset.

Of the six papers included in this section, the first two present single case studies in which the deliberate modification of parental behavior play an important role. In one of these studies (Johnson & Brown, 1969) parents were systematically reinforced by the therapist for correctly rewarding their child during observation sessions. Modelling was also found useful in this context.

Teaching parents how to implement appropriate responses to their children's deviant behavior is seen as an essential aspect of remedial strategies in which the re-programming of a patient's social environment is the aim. Nowhere is this strategy more appropriate than in dealing with a child showing multiple problem behavior.

The next two papers concern themselves with the modification of classroom behavior in "special education" settings. Again the corrective procedures are largely carried out by volunteers or, in one case, by an inexperienced teacher. Both studies employ token reinforcement systems. The paper by Staats *et al.* is based on an earlier single case study by the senior author. It is one of the rare examples in the literature describing the treatments of a large number of subjects who were treated for similar behavior deficits with the same reinforcement system. The paper is further remarkable for drawing attention to an instance of "malpractice" by a therapy-technician whose well intentioned but misguided encouragement of the child led to disturbance, hostility and threatened withdrawal of the child from the programme. Observations of this kind underscore the absolute necessity for effective supervison of non-professional helpers at all stages of a remedial programme.

As Broden *et al.* point out in their study, the principles of contingency management have probably always been used by good teachers everywhere. What is remarkable is their demonstration that a teacher who had not managed to control her class was helped to do so by a fairly simple manipulation of environmental contingencies.

That the outcome of behavioral treatment compares favorably with standard child guidance techniques is illustrated by the paper of Wahler and Erickson. Their study shows that the mean number of treatment weeks required in a child behavior therapy programme, staffed by public health nurses and other volunteers, was less than half of that required by traditionally-oriented professional therapists in the same setting.

In view of the social worker's professional concern with the social and physical environment of patients, surprisingly little has been written on his role in behavior therapy. The final paper in this section deals with that topic in the context of children's behavior problems. Not only trained social workers but also the increasing number of social case aides are likely to promote wider application of behavioral principles in the foreseeable future.

Producing Behavior Change in Parents of Disturbed Children*

STEPHEN M. JOHNSON† and RICHARD A. BROWN

Institute for Juvenile Research, Chicago, Illinois

Abstract: Out-patient clinic procedures for changing problematic parent–child relationships were described. These procedures were illustrated by the presentation of two cases in which parental behavior change was effected with resulting improvement in the parent–child interaction. Standard interactional situations were developed in each case in which a set of behavioral demands were made on the parent and the child. These demands elicited the problematic child behaviors for which treatment was required. Systematic behavioral observations were taken establishing a quantifiable measure of problematic child behaviors and related parental behaviors. Measures were then taken to modify the nature and frequency of parental behaviors while systematic observations on both parent and child continued. The techniques used in this parental training were described and their uses illustrated in the development of parental behavior change. The results indicated that these procedures can be effective in producing desirable changes in problematic parent–child relationships and that they are worthy of continued exploration.

INTRODUCTION

The focus of research reports on operant behavior modification appears to be changing as the field continues to develop. It no longer seems necessary to demonstrate that modification of behavioral contingencies can produce changes in the behavior of individuals who have shown marked behavioral deficits or excesses. It has also been documented that non-professionals with very limited training can serve as effective contingency managers (Allen & Harris, 1966; Allyon & Michael, 1959; Davison, 1965; Gericke, 1965; Risley & Wolf, 1966). In general, however, the methods necessary to affect change in these agents of contingency management have not been adequately described. Because writers have focused on changes in the target behavior of patients, few have given adequate information on how the new behaviors of the agents of change were produced. In our work with disturbed children and their parents, producing meaningful change in the parental component of the parent–child interaction has become the central therapeutic problem. The case reports which follow involve the examination of learning techniques used in producing effective contingency management behavior in the parents of disturbed children. The first report represents an example of parental instruction using many learning techniques more or less simultaneously. The second report represents the examination of only one learning technique in effecting parental behavior change.

Many of the learning techniques which are reported here have been used by other investigators in various combinations. One of the most common involves directing parental behavior

---

*Reprinted from the *Journal of Child Psychology and Psychiatry*, 1969, **10**, 107–121. Copyright 1969 with permission from Pergamon Press Publishing Company and Dr. Stephen M. Johnson.

†Now at the University of Oregon, Eugene, Oregon.

during parent–child interaction (O'Leary, O'Leary & Becker, 1967; Sanders, 1965; Welch, 1966). Some investigators have followed up this initial direction with some form of social reinforcement to the parents when they engage in effective contingency management on their own (Hanf, 1968; Wahler *et al.*, 1965). Although it has been infrequently recognized as a source of training, a number of endeavors in parental behavior change have included parental observations of child–therapist interaction (Hanf, 1968; Risley & Wolf, 1966; Russo, 1964; Straughan, 1964). While all of the above studies have employed some kind of didactic training and simple instruction, only the recent report by Walder *et al.* (1967) emphasizes and describes these procedures. In all other studies, the role of traditional interviewing techniques and the role of cognitive understanding of contingency management principles remain unclear.

The first case is presented to illustrate a wide variety of learning techniques in parental training. The case dramatizes rather well the problem of ascertaining the effective ingredients in an effective treatment.

CASE REPORT 1: THE USE OF MULTIPLE TECHNIQUES

Background

Judy was two years nine months when she was first referred for examination. Judy had been adopted shortly after birth and her parents felt that her development had been slower than average, especially in the language area, as she could say only two words. The child's most prominent behavioral difficulty was intense over-activity. Her mother was unable to control her during interviews prior to treatment and she responded with loud crying to every attempt by her mother to restrain her. At home she required constant supervision and control. Along with these difficulties, Judy's parents were most concerned about the fact that their daughter was not socially responsive. They reported that she would not respond to affection or punishment in any noticeable way and was oblivious to people around her.

The child was given a complete neurological and the results were negative in all respects. A Cattell Infant Intelligence Scale was attempted, but its validity was questioned due to the child's over-activity and her unwillingness to cooperate. The examiner's best estimate of IQ score was in the range sixty to seventy.

Judy's family included her parents, a nine-year-old brother and a grandmother. The father was employed as a white collar worker and this was an average middle-income family. Since the grandmother played an important role in the child's care, it was decided to involve her as well as the mother in the therapy programme. The father was not directly involved in the treatment.

PROCEDURES

Observational Diagnosis

Treatment began with two diagnostic observational sessions in which Judy, her mother and grandmother participated. Each session was divided into three periods. In Period 1, the mother was asked to get Judy to play with her in a playroom. In Period 2, grandmother was given the same task. In Period 3, both mother and grandmother were asked to converse together and require Judy to play by herself. Each period lasted five minutes. Systematic observations were made by the therapist from behind a one-way mirror. Past experience with over-active children suggested the following classes of behavior for observation:

1. Child changes activity — Every instance of redirection of activity (e.g., change from

playing with a doll to running across the room). Changes within one activity area (e.g., doll play) were not noted. One unit score was given for each instance of such behavioral redirection.

2. Child interacts — Child engages in the same activity as the adult within close proximity to the adult. One unit score for each ten-second period of such interaction.
3. Parent directs, pushes, holds, or carries child — Each instance of parental attempt to verbally or physically change the child's activity by directing, pushing, etc. In addition to one unit for each instance of such behavior, one unit was recorded for each ten-second period of continued restraint of the child.
4. Parent rewards child — Each instance of parental social praise to the child (e.g., "good girl," "that's right," etc.).

Observations were made as they occurred and dictated into a dictaphone. Timed variables (interaction and continued restraint) were measured by operating stop watches.

Figures 1 and 2 present data on these observations throughout the entire treatment course for Period 1 (5 minutes in which interaction was required between mother and child). Examination of the data for the first two baseline sessions clearly reveals that the behavior classes "child changes activity" and "parent directs, pushes, etc." are of high frequency, while the behaviors, "child interacts" and "parent rewards" are almost non-existent. In baseline

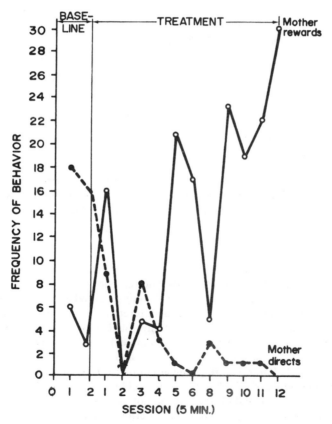

Fig. 1. Frequency of mother's recorded behaviors in five-minute mother–child interaction (Period 1) over sessions.

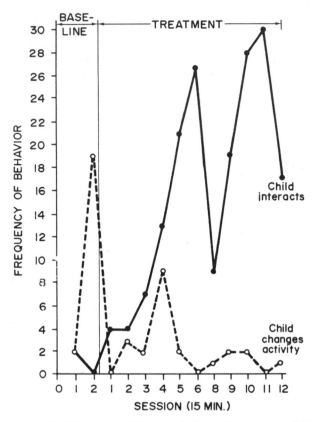

Fig. 2. Frequency of child's recorded behavior in five-minute mother–child interaction
(Period 1) over sessions.

Session 1, mother depressed Judy's over-activity by restraining her for a three-minute period.
Judy yelled and cried during this time. The data on grandmother and Judy were very similar in
baseline sessions although the grandmother had a slightly better relationship with the child.

Formulation

In the first two baseline sessions, both adults spent a good deal of time chasing Judy,
picking her up, returning her to the play area, and restraining her. All through this they talked
to Judy, never harshly but rarely with approval. Judy received almost constant attention from
the adults but it was non-contingent and undifferentiated. It would have been extremely
difficult for Judy to discriminate wanted from unwanted behavior under these circumstances.
The adults were told this at the beginning of treatment Session 1, and were shown recorded
data. They were told further that their pursuing and restraining behaviors appeared to be
ineffective because: (1) Parents were giving attention to Judy for undesired behavior and thus
were probably reinforcing it; (2) Parents were rarely punishing, as clear-cut disapproval was
hardly ever communicated; and (3) Parents did not label those behaviors which were desired.
The child seemed to do as she pleased in those periods when she was allowed to play by herself and it was clear that, as mother had reported, Judy did not find interaction with these
adults particularly rewarding.

Based on these observations and formulations, the immediate goal of the treatment programme was to reduce parental pursuit and restraint, and to increase parental reward for
desired behavior (interaction) in the child. Both adults were given a simple explanation of the
formulations and goals before the programme began. Treatment sessions were given twice
weekly and lasted approximately one and a half hours. The programme consisted of the
following techniques.

Direct Instruction

Parents were introduced to the central principles of learning theory and the presenting
problems were placed in that context. The presentation of the therapist's formulation represented one instance of direct instruction, as did subsequent discussions of reinforcement,
shaping, schedules of reinforcement and modelling. As part of the instructional programme,
the adults read programmed instruction materials on the principles of contingency management presented by Patterson *et al.* (1966). This programmed material has proved valuable in
short-cutting and clarifying the direct instruction process. The instruction appeared to
facilitate the realization by Judy's mother that chasing her daughter had become a "way of
life" for the family. This recognition occurred in treatment Session 2 and preceded one of the
mother's first dramatic behavior changes — her ability to completely ignore Judy's over-activity. Both adults seemed to grasp all the essential points of contingency management by
treatment Session 2 and most of the didactic training was completed by the end of this
session.

This direct instruction was among the less discreet and specifiable techniques in our treatment of this and similar cases. Experience seems to indicate, however, that all or most of this
instruction could be effectively done through sophisticated programmed instruction. The
existence of such materials would not only facilitate greater ease in this instructional step but
would also provide research tools to test the role of conceptual and theoretical understanding
in effecting appropriate contingency management behavior.

Group Discussion

Judy's family was seen together with another child's family, to whom the same general
principles and behaviors were being taught. All instruction and discussion were done in the
group context. Each of the parental groups observed the formal behavioral training of the
other and discussed it after the session. The group's discussion of punishment seemed most
valuable in opening Judy's family to the use of some mild aversive stimuli with her. Before
treatment, it was very apparent that she was rarely made aware of those behaviors which were
not desired. The parents of the second child provided a strong influence and probably accelerated learning in this area and others. Group discussion appears useful in spreading the base of
social influence to produce parental behavior change. In this case, for example, the report of
an experienced parent concerning the use of appropriate aversive control was of particular
value to Judy's parents who had been unable to show even clear-cut disapproval to their
child.

Behavioral Direction

The formal behavioral training took place in repeated sessions structured in the same
manner as the baseline sessions. Period 1 of each session involved mother–child interaction
for five minutes. Period 2 involved grandmother–child interaction for five minutes. Period 3
involved conversation between both adults with the child present, for the purpose of teaching

the child to play by herself without demanding adult attention. Behavioral direction was used only in the first two treatment sessions. The therapist, using a red light, signalled the adults to reward Judy when he felt it was appropriate. At first, parents were signalled to reward Judy whenever she approached them. By treatment Session 2, Judy was required to interact with the parents before receiving reinforcement. For the first four treatment sessions, candies (M & M's) were used and were always paired with verbal social rewards. About fifty per cent of the social rewards were accompanied by candy in these periods.

In many cases, behavioral direction appears to hasten parental learning by immediately raising the level of appropriate parental contingency management. When this occurs, the child may often begin to immediately reward such parental change by better behavior. In addition, this procedure may be of particular utility in the first stages of treatment where the parents must reward only approximations of the desired responses. Shaping procedures are perhaps among the most difficult to teach parents, and until parents understand behavior theory and have experienced some success with its techniques, it may be more useful to rely on behavioral direction.

Behavioral Reinforcement

Behavioral reinforcement was employed in Sessions 3–13 and consisted of signalling the parents by means of a signal light when they rewarded their child appropriately as well as when they missed a good opportunity to reward her. Thus, the signal light communicated the therapist's approval or disapproval of the adult's social reward behavior immediately after its occurrence. The light was not optimally effective, however, as the adults often missed seeing it. A device for administering an auditory stimulus to parents through a small receiver placed in the parent's ear may be used to eliminate the error experienced in this case (Welch, 1966).

Behavioral reinforcement has become a major technique in establishing effective contingency management behavior in parents. While other techniques may be valuable in eliciting appropriate contingency management, we believe that both specific behavioral reinforcement and generalized social reinforcement are vital in sustaining this new behavior over time. Of course, when the parental behavior becomes effective in maintaining desired behavior in the child, reinforcement from the therapist should no longer be necessary.

Modelling

In treatment Sessions 3–13 modelling sessions preceded the formal treatment interaction periods. During the modelling sessions, the therapist would attempt to play with Judy and demonstrate the desired behaviors to the parents who observed from behind a one-way mirror. During these periods, the therapist attempted to emphasize labelling the child's desired and rewarded behaviors, to accentuate positive affective expressions during reward, and to demonstrate a wide variety of socially rewarding behaviors including physical contact, etc. Although systematic observations of these periods were not made, the therapist was able to engage the child in play for the entire five-minute period on most occasions. In addition to these opportunities for modelling, a number of other opportunities were included in the treatment programme. Both adults had the opportunity to observe the other in interaction periods with the child. In addition, they viewed the formal treatment sessions of the other child and his parents. Modelling seems to be particularly useful in increasing the initial frequency and variability of contingency management behavior in parents. The rationale for this hypothesis will be discussed in the presentation of the second case.

DISCUSSION

Judy's case is rather typical in that improvement came suddenly and dramatically after a period of slow progress and change in parental behavior. This is reflected in the data on the mother–child interaction presented in Figs. 1 and 2. The data on the grandmother–child interaction are very similar although this interaction was somewhat better at all treatment stages. The results are of considerable interest for the striking agreement between verbal report of behavior, and the behavior shown in treatment sessions. A very real change in the problematic behaviors was evidenced in treatment Session 4, which began with an excited report of changes in Judy's behavior at home. It was reported that she was talking more and interacting with others more readily. Grandmother felt that Judy actually enjoyed playing with them and enjoyed receiving social rewards. In addition, she reported that Judy seemed to be affected by mild disapproval and punishment as never before—"it seems to hurt her feelings and she seems more sensitive to it." The adults reported that Judy had initiated numerous interactions with other people in various settings during the past week. Mother reported that her daughter was following many more direct commands and stated, "Before this, I really didn't think she understood what we said." While Judy interacted with her mother for only two minutes in this session, she interacted for the full five minutes with her grandmother. It seemed clear that the child–grandmother interaction was a much smoother one, and an additional five-minute session was added to involve child interaction with both adults. In this session, and those which followed, this period produced interaction at or near the five-minute maximum. Session 4 marked the first time when difficulty was experienced in the period in which the child was required to play by herself. She made bids for the adults' attention, and when she did not receive it, she became visibly frustrated and cried. This behavior is interesting in view of the fact that this child had previously been oblivious to others and not interested in interaction with them. After three sessions in which Judy's bidding for attention was ignored, it extinguished. In treatment Session 5, progress was further consolidated and mother further improved her relationship with Judy. In this session, mother indicated that her child was "more fun to live with" and stated "she seems more intelligent than we had thought." Sessions 4–6 showed marked improvement in all respects and this was a period of high optimism and rising expectations for the adults. Sessions 7[1] and 8, however, were characterized by a clear-cut reversal in progress as indicated by the behavior in the clinic and the adults' report of Judy's behavior. Although surprising at first, it quickly became apparent that the adults were requiring responses of which Judy was incapable, and thus, opportunities for rewarding success were infrequent. The parents indicated that they were once again disappointed by Judy's inability to do things usually expected of children her age. In short, the parents' expectations rose too rapidly. The adults were frustrated and communicated this to Judy through reducing the frequency and meaningfulness of their rewards. These points were discussed in Session 8 and the adults clearly agreed with and contributed to the above formulation. By Session 9, they appeared to have adjusted their expectations to a more realistic level and the quality of the interaction returned to its former level.

Between Sessions 11 and 12, the therapist visited the home during the morning hours. Judy was observed playing quietly by herself and intent on one activity. Her mother and grandmother were both successful in joining her play and interacting with her. The only behavior which upset the otherwise unremarkable observation of Judy and her parents was her repeated attempts to sit on the therapist's lap and relate to him.

The clinical observations of parental behavior change in Judy's case and others like it

---

[1]Data unavailable due to mechanical failure.

suggested that the modelling procedures used were quite powerful in contributing to successful outcome. Modelling seemed to be particularly valuable in effecting rapid initial change in parental behavior. There are a number of reasons to expect the success of modelling procedures in problems of this kind. Among the most apparent is the fact that, with most parents who require such training, the desired behaviors are of very low probability. Even when they can be evoked by instruction, they are often quite ineffective. Social rewards, for example, may be quite stereotyped, flat in affective tone, or they may be long and complex statements which make little sense to a small child. If the behavior problem constitutes parental over-involvement with the child, an instruction to ignore undesired child behaviors may well lead to cessation of verbal harangues, but intensification of non-verbal attention from parent to child. Thus, learning through behavioral direction and reinforcement alone may simply help to perpetuate ineffective behavior. Another powerful aspect of modelling would appear to be the vicarious reward provided the parent by his child's response to the model's behavior. It seems that many of these children respond in the desired ways more quickly to a strange model's contingency management behaviors than to those of his own parents. Thus, modelling procedures may strengthen the desired responses in the parents through vicarious reinforcement, when direct reinforcement is likely to be delayed. These clinical observations are consistent with the more systematic research on modelling which indicates that learning may often be greatly facilitated by observation, and that this facilitation may be far greater than that which is provided by additional learning trials (Adler, 1955; Hayes & Hayes, 1952; Rosenblith, 1959). The following case of David and his mother provided an opportunity to check the power of the modelling procedure used independently.

CASE REPORT 2: THE USE OF MODELLING

Background

David was a six-year-old child with a long history of poor development and adjustment. He was adopted at fourteen months and reportedly was rarely allowed to leave his crib during this first year. At the time of adoption he rolled constantly, crooned to himself and stiffened when touched. He was unable to walk, but soon learned to do so in his new home. Although his parents had considerable trouble in raising him, he was not referred for professional evaluation until it became apparent that he was unable to function in a regular school programme. His school teacher reported that he was over-active, distractible, tense, excitable, and given to frequent outbursts. He had attacked other children in school and was "defiant of authority," frequently responding to commands with "No, I won't," etc. David was dismissed from school because he was "too unpredictable to be safe." His behavior at home was also clearly problematical in that he was excessively demanding and manipulative, to the point that the organization of the household was largely determined by him. This process can be more readily understood by illustration than general description. The following excerpt of ongoing behavioral observation in the home will indicate the nature of the problem.[2]

> David, mother, Sue (twelve-year-old adopted sister), and baby brother are all in the family room in the basement. David annoys Sue and Sue complains to mother about David. Mother says to David, "Behave yourself." David complains in a whining voice, "The baby is wrecking my train set." Mother says, "No, he isn't." David whines and says, "Take him upstairs." Mother: "David, I'll take him if he bothers you, I'll take him." David whines again, "Do it now." Mother asks, "Are you going to work on your trains, now?" David replies in the affirmative and mother says, "Okay, I'll take him up." Mother then goes upstairs with the baby and David and Sue are left in the family

---

[2]The writers are grateful to Robert Phillips for his permission to use this excerpt of his observation.

room. David gets a small piece of rubber tubing, puts one end of the tubing in his mouth, goes up to Sue and blows air on her. Sue says "Stop!" in a loud annoyed voice. David does it again. Sue says "Stop!" again, but David continues. Sue yells upstairs to mother, "David has a tube in his mouth and he's blowing air in my face." Mother goes down into family room and tells David to stop that, sharply. David does it some more. Mother says to David, "I thought you were going to play with your trains, I took the baby upstairs so you could play." Mother leaves the room. David stays in the family room with Sue; he does not play with his trains, he keeps the tube in his mouth, but he doesn't bother her any more. He then goes into the laundry room. When David does this Sue calls, "Mother, David is going into the other room." Mother comes into the family room and says to Sue, "Let *me* handle that." Sue replies, "You always tell me to tell you when he goes into the laundry room." Mother talks to David in the laundry room and then takes him upstairs into the kitchen. Mother cooks in the kitchen and David fills a glass with soapy water and blows bubbles with his piece of tubing. Mother: "David, I said no bubble blowing." David laughs and stamps his feet in glee. Mother repeats in a stronger voice, "I said no blowing." David replies, "I didn't hear." Mother becomes angry and says, sharply, "Yes, you did." Mother then gives David a short lecture on bubble blowing.

In this, and a number of other observed interaction sequences, two relationships became apparent: (1) David's demands were very frequently followed by his mother's compliance which was frequently followed by further demands. (2) Behaviors by David which others found annoying almost always brought him attention. Following such attention, his annoying behaviors appeared to increase in frequency.

Psychological testing and a neurological examination were included in this child's evaluation. He earned an IQ score of 97 on the Stanford–Binet Intelligence Scale. Immaturity in visual-motor skills and absence of well-developed laterality were noted in the examination. The neurologist rejected the diagnosis of minimal brain damage while noting an element of immaturity in the functioning of the central nervous system. No chemo-therapy was recommended.

Enrolment in a day school for boys with severe behavior problems followed completion of this diagnostic study. His classroom was one in which contingency management principles were used extensively and it conformed in general design to the classrooms engineered and described by Birnbrauer *et al.* (1965). In addition, David's parents were seen in group treatment which could be described as fairly didactic in nature and oriented toward teaching the principles of contingency management. They had participated in this weekly therapy for a period of eight months before being referred for further individual intervention. During this time, David's behavior at school had improved considerably, but his behavior at home had been only minimally affected.

David's family included both parents, a twelve-year-old adopted girl, and a one-year-old non-adopted boy. The mother had a high school education and was not employed. The father was college educated and employed in a profession. This was an upper-middle income family.

PROCEDURES

Parental Interview

The child's mother was interviewed twice prior to observational diagnostic procedures. She indicated that she was very concerned because her son was "emotionally disturbed" and "sick." She was unable, however, to specify many of the behaviors which upset her, other than indicating that her boy would sometimes wave his arms when excited, and that he became overly involved with mechanical gadgets. At times he would withdraw for long periods to engage in this play. When pressed for more specific instances she reported that David would refuse to get ready for, or go to school, and that he would refuse to do simple assigned household chores. At these times mother would either "keep after" him, or do for David what he would not do for himself. She further reported that David could not tolerate having company in the home. This resulted in an almost total absence of visitors. In these and many other instances, mother revealed that she was most responsive to her son's undesired behaviors and compliant to his demands. She also manifested considerable resistance to the suggestions given her in the treatment group regarding the possibility of her ignoring David's undesirable behavior. She indicated that she felt it necessary to be constantly responsive to her son in order to avoid his becoming even more "out of control" and bizarre in his behavior. As the material on this child and his family accumulated, it became more apparent that his interaction patterns conformed rather closely to what Patterson and Reid (1968) refer to as "coercive interaction." In this pattern the behavior of the coercive member of the dyad is maintained by positive reinforcement (e.g., demands produce compliance), while the behavior of the coerced member is maintained by the withdrawal of an aversive stimulus (e.g., compliance produces the cessation of demands, whining, bizarre behavior, etc.). It was also apparent that the coerced member of this mother–child dyad (mother) was most reluctant to give up her habitual attentive and compliant behavior, due to her very reasonable fear that such a change would result in the exacerbation of her child's coercive behavior, which she found so unpleasant.

Observational Diagnosis

In order to create a situation which might elicit the problem behaviors, mother was asked to enter a room with David and was instructed to play with him for two minutes with a favored toy. She was then signalled to require him to do arithmetic problems for a five-minute period. This was followed by another two-minute play period and another five-minute arithmetic period. The arithmetic problems presented were well within his capabilities as determined by his teachers. Meanwhile, the therapists (T_1 and T_2) observed the interaction in the arithmetic periods for twenty seconds at a time, followed by ten-second breaks for recording the following behavior classes:

1. Mother rewards on-task behavior: Any verbal praise given to David for doing the arithmetic.
2. Mother criticizes off-task behavior: Any clearly critical remark by mother to David for his failure to do the arithmetic.
3. Mother attends to off-task behavior: Any non-critical verbal behavior by mother emitted when David is not doing arithmetic.
4. David's time on task. The cumulative time spend by David on arithmetic.

The observer agreement on the first three measures was computed by counting the agreements on the occurrence and non-occurrence of behaviors. Over the first four sessions (2 baseline and 2 treatment) composed of six five-minute arithmetic periods, observer agreement on mother's rewards was 100 per cent. Mother's attention to off-task behavior yielded ninety-seven per cent agreement, and mother's criticism of off-task behavior, ninety-five per cent agreement. T_1 observed the child's cumulative time on task in each session but no observer agreement was obtained on this measure.

Figure 3 shows that the average per cent of mother's attention to off-task behavior was ninety-eight per cent over two baseline sessions composed of four arithmetic periods. The average per cent of mother's criticism was 12.5 per cent. The child's cumulative arithmetic time, in these periods, was always below thirty seconds, and mother rewarded on-task behavior only twice in four sessions. When mother asked her son to do the arithmetic, a barrage of non-arithmetic behaviors was elicited. The first among these were, "I want a drink. . . . I have to go to the bathroom. . . . I won't do them with the lines on the paper. . . . How many do I have

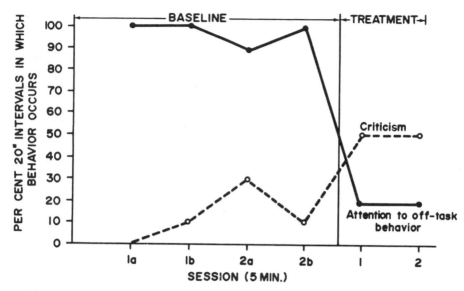

Fig. 3. Per cent of mother's attention to off-task behavior and criticism in five-minute baseline and treatment sessions.

to do?", etc. Mother responded to all these statements and many others like them, and little arithmetic was completed in the baseline sessions. While it was very easy for David to direct his mother's attention in these ways, it was observed that he could get even stronger responses from her by acting in more unusual ways, such as sucking his thumb, pouting, head banging, making machine-like noises, crawling on the floor, etc.

Formulation

The findings of the observational diagnosis further confirmed the formulation already outlined—namely that David's undesired behaviors appeared to be maintained by mother's compliance to his demands, and her rather intense attention to his unusual and manipulative behavior. In line with this formulation, the goal of intervention was the cessation of her compliance and attention. Weekly directive counselling and didactic group discussion had been employed to this end for eight months with limited success, and other measures seemed to be called for. It was decided to employ only the modelling procedure for a brief period for the purpose of producing the desired change. These treatment sessions were given twice weekly and lasted approximately one hour.

Modelling

In treatment Sessions 1 and 2, T_1 accompanied David into a room where he took him through the play periods and arithmetic periods just as mother had done. Meanwhile, mother and T_2 observed the interaction and both made systematic behavioral observations as already outlined. It was believed that this recording would direct the mother's attention to the relevant cues and model behaviors and thus facilitate learning.[3] She proved to be an accurate observer.

---

[3]Miller and Dollard (1941) found, for example, that when observation aided the subject in attending to relevant stimuli, learning was facilitated, but when observation led the subject to miss important cues, learning was retarded.

Observer agreement in treatment Sessions 1 and 2 were as follows: T_1 rewards, ninety-eight per cent agreement; T_1 attends to off-task behavior, ninety per cent agreement; T_1 criticizes, eighty-two per cent agreement.

T_1 engaged in contingency reversal procedures in the arithmetic periods and the child's time on task was noted. David's time on task was 4.5 minutes in the first arithmetic period during which T_1 rewarded on-task behavior, gave minimal criticism for off-task behavior, but otherwise did not respond to the child. The child's time on task was 0.5 minutes when T_1 responded to off-task behavior but did not reward on-task behavior or criticize off-task behavior. These results were observed by the mother and the data was shown to her immediately after the sessions. The therapists did *not* draw any conclusions from the data, nor did they require any conclusion from the mother. She was then sent into the room with her son and asked to use whatever methods she thought appropriate to get him to do the arithmetic. The same procedure was followed in treatment Session 2, except that T_1 attended to off-task behavior in the first arithmetic period, and rewarded on-task behavior with minimal criticism for off-task behavior in the second period. Under these conditions no reversal of the child's behavior was obtained.

As can be readily seen in Fig. 3, the mother's attention to off-task behavior dropped from an average ninety-eight per cent in the baseline session to an average of twenty per cent over the first two treatment sessions. Her critical comments rose from an average of 12.5 per cent in the baseline sessions to an average of fifty per cent in the treatment sessions. T_1 had modelled critical behavior at an average of twenty-five per cent and the child's mother apparently responded to the modelling. As treatment progressed, however, it became apparent that such criticism was ineffective in producing compliance even when used minimally. In later treatment of this child, mother was taught to restrict her use of verbal criticism. Her rewards of on-task behavior were at a uniformly low level throughout these first sessions. David's on-task behavior was very infrequent in these sessions, thus giving mother minimal opportunity for appropriate reward.

Extended Treatment

Having established the desired parental behavior through modelling procedures, the focus of the therapeutic intervention shifted slightly at this point in the direction of strengthening those behaviors and maintaining them, until the child himself could provide the needed reinforcement to sustain them. Two extended sessions with T_1 and David were carried out in which T_1 remained consistent in his contingency management behaviors. T_1 gave verbal approval for working on arithmetic but gave no attention for other behaviors. Mother and T_2 observed these sessions and recorded T_1's behavior. T_1 required David to stay in the situation until he had attended to the task for five minutes. In the first treatment session of this kind, forty-seven minutes were required for the child to reach this criterion. In the second session fifteen minutes were required.

The next four treatment sessions included mother–child interaction with David required to do arithmetic. The time required to reach the five-minute on-task criterion in each session was thirty minutes, fifteen minutes, 9.5 minutes, and thirteen minutes, respectively. In the final two sessions, David completed all the problems presented to him in ten minutes and fourteen minutes, respectively.

David's mother achieved very meaningful behavior changes during this time, both in and out of formal sessions. As in Judy's case, however, there was a good deal of fluctuation on the mother's part at various stages. Because procedures varied in the latter phase of treatment, it is impossible to determine which treatment ingredients helped maintain the new, more effective maternal behaviors. As in Case 1, direct instruction, discussion, modelling and social reinforcement were used to support mother's new behaviors and facilitate generalization to the home situation. In addition to the eight treatment sessions for which behavioral data is reported, the mother was given eight more counselling sessions to facilitate the effect of the behavior change programme in the home and to assist David's re-entry into public school. As she became more successful and positive in her relationship with her son she appeared more relaxed, and expressed feelings of confidence in "teaching" other family members more effective ways of interacting with David. Five months after the modelling procedure was initiated, David was successfully placed in a regular public school classroom.

DISCUSSION

The present case serves to demonstrate the effectiveness of brief modelling procedures in producing effective and novel contingency management behaviors in the parent of a disturbed child. It is significant that the success with modelling followed the relative failure of other more directive and instructional methods designed to produce such change. This fact seems to greatly enhance the interpretation that the modelling procedures were responsible for the changes observed. It is also interesting to note that, at the end of the treatment, David's mother perceived modelling as the most helpful technique in the treatment programme.

The vital problem in this case seemed to be the maintenance of the novel maternal behavior until the time when the child began to reinforce such behavior himself. Modelling was effective in producing behavior change; the maintenance of that change over this critical period then became the central problem. Because multiple techniques were employed to that end, the effective ingredients of this latter phase of treatment cannot be systematically ascertained.

The isolation of the modelling technique served to demonstrate its utility in effecting parental behavior change in the present case. Much more systematic research is required, however, to ascertain what effect each of these techniques may have in producing meaningful change in inter-personal behavior. In addition, follow-up data on cases such as these is vital to the continued development of the field.

Acknowledgments.   The first case reported in this paper was seen at the University of Oregon Medical School. The writers wish to express their appreciation to Frederick H. Kanfer for his assistance in this case. Thanks are also due to Frances Perce for her critical comments on the manuscript.

REFERENCES

Adler, E. A. (1955) Some factors of observational learning in cats. *J. gen. Psychol.*, **86**, 159–177.

Allen, Eileen K. & Harris, Florence R. (1966) Elimination of a child's excessive scratching by training the mother in reinforcement procedures. *Behav. Res. and Ther.*, **4**, 79–84.

Allyon, T. & Michael, J. (1959) The psychiatric nurse as a behavioral engineer. *J. exp. Analysis Behav.*, **2**, 323–334.

Birnbrauer, J. S., Bijou, S. W., Wolf, M. M. & Kidder, J. D. (1965) Programmed instruction in the classroom. In *Case studies in behavior modification* (Edited by Ullmann, L. and Krasner, L.), pp. 358–363. Holt, Rinehart & Winston, New York.

Davison, G. C. (1965) The training of undergraduates as social reinforcers for autistic children. In *Case studies in behavior modification* (Edited by Ullmann, L. and Krasner, L.), pp. 146–148. Holt, Rinehart & Winston, New York.

Gericke, O. L. (1965) Practical use of operant conditioning procedures in a mental hospital. *Psychiat. Stud. Proj.*, **3**, 2–10.

Hanf, Constance (1968) Modification of mother–child control behavior during mother–child interaction in standardized laboratory situations. Paper presented at meeting of the Ass. Behav. Ther. Olympia, Washington.

Hayes, K. J. & Hayes, Catherine (1952) Imitation in a home raised chimpanzee. *J. comp. physiol. Psychol.*, **45**, 450–459.

Miller, N. E. & Dollard, J. (1941) *Social learning and imitation.* Yale University Press, New Haven.

O'Leary, K. D., O'Leary, S. & Becker, W. C. (1967) Modification of a deviant sibling interaction in the home. *Behav. Res. and Ther.*, **5**, 113–120.

Patterson, G. R., Brodsky, G. D. & Gullion, E. (1966) *How did it happen to us and what can we do about it?* Unpublished mimeographed book, University of Oregon, Eugene, Oregon.

Patterson, G. R. & Reid, J. B. (1968) Reciprocity and coercion: Two facets of social systems. Unpublished manuscript, University of Oregon, Eugene, Oregon.

Risley, T. & Wolf, M. M. (1966) Experimental manipulation of autistic behavior and generalization into the home. In *Control of human behavior* (Edited by Ulrich, R., Stachnik, T. and Mabry, J.), pp. 193–198. Scott, Foresman, Chicago.

Rosenblith, Judy F. (1959) Learning by imitation in kindergarten children. *Child Dev.*, **30**, 69–80.

Russo, S. (1964) Adaptations in behavioral therapy with children. *Behav. Res. and Ther.*, **2**, 43–47.

Sanders, R. A. (1965) Behavior modification in a two-year-old child. Paper read at Midwestern Psychological Convention, Chicago.

Straughan, J. H. (1964) Treatment with child and mother in the playroom. *Behav. Res. and Ther.*, **2**, 37–41.

Wahler, R. G., Winkel, G. H., Peterson, R. F. & Morrison, D. C. (1965) Mothers as behavior therapists for their own children. *Behav. Res. and Ther.*, **3**, 113–124.

Walder, L. O., Cohen, S. I., Breiter, D. E., Dacton, P. G., Hirsch, I. S. & Liebowitz, J. M. (1967) Teaching behavioral principles to parents of disturbed children. Paper read at Eastern Psychological Convention, Boston.

Welch, R. S. (1966) A highly efficient method of parental counselling: A mechanical third ear. Paper read at Rocky Mountain Psychological Convention, Albuquerque, New Mexico.

A Behavior Modification Programme
for a Child with Multiple Problem
Behaviors*†

G. R. PATTERSON and G. BRODSKY

Department of Psychology, University of Oregon, Eugene, Oregon, U.S.A.

INTRODUCTION

Even now, in its infancy, the behavior modification movement has its full quota of pro- phets, critics and Don Quixotes (on both sides of the windmill). However, the present report is directed less to either crusaders or infidels, and more toward clinical psychologists who are in the process of deciding whether there may be something in behavior modification technology which is of practical value in changing the behavior of deviant children.

In considering this question, it seems to the present writers that there are at least three respects in which the behavior modification literature is deficient. The data which will be presented in the present report are a modest attempt to rectify some of these deficiencies.

In general, the literature has been deficient in reports which present "hard" data, describ- ing *successful* treatment of children who have *multiple* sets of problem behavior. All three deficiencies will have to be met before behavior modification technology can occupy a respec- table position. These deficiencies are illustrated in sources such as the excellent review by Grossberg (1964) or the presentation of cases in the edited volume by Ullmann and Krasner (1965). In some of the studies the data collected were excellent, and describe dramatic changes, but the behavior studied represents only "mild" or single classes of deviance. Illustrations of such investigations are to be found in the classic study by Jones (1924) on children's fears, Williams (1959) on tantrum behaviors; Harris *et al.* (1964) on crawling; and Jones' (1960) preview of the literature on the treatment of enuresis. These studies perform the necessary function of establishing the *possibility* that principles from learning theories do have practical implications for the treatment of deviant children. The fact is, however, that most children referred to clinics have four or five problem behaviors. There have been attempts to deal with children displaying multiple problems or highly aversive behavior, but these attempts have been limited in several important respects. In some studies of this kind the investigators unfortunately have followed the clinical tradition and provided only general descriptions, by the therapist or parent, of behavior change. The reports by Lazarus and Abramowitz (1962) and Patterson (1965a) are examples of studies which do not provide adequate criterion data. Lacking these, it is not possible to evaluate the effectiveness of the treatment. In a movement that is less than ten years of age, it is perhaps to be expected that

*This project was financed by USPH grant MH 08009-03. The writers gratefully acknowledge the cooperation of the nursery school teacher, Mrs. Ann Bradwell, who permitted these procedures to be carried out in her classroom and to the parents of Karl who generously gave their permission for the publication of this report.

†Reprinted from the *Journal of Child Psychology and Psychiatry*, 1966, 7, 277–295. Copyright 1966 with permission from Pergamon Press Publishing Company and Dr. G. R. Patterson.

the earlier studies will show many defects. However, it is to be hoped that contemporary studies will not continue to make the same errors. It is of critical importance that we provide criterion data we can use to evaluate the effect of our efforts.

Another group of investigators provide an example of the second style of deficiency. This group has dealt with the behavior patterns of the extremely aversive child, and they have provided excellent data describing the effects of their treatment programmes. However, these researchers have not as yet been *successful* in producing a remission of deviant behaviors in their subjects. This latter group of investigators have attempted to deal with "autistic" children; Ferster & DeMeyer (1961), Wolf, Mees & Risley (1963), Lovaas, Schaeffer & Simmons (1964), Bricker (1965), and Hingtgen, Sanders & DeMeyer (1965). When compared to the results produced by traditional treatment programmes, the efforts of the behavior modifiers are dramatic indeed. In spite of the fact that the data from these studies are of high quality and attest to significant changes in the behavior of these children, the primary patterns of deviant behavior persist for these subjects. If we hold to a rigorous definition of the term "successful" we cannot claim as an example the efforts of the behavior modifiers with autistic children.

The present report describes a set of conditioning programmes for the treatment of a pre-school boy who was referred for several behavior problems. The procedures are adaptations derived from the writings of Skinner (1958); in these procedures, both social and non-social reinforcers were used to shape the adaptive behaviors. The problem behaviors were "severe" in the sense that they were highly aversive to adults and to other children. In all respects he represented a typical case referred to child guidance clinics. In the study, an attempt was made to provide observation data showing the effect of the conditioning programmes for each set of deviant behaviors. In an effort to maximize the generalization and persistence of treatment effects, most of the conditioning procedures were introduced in the schoolroom and the home. For the same reason, much of the effort was directed toward re-programming the peer culture and the parents.

METHODS

The Child

Karl was a five-year-old boy whose parents had been asked to remove him from kindergarten. From the parent's report, it seemed that Karl was characterized by a multitude of deviant behavior. For example, when separated from his mother, he became intensely aggressive, biting, kicking, throwing toys, screaming and crying. The teacher's legs were a mass of black and blue marks; on several occasions he had tried to throttle her. The mother also reported sporadic enuresis. His speech pattern was immature, showing several minor articulation defects. There was a general negativism in his interaction with adults; for example, it was extremely difficult to get him to dress or feed himself. The mother thought he might be retarded, but his IQ tested at the end of the study was well within the normal range. The mother felt that the behavior pattern exhibited by Karl was so extreme and had persisted for such a period of time that it was extremely unlikely that he would change. As she said, Karl was very "strong headed." She was especially concerned about the behavior he exhibited when he was brought to school in the mornings. For example, on the previous week he had actually held on to her dress with his teeth in an effort to keep her at the school. At age two years, Karl was hospitalized for a few days' diagnostic study for suspected leukemia. The results of the diagnostic studies were negative; however, following the hospitalization it was increasingly difficult to leave him with baby-sitters.

At the close of the first interview, the mother smiled ruefully and said that she did not think that the programme we outlined would help Karl. However, his behavior was so aversive to her that she agreed to participate in it.

His play interaction with other children was limited in frequency and rather primitive in quality. Much of the time he ignored the other children. When he did interact with them, there was an awkward and frequently aggressive quality to his behavior which led the teacher to be concerned about their safety. As a result, much of the time he was followed about the room by an adult.

When presenting a report of a single case in which multiple problems are evident, it is very difficult to provide an adequate means for specifying the conditions under which replication could occur. By keeping the description of the child somewhat vague, the present writers could always claim that unsuccessful replication attempts by other investigators were involved with subjects that were "really" not like the one described by the writer. For this reason some effort was made to provide a careful description of the child; a procedure for doing this has been outlined by Patterson (1964). Karl was observed during the occasion of his first visit to the clinic for the presence, or absence, of 149 behavioral items. These behavioral items, plus the report by the parent and teacher as to "symptoms," constituted the description of Karl.

The behavioral items and symptom list had been previously used with a sample of 100 deviant boys to determine the factor structure which characterized this matrix. This analysis produced five oblique factors. The distribution of scores for each of the five factors had been transformed into deviation scores; and the distributions were normalized by the use of McCall's (1922) T score. The factor profile resulting from the combination of behavioral observation in Karl's first hour at the clinic, and the report by parents and teachers of his "symptoms," is shown (Fig. 1).

To summarize the description, Karl would be characterized as high on the Immaturity factor, and moderately high on the Hyperactivity and Anxiety-Psychotic factors. This profile was very similar to the mean profile for a class of deviant children obtained by Patterson

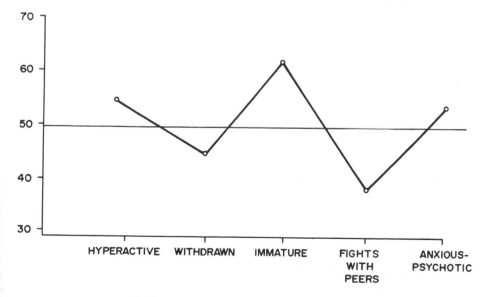

Fig. 1. The profile of factor scores describing Karl.

(1965).[1] The similarity of Karl's profile to that of the group indicated that he was a member of a class of patients that is often referred to clinics for treatment. As suggested earlier, these profile scores can serve as a basis of subject-comparison in attempts which might be made to replicate the present study.

The Parents

Karl's mother was an attractive woman, thirty years of age. She dressed appropriately and showed herself to be a reasonably well organized housekeeper and mother. She had received an eleventh grade education. A cursory investigation of her background and behavior did not reveal any marked psychopathology; this was in keeping with her MMPI profile of −97.

Karl's father was a husky, assertive man, thirty-one years of age. He had received a tenth grade education. A semi-skilled laborer, he was away from home much of the time. It was our impression that there was no obvious psychopathology characterizing the father; this was also corroborated by his MMPI profile of 13' 427−09. Both the parents agreed in stating that the father had better control over Karl's behavior than did the mother. They believed that the improved control was due to Karl's fear of the physical punishment which the father used on occasion.

Formulation

A paradigm such as the one currently being used by behavior modifiers may generate statements which lead to successful outcomes of treatment programmes. The fact that the data support statements about treatment outcomes does not necessarily lend support to other statements, made from the same paradigm, which purport to "explain" the *antecedents* for the deviant behavior. These are two separate sets of statements, and each require their own set of verification data. However, such tests will not be made until behavior modifiers explicate their "speculations" about probable antecedents for various classes of deviant behaviors. It is our intention to provide here a set of testable speculations about the antecedents for behaviors of the kind displayed by Karl.

After our initial observations in the school, we outlined the following formulation for the temper tantrum behaviors displayed at school.

Being left at school was a stimulus associated in the past with deprivation state.

$$S \dots \dots \dots \dots \dots \text{Depriv.}$$

This deprivation state, and cues associated with it, elicit an emotional state. This emotional state was labelled "separation anxiety."

Anxiety

The eliciting cues (S) and the anxiety state produce high amplitude behaviors which are reinforced in two ways. (1) These behaviors frequently terminate the presence of the aversive stimuli, and (2) they are also maintained by positive social reinforcers.

Temper tantrums: scream, bite, kick, cry, hold on to mother.

---

[1] The mean factor scores for this group were: Hyperactive 53; Withdrawn 39.5; Immature 65.0; Fights with Peers 38.0; and Anxious-Psychotic 59.3. In the earlier study four out of a hundred deviant boys has profiles of this kind. This group of four boys were highly homogeneous as evidenced by Haggard's R (1958), coefficient of profile similarity, of 0.73. The intraclass correlation took into account variations in level, scatter, and ranking of profiles for the group.

The key concept in this formulation was the use of a deprivation paradigm to explain the presence of anxiety in Karl. Such an approach is based upon the assumption that deprivation of social reinforcers creates an emotional state.[2] We assume that such deprivation must occur frequently in the lives of most children but that it is most likely to produce an intense emotional reaction in those children that we have labelled as "selective responders." Such a child has been conditioned to respond to social reinforcers dispensed by only a limited number of social agents.[3] The main result of selective responding is that the absence of the mother (parents) signifies that social reinforcers are no longer forthcoming. Thus when left at school or with a baby-sitter, he is, in effect, placed in an immediate deprivation state. The stimuli associated with the onset of this deprivation constitute a set of eliciting stimuli for the emotional state which typically accompanies this kind of deprivation. This complex of eliciting stimuli, deprivation and accompanying emotional state are usually labelled as anxiety.[4]

It would seem to be the case that not all deprivations led to anxiety states for Karl. For example, he could play by himself in the yard for extensive periods of time. We assume that the stimuli associated with some deprivation states would be more aversive than others. For Karl, it seemed to be the case that he was most anxious in deprivation conditions that he could not terminate upon demand. For example, being left at school was a stimulus associated with long periods of social deprivation; in addition, he had no control over the length of time which he was to be deprived. His playing in the yard by himself was a deprivation state which he could terminate at any time by simply going into the house. In summary, it was postulated that there was a relationship between deprivation of social reinforcers and anxiety; a relation between selective responsiveness and anxiety; and a relation between control over the period of deprivation and level of anxiety.

Karl has learned to avoid the onset of this anxiety by throwing temper tantrums, kicking, biting, etc. This behavior was reinforced either when the mother remained at the kindergarten in an attempt to comfort her son; or when the teacher interacted with Karl and attempted to quiet him by holding him or reading to him, etc. Thus, Karl's behavior was being maintained both by the presentation of these positive reinforcers and by the avoidance of the deprivation state. It is important in this respect to note that we assumed Karl to be responsive to the

---

[2] The existence of such a state, and the appropriateness of the label "anxiety" is attested to by a series of laboratory studies. A series of instrumental conditioning studies have shown that children who have been deprived of social contact for a time are more responsive to social reinforcers, Walters and Roy (1960), Walters and Karol (1960), Erickson (1962), Gewirtz and Baer (1958). There are also data showing the relation between deprivation of social reinforcers and physiological measures of anxiety. Unpublished data from our own laboratories showed that social deprivation produced a significant increase in "anxiety" as measured by skin conductance. A group of fifteen first and second grade girls were isolated while they responded to the apparatus (without being reinforced). There was a significant increase in skin conductance from the first to the second half of the trial ($p = 0.03$ level).

[3] Karl seemed to be a good example of the hypothesized relation between selective responding and deviant behavior outlined by Patterson and Fagot (1966). Their laboratory findings showed that some boys were responsive to social reinforcers dispensed by only one or two of the three major classes of social agents (mother, father, or peer). Such boys were more likely to be described as deviant when rated by teachers. In the present case we believe that Karl was responsive to social reinforcers dispensed by only a few people, e.g., his mother and his father. By and large, his behavior was not under the control of reinforcers dispensed by peers. Quite possibly this lack of control was due to the fact that Karl was raised in the country and had little opportunity to learn to be responsive to peers.

[4] The data reported in the Patterson and Fagot publication offered some support for these speculations. Boys who were shown to be responsive to social reinforcers dispensed by mothers, fathers, and by peers were described by teachers as being the most anxiety-free. On the other hand, boys who were electively responsive to only one or two of these agents were also rated as being more anxious.

teacher. Observations of Karl suggested that this was so; it also seemed to be the case that the presence of other children in the room making demands upon the teacher created a situation in which Karl was being minimally deprived most of the time.

In planning a treatment programme, it was assumed that the intense destructive behavior owed at least part of their amplitude to the presence of the emotion, anxiety. One of our behavior modification programmes must then deal with anxiety. However, reducing the anxiety will *not* necessarily extinguish the destructive behaviors; it may, for example, only reduce their level of intensity. For this reason, a second major component of the treatment programme involved the strengthening of socially adaptive behaviors which would compete with the occurrence of the behaviors associated with temper tantrums and other atavism. Presumably relatively permanent elimination of deviant behaviors may best be achieved by programmes that include the conditioning of socially adaptive behaviors which compete with their occurrence. This second point of focus involved the training of both the peer group and the parent to respond positively to socially adaptive behaviors displayed by Karl. In Karl's case, we suspected that the parents were using negative reinforcers to control his behavior and that there were few positive reinforcers dispensed by peers for socially adaptive behaviors. Most of the peer group seemed to find Karl's behavior quite aversive and avoided him as much as possible.

In addition to the temper tantrums, there was another class of deviant behavior which was of interest. The label used to characterize this second, broad class of response was "negativism." Karl seemed to precede many of the dramatic temper displays, both at kindergarten and at the clinic, with a verbal warning. For example, he would state that he was going to kick the experimenter or the teacher. On many occasions he would refuse to comply with any requests with a flat "No." Frequently such behaviors would be reinforced by the behavior of the adult. When faced with such "warnings," the adults would withdraw their requests. Perhaps the mother learned that such "warnings" were stimuli preceding subsequent temper tantrums. Mother could avoid what was most certainly, for her, a negative reinforcer, by withdrawing her request of Karl. In this way, Karl was being reinforced in a variety of settings each day for a complex of behaviors which we have labelled as "negativistic."

It is clear than an effective treatment programme will require several different conditioning procedures. It will be necessary to condition a new set of responses to the cues eliciting the anxiety reaction. It also will be necessary to extinguish the destructive behaviors and teach him some alternative mode of responding. We also must increase the frequency of the few socially adaptive behaviors he does demonstrate. The peers in turn must be re-programmed to provide more social reinforcers for Karl, particularly for the occurrence of his socially adaptive behaviors. The latter set of procedures is pivotal, for it partially insures the persistence of any change in Karl's behavior produced by our intervention. Finally an effective way must be found of altering the set of contingencies provided by the parents for Karl's anxiety responses, his temper tantrums, his immature behaviors, and his negativistic behaviors.

Treatment Procedures

There were four conditioning programmes used in the study. The procedures were as follows: (A) an extinction-counter conditioning programme for the temper tantrum behaviors; (B) an extinction-counter conditioning programme for the anxiety reactions elicited when being separated from mother; (C) a positive reinforcement programme to increase the frequency of positive initiations between Karl and the peer group; (D) and finally, a programme to change the schedule of reinforcements used by the parents to maintain negativistic and immature behaviors. As some of these programmes were used simultaneously, confusion will be minimized by outlining the development of each of these procedures on a day-to-day basis.

October 5: Programme A (temper tantrums).   Karl was brought to the door of the mobile laboratory to obtain a laboratory measure of his responsiveness to social reinforcers. He looked frightened (his pupils were dilated), and refused to come. When carried into the laboratory, he kicked the experimenter, screamed, cried, and attempted to destroy equipment. The experimenter brought him into one of the cubicles, closed the door and pinned Karl to the floor by the ankles. While Karl screamed, bit, and threw objects, E made every effort to prevent Karl from injuring him, and sat looking as bored as circumstances would permit. E looked at Karl and talked to him only when he was reasonably calm. Karl was told he could leave as soon as he quieted down. The episode lasted about thirty minutes.

Programme D (re-train the parents).   We had not planned beforehand to begin reprogramming the parents in this session. However, when Karl displayed his tantrum behaviors, the mother was brought to an adjoining room and observed the interaction through a one-way glass. A second experimenter explained to her that we were introducing a "timeout" procedure for Karl. As long as the destructive behavior lasted, he would be pinned down and effectively removed from all of the usual sources of positive reinforcement. The mother was told that such adult behaviors as "the mother stays in the classroom," "the teacher hugs him," "the teacher looks frightened or reads him stories" were powerful reinforcers for temper tantrums. The behavior of the experimenter with Karl served as a model for behaviors which the mother was to imitate.

October 6: Programme A (temper tantrums).   The mother had to drag Karl to the clinic today. Once inside, he refused to accompany E to play room and was picked up (kicking, clawing, screaming and crying). In the play room he was pinned to the floor by his ankles and cried for thirty seconds. As soon as he stopped the tantrum behaviors, he was released.

Programme B (anxiety).   Patterson (1965) described a technique in which dolls were used to represent situations in which a child would be separated from his mother. A similar procedure was used with Karl. After being presented with a situation in which the mother (doll) was separated from the boy (doll), Karl was asked if "the doll" would be afraid. If he said "No," he was reinforced with an M & M chocolate candy. He was also reinforced whenever he described behaviors which would compete with the occurrence of fear or temper tantrums, i.e. "I would play." The dropping of his M & M in his cup was preceded by an auditory signal coming from his "Karl Box." The "Karl Box" contained an electric counter, light, and a rather loud bell. Any one, or all, of these could be activated by E.

During this first session (15 minutes), Karl participated in a series of six doll sequences and received a total of thirty M & Ms.

Programme D (re-training the parents).   The mother and the second E observed Karl's play room behavior through an observation window. During the temper tantrum, the mother was shown the non-reinforcing (and non-punitive) behavior of the E holding Karl. She, in turn, was encouraged, to leave him quickly at school and thus reinforce the tantrum behaviors as little as possible. Mother was impressed with the fact that temper tantrums lasted only a few minutes today.

After the session in the play room, the two experimenters, Karl and the mother talked for ten minutes. Mother was instructed to reinforce him on those occasions in which he did not act in a frightened way when being separated from her, when he was cooperative, and when he behaved in a grown-up fashion. She was instructed to bring in notes describing four occasions on which she had reinforced Karl for any of these following behaviors: for not being afraid, for being cooperative, for being "grown up." Karl listened to this interchange with some interest.

Programme C (programme to increase positive interaction between Karl and peers). The "Karl Box" was used during the recess period at kindergarten. Karl was told that the buzzer would sound each time that he "played with another kid without hurting him." If Karl were within range, E dispensed social reinforcers for appropriate initiations, i.e. "That is good, Karl." He was also informed that the candy which he earned would be divided among all of the children and distributed during snack time. He earned seventy M & Ms in a ten-minute period; during this time he displayed no aversive behaviors.

October 7: Programme A (temper tantrums).   The same tantrum behaviors were observed at the clinic. The same procedures were applied as described for the previous day. However, today the behavior terminated as soon as Karl was carried into the play room.

Programme B (anxiety).   The same doll play procedure was used as described for the previous day; the session lasted about twenty minutes. Karl earned thirty M & Ms and a plastic ship. (The latter we "traded" for 10 M & Ms.) All of the reinforcers were delivered immediately and accompanied by the sound of the bell in the "Karl Box."

Programme D (re-train the parents).   The mother observed Karl's behavior in the play room. She was told of the necessity for reinforcing appropriate behavior immediately. She was also reminded of the importance of *not* reinforcing maladaptive behaviors, such as non-cooperation, temper tantrums or immature behaviors. The interactions of the experimenter and Karl were used to illustrate these points.

During the "group" interview which followed, the mother reported with pride that Karl was cooperative several times yesterday. Karl was very pleased with her remarks. She gave the following written examples of her efforts to reinforce him.

1. Karl put away his clothes for me and I told him that he was a good boy and hugged him.
2. Karl got a diaper for me and I told him how nice he was to help me take care of his baby brother.
3. Karl went to bed without any argument and didn't wet the bed and I told him how grown-up he was getting.
4. Karl picked up walnuts for me and I told him he was really getting to be such a big boy and kissed him.

Programme C (interaction of Karl and peers).   The other children had received their M & Ms from Karl's previous day's work and were curious when E again appeared with the box. They asked E what it was, and E told them that it was a "Karl Box." They asked, "What is a Karl Box?" E said, "It is a box that makes a noise, and gives candy whenever you talk to Karl." Immediately several children said "Hi Karl" to the box. E said, "No, you must say it to Karl, not to the box." The peers then received 150 reinforcers for initiating social contacts with Karl. He in turn was reinforced for responding appropriately and for initiating contacts of his own. The conditioning session lasted only about ten minutes. The M & M bonanza was again distributed to all of the children.

October 8: Programme A (temper tantrum).   Karl began to whimper as soon as he saw the experimenter's reception room and ran and hid. He then kicked and clawed as he was picked up and began to cry loudly. He was told that he could earn M & Ms by walking up the stairs himself.

He was placed at the bottom of the stairs; but he refused to move. The experimenter commented that Karl was not screaming, kicking or hurting people even though he was a little afraid. At this point the buzzer sounded on the "Karl Box." After a few seconds Karl was again asked to place his foot on the bottom step; but he refused. After a moment, the experimenter said, "Too bad, the next time the box went off you were going to earn one of these plastic boats. Guess I'll just have to keep the boat and carry you up the stairs again." There was a moment of silence at which point Karl said, "Suppose you touch my hand and see what happens." The experimenter touched Karl's hand. Karl immediately placed his feet on the stairs. The buzzer sounded and Karl was handed the plastic boat. At this point, he walked up the stairs and was reinforced by the bell for each step into the play room.

Programme B (anxiety). Karl and experimenter sat in the doorway of the play room. The mother was instructed to say "Goodbye, Karl," and Karl in turn was told to say goodbye to the mother while she walked across the room. As Karl said "Goodbye," he was reinforced by the bell and by the E saying "Very good, Karl." Karl was asked if he was afraid. He said that he was. E said "But you did sit there. You didn't run after her, and you didn't scream or kick. That is very good." (Bell sounded.) This was repeated several times with the mother moving further away each time until she walked across the lawn as Karl waved goodbye from the second-story window.

Programme D (re-training the parents). Mother reported that Karl was making good progress both in being able to tolerate her leaving him at school, and also in his increasingly cooperative and mature behavior at home. Both the Es and the mother praised Karl, who was obviously very pleased. Mother brought her "homework" with examples of how she had reinforced Karl for these behaviors on the previous day.

1. Karl took his bath without any argument at all and I told him how proud I was of him and let him sit in my lap in the rocking chair for a while.
2. Karl went to bed and I told him how big he was for it and kissed him.
3. Karl got into the car to come to the University without arguing and I told him how nice he was.

We pointed out to the mother that she still found herself doing for Karl things which he could do for himself; e.g., tying his shoes, buttering his bread. We practiced breaking such a behavior down into small steps and providing reinforcement for *any kind of progress* rather than waiting for terminal behavior before reinforcing. We also set up a point system so that each time Karl cooperated in one of these new behaviors he received a point, which mother recorded as part of her homework. When he had earned ten points, Karl could select any one of the plastic toys from our display.

Programme C (peer and Karl interactions). The school period was highly structured today. It was not possible to condition for peer interaction without disrupting the group. We left shortly; Karl was obviously disappointed, but remained in the group.

October 11: Programmes A and B (temper tantrums and anxiety). Karl walked up to the play room to the accompaniment of the bell and much praise from his parents and both Es. He said that now he only felt a little bit afraid when leaving his parents. We all agreed that he would no longer have to come to the clinic.

Programme D (training the parents). The father, who had been absent from home during the past week, had returned. The procedures were reviewed for him in the clinic with mother and Karl present. Arrangements were made for the remainder of the work with parents to take place in the home.

Programme C (peer interaction). Neither experimenter was able to go to the school today.

October 12: Programme D (training parents). One of the Es went to Karl's home along with an observer. Karl was extremely cooperative in following his parents' requests. E followed the mother around, offering suggestions on the best way to interact with Karl. When mother was slow in reinforcing him, E again explained the importance of the immediacy of reinforcement. In addition, the mother was again shown the principles of shaping successive approximations to a desired behavior. As an example, she asked Karl to comb his hair which he had not done before. She was then instructed to reinforce him for the *attempt* (which was actually a fairly good job). After several such successes it was explained to her that she was to reinforce Karl tomorrow only when he had done a better job. A similar procedure was begun in shaping the behaviors involved in tying his shoes.

Programme C (peer-Karl interaction).   The previous programme was continued. M & Ms were made contingent upon Karl's initiating social contacts and peers initiating contacts to Karl.

October 13: *Programme D* (re-train the parents).   Karl was again observed at home. He showed no deviant behavior. Mother reported that she had reinforced Karl for improving in tying his shoes, and for hair combing. E reviewed for mother the general principles under-lying the approach with Karl and explained how she might adapt them to use in future situa-tions, such as leaving Karl alone in the evenings with a baby-sitter. Mother reiterated that Karl was like a new boy and they were delighted with his progress.

Programme C (peer-Karl interaction).   Today there was no conditioning in the classroom.

October 14: *Programme B. C and D.*   The mother came to the school and operated the "Karl Box." She was instructed to reinforce Karl for playing with other children, or any socially appropriate behaviors which resulted in his staying away from the immediate vicinity of his mother.

Mother, teacher, and Karl agreed that there was no reason for continuing the programmes as there were no further behaviors that anyone believed should be changed. It was arranged with the parents, and the teacher, to follow up the effects of the programme by observing Karl in the school for several weeks following the study.

Procedures for Collecting Data

All of the observation data used in testing the effectiveness of the treatment programmes were collected in the classroom setting. In the first introduction to this setting, two observers, seated in the classroom, dictated narrative accounts of Karl's behavior, and the reactions of the teachers and the peer group. These initial impressions provided a basis for constructing a check list that was introduced during the second day's observation. Using the check list, observers tabulated the occurrence of the following behaviors: (1) the frequency of positive initiations, i.e. talking to another child, smiling, by peers to Karl; (2) the frequency of his positive initiations to peers; (3) the occurrence of withdrawal or isolation from the group, e.g., sitting three or four feet away from the group and not attending to or participating in the group activities; (4) the occurrence of negativistic behaviors, e.g., when asked to join the group, play a game, come into the room, etc., his behavior indicated noncompliance; (5) temper tantrums, when being left by parents behaviors occurred such as: cry, scream, kick, bite and hit.

The observations were made during periods ranging in length from twenty minutes to sixty minutes per day. The behaviors were tabulated by fourteen second intervals. To reduce the variability somewhat, the observations were collected during the same sixty-minute period each day (12:30 to 1:30). The data were collected each day during the time immediately prior to the conditioning procedures introduced in the classroom.[5]

During the study, the data were collected by three different observers, but chiefly by one. On several occasions she was accompanied by an untrained observer. On the first such occasion 300 separate events were recorded; but the two observers agreed only sixty-one per cent of the time. On the second occasion, 264 events were noted and the two observers agreed eighty-four per cent of the time. This suggests that with a minimum of training, comparatively unskilled observers can be used to collect these kinds of data.

RESULTS

Each day the observers in the school provided an estimate of the duration of Karl's temper tantrum; this information was combined with the data from his behavior at the clinic to form a "total" score for the day. A tantrum was said to have stopped when Karl had ceased to cry, kick, or scream for at least half a minute. During the three weeks previous to the study, the teacher told us that Karl had averaged about thirty minutes at the beginning of each school session. The data showing the effect of the programme on temper tantrum behaviors are presented in Fig. 2.

In many respects, both the data and the procedure are similar to those described by Williams (1959) in which tantrum behaviors were controlled by the withdrawal of positive social reinforcers. As shown in Fig. 2, there was a marked reduction in the duration of the temper tantrums by the second day of the programme. After the initial, dramatic reduction in duration, they were being emitted at a reasonably steady rate for a period of about four days. During this "plateau," he displayed a total of about ten minutes of tantrums per day. Most of these were occurring in the classroom on the occasion of the mother's leaving him with the teacher. In this setting, both of the adults were providing him with a good deal of reinforcement for tantrums. However, by the sixth day of the programme procedure, the adults no longer provided reinforcers for them and they terminated. They did not recur during the three-month follow-up.

The second set of data showed the change in frequency of occurrence of two classes of behaviors observed in the nursery school. The first category, "isolated," was defined by such behaviors as sitting several feet apart from the group.

Most of the time the children were engaged in a series of organized games, storytelling and group singing. These provided an occasion in which the teacher frequently made suggestions or demands to each of the children. Non-compliance with such demands was coded as "negativism."

If either of the behaviors occurred during a fifteen-second time interval, it would receive one entry on the data sheet. The ordinate in Fig. 3 indicates the per cent of the fifteen-second intervals in which they were observed to occur.

The data showed that by the second day of conditioning there was a dramatic drop in the occurrence for both classes of deviant behavior. In both cases, the rate of occurrence dropped to almost zero and stayed there during the remainder of the three-month follow-up period.

---

[5] It required three days of trial and error to construct the check list; at this point we had intended to collect a week's baseline data for each of the deviant responses. However, on the third day of our being in the classroom, the teacher informed us that she would have to drop him from the class unless he improved. It seemed to us that her toleration of these behaviors for three weeks had already been above and beyond the call of duty; consequently, we initiated our conditioning procedures. Being Good Samaritans, however, resulted in our obtaining only one day's baseline observation data.

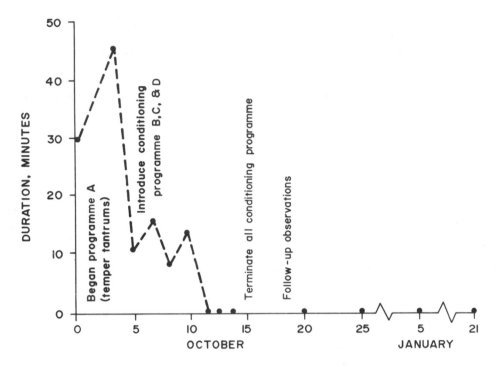

Fig. 2. Duration of temper tantrums.

In observing Karl, the baseline data showed that the other children tended to avoid him, probably as a result of the aversive quality of much of his behavior (pushing, elbowing, kicking, throttling, pinching). The prediction was that if Karl's aversive behaviors decreased in rate, the peer group would increase the frequency of their social reinforcers. Data presented in the report by Patterson & Ebner (1965) showed that when the aversive behaviors were decreased for two hyperactive children in different classrooms, the change was accompanied by a marked increase in the amount of social reinforcers provided (by peers) for one of the subjects *but not for the other subject.* This would suggest that the effect of a reduction in aversive behaviors is somewhat a function of the social group in which it occurs. To the extent that these variables are not understood, the final outcome of our treatment programme is determined in large part by chance factors. However, it should be possible to directly re-programme the schedule of reinforcement provided by the peer group, and the procedures innovated in the present study represented such an approach. If successful, the programme should result in an increase in the frequency of social initiations by peers and a corresponding increase in their use of positive social reinforcers contingent upon Karl's behaviors. The data to be presented here represented only a partial test of the hypothesis because the data were collected only for the occurrence of social *initiations* by peers to Karl. It was predicted that the conditioning programme would result in an increase in the frequency of initiations of positive social contacts made by the peer group to Karl and a corresponding increase in the frequency of positive initiations made by Karl to the peer group. The data for the frequency of social initiations consisted of such responses as: talking, smiling, playing, and touching. These events were also recorded by fifteen second intervals (Fig. 4).

Early in the conditioning period, the frequency of occurrence of positive initations by peers increased nine- or ten-fold. It should be kept in mind that these data were collected

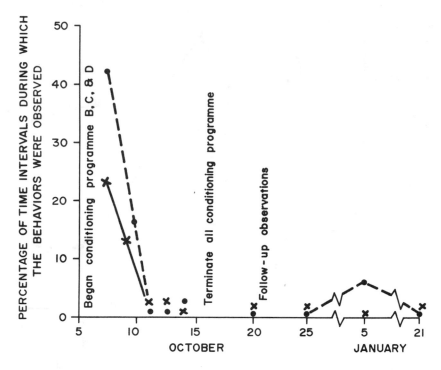

Fig. 3. Frequency of occurrence of negativistic and isolated behaviors. ×, frequency of negativistic behaviors; ●, frequency of isolated behaviors.

each day in the period immediately prior to the conditioning sessions; these data then reflect generalization, or transfer of conditioning effects.

There was a significant increase in frequency of social initiations by peers to Karl; there was also a significant increase in the frequency of positive social initiations by Karl to the peers. Both sets of initiations were at least doubled during conditioning. However, two months after the termination of the study it is clear that some of these earlier, more dramatic gains have been lost. The data from the end of the follow-up period show that the overall gain was only two- or three-fold for both sets of behaviors.

Discussions with both parents and with the teacher during the follow-up period indicate that Karl is "a changed boy." The casual observer in the classroom would have no reason to select Karl as showing particularly deviant behavior. His behavior is characterized by less avoidance of social controls and increased responsiveness to social reinforcers. Although still somewhat impulsive, Karl no longer displayed temper tantrums, nor did he isolate himself. During the baseline period, Karl would clutch a child by the arm and say such things to him as "I like you." He would then continue to hold the child's arm as he stared intently into the other child's face for a good ten seconds.[6] These primitive interactions no longer occurred. By any reasonable criteria, the changes in Karl constituted "successful treatment."

---

[6] This latter set of behavior was of particular concern to the writers because of its similarities to atavistic behaviors of this kind occasionally observed in schizophrenic children. Following the study, Karl was examined by an ophthalmologist who prescribed glasses. These "primitive" behaviors disappeared.

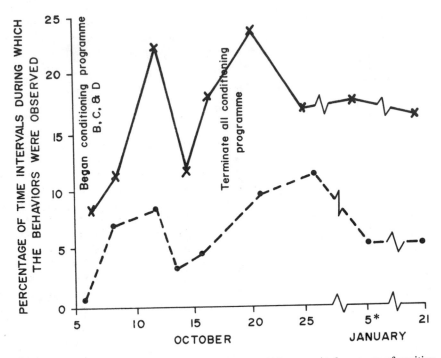

Fig. 4. Changes in the interaction between Karl and his peers. ×, frequency of positive
initiations by Karl; ●, frequency of positive initiations by peers.
*Based upon only twenty minutes of observation; the remainder of the period was too highly structured
to permit social initiations.

DISCUSSION

In some respects, data of the kind presented in this report are becoming commonplace.
They show that manipulation of reinforcement contingencies has a significant impact upon
behavior; these findings in turn have practical implications for the treatment of children
with deviant behavior problems. The first "rush" of data collecting activity served both to
reiterate our faith in the Law of Effect, and also to definitely place the promissory note
proferred by the behavior modifier in a place of prominence. However, at this point in the
development of the field, we should be able to raise questions which are more sophisticated
than those which characterized the earlier investigations. There is one set of questions which
have been encountered repeatedly in attempts to carry out behavior modification studies in
the laboratories here at Oregon. The general question concerns statements about the variables
which determine the persistence and generality of treatment effects. In our first studies we
were impressed by the fact that we were obtaining dramatic generalization of conditioning
effects (Patterson, 1965a; 1965b). In one of these studies the control over hyperactive behaviors quickly generalized from the conditioning periods to occasions in which the child was not
directly under the control of the apparatus. We assumed that the generalization occurred
because of the similarity in stimulus components present during conditioning and those present during the remainder of the day. In fact, our procedures had been constructed in an effort
to maximize just such transfer of effects. For example, in the series of studies using hyper-

active children as subjects, the conditioning was carried out in the classroom setting on occasions when the subject was engaged in routine classroom activities (Patterson, 1965b). The observation data obtained in this series of studies showed that not only did the conditioning effects generalize, but they persisted over extended periods of time. The data presented by Patterson & Ebner (1965) showed that a drop in the rate of production of deviant behavior can produce an effect on the social environment. In *some* groups, when the subject becomes less deviant, the peers begin to dispense more positive social reinforcers. Presumably, these reinforcers are contingent upon social behaviors which would compete with the occurrence of the deviant behaviors. However, as yet there are no data available which show that this latter hypothesis is indeed the case.

Our assumption is that the effect of the conditioning (or any successful treatment) produces a re-programming of the social environment; the altered programme of positive and negative reinforcers maintains the effect of the initial behavior modification. The fact that the peer group now responds by dispensing more social reinforcers also means that the effect would "generalize" to any social setting in which one would find members of this peer group. In effect the term "stimulus generalization" is an oversimplification. For this reason, in our own discussions about the process, we use the phrase "re-programming the social environment" rather than "stimulus generalization."

There are several implications which follow from such a reformulation. For example, if the social environment does not increase the frequency of social reinforcers for socially adaptive behaviors, then any "improvement" occurring from a treatment programme will be of short duration. *Or*, if the social environment continues to "pay off" for the deviant behavior at a very high rate, the likely outcome would be very little "improvement." An example of the latter would be the attempt to shape some socially adaptive behaviors in an institutional setting which is programmed to pay off heavily for deviant behaviors; e.g., institutions for delinquent adolescents have been shown to provide seventy per cent positive reinforcement for deviant behaviors (Patterson, 1963; Furness, 1964).

Taken together, the implications of these trends in the data are quite clear. The major focus of the behavior modifier should be upon the task of directly manipulating the reinforcement programmes being provided by the social environment, rather than upon the behavior of the individual subject. In effect, we are accusing the behavior modifier of following too closely the medical model. In the medical model, the behavior modifier would remove the "tumor" (change the deviant behavior) and then terminate his treatment programme. It is reasonable to believe that changing deviant behavior is simply not good enough; the goals for the behavior modifier must *also* be that of re-programming the social environment in which the subject finds himself.

Attempts to re-programme the social environment are only just beginning. The programmes described by Birnbrauer *et al.* (1965) and by C. Hanf (personal communication) are extremely provocative. In these attempts, the parent and child are observed interacting under relatively controlled laboratory conditions. The parent is reinforced for appropriately reinforcing the child. In our own laboratories, we have recently completed the development of a programmed teaching manual for use by parents and teachers. The main programme consisted of 120 frames which describe the concepts of social reinforcers, extinction, negative reinforcers, latency of reinforcement, and accidental reinforcement of deviant child behaviors. For each of the families which we are now investigating, the observation data in the home and the school are used to develop a branching programme for use by other mothers who have children with similar problems. For example, based upon our experience with Karl, we now have a fifty frame programme on separation phobia and temper tantrum behaviors in children. These programmes will be used in conjunction with our attempts to develop conditioning procedures to be used in re-training the parents *in the home*. This would mean devising new techniques to insure that the change in the programme of social reinforcers is provided both by adults and by peers. For example, it may be necessary to change our thinking about confining deviant children to groups in which they are mutually reinforcing each other's deviant behaviors. It is also necessary for us to re-consider the traditional clinical models which present the one to one relationship as *the* basis for behavior change. Our specula-tions lead us to believe that rather than improving the technology for changing behavior on a one to one basis, procedures in the future may rather completely differ from techniques for directly changing the behavior of the child and focus instead upon a technology which will re-programme the social environment.

This is one further point which should be made in setting behavior modification proce-dures in proper perspective. We might take the changes observed in Karl's behavior as a case in point. Presumably, the conditioning procedures strengthened socially adaptive behaviors which competed with the occurrence of deviant behavior. However, we do *not* believe that the conditioning procedures *shaped new* classes of socially adaptive behaviors, nor do we believe that the classes of deviant behaviors have been *extinguished*. In the present context, the terms "shaping," "conditioning," or "extinction" refer only to the fact that rankings have been changed in the hierarchy of response probabilities. The term extinction does not imply that such behaviors as "negativism" have vanished. By the same token, such socially adaptive behaviors as "smiling at a peer" are not in any sense completely novel to the child's reper-toire. "Conditioning" as it is used here implies only that a member of the class of responses such as "smiling at a peer" are more likely to occur. In a sense, we see the effect of most modification or treatment programmes as consisting of the re-arranging of social behaviors within *already existing hierarchies*.

In this perspective, the "therapist's" main function is to *initiate* the first link in a chain reaction. Such a chain reaction could *not* occur unless the child had been previously condi-tioned for socially adaptive behaviors. Also, the major changes occur outside the conditioning trials as the social environment begins to respond differently to the child who is being treated. It is the social environment which supports (or sabotages) the changes produced in treatment. In some cases this change in the schedule of positive social reinforcements results in the in-creased visibility of a whole spectrum of social behaviors which had previously been at very low strength. This latter phenomenon is familiar to both behavior modifiers and to traditional therapists.

REFERENCES

Birnbrauer, J. S., Bijou, S. W., Wolf, M. M. & Kidder, J. D. (1965) Programmed instruction in the classroom. In L. Ullmann and L. Krasner (Eds.), *Case studies in behavior modification*. Holt, Rine-hart & Winston, New York, pp. 358–363.

Erickson, Marilyn T. (1962) Effects of social deprivation and satiation on verbal conditioning in children. *J. comp. physiol. Psychol.*, 55, 953–957.

Eysenck, H. J. (1960) *Behaviour therapy and the neurosis*. Pergamon Press, Oxford.

Ferster, C. B. & DeMeyer, M. K. (1961) The development of performances in autistic children in an automatically controlled environment. *J. chron. Dis.*. 13, 312–345.

Furness, Jean M. (1964) Peer reinforcement of behavior in an institution for delinquent girls. Unpub. M.A. thesis, Oregon State University, Corvallis, Oregon.

Gewirtz, J. and Baer, D. (1958) Deprivation and satiation of social reinforcers as drive conditions. *J. abnorm. soc. Psychol.*, 57, 165–172.

Grossberg, J. M. (1964) Behaviour therapy: A review. *Psychol. Bull.*, 62, 73–88.

Haggard, E. A. (1958) *Intra class correlations and the analysis of variance*. Dryden, New York.

Harris, Florence, Johnston, Margaret, Kelly, Susan & Wolf, M. (1964) Effects of positive social rein-forcement on regressed crawling of a nursery school child. *J. educ. Psychol.*, 55, 35–41.

Hingtgen, J. N., Sanders, B. & DeMeyer, M. (1965) Shaping co-operative responses in early childhood schizophrenics. In L. Ullmann and L. Krasner (Eds.), *Case studies in behavior modification*. Holt, Rinehart & Winston, New York.

Jones, H. G. (1960) The behavioural treatment of enuresis nocturn. In H. J. Eysenck (Ed.), *Behaviour therapy and the neurosis*. Pergamon Press, Oxford, pp. 377–403.

Jones, Mary C. (1924) A laboratory study of fear: The case of Peter. *Pedag. Semin.*, **31**, 308–315.

Kanfer, F. H. & Phillips, Jeanne (1965) Behavior therapy: A panacea for all ills or a passing fancy? Mimeo paper, Univ. of Ore. Medical School, Portland, Oregon.

Lazarus, H. A. & Abramovitz, A. (1962) The use of "motive images" in the treatment of children's phobias. *J. Ment. Sci.*, **108**, 191–195.

Lovaas, I., Schaeffer, B. & Simmons, J. B. (1964) Experimental studies in childhood schizophrenia: Building social behaviors using electric shock. Paper read at Am. Psychol. Ass., Los Angeles.

McCall, W. A. (1922) *How to measure in Education*. Macmillan, New York.

Patterson, G. R. (1963) State Institutions as teaching machines for delinquent behavior. Unpublished mimeo paper, Child Study Center, University of Oregon.

Patterson, G. R. (1964) An empirical approach to the classification of disturbed children. *J. clin. Psychol.*, **20**, 326–337.

Patterson, G. R. (1965) A learning theory approach to the treatment of the school phobic child. In L. Ullmann and L. Krasner (Eds.), *Case studies in behavior modification*. Holt, Rinehart & Winston, New York. a

Patterson, G. R. (1965) The modification of hyperactive behavior in children. Paper read at *Soc. Res. Child Dev.*, Minneapolis, Minn. b

Patterson, G. R. & Ebner, M. (1965) Applications of learning principles to the treatment of deviant children. Paper read at *Amer. Psychol. Conv.*, Chicago, Ill.

Patterson, G. R. & Fagot, Beverly (1966) Children's responsiveness to multiple agents in a social reinforcement task. Mimeo paper, Child Study Center, University of Oregon, Eugene, Oregon.

Skinner, B. F. (1958) *Science of human behavior*. Macmillan, New York.

Ullmann, L. & Krasner, L. (Eds.) (1965) *Case studies in behavior modification*. Holt, Rinehart & Winston, New York.

Walters, R. H. & Karol, Pearl (1960) Social deprivation and verbal behaviour. *J. Personality*, **28**, 89–107.

Walters, R. H. & Roy, E. (1960) Anxiety, social isolation and reinforcer effectiveness. *J. Personality*, **28**, 358–367.

Williams, C. D. (1959) The elimination of tantrum behaviour by extinction procedures. *J. Abnorm. soc. Psychol.*, **59**, 269.

Wolf, M., Mees, H. & Risley, T. (1963) Application of operant conditioning procedures to the behavior problems of an autistic child. Paper read at *Western Psychol. Ass.*, Santa Monica, Calif. (Mimeo).

Wolpe, J. (1958) *Psychotherapy by reciprocal inhibition*. Stanford University Press, Stanford.

Cognitive Behavior Modification: "Motivated Learning" Reading Treatment with Subprofessional Therapy-Technicians*

ARTHUR W. STAATS,† KARL A. MINKE, WILLIAM GOODWIN
and JULIE LANDEEN

University of Wisconsin

Abstract: A method of treating reading deficits based upon an extrinsic motivational system previously employed successfully with a single subject was extended to eighteen additional subjects. The junior-high age subjects included retarded children in special classes, several emotionally disturbed children, and culturally deprived children. The method of training used in the original study was designed to be simple to administer and simple to record the performance of the child. Thus, it was hypothesized that subprofessional personnel could be employed to administer the treatment. Adult volunteers and high school seniors were used as the therapy-technicians,

The eighteen Ss were given 38.2 hours of training in daily half-hour sessions, during which period the average reinforcement earned was $22.29. The mean number of single word reading responses was 94,425. The rate of reading accelerated over the period of training even though the reading material became more difficult. This occurred during a period when progressively less (about one-fourth as much) reinforcement was given per reading response. A mean of 593.5 new words were learned and 70.9 per cent of these were retained in a long-term test. The attention, attendance, cooperation, and diligent work behavior of the various children were maintained in good strength throughout the duration of the study. The results suggest that research be conducted to develop methods for treatment of behavioral deficits that can be widely applied by subprofessional therapy-technicians supervised by clinical psychologists.

The first author (Staats, 1965; Staats & Staats, 1963) has outlined a learning approach to the study and treatment of behavior problems. In doing this it was suggested that behavior problems can arise, for example, because (1) there is a deficit of behavior necessary for adjustment in our society, (2) because behavior considered undesirable by the society is present in the individual's repertoire, or (3) because the individual's motivational (reinforcement system is inappropriate in some respect.

Actually, it should be indicated that there may be interaction between these classes of behavioral defects. Thus, the individual who has deficits in behavior may not as a consequence gain positive reinforcement — the receipt of which in contiguity with other stimuli would produce additional development of his motivational (reinforcement) system. For example, the male with deficits in social behavior may not be able to interact with normal women and thereby experience the sexual reinforcement necessary to develop his learned "sexual"

*Reprinted from *Behaviour Research and Therapy*, 1967, **5**, 283–299. Copyright 1967 with permission from Pergamon Press Publishing Company and Dr. Arthur W. Staats.

†Now on leave of absence at the University of Hawaii.

reinforcement system. As another example, certain deficits in behavior (e.g., the lack of intellectual or social skills) are punished socially and the punishment may help produce an inappropriate "social" reinforcement system.

On the other hand, a defective motivational system can lead to behavioral deficits. A child for whom learning something new, doing well in comparison to others, an adult's approval, and so on, are not positive reinforcers – a defect in achievement motivation – will not adjust well to one of his most crucial cognitive learning situations, the classroom. That is, his work and attentional behavior will not be maintained. As a consequence, he will later evidence deficits in his cognitive repertoires.

On the other hand, the individual with unpleasant inappropriate behavior may as a consequence be shunned and not obtain the social experiences necessary to learn an adequate social repertoire. Moreover, the deficit in social experience may leave deficits in his motivational system. Ordinarily, with severely abnormal individuals these various processes occur and interact producing inappropriate or deficit behavior.

The present study is concerned with demonstrating how a cognitive deficit, which it is suggested frequently arises from motivational deficits (*see* Staats & Butterfield, 1965; Staats, in press), may be treated by introducing a functional reinforcing system. In this case the cognitive deficit is reading, but the procedures have a wide applicability to the treatment of other behavioral deficits as well.

The first author and associates began this line of investigation first in basic studies (Staats, Staats, Schutz & Wolf, 1962; Staats, Minke, Finley, Wolf & Brooks, 1964; Staats, Minke, Finley & Wolf, 1964). Then the procedures developed were adapted for work with actual behavior problems (Staats & Butterfield, 1965). This latter study was a case involving a fourteen-year-old, culturally-deprived, juvenile delinquent. He had a long history of delinquency and maladjustment. Part of his difficulty in adjusting to school involved his previously acquired cognitive deficits, and part involved his inappropriate reinforcer system. That is, as was shown directly by his vandalism of a school, for which he was apprehended, he gave objective evidence of very "hostile" or negative school attitudes.

The method of treatment was based upon an extrinsic token-reinforcement system that had been developed in the basic studies. These methods achieved considerable success in the forty hours of training, given over a four and a half month period. The child, who was a severe behavior problem in a traditional classroom situation, worked and attended well in the experimental treatment programme, he made over 65,000 word reading responses, he received special training on 761 words he did not know, he retained 430 of those words (57 per cent) on a long-term retention measure, and he passed all his courses in school (the first time he had ever passed a course in his whole history), his misbehavior in school fell off markedly, and his general attitudes towards school and school work appeared to improve.

One of the major points of the treatment procedure, however, was the fact that it was designed to be easy to administer and record. The purpose of this design was to solve the practical problems involved in its widespread use for treatment and research. Thus, in the first study the procedure was applied by a probation officer. The suggestion that the behavior modification procedure could be employed standardly by subprofessional personnel has many implications for clinical psychology. Thus, it would seem that the procedure could be applied in many settings, involving various types of clinical, educational, and social problems.

However, this first study was based upon the results of a single subject. (Supporting case study evidence has been reported by Rachman, 1962 and by Whitlock, 1966.) The next step in this programme of research was a more general test of the procedure. In addition, the present study begins to assess the suggestion of the first study that learning problems can be treated by subprofessionals, supervised by a professional psychologist. In this case, literate high-school seniors and adult volunteers with high-school educations served as the therapy-technicians. The eighteen children who were the experimental subjects included under-achieving junior high school aged children with no special characteristics except their learning problem, children considered to be mentally retarded and in special classes, and several children with emotional or behavioral problems. Nine of the *S*s each had one of nine high school seniors as the instructional-technician, and the other *S*s each had one of nine adult volunteers as the instructional-technician.

It is important to note several additional points in introducing the present research. There is presently a great deal of interest in extending learning principles to clinical problems, both in behavior therapy and behavior modification studies. As the first author has outlined elsewhere (Staats, mimeo publication) most of these studies concern simple behavior, treated in short term procedures. Many of the behavioral repertoires that are most important to human adjustment are quite complex, however, and must be studied and treated over long periods. It is thus most important to a learning oriented clinical psychology that procedures be developed for dealing with complex behavior problems over the length of time necessary to understand and treat them. The present study attempts to demonstrate the possibilities for developing such research-treatment procedures and methods.

METHOD

Subjects

Eighteen experimental and eighteen control *S*s were selected for participation in the project in the following manner: Lists of students defined as poor readers on the basis of standard achievement tests and enrolled in seventh or eighth grade or in Special classes were obtained from five junior high schools in Madison, Wisconsin. These lists were then circulated to the teachers of various schools with the instructions to delete any names they felt were not reading problems and to add any students to the list whom they felt had been omitted. Final selection of *S*s for participation in the study was done on the basis of a 100-item word recognition test developed from the reading material. The thirty-six *S*s selected (twenty-eight male and eight female) were those most deficient on this oral test, reading eighty-one or fewer of the words contained. Subjects were grouped in thirds, from low to high, on the basis of their scores on the oral reading test, and subsequently divided into eighteen pairs, matched on the basis of their score on this word recognition test and, where possible, on the basis of IQ scores. The eighteen *S*s for the experimental group were obtained by randomly selecting one of the two students from each matched pair.

The average age at the start of the experiment was fourteen years, six months; the average IQ was seventy-four (sixty-nine Verbal and eighty Non-verbal). Seven of the experimental *S*s and seven control *S*s were enrolled in classes for the educable mentally retarded. A number of *S*s were classified as educationally (culturally) disadvantaged under provisions of the new Federal Education Act.

Experimenters (Therapy-technicians or Instructional-technicians)

Two types of experimenters were utilized in this study. Nine adult volunteers were obtained through the P.T.A.s of the participating schools and through the efforts of the individual principals. These volunteers were paid $2.00 a session to cover transportation, baby-sitting fees, and so on. The adult volunteers were all housewives with an average of four children living at home. Their average age was forty-two years, and their families earned approximately $7,500 per year.

In addition, nine high school seniors were obtained from East Senior High School and Central Senior High School. These students were selected by first circulating a list of the senior class among the teachers at the high school and having the teachers give the students a combined rating of above average, average, or below average on the characteristics of maturity, responsibility, and acceptable reading level. Students receiving a below average rating from any teacher were eliminated, and the remainder served as the pool from which volunteers were sought. These Es were paid $1.25 a session, and participated in the study during their regularly scheduled study halls. The seniors had a mean grade average of B for their four years in high school.

The instructional-technicians were trained in the use of the procedures in two one and a half-hour sessions just prior to the beginning of the project. This training included some experience in actually administering the materials. In addition, a brief third training session was held at the end of the second week to generally instruct the instructional-technicians on an error in procedure committed by one of the adult volunteers and to indicate some minor changes in procedure.

Instruments

The primary test used, both for grouping purposes and as a dependent variable, consisted of 100 words randomly selected from the reading materials used in the experimental sessions consisting of twenty words selected from each of five grade levels (1.2, 1.7, 2.3, 3.0, and 4.0). Subjects had to pronounce correctly the word shown them on a flash card in order to receive credit. The pre-test was given before assignment to treatment condition, and the post-test was administered by persons unfamiliar with the experiment.

Other tests. primarily of the standardized variety, were given during the screening of subjects, specifically the "Iowa Test of Basic Skills," Grade 7, Form 2, and the "Lorge–Thorndike Intelligence Test," Level D, Form 1. It was planned to give alternate forms of these tests as post-tests so the S's pre- and post-experimental performance could be compared. Many subjects, however, as will be discussed further on, appeared to be answering some of their tests randomly, and their chance scores substantiated this observation.

The same result was shown on the post-test where scores on the reading and vocabulary sub-tests of the Iowa Test of Basic Skills, Grade 7, Form 3, made it apparent that many of the subjects were still operating at chance expectancy. Accordingly, four additional sessions were utilized in which easier tests (the Lorge–Thorndike Intelligence Test, Level C, Form 2; and the California Reading Achievement Test, Elementary, Grades 4–6, Form W; and Forms 1 and X of the same two tests, respectively) were administered. As part of the attempt to salvage the test data, the extrinsic reinforcement method was extended to the testing situation during the last two sessions when the alternate forms were given. The alternate forms were thus given with the addition of the following reinforcement contingency instruction:

> The test you are to take now involves a procedure you should understand thoroughly. You will be able to earn money for doing this test, that is, by working hard, reading each item, and not guessing on items you do not know. You will get two cents for every question that you answer correctly, so the more questions you answer correctly the more you will make. However, you will lose one penny for every incorrect answer. Thus, if you do not read questions, and just guess at the answers, you will end up making nothing. Remember you get two cents for each question you answer correctly, and lose one cent for each incorrect answer.

Tests were scored, and students paid by envelopes a few minutes after these two contingency test sessions ended.

Reinforcer System for the Behavior Modification Procedure

There were three types of token, distinguished by color. The tokens were of different value in terms of the items for which the tokens could be exchanged. Initially, a blue token was valued at one-fifth of one cent, a yellow token at one-half of a cent, and a red token at one cent; however, at the end of the first week the tokens were devalued, and for the remainder of the study the value of the blue, yellow, and red tokens was one-tenth, one-fifth, and one-half of one cent respectively as in the original study.

During the eleventh week of the study a bonus system was introduced for a few slow children in order to maintain a $0.20 minimum in terms of S's daily earnings. From this point on, whenever S's earnings fell below $0.20 for any one session, he was given a bonus of $0.05, $0.10, or $0.15, whichever amount was needed in order to bring his earnings for that day up to between $0.20 and $0.25. When the bonus system was introduced, the child was told that he could not move as rapidly as before because the material upon which he was working was difficult, but if he continued to work hard he would be given a bonus at the end of the session.

The child's acquisition of tokens was plotted so that visual evidence of the reinforcers was available. The tokens could be used to purchase a variety of items. These items, chosen by the subject, could range in value from pennies to whatever the subject wished to work for. Records were kept of the tokens earned by S and of the manner in which the tokens were used.

Reading Materials

The reading material, as in the earlier study (Staats & Butterfield, 1965) was taken from the Science Research Associates (SRA) reading-kit materials, Reading Laboratories IA, IB, IC, and IIA. The SRA kits consist of stories developed for and grouped into grade levels. For the purpose of this study, stories were taken from the 1.2 (20 stories), 1.4 (60 stories), 1.7 (20 stories), 2.0 (32 stories), 2.3 (12 stories), 2.6 (12 stories), 3.0 (32 stories), 3.5 (32 stories), and 4.0 (10 stories) grade levels. Once a particular Reading Laboratory was selected for inclusion at a given grade level, all the stories at that grade level were presented in sequential order (with the exception of the 4.0 grade level, where only the first ten stories in Laboratory IIA were presented). The different numbers of lessons presented at each grade level were due to the use of different numbers of Reading Laboratories, in order to control somewhat the rate of introduction of new words.

Each story includes a series of questions which can be used to assess the reader's comprehension of the story. The reading training programme which again was that of the earlier study may be summarized as follows.

Vocabulary words. A running list was made of the new words that appeared in the series of stories. Each different form of a word was counted as a different word for this purpose; thus, *bring*, *brings*, and *bringing* were all counted as different words. The list finally included each different word that appeared in the stories, a total of 4253 words. From this list, the new vocabulary for each story was selected, and each word was typed on a separate three by five card.

The average number of new words introduced in each story was 18.5, the least number of new words being introduced in any one story being six, and the most being fifty. The new stories presenting over thirty new words occurred in the second half of the programme, after the children had already been presented a large number of lessons.

Oral reading materials. Each paragraph in the SRA stories was typed on a five by eight card. Each story could thus be presented to S paragraph by paragraph.

Silent-reading and comprehensive-question materials. Each SRA story and its comprehensive questions were typed on separate eight and a half by eleven sheets of white paper.

Procedure

Vocabulary presentation. The procedure for each story in the series commenced with the presentation of the new words introduced in that story. The words were presented individually on the cards, and S was asked to pronounce them. A correct response to a word-stimulus was eventually reinforced with a mid-value token. After a correct response to a word, the card was dropped from the group of cards yet to be presented. The S was instructed to indicate words that he did not know the meaning of, and this information was provided in such cases.

When an incorrect response to a word stimulus occurred, or when S gave no response, the instructional-technician gave the correct response. The S then repeated the word while looking at the stimulus word. However, the word card involved was returned to the group of cards still to be presented. A card was not dropped from the group until it was read correctly without prompting. After an error on a word stimulus, only a low-value token was given for finally reading the word correctly without prompting. The vocabulary-presentation phase of the training was continued until each word was read correctly without prompting.

Initially, the appropriate tokens were delivered immediately contingent upon each unprompted correct reading trial. However, by the end of the second week it was apparent that the instructional-technicians were having difficulty presenting materials, watching S, keeping data, and delivering tokens all at the same time. So at the beginning of the third week, all tokens were delivered at the end of each phase rather than after each reading response.

Oral reading. Upon completion of the vocabulary materials, each paragraph was individually presented to S in the order in which the paragraph occurred in the story. When correct reading responses were made to each word in the paragraph, a high-value token was given upon completion of the paragraph. When a paragraph contained errors, S was corrected, and he repeated the word correctly while looking at the word. The paragraph was put aside, and when the other paragraphs had been completed, the paragraph containing errors was again presented. The paragraph was repeated until it was read correctly in its entirety at which time a mid-value token was presented. When all paragraphs in a story had been completed correctly, the next phase of the training was begun.

When a few of the Ss had some difficulty in reading the words in sequential order, either failing to respond to one or more words in the sequence, or adding words for which no reading stimuli were presented, the instructional-technician would point to each word in turn and S would then read them. It was generally possible to drop this additional procedure later without any loss in the control over Ss' performance.

Silent reading and comprehensive questions. Following the oral reading, S was given the sheet containing the story. He was instructed to read the story silently, and he was told that it was important to read to understand the story so that he could answer the questions which would be presented later.

Initially, S was given reinforcement in the form of a yellow token on fifteen seconds variable interval schedule. That is, as long as S appropriately scanned the material he was given a mid-value token an average of every fifteen seconds. However, there was a great deal of variability in the abilities of the instructional-technicians to administer this type of schedule, and so at the beginning of the third week the procedure was changed such that four yellow tokens were delivered at the end of the silent reading of the story, regardless of the time needed to complete the task.

Upon completion of the story, *S* wrote his answers to the questions typed on a separate sheet and gave his answers to the instructional-technician. For each correct answer, *S* received a high-value token. For an answer with a spelling error, *S* was reinforced with a mid-value token when he had corrected the answer. For incorrect answers *S* had to re-read the appropriate paragraph, correct his answer, and he then received a low-value token.

Vocabularly review.   Some of the vocabulary words presented to *S* in the first phase of training were words he already could read. Many others, however, were words that the procedure was set up to teach. The oral-reading-phase performance indicated the level of *S*'s retention of the words he had learned and also provided further training trials on the words not already learned. A further assessment of *S*'s retention of the words that he did not know in the vocabulary training was made after each twenty stories of the SRA materials had been read. This test of individually presented words, for each story, was started immediately after completion of the twenty stories and constituted fairly long-term retention.

This test was also used as a review for *S*, and further training on the words was given. When *S* could not read a word, or missed one, he was prompted and had to correctly repeat the name of the word while looking at the word. This word-card was then put aside and presented later, at which time *S* was reinforced with a low-value token if he read it correctly. If not, the procedure was repeated until a correct unprompted trial occurred.

RESULTS AND CONCLUSIONS

Each of the eighteen subjects participated in the study over the period of the study with excellent cooperation, attention, and work behavior. In the original study, the juvenile delinquent subject made about 65,000 single word reading responses in forty hours of training. The mean number of hours of training in the present study was 38.2. During this period the mean number of word reading responses made by the subjects was 94,425.

The present sample of subjects included children with varying degrees of initial reading skill, as indicated by their ability to read the 100 individual words taken from the SRA materials in the way that has been described. Thus, the percentage of these words that could be read by the children prior to the training varied from a low of twenty-two per cent to a high of eighty-one per cent. In order better to see how the training affected the subjects as a function of their initial reading ability, some of the results to be presented will be grouped according to the level of the children's ability. Thus, the eighteen *S*s were grouped into three subgroups. The lowest had a mean percentage of reading the SRA words of 43.2 prior to the study. The mean IQ of these children on the Lorge–Thorndike Intelligence test was 71.9, ranging from fifty to ninety-one. The middle group had a mean percentage of 69.2 on the SRA words, and a mean IQ of 74.2 with a range from fifty-three to ninety-four. The high group had a mean percentage of 79.0 on the SRA words, and a mean IQ of 79.9, with a range of sixty-six to ninety-two.

The total number of words the child read during the training was tabulated. This included the words he read when singly presented on cards, the words he read aloud in the paragraph reading phase, the words he read in the silent reading phase, the words read in the comprehensive questions, as well as the words read in the vocabulary review. The cumulative record of the words read over the period of training for the three groups of *S*s is given in Fig. 1. In the original study of Staats & Butterfield the record produced indicated that the rate of reading accelerated slightly during the period of training even though the reading materials became steadily more difficult. A similar result is shown for the *S*s in the present study. (The later points on the curves, where indicated, do not include all the *S*s in the group, since some *S*s

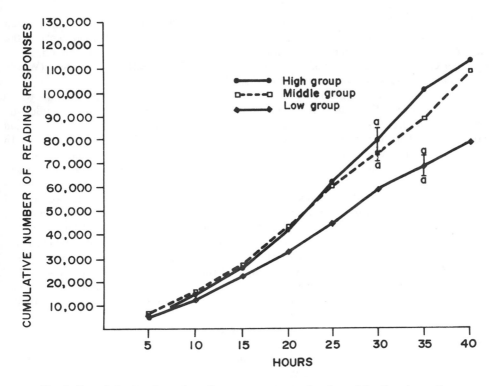

Fig. 1. Cumulative number of reading responses as a function of the time in reading training for low, middle, and high initial reading ability groups. The letter (a) on each curve represents the last point in which all *S*s in that group are represented.

did not read as many stories as others did.) The six *S*s with the highest reading ability show the greatest acceleration, the middle group the next highest, and the low group the least. This acceleration takes place even though the children advance from 1.2 grade reading materials to 3.5 grade level materials. It does appear, however, that the increase in difficulty does dampen the acceleration in reading rate of all the *S*s particularly those with low reading ability. In any event, as in the original study, the children's behavior of attending to the task and making the appropriate reading responses did not diminish throughout the period of training. Thus, the token reinforcement system employed was capable of maintaining the work behaviors of these children for a long period of time. During this time the attentional and cooperative behaviors instigated resulted in many, many, learning trials, a necessary aspect for the acquisition of achievement in any skill.

Records were kept of the number of words the children missed on first presentation, the number of these words which were then later missed in the oral reading of the paragraphs, as well as the number of the words originally missed that the child could not read on the review test presented at the later time. On the original study the juvenile delinquent missed 761 words on the first presentation, 585 (or about 77 per cent) of these were retained in the oral reading phase, and 430 (about 57 per cent) were retained in the review test when presented singly. The corresponding mean words missed on first presentation for the low ability group in the present study was 820.3. In the oral reading 686.5 (or 83.7 per cent) were retained. In the long-term retention test, where the words were presented singly, 433.5 (57.4 per cent) were retained. The performance of this group of *S*s was thus roughly comparable to that of the first subject. The middle ability group missed 535 words on first presentation, retained 483.8 (or 90.4 per cent) on second presentation, and retained 306.2 (or 69.1 per cent) on the long-term review test. The means for the high ability group were 425.2 first missed, 360.3 (or 84 per cent) retained on second test, and 291.0 (or 78.7 per cent) on review test. (Words from the last few sessions were not presented for long term review.)

Evidence indicated that the 100 word test taken from the SRA reading materials was a valid indicator of the *S*s' reading skill with the SRA materials. That is, the low, middle, and high groups on this measure (with original respective reading percentages of 43.2, 69.2, and 79.0) performed in that order of ability on the reading task itself, as indicated above. In addition, on the measure of the percentage of the words in the various stories that could be read on first presentation the means of the three groups were 67.7, 82.1, and 87.8 per cent.

In the original study there seemed to be some evidence that as the training progressed the subject missed fewer of the words on first presentation. This type of evidence would tend to indicate that the subject had been learning to sound out new words as a function of the training. Additional evidence (Staats, 1965) has shown that subjects "can" learn syllable reading units from training on whole word reading tasks. To test the possibility that improvement in sounding out new words occurred in the present study, the ratio of words missed the first time to the total presented was computed for each twenty stories presented. The results for the three groups are shown in Fig. 2. The later points on each curve do not include all the subjects in the group, since some *S*s did not read as many stories as others did. In any event, there does not appear to be evidence that the ratio decreased, but rather that it was constant throughout the training except for an increase in the ratio from the 1.2 grade level to the 1.4 grade level of the reading material. The question of whether phonetic reading skills emerge from this type of training may be considered to remain unanswered. More direct tests will probably be necessary.

One of the important aspects of the procedures involves the ratio of reinforcement for the reading responses. The procedures were designed to progressively reduce the amount of

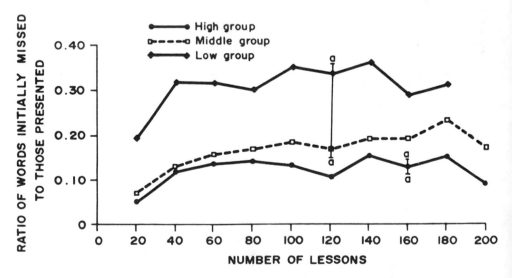

Fig. 2. The ratio of words missed upon initial presentation to the total number of words presented in the Individual Word Phase as a function of the number of SRA stories read for the three ability groups. The letter (a) on each curve represents the last point in which all *S*s in that group are represented.

reinforcement given per reading response as the training progressed or conversely to require more reading responses per unit of reinforcement. As was indicated in the original study, demonstration that this is possible in a long-term training programme has a number of important implications. Such a demonstration "is in part an answer to the question whether the use of extrinsic reinforcers in training will produce a child who is dependent upon these reinforcers" (Staats & Butterfield, 1965, p. 941).

Fig. 3 supports the original demonstration by showing that the ratio of the amount of reinforcement earned divided by the number of words read decreases as a function of number of training sessions. By the time sixty training sessions have been completed the children were receiving about one-fourth as much reinforcement for their reading behavior as they had at the beginning of the training. This was true of the three groups. This result is especially interesting in view of the acceleration of rate of reading response shown in Fig. 1. That is, in the period of time during which the reinforcement per reading response is cut in quarter, the rate of reading increases. Aside from its theoretical and practical implications for child learning, it is interesting to note that the result would be expected directly from basic laboratory research with lower organisms, on the effects of reinforcement schedules. Thus, it is important to see that the basic principles hold even in the context of such a complex and uniquely human behavior as reading.

As had been described, the test data concerning reading achievement appeared to be invalidated by the test-taking behavior of the children. In addition to that, midway through

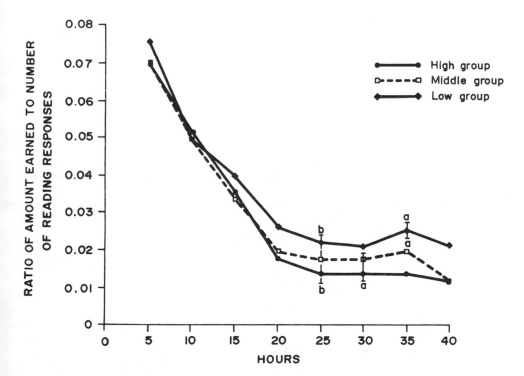

Fig. 3. Ratio of the monetary value of the tokens received divided by the number of reading responses made as a function of time in reading. The letter (a) on each ability group curve represents the last point in which all *S*s are represented, and the letter (b) indicates the time block in which the bonus was introduced for most *S*s.

the experiment special reading programmes were begun under the Elementary and Secondary Education Act Title I so that the control group could no longer be considered as such. The experiment, however, had been designed so that analyses of covariance could be made of the data. The main effects were the experimental treatment (experimental versus control) and the division into high, middle, and low groups on the basis of the first oral word reading (100 SRA words). The pre-tests were used as the covariates for the various post-test dependent variables. Although a detailed presentation of the design and analysis is not productive here, there are a few points that are relevant, as well as a few analyses of additional measures.

First, the analysis indicated that the test to be the main measure of reading achievement, the Iowa Test of Basic Abilities, was indeed not producing reliable results. There was not even a significant relationship between the Ss' pre- and post-test results, indicating that the Ss were randomly scoring their test items. It is also interesting to note that the I.T.B.A. was not related to the oral reading of the SRA words, a measure with considerable face validity as well as empirical validity in the study. There was a significant relationship between the pre- and post-test performance on the Lorge–Thorndike. However, there was no significant effect of the experimental treatment as compared to the control group's results. The "California Achievement Test" was given twice (alternate forms) in the post-test sessions in an effort to salvage the test results. There was not a significant relationship to the pre-test I.T.B.A. however, when the test was taken without reinforcers and only a significant relationship (at the 0.01 level) of the vocabulary part with the pre-test I.T.B.A. when the test was taken with reinforcers. However, the analysis of covariance did not reveal any effect on the "C.A.T." of the experimental treatment, when the pre-test I.T.B.A. was used as the covariate. The C.A.T. vocabulary part taken with no reinforcement was significantly related (0.01 level) to the oral reading measures (SRA words), however, the reading comprehension part was not. Under the reinforcement procedures both parts of the C.A.T. were significantly related to the pre-test oral reading measure, the vocabulary at the 0.001 level and the reading part at the 0.05 level.

The individually administered oral reading measure composed of the 100 SRA words appeared to be a reliable measure to the extent that the pre- and post-test measures were significantly related (at the 0.001 level). Furthermore, this measure did show a significant effect (at the 0.01 level) of the experimental treatment. The experimental groups subjects improved more on their ability to read the 100 words than did the control group. The experimental group had an original mean score of 63.8 on this measure and post-test score of 76.1; corresponding scores for the control group were 63.6 and 69.2.

Fourteen of the eighteen control Ss improved upon their oral reading, probably, at least in part, as a result of the special training programmes to which they also had been exposed, some of which used SRA materials. It is interesting to note that although each of the experimental Ss improved in this measure of reading ability, some by large amounts, the greatest improvement was shown by the Ss who were originally lowest in the oral reading ability. The mean improvement for the low, medium and high ability subgroups in the experimental group was respectively 18.3, 8.8, and 9.8. The mean improvement for all the groups combined was 12.2 words.

Another analysis of variance was conducted to analyze the effect of introducing the reinforcement contingencies upon the test-taking behaviors, and the test results, of the Ss for the California Achievement Test (both vocabulary and reading sections) and the Lorge–Thorndike on the verbal, non-verbal, and total scores. The main effects were the Experimental Treatment, Previous Oral Reading Ability (that is, the three groups, low, middle, and high) and the Reinforcement Contingency Condition. The results showed that the reinforcement procedure for the test administration produced significant effects upon the California Achievement Test. On the vocabulary the Ss advanced from a mean of 23.56 under no reinforcement to a mean of 26.00 with the reinforcement contingencies. This result was significant at the 0.05 level as was the next result. On the reading comprehension part the *S*s advanced from a mean of 35.53–38.50. The results for the Lorge–Thorndike were: on the verbal an advance from a mean of 67.83–71.36, on the non-verbal an advance from a mean of 80.89–85.89, on the total IQ an advance from 74.36–78.62. These three results were significant at the 0.001 level.

This improvement occurred even though seven fewer items, on the average for the two tests, were answered by the *S*s under the reinforcement contingency conditions. Thus, the children's scores under the no-reinforcement conditions were spuriously inflated since some of those seven additional items would have been correct by chance. At any rate, it may be concluded that the children's test behavior and test results were affected, and in a positive direction, when they were reinforced for correct test-taking behavior and punished for random responding.

Two types of instructional-technicians were employed in the study and it is of some interest to compare the results of their subjects for possible differences. As measured by the pre- and post-test on the 100-word oral reading measure the mean gain in words read was 12.56 for the adult-volunteer instructional-technicians and 12.11 for the highschool-student instructional-technicians. Thus, neither group of instructional-technicians was differentially effective.

DISCUSSION

The procedure and the reinforcer system appear to be generally functional. The attention, attendance, cooperation, and diligent work of the various children was maintained in good strength throughout the length of the study. In fact these behavior patterns appeared to be gaining strength. Thus, the methods have proved successful with an incorrigible juvenile delinquent and with the present group of eighteen children which included mentally retarded children and emotionally disturbed children. In addition, the procedures have also been tested with the same success in clinical work, with several psychiatrically disturbed children, one of whom was diagnosed as schizoid, as well as with culturally deprived problem learners, emotionally-disturbed children, and younger children with learning problems (this research which will be mentioned further on). Thus, the present study is one of the few in the field of behavior modification that has involved a substantial number of subjects treated for the same behavioral deficit with the same reinforcement system.

Moreover, not only was the behavior of these children very appropriate in the learning situation, but the behavioral measures indicated that the children covered a great deal of material and learned a number of new words. A mean of 593.5 words were presented that the children did not at first know. After training, in the long-term retention measure, the children retained a mean of 70.9 per cent of the words. This represents a straightforward indication that the children (including seven children in classes for the retarded) were learning the material on which they were being trained. In addition, the curves that indicate the rate at which the children were reading was accelerating even though the difficulty of the material was increasing.

These findings were supplemented by the differences between the experimental and control subjects on their ability to read the 100 SRA words when individually presented to each child. The experimental group increased in this index of reading ability to an extent that was significantly greater than the increase of the control group. Thus, when the measurement of reading ability was controlled and directly observed, and when the reading stimuli were among those on which the experimental group had received training, the affect of the experimental treatment was evident. This occurred even though the control group had begun to receive special training in reading during the study.

However, the standard test results did not show a difference between the pre- and post-test measures, for the experimental over the control group. Several alternative interpretations of this lack of effect on the tests are available. The training materials may not produce general skills that transfer to other tasks, such as taking an achievement test. If that was the case it would be an indictment against the SRA materials, at least when presented in the present fashion. This interpretation is difficult to accept, however. Provided the vocabulary included in the materials has generality, learning the words should by itself improve the child's reading ability for any verbal material that included the words. Nevertheless, it is possible that longer training would be necessary to be reflected on the tests, that the reading materials used might have been too elementary for any of these subjects.

Another possibility is that the tests themselves were insensitive dependent variables in the present instance. For example, the tests might have been too difficult. It is interesting to note that the California Achievement Test, but not the Iowa Test of Basic Abilities, was significantly related to the oral reading scores. Perhaps if the more elementary C.A.T. had been given in the pre-test instead of the I.T.B.A., the experimental effect might have been shown. It is even more likely, however, that the test-taking behavior of these children was at fault. The children all had long histories of unsuccessful (which means unreinforced) test-taking. It would be expected under those circumstances that the behavior would deteriorate and be replaced by less effortful behavior that is, indiscriminate marking of items. This weakness would have been amplified by the use of achievement tests that were too difficult for the children, since it would prevent the children from obtaining reinforcement at the time of taking the test. It should be noted in the Staats & Butterfield study, where the tests did reflect the success of the training, the testing was individually administered rather than a group procedure, which guaranteed better test-taking behavior to some extent, and the tests were easier and contained fewer items (both of which would enhance the reinforcement properties of the testing situation). As will be discussed, variations in test behavior because of variations in motivational variables are a general problem in clinical assessment. As has been noted, the special training given to the control group children probably helped obscure the positive affects of the experimental treatment.

In any event, these are matters for further research, some of which is now underway. The first two authors have a study now in progress in which the tests and testing circumstances have been improved. The study involves culturally-deprived children who are more homogeneously low in their reading deficits. The instructional-technicians are drawn from the same population as the subjects, except they are literate and have graduated from highschool. Adrian Van Mondfrans and the first author are also extending the methods and materials to younger children (4th, 5th, and 6th graders), with and without extrinsic reinforcement. And Judy McBurney and the first author have a study in which emotionally disturbed children are being individually tested in greater detail during the course of the treatment. Although these studies have not yet been completed, it is again evident that the procedures and reinforcer system work universally well with various children with various types of problems.

The reinforcement system used in the Staats & Butterfield study as well as the present study was designed so that the amount of reinforcement given per unit of behavior decreases over the period of the training. Thus, during the training each child was gradually getting less reinforcement for his reading. Nevertheless, his behavior was maintained in somewhat better strength as the training progressed. This result is in part an answer to the frequent question concerning the use of extrinsic reinforcement in child training, that is, that the child may become dependent upon the reinforcers. It may be suggested that sophisticated methods may be designed to produce the desirable behavior without lasting dependence upon an artificial system of reinforcement, although the full topic cannot be treated herein.

There are several points concerning the supervision of the training that should be mentioned. The procedure was set up so that the therapy-technicians were observed from time to time (especially in the beginning) in a systematic manner for the first, second, and fourth authors. This was done in general to supervise the correct application of the procedure. In addition, the monitoring provided observations concerning the information needs of the therapy-technicians as well as a means of assessing the manner in which the procedures and materials functioned with various subjects. In one case (which was unique) the first author observed practices of a therapy-technician in the first couple of weeks of training that were leading to deterioration in the training interaction. This led to replacement of this therapy-technician and to additional instructions to the other therapy-technicians. That is, they were instructed that they were not to urge the child to do better, or to expect better or faster performance in any case. The reinforcer system and materials were to take care of the child's good work, attention, and learning. When a child attended and worked well he was performing maximally regardless of his errors or rate of reading. The therapy-technicians were instructed that they could give positive social approval, but no aversive stimulation was to be given of either a direct kind or by implication through saying such things as "You can do better than that," "Try harder," "You knew that before," and so on.

The child who had been subjected to this type of urging, which was administered with very good intent and was so natural that it was not noticed by the other supervisors, was becoming more disturbed and hostile in action and difficult to control as the training progressed. (As it happened he was a child with acting-out problems.) He stated he was going to withdraw from the programme. When the difficulty was discovered, the second and third authors alternated as the therapy-technicians until another volunteer adult was obtained and trained. When the aversive training circumstances were removed by this adjustment, the child's behavior and learning improved quickly and he continued in the training in a normal manner throughout the experiment. It is suggested that an effective way to apply the present procedures is to have a child-clinical psychologist set up and supervise the programme, having direct training and supervisory contact with the therapy-technicians. Larger programmes could also be conducted in which the child-clinical psychologist had adjunct professional personnel (such as social workers, probation officers, prison personnel, special education teachers, and so on) who supervised the therapy-technicians. In any event, it would seem necessary to have the specialist in child learning and behavior problems in a position to handle the special problems of the children, or the therapy-technicians, which could be expected to arise on occasion.

An aspect not insignificant to the present treatment is its economy. Although a professional trained at the doctoral level, or even a lesser trained professional, cannot provide long-term individual treatment to children, it would be economical to have a professional train and supervise therapy-technicians in specific treatment responsibilities. Related to this is the cost of the treatment itself. In the first study the four and a half months of training cost $20.31 in reinforcers. This was closely paralleled in the present study. That is, the mean cost for the children over a similar period of time was $22.29. In many cases this would be a very minimal price to pay to insure that ordinarily untrainable children would not only be amenable to various types of training, but would also work diligently and learn well.

The reinforcement procedure which was introduced to produce better test taking behavior also has general significance. The children who had been randomly scoring items in the group testing procedure began to peruse the items more carefully under the extrinsic reinforcement procedure. The results showed that when the good test taking behavior was reinforced and poor test taking behavior punished the desired behavior increased in strength to a statistically significant extent. When reinforced, the children scored better on the tests even while answering fewer test items. This has theoretical implications; for differences in "motivation" are not usually controlled when testing different groups of subjects, even though there are many categories of disturbed individuals whose poor motivational circumstances would no doubt adversely affect their test results. For example, there are many, many studies that compare patient populations, such as schizophrenics, with normals on some cognitive (or other) task or test. The differences obtained in such studies could well be affected by differences in reinforcement variables and thus in the lesser extent to which the attention, cooperation, and diligent work behavior of the schizophrenics were maintained. It may be suggested that any group comparisons on tests or learning tasks made for theoretical purposes should take into account likely differences in behavior as a function of motivational differences. The present results suggest, of course, that this source of variation could be controlled by insuring that the subjects of the experiment are reinforced for good test-taking behavior.

These results also have similar significance for diagnostic testing. There are many cases in which test results are part of diagnosis and treatment and where the test-taking behavior of the subject prevents accurate appraisal because of motivational deficits. It is suggested that more valid test results could be obtained through the use of reinforcement to strengthen "good test behavior." If poor test performance is a function of motivational variables, it is important to know the source of the difficulty. The first author plans additional research in these areas of study.

It is suggested that the present general procedures are ready to be extended widely in research-treatment studies in clinical work with children with various problems. The methods have been tested sufficiently with various types of children to indicate that children who are otherwise untrainable will respond appropriately to the present type of training situation. When the procedures can be administered in a standard manner, subprofessional therapy-technicians can be employed. It may be suggested that clinical psychology must begin through research to develop procedures that can be administered by adjunct personnel in standard treatment programmes. The clinical psychologist would then set up the treatment programme and supervise the therapy and be an expert in dealing with any special problems that arise. Research to develop training procedures by which to treat deficits in various complex adjustive repertoires in patients who under traditional procedures are untrainable may be seen as an important task of learning oriented clinical psychology.

Clinical psychology in following the "illness model" that has pervaded the field of "mental health" has tended to concentrate on the intrapsychic life of the child, his gross social-emotional adjustment, and grossly aberrant behavior, sometimes neglecting consideration of his cognitive learning. If cognitive training is regarded "as it is in many mental health programmes, as something that can wait until the child gets better" (Hobbs, 1967, p. 1111), the disturbed child can develop severe cognitive deficits that will preclude later adjustment regardless of any diminution of other difficulties. The complex cognitive skills the child must learn require long periods of training and innumerable training trials. It is suggested that clearing up some other form of behavioral disturbance will not provide the child with those skills as one might erroneously assume from a "mental block" interpretation of cognitive deficit.

"Underachievement in school is the single most common characteristic of emotionally disturbed children" (Hobbs, 1967, p. 1110). It may be added that perhaps the most important significance of emotional disturbance in children is in the manner in which the difficulty prevents normal social learning, cognitive learning, sensory-motor learning, emotional learning, and so on. In general, it is thus suggested that clinical psychology in developing a "learning model" of human problems and their treatment must become interested in these problems for the part they play in producing repertoirial deficits. In addition, emphasis must be given to the development of methods of treatment of these deficits, methods which diverge from traditional psychotherapy procedures and involve an additional role for the clinical psychologist.

Acknowledgments. This study was made possible by the help and cooperation of Robert Gilberts, Superintendent of Madison Public Schools, and the principals of the schools involved, Homer Winger, Douglas Muller, Jack R. Stickels, George Maki, and Roger Cerutti. Mrs. Alice Inada of the University of Hawaii aided in the preparation of the manuscript. The study was conducted under the support of the U.S. Office of Education Center No. C-03, Contract OE 5-10-154.

REFERENCES

Hobbs, N. (1967) Helping disturbed children: Psychological and ecological strategies. *Am. Psychol.*, **21**, 1105–1115.

Rachman, S. (1962) Learning theory and child psychology. *J. Child Psychol. Psychiat.*, **3**, 149–163.

Staats, A. W. (1965) A case in and a strategy for the extension of learning principles to the problems of human behavior. In *Research in behavior modification* (Eds. Krasner, L. and Ullmann, L. P.). Holt, Rinehart & Winston, New York.

Staats, A. W. (1966) An integrated-functional learning approach to complex human behavior. Technical Rep. No. 28 between the Office of Naval Research and Arizona State University, 1965b. Reprinted in large part in *Problem solving: Research, method and theory* (Ed. Kleinmuntz, B.). Wiley, New York.

Staats, A. W. *Learning, language and cognition.* Holt, Rinehart & Winston, New York, 1968.

Staats, A. W. *Integrated-functional learning theory and clinical psychology; I. Human motivation and conditioning therapies.* Mimeo prepublication.

Staats, A. W. & Butterfield, W. H. (1965) Treatment of nonreading in a culturally-deprived juvenile delinquent: An application of reinforcement principles. *Child Dev.* **36**, 925–942.

Staats, A. W., Finley, J. R., Minke, K. A. & Wolf, M. (1964) Reinforcement variables in the control of unit reading responses. *J. exp. Analysis Behav.*, **7**, 139–149.

Staats, A. W., Minke, K. A., Finley, J. R., Wolf, M. M. & Brooks, L. O. (1964) A reinforcer system and experimental procedure for the laboratory study of reading acquisition. *Child Dev.*, **35**, 209–231.

Staats, A. W. & Staats, C. K. (1963) *Complex human behavior.* Holt, Rinehart & Winston, New York.

Staats, A. W., Staats, C. K., Schutz, R. E. & Wolf, M. (1962) The conditioning of reading responses utilizing "extrinsic" reinforcers. *J. exp. Analysis Behav.*, **5**, 33–40.

Whitlock, S. C. (1966) Note on reading acquisition: An extension of laboratory principles. *J. exp. Child Psychol.*, **3**, 83–85.

Effects of Teacher Attention and a Token Reinforcement System in a Junior High School Special Education Class*

MARCIA BRODEN, R. VANCE HALL, ANN DUNLAP
and ROBERT CLARK†

Abstract: Teacher attention and a token reinforcement system were used to bring about control in a disruptive junior high school special education classroom. Individual and group study levels were recorded during a baseline period. Subsequent experimental periods employing teacher attention and/or a token point system increased study levels and decreased disruptive behaviors of class members. Reinforcement of appropriate behaviors was withdrawn during short reversals producing lowered study rates. Reinstatement of contingencies again resulted in increased study levels.

A series of studies carried out in nursery schools (Harris, Wolf & Baer, 1964), special education classes (Hall & Broden, 1967; Zimmerman & Zimmerman, 1962), and regular public schools (Hall, Lund & Jackson, 1968; Hall, Panyan, Rabon & Broden, 1968; Thomas, Becker & Armstrong, 1968) have demonstrated that contingent teacher attention could be effective in increasing appropriate classroom behavior.

Similarly, token reinforcement systems backed up by food, field trips, toys, money, and grades were demonstrated to be effective in increasing academic behaviors of pupils in special education programmes including classrooms for the retarded (Birnbrauer, Wolf, Kidder & Tague, 1965), remedial classrooms for poverty area elementary age children (Wolf, Giles & Hall, 1968), and for elementary special education pupils (McKenzie, Clark, Wolf, Kothera & Benson, 1968; O'Leary & Becker, 1967).

With the exception of the study by Hall, Panyan, Rabon and Broden (1968), however, these studies were carried out by experienced teachers and dealt with preschool and elementary age children. Those using token reinforcement systems used reinforcers primarily extrinsic to the classroom, and most often there was more than one teacher available to conduct the class and carry out the experimental procedures.

In contrast, the present study was carried out in a public junior high school special education classroom by a first year teacher without prior teaching experience. When systematic

---

*Reprinted from *Exceptional Children*, 1970, **36**, 341–349. Copyright 1970 with permission from the Council for Exceptional Children and Marcia Broden.

†Marcia Broden is Research Assistant, Bureau of Child Research, University of Kansas, Lawrence; R. Vance Hall is Research Associate, Bureau of Child Research, and Associate Professor of Education and Human Development and Family Life, University of Kansas, Lawrence, and Coordinator, Juniper Gardens Children's Project, Kansas City; and Ann Dunlap is Teacher and Robert Clark is Principal, Bonner Springs Junior High School, Bonner Springs, Kansas. This research was partially supported by the National Institute of Child Health and Human Development (HD 03144 01-02) and the Office of Economic Opportunity (CG8180 to the Bureau of Child Research, University of Kansas). Reprints may be obtained from R. Vance Hall, 2021 N. 3rd Street, Kansas City, Kansas 66101.

teacher attention to appropriate behavior proved to be limited in its effect, a token reinforcement system backed by reinforcers available to most junior high school teachers was used to reduce extremely disruptive behavior and to increase appropriate study behavior.

SUBJECTS AND SETTING

The subjects were thirteen seventh and eighth grade students, eight boys and five girls, in a special education class in Bonner Springs Junior High School, Bonner Springs, Kansas. All students were several years behind in at least one major academic area and had other problems, including severe reading deficits, almost incoherent speech, emotional instability, and acts of delinquency. Some specific problem behaviors involved cursing the teacher; refusing to obey teacher requests or to do assignments; throwing pencils, pens, or paper; fighting; chasing each other about the room; and eating a variety of snacks.

The inappropriate behaviors described had persisted through the first four months of school although the teacher had used generally accepted methods for maintaining classroom control, including some praise for appropriate behavior and reprimands or a trip to the counselor or principal's office for misconduct.

The class met for five periods of the eight period day. The entire class was present for the first, fifth, and eight periods. Only the seven seventh graders were present for the second and sixth periods, and only the six eighth graders were present during the third and seventh periods.

Observations

The system used was essentially that developed by Broden (1968) for recording classroom study behavior. Daily observations were made by an observer equipped with a recording sheet and stop-watch. Data were recorded on the recording sheet at five-second intervals. At the five-second mark the behavior of the first pupil was recorded, at the ten-second mark the behavior of the second pupil was recorded, at the fifteen-second mark that of the third student, and so on until every student had been observed once; then the sequence was begun again. Thus the behavior of a different pupil was recorded every five seconds on a consecutive rotation basis.

As is shown in Fig. 1, the recording sheet was divided into triple rows of squares with a different pupil's name entered at the top of each column of three vertical squares. The middle row of squares was used to record whether or not the pupil was studying. An "S" (for study) was recorded if the pupil were attending to or oriented toward the appropriate book when he had been assigned reading to do, if he were attending to the teacher or another pupil who was speaking during class discussions, if he were writing spelling words during spelling period, or if he were otherwise engaged in a teacher assigned task. All other behaviors were designated as "N" except for the specific nonstudy behavior "out of seat" which was recorded as "O".

The top row of squares was used to record verbalizations by the teacher to subject or to the class. A "T" designated teacher verbalization directed to an individual pupil during that five-second interval.

The bottom row of squares was used to record pupil verbalizations. A "V" designated verbalizations recognized by the teacher.

Observations lasted from thirty to forty minutes during any given period.

Computing the percentage of the total five second intervals in which "S" had been recorded revealed the class study rate. It was also possible to compute individual study rates by dividing the number of "S" intervals for the pupil by the total number of intervals that the individual

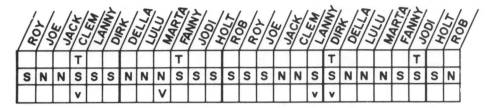

ROY	JOE	JACK	CLEM	LANNY	DIRK	DELLA	LULU	MARTA	FANNY	JODI	HOLT	ROB	ROY	JOE	JACK	CLEM	LANNY	DIRK	DELLA	LULU	MARTA	FANNY	JODI	HOLT	ROB
		T				T									T					T					
S	N	N	S	S	S	N	N	S	S	S	S	S	S	N	N	S	S	N	N	N	S	S	S	S	N
		v				V								v	v										

Row 1: T Teacher verbalization directed to pupil.
Row 2: S Study behavior.   N Nonstudy behavior.
Row 3: V Appropriate pupil verbalization.   v Inappropriate verbalization.

Fig. 1. Observer recording sheet and symbol key.

pupil was observed and multiplying the result by 100. Thus both class and individual study rates could be obtained.

Reliability checks were made periodically throughout the study. A second observer made independent, simultaneous observations. This record was compared with that of the primary observer, interval by interval. The percentage of agreement was then computed. Observer agreement for this study ranged from eighty-three to ninety-eight per cent.

EXPERIMENT 1

Initially, daily observations were begun during the fifth period when all thirteen pupils were present. Assigned study tasks included reading, writing, and participation in class discussions.

During the first (baseline) seven days of observation the teacher was asked to conduct class in her usual manner and to ignore the observer. Care was taken not to mention possible experimental procedures. Pupils were told someone would be coming in at various times to assist the teacher. All contact between the observer and teacher or pupils was avoided during class sessions.

Figure 2 presents the data for the seven baseline sessions. The broken horizontal line indicates that the mean rate of study behavior was twenty-nine per cent. During baseline sessions the teacher was observed giving attention to both study and nonstudy behaviors.

Prior to the eighth day of observation a conference was held with the teacher. She was shown the baseline study data and was asked to begin giving attention to study behavior only and to ignore all nonstudying. During the next eleven days the teacher went to pupils who were studying and commented on their good study behavior and work, called only on pupils who raised their hands, and complimented the entire group when all were studying quietly.

As can be seen in the Social Reinforcement$_1$ phase of Fig. 2, this procedure resulted in an increase in study behavior to a mean rate of fifty-seven per cent. Although an improvement over baseline rates, there were still frequent outbursts of inappropriate verbalizations, out of seat, and other disruptive behaviors. Therefore a new contingency for appropriate study was introduced.

During the next eighteen sessions a kitchen timer was placed on the teacher's desk and set to go off at random intervals averaging eight minutes. Pupils who were in their seats and quiet when the timer sounded were given a mark on a card taped to their desk tops. Each mark earned allowed them to leave one minute earlier for lunch. Teacher attention for study was continued during this phase.

As can be seen in the Timer₁ phase of Fig. 2, an immediate increase in study behavior resulted. Beginning in the twenty-fifth session ("Quiet Entire Interval" in Fig. 2) pupils were required to be quiet during the entire interval between timer rings in order to receive a mark. Beginning in the thirty-first session marks (grades) were continued as before, but a grade of E (excellent) was also given if the pupil had been engaging in study behavior. These conditions seemed to have little additional effect on study level.

The mean study rate for the entire Timer₁ phase was seventy-four per cent, and according to the subjective judgments of the teacher and observer there was noticeably less disruptive behavior.

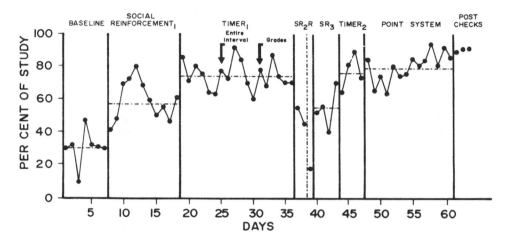

Fig. 2. A record of fifth period study behavior during Baseline₁, Social Reinforcement₁, Timer₁, Social Reinforcement₂ (SR₂), Reversal (R), Social Reinforcement₃ (SR₃), Timer₂, Point System, and Post Check conditions.

In order to see if the reinforcement procedures were the primary factors in increasing study, a brief return to prior conditions was made. For two days the timer early dismissal contingency was removed and only social reinforcement for study was given. This resulted in a drop in study behavior to fifty-five per cent the first day and to forty-five per cent the second (Social Reinforcement₂). The following day (Session 39) social reinforcement for study was also withdrawn. The teacher attended only to nonstudy behavior and ignored study behavior. The complete reversal of procedures resulted in a breakdown of study behavior and almost complete disruption of the class. As can be seen in Fig. 2 (R—Reversal) the study level during this one day reversal was only eighteen per cent.

During the next phase (Social Reinforcement₃) the teacher again attended to study behavior and ignored nonstudy. The level rose to fifty-five per cent. During the next four days the timer and marks for early lunch dismissal plus grades for study were reinstituted. Under these conditions (Timer₂) the mean study level was seventy-six per cent.

Beginning in Session 48, the timer condition was discontinued and pupils were put on a token point system described in Experiment II. The data presented in the Point System phase of Fig. 2 indicate that the higher study levels established with the timer were not only maintained but also slightly increased under the token point system. In fact, the mean study level rose to ninety per cent.

Postchecks taken over the next month and a half after conclusion of daily monitoring indicated that the higher study levels were maintained through the remainder of the school

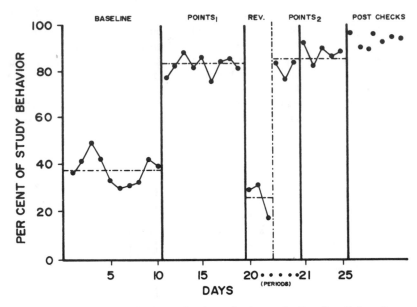

Fig. 3. A record of study behavior during the entire day, under Baseline, Points, Reversal (Rev.), Points₂ and Post Check conditions. Post Checks were taken periodically during the final six weeks of school after termination of regular observations.

year despite the fact the teacher was not informed prior to observation time when these checks would occur.

EXPERIMENT II

After a few days of higher study levels achieved by the procedures described above, the teacher and principal concurred in their judgment that pupil behavior during fifth period was indeed under much better control. However, they reported that the higher study rates had not transferred to the other five daily class periods. Therefore, an attempt to increase study during these periods also was made.

First, observations were made in order to determine the actual level of study during these five other periods. Nineteen thirty-minute observations were made on ten different days. Although the mean number of observations was a little less than two per day, the number on any one day ranged from one to all five (the number monitored on Days 7 and 8). As can be seen in Fig. 3 the mean levels of study for the ten days of observation ranged from thirty-three to forty-seven per cent. The mean baseline level as indicated by the dotted horizontal line was thirty-nine per cent.

Following baseline a token reinforcement system was instituted. A point system using a combination of available privileges and punishments was selected. (These periods were not followed by lunch and therefore earlier dismissal for lunch could not be utilized as it had been for period five.)

Each pupil was given a copy of the point system values similar to that shown in Table 1.

The "Earn Points" section was comprised of items suggested by the teacher, principal, and observer as desirable pupil behaviors. Earn Points were assigned so that a pupil could accumulate about twenty points per class period by engaging in reasonably appropriate behav-

Table 1. Point system.

Earn Points
5	in seat
5	quiet
5	doing assignment
2	extra credit (after regular assignment is complete)
3	an "A" on an assigned task
2	a "B" on an assigned task
1	a "C" on an assigned task
0	a "D" on an assigned task

Minus Points
15	out of seat without permission
1	talking out of turn: hand is not raised, teacher hasn't called on you
20	out of the room without permission
5	incomplete assignment (per period)
3	namecalling, swearing
20	throwing, hitting
20	arguing with the teacher
20	teacher must tell you more than once to stop

Spend Points
50	five minute pass to the rest room
50	permission to go five minutes early to lunch
10	permission to get out of your seat for one minute
50	permission to move your desk for one period
100	permission to move your desk for one day
300	permission to move your desk permanently
20	pass to get a drink of water
10	permission to talk to another person for five minutes
50	Friday snack
400	field trip
20	nonacademic activities approved by the teacher such as knitting, puzzles, games, records.

To Earn Off Minus Points
1	stay after school (per minute)
1	five earned positive points (earned off one minus point)
*	teacher assigned academic task
*	the teacher determines the task and the point value

ior such as remaining in his seat and being quiet. (Pupils were given the option of when and for what they would spend the points earned.)

The "Spend Points" section was comprised of activities and privileges which included those suggested by the pupils when they were asked, "What would you like to do if you had one free period?" Other Spend Point items were recommended by the teacher, principal, and the observer as probable reinforcers which could be administered within existing school policy. Spend Points were assigned so that behaviors thought to be highly desired were more costly than less desired ones.

The "Minus Points" section was comprised of undesirable pupil behaviors. Minus Points were assigned values so that the most disruptive behaviors cost the most. Pupils who accumulated twenty or more minus points were required to stay after school for one and a half hours on Thursday afternoon, which was the schoolwide detention period. Minus points could also be bought off by Earn Points at a ratio of five earned points to one minus point.

The teacher kept account of points during the period on a form at her desk which listed all pupils and had columns for posting point totals earned, spent, or lost. Point totals were posted on the chalkboard at the end of each period and pupils could see how many Earn Points and how many Minus Points each had acquired.

The results of instituting the point system were immediate and dramatic. As can be seen in the Points$_1$ phase of Fig. 3, the mean class study rate rose to eighty-three per cent on the first day. Study was maintained at high levels throughout the Points$_1$ phase of the experiment.

This increase in study level was recorded even though three pupils argued that it was childish, stated that they would refuse to cooperate, would quit school, and would complain to the principal and counselor. These remarks were largely ignored and the second day, two of the three showed increased study rates. Over the next four days the third objector, Rob, became extremely disruptive. He cursed the teacher, erased the board, tore up assignments, left the room, fought with other pupils, and said he wouldn't work and that no one could make him do it. When he was told to go to his seat or to the office he refused. Under the point system he soon accumulated 512 minus points and 19 positive points. By the fourth day other class members were spending increasing time watching Rob and laughing at his antics. Wolf, Risley & Mees (1964) had demonstrated that isolation procedures could be used effectively to reduce tantrum behaviors in a preschool child. Since much of Rob's behavior resembled tantrums these procedures were explained to both the teacher and the principal and a modified version of isolation was decided upon. It was agreed that if Rob refused to obey the teacher's direction to be quiet or sit down he would be sent immediately to the office. Unlike other times he had been sent there, he was not to be allowed back into the classroom until he had stated that he would be quiet and stay in his seat.

During the first period of the fifth day Rob refused to obey a teacher direction to be quiet and was sent directly to the principal's office. To reduce the chance that office procedures would reinforce him, the principal had an area screened off so that the student could not see who entered the office or what they were doing. He was not given work to do. He remained there until the end of the school day. The next day when he arrived at school he requested that he be returned to class and stated that he would stay in his seat and be quiet. When he returned to class his talking and out of seat behaviors decreased and his study behaviors increased. From that point on Rob presented no particular problem and obeyed the teacher. Though he refused to study for a time, he did begin to read a library book, then began to do individual work, and finally began to participate in group discussions. He began accumulating earn points and working off the minus points. He freely spent points, seldom accumulating enough for a field trip. By the end of school, however, he was able to participate in a field trip and an auction which was held to use up surplus earn points.

After nine days of increased study under the point system a reversal procedure was instituted. The experimenters agreed to allow reinstitution of the point system immediately if class behavior deteriorated to former levels and the teacher seemed to be losing control. It was thought that the effect of reversal might be observable over a three- or four-day period.

Reversal conditions were begun during first period of Day 20. The pupils were told that the point system was no longer in effect and the teacher discontinued giving attention for appropriate study although she provided verbal reprimands for nonstudy behaviors.

The data for Day 20 are shown on a period by period basis in Fig. 3 (Reversal). Study dropped to twenty-nine per cent in the first period. Second period it was thirty-one per cent and third period it dropped to sixteen per cent. Because of the extremely chaotic situation and the prior agreement to discontinue reversal if control was lost, the point system was put back into effect during the fourth period. As can be seen in Fig. 3 this resulted in a dramatic return to high study rates in the final three class periods of the day.

Period by period observations during the next five days showed that the mean study rate was above eighty per cent.

Observations taken intermittently beginning two weeks later showed that over the next one and a half months of the remainder of the school year, high study rates were being maintained under the point system (*see* Post Checks, Figs. 2 and 3).

The high Post Check rate (90 per cent) was maintained even though the system was changed so that Minus Points were subtracted from earned points on a one to one basis in the interest of simplifying the record keeping system.

The data indicated that in addition to study behavior, inappropriate talking and the number of times pupils were out of their seats were affected by the experimental procedures.

During baseline, inappropriate verbalizations were recorded in eighty-four per cent of the observed intervals. Under Points$_1$ conditions in appropriate talking dropped to ten per cent. It rose to forty-four per cent during Reversal. It dropped to five per cent when the point system was reinstated and was at seven per cent during the Post Check period.

Pupils were out of their seats an average of seventy seconds per period during baseline. When the point system was instituted the mean rate was ten seconds per period. In the brief and chaotic three period Reversal phase the time out of seats rose to mean rate of 215 seconds per period. Out of seats time returned to ten seconds per period during the Points$_2$ and Post Check phases. These data indicated that control of these specific inappropriate behaviors as well as increases in study had been achieved.

INDIVIDUAL DATA

Since a record was kept of which student was being observed during each five second interval it was possible to compute individual study rates for each experimental condition by dividing the number of study intervals by the total number of intervals that particular individual was observed and multiplying by 100.

An analysis of the data revealed that there was considerable individual variation in study rates and in the effects of the various experimental conditions on individuals. During the fifth period baseline phase, for example, study levels ranged from eleven to sixty-two per cent. Although teacher attention was effective in increasing study for all pupils, it was much more effective for some than for others. For instance, one girl's study level increased from fourteen to sixty-four per cent while one boy's study increased only from twelve to eighteen per cent. Similarly, though the Timer$_1$ condition backed by early dismissal for lunch resulted in further increases in study for all other pupils, it resulted in an actual decrease in study level for one.

Reversal effects varied from pupil to pupil also. During the reversal phase all showed decreased study levels, although study for six students remained at levels substantially higher than baseline rates while almost no study was recorded for the three pupils who had the lowest baseline study rates.

An analysis of the data for the point system also showed variations in study levels. Marked increases in study levels over baseline were achieved for all pupils under the points system. All pupils showed a marked decrease in study during the brief reversal phase when the point system was withdrawn. In the Points$_2$ and Post Check phases data indicated that even though the three pupils who had the lowest baseline study levels were still studying less than their classmates, all three were above the seventy per cent level, higher than the highest study rate recorded for any pupil during baseline.

DISCUSSION

This study showed that systematic reinforcement procedures using contingencies available in most junior high school classrooms could be used by a beginning teacher to gain control of an extremely disruptive junior high school special education class. Systematic teacher attention increased study levels but was limited in its effect. For most pupils classroom privileges, including such activities as early dismissal to lunch, getting a drink, sharpening a pencil, and talking to another pupil for five minutes, were more powerful than teacher attention alone for motivating desired behavior. Reversal procedures demonstrated the functional relationship between the reinforcement contingencies and the increases in appropriate behaviors.

The data also revealed that the effectiveness of a given procedure varied from pupil to pupil. In the case of one pupil it was necessary to institute a time out procedure to gain participation in the point system. Once participation was gained increases in study were dramatic.

In discussing the point system it should be mentioned that there was no rationale for the number of points assigned for particular activities or for the selection of the activities other than a seemingly suitable balance between the behaviors required to earn points and the reinforcing value of the activities and privileges for which they could be spent. Another teacher would doubtless have to adjust the system to fit his particular classroom group and the resources available to him.

Evaluating the point system in terms of value and convenience to the teacher is necessarily subjective but relevant to a discussion of the overall worth of the system. In her evaluation the teacher stated that the system was helpful for it gave both the student and the teacher "a black and white list of what is allowed in the classroom." She also stated that it was easier for her to be fair, since the clearly stated penalties and rewards stopped arguments over the teacher's handling of misconduct. She also reported that pupils did a great deal more classwork and made better grades. At times she had difficulty keeping up with the amount of extra credit work since pupils would choose extra work over any other activities if they were working for a highly prized privilege. She reported further that most pupils indicated they liked the order the system helped provide.

According to the teacher the system could be improved by establishing a simpler system for computing point totals. She felt it was important to post the totals every hour so pupils would have more immediate feedback on their status, but daily instead of hourly computations would reduce the amount of teacher time needed to figure points. She also suggested that the pupils should be more involved in establishing the point system. Such involvement might reduce the initial resistance to the system. She reported that allowing the class to take part in modifying the system when problems arose had helped them accept it.

It is understood by the authors that the procedures used to bring about classroom control in this study are not new or startling. Good teachers have used teacher attention and access to privileges to motivate appropriate pupil behavior for many years. The results reported here are of interest, however, for they demonstrate a means by which a teacher who had not managed to do so was helped to organize the environmental consequences available to her and bring about desired classroom behavior. In essence the point system acted as a convenient means for the teacher and the pupils to link desired study behavior with participation in desired activities.

It is conceded that a point system may not be necessary or appropriate in many junior high school classrooms. It may, however, be a valuable aid to teachers who have difficulty in maintaining classroom control over children with highly deviant and disruptive behaviors.

REFERENCES

Birnbrauer, J. S., Wolf, M. M., Kidder, J. D. & Tague, E. Classroom behavior of retarded pupils with token reinforcement. *Journal of Experimental Child Psychology*, 1965, **2**, 219–235.

Broden, M. Notes on recording. Observer's Manual for Juniper Gardens Children's Project, Unpublished manuscript, Bureau of Child Research, 1968.

Hall, R. V. & Broden, M. Behavior changes in brain-injured children through social reinforcement. *Journal of Experimental Child Psychology*, 1967, **5**, 463–479.

Hall, R. V., Lund, D. & Jackson, D. Effects of teacher attention on study behavior. *Journal of Applied Behavior Analysis*, 1968, **1**, 1–12.

Hall, R. V., Panyan, M., Rabon, D. & Broden, M. Instructing beginning teachers in reinforcement procedures which improve classroom control. *Journal of Applied Behavior Analysis*, 1968, **1**, 315–322.

Harris, F. R., Wolf, M. M. & Baer, D. M. Effects of adult social reinforcement on child behavior. *Young Children*, 1964, **20**, 8–17.

McKenzie, H., Clark, M., Wolf, M., Kothera, R. & Benson, C. Behavior modification of children with learning disabilities using grades as token reinforcers. *Exceptional Children*, 1968, **34**, 745–752.

O'Leary, K. D. & Becker, W. C. Behavior modification of an adjustment class: Token reinforcement system. *Exceptional Children*, 1967, **33**, 637–642.

Thomas, D. R., Becker, W. C. & Armstrong, M. Production and elimination of disruptive classroom behavior by systematically varying teacher's behavior. *Journal of Applied Behavior Analysis*, 1968, **1**, 35–45.

Wolf, M. M., Giles, D. K. & Hall, R. V. Experiments with token reinforcement in a remedial classroom. *Behaviour Research and Therapy*, 1968, **6**, 51–64.

Wolf, M. M., Risley, T. R. & Mees, H. L. Application of operant conditioning procedures to the behavior problems of an autistic child. *Behaviour Research and Therapy*, 1964, **1**, 305–312.

Zimmerman, E. H. & Zimmerman, J. The alteration of behavior in a special classroom situation. *Journal of the Experimental Analysis of Behavior*, 1962, **5**, 59–60.

Child Behavior Therapy:
A Community Programme in
Appalachia*†

ROBERT G. WAHLER

The University of Tennessee

and

MARIE ERICKSON

Bell County Health Center

Abstract: A community therapy programme based on reinforcement theory is described. The programme emphasizes the use of non-professional volunteer workers who were trained to function as behavior therapists in home and school settings. Essentially, these workers were trained to observe and to modify possible reinforcement contingencies between deviant child behavior and the behavior of those people who typically interact with the child. Data on the programme's effectiveness over a two-year period are presented.

Community psychology is a currently popular concept in the "mental health" field (e.g., Sarason *et al.*, 1966). It implies the notion that the clinician should concentrate his therapeutic and prophylactic efforts on the patient's immediate and not-so-immediate environment rather than on the patient *per se*. That is, instead of following the traditional dyadic treatment model, the clinician's role should be that of an agent for change in his client's community — community, meaning the client's relatives, friends, and working associates as well as the more impersonal aspects of his social and physical surroundings. It is clear that the clinician is seen from this point of view as an expert in human ecology; a practitioner who assumes that man's behavior is an important function of his current environment.

While a number of theoretical models could be employed to implement the community psychology concept, one is of particular relevance in view of its emphasis upon human ecology. Reinforcement theory has as one of its basic tenets the assumption that the development and maintenance of behavior is a function of stimulus contingencies set by one's environment. It is argued that man behaves as he does because of differential reinforcement, provided primarily by the social attention of other people. In the case of the child, people such as his parents, his peers, his siblings, his teachers, etc. are seen as selective dispensers of social attention; in a very real sense these social agents "teach" him which aspects of his behavior will be most instrumental in obtaining approval, reassurance, affection, nearness, and other forms of attention. From this view, then, the question of whether the child develops normal or deviant behaviors can be answered only through an assessment of his social community and how it interacts with him.

The above contention is an intriguing one and readily lends itself to research evaluation.

---

*The authors are grateful to Ira Weinstein for his helpful suggestions in the preparation of this manuscript. Thanks are also due to Norman Teeter for his statistical analysis of the data.

†Reprinted from *Behaviour Research and Therapy*, 1969, **7**, 71–78. Copyright 1969 with permission from Pergamon Press Publishing Company and Dr. Robert G. Wahler.

Thus far, attempts to isolate naturalistic events which may support or maintain deviant child behavior have proved promising. For example, evidence is now available to show that parents may inadvertently support their child's deviant behavior through their social attention to it (Wahler *et al.*, 1965). Similar studies of teacher–child interactions in preschool settings have demonstrated that teachers may also function in this capacity. That is, teachers have been found to function as powerful sources of reinforcement for child behavior such as excessive crying (Hart *et al.*, 1964), isolate play (Allen *et al.*, 1964), excessive passivity (Johnson *et al.*, 1966), regressive crawling (Harris *et al.*, 1964), and aggressive behavior (Scott *et al.*, 1967; Brown & Elliot, 1965). Finally, more recent studies have indicated that the preschool child's peer group adds a further component to these sources of control (Patterson *et al.*, 1967; Wahler, 1967).

In addition to demonstrating the roles which parents, teachers and peers may play in the maintenance of deviant child behavior, the above studies also brought to light a highly practical finding: In many cases the parents, teachers, and peers could be trained in the use of behavior modification techniques, enabling them to produce dramatic changes in the children's deviant behavior. The techniques, of course, were based on reinforcement theory and the previously discussed analyses of the adult–child interactions.

A community psychology programme based on reinforcement theory has several features to recommend it as far as child therapy is concerned: (1) the previously discussed research findings support the assumption that social agents in the child's immediate community may be responsible for the maintenance of his deviant behavior; (2) reinforcement contingencies set by these social agents may often be modified, and these modifications may produce therapeutic changes in the deviant child behavior; (3) the operations involved in modifying the social reinforcement contingencies are simple, and the T requires relatively little formal training to implement them. This latter point raises the possibility of training clinically unsophisticated community members as Ts. The present programme was initiated with these three points in mind.

Community and Clinic Settings

Pineville, Kentucky (population, 3000) is the county-seat of Bell County, and the location of the Bell County Health Center. This clinic is state supported and serves the medical and psychological needs of residents in Bell County (population 35,000) and in Harlan County (population 65,000). As far as psychological services are concerned, the Clinic represents the only source of this type in the two counties. The staff of the psychology unit is made up of one permanent member (a social worker) and one consulting member (a clinical psychologist) who visits the Clinic twice a month.

A picture of the two counties describes a rather typical cross-section of Appalachia. Poverty, unemployment, and low educational attainment are widespread among the residents, and many are dependent on social welfare for financial security. As might be expected, birth control is a serious problem among the poorer families.

Ninety-five per cent of the referrals to the psychological clinic are children. The majority of these are from the poorer families who generally bring their children in at the urging of public health nurses or public assistance workers. Presenting complaints range from retardation and autism to less serious problems such as low achievement motivation in school settings. At the present time the Clinic charges no fees for services rendered.

Programme Development and Current Functioning

The senior author's very limited contact with the Clinic was instrumental in the decision to develop a community programme. Not only were the senior author's consulting visits restricted to two a month, but because of travel time to and from Pineville, each visit was restricted to a period of about five hours. It seemed obvious that a clinician would find it difficult to work therapeutically with a patient, much less handle a large waiting-list of prospective patients, on such a contact basis. Therefore, it seemed advisable to consider a programme which emphasized the use of non-professionals as Ts—in this case, community members who could be trained in the use of child behavior therapy techniques.

Recruitment procedures were complicated by a lack of funds to hire new clinic staff members. Since it was then apparent that staffing the programme would require volunteer workers, efforts were made to obtain the cooperation of Pineville churches, the city school board, and the local mental health committee. The senior author provided these groups with mimeographed manuscripts which described the plight of the Clinic and the proposed behavior therapy programme. In addition, the manuscript stated that the educational background of the volunteers was immaterial and that they would be expected to serve no more than two hours per week.

Within a period of two months following the community group effort to recruit workers, a total of thirteen volunteers were available to the Clinic. Of this number, six were public health nurses from Bell and Harlan Counties, three were public assistance workers in Bell County and four were citizens in Pineville engaged in other occupations. In addition to these regular workers, several teachers and school counselors requested to assist the Clinic on specific cases.

Training of the workers was primarily of an in-service type. Although the authors did provide interested workers with reprints of several studies cited earlier in this paper, most of the workers did not find the material to be helpful. The following steps characterized the training and the regular functioning of the workers and the Clinic staff:

1. When a prospective child therapy case was seen at the Clinic, the child, his immediate family, and any other people who were closely involved with the child (e.g., teachers) were interviewed by the professional Clinic staff. These interviews were aimed at obtaining descriptions of the behavior which created problems at home, at school, or elsewhere. In addition, efforts were made to determine the usual consequences of such behavior-consequences provided by the child's parents, his teachers, his peers, etc. The interviews were diagnostic in the sense that their function was to provide a list of the child's deviant behavior and a list of probable reinforcers for the behavior.

2. A volunteer worker was then introduced to the interview data by the Clinic psychologist. Discussion of the case emphasized descriptions of those physical and verbal responses of the child which were considered deviant in his regular environment. Following this description, the clinician emphasized the notion that the behavior was probably being maintained by people in the child's environment. Then followed a brief essay on reinforcement theory, with emphasis on the concepts of reinforcement, extinction, and punishment. Finally, the clinician pointed to those social agents whom he suspected to be responsible for the maintenance of the deviant behavior; therapy for the child was described as a process of modifying the probable reinforcement contingencies currently provided by these social agents.

3. Prior to Step 3, the volunteer worker obtained at least two one-hour observations of the child's behavior within the problem setting (e.g., home or classroom). These observational procedures will be described later. Second interviews were then scheduled for those social agents who seemed to provide clear and potentially modifiable contingencies for the child's deviant behavior. The volunteer worker and the clinician conducted these interviews together. Essentially, these social agents were given descriptions of the child's deviant behavior and

they were then advised that their social attention to such behavior was a likely cause of their maintenance. The social agents were then told to ignore the child's deviant behavior but to respond as usual to his other behavior patterns, especially those which seemed incompatible with the deviant behavior. In cases where the deviant behavior involved highly aggressive or oppositional actions, a punishment procedure was suggested as well. In all instances this suggested procedure involved social isolation of the child for short periods of time following his deviant behavior. It was then made clear to the social agents that the volunteer worker would make weekly visits to observe interactions between them and the child and to point out needed corrections in social contingencies.

4. For an inexperienced volunteer worker, these interviews were continued on a twice a month basis until the clinician felt confident in the volunteer worker's understanding of the therapeutic process as it applied to the child. When this occurred, the clinician met only with the volunteer worker on the same time basis. Discussion centered around the child's progress and the progress of the social agents in maintaining their "therapeutic" contingencies for the child.

The following case study is cited to illustrate these procedures: Ricky (age 8) was referred to the Clinic by his school principal because of his disruptive behavior in the classroom. According to his teacher, Ricky would frequently tease the other children in a variety of ways. Following an interview with the teacher, numerous examples of Ricky's disruptive behavior were recorded; in addition, the interview revealed that the teacher's usual response to this behavior was to shout at Ricky, argue with him and at times to spank him. The teacher also admitted that her usual response to Ricky's infrequently cooperative behavior was to ignore him; she pointed out that Ricky irritated her so much of the time that she found it exceedingly difficult "to be nice to him" even when his behavior was appropriate. Since Ricky's parents were unwilling to come to the Clinic, the therapy programme focused on the school setting.

The volunteer behavior T was a young public health nurse who normally visited the school on a weekly basis. This was her first behavior therapy case. She and the psychologist discussed the interview data for about thirty minutes prior to the second meeting with Ricky's teacher. During the discussion, Ricky's disruptive classroom behavior was described in detail and the psychologist emphasized the possibility that the teachers' attention (admittedly negative) could be maintaining this behavior. The psychologist pointed out that the teacher could ignore it. However, it was evident that this procedure would be impractical in terms of maintaining any semblance of classroom routine. Therefore, a punishment technique was outlined by the psychologist. Essentially, the proposed procedure involved isolating Ricky from his peers and his teacher for short time periods following the occurrence of his disruptive behavior. The psychologist speculated that if the punishment procedure could suppress Ricky's disruptive behavior, the teacher might find it much easier to provide positive social attention following his appropriate behavior.

The second interview with Ricky's teacher included the volunteer behavior T. Prior to the interview, the psychologist urged the T to comment whenever possible on the therapeutic procedure. In beginning the interview, the psychologist reviewed Ricky's problem behavior and then briefly outlined the proposed behavior therapy programme for Ricky. During the ensuing discussion of the programme, Ricky's teacher offered suggestions for implementing the procedures — particularly the punishment portions. It was decided to use the teacher's lounge (a former cloakroom adjacent to the classroom) as the isolation area in the punishment programme. The teacher agreed to attempt the programme and to work closely with the volunteer T, who would visit the classroom twice weekly.

After the programme had been in effect for two weeks, a third Clinic meeting was scheduled for the teacher and the therapist. However, since the teacher was unable to attend, only the psychologist and the T were present. According to the T's report, little change had occurred in Ricky's disruptive behavior; both she and the teacher were quite discouraged. The T's reports revealed that the teacher had used the punishment procedure for five days with little success. At the end of that time she decided, "it wouldn't work" and discontinued its use.

A careful analysis of the T's classroom observations provided a possible explanation for the programme's failure. Two features of her report were of interest: (1) the teacher's use of the punishment procedure was inconsistent. That is, only about sixty per cent of Ricky's disruptive episodes were followed by social isolation; (2) when she did use the procedure, it was not used promptly upon the occurrence of the disruptive behavior. Often the teacher would first warn Ricky or argue with him before ordering him to the isolation room. The T agreed to discuss these problems with the teacher and to monitor the teacher's behavior more carefully in the next two weeks.

At the next interview, both the teacher and the T were present. Both were enthusiastic about the marked improvement in Ricky. According to the report, Ricky's disruptive behavior had dropped from about twenty episodes a day to only one or two. The teacher also reported that her attitude toward Ricky had changed to the point that she could now offer genuine approval for his appropriate behavior.

The T agreed to continue her observations on a weekly basis and to meet twice a month with the psychologist to describe her experiences. Two months later, therapeutic changes in Ricky were still in evidence and his case was closed.

Programme Effectiveness

The programme has now been in effect for over two years and fourteen volunteer workers are now actively involved in it. In all cases treated, the deviant behavior was in evidence either in the child's home or in his school. Therefore, most of the social agents were either the child's parents or his teachers, or both.

The major claims of the programme's effectiveness rest on observational reports of improvement by the volunteer workers, the number of cases seen by the Clinic, and the time spent treating these cases.

Observational data were collected in the following manner: after a volunteer worker became familiar with the behavioral problems presented by her case, she was introduced to a check-list method of recording the behavior. This method, similar to one described by Zeilberger *et al.* (1968), required the observer to make coded checks for the occurrence or non-occurrence of the problem behavior and the stimulus contingencies, within successive twenty-second intervals. For each case, the worker obtained two one-hour observations prior to treatment and two one-hour observations just after termination of treatment. These observations were made in the child's home or classroom or both, depending on the stimulus location of the presenting problem.

Because of time and scheduling problems, it proved possible to assess the scoring reliability of approximately half of the volunteer workers. In assessing observer reliability, observers worked in pairs; an agreement or disagreement was tallied for each twenty-second interval and the percentage of agreements for the two observers was computed for each response and stimulus class. All reliability tests showed agreement levels of eighty-five per cent or better; since all behavior categories were based on quite distinct physical and verbal behaviors, this kind of reliability is not particularly surprising.

It proved possible to classify the presenting problems for all cases in five general categories: (1) classroom disruptive behavior; this category included fighting with other children, shouting, and not obeying teacher instructions. (2) classroom study behavior; this category

Table 1. Mean number of problem behavior episodes before and after treatment.

	Mean variance				F-test	t-Test	Corrected t-test	Number of cases
	Pre-treatment		Post-treatment					
Classroom disruptive behavior	25.77	128.70	7.77	27.83	4.62*		4.03*	35
Classroom study behavior	51.68	660.22	95.12	1366.68	2.28*		10.70*	50
School absences (Days absent)	7.60	5.69	1.66	4.67	1.22	2.68*		15
Home study behavior	13.49	120.35	59.67	1075.00	8.93*		8.37*	45
Home disruptive behavior	29.87	259.10	9.88	76.40	3.39*		7.87*	52

$*p < 0.05$.

included attending (i.e., looking) to either the teacher or to the learning materials. (3) school absences; this record was obtained from teacher attendance records. (4) home disruptive behavior; this category included fighting with siblings, parents, or other people in the home, destruction of property, and not obeying parent instructions. (5) home study behavior; this category included attending to school homework materials.

Table 1 describes pre- and post-treatment measures of the above behavior problems over two years of the community programme. As this table indicates, many of the sixty-six cases handled during this time were deviant in terms of more than one of the problem categories. An examination of mean differences in the problem behavior categories before and after treatment revealed significant changes in the frequencies of these behaviors; all categories displayed marked changes in the therapeutic direction. Unfortunately, because of a lack of personnel, an appropriate control group was not included to evaluate the casual influence of the treatment procedures. Thus, although the children *did* show improvement, the role of the volunteer workers in producing the improvement is not clear.

Table 2. Mean number of treatment weeks per patient over three years.

	Number of cases	Weeks between screening and termination		Corrected	
		Mean	Variance	F-test	t-test
Traditional treatment year (T)	17	19.00	20.88		
First community programme year (C1)	31	8.63	5.08		
Second community programme year (C2)	35	9.17	5.00		
T vs. C1				4.11*	8.50*
T vs. C2				4.17*	8.40*
C1 vs. C2				1.02	0.01

*$p < 0.05$.

During the senior author's first year at the Clinic, he and the junior author engaged in fairly traditional techniques of diagnosis and therapy; no attempts were made to assess the effectiveness of these procedures. Table 2 presents a description of the number of cases seen during this initial year compared to the community programme years; in addition, the same comparison is made for time between the screening of a case and its termination. As Table 2 indicates, the mean treatment time for the community programme years was significantly shorter than that for the initial year—and a larger number of cases were seen during each programme year.

Although no great emphasis can be placed on the correlational improvement data, results based on the number of cases treated and on the time between screening and termination of cases must be considered compelling. There are certainly many treatment facilities in the United States which are similar to this Appalachian unit in terms of the undesirable ratio between patients and professional workers. Since it is unlikely that many of those units will obtain an adequate number of professional workers in the near future, programmes emphasizing the use of indigenous non-professional workers must be considered; as the present results show, a reinforcement theory based training programme can lead to highly desirable outcomes. Thus, in terms of efficient use of the professional clinician's time, such a community programme has much to recommend it.

REFERENCES

Allen, K. E., Hart, B. M., Buell, J. S., Harris, F. R. & Wolf, M. M. (1964) Effects of social reinforcement on isolate behavior of a nursery school child. *Child Dev.*, **35**, 511–518.

Brown, P. & Elliot, R. (1965) Control of aggression in a nursery school class. *J. Exp. Child Psychol.*, **2**, 103–107.

Harris, F. R., Johnson, M. K., Kelley, C. S. & Wolf, M. M. (1964) Effects of positive social reinforcement on regressed crawling of a nursery school child. *J. Educ. Psychol.*, **55**, 35–41.

Harris, F. R., Wolf, M. M. & Baer, D. M. (1964) Effects of adult social reinforcement on child behavior. *Young Child.*, **20**, 8–17.

Hart, B. M., Allen, K. E., Buell, J. S., Harris, F. R. & Wolf, M. M. (1964) Effects of social reinforcement on operant crying. *J. Exp. Child Psychol.*, **1**, 145–153.

Hawkins, R. P., Peterson, R. F., Schweid, E. & Bijou, S. W. (1966) Behavior therapy in the home: Amelioration of problem parent–child relations with the parent in a therapeutic role. *J. exp. Child Psychol.*, **4**, 99–107.

Johnson, M. K., Kelley, S. C., Harris, F. R. & Wolf, M. M. (1966) An application of reinforcement principles to development of motor skills of a young child. In *Control of human behavior*, pp. 135–136. (Eds. Ulrich, R., Stachnik, T. and Mabry, J.). Scott, Foresman and Company.

Patterson, G. R., Littman, R. A. & Bricker, W. (1967) Assertive behavior in children: A step toward a theory of aggression. *Soc. Res. Child Dev. Monogr.*, **32**, No. 5.

Sarason, S. B., Levine, M., Goldenberg, I., Cherlin, D. L. & Bennett, E. M. (1966) *Psychology in community settings: Clinical, educational, vocational, social aspects*. John Wiley, New York.

Scott, P. M., Burton, R. V. & Yarrow, M. R. (1967) Social reinforcement under natural conditions. *Child Dev.*, **38**, 53–63.

Wahler, R. G. (1967) Child–child interactions in free field settings: Some experimental analyses. *J. Exp. Child Psychol.*, **5**, 278–293.

Wahler, R. G., Winkel, G. H., Peterson, R. F. & Morrison, D. C. (1965) Mothers as behavior therapists for their own children. *Behav. Res. & Therapy*, **3**, 113–124.

Zeilberger, J., Sampen, S. & Sloane, H. (1968) Modification of a child's problem behaviours in the home with the mother as therapist. *J. app. Behav. Anal.*, **1**, 47–53.

The Role of Social Workers in
Behavior Therapy*†

DEREK JEHU

University of Leicester School of Social Work

Abstract: Social workers who use the behavioral model have the potentiality of giving substantial help in the treatment of many patients suffering from learned abnormalities of behavior. Their role provides the advantages of firsthand observation by a professional person of the patient's behavior in its natural environment. Upon identifying the stimuli that control unadaptive emotional behavior use can sometimes be made of learning principles within the environment to bring about diminution of this behavior. In other circumstances social workers can utilize operant conditioning principles to modify undesirable behavior by manipulating reinforcing contingencies. A number of specific proposals are made for the use of behavior principles by social workers, and some examples are given. In order to evaluate the extent of the contribution social workers might make, systematic controlled studies need to be carried out.

Traditionally, social workers have used a psychodynamic model in their assessment and treatment procedures and they are accustomed to collaborating with psychotherapists of a similar *orientation* as well as with general psychiatrists. Only recently has there been any exploration of the use of a behavioral model by social workers and of their role in behavior therapy (Jehu, 1967; Thomas, 1967).

The essential characteristic of the latter approach is an attempt to apply systematically certain principles established in experimental psychology to the treatment of abnormal behavior. This does not imply adherence to specific psychological theories or methods, but the study of learning is of particular importance. Treatment is regarded as a learning process, in which the principles accounting for the acquisition, performance and extinction of behavior are the same as in any other learning situation. These principles are utilized not merely to describe traditional treatment procedures in terms of learning concepts, but in an attempt deliberately to change and extend therapy so that it accords better with optimum learning conditions. This application is *a priori* rather than *post facto*.

As the approach does not imply commitment to any specific psychological theory, it follows that abnormal behavior may be conceptualized in as many ways as there are theories. However, in practice a stimulus–response analysis is used most commonly, and abnormal behavior is viewed as inappropriate ways of responding to certain stimuli. These may be external features of the patient's environment, including the ways other people behave towards him. They may also be internal stimuli, including those arising from his physiological and cognitive processes. The inappropriate responses may consist of any aspect of behavior

---

*Paper presented in section on "The Clinical Applications of Behaviour Therapy in Adult and Childhood Psychoses and the Anxiety Neuroses" at the Second International Congress of Social Psychiatry. London, August 1969.

†Reprinted from the *Journal of Behavior Therapy and Experimental Psychiatry*, 1970, **1**, 17–28. Copyright 1970 with permission from Pergamon Press Publishing Company and Professor Derek Jehu.

including physiological changes, motor activities, thoughts and feelings. Such abnormal behavior is seen as a function of past learning, current motivating and controlling conditions and individual biological differences between people, of a genetic or non-genetic kind. Thus abnormal behavior is a result of the same determinants as normal behavior. In particular the same *processes* of learning are common to both normal and abnormal behavior, but in the case of the latter the *conditions* of learning have been such as to produce deviant rather than normal stimulus–response relationships.

There does not seem to be anything in this approach to abnormal behavior to contra-indicate its use by social workers, and some apparent advantages of such a course will be mentioned later. However, there is little point in social workers merely replicating treatment by psychiatrists and psychologists, rather than making some special contribution from the viewpoint and experience of their own profession. In any case, social workers are not trained or oriented to intervene directly at an organic level, so that it would be inappropriate for them to use certain techniques such as those involving drug administration, muscular relaxation or physical aversive stimulation. In the longer term, their special contribution might be in the direction of modifying the life situations of patients as a means of treatment. This is insufficiently emphasized and exploited in the contemporary practice of behavior therapy, and it is a traditional social work function which might benefit from a fresh behavioral orientation. However, at present it seems wiser to avoid crystallizing interprofessional boundaries in behavior therapy until much more experience of collaboration is gained and evaluated. There-fore, the remainder of this paper will be devoted to a broad exploration of the possible role of social workers in the assessment and treatment of psychiatric disorders by behavior therapy.

ASSESSMENT PROCEDURES

Assessment for behavior therapy requires first of all precise identification of the patient's abnormal behavior. What is he doing or not doing which may need modification? Then it is necessary to identify the conditions controlling the abnormal behavior, that is the eliciting, discriminative and reinforcing stimuli which motivate, guide and maintain it. Information about the patient's life history may assist in the identification of these controlling conditions, and in a behavioral approach it is sought for this purpose rather than specifically to uncover the origins of the abnormal behavior. Next, assessment procedures must specify what modifi-cations in the patient's behavior it is desired to achieve by treatment. This involves important ethical considerations, that have been discussed elsewhere (Jehu, 1967). The feasibility of altering certain controlling conditions in order to produce the desired changes in behavior must be assessed also. Can certain aversive stimuli which are eliciting anxiety be removed? Will and appropriate verbal instruction serve as a discriminative stimulus for the suitable performance of certain responses? What positive reinforcers can be made available to main-tain desirable behavior, or withdrawn to extinguish abnormal behavior? Finally, any biological limitations which may restrict modification of a patient's abnormal behavior will need to be ascertained.

There are several features of assessment for behavior therapy which give it a different emphasis from that of more traditional procedures. One is specifying behavior and its con-trolling conditions in observable terms rather than inferred states, for example, what a mother *does* when her child *behaves* in a certain way, rather than "rejection" or "love." This facilitates the objective identification of the data needed for behavior therapy. A second and related feature is explaining behavior as a function of its antecedent and consequent controlling conditions. One advantage of this focus on these conditions as the "causes" of behavior is that they are potentially manipulable for treatment purposes. A third distinguishing feature is eliciting life history material to assist in identifying the conditions which control the abnormal behavior at the present time, rather than those which led to its acquisition in the first place.

Social workers might make a particular contribution towards assessment of behavior therapy which has been little realized to date, although it is a logical extension of their traditional functions and skills. This is the observation of patients' behavior in natural situations such as their home, school or work environments. The desirability of such observations is implied by conceptualizing abnormal behavior as deviant ways of responding to the controlling stimuli in the patient's current life situation. However, the assumption of this task by social workers would involve some modification of their more usual method of assessment by clinical interviews with patients and other informants. The data obtained in the customary way consists only of the interviewee's verbal report of what occurs in natural situations, together with the social worker's observations of the non-verbal reactions accompanying these verbal descriptions. There would be some obvious advantages in the firsthand observation by a professional person of the patient's behavior in his natural environment.

TREATMENT PROCEDURES

There are at least two possible general strategies for modifying abnormal behavior in patients, which may be implemented either singly or in combination. One is to alter the patient's responses to the controlling stimuli in his environment, without deliberately producing changes in the latter. Assuming a family environment to be essentially satisfactory, one might attempt to adjust a patient to it. The second strategy is to change the existing environmental stimuli which motivate, guide and reinforce the abnormal behavior, as a means of altering the behavior. One might arrange for a patient's material or social deprivations to be remedied, with consequent reduction in the anxiety or aggression elicited by them. Or a mother might be helped to respond to her child's reasonable requests rather than reinforcing his tantrum behavior with her attention.

These strategies may be implemented in interviews or in natural situations, which may be either the patient's usual environment or a special therapeutic situation such as a psychiatric ward. It is proposed now to review certain selected techniques of treatment in interviews or natural situations. They are by no means the only procedures which may be derived from experimental psychology, and the examples of their use are illustrative rather than exhaustive.

Reduction of Aversive Stimulation

One way of weakening responses such as anxiety, guilt, self-devaluation or aggression, is to reduce the aversive stimulation which elicits them.

This may be done in interviews if patients talk about matters which arouse such negative responses, without disapproval, criticism or punishment from the social worker. In a study of this process, anxiety over sexual matters decreased throughout a series of permissive therapeutic sessions (Dittes, 1957a). Moreover, the anxiety level varied systematically with the permissiveness of the therapist. It decreased when he was gentle and attentive, and increased when he reacted negatively (Dittes, 1957b).

In natural situations, aversive stimulation might be reduced by changing the behavior of other people towards the patient. A father might be helped to be less harshly punitive in order to weaken his child's fear and avoidance of him. A husband might be encouraged to be very controlled in his sexual behavior towards his frigid wife, so that her anxiety over sexual matters is not aroused and consequently reinforced while treatment is in progress.

Aversive stimulation might also arise from material or social deprivation, such as inadequate income or accommodation, or some lack of social care or opportunity. The mitigation of such deprivations is a traditional task of social workers, and it serves to highlight a special contribution they may make to behavior therapy by reducing excessive environmental stress on patients. Yet, oddly enough, such a procedure is scarcely mentioned in the behavior therapy literature, perhaps because of the absence of social work influence in the field.

Withdrawal of Positive Reinforcers

Abnormal behavior might be extinguished by withdrawing any positive reinforcers which are maintaining it. In interviews, social workers might withhold their attention and approval when patients talk in an excessively irrelevant or aggressive way.

An example of the use of this procedure in a natural situation is the treatment of a three-year-old child's tantrum crying on going to bed at night. This was being maintained by its retention of the mother in the bedroom until the child went to sleep. After full assessment, it was decided that the child should be put to bed in a kindly manner after ensuring that all her needs were met, and that the mother should then come downstairs and not return however hard the child cried. The social worker visited each bed-time and supported the mother in her difficult task by a variety of learning procedures including positive reinforcement, counter-conditioning and modelling. After seven nights the tantrums had ceased and the removal of their disruptive influence was followed by a general improvement in the family relationships. A short follow-up period revealed no evidence of symptom return or substitution in the child (Holder, 1969).

Positive Counter-Conditioning

The crux of all counter-conditioning procedures is the evocation of a response, which is incompatible with and stronger than an abnormal response to a particular stimulus, so that the latter response is inhibited, in consequence weakened and, with repetition, eventually eliminated. In the case of positive counter-conditioning, certain "positive" responses are used to eliminate "negative" responses, such as anxiety. The stimuli which arouse the negative response are presented in a gradually ascending sequence from the least to the most disturbing, so that the positive response is always the stronger of the two.

If in interviews social workers behave warmly and sympathetically, if they are concerned about patients' problems and hopeful for their solution, if they are known to respect confidences and to possess professional competence and prestige, then the patients may react with feelings of confidence, trust, optimism and positive self-regard, which will be counterposed against any anxiety, guilt or self-devaluation, and may serve to counter-condition these undesirable responses. This is most likely to occur if the stimuli which evoke the negative responses are discussed in a gradually ascending sequence of aversiveness, so that the incompatible positive responses evoked by the social worker remain the stronger.

A client's good relationship with his social worker has been used also in a natural situation to counter-condition school phobic responses in a ten-year-old boy. Each day for twenty days the social worker accompanied the boy and together they gradually approached the school, starting by sitting in the car in front of the school, and proceeding through several steps including getting out of the car, going to the door, entering the school and then the classroom, at first with only the teacher present, next a few children and finally the whole class (Garvey & Hegrenes, 1966).

Another type of positive response which is especially valuable in counter-conditioning social anxieties evoked in interpersonal situations, is self-assertiveness, including not only the overt expression of anger and resentment, but also of friendliness and affection. Stuart (1967) has reported an example of the use of this procedure in natural situations. The patient was a twenty-one-year-old girl, who presented with an anxiety state following her second abortion. She was markedly unstable both in her work history and in her relationships with men. Prior to dates, her anxiety over her imagined lack of physical attractiveness and intellectual and social skills mounted to panic level, and in order to distract the man from her imagined short-comings, she would have sexual intercourse with him as early as possible in the evening. The patient was helped to alter her behavior on dates, so that men would respond differently to her. She was instructed to behave as if she expected to be treated with respect, for example by waiting to be helped on with her coat and for doors to be opened and her cigarette lit. To avoid inappropriate sexual experiences, she was encouraged to meet her dates in public places, to remain with other people and not to invite the men into her flat at the end of the evening. These new ways of behaving were followed by more satisfying and continuous relationships with men, as well as by increased assertiveness and success in other sectors of her life.

Positive Reinforcement

Desired behavior can be strengthened in patients by positively reinforcing it, and this procedure is often combined with non-reinforcement of abnormal behavior so that it is extinguished.

There is now a good deal of evidence that therapists do influence the behavior of their patients in interviews, through processes of selective reinforcement, communicated by words, gestures, postural changes, facial expressions and other expressive acts. This occurs even when the therapist tries deliberately not to influence his patient. In one reported case treated by a Rogerian non-directive therapist, whose whole philosophy, theoretical orientation and train-ing was against influencing his patient, it was demonstrated that in various subtle ways the therapist approved of statements indicating independent behavior by the patient and that these increased during therapy, while he disapproved of statements relating to dependence, sex and intellectual defences, all of which decreased (Murray, 1956). Recordings of a series of treat-ment sessions with a single patient, conducted by Carl Rogers himself, have been analyzed by Truax (1966). Three reinforcers were identified: empathy, non-possessive warmth or accep-tance, and directiveness. If Rogers had succeeded in being completely non-directive, then these reinforcers would have been distributed equally over all nine classes of patient behavior used in Truax's analysis of the data. In fact, Rogers selectively reinforced five of these nine classes to a significant degree, and the behavior in four of these five increased during therapy, while behavior in three of the four non-reinforced classes did not vary. Thus the patient's behavior was consistent with predictions from Rogers' pattern of reinforcement in seven out of nine classes. In a further study of the group treatment of thirty patients, Truax (1967) found a significant relationship between therapist reinforcement (empathy, warmth and genuineness) for self-exploration by the patients, and their actual level of self-exploratory behavior during treatment. Moreover, the outcome of treatment for patients in groups in which self-explora-tion was highly reinforced, was better than for patients in groups where this was not the case. This last finding bears upon the important issue of the generalization of changes in patient behavior within interviews to their real life situations outside. At present, the available evi-dence is not very adequate on this point, although some studies, such as the one just cited, do offer some support for such generalization.

Social workers are not necessarily restricted to using social reinforcers. Instead, or in addition, they may employ material reinforcers and the latter may be especially valuable with clients for whom the social worker is not yet established as an effective social reinforcer. An example involving the combination of social and material reinforcers, is the treatment of a five-year-old electively mute girl. For about a year the patient had refused to speak to anyone, although soon after referral she spontaneously resumed talking to her family, while remaining mute with other people both inside and outside her home. Part of the treatment consisted of her being reinforced for achieving certain levels of performance, commencing with whispering a line of a book to her mother in the remote presence of the social worker, and progressing through reading at greater length, with increasing audibility and at decreasing distance from the social worker. At a suitable stage, the family tape-recorded the child talking and singing, and subsequently she played these recordings to the social worker and her headmistress. Finally, the child was reinforced for reading to the social worker in the absence of the mother. The reinforcers used in the treatment included sweets and colored stars to be stuck in a special book, as well as attention and approval from the parents, social worker and head-mistress. The patient began speaking to other adults and children again, and follow-up over a year showed her to be behaving normally at home and at school with no sign of symptom return or substitution (Sluckin & Jehu, 1969).

The problem of achieving generalization and persistence of desired changes from interviews to clients' real life situations has been mentioned, and one way of by-passing it, is to intervene directly by altering the reinforcement contingencies in the real life situation itself. A social worker might help parents to modify their reinforcement practices toward their child, as a means of changing and maintaining his behavior in the desired direction. Patterson *et al.* (1967) have reported an application of this approach. The patient, a five-year-old boy, was extremely isolated, socially unresponsive, negativistic and subject to outbursts of bizarre behavior. His stepmother was using aversive means of control, and the child's behavior was being maintained as an avoidance and escape reaction to this. It meant also that the present parents received no reinforcement from the boy for their attempts to establish social contact with him. The treatment was aimed first at increasing the positive reinforcement value of the child and his parents for each other. Attention and smiling responses to the parents were shaped up in the child, using sweets and praise as reinforcers. In turn, the parents were rein-forced by a reduction in the clinic fee, for reinforcing the child appropriately. As treatment proceeded, in order to reduce his isolation the boy was reinforced for approaching and spending time with his stepmother, and to increase his cooperativeness he was reinforced for carrying out tasks as requested. The authors offer evidence in support of their conclusion that these systematic alterations in the reinforcing practices of the parents were followed by attainment of the treatment goals.

The procedure of changing the reinforcement contingencies in natural situations seems to have considerable potential for use by social workers in behavior therapy.

Observational Learning

Desired behavior may be strengthened and abnormal behavior weakened by exposing patients to real life or symbolic models whom they may imitate (Bandura, 1968).

Social workers may provide models of desired behavior in interviews, either in their personal conduct or symbolically by verbal prescription and proscription. Their own behavior may constitute a model of effective personal problem solving for patients to imitate in dealing with current and future difficulties. Many social workers have a parental role which requires them to be an appropriate model to children and adolescents, in matters such as interpersonal relationships, moral behavior, dress and the management of money. They also sometimes promote good child rearing practices in parents by actually demonstrating appropriate behavior toward the children, perhaps by remaining calm in the face of hostility, by expressing affection, or by praising achievement. Symbolically, by verbal prescription and proscription, social workers provide models each time they suggest, advise or advocate a course of action to a patient.

In the natural situation of a patient's own environment a social worker might seek to establish suitable models for the patient to imitate. Examples of this procedure are the promotion in parents of reasoning as a method of socialization instead of excessive physical punishment, so that they constitute rational controlled models for their children to imitate rather than aggressive ones; and the provision of substitute male or female models so that children who are separated from their own parents may learn the appropriate role.

Cognitive Learning

In interviews with social workers, patients may be helped to perceive their problems differently and to understand how to deal with them more effectively. They may be assisted to identify and focus their problem behavior and to recognize the stimulus conditions controlling it. In this way the situation may be presented in a manner most likely to lead to its solution.

Patients may be encouraged also to verbalize their problems — and if necessary provided with the words to do so. This acquisition and application of relevant language processes may have several advantages. Patients can communicate their difficulties to other people and receive information, advice and help from them. The application of logical reasoning in personal problem solving may be improved because gaps, distortions and incompatibilities become more obvious. Finally, control over overt behavior may be enhanced in several ways. Possible courses of action may be rehearsed symbolically so that their consequences are appreciated and impulsive maladaptive behavior avoided. Long-term goals may be maintained by interim symbolic reinforcement. Adaptive discrimination learning and generalization may be facilitated by verbal cues. As an example of the former, a social worker might help a patient to see that he is overgeneralizing responses learned in relation to his parents in childhood to his adult life. Fear of parents may be generalized to later authority figures, and the patient may be helped to recognize that fear of a perfectly reasonable boss is quite unnecessary. Sexual guilt in childhood may be overgeneralized to marital relationships, and the social worker may try to communicate that no guilt need attach to sexual relationships within marriage. Dependence on parents may be generalized to the patient's wife and children, so that he needs to recognize that overdependence on other people is inappropriate in a mature adult with a family dependent on him. Such therapeutic tasks are of course common to many forms of treatment, and the specific contribution of a behavioral approach is the deliberate exploitation of knowledge about discrimination learning.

Verbal instruction is one way of helping patients to perceive accurately the relationships between their problems, the stimulus conditions controlling them and the means of solution. If the required responses exist in the patient's repertoire and appropriate reinforcement is available in his environment, then the instruction may provide discriminative stimuli for appropriate problem solving behavior, thus enhancing the patient's learning and performance.

Two other procedures for promoting understanding and problem solving behavior in patients, are "behavior rehearsal" and "behavior assignment." The former consists of the patient performing in the treatment situation the behavior he would like to perform in his life situation, and it is accompanied often by some form of modelling of the desired behavior. Following such rehearsals, behavioral assignments to perform the desired behavior in real life may be given. Rose (1967b) has described the use of these procedures with the parents of disturbed children.

SELECTED ISSUES

In the professional education and reorientation of social workers for a role in behavior therapy, there are certain issues which arise repeatedly. These include the nature of the treatment goals and the respective functions of insight and a therapeutic relationship in behavior therapy. As accurate communication and comprehension of a behavioral viewpoint on these matters seems to be the major hurdle to be surmounted in introducing social workers into behavior therapy, it is proposed to discuss them briefly now.

Goals of Treatment

Traditionally, social work theorists have emphasized a "medical" model of abnormal behavior, by which it is seen as resulting from underlying causes such as needs, motives and conflicts. These processes are regarded as analogous to the germs, viruses, lesions and other factors foreign to the normal working of the organism, which lead to the production of symptoms in physical medicine. An important implication of the utilization of this model is that the direct modification of the symptomatic abnormal behavior without removal of its underlying causes, will be followed either by the return of the same behavior or by the substitution of other abnormal behavior in its place. It follows that the goal of treatment should be the modification of the presumed underlying causes of problem behavior, just as an attack on the disease process rather than the symptom is often preferred in physical medicine. When discussing the conceptualization and explanation of abnormal behavior within a behavioral approach, we saw that it is regarded as a function of biological factors, learning experiences, and eliciting discriminative and reinforcing stimuli in the current environment. This is an alternative to conceiving hypothetical needs, motives and conflicts as the underlying causes of abnormal behavior. It leads also to an alternative approach in treatment, that is instead of attempting to modify these presumed underlying causes, one may aim at modifying the abnormal behavior directly, and this may or may not involve altering a patient's natural environment.

Thus in a behavioral approach treatment goals are framed in terms of the reduction of deviant responses, and the acquisition and maintenance of appropriate responses to certain stimuli. As we saw earlier, the term "behavior" is used to include physiological, motor, cognitive and affective responses. It is deemed deviant when it is performed in a manner or in circumstances which are unacceptable to the patient or to the society in which he lives. Thus an inadequate father may work or pay his rent too infrequently. A chronic invalid may be overdependent on others. The normal response of fear is triggered off by inappropriate stimuli in the phobic patient. The exhibitionist performs the normal response of unclothing himself in the unusual circumstances of public observation. This last example perhaps illustrates the culture-bound nature of problem definition, for what is "exhibitionism" in western society, is conventional in certain other societies. Similarly, homosexuality between consenting adults in private, was unacceptable legally in Great Britain until recently, thus illustrating the changing nature of what is deemed to be deviant.

In formulating goals for behavior therapy, the modification of behavior to be aimed at is stated as precisely as possible in observable terms, rather than as broad, abstract and inferred subjective states, such as self-knowledge or self-fulfilment. This does not mean that behaviorally defined goals are excessively narrow or limited, as can be seen from some of the illustrative cases cited in this paper. Moreover, there is evidence that quite small changes in particular aspects of behavior can precipitate an avalanche of much more widespread beneficial effects (Patterson *et al.*, 1967).

There are indications that symptom substitution is infrequent following the direct modification of abnormal behavior, but when it does occur, this does not necessarily entail support for the medical model, for such substitution may be accounted for within a behavioral approach (Cahoon, 1968). In the first place, the patient may be subjected to fresh stresses which evoke fresh abnormal responses – there is no more reason to regard this as arising from continuing underlying causes that the case of a person who twice breaks his leg while skiing – it is a new problem rather than a return of the original one. Second, all relevant abnormal responses may not have been modified, for example, if avoidance responses are removed but the anxiety they serve to reduce is left untouched, then fresh avoidance responses may appear. Third, problem responses may not have been modified to all relevant stimuli, for example, anxiety and avoidance responses need to be eliminated in relation to all the phobic stimuli which elicit them. Fourth, correcting a deficit in behavior means adding responses to the patient's repertoire which in turn may be either normal or abnormal. An example of the latter occurred in the treatment of an autistic child, which involved teaching him to wear spectacles. When this was accomplished by positive reinforcement, he began throwing the spectacles away with great frequency, so that this new response required modification. Clearly the correction of the original problem was a necessary precondition for the appearance of the second one (Wolf *et al.*, 1965). Fifth, where problem behavior has obtained reinforcement for the client, removal of this behavior may be followed by other means of gaining reinforcement which may in turn be either normal or abnormal. Goldiamond (1965) has described the case of a woman who assumed a foetal posture for three days after an argument with her husband. She was restored to mobility in two hours by direct treatment, but Goldiamond comments that new childish means of influencing her husband are likely unless she learns more appropriate means of doing so. Finally, potential responses may be arranged in a hierarchy according to their respective probabilities of occurrence. The removal of one abnormal response high in a hierarchy may facilitate the appearance of others which in turn will require treatment. An example of this is cited by Ullmann & Krasner (1965). A boy at a summer camp exhibited a series of abnormal responses, including self-punishment behavior, tantrums, taking his clothes off in public, stealing food, smearing faeces and finally mixing up all the children's shoes in one pile. Each of these responses had to be extinguished in turn by non-reinforcement.

Some time has been spent on the topic of symptom substitution, not only because of its theoretical and therapeutic importance, but also because it highlights the need for accurate and comprehensive assessment of abnormal behavior and its controlling conditions, as a necessary basis for the choice and planning of treatment.

Role of Insight

The term "insight" may refer to a patient's awareness of four aspects of his abnormal behavior: recognition that it is abnormal, in that it is in some way unacceptable to himself or society; appreciation of the nature of the behavior, in particular of the consequences it has for himself and others; knowledge of the factors which currently motivate and control his abnormal behavior; and, knowledge of its origin. A distinction is commonly made between "intellectual" and "emotional" insight. All insight has an intellectual component in that it involves awareness of the problem at a cognitive level, but some has the additional emotional component of being accompanied by the expression of appropriate feeling. It is this emotional insight which often is considered to be an essential precondition for therapeutic change. (An unfortunate tendency toward circular definition is not uncommon, in which insight is judged to be intellectual if no therapeutic change occurs, and to be emotional if it does.)

In fact, the relationships are complex between insight and therapeutic change. It seems that insight is neither a necessary nor a sufficient cause of change, in that change can occur without prior insight and insight is not always followed by change. Indeed, it may be that insight is sometimes a result rather than a cause of change. As a patient's difficulties begin to be resolved directly, he may increasingly be able to confront and verbalize disturbing material. This in turn may contribute to problem solution so that change has led to insight, and this insight to further change.

Because of this empirical complexity as well as certain historical and theoretical reasons, there is an emphasis in behavior therapy on the direct modification of abnormal behavior and its controlling conditions, rather than on the production of insight on patients as a means to change. It should be noted that this is a matter of emphasis rather than the complete exclusion of insight from any role in behavior therapy. Indeed, there are several ways in which it may play an important part in contributing to therapeutic change. It may provide the patient with an explanation of his abnormal behavior which previously seemed inexplicable, mysterious, bizarre and therefore frightening, and any explanation that reduces chaos to order is likely to diminish anxiety. This particular contribution is not specific to behavior therapy, for it occurs in many forms of treatment, although the nature of the insight given varies between them. Secondly, increasing awareness of his problem enables a patient to symbolize it in words, so that the negative emotional responses this arouses, such as anxiety, can be extinguished by non-reinforcement or positive counter-conditioning by the social worker. Thirdly, high emotional arousal commonly impairs adaptive stimulus discrimination; therefore to the extent that insight reduces anxiety it is likely to facilitate the sort of appropriate discriminations described in the earlier section on cognitive learning. Also in that section, it was suggested that increasing awareness might promote learning and problem solving in patients by assisting them to organize, supplement and verbalize information about their problems, and to apply logical reasoning and adaptive behavioral control toward their solution. Thus, insight into the existence and nature of abnormal behavior and the conditions which evoke, guide and reinforce it, may help patients to perceive their difficulties differently and to understand how to deal with them more effectively.

The Casework Relationship

Traditionally, the relationship between patient and social worker has been emphasized as an important factor in treatment, but the precise nature of the relationship and the critical factors by which it produces beneficial change have been very inadequately defined. In behavior therapy the importance of the relationship is in no way devalued, and an attempt is made to conceptualize it more adequately and to identify and exploit the mechanisms by which it produces changes in patients.

The social worker is conceived as a source of eliciting, discriminative and reinforcing stimuli, of a verbal and non-verbal kind, which may serve to modify the abnormal behavior of patients. Some of the ways in which this may occur were described earlier. Positive reinforcers, such as attention, approval and praise, may be withheld or dispensed in order to weaken abnormal behavior or to strengthen desired responses. Aversive stimulation, such as disapproval, criticism or punishment, may be withheld so that anxiety and similar negative feelings are extinguished. The social workers' warmth, sympathy, attention, interest, concern and professional discretion and competence may elicit positive feelings in patients, such as confidence, trust, optimism and self-regard, which may counter-condition certain problem responses including anxiety, guilt and self-devaluation. Observational learning procedures depend upon the social worker exhibiting appropriate behavior for the patient to imitate, and the extent to which he will do this is known to be influenced by the warmth, nurturance, expertise and prestige of the model. Cognitive learning calls upon the social worker's knowledge, intelligence, ability to communicate and systematic, rational and controlled approach to problems. Thus the role of the social worker in behavior therapy is by no means an impersonal one, and it involves an attempt to exploit deliberately any mechanisms by which the therapeutic relationship achieves its effect so that this is maximal.

CONCLUSION

The model of abnormal behavior and the procedures for its assessment and treatment described in this paper, seem to present certain opportunities to social workers in behavior therapy.

In the first place, there may be some merit in focusing on *observable* responses and their *contemporary* controlling conditions. These observable responses are more accessible to social work assessment and diagnosis, than hypothetical internal states such as needs, motives or conflicts. Similarly the conditions controlling the responses in the current situation are more susceptible to social work modification, than any past conflicts in which the patient's present problems might have originated. The emphasis is on the conditions which elicit and maintain the abnormal behavior at the present time, rather than on those which led to its acquisition in the first place. Thus behavior therapy concentrates on the "here and now" instead of on an historical working through of past experiences, and this may be a more practicable and appropriate strategy for many problems, patients and social workers.

Behavior therapy is derived from, and deliberately exploits, a large body of empirical, systematic and cumulative knowledge from a broad field of experimental psychology. The potential advantages of this are obvious, although there are also certain restrictions, including: limitations in the finding, principles and theories which constitute contemporary psychology; inadequate and inaccurate derivation of knowledge from general psychology for therapeutic purposes; and practical difficulties in converting such knowledge into usable treatment techniques.

Nevertheless, on the basis of knowledge derived from experimental psychology, an attempt is made in behavior therapy to modify particular classes of abnormal behavior with certain specific techniques. This contrasts with the more traditional approach of treating all types of problems with relatively nonspecific techniques, such as an inadequately defined therapeutic relationship. For many social workers behavior therapy may offer more systematic direction to their treatment.

Behavior therapy has the additional advantage of being applicable with certain categories of patient whom it may be difficult to help with the more traditional approach. These might include the less verbal and well-educated patients, who might profit from the more direct modification of their behavior with less reliance on their understanding and verbalization to mediate change. Similarly, because of the greater use of material controlling stimuli in behavior therapy, it may be useful with patients who are little influenced by social stimulation, including some psychotics or psychopaths. Some such patients may become more susceptible to social motivation and reinforcement, following the use initially of material controlling stimuli. Conversely, it is difficult at present to see how to apply behavior therapy to certain types of problems, which are hard to analyze into particular dysfunctional behavior, however broadly defined. These conditions might include so-called "existential problems" such as general unhappiness or lack of meaning or purpose in life. They are more appropriately conceptualized as problems of meaning rather than functioning, and although it is theoretically possible to see how certain aspects of experimental psychology, such as cognitive learning and attitude change, might provide suitable treatment approaches, this has not been much explored to date. The scope of behavior therapy is limited also to the extent that a patient is unable to learn because of any biological constraining factor, or where abnormal behavior is not under recognizable stimulus control: for example in pervasive anxiety states, depression and character disorders.

Finally, behavior therapy includes the formulation of specific and observable treatment goals, so that outcome can be assessed and treatments changed both for the individual patient and in the approach generally. Thus the data for the proper evaluation of the contribution of social workers in behavior therapy is potentially available, but this demands systematic controlled studies which so far have not been carried out. Until they are, judgment must be suspended, and the cases described in this paper are to be regarded as illustrative only, and not as constituting adequate support for the efficacy of a behavioral approach by social workers.

REFERENCES

Bandura, A. (1968) Modelling approaches to the modification of phobic disorders. In *The role of learning in psychotherapy*. (Ed., R. Porter) pp. 201–207. J. & A. Churchill, London.

Cahoon, D. D. (1968) Symptom substitution and the behavior therapies: a reappraisal. *Psychol. Bull.*, **69**, 149–156.

Dittes, J. E. (1957) Extinction during psychotherapy of G.S.R. accompanying "embarrassing" statements. *J. abnorm. soc. Psychol.*, **54**, 187–191. a.

Dittes, J. E. (1957) Galvanic skin responses as a measure of patient's reaction to therapist's permissiveness. *J. abnorm. soc. Psychol.*, **55**, 295–303. b.

Garvey, W. P. & Hegrenes, J. R. (1966) Desensitization techniques in the treatment of school phobia. *Am. J. Orthopsychiat.*, **36**, 147–152.

Goldiamond, I. (1965) Self-control procedures in personal behavior problems. *Psychol. Rep.*, **17**, 851–868.

Holder, C. E. (1969) Temper tantrum extinction. *Social Work*. (Lond.), **26**, 8–11.

Jehu, D. (1967) *Learning theory and social work*. Routledge & Kegan Paul, London.

Murray, E. J. (1956) A content-analysis method for studying psychotherapy. *Psychol. Monogr.*, **70**, (Whole No. 420).

Patterson, B. R., McNeal, S., Hawkins, N. & Phelps, R. (1967) Reprogramming the social environment. *J. Child. Psychol. Psychiat.*, **8**, 181–195.

Roses, S. D. (1967) A behavioral approach to group treatment in children. In *The socio-behavioral approach and applications to social work*. (Ed., E. J. Thomas) pp. 39–54. Council on Social Work Education, New York. a

Rose, S. D. (1967) A behavioral approach to the group treatment of parents. Revision of a paper presented at the 94th Annual Forum of the National Conference of Social Welfare, Dallas, Texas. (Mimeographed). b

Sluckin, A. & Jehu, D. (1969) A behavioral approach in the treatment of elective mutism. *Br. J. Psychiat. Soc. W.*, **10**, 70–73.

Stuart, R. B. (1967) Analysis and illustration of the process of assertive conditioning. Paper read at the 94th Annual Forum of the National Conference on Social Welfare, Dallas, Texas. May 1967.

Thomas, E. J. (1967) *The socio-behavioral approach and applications to social work*. Council for Social Work Education, New York.

Truax, C. B. (1966) Reinforcement and non-reinforcement in Rogerian psychotherapy. *J. abnorm. soc. Psychol.*, **71**, 1–9.

Truax, C. B. (1967) *Toward effective counselling and psychotherapy*. Aldine, Chicago.

Ullmann, L. P. & Krasner, L. (1965) *Case studies in behavior modification*. Holt, Rinehart & Winston, New York.

Wolf, M. M., Risley, T. & Mees, H. (1965) Application of operant conditioning procedures to the behavior problems of an autistic child. In *Case studies in behavior modification*. (Eds. L. P. Ullmann and L. Krasner) pp. 138–145. Holt, Rinehart & Winston, New York.

Conclusion

EVALUATION AND FUTURE PROSPECTS

The Significance of Behavior Therapy for Community Psychology

The evaluation of any therapy must, in the final analysis, base itself on data obtained from those members of the community who have experienced it. Few authoritative, long-term assessments comparing the effects of different treatments upon the behavior disorders of children have so far appeared. In fact, outside of those studies concerned with the treatment of enuretics (e.g., Werry & Cohrssen, 1965) it is difficult to find comparative outcome studies contrasting behavioral with traditional approaches to the treatment of children. For the disorders concerned, these studies support the conclusion that behavior techniques are more effective than dynamically-oriented approaches.

Studies with normal children generally show a greater occurrence of change in target behaviors when behavior modification techniques are introduced. Comparative data is needed to determine whether these methods are significantly better than a vast array of other methods which might have been employed.

However, many of the articles included in this book indirectly provide some data as to the efficacy of behavior techniques in contrast to other therapies. Frequently authors make reference to a number of treatments to which the child was exposed prior to receiving behavior therapy. Improvements described resulted from behavioral methods. One must conclude that, in many cases, behavior therapy should be applied before other treatments and not as a last resort after other treatments have failed.

In our experience response from institutions employing behavior therapy techniques with children has been most favorable. After years of experimentation with other therapies, many day nurseries and schools for emotionally disturbed children are prepared to forego these treatments in favor of behavioral approaches.

The involvement of parents in their children's treatment programme has also had desirable effects. From the therapist's point of view this involvement is essential. At no stage of treatment is parental cooperation more vital than at the point where out-patient or institutional treatment leaves off and the child's natural environment takes over again. If, at that crucial time, the parents or parent surrogates cannot be enlisted as "allies in reinforcement" relapse may result. The benefit parents of normal children can and do derive from a better understanding of behavioral principles should require no special emphasis. Yet informal observation of parental behavior at playgrounds, school openings, ice cream parlors or wherever child–parent confrontations are commonly seen, convince one that even the most basic principles of behavioral management are often ignored. Such parental "malpractice" is sometimes explained on the grounds that systematic application of contingency principles would be tantamount to mind control or brainwashing. That non-contingent reinforcement, or for that matter random parental behavior, also "controls" children's conduct, albeit in unpredictable and often undesirable ways, is seldom taken into consideration.

To ensure that parents of emotionally disturbed children become proficient in contingency management, we have found it useful to conduct regular parent education groups in which the basic principles of operant conditioning are discussed. Social workers dealing with these families report that they have rarely seen parents so communicative, eager and helpful. Discussions which de-emphasize feelings and deal instead with improved strategies for changing the very difficult behavior of their children appear to arouse parental involvement. Previously parents were often inhibited by the mobilization of guilt feelings arising from self-blame and a sense of personal insufficiency.

The use of parents, or other non-professional helpers, as co-therapists can pose certain problems. One of these is that behavior therapy may appear to be little more than a bag of tricks for those who have no understanding of the conceptual framework on which it is based. Principles of reinforcement theory can be misinterpreted and, consequently, abused. It is a therapist's nightmare that aversive conditioning in the hands of uninformed non-professionals, or for that matter in the hands of unethical professionals, could cause greater ills than are alleviated. These risks cannot be totally avoided. One can only recommend that if negative reinforcement or aversive conditioning is to be used it must be done only under supervision or after a great deal of supervised training. We are speaking here of the more drastic forms of aversive conditioning. Certainly, the more usual forms of aversive control employed by parents or teachers will continue to be used — contingently or otherwise!

Questions for Future Training and Research

Within the past few years the success of applied behavior modification programmes has had considerable impact on graduate and undergraduate teaching in clinical psychology. Whereas heavy emphasis was once placed upon training in diagnostic techniques and dynamically-oriented therapies many schools now place equal or greater emphasis on behavior modification. This new trend derives largely from the repeated demonstration that principles of learning, tested in the laboratory, are highly relevant to the modification of human behavior, both normal and deviant.

With this change in emphasis from behavior classification to behavior modification, the former preoccupation with psychological testing is now also on the decline. The discovery that an autistic or brain damaged child "tests out" at IQ 50, "lacks conceptual ability" or "shows syncretic thinking" becomes less important when it is demonstrated that the child *can* learn. More meaningful would be tests to evaluate the child's capability (not capacity) for learning at a very fundamental level. Moreover, tests which would indicate changes that occur as a consequence of therapeutic intervention are now needed.

As one might expect, work in behavior therapy with children has given rise to a multitude of problems which must be the subject of future research. The first of these concerns speech development. How is speech acquired and organized in normal infants? As far as is known very little systematic investigation of this process has been undertaken. Clearly, organization of speech by college students may be totally different from the child's organization and sequencing of newly acquired words. When conditioning speech in the non-verbal child, is it more effective to condition the developmental sequence or to impose the adult form? Is "meaning" comprehended more quickly if the developmental sequence is followed?

Another problem concerns the relative merits of positive and negative reinforcers and the use of aversive conditioning in dealing with maladaptive behaviors. When should positive reinforcement and *not* aversive or negative reinforcement be used? If aversive stimulation is used what is its purpose? The whole question of what the negative reinforcer produces in a child is one with which behavior therapists have not come to grips. Does an aversive stimulus necessarily produce anxiety? To change inappropriate behavior is it necessary to produce anxiety? Are there certain diagnostic categories which require specific anxiety conditioning while others do not? Are there alternatives to anxiety conditioning? Covert sensitization (the pairing of nauseous images with pleasurable but maladaptive ones) has proved effective with adults. Its use with children needs to be further explored.

The theoretical and applied literature offers very little in the way of guidelines whereby therapists might decide whether to use anxiety conditioning for behavior modification. If it is to be used, the matter of when, under what circumstances, and for how long is still essentially a matter of clinical judgment. Nor is there any clear indication of what particular aspect of the stimulus configuration a child perceives to be anxiety arousing. Some levels of pain can be unpleasant, without necessarily provoking anxiety. It is very likely that factors related to reinforcement contingencies or stimuli associated with an aversive reinforcement, i.e. a slap, are more anxiety provoking than the pain associated with it. Again, if punishment is administered inconsistently, anxiety may be produced. Physical punishment may be less anxiety provoking than withdrawal of attention (a very common practice in behavior modification). Timeout procedures may well produce phobias, or, under certain circumstances, fears of parental rejection.

For these reasons one wonders whether there is justification for anxiety conditioning in a child to modify even the most undesirable behaviors. At our present state of knowledge it seems doubtful that aversive conditioning is equally beneficial for all children. If it is necessary for some children, then research is needed to specify selection criteria to identify those children for whom it is the optimal method. Alternatives to anxiety conditioning also need to be investigated.

The vast area of modelling as a vehicle of behavior change, so ably pioneered by Bandura (1969) and his colleagues, has raised many exciting possibilities in need of further research. Particularly challenging in this regard is the application of these techniques to the acquisition of moral and ethical values. As educators come to accept greater responsibility for the facilitation of social learning, studies examining children's interpersonal behavior, as those of Bryan & Midlarsky (1967), will become increasingly relevant. There is clearcut evidence that the modification of children's verbal behavior has demonstrable effects on their non-verbal behavior (Lovaas, 1961; Risley & Hart, 1968). If it can be verified that instruction in situational ethics will generalize to a wide spectrum of other, not necessarily, similar situations by making their ethical implications more salient for the child (Loukes, 1969), promising vistas are opened to the much neglected area of character education.

Perhaps the most unique contribution the behavioral approach could make to the mental health of children is in the area of primary prevention. There is much evidence to suggest that not all forms of psychopathology result from early traumatic experiences. Some behavior disorders may well arise from an absence of those learning experiences which promote healthful development. In preventative work until now attention has been paid almost exclusively to the former source of impairment and then only in terms of remediation.

However, it is possible to arrange for the occurrence of certain "immunizing" experiences if there is reason to believe that these would not naturally occur in the child's environment. Deliberate exposure of children to potentially anxiety provoking situations in the presence of stimuli antagonistic to anxiety may well prevent the subsequent development of maladaptive responses to stress. In one animal study supporting this conclusion (Poser, Baum & Skinner, 1970) rats were systematically pre-exposed to the cage in which they were later taught to perform an avoidance response. By comparison to a non pre-exposed control group the experimental animals took longer to learn the avoidance response and required fewer trials to achieve extinction. Some studies of human subjects supporting the notion of "behavioral prophylaxis" are reviewed by Poser (1970).

It must be recognized that every new approach to treatment implies a critique if not a rejection of what went before. Behavior modification is no exception to this trend. At the same time it would be misleading to conclude that the methods and principles discussed in this book are incompatible with the insights gained from other schools of thought. Whether a therapist thinks in terms of behavioral or dynamic formulations, uses desensitization rather than insight or prefers verbal conditioning to non-directive counselling may be a matter of personal preference. But ultimately these distinctions resolve themselves into differences in means rather than ends. For whatever strategy a therapist may choose must be justified by the outcome of his efforts.

REFERENCES

Baer, D. M., Wolf, M. M. & Risley, T. R. Some current dimensions of applied behavior analysis. *Journal of Applied Behavior Analysis*, 1968, **1**, 91–97.

Bandura, A. *Principles of behavior modification.* New York: Holt, Rinehart & Winston, 1969.

Bryan, J. & Midlarsky, Elizabeth. Training charity in children. *Journal of Personality and Social Psychology*, 1967, **5**, 408–415.

Loukes, H. What is moral education? In C. Macy (Ed.), *Let's teach them right.* London: Pemberton, 1969.

Lovaas, O. I. Interaction between verbal and non-verbal behavior. *Child development*, 1961, **32**, 329–336.

Poser, E. G. Training behavior therapists. *Behaviour Research and Therapy*, 1967, **5**, 37–41.

Poser, E. G. The teaching of behavior modification in an interdisciplinary setting. In R. D. Rubin and C. M. Franks (Eds.), *Advances in behavior therapy.* New York: Academic Press, 1969.

Poser, E. G. Toward a theory of "Behavioral Prophylaxis". *Journal of Behavior Therapy and Experimental Psychiatry*, 1970, **1**, 39–43.

Poser, E. G. & Ashem, Beatrice A. Establishing a behavior therapy teaching unit. *Canada's Mental Health*, 1969, **17**, 17–21.

Poser, E. G. Baum, M. & Skinner, Carole. CS Pre-exposure as a means of "Behavioral Prophylaxis". Proceedings of 78th Annual Convention of American Psychological Association, Miami, 1970.

Risley, T. R. & Hart, Betty. Developing correspondence between the non-verbal and verbal behavior of pre-school children. *Journal of Applied Behavior Analysis*, 1968, **1**, 267–281.

Schofield, W. *Psychotherapy: The purchase of friendship.* Englewood Cliffs: Prentice Hall, 1964.

Werry, J. S. & Cohrssen, J. Enuresis—An etiologic and therapeutic study. *Journal of Pediatrics*, 1965, **67**, 423–431.

Subject Index

Author Index

435

TITLES IN THE PERGAMON GENERAL PSYCHOLOGY SERIES

**CLASSROOM MANAGEMENT: THE SUCCESSFUL
USE OF BEHAVIOR MODIFICATION**

Pergamon General Psychology Series, Volume 27
**By K. Daniel O'Leary and Susan G. O'Leary, State University of
New York at Stony Brook**

"The authors/editors are experts in the field, they write clearly and
accurately, the articles selected are excellent . . . absolutely essential
for all school psychologists and certainly very important for those
interested in research and improvement in the schools."

—Behavior Therapy

THE EARLY WINDOW: EFFECTS OF TELEVISION ON CHILDREN AND YOUTH

Pergamon General Psychology Series, Volume 32
**By Robert M. Liebert, John M. Neale, and Emily S. Davidson,
State University of New York at Stony Brook
Foreword by Alberta E. Siegel, Stanford University**

The Early Window provides a brief and readable account of the extensive research which now bears on television and children's social behavior — violence, advertising, social stereotypes, and educational programs as well as on the social and political questions raised by possible regulation of the medium. **The Early Window** will constitute the most up-to-date and authoritative review of the effects of television ever published. Included are clear explanation of: all the major theoretical issues (catharsis, modeling, and instigation effects), each of the significant findings of the Surgeon General's investigation, and the political history of FCC and Congressional investigation — including decisions and events not previously brought before the public eye.

CHILD BEHAVIOR MODIFICATION: A MANUAL
FOR TEACHERS, NURSES, AND PARENTS
Pergamon General Psychology Series, Volume 24
By Luke S. Watson, Jr., Columbus State Institute, Columbus, Ohio

Written in laymen's language, this book is designed to teach principles of behavior modification based on the operant conditioning
approach to teachers, occupational therapists, nurses, psychiatric
aides, parents, and other para-professionals who work with mentally
retarded, psychotic, and emotionally disturbed children. It provides
sufficient information to deal with all problems that such persons
encounter with children of this type in educational, institutional, and
home settings. Testing materials are included to assure that the
reader understands the essential points of the book.

CHILD WITHOUT TOMORROW

Pergamon General Psychology Series, Volume 36
By Anthony M. Graziano, State University of New York at Buffalo

Reports the development of a community program for modifying the behavior of severely disturbed children. The program described was initiated by the author in the early 1960's and was recently completed. The emphasis is on problems involved *vis à vis* the community and its reaction to the program.

A GUIDE TO BEHAVIORAL ANALYSIS AND THERAPY

Pergamon General Psychology Series, Volume 19
By Robert Paul Liberman, M.D., Camarillo, California

". . . a rather comprehensive introduction to the field of behavior therapy and behavior modification . . . The most commendable feature of the text is its method of presentation. As the book is orientated towards giving the reader an intellectual understanding of behavior therapy and whetting his appetite for learning to use the techniques through more intensive training . . . The overall effect is to insure the quick and accurate appropriation of both theoretical and methodological information."

—The American Journal of Occupational Therapy

STUDIES IN VERBAL BEHAVIOR: AN EMPIRICAL APPROACH

Pergamon General Psychology Series, Volume 16
Edited by Kurt Salzinger and Richard S. Feldman, both Biometrics Research, New York, New York

The editors show, by example, the wisdom of viewing language as behavior, produced, modified, and maintained in accordance with known principles of behavior theory. These previously unpublished papers in verbal behavior include an early pioneering study by William M. Schoenfeld and the late William W. Cumming as well as more recent work by the editors and others. The papers are organized into three detailed sections: (1) Some Basic Issues in Studies of Verbal Behavior, (2) Some Stimulus Properties of Verbal Behavior, and (3) Some Response Properties of Verbal Behavior: The Sentence Unit. Each section is preceded by an extensive introduction placing the papers in their broader context. A fourth section contains statistical compilations and other materials, some previously unpublished, useful in a variety of verbal behavior studies.

PERSONALITY: THE HUMAN POTENTIAL

Pergamon General Psychology Series, Volume 33
By M.L. Weiner

This important new volume demonstrates how real-life, down-to-
earth personalities, individuals like ourselves and the people we relate
to in our everyday lives, may be better understood. The author strikingly recounts in a non-technical manner the fundamental dynamics
of personality functioning. The book is unique in that it explores the
major emotional problems and crises confronting mankind today. It
concludes that the reforms man must undertake are in himself and in
his values so that a new era of mankind may evolve — THE PSYCHO-
LOGICAL ERA, where human values are given first priority.

COLLEGE AND STUDENT
Selected Readings in the Social Psychology of Higher Education
Pergamon General Psychology Series, Volume 28

Edited by **Kenneth A. Feldman,** *State University of New York at Stony Brook*

The thirty-two readings that comprise this source book are concerned with the student in college and, in a sense, the college in the student. Focusing on the connections between students' *intra*personal and *inter*personal processes (whether these latter occur in a friendship dyad or among the members of a multiversity of 40,000 students), the selections in *College and Student* include recent, provocative theoretical efforts, scholarly analyses, and reports of recent research.

College and Student will also provide an excellent supplementary textbook for courses in social psychology, socialization, culture and personality, the sociology (psychology) of youth, and the numerous new courses devoted specifically to higher education that are currently being added to college curricula.

STUDIES IN DYADIC COMMUNICATION: Proceedings of a Research Conference on the
Interview
Pergamon General Psychology Series, Volume 7
Edited by Aron W. Siegman, University of Maryland (Baltimore County Campus) and the
Psychiatric Institute, University of Maryland School of Medicine and Benjamin Pope,
The Sheppard and Enoch Pratt Hospital, Towson, Maryland

The result of a special conference held at the Psychiatric Institute of the University of
Maryland in 1968, this volume includes a number of diverse studies based on both experimental and naturalistic interviews, experimental dialogues and free speech samples. The
papers explore such aspects of the interview as the effectiveness of various interviewing
styles, the role of the interviewer-interviewee relationship, the synchrony phenomenon
or reciprocal modeling, the role of auditory feedback in the control of spontaneous speech,
and speech patterns in patient groups. **Studies in Dyadic Communication** will be a valuable
textbook and reference source for graduate students and research workers in psychology,
communication, psycholinguistics, interviewing, psychotherapy, and counseling.

CLIMATE FOR CREATIVITY
Report of the Seventh National Creativity Research Conference held in Greensboro,
North Carolina. Supported Jointly by the National Science Foundation and the Smith
Richardson Foundation, Inc.
Pergamon General Psychology Series, Volume 9
Edited by Calvin W. Taylor, the University of Utah

This volume offers a multidimensional investigation of the problems of identifying and
establishing proper "climates" or settings for creativity. Part I concentrates on organizational
settings for creativity, including papers on the identification and use of creative abilities
in industry, scientific organizations, major weapon systems innovations, and the U.S. Civil
Service Commission. Part II examines more general creativity climates and studies, discussing
predictors and criteria of creativity; the maintenance of creative output through the years;
programming creative behavior; intellective, non-intellective, and environmental correlates
of mechanical ingenuity; and a holistic approach to creativity.

EMOTION IN THE HUMAN FACE: Guidelines for Research and an Integration of Findings
Pergamon General Psychology Series, Volume 11
By Paul Ekman, University of California, San Francisco and Langley Porter Neuropsychiatric Institute, Wallace V. Friesen, Langley Porter Neuropsychiatric Institute, and Phoebe Ellsworth, Stanford University

Can facial behavior be controlled or disguised? Can two or more emotions be shown simultaneously? Can judgements of emotion from facial behavior be accurate? What are the similarities and differences in facial behavior across cultures? These and other major questions which have been asked about human facial expression of emotion are examined here in **Emotion in the Human Face**, the first volume to evaluate and integrate critically all quantitative research conducted since 1914 on this particular psychological phenomenon. Including results from yet unpublished studies, the volume also provides conceptual and methodology guidelines for future research.

PHYSICAL DISABILITY AND HUMAN BEHAVIOR
Pergamon General Psychology Series, Volume 3
By James W. McDaniel, University of Colorado

This textbook and reference concerning the psychological effects of chronic illness and physical disability covers all important aspects of human behavior influenced by illness and physical impairment, as well as the implications of behavioral factors for treatment and rehabilitation processes. Unique in his approach to the subject, the author treats basic psychological processes such as learning, perception, motivation, and emotion as central characteristics which all human beings have in common, and which are subject to predictable changes with illness and permanent disability. The volume collates and critically evaluates for the first time both the theoretically and experimentally relevant work on these problems from the medical and behavioral sciences. Also included are several novel definitions and conceptual models for the study of human behavior in relation to physical disability.

THE PSYCHOLOGICAL EXPERIMENT: A Practical Accomplishment
Pergamon General Psychology Series, Volume 22
Edited by Harold B. Pepinsky, The Ohio State University, and Michael J. Patton,
University of Utah

Based on the thesis that the reality of an empirical world exists for the participant only
through the methods he and others use to make that world evident to each other, this
volume focuses on reports of six psychological experiments involving counseling processes
and negotiation. The editors examine each of these experiments in retrospect and analyze
how the experimenter and fellow participants contrived to develop the experiment from
its original prospectus into a completed, published document.

PERGAMON JOURNALS OF RELATED INTEREST . . .

JOURNAL OF BEHAVIOR THERAPY AND EXPERIMENTAL PSYCHIATRY
BEHAVIOUR RESEARCH AND THERAPY
JOURNAL OF CHILD PSYCHOLOGY AND PSYCHIATRY